# Arab Gulf States

## Bahrain, Kuwait, Oma~~n, Qatar, Saudi Ara~~bia
## & the United A~~rab~~

### Gordon

**Arab Gulf States:**
**Bahrain, Kuwait, Oman, Qatar, Saudi Arabia & the United Arab Emirates – a travel survival kit**

**1st edition**

**Published by**

**Lonely Planet Publications**
Head Office:   PO Box 617, Hawthorn, Vic 3122, Australia
Branches:      PO Box 2001A, Berkeley, CA 94702, USA
               12 Barley Mow Passage, Chiswick, London W4 4PH, UK

**Printed by**
Singapore National Printers Ltd, Singapore

**Photographs by**
Gordon Robison (GR)

Front cover: Tombs at Madain Salah, Saudi Arabia (GR)

**First Published**
March 1993

National Library of Australia Cataloguing in Publication Data

Robison, Gordon
    Arab Gulf States – a travel survival kit.

    1st ed.
    Includes index.
    ISBN 0 86442 120 6.

    1. Arabian Peninsula - Guidebooks. 2. Persian Gulf Region – Guidebooks. I. (Series: Lonely Planet travel survival kit).

915.304

## Gordon Robison

Gordon Robison is an American who has been living, travelling, working and studying overseas since 1985. After working for a year in Saudi Arabia, he decided that there had to be more to life than earning a living so, in 1988, he moved to Cairo and became a freelance journalist. Gordon now reports regularly for the American ABC Radio News and *The Irish Times*. His work has also appeared in the London *Sunday Times* and the *Miami Herald* and he has worked for the English service of Radio France International. Gordon attended Westminster School in London and graduated from Pomona College in Claremont, California, with a degree in government. He later studied Arabic at Cairo's International Language Institute. Gordon also wrote the Saudi Arabia, Bahrain and Kuwait chapters of Lonely Planet's *West Asia on a Shoestring*.

## From the Author

No book is the work of just one person. First and foremost, thanks go to all my friends and colleagues in Cairo and my editors in the USA, Ireland, Britain and France. The latter put up with my long absences from Egypt while the former were remarkably indulgent of my monologues on the subject of travel in the Gulf.

Some people deserve specific mention. In Cairo, I would like to thank Mae Ghalwash who helped with the translation of Arabic-language documents and looked after my apartment during the last, long research stint in the Gulf. Thanks also to Patrick Werr for his files on the Asir National Park and the Hejaz Railway and his insights on Saudi Arabia and Kuwait; to Sarah Gauch for her helpful comments on the Kuwait chapter; and to John West for fact-checking above and beyond the call of friendship.

In Bahrain, I am grateful to Ahmed Sherooqi and his staff in the Ministry of Information for their help with visas. I am also greatly indebted to Dorothee Ramadan for accommodation, use of the office and innumerable phone messages taken and facts checked in both Cairo and Bahrain. She, too, was remarkably tolerant. Thanks also to Mohammed Fadael of *Al-Ayam* and Don Hepburn of BAPCO, who were both generous with their time and insights into life in Bahrain, and to Tony Taylor and Athena Bettino who put me up during my 1989 visit to the island.

In Kuwait, I have always appreciated the helpfulness and efficiency of Amal Al-Hamad and her staff at the Ministry of Information, especially Hala Al-Ghanim and Rifa'a Al-Sayer. Thanks also to Miriam Amie for her friendship and assistance over the years in Cairo, Bahrain and Kuwait.

In Oman, thanks go to Anthony Ashworth and Rosemary Hector at the Ministry of Information and to Connie Miller, then of Muscat and now of Abu Dhabi, for her helpful comments on the Oman chapter.

In Qatar, I am indebted to Abdullah Sadiq and his successor, Moustafa Alaydi, at the Ministry on Information; to John Berry at the US embassy and to Ambassador Mark Hambley for two wonderful Thanksgiving dinners in Doha.

I wish I could name all of the people who

helped me in Saudi Arabia but many of them have asked me to leave their names out of this book. They know who they are and, I hope, of my gratitude. I owe a special thank you to Mark Thomas in Riyadh, who put up with my comings and goings from his villa during both 1989 and 1992 and to Khalid Ali Alturki in Alkhobar, whose assistance and advice over the years have been invaluable. I am deeply grateful to the Saudi Arabian ambassador to the USA, Prince Bandar Bin Sultan, who sponsored my visa for the 1992 research trip to the Kingdom and to the Director-General of the Royal Commission for Jubail & Yanbu, Prince Abdullah Bin Faisal Bin Turki, who sponsored my visa for the 1989 research trip. Thanks also to Prince Bandar's staff at the Saudi embassy in Washington and to Ali Al-Moghanim at the Dammam Museum.

In the UAE, my thanks go to Abdul Aziz Abdel Hodi at the Information Bureau in Dubai.

Finally, I'd like to thank Lonely Planet for their efforts to track me down when they thought I had been trapped in Kuwait during the Iraqi invasion. As it happened, I was in Dubai by then, but it was nice to know that the folks in Melbourne cared.

## From the Publisher

This book was edited and proofed by Diana Saad, with additional proofing by Simone Calderwood and James Lyon. Trudi Canavan drew the maps and also did the layout, illustrations and cover design. Thanks to Sharon Wertheim for indexing.

## Warning & Request

Things change – prices go up, schedules change, good places go bad and bad places go bankrupt – nothing stays the same. So if you find things better or worse, recently opened or long since closed, please write and tell us and help make the next edition better. Your letters will be used to help update future editions and, where possible, important changes will also be included in a Stop Press section in reprints.

We greatly appreciate all information that is sent to us by travellers. Back at Lonely Planet we employ a hard-working readers' letters team to sort through the many letters we receive. The best ones will be rewarded with a free copy of the next edition or another Lonely Planet guide if you prefer. We give away lots of books, but, unfortunately, not every letter/postcard receives one.

# Contents

# THE UNITED ARAB EMIRATES ................................................................... **275**

# INDEX ................................................................................................... **340**

# Map Legend

## BOUNDARIES

— · — · — · — ........ International Boundary

— · — · — ................ Internal Boundary

+++++++++ .... National Park or Reserve

— — — — — ......... The Equator

·················· ......... The Tropics

## SYMBOLS

◉ NEW DELHI ...................... National Capital

● BOMBAY ......... Provincial or State Capital

● Pune ............................. Major Town

● Barsi ............................. Minor Town

■ ............................. Places to Stay

▼ ............................. Places to Eat

⊠ ................................. Post Office

✈ ..................................... Airport

i ........................... Tourist Information

⊖ ............. Bus Station or Terminal

66 ............. Highway Route Number

☪ ✝ ⛪ ✝ ...... Mosque, Church, Cathedral

∴ ........................... Temple or Ruin

✚ ..................................... Hospital

✳ ..................................... Lookout

▲ .......................... Camping Area

⊓ .............................. Picnic Area

⌂ ............................. Hut or Chalet

▲ .......................... Mountain or Hill

⊢■⊣ .......................... Railway Station

═ ............................. Road Bridge

+++ .......................... Railway Bridge

⇒ ⇐ ............................. Road Tunnel

→) (← .......................... Railway Tunnel

⁓⁓⁓ ................... Escarpment or Cliff

‿ ............................................ Pass

ⴖⴖ ............. Ancient or Historic Wall

## ROUTES

————— ...... Major Road or Highway

— — — — — ......... Unsealed Major Road

————— ...................... Sealed Road

— — — — — ..... Unsealed Road or Track

═══════ ........................... City Street

+++++++ .................................. Railway

●━━━◉━━━● ................................. Subway

················· ...................... Walking Track

— — — — — .......................... Ferry Route

+++++++ ........ Cable Car or Chair Lift

## HYDROGRAPHIC FEATURES

.................... River or Creek

............... Intermittent Stream

........ Lake, Intermittent Lake

.......................... Coast Line

................................ Spring

............................. Waterfall

................................ Swamp

................ Salt Lake or Reef

.................................. Glacier

## OTHER FEATURES

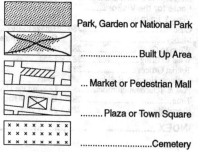

Park, Garden or National Park

...................... Built Up Area

... Market or Pedestrian Mall

......... Plaza or Town Square

............................. Cemetery

Note: not all symbols displayed above appear in this book

# Introduction

What moved thee, or how couldst thou take such journeys into the fanatic Arabia?

**Doughty,** *Travels in Arabia Deserta*

In our age of space shuttles and satellite telephones, at a time when mass tourism has penetrated even such famously remote places as Siberia and the Amazon, few regions of the world have remained as mysterious as Arabia. Misconceptions about travel in Arabia and the Gulf abound. The caricature of the region as inaccessible, expensive and dull has little in common with the reality of the place.

Many people believe that travel in the Gulf is effectively impossible. Wrong. For several years now Arabia has been a fairly easy place to visit. Bahrain, Oman, Qatar and the United Arab Emirates (UAE) are all working to promote tourism and visits to Kuwait can be arranged relatively easily. Only Saudi Arabia lives up to the region's reputation for inaccessibility.

Myth number two is that any visit to the Gulf will be astronomically expensive. Wrong again. Moderately priced hotels and cheap meals can be found almost everywhere in the Gulf. If Egypt or Thailand is your sole definition of 'cheap' well, yes, the Gulf is rather expensive, but (with the exception of Kuwait) it is hardly in the same price category as London, Paris or Geneva.

Myth number three is that the first two myths don't matter because there is nothing to see or do anyway. This myth is the silliest and the most enduring of the lot. For 5000

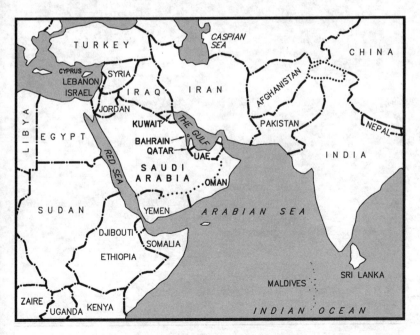

years the Gulf has lain along some of the most heavily travelled trade routes on the planet. If the region's archaeology – from 3rd millennium BC temples and tombs to Portuguese forts – is not enough for you then what about its scenery? There is more to Arabia than the desert: Saudi Arabia has forests, the mountains of Oman are stunning and oases throughout the region offer cool greenery in the midst of the desert. The desert itself can be an attraction – for years expatriates have spent their weekends camping there, and desert safaris are one of the main selling points of package tours to the Gulf.

Even the Gulf's somewhat sterile cities are fascinating contrasts of the old and the new. Over the last 25 or 30 years the Gulf countries have experienced a degree of development which the West eased itself through over a period of nearly two centuries. The resulting juxtaposition of tradition and modernity is arguably the region's single most fascinating feature.

Travelling in the Gulf is not always easy but it is invariably interesting. Go beyond the easy myths and make an attempt to see and understand the Gulf on its own terms. You may be surprised at what you find.

# Facts about the Region

## HISTORY

The most surprising thing about the Gulf states is the degree to which their histories differ. While it might seem fair to assume that a group of tiny countries sharing a single, relatively small, region would also share a great deal of their history, this has been the case in the Gulf in only the broadest terms. What follows is a very general summary of the region's history. Detailed histories of the six countries covered in this book appear in the relevant Facts about the Country sections.

### Beginnings

Ten thousand years ago Arabia probably looked much the way East Africa does today, with huge stretches of savannah land and

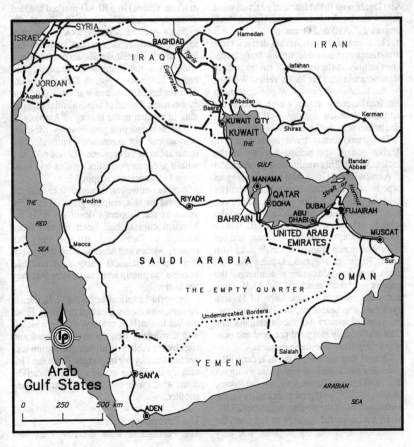

**Arab Gulf States**

0    250    500 km

abundant annual rainfall. It is not known when Arabia was first settled, but excavations at Thumamah, in central Saudi Arabia, have shown that the peninsula has been inhabited at least since Neolithic times – about 8000 years ago. The earliest known settlements on or near the Gulf coast date from about 5000 BC.

In Bahrain a civilisation known as Dilmun arose during the 3rd millennium BC which eventually became a powerful empire controlling much of the central and northern Gulf. The same period also saw significant settlements at Umm An-Nar, near modern Abu Dhabi, and in the Buraimi oasis on what is now the border between the United Arab Emirates (UAE) and Oman.

The cities of ancient Arabia derived their sometimes considerable wealth from trade. The Gulf lay on the main trade routes linking Mesopotamia with the Indus Valley. Western Arabia flourished through its position along the frankincense route which linked the southern Arabian regions of Dhofar and Hadhramaut to the Levant and Europe.

The frankincense trade made southern Arabia one of the richest regions of the ancient world. This wealth drew the attention of Alexander the Great who was planning an expedition to the frankincense lands when he died in 323 BC. One of his admirals, Nearchus, established a colony on Failaka Island, off the coast of Kuwait, which became an important trading centre and for several centuries maintained trade links with India, Rome and Persia. During the 950 years between Alexander's death and the coming of Islam much of the Gulf came under the sway of a succession of Persian dynasties: the Seleucids, the Parthians and, from the 3rd century AD, the Sassanians. The Gulf was of only marginal political and economic importance to these empires.

Central and western Arabia, meanwhile, became a patchwork of city-states living off the frankincense trade and, in the oases, farming. A Roman legion marched down the western coast of the peninsula around 25 BC in an unsuccessful attempt to conquer the frankincense-producing regions, but they

seem to have left remarkably little behind them. Between about 100 BC and 100 AD the Nabataean empire controlled most of north-western Arabia and grew extremely rich by taxing the caravans travelling between southern Arabia and Damascus. The remains of the Nabataean civilisation can be seen today at Madain Salah in Saudi Arabia where, as at their capital at Petra (in modern Jordan), the Nabataeans carved spectacular tombs into the desert cliffs.

## A New Era

The destruction of the great dam at Marib (in modern Yemen) in 570 AD marked the end of southern Arabia's prosperity, though the region's decline actually took place over several generations. Arabian tradition has long attached great significance to the dam, which was the symbol of Arabia's 'old order'. In the same year that the dam broke the Prophet Mohammed was born. The two events mark the end of one era and the beginning of another in the history of Arabia.

The new religion preached by Mohammed spread out across the peninsula with remarkable speed between 622 and 632, and within a century Muslim armies had conquered an enormous empire.

Arabia, however, became increasingly marginal as this empire grew. Within 30 years of the Prophet's death (in 632) the Muslim capital had been moved from Medina to Damascus. By the early 9th century Mecca and Medina were stripped of their earlier political importance and had become the purely spiritual centres that they are today.

In world-historical terms the Gulf, during this era, was the back end of nowhere. From the 9th to the 11th century, during which it was dominated first by the Umayyad and later by the Abbasid empires, the region was neither wealthy nor important. From the 11th century it became an area of petty sheikhdoms which were constantly at war with one another.

## The Europeans Arrive

The Portuguese were the first European

power to take an interest in the Gulf. In 1498 the explorer Vasco de Gama visited Oman's northern coast, the Strait of Hormuz (then the seat of an independent kingdom) and the sheikhdom of Julfar, in what is now the United Arab Emirates. Within 20 years the Portuguese controlled much of the lower Gulf. Their power eventually extended as far north as Bahrain and lasted until the 1630s. Throughout this period the Portuguese were trying to build an empire in India and they realised that control of the sea routes linking Lisbon to Bombay and Goa, in other words control of the Gulf, was the key to their success or failure.

The Portuguese gradually gave way to Britain's seemingly omnipresent East India Company, which had trading links with the Gulf as early as 1616. During the 17th and early 18th centuries the British concentrated on driving their French and Dutch competitors out of the region, a task they had largely accomplished by 1750. By 1770 the Royal Navy was much in evidence in the Gulf and in 1798 the British signed a treaty with the sultan of Muscat. The treaty was specifically aimed at keeping the French away from Oman and safeguarding Britain's route to India. It was around this time – the early to mid-18th century – that all of the families which today rule the Gulf states first came to prominence.

In the Gulf states (but not in Saudi Arabia or Oman) the power of these families was entrenched during the 19th century when they signed protection treaties, known as Exclusive Agreements, with the British. Under these agreements the local rulers gave Britain control of their dealings with the outside world and agreed not to make treaties with, or cede land to, any other foreign power without first receiving Britain's permission. In exchange the Royal Navy guaranteed their independence from Turkey, Persia and anyone else who might pose a threat.

The British administration in the Gulf fell under the jurisdiction of the British Raj in India. (Until India became independent the rupee was the common currency of all the Gulf states; after 1948 it was replaced by a 'Gulf rupee' which was in circulation until 1971.) The chief British officer in the region was the Political Resident, who was based in Bushire, on the coast of what is now Iran. The Resident supervised the Political Agents, usually junior officers, stationed in the various sheikhdoms of the Gulf. The system was designed to be low-key while allowing the British to make their presence felt quickly when they wanted to.

In the early years of this century the British were concerned about two main threats to their interests in the Gulf. The first came from the north, where the Ottomans were working to boost their own presence in the region in cooperation with the Germans. The second threat came from within Arabia itself. In 1902 Abdul Aziz Bin Abdul Rahman Al-Saud, known as Ibn Saud, began a series of conquests which eventually led to the formation of Saudi Arabia. By 1912 the Saudis posed a serious threat to the Gulf sheikhdoms. Had it not been for British promises of protection there is little doubt that Saudi Arabia would today include most or all of Kuwait, Qatar and the UAE.

When WW I broke out the British encouraged and funded a revolt against the Ottoman rule in the western part of the peninsula known as the Hejaz. The Ottoman presence in Arabia was limited and the revolt involved little more than bottling up a Turkish garrison at Medina. The overly romantic (and rather self-serving) account of the revolt later written by T E Lawrence, who came to be known as Lawrence of Arabia, concerned events which mostly took place in Syria and what is today Jordan.

After the war the Sherif (governor) of Mecca declared himself 'King of the Arabs'. The British, however, did not honour their promise of support for the Sherif's pan-Arab dreams and forced him to confine his kingdom to the Hejaz where, less than a decade later, it was overrun by Ibn Saud, who became 'King of the Hejaz and Sultan of Najd'. In 1932 Ibn Saud combined these two crowns and renamed his country the 'Kingdom of Saudi Arabia'.

## Oil

The search for oil in the Gulf began shortly after WW I. The most famous early prospector was a New Zealander named Frank Holmes, who obtained the first oil concessions in Saudi Arabia and Bahrain in 1923 and 1925, respectively. Holmes let the Saudi concession lapse after failing to find backing for his exploration projects but he eventually secured funding for his Bahrain venture. The British and the local rulers were initially skeptical about the prospects for finding oil in the Gulf. Their interest only picked up after oil was found in commercial quantities in Bahrain in 1932.

This interest was spurred on by the collapse, around 1930, of the pearling industry which for centuries had been the mainstay of the Gulf's economy. The pearl trade fell victim to both the worldwide depression that began in 1929 and to the Japanese discovery, about the same time, of a method by which pearls could be cultured artificially.

Within a few years almost every ruler in the Gulf had given out an oil concession in a desperate attempt to bolster his finances. By the time WW II broke out, a refinery was operating in Bahrain and exports of Saudi crude oil had also begun. Saudi and Kuwaiti operations had to be suspended because of the war, though by the time the fighting began the companies were well aware of how valuable their concessions were. Export operations in both countries took off as soon as the war was over.

The first enormous jump in the region's wealth came in the early '50s when Iran's Prime Minister, Mohammed Mossadiq, nationalised the Anglo-Iranian Oil Company, which was then the world's biggest producer. The oil companies stepped up production in the Arab Gulf, particularly Kuwait, to make up for the supplies they had lost in Iran. By 1960 the Middle East was producing 25% of the non-Communist world's oil.

In 1968 Britain announced that it would withdraw from the Gulf by the end of 1971, a move which came as a shock to the rulers of the small sheikhdoms of the middle and lower Gulf. (Kuwait had already become independent in 1961.) In late 1971 Bahrain and Qatar became independent states. A few months later the small sheikhdoms of the lower Gulf combined to form the UAE.

## The Oil Weapon

What came to be called the 'oil weapon', ie the embargo by the Gulf states of oil supplies to the West, was first used during the 1967 Arab-Israeli war. At that time the cutoff lasted only a few days and proved ineffective, a result which may have lulled the West into a false sense of security. By the time the Arabs and Israelis went to war again in 1973 things had changed. On 17 October 1973, 11 days after the war began, Arab oil producers, led by Saudi Arabia, cut off oil supplies to the USA and Europe in protest at the West's support for Israel. Within a few days the embargo had been lifted on all countries except the USA and Holland. The embargo was relatively short-lived (supplies were resumed to the USA in March 1974, and to Holland in July 1974) and its effects proved to be more psychological than practical, but if the goal was to get the West's attention then it certainly worked.

Ironically the long-term result was to tie the USA and the Gulf states, particularly Saudi Arabia, more closely to one another. In the final analysis the West needs the oil and the Gulf states need the revenue that the oil generates. The embargo drove home to both sides the degree to which their economies had become dependent upon each other.

## The Oil Boom

With the surge in oil prices that followed the embargo, an enormous building boom began in the Gulf. The mid-70s to the early '80s was a time when almost anything seemed possible. In 1979 the Iranian revolution shook the Gulf states, but it also made them even richer as the oil companies increased their production to fill the gap left first by the revolution and later by the outbreak of the Iran-Iraq war in 1980. This gap also caused prices once again to soar – fuelling yet another surge of building throughout the region.

Obviously this could not go on forever. In 1985 the bottom fell out of the oil market and everything changed. To varying extents all of the Gulf countries had trouble keeping up their building programmes while maintaining the generous welfare states which their people had come to expect. The Iran-Iraq war continued to drag on, scaring away potential foreign investors and becoming a constant source of concern throughout the region. This was particularly the case in Kuwait, which was only a few km from the front line.

In May 1981 Saudi Arabia, Kuwait, Bahrain, Qatar, the UAE and Oman formed the Gulf Cooperation Council (GCC) in an effort to increase economic cooperation but also in response to the threat from Iran.

### Recent History

When Iran and Iraq grudgingly agreed to a cease-fire in August 1988 the Gulf breathed a collective sigh of relief. After Ayatollah Khomeini, the spiritual leader of Iran's Islamic revolution, died in the summer of 1989 Iran began to seem a bit less frightening. The economic climate in the Gulf looked reasonably good during late 1989 and the spring and summer of 1990.

In retrospect this period appears to have been the calm before the storm. On 2 August 1990 Iraq invaded Kuwait, which it annexed a few days later. Within days King Fahd had asked the USA to send troops to defend Saudi Arabia against a possible Iraqi attack. The result was Operation Desert Shield, the formation of a US-led coalition in Saudi Arabia and the Gulf which eventually numbered over 500,000 troops. On 17 January 1991 the coalition launched Operation Desert Storm to drive Iraq out of Kuwait. This was accomplished after a six-week bombing campaign and a four-day ground offensive. Kuwaitis returned to their country to find hundreds of burning oil wells blackening the sky.

A year after the war Kuwait's oil fires had been extinguished and the government was working feverishly to erase every trace of Iraq's seven-month occupation of Kuwait

City. As a result, building materials companies in eastern Saudi Arabia were having their best year in a decade. In the UAE bookings for package tours were up 200% on the 1989-90 travel season. Since the 3rd millennium BC prosperity in the Gulf has been built on trade. With the region's latest war over, people returned to the normal business of life in the Gulf – making money.

### GEOGRAPHY

The Gulf states (Kuwait, Bahrain, Qatar and the UAE) have relatively similar geography. They consist almost entirely of low-lying desert areas and salt flats. Bahrain, which has an abundance of underground springs, has a lot more natural greenery than the others, though the cities of all these countries have created parks and gardens over the last generation through modern irrigation. The east coast of the UAE and the areas around Ras Al-Khaimah and Al-Ain provide some break from the monotonous landscape with striking mountain scenery.

Saudi Arabia and Oman both have much more varied landscapes (see under Geography in the Saudi Arabia and Oman chapters).

### CLIMATE

From April to October much of the Gulf experiences daytime highs of 40°C or more almost daily. In Bahrain, Qatar, the coastal areas of Saudi Arabia and most of the UAE the humidity during summer is stifling. During high summer the central deserts of Saudi Arabia are spared this humidity while in the west of the Kingdom many people retreat to the Asir mountains.

Winter in the Asir mountains can be bitterly cold, and fog in some places cuts visibility to near zero. Saudi Arabia's central deserts also experience near-freezing overnight temperatures from November to early March. The climate along the Gulf coast, from Kuwait to the UAE, is milder but still chilly enough to warrant a sweater (sometimes even two) in the evenings.

Oman, separated from the rest of Arabia by the Hajar mountains, is just as hot and humid as the Gulf during the summer but it also catches the Indian monsoon, leaving portions of the south of the country lush each September. The Indian Ocean breezes also guarantee Muscat a slightly warmer climate than Bahrain, Kuwait or Riyadh in mid-winter.

## CULTURE
### Traditional Dress

The majority of men in the Gulf states wear traditional dress. This consists of a floor-length shirt-dress which in Saudi Arabia, Bahrain and Qatar is called a *thobe* and in Kuwait and the UAE is called a *dishdasha*. These are usually white though blue, brown and black ones are common during winter. Omanis also call their national dress dishdasha, though Omani dishdashas tend to be less tightly cut than those worn by the Gulf Arabs. Omani dishdashas also come in a wider variety of colours, though white is still the most common.

Omani dishdashas tend to be fairly traditional in their styling (eg there are no pockets), and aficionados can even tell where the wearer is from by examining the garment's cut and collar design. In the Gulf states, thobes and dishdashas have adopted many of the conventions of Western men's shirts, particularly among wealthier people. Thobes and dishdashas sold outside of Oman now routinely have side and breast pockets. Expensive thobes in Saudi Arabia and the northern Gulf may even have Western-style collars and French cuffs.

In all the Gulf countries except Oman men wear a loose headscarf called a *gutra*. This is usually white, though (particularly in Saudi Arabia) it may also be red-and-white check. The black headropes used to secure the gutra are called *agal* and are said to have originated with the rope which Bedouins would use to hitch up their camels at night. Men from Qatar and the UAE often have two long cords hanging from the back of their agals by way of decoration. Omanis usually wear a solid-coloured turban with intricate and brightly coloured embroidery around its edges.

In south-western Saudi Arabia, particu-larly in areas near the Yemeni border, men often wear the skirts which are common in northern Yemen and usually wrap their gutras turban-like around their heads without using an agal.

Traditional women's dress, at least in public, is little more that an enormous, all-covering black cloak. This may completely obscure the wearer's face, in which case the portion of the cloak which covers the face will be made from a thin black gauze that allows the wearer to look out but prevents the world from looking in. Alternatively, the woman's eyes may be visible between her headscarf and veil. Small masks covering the nose, cheeks and part of the mouth are most often seen in rural areas or among old women in the cities. What a woman wears beneath her cloak may be anything from a traditional caftan to the latest haute couture from Paris or Milan.

Arab women walking around a Gulf city with their faces, or even their heads, uncovered are almost always not from the Gulf but rather Egyptian, Palestinian, Jordanian, etc. The only countries in the region where significant numbers of local women no longer wear veils or headscarves are Kuwait and, to a lesser extent, Bahrain.

### Architecture
**Wind Towers** Wind towers, *barjeel* in Arabic, are the Gulf's unique form of non-electrical air-conditioning. In most of the region's cities a handful are still in existence, sometimes on people's homes and sometimes carefully preserved or reconstructed at museums. In Sharjah a series of massive wind towers are used to cool the modern Central Market building.

Traditional wind towers rise five or six metres above a house. They are usually built of wood or stone but can also be made from canvas. The tower is open on all four sides and catches even small breezes. These are channelled down around a central shaft and into the room below. In the process the air speeds up and is cooled. The cooler air already in the tower shaft pulls in, and sub-

Windtower, Doha Ethnographic Museum, Qatar.

sequently cools, the hotter air outside through simple convection.

The towers work amazingly well. Sitting beneath a wind tower on a day when it is 40°C and humid you will notice a distinct drop in temperature and a consistent breeze even when the air outside feels heavy and still.

**Barasti** The term *barasti* describes both the traditional Gulf method of building a palm-leaf house and the completed house itself. Barastis consist of a skeleton of wooden poles onto which palm leaves are woven to form a strong structure through which air can still circulate. They were extremely common throughout the Gulf in the centuries before the oil boom but are now almost nonexistent. The few examples which survive are fishers' shacks, storage buildings in rural areas and a few examples sitting in the courtyards of museums. For a detailed description of how a barasti is constructed see Geoffrey Bibby's book *Looking for Dilmun*.

### Taboos & Avoiding Offence

Etiquette is very important in Arab culture and you will find that your time in the Gulf goes much more smoothly if a few simple rules and rituals are followed.

**General Etiquette** Always stand when someone (other than the coffee boy) enters the room. Upon entering a room yourself shake hands with everyone, touching your heart with the palm of the right hand after each handshake. This goes for both Arab men and women, though men finding themselves in the presence of Arab women should not offer to shake hands unless the woman takes the lead by extending her hand first. When two men meet it is considered polite for them to enquire after each other's families but *not* each other's wives.

Western men should not wear thobes or dishdashas because traditional dress has become an unofficial national uniform throughout the Gulf, visually setting natives of the region apart from the foreign population. Many Gulf Arabs will think that you are making fun of them if you adopt Arabian dress.

Do not sit in such a way that the soles of your feet are pointing at someone else and do not eat or offer things with your left hand.

**Forms of Address** Throughout the Arab world it is common to attach forms of address to people's given, as opposed to their family, names. Just as Arabs refer to each other as 'Mr Mohammed' or 'Mr Abdullah', they will refer to you as 'Mr John', 'Mr Stephen', 'Miss Simone' or 'Mrs Susan'.

The word 'shaikh' (or sheikh) has two quite different meanings in the Gulf. In Saudi Arabia it is a general term of respect and is commonly applied to senior businessmen, high government officials and older men to whom one is not related. It is only rarely applied to men who are not Gulf Arabs, and it is *never* applied to male members of the royal family (who are called 'princes').

By contrast, in Kuwait, Bahrain, Qatar and the UAE the term 'shaikh' applies *only* to members of the ruling family. The rulers themselves carry the formal title of 'Emir' (literally, 'Prince'), but are usually referred to as 'shaikhs', as in 'The Emir of Bahrain, Shaikh Isa Bin Salman Al-Khalifa'.

If, for example, you work for a trading company in Saudi Arabia it would be normal for employees to address the company's Saudi owner as 'Shaikh Ahmed'. In Kuwait you would only refer to the owner as Shaikh Ahmed if he also happened to be a member of the ruling Al-Sabah family.

The feminine form of shaikh is 'shaikha' (or sheikha). This word is rarely, if ever, used in Saudi Arabia. In the other Gulf states it applies to all female members of the ruling family.

**Coffee & Tea** It is considered very impolite to refuse an offer of coffee or tea in any social or business setting. If you are the host it is considered equally impolite to fail to make such an offer. Throughout the Gulf, but particularly in Saudi Arabia, you may be offered Arabian coffee (sometimes called Arabic or Bedouin coffee) and this involves a certain ritual all its own. Arabian coffee is served in tiny handleless cups which hold only two or three sips of coffee. The coffee is flavoured with cardamom which makes it green, or sometimes greenish-brown, in colour. The version served in the cities is fairly tame but should you ever find yourself out in the desert with Bedouins be prepared for an extremely bitter taste. After finishing your coffee hold out the cup in your right hand and either rock it gently back and forth to indicate that you want more, or cover it with your hand to indicate you're through. (At all other times act as though the coffee boy is invisible.) It is considered impolite to drink more than three cups.

**Ramadan** Ramadan, the month during which Muslims fast from dawn until dusk, is observed more strictly in the Gulf than in many other parts of the Muslim world. Those Gulf countries in which alcohol is legal usually ban its sale during Ramadan. Discos, where they exist, are closed throughout the month. In all Gulf countries everyone, regardless of their religion, is required to observe the fast in public. That not only means no eating and drinking but no smoking as well. The few restaurants open during the daytime will invariably be ones that passers-by cannot see into. The penalties for publicly breaking the fast vary – in Saudi Arabia you can go to jail for merely smoking a cigarette while driving down the freeway in your own car.

Non-Muslims offered coffee or tea when meeting a Muslim during the daytime in Ramadan should initially refuse politely. If your host insists, and repeats the offer several times, you should accept so long as it does not look as though your doing so is going to anger anyone else in the room who may be fasting.

The month of Ramadan varies from year to year as the Islamic calendar is 11 days shorter than the Gregorian calendar. For dates see the table of holidays on page 28.

## RELIGION
### Islam

Life in the Gulf revolves around the Islamic religion. Muslims believe the religion preached in Arabia by the Prophet Mohammed to be God's final revelation to humanity. For them the Koran, God's words revealed through the Prophet, supplements and completes the earlier revelations around which the Christian and Jewish faiths were built and corrects human misinterpretations of those earlier revelations. For example, Muslims believe that Jesus was a prophet second only to Mohammed in importance but that his followers later introduced into Christianity the heretical idea that Jesus was the son of God. Adam, Abraham, Moses and a number of other Christian and Jewish holy men are regarded as prophets by Muslims. Mohammed, however, was the 'Seal of the Prophets' – the last one who has, or will, come.

**The Prophet** Mohammed was born at Mecca, a prosperous centre of trade and pilgrimage, in 570 AD. He came from a less well-off branch of the Quraysh, the ruling tribe of Mecca, and his father died before he was born. When Mohammed was seven his mother died and he was subsequently raised first by his grandfather and later by an uncle. As a young man he worked as a shepherd and accompanied caravans to Syria on at least two occasions. At the age of 25 he married a wealthy and much older widow named Khadija by whom he had four daughters and two sons (both of the boys died in infancy).

Mohammed received the first revelation in 610 at the age of 40. He was meditating in a cave near Mecca when a voice commanded him to 'Recite'. This first revelation is preserved in the Koran as Sura 96:1-8

Recite: In the Name of thy Lord who created,
    created Man of a blood-clot.
Recite: And thy Lord is the Most Generous,
    who taught by the Pen,
    taught Man that he knew not.
No indeed; surely Man waxes insolent,
    for he thinks himself self-sufficient.
Surely unto thy Lord is the returning.

After an initial period of doubt Mohammed came to believe that this, and the many later revelations he received, was the actual speech of God, conveyed to him through the archangel Gabriel. He had been commanded to preach the religion of the one true God (allah in Arabic) whose messages sent through earlier prophets had been distorted and misunderstood.

Mohammed did not begin to preach in public until 613, three years after this first revelation. When he did reveal himself as God's prophet to the Arabs the people of Mecca did not exactly rush to embrace the new religion – after four years of preaching Mohammed is said to have had only about 70 followers. The reason for this lay partly in the fact that in attacking the paganism and corruption he saw around him Mohammed was attacking the foundation of his native city's wealth. Much of Mecca's prosperity was built on its status as a pagan pilgrimage centre.

Eventually Mohammed's verbal assaults on the pagan pilgrim trade so angered the local establishment that they plotted to murder him. Hearing of this the Prophet, in June 622, secretly fled Mecca for Yathrib (present-day Medina), a largely Jewish city in an oasis 360 km to the north. This date marks the starting point of the Muslim calendar which also takes its name, Hejira, from

the Arabic word hijrah meaning 'migration', the term given to the Prophet's journey.

Mohammed quickly established himself in Yathrib, where he already had a substantial following, and the name of the city was changed to Medinat An-Nabi – the City of the Prophet. Medina became the Prophet's model community. Over the next eight years Mohammed's following increased dramatically in Medina and in the rest of Arabia.

The Medina-based Muslims and the still-pagan Meccans fought a series of battles, both military and political, throughout the 620s. Finally, in January 630, the Muslims marched on Mecca with an army of 10,000. The city surrendered without a fight and the next day the Prophet entered the pagan temple which is now the Grand Mosque, removed 365 idols from the Kaaba, the shrine at its centre, and declared it cleansed. Later that year he returned to Medina, where he continued to live. In 632 he travelled again to Mecca to perform the pilgrimage and established in their final form the rituals which are still performed by Muslim pilgrims today. After his trip to Mecca, Mohammed returned to Medina where he died later that year.

**The Faith** The essence of Islam is the belief that there is only one God and that it is the people's duty to believe in and serve Him in the manner which He has laid out in the Koran. In Arabic, islam means submission and a muslim is one who submits to God's will.

In the first instance, one does this by observing the five pillars of the faith:

1. The profession of faith (shahadah). To become a Muslim one need only state the Islamic creed, 'There is no God but God, and Mohammed is the messenger of God', with conviction.

2. Prayer (salat). Muslims are required to pray five times every day: at dawn, midday, mid-afternoon, sunset and 1½ hours after sunset. Prayers follow a set ritual pattern which varies slightly depending on the time

of day. During prayers a Muslim must perform a series of prostrations while facing in the direction of the Kaaba, the ancient shrine at the centre of the Grand Mosque in Mecca. Before a Muslim can pray, however, he or she must perform a series of ritual ablutions, and if no water is available for this purpose sand or dirt may be substituted.

3. Charity or Alms *(zakat)*. Muslims must give a portion of their income to help those poorer than themselves. How this has operated in practice has varied over the centuries: either it was seen as an individual duty or the state collected zakat as a form of income tax to be redistributed through mosques or religious charities.

4. Fasting *(sawm)*. It was during the month of Ramadan that Mohammed received his first revelation in 610 AD. Muslims mark this event by fasting from sunrise until sunset throughout Ramadan each year. During the fast a Muslim may not take anything into his or her body. This means that not only food and drink but also smoking and sex are banned. Young children, travellers and those whose health will not permit it are exempt from the fast, though those who are able to do so are supposed to make up the days they missed at a later time.

5. Pilgrimage *(hajj)*. All Muslims who are able to do so are required to make the pilgrimage to Mecca at least once during their lifetime. However, the pilgrimage must be performed during a specific few days in the first and second weeks of the Muslim month of Dhul Hijja. Visiting Mecca and performing the prescribed rituals at any other time of the year is considered spiritually desirable, but it is not hajj. Such visits are referred to as *umrah*, or 'little pilgrimage'.

Beyond the five pillars of Islam there are many other duties incumbent on Muslims. In the West the best known and least understood of these is *jihad*. This word is usually translated into English as 'holy war', but literally means 'striving in the way of the faith'.

Exactly what this means has been a subject of keen debate among Muslim scholars for the last 1400 years. Some scholars have tended to see jihad in spiritual, as opposed to martial, terms.

Muslims are forbidden to eat or drink anything containing pork, alcohol, blood or the meat of any animal which died of natural causes (as opposed to having been slaughtered in the prescribed manner). Muslim women may not marry non-Muslim men, though Muslim men are permitted to marry Christian or Jewish women (but not, for example, Hindus or Buddhists).

**The Law** The Arabic word *sharia* is usually translated as 'Islamic Law'. This is misleading. The sharia is not a legal code in the Western sense of the term. It refers to the general body of Islamic legal thought. At the base of this lies the Koran itself, which Muslims believe to be the actual speech of God, revealed to humankind through Mohammed. Where the Koran itself does not provide guidance on a particular subject Muslim scholars turn to the Sunnah, a body of works recording the sayings and doings of the Prophet and, to a lesser extent, his companions as reported by a string of scholarly authorities. There are many Sunnah authorities and their reliability is determined by the school of Islamic jurisprudence to which one subscribes. There are four main Sunni and two principal Shiite schools of Islamic jurisprudence.

The Koran and Sunnah together make up the sharia. In some instances the sharia is quite specific, such as in the areas of inheritance law and the punishments for certain offences. In many other cases it acts as a series of guidelines. Islam does not recognise a distinction between the secular and religious lives of believers. Thus, a learned scholar or judge can with enough research and if necessary, through use of analogy, determine the proper 'Islamic' position on or approach to any problem.

**Sunnis & Shiites** The schism which divided the Muslim world into two broad camps took place only a few years after the death of the Prophet. In 644, 12 years after the Prophet's death, a serious dispute arose over the leadership of the Muslim community. Those who took the side of Ali, Mohammed's cousin and son-in-law and one of the first converts to Islam, became known as the *shi'a*, or 'partisans (of Ali)'. Ali eventually became the leader, or *khalif* (Caliph), of the Muslims in 656 but his assassination five years later by the Governor of Syria, who set himself up as Caliph, split the Muslim community into two competing factions. The Sunnis favoured the succession from the Caliph, while the Shiites favoured the descendants of Ali. The split widened and became permanent when Ali's son, Hussein, was killed in brutal circumstances at Karbala (now in southern Iraq) in 680.

Most of the world's Muslims are Sunnis. In the Gulf, Shiites are a majority only in Bahrain (though Bahrain's ruling family are Sunnis). There are significant Shiite minorities in Kuwait, the UAE and Saudi Arabia's Eastern Province.

As with any religion embracing about one billion people, Islam has produced many sects, movements and offshoots both within and beyond the traditional Sunni-Shiite division. The two most important Sunni sects in the Gulf states are the Wahhabis, whose doctrines are the official form of Islam in Saudi Arabia, and the Ibadis, who are the dominant sect in Oman. See the religion sections of the Saudi Arabia and Oman chapters for more information on Wahhabis and Ibadis, respectively.

## LANGUAGE

English is widely spoken throughout the Gulf, but a few words of Arabic can do a lot to ease your passage through the region. There are several different varieties of Arabic. Classical Arabic, the language of the Koran, is the root of all today's dialects of spoken and written Arabic. A modernised and somewhat simplified form of Classical Arabic is the common language of the educated classes in the Middle East. This language, usually known as Modern Standard Arabic, is used in newspapers and by television and radio newsreaders. It is also used as a medium of conversation by well-educated Arabs from different parts of the region. Such a written language is necessary because the dialects of spoken colloquial Arabic differ to the point where a few of them are mutually unintelligible.

Mercifully, the words and phrases a traveller is most likely to use are fairly standard throughout the Gulf. The glossary which follows should be understood anywhere in the region. Local variants, where applicable, have been noted.

## Greetings & Civilities

Hello.
*as-salaamo alaykum*
Hello.(response)
*wa alaykum e-salaam*
Goodbye.
*ma'al salaama*
Goodbye. (response)
*alla ysalmak* (to a man)
*alla ysalmich* (to a woman)
*alla ysallimkum* (to a group)
Goodbye.
*hayyaakallah* (to a man)
*hayyachallah* (to a woman)
*hayyakumallah* (to a group)
Goodbye. (response)
*alla yhai'eek* (to a man)
*alla yhai'eech* (to a woman)
*alla yhai'eekum* (to a group)
Goodbye. (UAE only)
*fi aman ullah*
Good morning.
*sabah al-kheir*
Good morning. (response)
*sabah an-nur*
Good afternoon/evening.
*masa' al-kheir*
Good afternoon/evening. (response)
*masa' an-nur*
Good night.
*tisbah ala-kheir* (to a man)
*tisbihin ala-kheir* (to a woman)
*tisbuhun ala-kheir* (to a group)

Good night. (response)
*wa inta min ahlil-kheir* (to a man)
*wa inti min ahlil-kheir* (to a woman)
*wa intu min ahlil-kheir* (to a group)

Welcome.
*ahlan wa sahlan* or *marhaba*
Welcome to you.
*ahlan feek* (to a man)
*ahlan feech* (to a woman)
*ahlan feekum* (to a group)
Pleased to meet you. (also said to people as they are leaving)
*fursa sa'ida*
Pleased to meet you. (response)
*wa ana as'ad* (by an individual)
*wa ihna as'ad* (by a group)

Please.
*min fadhlik* or *lau samaht* or *lau tismah* (to a man)
*min fadhlich* or *lau samahti* or *lau tismihin* (to a woman)
*min fadhelkum* or *lau samahtu* or *lau tismuhun* (to a group)
Thank you.
*shukran* or
*mashkur* (to a man)
*mashkura* (to a woman)
*mashkurin* (to a group)
You're welcome.
*afwan* or *al-afu*
Excuse me.
*lau samaht* (to a man)
*lau samahti* (to a woman)
*lau samahtu* (to a group)
After you.
*atfaddal*
How are you?
*shlonik* or *kef halak* (to a man)
*shlonich* or *kef halik* (to a woman)
*shlonkum* or *kef halkum* (to a group)
Fine, thanks. (response)
*bkheir al-hamdulillah* or
*zein al-hamdulillah* (by a man)
*zeina al-hamdulillah* (by a woman)
*zeinin al-hamdulillah* (by a group)

## Small Talk

What is your name?
*shismak* (to a man)
*shismich* (to a woman)
*shisimkum* (to a group)
My name is...
*ismi...*
I am...
*ana...*
I am from...
*ana min...*
　　　Australia
　　　　*usturalia*
　　　France
　　　　*faransa*
　　　Germany
　　　　*almania*
　　　Netherlands
　　　　*holanda*
　　　Switzerland
　　　　*swissra*
　　　the UK
　　　　*britania*
　　　the USA
　　　　*amrika*

## Useful Words & Phrases

Yes.
*ai* (rhymes with the English word 'hay') or *aiwa* or *na'am*
No.
*la'*
Maybe.
*mumkin*
OK.
*zein* or *kwayyis* or *tayib*
No problem.
*mafeesh mushkala*
Impossible.
*mish mumkin*
It doesn't matter/I don't care.
*ma'alish*
Go/Get lost!
*imshi*

I understand.
*ana fahim* (by a man)
*ana fahma* (by a woman)
We understand.
*ihna fahmeen*

I do not understand.
*ana mu fahim* (by a man)
*ana mu fahma* (by a woman)
We do not understand.
*ihna mu fahmeen*
Do you speak English/French/German?
*titkallam ingleezi/fransawi/almaani*
I don't speak Arabic.
*ma-atkallam arabi*

## Getting Around

How far is...?
*cham yibe'id...*
the bus stop
*mokaf al-bas*
the bus station
*mahattat al-bas*
the train station
*mahattat al-qatar*
a taxi stand
*mahattat tax* or *mahattat ajara*
the airport
*al-mataar*

Where is the...?
*wein al...*
boat
*markab*
bus
*bas*
camel
*jamal*
car
*sayyara*
donkey
*hmaar*
horse
*hsan*
taxi
*tax* or *ajara*
ticket office
*maktab al-tathaaker*

I want to go to...
*abga arouh li...*
When does the... leave?
*mata yamshi il...*
*muta yamshi il...* (in Kuwait)

When does the...arrive?
*mata tosal il...*
*muta tosal il...* (in Kuwait)
What is the fare to...?
*cham il tathkara li...*

Which bus/taxi goes to...?
*ai bas/tax yrouh il...*
Does this bus/taxi go to...?
*hathal bas yrouh il...*
How many buses go to...?
*cham bas yrouh li...*

Please tell me when we arrive at...
*lau samahtit goul li mata nosal li...*
May I sit here?
*mumkin ag'id hina*
May we sit here?
*mumkin nag'id hina*
Stop here, please.
*'ogaf hina, law samaht*
Please wait for me.
*law samaht, intitherni*

## Directions

to or for
*lil*
left
*shimal* or *yasaar*
right
*yimeen*
straight
*ala tool*
*seeda* (in Kuwait only)
*doghri* (in the UAE only)
street
*shaari'*
number
*raqam*
city
*madina*
village
*qaria*

## Around Town

Where is the...?
*wein al...*
Can you show me the way to (the)...?
*mumkin tdallini mukaan ...*

bank
*el-bank*
barber
*el-hallaq*
beach
*il-shatt* or *il-shaat'i*
embassy
*es-safara*
hotel
*el-funduq*
market
*es-souk*
mosque
*el-masjid*
museum
*el-mathaf*
old city
*el-madina il-qadima*
palace
*el-qasr*
police station
*el-makhfar*
post office
*maktab al-bareed*
restaurant
*el-mataam*
telephone
*el-telefon* or *el-hataf*
toilet
*el-hammam*
university
*il-jam'a*
zoo
*hadiqat il-haywan*

## Accommodation
May I see the room?
*mumkin ashuf al-ghurfah*
May I see other rooms?
*mumkin ashuf ghuraf thaania*
How much is this room per night?
*cham ujrat haathil ghurfah fil-leila*
Do you have any cheaper rooms?
*fih ghuraf arkhas*
This is very expensive.
*wai'd ghali*
*hatha ghali jeddan* (in Saudi Arabia)
This is fine.
*hatha zein.*

## Food
bread
*khubz*
chicken
*dajaj*
coffee
*qahwa*
fish
*samak*
meat
*lahma*
milk
*laban*
pepper
*felfel*
potatoes
*batatas*
rice
*roz*
salt
*sel* or *melah*
sugar
*suker*
tea
*chai*
water
*mayya*

## Shopping
I want...
*abga...*
*abi...* (Kuwait & Bahrain only)
Do you have...?
*indik* (to a man)
*indich* (to a woman)
Where can I buy...?
*wein agdar ashtiri*
How much is this?
*bcham hatha*
How much is that?
*bcham hathak*
How much are those?
*bcham hathol*
How much...? (Saudi Arabia, Qatar & UAE only)
*qedaish*
It costs too much.
*ghalia wai'd*

I want to change...
*abga asrif...*
  money
    *floos*
  US$
    *dolarat amrikiia*
  UK£
    *jneihat isterlini*
  A$
    *dolarat usturaliia*
  FF
    *frankat fransi*
  DM
    *markat almani*
  travellers' cheques
    *sheikat syahiia*

## Time & Date

What time is it?
  *as-sa'a kam*
It is...
  *as-sa'a...*
    one o'clock
      *wahda*
    1.15
      *wahda wa rob'*
    1.20
      *wahda wa tilt*
    1.30
      *wahda wa nus*
    1.45
      *ithneen illa rob'* (literally, quarter to two)

Monday
  *yom al-ithneen*
Tuesday
  *yom al-thalath*
Wednesday
  *yom al-arbaa'*
Thursday
  *yom al-khamis*
Friday
  *yom al-jama'a*
Saturday
  *yom as-sabt*
Sunday
  *yom al-had*

## Numbers

| 0 | *sifir* |
|---|---|
| 1 | *wahid* |
| 2 | *ithneen* |
| 3 | *thalatha* |
| 4 | *arba'a* |
| 5 | *khamsa* |
| 6 | *sitta* |
| 7 | *sab'a* |
| 8 | *thimania* |
| 9 | *tis'a* |
| 10 | *ashra* |
| 11 | *Hda'ash* |
| 12 | *thna'ash* |
| 13 | *thalathta'ash* |
| 14 | *arba'ata'ash* |
| 15 | *khamista'ash* |

daily
  *kil yom*
today
  *al-yom*
yesterday
  *ams*
tomorrow
  *bukra*
early
  *mbach'ir* or *badri*
late
  *mit'akhir*

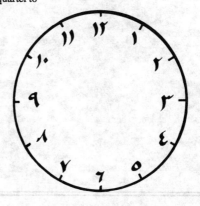

| | | | | |
|---|---|---|---|---|
| 16 | *sitta'ash* | | 102 | *imia wa-ithneen* |
| 17 | *sabi'ta'ash* | | 103 | *imia wa-thalatha* |
| 18 | *thimanta'ash* | | 200 | *imiatain* |
| 19 | *tisi'ta'ash* | | 300 | *thalatha imia* |
| 20 | *'ishreen* | | 1000 | *alf* |
| 21 | *wahid wa 'ishreen* | | | |
| 22 | *ithneen wa 'ishreen* | | | |
| 23 | *thalatha wa 'ishreen* | | 1st | *awwal* |
| 30 | *thalatheen* | | 2nd | *thaani* |
| 40 | *arbi'een* | | 3rd | *thaalith* |
| 50 | *khamseen* | | 4th | *raabi'* |
| 60 | *sitteen* | | 5th | *khaamis* |
| 70 | *saba'een* | | 6th | *saadis* |
| 80 | *thimaneen* | | 7th | *saabi'* |
| 90 | *tis'een* | | 8th | *thaamin* |
| 100 | *imia* | | 9th | *taasi'* |
| 101 | *imia w-ahid* | | 10th | *'ashir* |

# Facts for the Visitor

## VISAS

The visa situation in the Gulf ranges from fairly simple and straightforward (Bahrain) to nightmarishly complicated (Saudi Arabia). Bahrain, Qatar, the UAE and Oman all issue tourist visas. Saudi Arabia and Kuwait do not, so you have to get a transit or a business visa to visit them.

Bahrain issues visas to most native-born Western nationals at the airport and on the causeway connecting Bahrain to Saudi Arabia. Oman sometimes issues tourist visas through its embassies in some countries. Saudi Arabia issues transit visas for people travelling overland between Jordan and Bahrain, Kuwait, Oman, Qatar, the UAE or Yemen. The transit visas are issued at Saudi Arabian embassies in these countries. For more details on each country's visa regulations see the Visa heading in the individual country chapters.

### Visa Sponsorship

If you cannot obtain a visa to the Gulf states through an embassy, you can get it through a sponsor. A sponsor is a national of the country you are visiting who is willing to vouch for your good behaviour while in the country and take responsibility for your departure when you're supposed to leave. How easy it is to get a sponsor, and what you must do once you have found one, varies from country to country.

In Kuwait, Qatar, the UAE and Oman all the larger hotels can sponsor visas for travellers. The documentation required varies from one country to the other and its processing can take anything from a few days to a few weeks. In Bahrain, hotels can arrange sponsorship for those unable to obtain a visa on arrival.

### Collecting Visas

Once approved, Kuwaiti and Saudi visas have to be picked up at a Kuwaiti or Saudi embassy before you travel. Visas for the other Gulf states are issued for pick-up at the destination airport or port. If you are travelling to one of these countries be sure to have some proof (a fax or telex with a visa number) that you have a visa waiting for you at your destination or you may not be allowed to board the aeroplane.

## WHEN TO GO

Avoid the Gulf from April to early October if possible. The tourist season, in those countries which admit tourists, is November to February.

The monsoon season in southern Oman is June to September, and this is a good time to avoid that part of the country. However, late September when everything is green in the wake of the rains is one of the best times to visit the Salalah area.

You should avoid visiting the Gulf during Ramadan (see the table of holidays on page 28). At hajj time it would also be a good idea to avoid Jeddah unless you have a pressing reason to be there.

## WHAT TO BRING

A good hat and sunglasses are essential even if you do not plan to spend time travelling in the desert. Long, loose clothing is always the best idea in conservative Islamic countries and the Gulf is no exception.

Almost anything you can get in the West can easily be purchased in any of the Gulf's bigger cities, though voracious readers of anything other than spy novels should note that there are few really good bookstores in the Gulf. Also, most Western works on the history and politics of the Middle East are unavailable in the Gulf states.

## BUSINESS HOURS & HOLIDAYS

The end of week holiday throughout the Gulf is Friday. Most embassies and government offices are also closed on Thursday, though private businesses and shops are open on

**Table of Holidays**

| Hejira Year | New Year | Prophet's Birthday | Ramadan Begins | Eid Al-Fitr | Eid Al-Adha |
|---|---|---|---|---|---|
| 1413 | 02.07.92 | 10.09.92 | 23.02.93 | 26.03.93 | 01.06.93 |
| 1414 | 21.06.93 | 30.08.93 | 12.02.94 | 15.03.94 | 21.05.94 |
| 1415 | 10.06.94 | 19.08.94 | 01.02.95 | 04.03.95 | 10.05.95 |
| 1416 | 31.05.95 | 09.08.95 | 22.01.96 | 22.02.96 | 29.04.96 |
| 1417 | 19.05.96 | 28.07.96 | 10.01.97 | 10.02.97 | 18.04.97 |
| 1418 | 09.05.97 | 18.07.97 | 31.12.98 | 31.01.98 | 08.04.98 |
| 1419 | 28.04.98 | 07.07.98 | 20.12.99 | 20.01.99 | 28.03.99 |
| 1420 | 17.04.99 | 26.06.99 | | | |

Thursday mornings and many stores will reopen in the evening on Friday.

The Gulf states observe the main Islamic holidays of Eid Al-Fitr, which marks the end of Ramadan, and Eid Al-Adha, which marks the pilgrimage to Mecca. All observe both the Gregorian and the Islamic new year holidays, except for Saudi Arabia which only celebrates the Muslim new year. A list of the dates for Muslim holidays up to the year 1999. These dates may vary by several days in either direction as the Islamic calendar is based on cycles of the moon. The Islamic calendar is 11 days shorter than the Gregorian calendar and the holidays mentioned will move back accordingly in subsequent years.

## BOOKS

The books listed here contain general information about the Gulf or the Middle East. Many of these books may also be listed in the country chapters.

### People & Society

Possibly the best single overview of life, business and culture in the Gulf is *The Merchants* by Michael Field (Overlook Press, Woodstock NY, 1985). While ostensibly focusing on the rise of nine of the Gulf's prominent merchant families it is really a book about Arabian society, how it works and how it has changed since the discovery of oil. *The New Arabians* by Peter Mansfield (Ferguson, Chicago, 1981) is an introduction to both the history and society of the Gulf,

though the focus is mostly on Saudi Arabia and the general tone of the book is fairly uncontroversial.

Peter Theroux gives a witty, candid portrait of culture and politics in the Middle East in his book *Sandstorms – Days and Nights in Arabia* (Norton, New York, 1990).

For travel literature try Jonathan Raban's *Arabia Through the Looking Glass* (Picador, London, 1981). Raban's observations on expatriate life in the region are as valid today as they were during the oil boom (he visited in early 1979) and, unlike many travel writers, he found the time to speak with a lot of Gulf Arabs in addition to the expats. Another good read is Christopher Dickey's *Expats* (Atlantic Monthly Press, New York, 1990), which explores the interaction between the Arabs and the expats in the Middle East.

### History

Most books on the history of the Gulf tend to be either heavy academic works or propagandist in tone. Books on the broader history of the Middle East pass only fleetingly over the Gulf. An exception is Peter Mansfield's *The Arabs* (Penguin, London, 2nd edition 1985), which is also one of the better books with that particular catch-all title. In addition to a broad-brush history of the Middle East Mansfield comments on the individual countries in the region. Dilip Hiro's *Inside the Middle East* (Routledge & Keegan Paul, London, 1982) is also quite good on the Gulf.

If you are genuinely serious about the region's history, politics and economics (and you like books that are heavy on statistical charts), there's the *Area Handbook for the Persian Gulf States* by Richard Nyrop, et al (US Government Printing Office, Washington, 1977). This is a manual compiled by a team of researchers at the American University in Washington DC and used for training US diplomats and soldiers headed for the region. It covers Kuwait, Bahrain, Qatar, the United Arab Emirates (UAE) and Oman. Another book in the same series covers Saudi Arabia. You will almost certainly have to go to a specialist bookstore to find it, or order a copy directly from the USGPO. The handbooks are available only in hard cover.

Among the best general histories of the Middle East is Albert Hourani's *A History of the Arab Peoples* (Belknap-Harvard, Cambridge, Massachusetts, 1991). There's not a lot of information specifically on the Gulf in Hourani's book, but as a general introduction to the region's history and philosophy you could hardly do better. Among the old-line Orientalists John Bagot Glubb's *A Short History of the Arab Peoples* (Quartet, London, 1969) is still worth reading today.

## Islam

You cannot hope to understand the Gulf without some understanding of Islam and its history. If you are looking for a relatively short book on Islamic beliefs and practices which is aimed at the general reader one of the best is *Mohammedanism – An Historical Survey* by H A R Gibb (Oxford University Press, London, 1952). If, on the other hand, you want to immerse yourself in the minutiae of Islamic history, culture and civilisation the best work on the subject in English is Marshall G S Hodgson's *The Venture of Islam* (three volumes, University of Chicago Press, 1974). Even if you have no intention of wading through 1500 pages of Hodgson, the first 100 pages of volume one (the 'Introduction to the Study of Islamic Civilization' and the 'General Prologue') is required reading for anyone headed for the Middle East.

The Koran itself is notoriously difficult to translate. Pious Muslims insist that it cannot be translated, only rendered or interpreted, into other languages. A J Arberry's *The Koran Interpreted* (Macmillan, New York, 1955) is generally accounted to be the best version available in English.

Those interested in Islamic literature should try another of Arberry's works, *Aspects of Islamic Civilization* (George Allen & Unwin, London, 1964), or James Kritzeck's *Anthology of Islamic Literature* (Meridian, New York, 1964).

## FILM & PHOTOGRAPHY

The basic rules in the Gulf are simple – do not photograph anything even vaguely military in nature (this always includes airports), do not photograph people without their permission, and never photograph women.

Bahrain and the UAE are the most relaxed countries in the Gulf when it comes to photography, while Kuwait and Oman seem to have the broadest definitions of what constitutes a 'strategic' site. Few officials in the Gulf will be pleased by photographs of tents, run-down houses or anything which resembles poverty, as the tendency is to emphasise what the country has achieved in the last few decades.

## HEALTH

Travel health depends on your pre-departure preparations, your day-to-day health care while travelling and how you handle any medical problem or emergency that does develop. While the list of potential dangers can seem quite frightening, with a little luck, some basic precautions and adequate information few travellers experience more than upset stomachs.

Throughout the Gulf the quality of health care is very high. When the Gulf states began to prosper, their rulers invested huge sums of money into hospitals, clinics and long-term health programmes. The result is that countries which only a generation or two ago were ridden by famines and epidemics (which the Bedouin traditionally used as a way of marking time – for example, a child would be said to have been born 'in the year after the year of measles') now enjoy a standard of health care which equals that of the richest countries in the West. In some Gulf countries medical care is free; in others the costs are relatively nominal. For details see the Health section in the individual country chapters.

The flip side of this is that some Gulf countries, particularly Saudi Arabia, are very reluctant to acknowledge outbreaks of infectious disease. Western embassies tend to be the best sources of up-to-date information on any local contagious diseases.

## Travel Health Guides

There are a number of books on travel health. *Staying Healthy in Asia, Africa & Latin America* (Volunteers in Asia) is probably the best all-round guide to carry, as it's compact but very detailed and well organised.

*Travellers' Health* by Dr Richard Dawood (Oxford University Press) is comprehensive, easy to read, authoritative and also highly recommended though it's rather large to lug around. *Where There is No Doctor* by David Werner (Hesperian Foundation) is a very detailed guide intended for someone, like a Peace Corps worker, going to work in an undeveloped country, rather than for the average traveller. *Travel with Children* by Maureen Wheeler (Lonely Planet Publications) includes basic advice on travel health for younger children.

## Pre-Departure Preparations

**Health Insurance** A travel insurance policy to cover theft, loss and medical problems is a wise idea. There are a wide variety of policies and your travel agent will have recommendations. The international student travel policies handled by STA or other student travel organisations are usually good value. Some policies offer lower and higher medical expenses options but the higher one is chiefly for countries like the USA which have extremely high medical costs. Check the small print:

1. Some policies specifically exclude 'dangerous activities' which can include scuba diving, motorcycling, even trekking. If such activities are on your agenda you don't want that sort of policy.

2. You may prefer a policy which pays doctors or hospitals direct rather than you having to pay on the spot and claim later. If you have to claim later make sure you keep all documentation. Some policies ask you to call back (reverse charges) to a centre in your home country where an immediate assessment of your problem is made.

3. Check if the policy covers ambulances or an emergency flight home. If you have to stretch out you will need two seats and somebody has to pay for them!

4. Make sure that the policy you have in mind covers the Gulf. Some insurers, particularly in the USA, still consider the Gulf a danger zone and either will not cover travel there or will insist on exorbitant premiums. It pays to ask these sort of questions in advance rather than discover too late that your policy does not cover the country you are in. If you are working in the Gulf your job will almost certainly include medical coverage of some sort but be sure to find out its exact extent – it may include business trips but not holiday travel, for example.

**Medical Kit** A small, straightforward medical kit is a wise thing to carry. A possible kit list includes:

1. Aspirin or Panadol – for pain or fever.
2. Antihistamine (such as Benadryl) – useful as a decongestant for colds, allergies, to ease the itch from insect bites or stings or to help prevent motion sickness.
3. Antibiotics – useful if you're travelling well off the beaten track, but they must be prescribed and you should carry the prescription with you.
4. Kaolin preparation (Pepto-Bismol), Imodium or Lomotil – for stomach upsets.
5. Rehydration mixture – for treatment of severe diarrhoea, this is particularly important if travelling with children.
6. Antiseptic, mercurochrome and antibiotic powder or similar 'dry' spray – for cuts and grazes.

7. Calamine lotion – to ease irritation from bites or stings.

8. Bandages and Band-aids – for minor injuries.

9. Scissors, tweezers and a thermometer (note that mercury thermometers are prohibited by airlines).

10. Insect repellent, sunscreen, suntan lotion, chap stick and water purification tablets.

Ideally antibiotics should be administered only under medical supervision and should never be taken indiscriminately. Overuse of antibiotics can weaken your body's ability to deal with infections naturally and can reduce the drug's efficacy on a future occasion. Take only the recommended dose at the prescribed intervals and continue using the antibiotic for the prescribed period, even if the illness seems to be cured earlier. Antibiotics are quite specific to the infections they can treat, stop immediately if there are any serious reactions and don't use it at all if you are unsure if you have the correct one.

In many countries if a medicine is available at all it will generally be available over the counter and the price will be much cheaper than in the West. However, be careful of buying drugs in developing countries, particularly where the expiry date may have passed or correct storage conditions may not have been followed. It's possible that drugs which are no longer recommended, or have even been banned, in the West are still be being dispensed in many Third World countries.

**Health Preparations** Make sure you're healthy before you start travelling. If you are embarking on a long trip make sure your teeth are OK; there are lots of places where a visit to the dentist would be the last thing you'd want to do.

If you wear glasses take a spare pair and your prescription. Losing your glasses can be a real problem, although in many places you can get new spectacles made up quickly, cheaply and competently.

If you require a particular medication take an adequate supply, as it may not be available locally. Take the prescription, with the generic rather than the brand name (which may not be locally available), as it will make getting replacements easier. It's a wise idea to have the prescription with you to show you legally use the medication – it's surprising how often over-the-counter drugs from one place are illegal without a prescription or even banned in another. If you are travelling to Saudi Arabia it is particularly important that you do this as the Saudis are very strict on the import of prescription drugs. Consult someone at a Saudi embassy beforehand though be warned that this can be a rather frustrating experience.

**Immunisations** Vaccinations provide protection against diseases you might meet along the way. None of the Gulf countries require particular vaccinations unless you are arriving from an infected area. In practice this means an area infected with yellow fever and/or cholera, though Saudi Arabia sometimes requires people arriving in the country by sea to submit to meningitis jabs (even if you can show that you've already had them). Otherwise no particular immunisations are necessary for travel in the Gulf though precautions are always in order, particularly if you are planning to venture far off the beaten track. All vaccinations should be recorded on an International Health Certificate, which is available from your physician or government health department.

Plan ahead for getting your vaccinations: some of them require an initial shot followed by a booster, while some vaccinations should not be given together. Most travellers from Western countries will have been immunised against various diseases during childhood but your doctor may still recommend booster shots against measles or polio. These diseases are now very rare in the Gulf but they do still occur (usually in remote areas, very rarely in the cities). The period of protection offered by vaccinations differs widely and some are contraindicated if you are pregnant.

In some countries immunisations are available from airport or government health centres. Travel agents or airline offices will tell you where. The possible list of vaccinations includes:

*Cholera* Some countries may require cholera vaccination if you are coming from an infected area, but protection is not very effective, only lasts six months and is contraindicated for pregnancy.

*Tetanus & Diptheria* Boosters are necessary every 10 years and protection is highly recommended.

*Typhoid* Protection lasts for three years and is useful if you are travelling for long in rural, tropical areas. You may get some side effects such as pain at the injection site, fever, headache and a general unwell feeling.

*Infectious Hepatitis* Gamma globulin is not a vaccination but a ready-made antibody which has proven very successful in reducing the chances of hepatitis infection. Because it may interfere with the development of immunity, it should not be given until at least 10 days after administration of the last vaccine needed; it should also be given as close as possible to departure because of its relatively short-lived protection period of six months.

*Yellow Fever* Protection lasts 10 years and is recommended where the disease is endemic, chiefly in Africa and South America. You usually have to go to a special yellow fever vaccination centre. Vaccination is contraindicated during pregnancy but if you must travel to a high-risk area it is probably advisable.

### Basic Rules

Care in what you eat and drink is the most important health rule; stomach upsets are the most likely travel health problem but the majority of these upsets will be relatively minor. Don't become paranoid; trying the local food is part of the experience of travel after all.

**Water** The number one rule is *don't drink the water* and that includes ice. If you don't know for certain that the water is safe always assume the worst. The quality of tap water varies widely in the Gulf. In Oman it is

absolutely OK, but in Bahrain it is absolutely off limits. The Health section of each individual country gives a general idea of the quality of the local tap water but be warned that it varies from place to place within each country – particularly in Saudi Arabia. Reputable brands of bottled water or soft drinks are generally fine though you should make sure that the seal on your bottle of mineral water has not been broken. Take care with fruit juice, particularly if water may have been added. Dairy products in the Gulf are generally manufactured to Western standards, though in more remote places you might want to check the 'use by' date and see whether the products are pasteurised and have been stored properly. Boiled milk is fine if it is kept hygienically and yoghurt is always good. Tea or coffee should also be OK since the water should have been boiled.

**Water Purification** The simplest way of purifying water is to boil it thoroughly. Technically this means boiling for 10 minutes, something which happens very rarely! Remember that at high altitude water boils at lower temperature, so germs are less likely to be killed.

Simple filtering will not remove all dangerous organisms, so if you cannot boil water it should be treated chemically. Chlorine tablets (Puritabs, Steritabs or other brand names) will kill many but not all pathogens. Iodine is very effective in purifying water and is available in tablet form (such as Potable Aqua), but follow the directions carefully and remember that too much iodine can be harmful.

If you can't find tablets, tincture of iodine (2%) or iodine crystals can be used. Two drops of tincture of iodine per litre or quart of clear water is the recommended dosage; the treated water should be left to stand for 30 minutes before drinking. Iodine crystals can also be used to purify water but this is a more complicated process, as you have to first prepare a saturated iodine solution. Iodine loses its effectiveness if exposed to air or damp so keep it in a tightly sealed container. Flavoured powder will disguise the taste of treated water and is a good idea if you are travelling with children.

**Food** Salads and fruit should be washed with purified water or peeled where possible. Ice cream is usually OK if it is a reputable brand name, but beware of ice cream that has melted and been refrozen. Thoroughly cooked food is safest but not if it has been left to cool or if it has been reheated. Take great care with shellfish or fish and avoid undercooked meat. If a place looks clean and well run and if the vendor also looks clean and healthy, then the food is probably safe. In general, places that are packed with travellers or locals will be fine, while empty restaurants are questionable.

**Nutrition** If your food is poor or limited in availability, if you're travelling hard and fast and therefore missing meals, or if you simply lose your appetite, you can soon start to lose weight and place your health at risk.

Make sure your diet is well balanced. Eggs, tofu, beans, lenils and nuts are all safe ways to get protein. Fruit you can peel (eg bananas, oranges or mandarins) is always safe and a good source of vitamins. Try to eat plenty of grains (rice) and bread. Remember that although food is generally safer if it is cooked well, overcooked food loses much of its nutritional value. If your diet isn't well balanced or if your food intake is insufficient, it's a good idea to take vitamin and iron pills.

In hot climates make sure you drink enough – don't rely on feeling thirsty to indicate when you should drink. Not needing to urinate or very dark yellow urine is a danger sign. Always carry a water bottle with you on long trips. Excessive sweating can lead to loss of salt and therefore muscle cramping. Salt tablets are not a good idea as a preventative, but in places where salt is not used much adding salt to food can help.

**Everyday Health** A normal body temperature is 98.6°F or 37°C; more than 2°C higher is a 'high' fever. A normal adult pulse rate is 60 to 80 per minute (children 80 to 100, babies 100 to 140). You should know how to take a temperature and a pulse rate. As a general rule the pulse increases about 20 beats per minute for each °C rise in fever.

Respiration(breathing) rate is also an indicator of illness. Count the number of breaths per minute: between 12 and 20 is normal for adults and older children (up to 30 for younger children, 40 for babies). People with a high fever or serious respiratory illness (like pneumonia) breathe more quickly than normal. More than 40 shallow breaths a minute usually means pneumonia.

Many health problems can be avoided by taking care of yourself. Wash your hands frequently – it's quite easy to contaminate your own food. Clean your teeth with purified water rather than straight from the tap. Avoid climatic extremes: keep out of the sun when it's hot, dress warmly when it's cold. Unfortunately, life in the Gulf often involves walking through truly ferocious heat between heavily air-conditioned buildings or cars. This is not good for you but, like the air-conditioner colds from which every other person in the Gulf often seems to be suffering, there is little you can do about it.

Some potential diseases, however, can be avoided by dressing sensibly. You can get worm infections through walking barefoot or dangerous coral cuts by walking over coral without shoes. You can avoid insect bites by covering bare skin when insects are around, by screening windows or beds or by using insect repellents. Seek local advice: if you're told the water is unsafe due to jellyfish (and this is often a problem in both the Gulf and the Red Sea) don't go in. In situations where there is no information, discretion is the better part of valour.

## Medical Problems & Treatment

Potential medical problems can be broken down into several areas. First there are the climatic and geographical considerations – problems caused by extremes of temperature, altitude or motion. Then there are diseases and illnesses caused by insanitation, insect bites or stings, and animal or human contact. Simple cuts, bites or scratches can also cause problems.

Self-diagnosis and treatment can be risky, so wherever possible seek qualified help. Although we do give treatment dosages in this section, they are for emergency use only. Medical advice should be sought before administering any drugs.

An embassy or consulate can usually recommend a good place to go for such advice. So can five-star hotels, although they often recommend doctors with five-star prices. (This is when that medical insurance really comes in useful!) You can, however, take some comfort from the fact that the standard of medical care throughout the Gulf is among the highest in the world.

**Climatic & Geographical Considerations**
**Sunburn** It should hardly need saying that this is a potential problem in the Gulf. In the desert or at high altitude you can get sunburnt surprisingly quickly, even through cloud. Use a sunscreen and take extra care to cover areas which don't normally see the sun – eg, your feet. A hat provides added protection and in the Gulf can be considered a necessity. You should also use zinc cream or some other barrier cream for your nose and lips. Calamine lotion is good for mild sunburn.

**Prickly Heat** Prickly heat is an itchy rash caused by excessive perspiration trapped under the skin. It usually strikes people who have just arrived in a hot climate and whose pores have not yet opened sufficiently to cope with greater sweating. Keeping cool but bathing often, using a mild talcum powder or even resorting to air-conditioning may help until you acclimatise.

**Heat Exhaustion** Dehydration or salt deficiency can cause heat exhaustion. However, life in the Gulf is now so universally air-conditioned that this is less of a problem than you might think. Still, it pays to take time to acclimatise to high temperatures and make sure you get sufficient liquids. Salt deficiency is characterised by fatigue, lethargy, headaches, giddiness and muscle cramps and

in this case salt tablets may help. Vomiting or diarrhoea can deplete your liquid and salt levels. Anhydrotic heat exhaustion, caused by an inability to sweat, is quite rare. Unlike the other forms of heat exhaustion it is likely to strike people who have been in a hot climate for some time, rather than newcomers.

**Heat Stroke** This serious, sometimes fatal, condition can occur if the body's heat-regulating mechanism breaks down and the body temperature rises to dangerous levels. Long, continuous periods of exposure to high temperatures can leave you vulnerable to heat stroke. You should avoid excessive alcohol or strenuous activity when you first arrive in a hot climate.

The symptoms are feeling unwell, not sweating very much or at all and a high body temperature (39°C to 41°C). Where sweating has ceased the skin becomes flushed and red. Severe, throbbing headaches and lack of coordination will also occur, and the sufferer may be confused or aggressive. Eventually the victim will become delirious or convulse. Hospitalisation is essential, but meanwhile get patients out of the sun, remove their clothing, cover them with a wet sheet or towel and then fan continually.

**Fungal Infections** Hot weather fungal infections are most likely to occur on the scalp, between the toes or fingers (athlete's foot), in the groin (jock itch or crotch rot) and on the body (ringworm). You get ringworm (which is a fungal infection, not a worm) from infected animals or by walking on damp areas, like shower floors.

To prevent fungal infections wear loose, comfortable clothes, avoid artificial fibres, wash frequently and dry carefully. If you do get an infection, wash the infected area daily with a disinfectant or medicated soap and water, and rinse and dry well. Apply an anti-fungal powder like the widely available Tinaderm. Try to expose the infected area to air or sunlight as much as possible and wash all towels and underwear in hot water as well as changing them often.

**Motion Sickness** Eating lightly before and during a trip will reduce the chances of motion sickness. If you are prone to motion sickness try to find a place that minimises disturbance – near the wing on aircraft, close to midships on boats, near the centre on buses. Fresh air usually helps; reading or cigarette smoke doesn't. Commercial anti-motion-sickness preparations, which can cause drowsiness, have to be taken before the trip commences; when you're feeling sick it's too late. Ginger is a natural preventative and is available in capsule form.

## Diseases of Insanitation
**Diarrhoea** A change of water, food or climate can all cause the runs; diarrhoea caused by contaminated food or water is more serious. Despite all your precautions you may still have a bout of mild travellers' diarrhoea but a few rushed toilet trips with no other symptoms is not indicative of a serious problem. Moderate diarrhoea, involving half-a-dozen loose movements in a day, is more of a nuisance. Dehydration is the main danger with any diarrhoea, particularly for children, so fluid replenishment is the number one treatment. Weak black tea with a little sugar, soda water, or soft drinks allowed to go flat and diluted 50% with water are all good. With severe diarrhoea a rehydrating solution is necessary to replace minerals and salts. You should stick to a bland diet as you recover.

Lomotil or Imodium can be used to bring relief from the symptoms, although they do not actually cure the problem. Only use these drugs if absolutely necessary – eg, if you *must* travel. For children Imodium is preferable, but do not use these drugs if the patient has a high fever or is severely dehydrated.

Antibiotics can be very useful in treating severe diarrhoea especially if it is accompanied by nausea, vomiting, stomach cramps or mild fever. Ampicillin, a broad-spectrum penicillin, is usually recommended. Two capsules of 250 mg each taken four times a day is the recommended dose for an adult. Children aged between eight and 12 years should have half the adult dose; younger children should have half a capsule four times a day. Note that if the patient is allergic to penicillin ampicillin should not be administered.

Three days of treatment should be sufficient and an improvement should occur within 24 hours.

**Giardia** This intestinal parasite is present in contaminated water. The symptoms are stomach cramps, nausea, a bloated stomach, watery, foul-smelling diarrhoea and frequent gas. Giardia can appear several weeks after you have been exposed to the parasite. The symptoms may disappear for a few days and then return; this can go on for several weeks. Metronidazole known as Flagyl is the recommended drug, but it should only be taken under medical supervision. Antibiotics are of no use.

**Dysentery** Dysentery is not generally a problem in the Gulf, but should you come down with it, it should be treated seriously. It is caused by contaminated food or water and is characterised by severe diarrhoea, often with blood or mucus in the stool. There are two kinds of dysentery. Bacillary dysentery is characterised by a high fever and rapid development; headache, vomiting and stomach pains are also symptoms. It generally does not last longer than a week, but it is highly contagious.

Amoebic dysentery is more gradual in developing, has no fever or vomiting but is a more serious illness. It is not a self-limiting disease: it will persist until treated and can recur and cause long-term damage.

A stool test is necessary to diagnose which kind of dysentery you have, so you should seek medical help urgently. In case of an emergency, note that tetracycline is the prescribed treatment for bacillary dysentery, metronidazole for amoebic dysentery.

With tetracycline, the recommended adult dosage is one 250 mg capsule four times a day. Children aged between eight and 12 years should have half the adult dose; the dosage for younger children is one-third the adult dose. It's important to remember that tetracycline should be given to young children only if it's absolutely necessary and only for a short period; pregnant women should not take it after the fourth month of pregnancy.

With metronidazole, the recommended adult dosage is one 750 mg to 800 mg capsule three times daily for five days. Children aged between eight and 12 years should have half the adult dose; the dosage for younger children is one-third the adult dose.

**Cholera** Cholera is another disease which is now quite rare in the Gulf. Cholera vaccination is not very effective. The disease is characterised by a sudden onset of acute diarrhoea with 'rice water' stools, vomiting, muscular cramps, and extreme weakness. You need medical help – but treat for dehydration, which can be extreme, and if there is an appreciable delay in getting to hospital then begin taking tetracycline. See the Dysentery section for dosages and warnings.

**Viral Gastroenteritis** This is caused not by bacteria but, as the name suggests, by a virus. It is characterised by stomach cramps, diarrhoea, and sometimes by vomiting and/or a slight fever. All you can do is rest and drink lots of fluids.

**Hepatitis** Again, this is no longer common in the Gulf but it is not unheard of. It *is* common in a number of popular holiday destinations for Gulf-based expats: Egypt, Kenya and India, for example.

Hepatitis A is the more common form of this disease and is spread by contaminated food or water. The first symptoms are fever, chills, headache, fatigue, feelings of weakness and aches and pains. This is followed by loss of appetite, nausea, vomiting, abdominal pain, dark urine, light-coloured faeces and jaundiced skin; the whites of the eyes may also turn yellow. In some cases there may just be a feeling of being unwell or tired, accompanied by loss of appetite, aches and pains and the jaundiced effect. You should seek medical advice, but in general there is not much you can do apart from

resting, drinking lots of fluids, eating lightly and avoiding fatty foods. People who have had hepatitis must forego alcohol for six months after the illness, as hepatitis attacks the liver and it needs that amount of time to recover.

Hepatitis B, which used to be called serum hepatitis, is spread through sexual contact or through skin penetration – it can be transmitted via dirty needles or blood transfusions, for instance. Avoid having your ears pierced or injections where you have doubts about the sanitary conditions. The symptoms and treatment of type B are much the same as for type A, but gamma globulin as a prophylactic is effective against type A only.

**Typhoid** Typhoid fever, rare in the Gulf, is another gut infection that travels the fecal-oral route – ie, contaminated water and food are responsible. Vaccination against typhoid is not totally effective and it is one of the most dangerous infections, so medical help must be sought.

In its early stages typhoid resembles many other illnesses: sufferers may feel like they have a bad cold or flu on the way, as early symptoms are a headache, a sore throat, and a fever which rises a little each day until it is around 40°C or more. The victim's pulse is often slow relative to the degree of fever present and gets slower as the fever rises – unlike a normal fever where the pulse increases. There may also be vomiting, diarrhoea or constipation.

In the second week the high fever and slow pulse continue and a few pink spots may appear on the body; trembling, delirium, weakness, weight loss and dehydration are other symptoms. If there are no further complications, the fever and other symptoms will slowly go during the third week. However you must get medical help before this because pneumonia (acute infection of the lungs) or peritonitis (burst appendix) are common complications, and because typhoid is very infectious.

The fever should be treated by keeping the victim cool and dehydration should also be watched for. Chloramphenicol is the recommended antibiotic but there are fewer side effects with ampicillin. The adult dosage is two 250 mg capsules, four times a day. Children aged between eight and 12 years should have half the adult dose; younger children should have one-third the adult dose.

Patients who are allergic to penicillin should not be given ampicillin.

**Diseases Spread by People & Animals**
**Tetanus** Tetanus can strike you down just about anywhere in the world. It is potentially fatal and difficult to treat but is preventable with immunisation. Tetanus occurs when a wound becomes infected by a germ which lives in the faeces of animals or people, so clean all cuts, punctures or animal bites. Tetanus is known as lockjaw, and the first symptom may be discomfort in swallowing, or stiffening of the jaw and neck; this is followed by painful convulsions of the jaw and whole body.

**Rabies** Rabies is found in many countries and is caused by a bite or scratch by an infected animal. Dogs are a noted carrier, though there aren't a lot of dogs in most Gulf countries in keeping with the Muslim belief that the dog is an unclean animal. Any bite, scratch or even lick from a mammal should be cleaned immediately and thoroughly. Scrub with soap and running water, and then clean with an alcohol solution. If there is any possibility that the animal is infected medical help should be sought immediately. Even if the animal is not rabid all bites should be treated seriously as they can become infected or can result in tetanus. A rabies vaccination is now available and should be considered if you are in a high-risk category – eg if you intend to work with animals.

**Meningococcal Meningitis** Sub-Saharan Africa is considered the 'meningitis belt' but the disease has appeared in the Gulf several times in recent years. The most serious of these occurrences was in 1987 and appears to have originated with pilgrims who accidentally infected other pilgrims in Mecca during the hajj. Within weeks it was a problem throughout the Gulf, though not every country was willing to acknowledge it. For several years after this outbreak the Saudi authorities required everyone arriving in the country by ship to submit to meningitis jabs before disembarking at Jeddah.

This very serious disease attacks the brain and can be fatal. A scattered, blotchy rash, fever, severe headache, sensitivity to light and neck stiffness which prevents forward bending of the head are the first symptoms. Death can occur within a few hours, so immediate treatment is important.

Treatment is large doses of penicillin given intravenously, or, if that is not possible, intramuscularly (ie, in the buttocks). Vaccination offers good protection for over a year, but you should also check for reports of current epidemics.

**Tuberculosis** Although this disease is widespread in many developing countries, it is not a serious risk to travellers. Young children are more susceptible than adults and vaccination is a sensible precaution for children under 12 travelling in endemic areas. TB is commonly spread by coughing or by unpasteurised dairy products from infected cows. Milk that has been boiled is safe to drink; the souring of milk to make yoghurt or cheese also kills the bacilli.

**Diptheria** Diptheria can be a skin infection or a more dangerous throat infection. It is spread by contaminated dust contacting the skin or by the inhalation of infected cough or sneeze droplets. Frequent washing and keeping the skin dry will help prevent skin infection. A vaccination is available to prevent the throat infection.

**Sexually Transmitted Diseases** Sexual contact with an infected sexual partner spreads these diseases. While abstinence is the only 100% preventative, using condoms is also effective. Gonorrhoea and syphilis are the most common of these diseases; sores, blisters or rashes around the genitals, discharges or pain when urinating are common symptoms. Symptoms may be less marked or not observed at all in women. Syphilis symptoms eventually disappear completely but the disease continues and can cause severe problems in later years. The treatment of gonorrhoea and syphilis is by antibiotics.

There are numerous other sexually transmitted diseases, for most of which effective treatment is available. However, there is no cure for herpes and there is also currently no cure for AIDS. Using condoms is the most effective preventative.

AIDS can be spread through infected blood transfusions; blood is said to be screened for AIDS in Gulf countries, but most Gulf countries also play down the incidence of AIDS locally. It can also be spread by dirty needles – vaccinations or acupuncture can potentially be as dangerous as intravenous drug use if the equipment is not clean. If you do need an injection you should be absolutely certain that the doctor is using a clean (preferably a sterile, disposable) syringe.

### Insect-Borne Diseases

**Malaria** This serious disease is spread by mosquito bites. If you are travelling in endemic areas it is extremely important to take malarial prophylactics. Symptoms include headaches, fever, chills and sweating which may subside and recur. Without treatment malaria can develop more serious, potentially fatal effects.

Antimalarial drugs do not actually prevent the disease but suppress its symptoms. Chloroquine is the usual malarial prophylactic; a tablet is taken once a week for two weeks prior to arrival in the infected area and six weeks after you leave it. Chloroquine is quite safe for general use, side effects are minimal and it can be taken by pregnant women. Chloroquine is also used for malaria treatment but in larger doses than for prophylaxis.

Malaria has virtually been eradicated in much of the Gulf. The main area where it has continued to be a problem is southern Oman, though there were reports as this book went to press of significant outbreaks of malaria in northern Oman as well. Travellers to

Oman should contact a doctor and/or the Omani embassy in their home country for up-to-date information on the situation.

In the Saudi portion of the Tihama (ie, in Jizan) the disease is not a problem and antimalarial drugs are not necessary.

Mosquitoes appear after dusk. Avoiding bites by covering bare skin and using an insect repellent will further reduce the risk of catching malaria. Insect screens on windows and mosquito nets on beds offer protection, as does burning a mosquito coil. Mosquitoes may be attracted by perfume, aftershave or certain colours. The risk of infection is higher in rural areas and during the wet season.

### Cuts, Bites & Stings

**Cuts & Scratches** Skin punctures can easily become infected in hot climates and may be difficult to heal. Treat any cut with an antiseptic solution and mercurochrome. Where possible avoid bandages and Band-aids, which can keep wounds wet. Coral cuts are notoriously slow to heal, as the coral injects a weak venom into the wound. Avoid coral cuts by wearing shoes when walking on reefs, and clean any cut thoroughly.

**Bites & Stings** Bee and wasp stings are usually painful rather than dangerous. Calamine lotion will give relief or ice packs will reduce the pain and swelling. There are some spiders with dangerous bites but antivenenes are usually available. Scorpion stings are notoriously painful. Scorpions often shelter in shoes or clothing.

There are various fish and other sea creatures which can sting or bite dangerously – in the Gulf and Red Sea, jellyfish are the most common problem. Stings from most jellyfish are simply rather painful. Dousing in vinegar will deactivate any stingers which have not 'fired'. Calamine lotion, antihistamines and analgesics may reduce the reaction and relieve the pain.

**Snakes** To minimise your chances of being bitten always wear boots, socks and long trousers when walking through undergrowth where snakes may be present. Don't put your hands into holes and crevices, and be careful when collecting firewood.

Snake bites do not cause instantaneous death and antivenenes are usually available. Keep the victim calm and still, wrap the bitten limb tightly, as you would for a sprained ankle, and then attach a splint to immobilise it. Then seek medical help, if possible with the dead snake for identification. Don't attempt to catch the snake if there is even a remote possibility of being bitten again. Tourniquets and sucking out the poison are now comprehensively discredited.

**Bedbugs & Lice** Bedbugs live in various places, but particularly in dirty mattresses and bedding. Spots of blood on bedclothes or on the wall around the bed can be read as a suggestion to find another hotel. Bedbugs leave itchy bites in neat rows. Calamine lotion may help.

All lice cause itching and discomfort. They make themselves at home in your hair (head lice), your clothing (body lice) or in your pubic hair (crabs). You catch lice through direct contact with infected people or by sharing combs, clothing and the like. Powder or shampoo treatment will kill the lice and infected clothing should then be washed in very hot water.

**Women's Health**
**Gynaecological Problems** Poor diet, lowered resistance due to the use of antibiotics for stomach upsets and even contraceptive pills can lead to vaginal infections when travelling in hot climates. Keeping the genital area clean, and wearing skirts or loose-fitting trousers and cotton underwear will help to prevent infections.

Yeast infections, characterised by a rash, itch and discharge, can be treated with a vinegar or even lemon-juice douche or with yoghurt. Nystatin suppositories are the usual medical prescription. Trichomonas is a more serious infection; symptoms are a discharge and a burning sensation when urinating. Male sexual partners must also be treated,

and if a vinegar-water douche is not effective medical attention should be sought. Flagyl is the prescribed drug.

**Pregnancy** Most miscarriages occur during the first three months of pregnancy, so this is the most risky time to travel. The last three months should also be spent within reasonable distance of good medical care, as quite serious problems can develop at this time. Pregnant women should avoid all unnecessary medication, but vaccinations and malarial prophylactics should still be taken where possible. Additional care should be taken to prevent illness and particular attention should be paid to diet and nutrition.

**WOMEN TRAVELLERS**
Travel in the Gulf poses a special set of problems for women – especially unaccompanied women. Many imagine the situation to be much worse than it actually is. This is partly because the strictest country in the region, Saudi Arabia, is the one which receives the most publicity. Outside of Saudi Arabia women can drive cars, eat in restaurants alone or with men to whom they are not either married or related, shop in stores where men are also present, etc. Any specific restrictions on visas, travel or general movement are covered in the Women Travellers section of the individual country chapters.

Sexual harassment is a problem almost everywhere in the world. Some women say that this is less of a problem in the Gulf than in other Middle Eastern countries. Certainly the situation in the Gulf is no worse than in, say, Egypt, Tunisia or Morocco. Unaccompanied women will routinely be stared at and will often have lewd comments directed at them. They may be followed and may find strange and unwanted visitors turning up outside their hotel rooms.

A few simple rules should be followed whenever possible. Try to stay in better hotels (possibly a moot point – many bottom-end hotels in the Gulf will not rent rooms to single women), do not flirt or make eye contact with strange men, dress conservatively and do not ride in the front seat of taxi cabs. If a person or a situation is becoming troublesome head for a busy place, preferably where a lot of other foreigners and a few policemen are gathered (a shopping mall or the lobby of a big hotel, for example).

Expat women who have lived for many years in the Middle East say that the most important thing is to retain both your self-confidence and your sense of humour. Saying that you should not make eye contact with strange men is not the same as saying that you should act timid and vulnerable, and there are obviously times when a cold glare is an effective riposte to an unwanted suitor.

## ACCOMMODATION
### Camping
The Gulf's only formal camping grounds are those in Saudi Arabia's Asir National Park. It is also possible to camp out in the desert in some of the Gulf countries (see the individual country chapters).

### Hostels
Bahrain, Qatar, Saudi Arabia and the UAE all have youth hostels. All these countries are IYHF members and hostel cards are required (though sheet sleeping sacks are not).

### Hotels
There are very few truly horrible hotels in the Gulf. Even in the cheapest places it is rare to find rooms which are not air-conditioned or that lack hot water. Mini-fridges and other extras are often standard. The worst hotels listed in this book may seem quite decent if you have recently arrived from Egypt or India. The flip side of this is that no place in the Gulf is really cheap – outside the youth hostels you are going to find few beds for less than US$15 a night. Most places in the Gulf are amply supplied with mid-range (US$25 to US$50) hotels and all of the bigger cities are utterly awash in four and five-star accommodation.

## FOOD
At the turn of the century half the population of Kuwait was said to be living exclusively on dates and camel milk. The Gulf has never been known for its cuisine. Whenever you see Arab or Arabian food advertised you can safely assume that the place is offering a Lebanese menu.

Eating cheaply in the Gulf usually means either eating Western-style fast food or eating in small Indian/Pakistani restaurants. The menu at these places tends to be very limited: usually *biryani* dishes (chicken, mutton or fish cooked in a pile of mildly spiced rice) and chicken and/or mutton tikka. That's it. In Saudi Arabia, outside of the main cities the only options are usually small, Turkish-run places offering only kebabs and/or chicken with rice. In some places it is possible to get quite cheap Oriental food, Thai and Filipino being the most common.

Street food consists mainly of *shawarma*, which is lamb or chicken carved from a huge rotating spit and served in pita bread, often with lettuce, tomatoes or potatoes. In many places you can also find *foul* (pronounced 'fool'), a paste made from fava beans, and *ta'amiya* (or falafel), a mixture of beans deep-fried into a small patty.

For those with more money to spend almost anything from fish & chips to burritos to sushi is available in the larger cities.

## DRINKS
Again, there are practically no indigenous or traditional Arabian drinks, though if you want to try camel's milk you can often find it in supermarkets. Western soft drinks, mineral water and fruit juice are the standard fare. In small Indian/Pakistani restaurants, however, tap water may well be the only liquid available.

For religious reasons there are no local alcoholic drinks either. Where alcohol is available it has been imported from the West.

# Getting There & Away

There are often many more travel agents in the Gulf than the local market can support and their staffs are often of, at best, marginal competence. The problem is the high degree of turnover among the people who staff most of the agencies (which is why I have not recommended any particular travel agencies). Combine this with the fact that most of the agencies make their money from high-volume corporate clients and have little time for people walking in off the street and you can understand why shopping for plane tickets in the Gulf can be a life-shortening experience.

In any Gulf city your best bet is to ask around. If you shop around for tickets expect to get similar prices everywhere – they are usually controlled by the local government. Shopping around will probably save you some, but not a lot of, money.

## AIR

All of the main cities in the Gulf have excellent air links with Europe, India, Pakistan and the Far East. The Gulf, however, is still seen by the travel industry primarily as a business destination and, as such, there are very few discount airfares available. Your best bet for cheap plane tickets to or from the Gulf will be to buy them in countries like Egypt, India and Pakistan, which send masses of workers to the region.

The cheapest way to visit the Gulf is often to stop over there when travelling between Europe and Asia, or to include it in a Round-the-World ticket. It is also possible to stop over in a Gulf capital at little or no extra cost when travelling to another Gulf city. Otherwise, there are very few special fares to the area (for details see the Getting There & Away sections in the individual countries).

Note that over the next few years this may change. At this writing a handful of charter flights were arriving each week in Oman and the United Arab Emirates (usually Sharjah). If tourism picks up in these countries and in Bahrain it may soon become much easier to make your way to the Gulf at a reasonable cost.

## LAND

It is possible to cross the desert by bus from Turkey, Syria, Jordan and Egypt (via a ferry to Jordan) to Saudi Arabia and Kuwait. See the Getting There & Away sections of the Saudi Arabia and Kuwait chapters for details.

Those wishing to continue beyond Saudi Arabia will need to cross to Dammam in the Kingdom's Eastern Province for bus connections. From Dammam, buses go directly to Bahrain and Abu Dhabi. To travel onward to Oman from the UAE you need to go by service taxi from Abu Dhabi to Dubai where you can catch a bus to Muscat. To go to Qatar from Dammam you'll have to catch a bus to Hofuf and from there a private taxi to Doha.

## SEA

There are ferries from Egypt, Jordan and Sudan to Jeddah. See the Saudi Arabia chapter for more details.

There are also boats from Iran to Bahrain and the UAE. For more details see the Getting There & Away sections of those two countries.

## TOURS

There are Bahrain stopover packages (sold through the airlines) and package holidays in the UAE and Oman. There are plans for tour packages encompassing several Gulf states, but at the time of writing none had been organised.

# Getting Around

Although the Gulf is a relatively small area the visa regulations of the region's various countries often make air the only practical way for anyone other than Gulf Cooperation Council nationals to travel. Qatar and the United Arab Emirates, for example, issue virtually all visas for business travellers and tourists at the airport only. Most Omani visas are now issued at Muscat airport though this may change as the country becomes more accustomed to tourism and visas are issued at Omani embassies more often.

This is not to say that overland travel in the Gulf is impossible. There are buses between Dubai and Muscat and from eastern Saudi Arabia to Bahrain and Abu Dhabi. The problem is getting a visa which allows you to make the crossing.

For example, Saudi Arabian visas must be obtained in advance. Once you have the visa you can enter the country by whatever means you choose. But UAE visas are almost always issued for pick-up at an airport. Thus, if you can get a Saudi visa (no mean feat), taking the bus from Abu Dhabi to Dammam is easy. If, however, you are in Saudi Arabia and want to go to Abu Dhabi, the situation is much more complicated. UAE visas are not usually issued through UAE embassies. Instead, a hotel sponsors your visa and deposits it at one of the country's international airports (Abu Dhabi, Dubai, Sharjah, Ras Al-Khaimah or Fujairah). This system makes no allowances for people travelling by bus, so you'll probably have to fly. Much the same can be said for travel in either direction between Dubai and Muscat.

This system of airport-issued visas also means that hitching across borders with long-distance trucks is not an option.

The main exception to this rule is Bahrain, which issues tourist and business visas on the Saudi-Bahrain causeway.

Crossing borders by land is easier with your own vehicle; it simply involves filling out lots of papers at lots of embassies to get your carnet validated. For more details refer to the individual country chapters.

## AIR

In addition to the region's six capitals (Riyadh, Kuwait City, Bahrain, Doha, Abu Dhabi and Muscat), there are international regional flights to Jeddah and Dhahran in Saudi Arabia and to Dubai, Sharjah, Ras Al-Khaimah and Fujairah in the UAE. For costs see the fares table in the individual country chapters.

## BUS

There are three regional bus routes in the Gulf: Saudi Arabia (Dammam/Al-Khobar) to Bahrain (Manama), Saudi Arabia to the UAE (Abu Dhabi) and the UAE (Dubai) to Oman (Muscat).

The Saudi Arabia to Bahrain route offers five daily departures and, as long as you have organised your Saudi visa in advance, is straightforward.

Travel to Abu Dhabi overland is a problem because there is nowhere to pick up your UAE visa. However, going from Abu Dhabi to Dammam is not a problem once you have a Saudi visa.

Travelling to Dubai from Muscat poses the same visa problem as travelling to Abu Dhabi from Dammam. Going in the other direction should not be a problem if, as is sometimes possible, you can get an Omani visa from an Omani embassy instead of picking it up at the airport. If you do obtain such a visa make sure it is not stamped 'Not valid for entry by road'. Look at the very bottom of the visa.

If you have an Omani visa which allows you to cross by land it is also possible to travel between Muscat and Abu Dhabi by crossing the border at Al-Ain/Buraimi and taking a domestic bus from Buraimi to Muscat or from Al-Ain to Abu Dhabi. Doing this in either direction you will clear customs in Oman about 12 km from Buraimi. In the

## Wadi Bashing

'Wadi bashing' is expat-speak for zooming around the desert in a 4WD vehicle with stops for food and merriment. It is usually a day activity, though many also camp out, especially in Saudi Arabia and Oman. Wadi bashing is a great way to see some spectacular scenery and get away from the rather sterile atmosphere of many of the Gulf's cities. That said, it can also be dangerous. Never head out into the desert without a first aid kit, extra food and fuel, a spare tyre (or two) and an idea of where you are going. You should also let someone who is staying behind know where you are going and when you are expected back. It goes without saying that you should not just hop into a Land Rover and head off on your own if you have no experience at this sort of thing. Anyone planning an overnight trip in the desert should pick up *Staying Alive in the Desert* by K E M Melville (Roger Lascelles, London, 2nd edition 1981). ■

---

Al-Ain/Buraimi oasis itself there is no customs check at the border nor is there any other check on the UAE side.

### CAR

Most of the main roads in the Gulf are high-quality two or four-lane highways. Very few roads are unpaved and 4WDs are only necessary for driving around the desert or other 'off-road' activities.

That said, even though it does not rain often in the Gulf, avoid driving when it does rain, as few of the region's city streets have proper drainage with the result that they often turn into rivers.

### HITCHING

Hitching is legal throughout the Gulf and in some places it is extremely common. If, however, you are a White person bear in mind that trying to hitchhike may attract the attentions of the police. This is because

hitching throughout the region tends to be the preserve of Gulf Arabs and people from Asia. A White person hitching would be regarded as unusual, and therefore suspicious, by police.

The most common way of signalling that you want a ride is to extend your right hand, palm down. Drivers will usually expect you to pay the equivalent bus or service-taxi fare, though you should be sure of whether, and how much, money is expected before you get in.

### TOURS

Tour companies in the UAE and Oman run professional desert safaris. They range from simple dinner excursions which include a barbecue dinner in the desert followed by local music and dancing, to several nights camping out in the desert and visiting sites around the country.

# Bahrain

The only island-state in the Arab world, this tiny country (about the size of Singapore but with a fraction of its population) is unique in several ways. Gulf Arabs and expats mix more easily here than anywhere else in the region. Altough Bahrain comprises about 33 islands the country is often referred to simply as 'the island'. Bahrain has a relaxed self-confidence about it which shows in, among other things, its active promotion of tourism. It is the easiest of the Gulf countries to visit, and one of the best values for those on a budget.

But while Bahrain is certainly one of the most liberal countries in the Gulf it remains, by Western standards, a very conservative place. In comparison to other Arab countries it is less open than Egypt, Jordan or Tunisia, and it certainly does not share those countries' long experience with tourism. Bahrain is a good introduction to the Gulf, though those making their first trip to an Arab country should still be prepared for more than a little culture shock.

In Arabic, *bahrain* means 'two seas'. It is an appropriate designation. Since the dawn of history Bahrain has been a trading centre and until about a generation ago virtually all trade came and went via the sea. Occupying a strategic position on the great trade routes of antiquity, with good harbours and abundant fresh water, the Bahrainis are natural traders. And they have a reputation for being the hardest bargainers in the region.

---

# Facts about the Country

## HISTORY

The island's position has proved to be both a blessing and a curse. It has made Bahrain an outward-looking place and the Bahrainis an open-minded people. It has also meant a lot of other people have been interested in Bahrain. At one time or another Sumerians, Greeks, Persians, Portuguese, Turks, Wahhabis, Omanis and, of course, the British have all taken an interest in the island.

### Dilmun

Bahrain's history goes back to the roots of human civilisation. The main island is thought to have broken away from the Arabian mainland sometime around 6000 BC and it has almost certainly been inhabited since prehistoric times.

The Bahrain islands first emerged into world history in the 3rd millennium BC as the seat of what became one of the great trading empires of the ancient world. This was Dilmun, a civilisation founded during the Bronze Age and which continued in some form or other for more than 2000 years. Dilmun evolved here because of the islands' strategic position along the trade routes linking Mesopotamia with the Indus Valley.

What we now call the Middle East had a much more temperate climate 4500 years ago than it does today. But even then the land was becoming increasingly arid and Dilmun, with its lush, spring-fed greenery, became known as a holy island in the mythology of Sumeria, the area of what is now southern

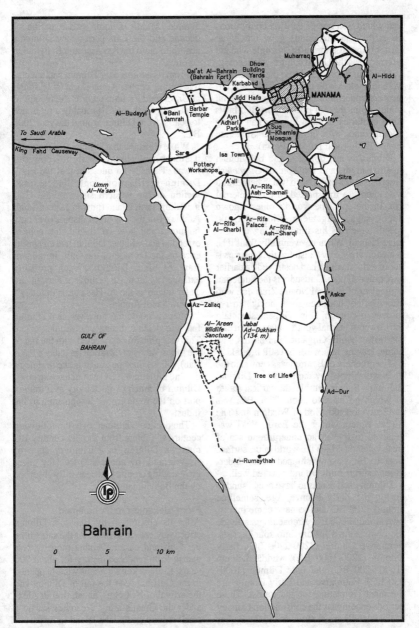

Bahrain

0    5    10 km

Iraq which was one of the first civilisations on earth. The Sumerians grew out of an earlier (4th millennium BC) people who are referred to as the Ubaid culture. Archaeological finds in Bahrain indicate that the islands were in contact with the Ubaids. Those contacts continued after the founding of Dilmun, sometime in the 3rd millennium BC. In its early centuries Dilmun already had strong trading links with the powerful Sumerian city of Eridu (near modern Basra).

Dilmun is mentioned in the Babylonian creation myth, and the *Epic of Gilgamesh* describes it as a paradise to which heroes and wise men are transported to enjoy eternal life. In the epic, the world's oldest known poetic saga, Gilgamesh, King of Uruk, spends much of his time seeking out this sacred island. When he eventually finds it he is met on arrival by Ziusudra, the lone survivor of a flood which had destroyed an earlier generation of men. (Ziusudra is the Sumerian equivalent of Biblical Noah.) Ziusudra, who after the flood had been given the right to live forever in Dilmun, helps Gilgamesh obtain the flower of eternal youth, but a serpent eats the flower while Gilgamesh is on his way home, leaving him wiser but still mortal.

The greenery of Bahrain was central to the gods worshipped by the people of Dilmun. Bahrain's Barbar Temple, the earliest stages of which go back to about 2250 BC, was dedicated to Enki, God of Wisdom and The Sweet Waters Under the Earth. Enki was believed to live in an underground sea of fresh water on which the world of the surface floated. He was worshipped at an underground shrine built around a sacred well.

Dilmun itself seems to have been founded during the Early Bronze Age, sometime around 3200 BC, and to have come into its own around 2800 BC. Archaeologists divide the civilisation's history into four periods: Formative Dilmun (3200-2200 BC), Early Dilmun (2200-1600 BC), Middle Dilmun (1600-1000 BC) and Late Dilmun (1000-330 BC). Formative and Early Dilmun are the most interesting for the tourist. These periods encompass the construction of many of the island's grave mounds and the Barbar

Temple. Middle Dilmun was a period of decline and the Late period saw Dilmun's absorption into the Assyrian and Babylonian empires.

From its earliest days Dilmun was a lucrative trading centre. A cuneiform tablet found at Ur, in modern Iraq, records the receipt of 'a parcel of fish eyes' (probably a reference to pearls) from Dilmun around the year 2000 BC.

While we know that Dilmun was powerful it is much harder to say exactly how powerful it was. There is no question that the Early Dilmun civilisation controlled a large section of the western shore of the Gulf including Tarut Island (now in eastern Saudi Arabia). But there is much dispute over how far north and how far inland that control extended and whether Dilmun had any influence on the far side of the Gulf, in modern Iran. At times Dilmun's reach probably extended as far north as modern Kuwait and as far inland as the Al-Hasa oasis in today's eastern Saudi Arabia.

There is no doubt, however, that Dilmun fell into decline during the Middle period. This was probably connected with the fall of the Indus Valley civilisation (in today's Pakistan), whose disappearance in the middle of the 2nd millennium BC would have stripped Dilmun of much of its activity as a trading port on the route from Mesopotamia to the Indus.

The decline continued over the following centuries. Tablets from the 8th century BC mention Dilmun as a tributary state of Assyria and, by about 600 BC, the once-great trading empire had been fully absorbed by the Babylonians.

### From Alexander to Mohammed
After its absorption by Babylon, Dilmun effectively ceased to exist. At the same time the Gulf and eastern Arabia more or less vanish from recorded history for about 200 years. Little is known about what happened in the Gulf between the fall of Dilmun and the arrival of Nearchus, an admiral in Alexander the Great's army. Nearchus set up a small colony on Failaka Island (now part of

Kuwait) in the late 4th century BC and is known to have explored the Gulf at least as far south as Bahrain. From the time of Nearchus until the coming of Islam in the 7th century AD Bahrain was generally known by its Greek name of Tylos.

The period from about 300 BC to 300 AD appears to have been reasonably prosperous. Pliny, writing in the 1st century AD, noted that Tylos was famous for its pearls. However, few ruins remain from this period. The Bahrain islands seem to have fallen under the sway of the Seleucid empire, one of the three principal successor states into which Alexander's realm broke up after his death in 323 BC. The Seleucids controlled the swath of land running from modern Israel and Lebanon through Mesopotamia to Persia. Bahrain lay on the outermost edge of this area and may or may not actually have been run by the Seleucids.

The Seleucid empire, however, was relatively short-lived. Its successor, in what had been the eastern part of the Seleucid lands, was the Parthian empire. The Parthians were a more explicitly Persian dynasty though they presented themselves as the protectors of Hellenic culture and Alexander's legacy. Bahrain almost certainly fell under the Parthians' sway and later drifted into the empire of the Sassanians, who succeeded the Parthians in Persia around the 3rd century AD. The Sassanians formally annexed the islands in the 4th century AD.

It was around this time, the 3rd or 4th century AD, that many of Bahrain's inhabitants appear to have adopted the new Christian faith. Exactly how many, or what percentage of the population they represented, is impossible to determine. The Sassanian empire was also a centre for Zoroastrianism and, for a time, Manicheism. Zoroastrianism became the empire's official religion in the late 3rd century AD and dissenters were officially persecuted. Though such persecution is known to have continued into the late 6th century Bahrain seems to have avoided the worst of it. It is certain that the Nestorian sect of Christianity was firmly established in Bahrain, and along much of

the Arabian side of the Gulf, by the early 5th century. Church records show that Muharraq and Manama, then known as Samahij and Tilwun respectively, were the seats of two of the five Nestorian bishoprics which existed on the Arabian side of the Gulf at the time of the coming of Islam. Muharraq also housed a Nestorian monastery. It is uncertain when the two Bahraini bishoprics were finally dissolved, though they are known to have survived until at least 835 AD.

There is also some evidence that during this period the Bahrain islands controlled at least part of the adjacent coast. Sassanian chronicles state that the king settled some of the members of a conquered tribe in Bahrain, namely in Darin. Darin is the main town of Tarut Island which lies north of Bahrain and is much closer to the Arabian mainland. It is also around this time that Bahrain island came to be known as 'Awal', a name which Bahrainis used for the main island until the early years of this century.

### The Coming of Islam

Bahrainis pride themselves on the fact that they were one of the first territories outside the Arabian mainland to accept Islam. Around 640 AD the Prophet Mohammed sent a letter to the ruler of Bahrain (possibly a Christian Arab who served as governor on behalf of the Sassanian Persians) inviting him to adopt Islam. In fairly short order the ruler did so though Christians and Muslims lived peacefully together in Bahrain for another two centuries. Even today Bahrain has a tiny community of indigenous Christians.

From the 9th to the 11th century Bahrain was part of the Umayyad and, later, Abbasid empires. Its reputation as a stronghold of Shiite Islam was firmly established under the Abbasids whose capital was Baghdad but who derived much of their culture from predominantly Shiite Persia. Though Bahrain in this period had neither the wealth nor the importance it had enjoyed some 2000 years earlier, it appears to have been reasonably prosperous and well run. It was once again on the trade routes between Mesopotamia and the Indian subcontinent. In the middle of the 12th century the great Arab/Spanish geographer Al-Idrisi described the people of Bahrain as being satisfied with their ruler, who was apparently an independent king owing nominal allegiance to the Caliph in Baghdad. Al-Idrisi referred to the Bahrainis as the people of 'the two banks', which might be a reference to Bahrain and Muharraq islands, or may indicate that Bahrain's ruler still controlled a portion of the mainland coast.

During the Middle Ages Bahrain appears to have changed hands fairly frequently, which is hardly surprising considering its position as a trading centre on the geographical fringe between two or more competing empires. In addition, the entire Gulf during this period was run by various petty sheikhs who seem to have been constantly at war with one another.

The Omanis were the next major power to take an interest in Bahrain. They conquered Bahrain and Muharraq islands around 1487

## Pearls & Pearl Diving

A report filed in 1900 by a British official in Bahrain stated that half of the island's male population was employed in the pearling industry. This is hardly surprising. Pearling had been a part of the local economy since the 3rd millennium BC. By the early 1800s, when most of the trade routes that had straddled the Gulf were ancient history, pearls and dates were virtually the only things which the region had to offer to the rest of the world.

Today pearling has come to be viewed through something of a rose-coloured mist. The fact is that pearl diving was a truly terrible way to make a living. The pearl trade made a few 19th century Arab families spectacularly rich but for just about everyone else involved it was both physically and economically brutal. One can only conclude that it survived as long as it did largely by default – there simply was no other way for most people in the Gulf to earn enough to live.

The pearling season began each year in late May when the boats would leave Bahrain and the other settlements around the Gulf for the offshore pearl banks. They remained constantly at sea until mid-October. Supplies were ferried out by dhow.

The workers were divided into divers and pullers. A diver's equipment consisted only of a nose-clip and a bag. More fortunate divers might also have had some sort of thin cotton garment which, it was hoped, would provide protection against jellyfish. Rocks were tied to the divers' feet as weights. They would leap into the water with a rope tied around their waists and usually stayed under for about a minute at depths of up to 15 metres. A tug on the rope meant it was time for the pullers to return the diver to the surface.

Neither the divers nor the pullers were paid wages. Instead they would receive shares of the total profits for the season and a puller's share was half to two-thirds that of a diver's. Boat owners would advance money to their workers at the beginning of the season. The divers often were unable to pay back these loans, got further into debt with each year and, as a result, were often bound to a particular boat owner for life. If a diver died his sons were obliged to work off his debts. It was not unusual to see quite elderly men still working as divers. British attempts in the '20s to regulate and improve the lot of the divers were resisted by the divers themselves, most of whom did not understand the complex accounting system the British had imposed. Riots and strikes became a regular feature of the pearling seasons in the late '20s and early '30s.

In addition to its own, long-established pearl trade, by the 19th century Bahrain was also serving as the main trans-shipment point for almost all the pearls produced in the Gulf. From Bahrain pearls were shipped to Bombay where they were sorted, polished and drilled. Most of them were then exported to Europe.

Around 1930 the Japanese invented a method of culturing pearls and this, combined with the Great Depression, caused the bottom to fall out of the international pearl market. Bahrain has never quite forgiven the Japanese and even now it bans the importation of cultured pearls.

The pearl merchants could all instantly tell the difference between natural and cultured pearls but most other people could not, and didn't care anyway. Today pearls are more common – and far less valuable – than they were 75 years ago. Even if someone wanted to revive the traditional pearling industry today it is doubtful that it would be economically viable. ∎

and built Arad Fort on Muharraq. This was to supplement the earlier fortifications (the ruins known today as the Islamic Fort at the Qal'at Al-Bahrain site) they had taken over on the north coast of Bahrain Island. Two years earlier the first European known to have visited the islands, a Portuguese explorer named Duarte Barbosa, had noted both the number and quality of the pearls of Bahrain (he called Bahrain, 'Barem').

## The Portuguese & the Persians

It was another 36 years before the Portuguese navy conquered the islands as part of their procession up the Gulf from Muscat and Hormuz. As one of the main pearling ports in the Gulf the islands clearly had economic value. Bahrain's ample freshwater supply and position about halfway between the Strait of Hormuz and the head of the Gulf gave it military value in the ongoing struggle for control of the area. In the first half of the 16th century Bahrain was on the front line as Portugal and the Ottoman Turks battled for control of the Gulf. The second half of the century was somewhat quieter, as the Portuguese were by then firmly in control.

In the end it was the Bahrainis themselves, not the Turks or the Omanis, who drove the Portuguese from the islands in 1602.

In that year the Portuguese governor made the critical mistake of executing the brother of one of the island's richer traders. The trader, Rukn El-Din, proceeded to lead an uprising which soon drove the Europeans from Bahrain. Rukn quickly appealed to Persia for protection, which was a shrewd political move. Aside from the need for help in case the Portuguese decided to come back and punish the Bahrainis, the Portuguese were in competition mainly with the Turks for influence in the Gulf, so appealing to Persia for help seemed less provocative. On the other hand it brought Bahrain, once again, firmly back into a Persian empire, which was where it stayed for the rest of the 17th century.

## The 18th & 19th Centuries

The Al-Khalifa, Bahrain's ruling family, first arrived in the archipelago in the mid-18th century. They came to Bahrain from Kuwait where they had helped their distant relatives, the Al-Sabah family, become the established power. The Al-Khalifa settled in Zubara, on the north-western edge of the Qatar peninsula, apparently with a mind towards getting involved in the region's lucrative pearling trade. Zubara quickly grew into a large town, the ruins of which can still be seen today.

In 1782 or 1783, Shaikh Ahmed Al-Fatih, a member of the Al-Khalifa family, drove out the Persian garrison and occupied the main islands of the Bahrain group, apparently with some help from his Al-Sabah cousins in Kuwait. Bahrain and Muharraq islands were particularly important prizes because their position off the Arabian mainland made them relatively immune to the Wahhabi raids. These raids, led by the ancestors of the present Saudi royal family, seem to have been a regular feature of life in Zubara from the late 18th century until the Ottoman suppression of the Wahhabis in 1818. Ahmed ruled until his death in 1796 when his two sons, Abdullah and Salman, took over as joint rulers. Three years later, however, the Omanis returned in force to the islands from which the Portuguese had driven them over 275 years earlier. Salman was forced to retreat to Zubara while Abdullah went into exile on the Arabian mainland.

In 1820 the brothers managed to retake the islands and a few years of relative tranquillity ensued. Shortly thereafter a treaty was signed with the British, who had by then already been present in the region, in the form of the ubiquitous East India Company, for over 200 years. This treaty, in which the Bahrainis agreed to abstain from what the British defined as piracy, became the model for similar treaties signed or imposed by the British throughout the Gulf over the next generation. Salman died in 1825 and his son Khalifa continued to rule jointly with Abdullah until 1834 when Khalifa died.

Abdullah ruled alone for a few years. It was during this period that the British began to formalise their presence in the Gulf. India was becoming an increasingly important element of the British empire and Britain saw security in the Gulf as vitally important to its trade and supply routes to the Indian subcontinent. In 1835 the rulers of Bahrain and the other sheikhdoms of the Gulf had a peace treaty more or less dictated to them by the Royal Navy. Like the earlier treaty signed with Bahrain, the purpose of this agreement was to end piracy (ie any threat to British shipping) in the region. The British also pressured the sheikhs into outlawing slavery.

But despite the best efforts of the Royal Navy, things did not stay quiet and around 1840 a string of events began which led to three turbulent decades in Bahrain. A few years after Khalifa's death his son, Mohammed Bin Khalifa, began to challenge Abdullah's authority. Eventually he set himself up in Muharraq as a co-ruler and a rival. In 1843 he conquered Zubara and deposed Abdullah, who died in exile five years later. Mohammed ruled unopposed for a few years and, in 1861, signed a Treaty of Perpetual Peace and Friendship with the British. This was the first of the so-called Exclusive Agreements, under which he (and other Gulf rulers who later signed similar documents) ceded to Britain control of foreign affairs in exchange for protection from attack. Other agreements with the British were signed in 1881 and 1891.

Mohammed Bin Khalifa was soon challenged by his cousin Mohammed Bin Abdullah (Shaikh Abdullah's son). Seeking revenge for his father's deposition, Mohammed Bin Abdullah began raiding Bahrain from a base on the mainland. In the midst of this already turbulent situation a war broke out between Bahrain and Qatar, which ended in 1868 with Mohammed Bin Khalifa fleeing to Qatar while his brother Ali proclaimed himself ruler of Bahrain.

In Qatar Mohammed Bin Khalifa built a new fleet, invaded Bahrain again and killed Ali in 1869. In this, however, he made one key mistake. He buried the hatchet with his cousin, Mohammed Bin Abdullah, and gave him a post in the reconquering force. Once they were back in control of Bahrain Mohammed Bin Abdullah, who apparently had not forgotten who deposed his father, promptly overthrew and imprisoned Mohammed Bin Khalifa.

From their base in Bushire, on the coast of present-day Iran, the British watched with, what one can only assume, a combination of annoyance and alarm. The topsy-turvy Bahraini politics of 1869 were the last straw. Soon after Mohammed Bin Abdullah's coup, the Royal Navy sailed down from Bushire, deported both of the Mohammeds to Bombay and installed Ali's 21-year-old son Isa as Emir. They also leaned on Isa (who reigned until 1932) to appoint a crown prince so as to remove any doubts about the succession. Shaikh Isa's line has ruled Bahrain ever since. The current Emir, also named Isa, is his great-grandson.

After installing Isa as Emir the British largely stayed out of local politics for the remainder of the 19th century. Their main concern was to keep the Turks, who then controlled eastern Arabia, out of the region. (This was also a concern for the sheikhs, which was one reason why they had signed those agreements in the first place.) Both Turkey and Persia continued to claim Bahrain as part of their respective empires well into the 20th century but neither was willing to challenge the British for control of the islands.

This threat to Bahrain's sovereignty from its larger neighbours continued up until 1970. After Persia became Iran, it continued to refuse to recognise Bahrain's existence as anything other than an Iranian province. Tehran threatened military action several times in the 1950s and '60s and refused entry to Iran to travellers whose passports showed evidence of travel to Bahrain. The claim was finally dropped in 1970 after Britain talked the Shah of Iran into accepting the results of a United Nations mission to the island to determine whether or not the inhabitants wanted to be part of Iran. In the wake of Iran's 1979 Islamic revolution, one of Tehran's senior clerics briefly revived the issue, but Iran's spiritual leader, Ayatollah Khomeini, disapproved and the Islamic Republic let the matter drop.

## The Discovery of Oil

Ancient texts contain the occasional reference to oil being found in natural pools, or seepages, in Bahrain. It was traditionally used to fuel lamps and to help make boats waterproof. Seepages, however, do not necessarily imply the presence of crude oil in exploitable quantities.

In 1902 a British official wrote to his superiors that he had heard stories about oil spouting from the sea bed at a point close to Bahrain's shoreline. An engineer was sent to investigate but his report was not promising. Interest among British officials revived in 1908 after oil was found in large quantities in Iran. Still, the Anglo-Persian Oil Company, which then dominated the Middle East's nascent oil industry, seemed more interested in litigation than exploration. They sought to guarantee that no one else had the opportunity to prospect for oil in Bahrain, but at the same time made no attempt to look for it themselves.

The man who spurred the search for oil, not only in Bahrain but also in eastern Saudi Arabia, was Frank Holmes, a New Zealander who had recently retired from the British Army (hence the habit of referring to him as Major Holmes). Virtually every book ever written on oil and the Gulf describes Holmes as eccentric, though few make it clear what was so eccentric about him except for his firm conviction that oil was to be found underneath Arabia. After a great deal of convoluted toing and froing, Holmes' tiny Eastern and General Syndicate was granted a concession to drill for oil in Bahrain in late 1925. The only problem was that neither Holmes nor the syndicate had the sort of money required to launch such an operation.

Holmes spent the next five years trying to round up the necessary funds. When he found a backer in Standard Oil of California (SOCAL, the precursor of today's Chevron) he was then forced to embark on another series of legal contortions. The terms of the concession agreement stipulated that it could not be assigned to any 'foreign' (meaning non-British) company. Eventually SOCAL set up a subsidiary in Canada, which was

apparently British enough to get the foreign office in London to agree, and exploration went ahead. Oil in commercial quantities was found in June 1932, the first such strike on the Arab side of the Gulf. Exports began soon afterward and a refinery opened in 1936.

The discovery of oil could not have come at a better time for Bahrain, as it roughly coincided with the collapse of the world pearl market. Until that time pearling had been the mainstay of the Bahraini economy.

Equally important was the fact that oil was discovered in Bahrain before it was discovered elsewhere in the Gulf. The Bahrainis were the first to enjoy the benefits that came from the oil revenues – notably a dramatic improvement in the quality of education and health care. This led to the island assuming a larger role in Britain's operations in the Gulf. The main British naval base in the region was moved to Bahrain in 1935. In 1946 the Political Residency, the office of the senior British official in the region, was moved from Bushire to Bahrain.

The island's oil reserves are quite small and its revenues from oil sales have never approached those of Kuwait, Saudi Arabia or the United Arab Emirates (UAE) on a per capita basis. Today Bahrain produces, by Gulf standards, only a token quantity of oil. In one sense, this has been a boon. Lacking the resources for extravagance Bahrain has proceeded into the 20th century in a reasonable, measured way. The Bahrainis were forced to think about diversifying their economy far earlier than any of the other Gulf states and this, combined with their long history as a trading nation and lengthy contact with the outside world, has proved an admirable blend of circumstances.

## The 20th Century

Shaikh Isa Bin Ali, whom the British had installed in 1869, reigned until his death in 1932. In 1923, however, the British forced him to hand over the day-to-day running of the country to his son, Hamad. Isa, who was then in his mid-70s, was notoriously conservative and opposed even modest reform or modernisation. After his father's death Hamad ruled in his own right from 1932 to 1942.

Almost immediately upon Hamad's taking power in 1923, modernisation in Bahrain took off. A decade later, when the oil money started coming in, the pace quickened. Schools, hospitals and new mosques were built, much of the country received electricity and an airport was constructed to serve as a stop on Imperial Airways' London to India route.

In addition to the discovery of oil, the years after WW I also saw another event with long-term significance for Bahrain – the arrival, in 1926, of a new British advisor to the Emir, Charles Belgrave. Described in later years by the archaeologist Geoffrey Bibby as 'tall, cool, cheroot-smoking, very, very efficient', Belgrave (who got the job, believe it or not, by answering an ad in a London newspaper!) was to remain for over 30 years. He was instrumental in setting up the island's educational system and he appears to have overseen much of Bahrain's early infrastructural development. Because he was, for a time, so powerful Bahraini officialdom tends to treat him as something of a nonperson these days.

In true empire style Bahrain declared war on the Axis powers one day after Britain in 1939. The Bahrain refinery was then one of only three in the Middle East and its continued functioning was regarded as crucial to the war effort, particularly as both Japan and Germany had been trying to gain toeholds in the Gulf during the 1930s. The war years in Bahrain were generally quiet, the main exception being a botched attempt by the Italian Air Force to bomb the oil refinery on 19 October 1940. They missed.

Shaikh Hamad died in 1942 and was succeeded as Emir by his son, Salman. Salman's 19 years on the throne saw a vast increase in the country's standard of living as oil production boomed in Saudi Arabia, Kuwait and Qatar. At that time none of these other areas could match Bahrain's level of development, health or education. As a result, though the

country's oil output was tiny compared to that of its neighbours, Bahrain was well positioned to serve as the Gulf's main entrepôt.

The 1950s were unsettled years throughout the Arab world. The rise of the Egyptian leader, Gamal Abdel Nasser, his fiery rhetoric and his assaults on the colonial privileges enjoyed by Britain and other Western countries in the Arab world, including most areas which were at least nominally independent, galvanised people throughout the Middle East. In the years immediately after WW II, wealthy Bahrainis had begun sending their sons (not, usually, their daughters) abroad to further their education. They studied in Cairo, Beirut or, for the very rich and/or well-connected, London. This new class of well-educated technocrats proved to be particularly resentful of British domination.

In 1952, reform-minded members of the country's Sunni and Shiite communities formed an eight-man Higher Executive Committee. They sought Western-style trade unions, a parliament and, more to the point, demanded that the Emir sack Belgrave. Their demands for a more open political system even received some tacit support from the British government (though not, presumably, from Belgrave). Belgrave stayed, but the Emir agreed to some of the Committee's demands – a victory which seems to have encouraged them to ask for more.

Matters came to a head in 1956. Early that year stones were thrown at the British Foreign Secretary, Selwyn Lloyd, while he was visiting Bahrain. In retaliation, several members of the Committee of National Union (the Higher Education Committee's successor) were deported. Several people were killed in anti-British riots in Bahrain in November of that year, held during the Suez crisis. The British landed troops to protect the oilfields, but at about the same time the Saudis, regarding Bahrain as too closely under Britain's thumb, cut off the supply of oil to the refinery (which even then refined significantly more Saudi oil than Bahraini oil). Not long afterwards Belgrave 'retired'. Though the Emir appointed another Briton to replace him, the crisis had passed, calm prevailed and Bahrainis went back to their first love – making money.

Shaikh Salman died in 1961 and was succeeded by his son, the present Emir, Shaikh Isa Bin Salman Al-Khalifa.

After Britain announced its intention to withdraw from the Gulf by the end of 1971, Bahrain participated in the attempts to form a federation with Qatar and the seven Trucial States (now the UAE). As the most populous and advanced of the nine emirates, Bahrain demanded greater representation on the council which was to govern the proposed federation. When the other rulers refused, Bahrain decided to go it alone and declared independence on 14 August 1971 – a decision which also prompted Qatar to pull out of the proposed federation.

A Constituent Assembly charged with drafting a constitution was elected at the end of 1972. The Emir issued the constitution in May 1973 and another election was held later that year for a National Assembly which convened in December. But the Assembly was dissolved only 20 months later when the Emir decided that radical assembly members were making it impossible for the executive branch to function. Governing is now done by Emiri decree, exercised through a cabinet. In 1975 trade unions were disbanded. Although allowed to exist under the constitution, the government had never actually sanctioned their formation. All strikes were banned as well.

Since then things have generally been quiet. During the '70s and '80s Bahrain experienced a huge degree of growth, partly from the skyrocketing price of oil but also because it was still, in the mid to late '70s, well ahead of much of the rest of the Gulf in terms of infrastructure. In recent years its status as an entrepôt has declined somewhat, but its economy has also become more diversified and less oil-dependent. In particular, since the demise of Beirut in the late '70s, the island has established itself as one of the region's main banking and finance centres. Though there were a few violent pro-Iranian demonstrations in late 1979 and early 1980 the country has been quiet since then.

Despite the economic downturn felt throughout the Gulf in the late '80s, Bahrain has remained both calm and prosperous. The country's main shipyard did a roaring trade during the mid-80s, patching up tankers that had been hit by one side or the other in the Iran-Iraq war, and the opening of the Saudi-Bahrain causeway in late 1986 gave a boost to both business and tourism.

The '90s have seen a vast improvement in Bahrain's relations with Iran and the resumption of air service between Bahrain and Tehran. Relations with Iraq have gone sharply downhill – Bahrainis will not soon forget that Iraq's Saddam Hussein ordered a Scud missile attack on their country during the Gulf War (the missile landed harmlessly in the sea). A dispute with Qatar over ownership of the Hawar Islands, of which Bahrain has de jure control, has dragged on for years and remains a diplomatic sore spot between the two countries.

In general, however, Bahrain remains relaxed and open. Politics are a sidelight and trade, as has been the case for the last 5000 years, is the mainstay of life in the Arab world's only island-state.

## GEOGRAPHY

The country is a low-lying archipelago of about 33 islands (including the disputed Hawar group) of which Bahrain Island is the largest at about 50 km long and 16 km wide. The total area of the country is 583 sq km. Jabal Ad-Dukhan, the highest point in the country at 134 metres above sea level, is in the centre of Bahrain Island. The country's population is heavily concentrated in the northern third of Bahrain Island and on the southern edge of Muharraq Island, the only one of the outlying islands to be inhabited by any significant number of people. Sitra Island has been largely given over to industry. Land reclamation on Sitra and around downtown Manama has been extensive.

Bahrain, Muharraq, Sitra and Umm Al-Na'san are the only islands in the group of any significant size. Many of the smaller islands are little more than outcrops of rock, with or without an accompanying sandbar.

White Arabian Oryx

Several have been tied to Bahrain Island or Muharraq by roads and causeways in such a way that they are now really extensions of the main islands rather than separate entities.

## CLIMATE

This is one area in which Bahrain exactly duplicates all of its neighbours. It can get extremely hot and humid from April to October with temperatures rarely dropping below 30°C at night and running up to 40°C or more during the day. November to March tends to be quite pleasant with warm days and cool (though not really cold) nights. Temperatures vary between a minimum of 14°C to a maximum of 24°C.

## FLORA & FAUNA

Bahrain has long been famous for its greenery in the midst of the region's deserts. Recently, however, this has been changing. Though parts of the island are still thickly covered in date palms, the island is a lot less green than it used to be. Some of the trees have been cut down and others have died as increasing demands are made on the underground springs which water them.

As for the fauna, aside from domesticated donkeys and camels you are not going to see many animals outside of the Al-'Areen park.

## Al-'Areen Wildlife Sanctuary

The park, a 10-sq-km area in the south-west of Bahrain Island, serves as a conservation area for endangered species indigenous to Arabia, such as the Arabian oryx, though other animals not native to Arabia (eg zebras) have been introduced as well. Access is strictly controlled and there is a limit on the number of people allowed to visit each day. Generally you have to go through the park in a government bus after parking at the entrance. See the tourist office or the municipality for tickets and details of the tour times.

## GOVERNMENT

Bahrain is an absolute monarchy though the Emir, Shaikh Isa Bin Salman Al-Khalifa, consults often with government ministers and is readily available to citizens. The Emir's health has suffered in recent years and much of the day-to-day governing has been carried out by his brother the Prime Minister, Shaikh Khalifa Bin Salman Al-Khalifa. The Crown Prince, Shaikh Hamad Bin Isa Al-Khalifa, is also the head of the Bahrain Defence Forces. Bahrain is the only Gulf state to have adopted a strict rule of primogeniture within the royal family.

## ECONOMY

Bahrain produces fewer than 50,000 barrels of oil per day (for comparative purposes the UAE pumps about two million barrels a day) and refines a large quantity of Saudi oil which arrives via an undersea pipeline. With relatively limited oil reserves the island has developed a somewhat more diversified economy than many other Gulf states. Bahrain is home to the largest aluminium smelter in the Middle East, a large shipbuilding and repair yard and one of the region's busiest airports.

When Lebanon imploded in the late '70s the Bahraini government made a conscious effort to lure the region's bankers (until then mostly based in Beirut) to Manama and met with a great deal of success. In the late '80s Bahrain's large financial services sector branched out into offshore banking, though it has met with stiff competition from Cyprus and Abu Dhabi in this field.

In recent years the government has also begun a calculated drive to attract tourists to the country, focusing its attention on the high volume of transit traffic at the airport.

Economically, the Gulf War proved to be a mixed blessing. On one level business was great: Manama's hotels and bars were filled for many months, first by soldiers and sailors on leave and journalists at work, and later by a string of entrepreneurs hoping to cash in on post-war reconstruction work in Kuwait. But in the longer term the war damaged the country's financial services industry. In addition, the recession which hit the West in the early '90s combined with the fallout of the war to leave the country's financial services industry in a fragile, if slowly recovering, state.

## POPULATION & PEOPLE

At the last count, Bahrain had a population of about 550,000 people, of whom some 150,000 are foreign workers. There are many North Americans and Britons working in the island's oil and financial industries. Services are dominated by Filipinos. That said, Manama is probably the most cosmopolitan city in the Gulf.

The Bahrainis themselves are Arabs, though many are at least partially of Persian ancestry. The population is 85% Muslim with indigenous Christian, Jewish, Hindu and Parsee minorities (according to the Ministry of Information). Islam is the state religion. The majority of the Muslims, probably upwards of 70%, are Shiites. The Sunni Muslim minority includes the royal family and most of the leading merchant families.

While there has been no civil unrest in Bahrain for well over a decade the government remains sensitive about the Shiites, who are generally not as well off economically as the country's Sunnis. You are apt to find that Bahrainis, particularly those working for the government, are not comfortable discussing religion. This is reinforced by the fact that many of the Shiites are at least partially of Persian ancestry,

another fact with which the government seems a bit uncomfortable, despite the recent improvement in relations with Iran.

## EDUCATION

As in most of the other Gulf countries literacy was not widespread until fairly recently. Bahrain now provides free education for all Bahrainis and its American-system international school is considered one of the best in the region – there are even Saudi families from the Eastern Province who send their children across the causeway every day to attend classes there! Though many young Bahrainis still travel abroad to further their education, particularly in the UK and the USA, Bahrain itself has two universities: Bahrain University and the Arabian Gulf University. The latter is managed and funded jointly by the six Gulf Cooperation Council (GCC) states and Iraq.

## ARTS

Traditional craftwork continues in several places around Bahrain: dhow building on the outskirts of Manama, basket weaving in Karbabad near the Bahrain Fort, cloth weaving at Bani Jamrah and pottery making at A'ali. The tourist office in Manama has a selection of all of these (except the dhows!) on sale and you can also drive out and bargain with the craftspeople yourself. The Heritage Centre in central Manama has a number of displays which put these crafts into their original context. As for more expensive traditional arts and crafts, a few goldsmiths still operate in the Manama souk, though a lot of the work is now done abroad.

Public performances of traditional music and dancing have largely died out, though the tourist office is said to be considering organising shows to keep alive this aspect of Bahraini culture.

## CULTURE

As flashy and modern as downtown Manama may be, the basic rhythms of life in the island's many villages, and in parts of

Manama itself, remain remarkably traditional. Starting from Bab Al-Bahrain in Manama, the further you go back into the souk the more traditional life gets. The same can be said for much of the rest of the country. It is a side of Bahrain that visitors all too often miss.

### Taboos & Avoiding Offence

Though traditional life can still be seen in Bahrain you should not make the mistake of assuming that you can join in it. Bahrain is relatively liberal as Gulf countries go, but the Gulf itself remains one of the most conservative places on earth. In Bani Jamrah, for example, nobody will object to your taking a photograph of the weavers sitting near the entrance to the village, but that does not necessarily mean that the villagers will be happy if you and your camera go wandering through the village itself. As is the case almost everywhere in the Arab world you should not attempt to photograph women.

Bahrain is still a conservative country where dress is concerned, at least by Western standards. In general apply common sense: for women; no miniskirts, short shorts, bikini tops, etc. Men should not walk around barechested or in overly tight clothing. Women should probably stick to one-piece bathing suits at the beach, though bikinis are OK around the pool at big hotels. Conservative dress is particularly in order in rural areas. That means long, loose clothing. Short sleeves are OK, even for women, but sleeveless clothes (especially on women) may cause offence in more traditional areas.

Non-Muslims may enter mosques except during prayer time. As in any mosque both men and women are expected to be well covered (for women this includes covering the head, though a veil is unnecessary) and to take off their shoes at the door.

See the Taboos & Avoiding Offence heading in the Facts about the Region chapter for a more detailed description of Gulf do's and don'ts.

### LANGUAGE

Arabic is the official language but English is very widely spoken. As in Saudi Arabia most of the service personnel are Asian and you can safely assume that they speak English (otherwise they would not be working here). Farsi is also widely spoken, though it is most often used in the home rather than in public.

See the Facts about the Region chapter for a glossary of Arabic words and phrases.

# Facts for the Visitor

### VISAS & EMBASSIES

British citizens do not need a visa to enter Bahrain for periods of up to one month. People of most other Western nationalities can obtain a 72-hour transit visa or a seven-day tourist visa on arrival at Bahrain Airport or at the Bahraini customs post on the Saudi Arabia-Bahrain causeway. The three-day visa costs BD 4 and the seven-day visa BD 8. Fees can be paid in Bahraini dinars or Saudi riyals. There is an exchange desk in the transit lounge at the airport. For those not driving their own vehicle across the causeway, possession of an onward or return plane or bus ticket is not formally required, but travellers are often asked to produce these and you should expect some delays if you are unable to show one.

A difficulty that some travellers may encounter is that Bahrain does not recognise the concept of naturalisation. For example, an Indian-born Australian or an American who immigrated from Lebanon are still, as far as the Bahraini government is concerned, Indian and Lebanese, respectively, and that means they can't get visas at the airport. Bahraini customs officials are especially strict with nationals of Iran, the Arab world outside the Gulf (especially Lebanon, Palestine and Iraq) and the Indian subcontinent. If your paternal grandparents came from one of these areas of the world you may be OK, but it's a hit-or-miss situation. Calling a Bahraini embassy for advice is of little use as the embassies are often unaware of airport-issued visas regulations.

If you fall into one of the above categories

your best bet is to have one of the larger hotels arrange your visa as outlined in the following section.

Whatever your ethnic background, people listing their occupation as writer, journalist, editor, etc are generally not admitted to Bahrain unless the Ministry of Information has sponsored their visa. This includes British citizens and the fact that you may only be on holiday or in transit overnight makes no difference! The ministry usually needs about a week to arrange visas.

Women travelling alone should be aware that the rules on granting visas at the airport to unaccompanied females seem to change fairly frequently. Pensioners probably won't have any problems, but for younger women the safest course is to book a room at a medium-size (or larger) hotel in advance and have the hotel arrange the visa.

Drivers arriving from Saudi Arabia must sign a Personal Guarantee promising to take the car back out of Bahrain within a specified period of time. Be sure to keep this piece of paper as it must be turned in at customs on the way out. A mandatory insurance fee of BD 1.500 or SR 15 is collected from the driver of every car crossing the causeway.

If your passport has an Israeli or South African stamp you will be denied entry (and they do check).

## Hotel-Sponsored Visas

To organise a hotel to arrange a visa for you, send them a telex or, better still, a fax about three weeks prior to arrival with all your passport data as well as arrival and departure dates and the purpose of your visit ('tourism' is fine). You'll also need to specify the exact flight on which you plan to arrive (airline, flight number, day and time) and include a telephone, fax or telex number where you can be reached. It might be a good idea to double-check everything by telephone. The hotel will act as your sponsor and make all of the visa arrangements for a small fee (usually BD 2 to BD 4, which will be added to your bill). You can then pick up the visa at the airport, port or on the causeway.

However, as visa rules have loosened up

a lot in the last few years, hotels are becoming increasingly reluctant to go through the hassle of arranging visas unless you can give them a good reason to do so. They will gladly extend visas once you are in the country provided, of course, you are staying in their hotel.

## Bahraini Embassies

Bahraini embassies overseas are of little use to the traveller. They usually handle only residence and work visas, which are only issued after approval has been received from Manama. Addresses of some Bahraini embassies around the world follow:

Iran
  Kheyabun-é Sarvan Khaled Eslamboli, 123 Kuché-yé Nozdahom (☎ 626202, 626203)
UK
  98 Gloucester Rd, SW7 (☎ (071) 370 5132)
USA
  3502 International Drive NW, Washington DC 20008 (☎ 342-0741)

## Visa Extensions

Hotels that can issue visas can also get your visa extended once you are in the country. They generally prefer to have you pick up a 72-hour transit visa on your own at the airport and then, if you want to stay a few more days, they will handle the extension. If you are staying in a cheap hotel and want to extend your stay your only practical option is to move up-market and stay there. The procedure for extending visas through a hotel is painless and requires nothing from you except a few extra dinars (usually BD 8 for a one-week extension plus a hotel charge of BD 2 to BD 4). It usually takes about two days so don't wait until the morning your visa runs out to hand your passport to the desk clerk at the hotel! Getting a one-week extension of your tourist visa once or even twice should not be a problem but after that things could change. Bahrain is a small place and while it is packed with things to see it still does not take too long to see all of them. The government is very wary of people trying to stay in the country and work on tourist visas. If you came in on a tourist visa and want to stay for more than two weeks you had better be prepared to explain why, because someone is almost sure to ask.

### Exit/Re-Entry Visas

These are not issued for tourists. Resident foreigners must obtain a re-entry visa before leaving the country on business or holiday. If you live in Bahrain your company ought to take care of this. Resident foreigners who travel frequently can obtain multiple re-entry visas valid for six months.

### Foreign Embassies in Bahrain

Embassies in Bahrain are listed in the Manama section.

## DOCUMENTS

No special documents are needed to enter or move about the country. Health certificates are not required to enter Bahrain unless you are coming from one of the areas of endemic yellow fever, cholera, etc (eg Sub-Saharan Africa). If you plan to rent a car you will need an International Driving Permit.

## CUSTOMS

You can expect a thorough, though not particularly intrusive, search at Bahrain Airport. Non-Muslims are allowed to import two litres of alcoholic beverages. All passengers are allowed to bring in 400 cigarettes or 50 cigars and 250 grams of loose tobacco. You are also allowed eight ounces (227 ml) of perfume.

For some reason it is forbidden to bring portable computers into the country unless you have a Bahraini sponsor prepared to guarantee that you will take the machine back out. The sponsor must file a paper to that effect with the customs service prior to your arrival. It is possible to get around this by leaving a deposit equal to 10% of the machine's value with the customs authorities, though the customs officers do not always volunteer that particular piece of information. If you choose to leave a deposit you will be given a receipt and can collect your money on the way out.

That said, this rule is not enforced with any uniformity. I know lots of people (myself included) who have taken laptop computers in and out of the country without any problem. On the other hand, my computer was once confiscated under these regulations and it took me two days to get it back.

This rule seems to apply to consumer electronics. The last time I came into Bahrain they asked whether I was carrying a video camera. You can expect items like this to be written down in your passport to guarantee that you take them out again.

Beyond that, the items on the forbidden list include pornographic material, guns and ammunition and cultured pearls.

## MONEY
### Currency

The Bahraini dinar (BD) is divided into 1000 fils. Notes come in denominations of BD ½, 1, 5, 10 and 20. Coins are 5, 10, 25, 50 and 100 fils. For small transactions most businesses will accept Qatari or Saudi riyals at a flat rate of BD 1 = QR/SR 10. The Bahraini dinar is a convertible currency and there are no restrictions on its import or export.

### Exchange Rates

| | | |
|---|---|---|
| US$1 | = | BD 0.377 |
| UK£1 | = | BD 0.572 |
| FF1 | = | BD 0.070 |
| DM1 | = | BD 0.235 |
| A$1 | = | BD 0.260 |

Banking hours are Saturday to Wednesday from 7.30 am to noon. Most banks close at 11 am on Thursday. Some moneychangers keep slightly longer hours and may be open for a while in the late afternoon. Changing money on a Friday will be difficult anywhere except at a big hotel, where the rate is certain to be pretty bad.

The exchange rates on offer at banks and moneychangers, as well as the commissions they charge, can vary widely. Particularly if you are in the centre of Manama (where a large number of banks and moneychangers are concentrated on Government Ave between Bab Al-Bahrain and the Standard & Chartered Bank building) it can pay to spend a few minutes shopping around.

American Express provides its usual range of cheque-cashing services for card holders and this is probably the easiest way to get money in Bahrain, though some banks will advance cash against Visa cards.

### Costs

If you stay in the souk, walk a lot and have no huge appetite for either food or booze, it is quite possible to get by on BD 10 per day. It is possible to eat for under BD 2. Alcohol will bust your budget quickly – a beer usually costs at least BD 1, hard liquor BD 1.500 or more per shot.

### Tipping

A service charge is added to almost every bill in Bahrain but it goes to the shop, not the waiter or waitress. If you're in a good restaurant an appropriate tip would be about 10%. While tips are not expected, especially in cheap places, foreign waiters and waitresses are often paid appalling wages, especially in the smaller places that cater largely to, say, Indian or Sri Lankan labourers. A tip, even a small one, will be much appreciated.

### Bargaining

Almost all prices in Bahrain are negotiable up to a point. The trick is finding that point. You might be able to talk the price of souvenirs on sale in the souk down by 10% or so (but not the ones in the Bab Al-Bahrain government tourist shop; the prices there are fixed). The bargaining range on things like electronics varies a lot depending on the market at the time, from almost nothing up to maybe 15%. Hotel rates are almost always negotiable though, again, to what extent depends a lot on how business has been over the last few days. There is usually a certain, if small, amount of leeway on plane tickets. This is rarely more than 5%.

Prices of meals, books and organised tours are generally not negotiable.

### WHEN TO GO

The best time to visit Bahrain is between November and February, when it's not too hot. Avoid visiting during Ramadan when things slow down significantly. You might also want to stay away during the Muslim festivals marking the end of Ramadan and the annual pilgrimage to Mecca (see Business Hours & Holidays) or over New Year's Eve. At these times the country is swamped, particularly with merrymakers (both Arab and foreign) from Saudi Arabia and Kuwait and hotel rooms become very difficult to find, especially at the bottom end of the scale where the prices sometimes double.

### WHAT TO BRING

As is the case everywhere in the Gulf, sunglasses are an absolute necessity for much of the year. Other things you might want to bring include a hat, sunscreen and a very loose long-sleeved shirt or blouse in case your arms get sunburnt and you need to cover them. Something that covers up short sleeves will also be necessary if you plan to visit any mosques. These items, or anything else you might forget or find a sudden need for, are all readily available in Manama.

### TOURIST OFFICES

There's a tourist office in Bab Al-Bahrain in Manama. They organise tours of the city and have a shop selling maps, postcards, Bahraini handicrafts and assorted touristy kitsch. There is also a tourist information desk at Bahrain Airport.

### USEFUL ORGANISATIONS

While things have been developing quite quickly in recent years, Bahrain is still relatively new to tourism and, as a result, there is very little in the way of travel infrastructure. Bahrain's tourist organisations are still geared mostly to people visiting from Saudi Arabia for the weekend and groups who stay in five-star hotels and arrive with everything already organised. Should you find yourself in need of a youth hostel card one can be obtained from the Bahrain Youth Hostels Association for BD 7. (See the Manama section for more details.) Aside from that, however, Bahrain has little in the way of budget travel infrastructure. There are no bucket shops, no place that sells student cards to outsiders and you shouldn't waste too much time looking around for youth or student discounts.

## BUSINESS HOURS & HOLIDAYS

Shops and offices are generally open from around 8 am until 1 pm. Many shops, particularly in the Manama souk, reopen in the late afternoon from 4 or 5 until 7 pm. Friday is the weekly holiday and many businesses also close early on Thursday. Most Western embassies and virtually all government offices are closed all day Thursday (though many Arab embassies will be open on Thursday mornings).

The Islamic holidays of Eid Al-Fitr (the end of Ramadan), Eid Al-Adha (Pilgrimage) and the Islamic New Year are all observed; for dates see the table of holidays page 28. Bahrain's large Shiite community also marks Ashoora (see Cultural Events) though this is not an official government holiday.

Bahrain also celebrates New Year's Day (1 January) and National Day (16 December).

## CULTURAL EVENTS

*Ashoora* is a Shiite Muslim festival marking the death of Hussein, the grandson of the Prophet, at the battle of Karbala in 680 AD. It is the most important religious festival celebrated in Bahrain after the more universal Islamic holidays of Eid El-Fitr and Eid Al-Adha. Processions, led by men flagellating themselves, take place in many of the country's predominently Shiite areas. In Manama, the main procession takes place on a series of relatively small streets in the souk about five blocks directly back from Bab Al-Bahrain. You can expect heavy security. The festival takes place every year on the 10th day of the Muslim month of Muharram, the first month of the Hejira year (around 1 July in 1993).

## POST & TELECOMMUNICATIONS
### Postal Rates

Sending letters to Europe costs 155 fils per 10 grams, to North America and Australia it's 205 fils per 10 grams. Postage for postcards is 125 fils to Europe and 155 fils to North America and Australia. Sending parcels costs BD 3 for the first half kg. Additional half kg cost BD 1 to Europe and BD 1.500 to North America and Australia.

### Sending Mail

Mail to and from Europe and North America takes about a week. Allow 10 days to Australia. The main post office is across Government Ave from Bab Al-Bahrain.

### Receiving Mail

The GPO on Government Ave has poste restante facilities. Address letters to: Your Name, c/o Poste Restante, Manama Post Office (Counter Section), Manama, Bahrain.

### Telephone

Bahrain has an excellent telecommunications system. You can direct-dial just about anywhere. When calling Bahrain from the outside world the country code is 973, followed by the local six-digit number. There are no area or city codes.

Bahrain also has one of the most extensive sets of Home Country Direct services in the world. By dialling a special number these connect you directly to an operator in the country in question. You may then make a collect (reverse charges) call or bill the call to a phone company credit card issued in that country. Home Country Direct services available from any phone in Bahrain include:

| | |
|---|---|
| Australia | 800-061 |
| Canada | 800-100 |
| Denmark | 800-045 |
| Hong Kong | 800-852 |
| Japan | 800-081 |
| Malaysia | 800-060 |
| Netherlands | 800-031 |
| Philippines | 800-163 |
| Singapore | 800-065 |
| South Korea | 800-082 |
| UK | 800-044 |
| USA | 800-001 (AT&T) |
| USA | 800-002 (MCI) |

Payphones take coins, though card phones are increasingly common. You need to insert a minimum of 100 fils. Local calls are charged in 50 fils increments. You can make calls and purchase phonecards at the Telecommunications Office on Government Ave in Manama.

BATELCO, the Bahrain Telephone Company, also has a wide range of information-by-phone services. These run the gamut from the conventional to the bizarre. The conventional ones include Time (☎ 140) and Weather (☎ 268700). Among the more interesting and novel services are Money Line (for financial news, ☎ 268914), News (☎ 268912), Sports (☎ 268222) and What's On (☎ 268444). The stranger ones include Video Line (☎ 268888), a number that gives advice on what video tape you might want to rent tonight, and a Recipe Line ('Your recipe of the day is cream of mushroom soup...', ☎ 268300).

### Fax, Telex & Telegraph

Fax, telex, and telegraph services are available from the Telecommunications Office on Government Ave in Manama. See the Manama section for more details.

### TIME

Time in Bahrain is GMT plus three hours. The clocks are not changed for summer time. When it's noon in Manama, the time elsewhere is:

| City | Time |
|---|---|
| Paris, Rome | 10 am |
| London | 9 am |
| New York | 4 am |
| Los Angeles | 1 am |
| Perth, Hong Kong | 5 pm |
| Sydney | 7 pm |
| Auckland | 9 pm |

### ELECTRICITY

The current in Bahrain is 230 volts AC. British-style three-pin electrical sockets are standard.

### LAUNDRY

Laundromats are virtually unknown in Bahrain, as is the case pretty much everywhere in the Gulf. If you don't feel like doing your washing in the hotel room, the best way to get your clothes cleaned is through your hotel. Even the small ones often have a laundry service of some sort and in the cheapies, washing a medium-sized load should not cost more than BD 2.

### WEIGHTS & MEASURES

Bahrain uses the metric system.

### BOOKS & MAPS
#### History, People & Society

Possibly the best book on Bahrain is *Looking for Dilmun* by Geoffrey Bibby (Penguin Travel Library, 1972), an Anglo-Danish archaeologist who supervised the early professional archaeological work on the island. This is an account of Bibby's digs in Bahrain (which later branched out to include Qatar, Kuwait, Abu Dhabi and eastern Saudi Arabia) and the slow discovery and reconstruction of the history of the ancient Dilmun civilisation. But it also provides a fascinating picture of life in Bahrain and the rest of the Gulf in the '50s and '60s. It's also a pretty good primer on basic archaeological technique. Archaeology buffs might also want to pick up *Bahrain Through the Ages – The Archaeology* by Shaikha Haya Ali Al-Khalifa & Michael Rice. Hotel bookshops in Bahrain are the easiest place to find this one, which is only available in hardback.

*The Merchants* by Michael Field (Overlook Press, Woodstock NY, 1985) includes an interesting chapter on the rise of the Kanoos, Bahrain's most prominent merchant family.

The Bahrain chapter in Jonathan Raban's *Arabia Through the Looking Glass* (Picador, London, 1981) is quite a good read and contains some pointed observations on expatriate life on the island during the oil boom. He visited in early 1979.

### Travel Guides

The best all-around guide to the country's architecture, archaeology and curiosities is *Bahrain: A Heritage Explored* by Angela Clark (MEED Books, London, 1986). It can be found at all hotel bookshops and costs about BD 5. The book, an updated version of Clark's 1981 book, *The Islands of Bahrain*, includes the best general descriptions of the country's archaeological sites (outside of the Al-Khalifa/Rice book which is a bit bulky to haul around). Clark covers every conceivable place of interest though there is nothing on hotels, restaurants, visa regulations, etc. Her driving instructions to the sites outside of Manama are sometimes a bit out of date, but one can usually manage to follow them.

*Bahrain – A MEED Practical Guide*, like the other books in the MEED series, is indispensable for those planning to live in Bahrain. *The Economist Business Traveller's Guides – Arabian Peninsula* is, along with the MEED guide, the best among the many how-to-do-business-with-the-Arabs sort of books on the market.

### Maps

The best map is the blue *Bahrain Map* published by the Ministry of Information and sold at the tourist office for BD 1.500. It has a comprehensive map of the country and good inset maps of Manama and Muharraq. Note that some of the roads shown as 'under construction' are now finished.

## MEDIA
### Newspapers & Magazines

The *Gulf Daily News* is Bahrain's English-language newspaper. It's a bit disappointing in terms of news but hugely useful as a source of 'What's On' information. There is no Friday edition.

All of the larger hotels stock the usual array of international publications: the *International Herald Tribune*, all the main British newspapers, *Time*, *Newsweek*, the *Economist*, as well as major French and German newspapers and magazines. Foreign newspapers and magazines are usually available one or two days after publication.

### Radio & TV

Radio Bahrain broadcast 24 hours a day on several FM and MW frequencies, of which the main one is 98.5 FM. The fare consists, broadly, of pop music in the mornings, feature programmes in the afternoons and light music at night with quiz shows and documentaries (some locally made, some foreign, which usually means British) mixed in throughout the day. As a community bulletin board and 'What's On' source it can't be beaten.

Channel 55 is Bahrain TV's English programme service. They carry a mix of British and US programmes every day from 5 or 6 pm until around midnight and then broadcast CNN until the programme service resumes the following evening. Bahrain TV also broadcasts BBC World Service TV 24 hours a day on a local UHF frequency.

## FILM & PHOTOGRAPHY

The general rules outlined in the Facts about the Region chapter apply to Bahrain. Bahrain is fairly relaxed about both tourists and cameras and as long as you don't try to take a picture of something obviously military or obviously taboo (for example women, especially in rural areas) you should have no problems.

Film is easily available anywhere in Manama, as is processing for colour prints. Slides can often take a few days to get developed and B&W film can be a problem. It might be best to wait and get B&W film developed somewhere else.

## HEALTH

Bahrain has a quite highly developed health-care system and while treatment is not free it is, by Western standards, moderately priced. The quality of medical care in Bahrain is very high and there would be no need to evacuate a patient abroad for anything other than fairly serious, specialised procedures. If you are staying in a medium-sized or larger hotel they will almost certainly have a doctor on call or on staff to deal with minor ailments. Otherwise, or for more serious care, contact your embassy for advice. They may refer you to their own doctor or provide you with a list of doctors who speak English. Several of Bahrain's hospitals also offer patient consultations on a walk-in basis. See the Medical Services entry in the Manama section for more details.

Hygiene standards for food preparation in Bahrain are quite high except in a few of the darker corners of the souk. Cases of travellers diarrhoea almost always originate in the cheaper parts of the souk and if you avoid these sort of places and exercise a little common sense you will probably be alright.

The tap water in Bahrain is not suitable for drinking. It won't kill you, but you won't feel so great after drinking it either. In general stick to bottled water, though coffee or tea made with tap water which has been thoroughly boiled is generally OK.

## WOMEN TRAVELLERS

Bahrain is without a doubt one of the easiest countries in the Gulf for women to travel in. The country's long trading history and traditional openness account for its relatively progressive attitude toward women. Though some restaurants have 'family sections' these tend to be used only by Bahraini and Saudi families. Foreigners who do not want to sit there will not usually be forced to do so. Women may drive in Bahrain. Should you find yourself on the receiving end of unwanted advances, remain calm and be firm. If you are not in a public place, seek one out, particularly where someone in authority (a police officer, hotel security person, etc) is in evidence.

Women (and men) should still, of course, be aware that Bahrain is a conservative, Muslim country and that many things which would be acceptable in the West will be frowned upon here. Clothing that is overly tight or revealing (miniskirts, halter tops, etc) may offend Bahrainis and attract unwanted attention.

Outside of mosques, however, it is never necessary for female visitors to Bahrain to cover their heads, though extra caution should be taken in village areas. Modest shorts or above-the-knee skirts which would be perfectly acceptable in Manama will not go down well in the villages.

## DANGERS & ANNOYANCES

Bahrain is a very safe place. Violent crime is quite rare and you can walk around the centre of Manama late at night without fear. However, men travelling in Bahrain should brace themselves for a certain amount of sexual harassment, particularly if they plan to hang around in the cheap hotel area. I have lost track of the number of times I've been propositioned by Arab men (though rarely Bahrainis) in this area.

The biggest local annoyance is the unshakeable conviction of every taxi driver in the country that any foreign person on foot must want a taxi. Particularly at times when the streets are relatively empty, such as mid-afternoon, it can be really annoying to walk down Government Ave and have one's thoughts interrupted every 10 seconds by yet another taxi driver slowing down and leaning on his horn to attract your attention.

## WORK

Throughout the Gulf regulations controlling work visas are quite strict. Converting a tourist visa to a work permit can, at least in theory, be done but it is not easy and you might well have to go back home first and pick up your work visa there. It is rather easier for the spouse of a foreigner working in Bahrain to get permission to work. Ultimately, however, working in the country requires that you have a Bahraini sponsor and it is not the sort of place where the casual traveller can expect to pick up short-term work, either legally or illegally.

## ACTIVITIES

Most activities on the island are centred on clubs, societies and sports organisations. The *Gulf Daily News* and Radio Bahrain are good sources of information for events and gatherings around the island. Although Bahrain is surrounded by water the public beaches are pretty crummy, mainly because the Gulf is so shallow that you can wade as much as half a km out and the water's still only up to your knees. (The clubs dredge their beaches.) There's no problem for women to swim at the public beaches but they might feel more comfortable at clubs or hotel pools. Otherwise, social life on the island consists mainly of eating and/or drinking out.

## HIGHLIGHTS

A tour of Bahrain should start at the National Museum and include a trip to the Heritage Centre. Try to visit these before going to the archaeological sites as both, particularly the museum, will help you understand the country. Qal'at Al-Bahrain, aka the Portuguese Fort, is at the top of most people's lists of things to see. It is the country's main archaeological site and one of the more important digs in the Gulf. The large burial mounds at A'ali are also worth visiting.

## ACCOMMODATION
### Hostel

Bahrain's youth hostel is in Al-Jufayr suburb south-east of Manama's centre. If you are not an IYHF member, membership cards are available to foreigners for BD 7. See the Manama section for more details.

## Hotels

Hotel rooms bottom out at about BD 7/10 for singles/doubles with bath. Rooms without private baths are a dinar or two less. These rates are negotiable, especially for stays of more than three days. In the cheaper hotels, rates go up on the weekends (Wednesday and Thursday nights) when all of the Saudis flow across the causeway. If you arrive before and stay through the weekend you should only be charged the weekday rate for the Wednesday to Friday period, though it might be a good idea to double-check this with the hotel management first to avoid any misunderstandings. Bottom-end hotel space can be a bit hard to come by on weekends, especially during the Eid Al-Fitr holiday which marks the end of Ramadan.

Like most places in the Gulf Bahrain has a glut of five-star hotels and this can lead to some unusual surprises for the budget traveller. The Bahrain Hilton, for example, has a weekend package (available every Thursday, Friday and Saturday) of one night's accommodation, use of the swimming pool and health club and a free drink at the bar for BD 24 for two people, including the service charge. When you consider that the Hilton will pick you up at, and return you to, the airport for free (saving you a BD 3 taxi fare in each direction) this works out to be almost as cheap as the weekend rates at many of the places in the souk. The Holiday Inn and Delmon Hotel often have similar packages, and they all have to be booked in advance.

## FOOD

While a bit thin on Arabic food Bahrain is a bonanza of Asian specialities. From Indian and Pakistani to Thai and Filipino you can find almost any sort of cuisine in the area around Al-Khalifa Rd. Good meals are usually about BD 3.

### Cafes & Bars

Cafes tend to be modern, Western-style establishments, usually located in the larger shopping centres. A few traditional coffee houses remain, including a particularly good one on Government Ave near the Delmon

Top: Al-Fatih Mosque, Bahrain's largest, Manama
Bottom: View of Al-Khalifa Avenue, Manama, Bahrain

Top: Water Towers, Al-Jahra, Kuwait
Bottom: Kuwaiti family, Kuwait

Hotel, but there are far more places offering cappuccino and cakes than sweet tea and water pipes.

The traditional coffee houses serve mostly tea. Coffee at these establishments usually means Turkish coffee. Traditional Arabian coffee has largely retreated to the hospitality carts of five-star hotels.

Bars are almost all located in hotels, though a few free-standing restaurants also have bar sections.

### Snacks

Bahrain's selection of street food and snacks runs from the traditional to the modern. At the traditional end are shawarma and *sambousa* (samosa) which you are likely to find sold alongside such Western fare as burgers, french fries, ice cream and popcorn.

### Main Dishes

Among the cheap restaurants the market is dominated by Indian and Chinese food. Many of the tiny Indian places have an extremely limited menu, often consisting mostly of biryanis. Oriental food is a bit more expensive but tends to be a better bet. For one thing the Oriental restaurants often look a lot cleaner. Most of these restaurants offer standard Chinese fare with whatever variations are in order on the basis of the staff's origin (Thai, Filipino, etc). Desserts don't amount to anything special. Do as the locals do: order ice cream.

### Self-Catering

The main problem with self-catering on a budget in Manama is that there are not a lot of places to shop for bread, meat, etc in the centre. The small food stores which dot Al-Khalifa Ave and Municipality Ave sell mostly uncooked food (eg rice) and canned or other food requiring some sort of preparation. In other words, this is not a country where buying a loaf of bread and a hunk of cheese is really much of an option. My advice is to spend the extra dinar and get a decent dinner.

### DRINKS

Nonalcoholic drinks consist of Pepsi, Seven-up, orange soda or fruit juice (not usually fresh unless you are in a big hotel). Alcohol is draft beer and the same selection of the harder stuff that you would find in any bar. Booze is not cheap. Expect to pay at least BD 1 for a can of beer and BD 1.500 for an English pint. Mixed drinks start at around BD 1.500 and head for the sky from there.

### THINGS TO BUY

Bahrain's specialities, pearls and gold, are good value. Good handicrafts are on sale at the tourist office at Bab Al-Bahrain, which has displays showing where various items come from on the island. This gives you the option of going out to the village in question and hunting down the craftspeople yourself (though don't expect to save a lot of money this way). See Things to Buy in the Manama section for details.

# Getting There & Away

### AIR

#### To/From the USA, Europe & Asia

Though a cheap stopover, Bahrain is a pretty expensive end-destination. Fares to and from the island have recently reached absolutely absurd levels. From the USA you can expect to pay as much as $1400 return from New York. It's often a bit cheaper to originate such a trip in Bahrain, and if some airline or other has a special offer going it will be widely advertised by travel agencies. But even the special fares are not great: for example, BD 340 to London and BD 325 to Frankfurt (return). Routes to India and South-East Asia tend to be a bit more competitive because of the large number of Asian workers in the country, but you're still looking at special fares of BD 260 or more to Bangkok.

#### To/From Other Gulf States

Don't look for bargains here either, especially when you consider the tiny distances involved. Here's a sample of one-way and cheapest return fares from Bahrain, with minimum and maximum stay requirements:

| To | One-Way | Return | Min/Max |
|---|---|---|---|
| Dhahran | BD 24 | BD 32 | 3/14 days |
| Doha | BD 25 | BD 26 | 3/7 days |
| Dubai | BD 56 | BD 60 | 3/7 days |
| Kuwait | BD 41 | BD 57 | 3/7 days |
| Muscat | BD 88 | BD 92 | 3/7 days |
| Jeddah | BD 70 | BD 97 | 3/14 days |
| Riyadh | BD 29 | BD 41 | 3/14 days |

## LAND

Land travel to/from Bahrain is via the causeway to Saudi Arabia, the opening of which, in 1986, spelled the end of passenger dhow service between Bahrain and Alkhobar. You may hear rumours to the effect that only Saudis and Bahrainis can use the causeway. This is nonsense. I've been back and forth over it at least half a dozen times both by bus and car. Except at the weekend crunch periods (Thursday afternoon for traffic to Bahrain, Friday evening for traffic to Saudi Arabia) it tends to be quick and easy. During the weekend crush the bus is a particularly good bet as it has a special lane at customs.

To enter the causeway you must pay a toll of BD 2 or SR 20, regardless of whether you are travelling to Saudi Arabia or only to the island halfway across (where there is a restaurant). At the toll booth on either side you will be asked whether or not you are crossing the border and, if necessary, will be given a landing card to fill out. Drivers entering Bahrain from Saudi Arabia must purchase temporary Bahraini insurance and sign a personal guarantee. For more details see under Visas & Embassies in the Facts for the Visitor section earlier in this chapter.

The Saudi-Bahraini Transport company runs five buses daily to and from Dammam via Alkhobar. The fare is BD 4 one-way, BD 7 return. Bahrain to Dammam and vice versa takes about three hours. For more details see the Manama section.

## SEA

There are passenger services between Iran and Bahrain. The boats leave from Mina Sulman on the outskirts of Manama, and there is only one class of service. The trip takes 16 hours and costs BD 36 one-way, BD 63 return, plus a BD 3 port tax. Contact Internationat Travel (☎ 250883) on Al-Khalifa Ave for tickets and details. They also arrange visas.

## TOURS

Bahrain's tourist industry is still largely aimed at stopover and transit passengers and weekend visitors from Saudi Arabia. A number of airlines, starting with Gulf Air, offer short-stay stopover packages in Bahrain aimed at people travelling between Europe and Asia. These generally include a one or two-night stay, some meals and one or more half-day tours. Some of these cost less than US$100, including accommodation, and are pretty good deals. The usual method of booking a stopover holiday is through the airline on which you will be travelling. Alternatively, you can enter Bahrain on a transit visa and contact a tour company directly. See the Manama section for a complete listing of tour companies.

## LEAVING BAHRAIN

If you depart by air there is an Airport Usage Fee of BD 3. This must be paid in cash in Bahraini dinars (Saudi or Qatari riyals are not accepted). Some of the five-star hotels sell pre-paid Airport Usage Fee vouchers which spare you having to stand in an extra line at the airport to hand over your BD 3.

There is BD 2 toll for leaving the country via the causeway to Saudi Arabia and a BD 3 port tax if you leave by boat.

# Getting Around

## BUS

Bahrain has a fairly straightforward bus system linking most of the major towns to terminals on Manama and Muharraq. The fare is a flat 50 fils per trip. For a complete list of bus routes see the Manama and Muharraq sections.

## TAXI

If you do not have a car and want to make a quick tour of some of the sights closer to Manama, hiring a taxi by the hour may be a reasonable option, particularly if you can split the cost among several people. The method is simple; just walk up to a taxi rank and start bargaining. A fare of BD 5 per hour to go anywhere is reasonable. I've never had any trouble doing this, though the drivers still find the concept a bit novel and they may want a complete list of the places you plan to see. Do not give in to this, as it only provides them with an excuse to demand more money. Few places in Bahrain are much more than half an hour's driving time from anywhere else in the country and BD 5 per hour is perfectly reasonable, particularly if the cab is going to be standing still while you walk around the site.

## CAR

Everything in Manama can be seen on foot, but outside of the capital getting around can be a problem if you do not have a car. After all the obligatory extras, you can count on car hire running to BD 15 per day.

Bahraini law requires people driving cars or riding in the front seat to use seat belts. There is a BD 10 fine if the police catch you without your seat belt on. Speed limits are rigorously enforced and drunk driving laws are also quite strict.

Bahrain is the only country in the Gulf where you cannot rent a car on a foreign driving licence. An International Driving License is required and must be obtained before you arrive in Bahrain. For more detailed rental information see the Manama section.

## BICYCLE, HITCHING & WALKING

While most of Manama and Muharraq can be seen on foot, for about seven months a year it is impractical. You can walk from the Pearl Roundabout to the Diplomat hotel (ie from one end of Manama to the other) in about 30 to 45 minutes and from the Diplo-

mat to the Muharraq souk in another 20 to 30 minutes. When it is 45°C and humid, however, you may want to think twice about doing this.

Bicycles are not common. Hitchhiking is a bit more problematic. It is not common, but it is not unheard of either. If you find yourself stranded outside of Manama, drivers will often stop and give you a lift. They may or may not expect payment for this but it is considered polite to offer to pay.

## LOCAL TRANSPORT

### Taxi

Most of Bahrain's taxis have no meters. There is a set table of fares to which the drivers are supposed to adhere but, like most taxi drivers everywhere in the world, they'll take whatever they can get. If you bargain or ask the fare in advance, you will pay too much. On the other hand, agreeing on the fare in advance is a good way to avoid misunderstandings. The only way, really, to pay the official fares is simply to get into the cab, tell the driver your destination and hand him the right sum of money when you get out. If you do not look like you know what you are doing then be prepared for an argument.

Before attempting this you should pick up a copy of *Taxi Fares & Tourist Information Guide*, a very useful booklet which contains a complete list of the official taxi tariffs printed in both English and Arabic. It is available free at the tourist office. Though they are loathe to admit it, taxi drivers almost always have a copy of the fare booklet in the glove box. If you get into an argument with a driver you should insist on seeing it. Following is a selection of fares from the official table (while these fares were current at this writing this table has not been revised since 1988, so it may be due for an increase).

Within Manama (the area between King Faisal Highway in the north and west, Al-Sulmaniya Ave in the south and Al-Fateh Highway in the east): 500 fils

Manama to Muharraq Town Police Station or Central Market or vice versa: 700 fils

Manama to any of the following: inside Muharraq Town, Mina Sulman (main gate), Al-Jufayr, Umm Al-Hassam, Al-Mahuz, Al- Zinj, Bilad Al-Qadim, Al-Khamis, Ayn Adhari, Al-Sehla, Salmabad, Tubli, Isa Town, Jurdab, Sanad, Sanabis, Jidd Hafs or vice versa: BD 1
Manama to Arad or vice versa: BD 1.200
Manama to Barbar or vice versa: BD 1.400
Manama to A'ali or vice versa: BD 1.700
Manama to Ad-Diraz, Bani Jamrah or vice versa: BD 1.800
Manama to Rifa East or West or vice versa: BD 2
Manama to Awali or vice versa: BD 2.500

Having a taxi wait costs 500 fils for half an hour, BD 1 for an hour and beyond that you have to agree on a price with the driver. The official fares increase by 50% between midnight and 5 am. Taxis hired at the airport cost an extra dinar. One might note, on that score, that while it theoretically costs BD 1.200 from Manama to the airport you can almost certainly forget about getting that trip at the official rate. The accepted standard fare to or from the airport is BD 3, whatever the fare booklet says.

Unofficially, hiring a taxi by the hour goes for about BD 5 after some hard bargaining. For this price the driver should take you anywhere you want to go and wait for as long as you want, though he will probably insist on knowing how much time you have in mind before you set off.

### Service Taxis
Unlike other Middle Eastern countries, service taxis in Bahrain do not follow set routes. Most of the service taxis are small pick-up trucks. Look for the yellow circle on the side with a license number painted in black-coloured Arabian numerals. They will take five people plus luggage and go wherever the driver decides he would like to go, or wherever the passengers express an interest in going. Fares are generally a few hundred fils per person – a lot more than a bus but a lot less than a private taxi.

# Manama

Manama is the very new capital of a very old place – many of the hotels and official buildings along Government Ave sit on reclaimed land. But don't be fooled – only a few blocks inland from the shiny new hotels are sections of the city which have changed little in the last 50 years.

### Orientation
Manama's main street is Government Ave, which runs roughly east-west through the city. The central section of this street is the stretch from the Delmon Hotel to the large roundabout by the Hilton and Sheraton hotels. Al-Khalifa Ave runs more or less parallel to, and one block south of, Government Ave. Here you will find many of Manama's cheaper hotels and numerous small restaurants. The hub of all activity is Bab Al-Bahrain and the small roundabout in front of it. The area between Government Ave and the King Faisal Highway contains a collection of government office buildings, banks and hotels. The area south of Government Ave is the souk, or marketplace. The King Faisal Highway runs along the city's (and the island's) northern coast and turns south around the Holiday Inn, changing its name to the Al-Fatih (or Al-Fateh) Highway. The western limit of the centre is the Pearl Monument Roundabout, while the National Museum and the causeway to Muharraq mark the centre's eastern boundary.

### Information
**Tourist Office** The tourist office (☎ 231375) and a government-run souvenir shop are both in Bab Al-Bahrain and are entered from the Al-Khalifa Ave side. They are open daily, except Fridays and holidays, from 8.30 am to noon and from 4.30 to 6.30 pm. The shop sells an excellent map of both Bahrain and Manama for BD 1.500 (the blue *Bahrain Map*; avoid the 800 fils *Bahrain Tourist Map*). The map is available in both English and Arabic versions. The office also sells

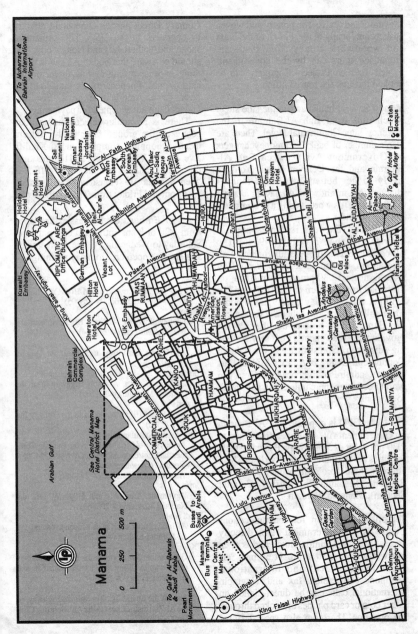

Manama

0   250   500 m

Arabian Gulf

To Muharraq &
Bahrain International
Airport

To Gulf Hotel
& Al-Jufair

El-Fateh
Mosque

To Qal'at Al-Bahrain
& Saudi Arabia

Pearl
Monument

To Al-Busem Highway

King Faisal Highway

souvenirs and crafts. The pottery and woven baskets are locally made, but all of the brass and woodwork comes from Pakistan. Organised tours run by the government-owned Tourism Projects Company can be booked through the tourist office.

**Money** Several banks are on the side street which runs from Bab Al-Bahrain to the Regency Inter-Continental Hotel. There are also a number of banks and moneychangers on Government Ave between Bab Al-Bahrain and the Delmon Hotel. You are likely to get better rates from money-changers but might wind up paying a larger commission. It's worth taking a few minutes to shop around.

American Express is represented in Bahrain by Kanoo Travel (☎ 249346). The office, on Al-Khalifa Ave just behind Bab Al-Bahrain, is open Saturday to Wednesday from 8 am to 12.30 pm and 3 to 6 pm, on Thursday from 7.30 am to 12.30 pm and 3 to 5.30 pm and on Friday from 9 am to noon. They will cash personal cheques for American Express card holders but they do not provide the Amex client's mail service. The big American Express office in the Bahrain Commercial Centre is Amex's Middle East regional administrative headquarters; you won't need to go there unless you have a bill to pay.

**Post** The GPO is opposite Bab Al-Bahrain on Government Ave. It is open from 7 am to 7.30 pm daily except Friday. Poste Restante facilities are available. To receive letters here address them to: Your Name, c/o Poste Restante, Manama Post Office (Counter Section), Manama, Bahrain.

**Telephone** The main Telecommunications Centre is on Government Ave, directly across from the Delmon Hotel, and is open every day from 6.30 am to 11.30 pm. Services include local and international telephone calls, telex, fax and telegraph. International calls can be direct-dialled on either coin or card phones or booked through the operator. There are also special Home

Country Direct phones connecting directly to operators in the USA, UK, Australia, Japan, the Netherlands and Hong Kong. You should be aware that booking a call is much more expensive than calling direct on the card phones. Phonecards are on sale at the desk. Cash, American Express, Visa and Diners Club are accepted for payment.

There is a smaller telecommunications centre on the ground floor of the Yateem Centre shopping complex on Al-Khalifa Ave. Home Country Direct and international direct-dial calls are available. The office is open Saturday to Thursday from 7 am to 11.30 pm and Friday from 7 am to 10.30 pm.

**Foreign Embassies** Embassies are open from 7.30 or 8 am until noon or 1 pm from Saturday to Wednesday. Some Arab embassies are also open on Thursday mornings.

Egypt
    Kuwait St, just beyond the Al-Hora Cold Store in the Al-Mahuz District (☎ 720005)
France
    Diplomatic Area, Al-Fatih Highway, near the National Museum (☎ 291734)
Germany
    Al-Hassaa Building, near Beit Al-Qur'an (☎ 530210)
Jordan
    Diplomatic Area, Al-Fatih Highway, near the National Museum (☎ 291109)
Kuwait
    King Faisal Highway, opposite the Holiday Inn (☎ 242330)
Netherlands (consular agency)
    At the ABN-AMRO Bank, in the Bahrain Commercial Centre, on Al-Furdah Ave (☎ 255420)
New Zealand (consular agency)
    Yateem Centre, Level 2 (☎ 271600)
Oman
    Diplomatic Area, Al-Fatih Highway, near the National Museum (☎ 293663)
Saudi Arabia
    Al-Jufayr, near the Great Mosque, behind the Al-Hamra Building (☎ 727223)
UK
    Government Ave, opposite the Bahrain Commercial Complex. They also handle Canadian and Australian affairs (☎ 534404)
USA
    Just off the Shaikh Isa Bin Sulman Highway, in the Al-Zinj district, next to the Ahli Sporting Club (☎ 273300)

**Cultural Centres** The main Western cultural centres in Bahrain are:

Alliance Française (☎ 683295), in Isa Town, behind Bahrain University's Polytechnic College, off the 16th December Highway. Look for the only building without a wall around it.
British Council (☎ 261555), in the Ahmed Mansour Al-Ali Building (opposite the BMW showroom) on the Shaikh Salman Highway.
USIS (☎ 273300) has a library (open to all) at the US embassy with US newspapers and magazines.

**Travel Agencies** More travel agents than one would think the market could possibly support have offices on either Government Ave or Al-Khalifa Ave. As in most Gulf countries, aeroplane tickets are usually cheaper if purchased through a travel agent, provided you don't mind locking yourself into particular travel dates at the time of purchase. Also, as in other Gulf states, prices are government controlled and do not vary enough to be worth mentioning individual travel agents. However, since not every agent offers every fare you should go to three or four places before making up your mind as to what really is the cheapest fare. Many of the travel agents in the Al-Khalifa Ave area have signs advertising special deals which change from month to month. London, Bangkok and India (usually Delhi or Bombay) are the most common destinations for these cut-rate fares.

**Bookshops** The Al-Hilal Bookshop on Tujjaar Ave has a rather eclectic selection of English books ranging from romance novels to technical books to the occasional out-of-print account of some 18th or 19th century explorer's voyages. The books are not cheap but it's as good as the selection gets. Try also the Family Bookshop, near the roundabout next to the UK Embassy.

**Medical Services** If you get sick, medical treatment is relatively easy to obtain. The American Mission Hospital (☎ 253447) offers walk-in consultations for BD 5 plus the cost of any medicine or X-rays required. Similar services are available at the Awali

Hospital (☎ 753434) and the International Hospital (☎ 591666).

**Emergency** For fire, police or ambulance services dial 999 from any telephone.

**Dangers & Annoyances** Bahrain is not a dangerous place. That said, young unaccompanied males (that's right, males) should steel themselves for a certain amount of petty harassment. Several years ago, on my first visit to Bahrain, I was surprised when a large car (which did not have Bahraini number plates) pulled up beside me as I walked across a vacant lot near the Delmon Hotel. The driver, a middle-aged Arab man wearing an expensive thobe, rolled down the window and said in broken English, 'You. Me. We go fuckey fuck. Good?' The next day I received similar comments from a group of young men on a balcony as I walked down a side street off Al-Khalifa Ave. In both cases I ignored it and just kept walking. It is highly unlikely that any such incident will go beyond that. It seems that foreign women encounter far less of this sort of thing than they would in, say, Cairo or Athens, which is not to say that it does not happen. Be firm but maintain your composure and everything will probably be OK.

**National Museum**
This is the large white building at the northern end of the Al-Fatih Highway, near the Bahrain Island end of the Muharraq causeway. The museum is open Saturday to Wednesday from 8 am to 2 pm, and Thursday from 10 am to 5 pm. It is closed on Friday. Admission is 500 fils. Photography is permitted except in the Document Hall and the Dilmun Gallery. The collection is exceptionally well displayed, and most exhibits are marked in both English and Arabic. The archaeological displays are particularly good at explaining in lay terms exactly how archaeologists can tell so much from what, to some of us, looks like a bunch of rocks or bones.

The museum, which opened in December 1988, consists of three diamond-shaped halls, each with galleries on both the ground floor and the upper level. These are connected to the large, rectangular building which houses the entrance, an art gallery (to your left as you enter the building), auditorium, classroom, cafeteria and a shop.

The museum divides Bahrain's history into the Stone Age (5000-3200 BC), Formative Dilmun (3200-2200 BC), Early Dilmun (2200-1600 BC), Middle Dilmun (1600-1000 BC), Late Dilmun (1000-330 BC), Tylos (330 BC-630 AD) and Islam (630 AD-Present).

The organisation of the galleries reflects this division. The easiest way to approach the museum is to start in the Hall of Graves (the gallery nearest the entrance, on the ground floor), work your way through the Dilmun to the Costumes & Traditions galleries and then go directly upstairs and work your way back (from the Travel, Trades & Crafts to Tylos and Islam to the Document Hall galleries). Sticklers for chronological order may want to move upstairs to Tylos and Islam after viewing the Dilmun gallery, view ethnographic exhibits in the third hall and then finish up in the Document Hall which contains most of the modern material.

**Hall of Graves** This gallery is dedicated to Bahrain's best known tourist attraction: its grave mounds. There are some 85,000 mounds in the country, covering about 5% of Bahrain's total area. Mound burials in various forms took place from 2800 BC until the coming of Islam in the 7th century AD. The centrepiece of the room is a cross-section of a large 'late type' burial mound. There are also several smaller reconstructed burial sites of other types. Printed displays explain the various types of grave mounds and the differences between them. Grave contents are also on display with signs detailing their functions.

**Dilmun** The Dilmun gallery has more displays on archaeological technique. It also includes exhibits on seals and engraving, metal casting, pottery, and a thorough outline of temples and temple building.

**Costumes & Traditions** The displays in this gallery cover birth, childhood, marriage, traditional ceremonies, toys and games. The education display highlights the differences between traditional Koranic schools and the 20th century government schools (founded in 1919). The displays are generally a combination of old photographs, text and life-size dioramas.

**Traditional Trades & Crafts** This is largely an extension of the Costumes & Traditions gallery on the lower floor. There are large displays on pearling and fishing and smaller ones on weaving and pottery. There's also a reconstruction of an old street in the souk.

**Tylos & Islam** This gallery is a bit sparse compared with the Dilmun exhibit on the lower floor. Most of the material is from Islamic times, reflecting a dearth of finds from Bahrain's Tylos (Greek) period. A lot of space is devoted to graves and grave architecture (especially gravestones). Note that this gallery has less explanatory material than some of the others. All of the grave inscriptions are translated but little else is. Be sure to see the section on the *qanats*, the large system of underground irrigation canals which were used to transport water from the islands' numerous springs to fields elsewhere. There is also a big display on the country's various forts.

**Documents & Manuscripts** Most of the signs on the walls (biographies of the rulers of Bahrain, etc) are in English but a lot of the material in here is not translated. There is also an interesting display on Arabic writing and calligraphy.

**Heritage Centre**
The centre occupies a villa on Government Ave across from the Bahrain Commercial Centre. The villa was built in 1937 to house the law courts. The centre is open Saturday to Wednesday from 8 am to 2 pm and Thursday from 9.30 am to 5 pm, but it's closed Friday. Admission is free and photography is prohibited.

In the parking lot by the main door are displayed an old-style canoe and a scale model of an ocean-going dhow. The courtyard features a reconstruction of a traditional diwan under the staircase. The rooms surrounding the courtyard contain photographs of state occasions and the comings and goings of numerous Arab and foreign dignitaries from the island throughout the 20th century. There are also displays on pearl diving, sea hunting, folk music instruments, the various uses of the date palm and a reconstruction of the High Court whose sessions used to be held in the building.

The upper level of the centre houses a series of one-room displays of antique weapons, games, folk medicine, traditional costumes and 'scenes' from everyday life.

## Wind Towers
Bahrain's pre-electricity form of air-conditioning can be seen in several places in the older part of town. The towers are designed to catch even slight breezes and funnel the air down into the house. The easiest one to find is 10 to 15 minutes walk from the Hilton/Sheraton roundabout. With your back to the two hotels follow Palace Ave. Turn right on Rd 609 (at the corner with a large Bridgestone sign). Follow this street for about 200 metres; it is on the left. The same house also has a well-preserved covered balcony (if driving, note that Palace Ave is a limited access road and you cannot turn on Rd 609 from either lane).

## The Friday Mosque
This mosque, built with the island's first oil revenues in 1938, is easily identifiable by its colourful mosaic minaret. The minaret is, in fact, the mosque's most interesting architectural feature, and you're not missing much if you just look at the mosque from the outside. The mosque is at the intersection of Al-Khalifa and Shaikh Isa Aves.

## Bab Al-Bahrain
Built by the British in 1945 to house government offices and serve as a formal entryway to the city, the Bab, as it is known locally,

now is the home of the tourist office. The gateway was designed by Sir Charles Belgrave, the long-time British adviser to the rulers of Bahrain. The small square in front of the Bab was once the terminus of the customs pier (which gives some idea of the extent of land reclamation in the area).

## The Souk
The Bab serves as the main entrance to the souk, which covers roughly the area between Al-Khalifa Ave and Shaikh Abdulla Ave, from Municipality Ave to Bab Al-Bahrain Ave. Electronics and women's clothing seem to be the souk's main stock in trade, aside from gold, but in the great tradition of Middle Eastern bazaars almost anything can be found if you look long and hard enough. Opening hours are from 8.30 am to 12.30 or 1 pm and from 3 to 6 pm daily with everything closed on Friday.

## Beit Al-Qur'an
A striking bit of architecture at the eastern end of Government Ave, Beit Al-Qur'an (Koran House) was opened in 1990 as a museum and research centre. The museum, which is open Saturday to Thursday from 9 am to noon and 4 to 6 pm, houses a large, and quite striking, collection of Korans, manuscripts, wood carvings, etc. Not everything is labelled in English, and a few of the displays are not even labelled in Arabic, but it is definitely worth the trip. If you are unfamiliar with Islam, this centre is a particularly good introduction to the art of Islamic calligraphy. Admission is free, but a donation is requested.

## Dhow Builders
The most interesting dhow building yard on the Arabian side of the Gulf is in the nondescript-looking sheds just west of the Pearl Monument Roundabout. In the same area you can also see fish traps being woven from wire. No admission fee is charged but ask before taking photographs or climbing on the half-built dhows, the latter being a matter of safety as well as courtesy.

Working on a dhow hull

## The Al-Fateh Mosque

The Al-Fateh Mosque, also known as the Great Mosque, dominates the Al-Fatih Highway on the coast south of central Manama. You can't miss it; it's the largest building in the country and is said to be capable of holding up to 7000 worshippers.

## Organised Tours

Bahrain Explored (☎ 246266) is the best established tour company on the island, offering half-day tours of Manama and other parts of the country. Their brochures are on display at many medium-size and larger hotels. Tours cost BD 9 per person if two or more people are on the tour or BD 30 for a private (solo) tour. Tours go only when there are enough people expressing interest, so call ahead. If you book a trip they will usually meet you at one of the big hotels.

Al-Dur Travel & Tourism (☎ 695876, 695877) offers morning or afternoon half-day tours for BD 3.500 and full-day tours for BD 6.

The government-run Tourism Projects Company (☎ 211025) offers a number of itineraries around Manama and the main archaeological/historical sites. These cost BD 3 to BD 5 (special rates are available for children under 12 on some tours) and most of them last three hours. Different tours go on different days. The best idea is to drop by the tourist office, which also doubles as the

Tourism Projects Company's office, to look at the brochures. They also organise excursions ranging from walking trips of the souk at BD 1.500 and dhow trips (BD 3) to scuba diving (between BD 13 and BD 32, depending on where you go and for how long).

## Places to Stay – bottom end

The *Youth Hostel* (☎ 727170) is at No 1105, Rd 4225 in Al-Jufayr, south-east of the city centre. It is opposite the Bahrain School and just beyond the United Nations Development Programme (UNDP) and UNICEF offices. Beds are BD 1 per night. This is a bit out of the way and if you've got luggage it might be a good idea to take a cab.

All of the following hotels have air-conditioning. Service charges, where applicable, are included in the rates quoted here. Also note that the rates listed are initial quotes and are definitely negotiable, at least during the week. Most of Bahrain's cheap hotels raise their rates over the weekend, which usually means on Wednesday and Thursday nights. If you check in before the weekend and stay through it, you should only be charged the weekday rate, but check first with the management to avoid any misunderstandings.

The *Central Hotel* (☎ 233553) remains one of the better values in Bahrain, though it is a bit out of the way. It's in an alleyway off the east side of Municipality Square. The rooms are small and simple but fairly clean, all with private bath, TV and fridge. The rates are BD 10/15 for singles/doubles. Another decent buy is the *Al-Sakir Hotel* (☎ 210801) on a small street that runs along the west side of the Al-Jazira Hotel and Al-Kuwait Guest House. Rooms are BD 6/12 a single/double, some with bath, some without. The rooms are a bit musty, but the price can't be beaten. They do not hire out singles on weekends. Nearby, the *Al-Kuwait Guest House* (☎ 210781) has small, spartan, uncarpeted rooms, some with Turkish toilets, for BD 7/12. Some of the rooms have attached baths and some don't. The clientele seems to be mostly low-income Saudis. Unaccompanied women might want to look somewhere else.

A number of what used to be the better

budget hotels have gone into decline. This category includes *Hotel* (formerly the Al-Afrah Hotel; ☎ 211549), on Al-Khalifa Ave. Once the best deal in town it has been in a tailspin since new management took over. The rooms are bare and the toilets so-so. They charge BD 8/10 for singles/doubles with bath, BD 6/10 without and the rates do not change on weekends. The *Abu Nawas Hotel* (☎ 213163) on Municipality Ave has also seen better days but is still a pretty good deal at BD 8/10 with bath, BD 6/8 without. The rooms are OK but the shared toilets could stand to be cleaned a bit more often.

The *Seef Hotel* (☎ 244557) is just off Government Ave behind the Standard & Chartered Bank building. Singles/doubles cost BD 8/12, all with bath, TV and fridge. The rooms are OK but nothing to write home about. The toilets are all Turkish-style – the hole-in-the-floor variety.

Heading for the bottom of the barrel, the *Al-Gindoul Hotel* (☎ 210353) on Municipality Ave (the entrance is in the alley across the street from the National Bank of Bahrain) is not quite as bad as it used to be, but that's not saying much. Beds are between BD 5 and BD 6.500 per person depending on what the manager thinks you might be able to afford. They say the rates don't change on the weekend, but this is the sort of place where they might change for some people and not for others. When all is said and done it's still Bahrain's last resort.

Further afield, the recently spiffed-up *Bahrain Hotel* (☎ 253478) is good value at BD 12/22 a single/double for simple but very clean rooms, all with private baths, telephones and TVs. The hotel is in two old houses which have been reconstructed, which makes for nice surroundings, but also a lot of walking up and down staircases to get to your room. The hotel is on Al-Khalifa Ave, near the intersection with Rd 453 (two blocks east of the Tylos Hotel).

## Places to Stay – middle

Bahrain's mid-priced hotels are a varied lot. A 15% service charge (included, where applicable, in the prices quoted here) can be assumed at this level, as can such amenities as a fridge, TV and telephone. During slow periods you may be able to bargain a dinar or two off the rates quoted here, but don't count on it. Most hotels in this category do not raise their rates on weekends.

If you want or need to have your entry visa sponsored by a hotel the two cheapest places that provide this service are among the better values in this price category. The *Al-Jazira Hotel* (☎ 258810, telex 8999 JAZOTL BN, fax 233910) on Al-Khalifa Ave in the souk is the landmark by which you know you have reached the cheap hotel district. It is quite a good hotel, catering largely to business travellers with small expense accounts. Rooms in the hotel are BD 20.700/27.600 for singles/doubles. Another good bet is the *Oasis Hotel* (☎ 259979, telex 8970 OASIS BN, fax 259735) on Government Ave opposite the Delmon Hotel. Rooms cost BD 20.700/28.750. This two-star hotel is very good value and I would recommend it for unaccompanied women. Further west along Government Ave, moving away from the town centre, is the *Tylos Hotel* (☎ 252600, telex 7482 TYLOS BN, fax 252611) with rooms at BD 23/32.200 a single/double. They also arrange visas.

If you are looking only for a central location it is hard to beat the *Bab Al-Bahrain Hotel* (☎ 211622), on Government Ave right next to the Bab itself. It is an extremely clean place with good, medium-sized rooms at BD 23/28.750. The *Sahara Hotel* (☎ 250850) on Municipality Square also has a good spot. Singles/doubles are BD 20.700/28.750. The *Adhari Hotel* (☎ 271424) across the square charges BD 23/28.750 but will readily discount their prices. Their bar, the Hunter's Lounge, is popular with US sailors on shore leave. The *Aradous Hotel* (☎ 241011) on Wali Al-Ahed Ave is under the same management as the Adhari and has roughly the same prices. At the southern end of the square the *Al-Dewania Hotel* (☎ 263300) at BD 12/15 a single/double is a definite step down (the air-conditioner drains into the basin).

On Tujjaar Ave in the souk the *Capital*

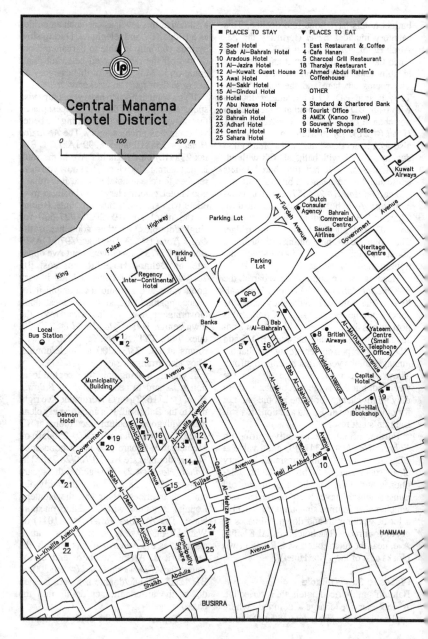

## Central Manama Hotel District

0    100    200 m

■ PLACES TO STAY
2 Seef Hotel
7 Bab Al–Bahrain Hotel
10 Aradous Hotel
11 Al–Jazira Hotel
12 Al–Kuwait Guest House
13 Awal Hotel
14 Al–Sakir Hotel
15 Al–Gindoul Hotel
16 Hotel
17 Abu Nawas Hotel
20 Oasis Hotel
22 Bahrain Hotel
23 Adhari Hotel
24 Central Hotel
25 Sahara Hotel

▼ PLACES TO EAT
1 East Restaurant & Coffee
4 Cafe Hanan
5 Charcoal Grill Restaurant
18 Tharaiya Restaurant
21 Ahmed Abdul Rahim's
   Coffeehouse

OTHER
3 Standard & Chartered Bank
6 Tourist Office
8 AMEX (Kanoo Travel)
9 Souvenir Shops
19 Main Telephone Office

Kuwait
Airways

Dutch
Consular
Agency

Bahrain
Commercial
Centre

Saudia
Airlines

Heritage
Centre

Al–Furdah Avenue

Government Avenue

Parking Lot

Highway

Faisal

King

Parking
Lot

Parking
Lot

Regency
Inter–Continental
Hotel

GPO

Banks

Local
Bus Station

Bab
Al–Bahrain

British
Airways

Yateem
Centre
(Small
Telephone
Office)

Avenue

Municipality
Building

Capital
Hotel

Al–Hilal
Bookshop

Al–Mutanabi Avenue

Bab Al–Bahrain

Abu Obidah Avenue

Al–Muthanna Avenue

Delmon
Hotel

Government Avenue

Municipality Avenue

Saleh Al–Deen

Al–Khalifa Avenue

Al–Ayoobi

Qassim Al–Mehza Avenue

Tujjaar Avenue

Avenue

Wali Al–Ahed Ave

Avenue

HAMMAM

Al–Khalifa Avenue

Municipality Square

Avenue

Shaikh Abdulla

BUSIRRA

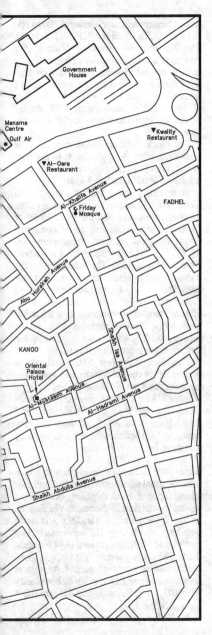

*Hotel* (☎ 255955) is quite good value at BD 14/19 a single/double. The somewhat pricier *Oriental Palace Hotel* (☎ 233331), with rooms at BD 24/37, is just around the corner. Back on Al-Khalifa Ave, near Al-Jazira Hotel, the *Awal Hotel* (☎ 211321) is overpriced at BD 15/22. The rooms are large but rather musty, and for that sort of money one expects much cleaner bathrooms. Nearby, the *Ambassador Hotel* (☎ 277991) costs BD 20.700/25.300 a single/double.

There are also several options in this category outside central Manama. The *Albustan Hotel* (☎ 713911), just off Bani Otbah Ave near Guddies Supermarket, is slightly dowdy and a bit out of the way but decent enough. Singles/doubles cost BD 13.800/19.550. The *Maryland Hotel* (☎ 290295), off Exhibition Ave opposite the Abu Bakr Al-Sadiq Mosque, has spacious, comfortable rooms for BD 17.250/28.750. The *Omar Khayam Hotel* (☎ 713941) on Abdul Rahman Al-Dakhel Ave, off Exhibition Ave, charges BD 23/28.750 for singles/doubles.

### Places to Stay – top end

Bahrain has the usual array of top-line hotels. For five-star accommodation you can expect to pay at least BD 35, and probably closer to BD 50, even before the 15% service charge is added on. 'Corporate' discounts of up to 30% are available, but the hotel's generosity in this regard depends on the occupancy rate at the time. Most of these places offer weekend discount packages (see Accommodation in the Facts for the Visitor section earlier in this chapter) for which you have to book in advance. They all arrange visas.

People with money to spend who want something with a bit more character than the average four or five-star hotel should try the *Delmon Hotel* (☎ 234000, telex 8224 DELHTL BN, fax 246236). At BD 31/41.400 a single/double it's a bit cheaper than the other top-end hotels and good weekend packages are often available on Wednesday, Thursday and Friday nights. The Delmon opened in 1967, which makes it one of the older hotels on the island and something of a local institution. Its Indian restaurant has a very good reputation.

The main four and five-star hotels in Bahrain are:

*Bahrain Hilton* (☎ 535000, telex 8288 HILTON BN, fax 533097), Palace Ave, just north of Government Ave

*The Diplomat* (☎ 531666, telex 9555 BN, fax 530843), across King Faisal Highway from the National Museum

*Gulf Hotel* (☎ 233000, telex 8241 GULFTL BN, FAX 713040), Bani Otbah Ave, near the intersection with the Al-Fatih Highway

*Holiday Inn* (☎ 531122, telex 9000 HOLINN BN, fax 530154), King Faisal Highway, near the causeway to Muharraq

*Ramada Hotel* (☎ 714921, telex 8855 RAMADA BN), Bani Otbah Ave

*Regency Inter-Continental Bahrain* (☎ 231777, telex 9400 REGENT BN, fax 240028), King Faisal Highway, near Bab Al-Bahrain

*Sheraton Bahrain* (☎ 533533, telex 9440 SHERAT BN, fax 534069), Palace Ave at the intersection with Government Ave

### Places to Eat

**Cheap & Medium-Priced** Very few restaurants in this price category serve alcohol and most of them have the same basic mix of Arabic appetisers and Indian and Far Eastern main dishes. A few Western specialities (usually steaks) fill out the menu. While the selections on the menu don't vary much you'll probably find that places staffed by Indians tend to push Indian food, places staffed by Thais will feature Chinese and Thai food, etc.

Western-style fast food is also plentiful and affordable; at breakfast time this may be one of your better options. The Western fast-food joints are also your best bet if you need a midnight snack – several of the ones around Bab Al-Bahrain are open 24 hours a day.

There are lots of cheap places to eat in the centre, especially on Government and Al-Khalifa Aves around Bab Al-Bahrain. If your taste does not run to burgers and fries try the *Charcoal Grill* restaurant next to Bab Al-Bahrain. They feature a wide selection of Indian, Chinese and Filipino food. Try the mixed fried rice at BD 1.600. Nearby, also on Government Ave, *Cafe Hanan* offers a

mix of burgers and sandwiches at 300 to 700 fils and Filipino food for BD 1 to BD 1.200. The *Tharaiya* restaurant on Municipality Ave, next to the Abu Nawas Hotel, is slightly more expensive. The menu is heavy on Thai and Chinese noodle dishes. A meal at any of these places costs BD 2 to BD 3. A number of small Indian restaurants, with similar prices, are in the area around the Al-Jazira Hotel.

One block north of Government Ave, the *East Restaurant & Coffee*, next to the Seef Hotel, has Thai food but not much of a selection. Meals cost BD 3 to BD 4.

Immediately across from the entrance to Government House on Government Ave, the *Al-Osra Restaurant* has the usual blend of 'Arabic, Indian, Chinese and Continental Foods' (to quote its sign). Starters cost 300 to 500 fils and main dishes cost anywhere from 500 fils to BD 3. The Indian food is the cheapest, while steaks are the most expensive. The *Kwality Restaurant*, further along Government Ave in the direction of the Hilton/Sheraton roundabout, has a similar menu but with more emphasis placed on the Indian food. The surroundings are nicer, but the prices are pretty much the same.

There are very few traditional coffee houses left in central Manama. A good one, however, is *Ahmed Abdul Rahim's Coffee House* on Government Ave, west of the Oasis Hotel. The sign is only in Arabic but you'll find it hard to miss with all those old men sitting on blue benches sipping tea. You may join them for 25 fils per cup.

**Expensive** Outside of the big hotels, which offer the usual selection of Arabic, Continental and Japanese food, there are not too many top-end restaurants in the centre. *The Saddle*, in the Tylos Hotel, a Tex-Mex restaurant popular with off-duty US servicemen, is a pretty good Mexican restaurant by Gulf standards. They have good enchiladas, very good nachos and excellent margaritas. Appetisers start from around BD 1; main dishes mostly from BD 3. Figure on paying BD 6 to BD 8 for a good meal.

*Baalbek*, adjacent to the Tylos Hotel on

Government Ave, is a very good Lebanese restaurant. Mezza range from 850 fils to BD 1.500 and main dishes are BD 3.500 to BD 5. They also feature live music in the evenings.

Popular up-market places outside the centre include *Upstairs, Downstairs* in Al-Adliya near the Ramada hotel for English food and *Señor Paco's* in Al-Mahuz near the British Club for Tex-Mex.

You should also keep an eye on the *Gulf Daily News* for cheap lunch specials at the big hotels (or just stick your head into a five-star hotel's bar at lunch time). A typical offer is a buffet lunch (frequently served in the bar) including a beer or soft drink and dessert for anywhere between BD 2.500 and BD 5.500, service included. The *Clipper Bar* at the Regency Inter-Continental Hotel is a good bet.

On Fridays most of the big hotels put on all-you-can-eat buffet brunches for BD 6 to BD 8 plus a service charge. If you have an appetite these can be good for a splurge. The best established is the *Jazz Brunch* at the Diplomat Hotel, featuring live music by the Bahrain Jazz Quartet from 11.30 am to 2.30 pm. Use of the swimming pool for the afternoon is included in the price.

### Entertainment
Bahrain's nightlife revolves around the bars and lounges in the large and medium-size hotels. These range from comfortable-but-generic (the Clipper Bar at the Regency Inter-Continental) to the bizarrely thematic (the Sherlock Holmes Bar at the Gulf Hotel and the 1st-floor bar at the Al-Jazira Hotel, featuring Tudor decor) to the carefully targeted (the Hunter's Lounge at the Adhari Hotel). Western rock stars occasionally drop in for one-off performances and the five-star hotels regularly bring theatre companies out from the UK (and occasionally France) for three or four-night runs. Arab singing stars show up now and then.

On a weekly basis, however, it is mostly lounge bands (a man, a woman and a drum machine) and a lot of loud drunks, most of them from out of town.

There are a couple of small cinemas in town which show only Indian films.

### Things to Buy
A wide selection of local crafts are on sale at the tourist office in Bab Al-Bahrain. The shop also stocks some quite striking wood and brasswork, though most of it is not locally made. Prices in the tourist office shop are fixed.

For interesting antiques and regional (though rarely Bahraini) crafts try the Badran Trading House Persian Store on Rd 467 (an alley off Government Ave near the Bahrain Islamic Bank). They have a selection of Iranian, Indian and Chinese goods. The printed tablecloths from Isfahan in Iran are especially nice. These sell from BD 2 to BD 20, depending on size.

### Getting There & Away
**Air** The development of longer range aircraft in recent years has caused Bahrain's once booming stopover trade to drop off a bit, but Bahrain International Airport is still one of the busiest in the Gulf. Remember to reconfirm your flight 72 hours in advance, particularly if you are travelling with Gulf Air, Saudia or Kuwait Airways. Most airline offices are open Saturday to Wednesday from 8 or 8.30 am to 12.30 pm and 3 pm to 5 or 5.30 pm (morning hours only on Thursday). The addresses and phone numbers of some of the carriers serving Bahrain are:

Air France
    Manama Centre, Government Ave (☎ 255375)
British Airways
    Al-Khalifa Ave, next to Kanoo Travel/American Express (☎ 253503)
Cathay Pacific
    Government Ave, just west of Bab Al-Bahrain (☎ 250676)
Gulf Air
    Manama Centre, Government Ave (☎ 530044)
KLM
    Manama Centre, Government Ave (☎ 234234)
Kuwait Airways
    Manama Centre, Government Ave (☎ 230390)
Lufthansa
    Manama Centre, Government Ave (☎ 210026, 210505)

Royal Jordanian
  Off the alley that intersects Al-Furdah Ave between the Dairy Queen and the Al-Ahli Centre (☎ 258616)
Saudia
  Bahrain Commercial Centre at the corner of Government Ave and Al-Furdah Ave (☎ 211550)

**Bus** The Saudi-Bahraini Transport company runs five buses daily to and from Dammam via Alkhobar. The fare is BD 4 one-way, BD 7 return. Buses leave Bahrain for Saudi Arabia at 8.30 am, noon, and at 3, 6 and 8.30 pm. Buses leave Dammam for Bahrain at 8 and 11 am and at 2, 5 and 8 pm.

The trip between Bahrain and Alkhobar takes about two hours with the bus arriving in Dammam about 45 minutes later.

The buses arrive at the Manama Bus Terminal, just east of the Central Market buildings on Lulu Ave, between King Faisal Highway and Government Ave. The ticket office and departure station is in the commercial centre across the street. There are fewer buses each day during Ramadan and more during Eid Al-Fitr and Eid Al-Adha. There are no lockers in the waiting room at the ticket office but if you ask nicely they might let you stow your gear for a few hours if you are travelling out by bus later that day.

**Car** All of the big hotels have car rental desks representing the major chains. Rates for compact cars start at around BD 13 per day or BD 78 for a week, including unlimited mileage. The insurance included usually leaves the renter liable for the first BD 200 of damage in the event of an accident, but you can get around this by purchasing a collision damage waiver for BD 2 per day. Personal accident insurance will probably add another BD 1. To rent a car in Bahrain you need an International Driving License. This cannot be obtained in Bahrain if you do not already have one. Foreigners resident in another GCC country can rent a car using a license from that country.

If you want to save some money, Fakhrawi Car Hiring & Construction Establishment (☎ 712628) on Bani Otbah Ave, near the Ramada Hotel, has some old Datsuns which they will rent out for BD 7 per day, but they won't sell you any insurance to go with them. They have newer cars as well, for which insurance is available. These are a little bit cheaper than the ones available from the bigger firms, but not much.

### Getting Around

**To/From the Airport** Bahrain International Airport is on Muharraq Island, six km from the centre. There is no direct bus service between Manama and the airport. Getting there from Manama by bus involves taking bus Nos 2, 3, 7, 16 or 19 to Muharraq and changing there to bus Nos 4, 6 or 10. To reach Manama from the airport do this in reverse. At 50 fils per bus (ie, 100 fils from the airport to town) this is cheap. It is also a very slow way to travel six km. There is usually only one bus every 40 to 60 minutes on each route and the buses stop running in the early evening. That means that if you clear customs any time after about 8 pm you might as well resign yourself to paying for a taxi. It also means that you cannot count on getting out to the airport by bus anytime after about 9 pm, which is not very convenient if you are catching a 2.30 am flight. A taxi between Manama and the airport is a flat BD 3 in either direction.

**Bus** Bahrain's bus system links routes around Greater Manama and to the outlying towns. Fares are a flat 50 fils per trip. The buses run from about 5.30 or 6.30 am until 7.30 or 9.30 pm depending on the route. There is usually a bus every 40 to 60 minutes (except on Route 18 which only has service every 90 minutes). Manama's main bus terminal is on Lulu Ave by the Central Market. See the Muharraq section for routes based on Muharraq Island. Manama-based routes are:

Route 1 – Manama Bus Terminal, Water Garden, Sulmaniya, Police Fort, American Mission Hospital, Ras Rumman, Muharraq
Route 2 – Isa Town, Al-Sehlah, Al-Khamis, Sulmaniya, Manama Bus Terminal, Manama Municipality, Ras Rumman, Muharraq

Route 3 – Manama Bus Terminal, Manama Municipality, UK Embassy, American Mission Hospital, Kuwaiti Building (Shaikh Isa Ave), Radio Station, Al-Jufayr, Mina Sulman

Route 5 – Al-Budayyi', Ad-Diraz, Abu Saybi, Jidd Hafs, Al-Budayyi' Rd, Manama Bus Terminal, Manama Municipality, Ras Rumman, Old Palace Rd, Al-Sulmaniya Ave

Route 7 – East Rifa, West Rifa, Isa Town, Al-Sehlah, Al-Khamis, Al-Sulmaniya Ave, Manama Bus Terminal, Manama Municipality, Ras Rumman, Muharraq

Route 12 – Manama Bus Terminal, Water Garden, Sulmaniya, Al-Mahuz, Umm Al-Hassam, Sitra

Route 16 – Manama Bus Terminal, Manama Municipality, Ras Rumman, Muharraq

Route 18 – Manama Bus Terminal, Ras Rumman, Gudabiya Rd, Radio Station, Umm Al-Hassam, Al-Jufayr, Mina Sulman, Nabih Salih Island

Route 19 – Isa Town, Tubli, Al-Sehlah, Jidd Hafs, Al-Budayyi' Rd, Manama Bus Terminal, Manama Municipality, Ras Rumman, Muharraq

**Taxi** If you opt to bargain with taxi drivers, trips in Manama should cost BD 1; this includes more far-flung places like the Gulf Hotel. Short runs around downtown are 500 to 700 fils. Even a trip to Isa town should not be more than BD 3 each way. If you want to stick to the official rates, however, first go to the tourist office and get a copy of the official fare list, *Taxi Fares & Tourist Information Guide*. Tips are not expected if you bargained the fare in advance, but a small tip might be in order if you are sticking to the set tariff. See the Getting Around section earlier in this chapter for a selection of official taxi fares.

# Around Bahrain Island

### Qal'at Al-Bahrain

Bahrain's main archaeological site, also known as Bahrain Fort or the Portuguese Fort, is a complex containing four separate excavations. The site is about five km west of Manama and is easy to reach by car: keep driving on King Faisal Highway past the Pearl Monument roundabout. Look for a sign saying 'Bahrain Fort' about two to 2.5 km past the roundabout. The site is not on any bus route. The closest that the buses come is the Al-Budayyi' Highway, from which it would be a very long walk. The site is open every day during daylight hours. Admission is free. If you hire a taxi to take you out to the fort do not let the driver leave you there and 'come back in an hour'. The fare from Manama should be between BD 3 and BD 5.

This was the site of the earliest professional archaeological digs in Bahrain, the ones described so wonderfully in Geoffrey Bibby's *Looking for Dilmun*. When Bibby began digging here in the winter of 1953-54, the Portuguese Fort was the only thing visible. It was obvious, however, that the Portuguese structure was sitting on a tell, a hill formed from the rubble of previous cities. The digging went on well into the '80s and what emerged was a much broader and more complex pattern of settlement than had been expected. In all, seven layers of occupation were discovered. Bear in mind when looking at both the fort and the excavated areas that the coastline would then have been closer to the ruins than it is today.

The site appears to have been occupied from about 2800 BC, the time when Dilmun was coming into its own as a commercial power. The settlement here was then fairly small. The oldest excavated part of the site is the portion of a defensive wall from the City II period (circa 2000 BC). This was the Early Dilmun period during which the Dilmun civilisation was at the height of its power. The wall ruins are now all that survive from this era of the site's history. They indicate, however, that this spot on the north coast of the island had come to be regarded as important. (Why else would the previously undefended site have been surrounded with a wall?) The largest visible section of the wall lies just east of the Portuguese ruins.

The excavated remains of Cities III and IV are referred to as the Kassite and Assyrian Buildings. These date from 1500 to 500 BC and lie just south of the Portuguese fortress. The main thing you can see in this area is the remains of a house with a three-metre-high entryway in the over-monumental style familiar to anyone who has ever spent a few minutes in the British Museum's Assyrian gallery. The house probably dates to the latter part of the City IV period.

City V was a Hellenistic settlement of which no excavated remains are visible. The area toward the sea contains City VI, the Islamic Fort, of which little remains. This is generally thought to have been built in the 11th century AD though some archaeologists believe it shows characteristics of much earlier construction. It is thought that it may have been built on top of (or by making significant alterations to) an earlier structure.

Then there is City VII, the mid-16th century Portuguese fort surrounded by a dry moat. Two of the bastions are in decent shape and restoration work is in progress.

## Karbabad

As you approach Qal'at Al-Bahrain from Manama and pass through an area of gardens and trees, you will probably see some old men sitting along the side of the road. They are basket weavers from the village of Karbabad and the baskets are for sale. You can also buy the baskets in the shop at the tourist office.

## Ad-Diraz & Barbar Temples

These sites are west of Qal'at Al-Bahrain and are easily accessible from the Al-Budayyi' Highway. Both are north of the highway and are clearly signposted as you come from Manama (but not if you are driving in the other direction). They are open during daylight hours and admission is free. Bus No 5 stops very close to the Ad-Diraz Temple. If you do not have a car you will have to walk from there to the Barbar Temple, which could take 20 to 30 minutes.

The Ad-Diraz Temple is adjacent to the Al-Budayyi' Highway. It was excavated in the mid-70s. Less is known about it than some of the other contemporary Dilmun temples. It dates from the 2nd millennium BC, and is several centuries younger than the Barbar Temple, from which it differs significantly.

The site is quite small. Its centrepiece is a stone base standing in an area where it would have been almost surrounded by columns. Many of the column bases are still intact. It is thought that the stone base originally supported either an altar or a statue of the god to whom the temple was dedicated. In the centre of the temple is another stone which was almost certainly an altar of some sort. Note the drain hole in the floor, thought to have been used to channel the offerings away from the altar.

Barbar is a complex of three 2nd and 3rd millennium BC temples. These were probably dedicated to Enki, the God of Wisdom and The Sweet Waters Under the Earth. In a country as blessed with natural springs as Bahrain is, this god of fresh waters was, understandably, an important one to the people who lived here.

The excavated complex is viewed from a series of walkways. These give you a great view of everything, though even with a detailed map (such as those in Carter's *Bahrain – A Heritage Explored* or the site guide published by the Ministry of Information) you'll have trouble distinguishing one period from another.

Temples I and II are both from the 3rd millennium BC. In general, the oldest portions of the complex are those closer to the centre, though the entire site was enclosed by a wall during the Temple II period. The thick wall areas, including the rounded corner one, are from Temple III (early 2nd millennium BC).

## Bani Jamrah

This village, just south of the Al-Budayyi' Highway, near the road's western end, is known for its cloth weavers. They sit in small open shacks weaving from skeins placed in a bag secured to a wooden post eight to 10 metres away. Taking pictures is no problem though the location of the weavers' shacks which is away from the village and near the main road implies that tourists are welcome at the shacks but not in the village itself.

## Al-Budayyi' (Budaiya)

This small village marks the western edge of

Bahrain Island. The beach where the road ends has nice views at sunset and also gives you some idea of the scale of the Saudi-Bahrain causeway.

## Suq Al-Khamis Mosque

Approximately 2.5 km south of Manama on the Shaikh Salman Highway, this is the oldest mosque in Bahrain. The mosque is a ruin but restoration work has begun in recent years. The site is open Saturday to Wednesday from 7 am to 2 pm and Thursdays and Fridays from 8 am to noon. Admission is free.

It is possible to climb the minarets, though I wouldn't recommend this for anyone who is either tall or claustrophobic. The original mosque is believed to have been built in the late 7th century by Umar, one of the first Caliphs. As for what you see today, an inscription puts the construction in the second half of the 11th century. It is possible, however, that some fragments of the original mosque remain. Experts say that the building has some architectural features generally unique to 7th and 8th century mosques.

To reach the mosque leave Manama via the Shaikh Salman (or Sulman) Highway. Once in the village of Al-Khamis (the site, until the 1960s, of Bahrain's donkey market) you'll see the mosque on the right side of the road as you come from Manama.

## Ayn Adhari Park

The spring *(ayn)* for which the park is named, and the entrance to the park itself, are a few km south-west of the Suq Al-Khamis mosque along the Shaikh Salman Highway. You can also approach the park from the south via the Shaikh Isa Bin Sulman Highway. The park is part formal garden, part amusement park (complete with a tiny train chugging among the hedges) and a pleasant respite from Manama's traffic.

## A'ali Burial Mounds

There are about 85,000 burial mounds in Bahrain. They are, literally, all over the island, though many are concentrated in about half a dozen major mound fields. If you want to look at some excavated ones a permit, though not technically necessary, is a good idea as it makes the guards and/or archaeologists rather more amenable to the presence of your camera. The tourist office can offer advice on this formality. Before visiting a mound field you might also want to visit the National Museum and look at the reconstructed mound in the Dilmun gallery.

The most impressive group of mounds are the so-called 'Royal Tombs' in the village of A'ali, south-west of Manama. These are the largest burial mounds in Bahrain and may or may not have been the tombs of kings. It was one of the great fallacies of 19th century Western archaeology to impose European notions of kingship on almost every ancient society. The mounds were originally pronounced 'royal' simply because of their size. The largest are 12 to 15 metres high and up to 45 metres in diameter.

A'ali is also the site of Bahrain's best known pottery workshop. A'ali pottery is on sale in the tourist office shop or at several stalls around the village.

To reach A'ali from Manama, take the Shaikh Salman Highway south past Isa Town, then turn west on A'ali Highway. Once you reach the village turn right on Ave 42 (there's a small blue street sign) to reach both the mounds and the pottery workshop. If you would like to see some mounds which are not surrounded by lots of houses and a few slag heaps, get back on the A'ali Highway and drive out beyond the edge of town. You'll see one of the island's larger mound fields immediately to your left. Another large mound field is a few km to the north-west at Sar. The Causeway Approach Rd runs straight through it.

## King Fahd Causeway

The causeway connecting Saudi Arabia and Bahrain was conceived during the oil boom of the mid-70s and finally opened in late 1986. It is an impressive piece of engineering. Customs and immigration formalities are carried out on an artificial island halfway across in the centre of the causeway. Two needle-like towers dominate the island, one

## The Garden of Eden?

And the Lord God planted a garden eastward in Eden; and there he put the man whom he had formed.
And out of the ground made the Lord God to grow every tree that is pleasant to the sight, and good for food; the
tree of life also in the midst of the garden, and the tree of knowledge of good and evil.

*Genesis 2:8-9*

Bahrain's greenery and its depiction in Sumerian mythology as an enchanted place where people lived a life free of death and disease has led some archaeologists and scholars to conclude that it may have been the geographical location of the biblical Garden of Eden. This idea is reinforced by the Tree of Life, the traditional name given by Bahrainis to the lone tree, fed by an underground spring, which stands in the centre of the southern, largely desert, part of Bahrain Island.

On one level the identification of Bahrain with Eden may not be as implausible as it seems. Most scholars believe that what we now know as the Old Testament is a product of the mingling of centuries of mostly oral traditions from throughout the Middle East. Trade routes and conquering kings brought the religious traditions of many societies into contact with one another. In the *Epic of Gilgamesh*, Dilmun (Bahrain) is portrayed as an Eden-like paradise. When he arrives there Gilgamesh is met by the Sumerian equivalent of Noah. It is not unreasonable to suppose that in the centuries before the Book of Genesis was written, the Hebrew and Sumerian traditions of paradise and the creation became, to some extent, intermingled. Genesis itself actually combines two separate creation stories and includes (chapter 2, verses 10-14) an account of Eden's location which most modern scholars believe to be a later addition, probably by an ancient scholar who was trying to clarify the text.

Those verses say that 'a river went out of Eden...and from thence it was parted and became into four heads' (2:10). It then names the four rivers. One is the Euphrates and another is obviously the Tigris but the identification of the other two is much less clear. Some scholars have identified the other two rivers, named Pison and Gihon, with the Indus and the Nile respectively. Granted ancient conceptions of geography the idea of those four rivers having a common source would not have seemed as weird at the time as it does now, though that would put Eden somewhere in either southern Turkey or north-central Iraq. Even with an ancient map it is a little hard to see those (or any other) four rivers having a common source at Bahrain.

As the Encyclopaedia Britannica's entry on Eden notes, drily: 'The attempt to locate a mythological garden is bound to be attended by considerable difficulty'. ■

in Saudi Arabia and the other in Bahrain. A restaurant in the Bahraini tower offers views splendid enough to make up for the mediocre food. The causeway is well worth both the trip and the BD 2 causeway toll.

### The Tree of Life

This lone tree, apparently fed by an underground spring, has been the subject of much speculation. It is the centrepiece of the 'Bahrain-was-the-Garden-of-Eden' theory advanced by some archaeologists, scholars and, most enthusiastically, by the tourist office. For the record no angel, flaming sword in hand, has recently been spotted guarding the tree though the military occasionally uses the area for manoeuvres. It's very hard to find and your best bet is either a resident with a car, a map and a lot of

patience or the Bahrain Explored's Southern Region Tour.

# Muharraq Island

There is no place to stay on Bahrain's second most important island, but there is a lot to see. Most of it is within walking distance of Muharraq's bus terminal. The bus terminal is near the end of the causeway to Manama and there are several tea stalls and restaurants in the neighbourhood, as well as a post office. To reach the bus terminal as you come off the causeway turn right at the first roundabout. The station will be on your right after about 100 metres.

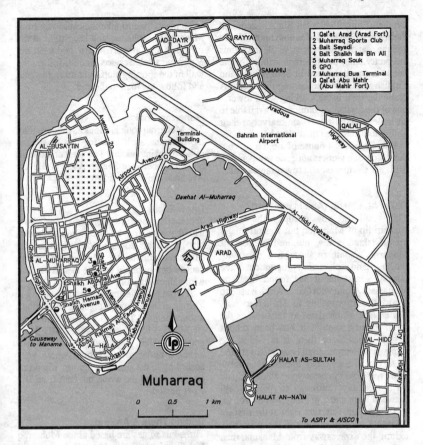

1 Qal'at Arad (Arad Fort)
2 Muharraq Sports Club
3 Bait Seyadi
4 Bait Shaikh Isa Bin Ali
5 Muharraq Souk
6 GPO
7 Muharraq Bus Terminal
8 Qal'at Abu Mahir
  (Abu Mahir Fort)

## Bait Shaikh Isa Bin Ali & Bait Seyadi

These two traditional houses are well worth visiting for a look at pre-oil life in Bahrain. To reach them go straight through the roundabout as you come off the causeway from Manama. Follow the road as it swings around to the left, then turn right on Shaikh Abdulla Bin Isa Ave (you should see two small blue-and-white signs pointing the way to the houses). Further up Shaikh Abdulla Bin Isa Ave you will see another set of signs pointing to the left. After turning left take the first right to reach Bait Shaikh Isa Bin Ali. To reach Bait Seyadi continue in the direc-

tion of the signs until the road forks. Keep right and then follow the road around to your left. The house will be immediately in front of you, next to a small mosque. The entrance is around the far side. Both houses are open Saturday to Wednesday from 8 am to 2 pm and Thursday from 9.30 am to 5 pm. It is closed Friday and admission is free.

Walking to either house from Muharraq Bus Terminal should not take more than 10 or 15 minutes.

Bait Shaikh Isa Bin Ali was built around 1800, presumably by one of Muharraq's wealthier citizens. Later in the 19th century the then-Emir, Shaikh Isa Bin Ali, acquired the house which he used as both his residence and the seat of government. While the rooms are pretty bare, the different sections of the house are well marked in both Arabic and English with signs explaining their uses. A particular treat is the working wind tower – one of the few opportunities still available to sit under a wind tower and marvel at their ability to catch even the tiniest breeze.

Bait Seyadi is a house of similar age but the restoration work is not quite as advanced. Still, it's worth the extra few minutes walk.

### Qal'at Abu Mahir (Abu Mahir Fort)
This small fort now occupies the southwestern tip of Muharraq but was originally on an island a few hundred metres off Muharraq's southern shore. It is only with the huge land reclamation programme of the last 40 years that it has found itself on Muharraq. Along with Qal'at Arad, it used to guard the approaches to Muharraq bay. Qal'at Abu Mahir dates as far back as the 16th century, though it has been rebuilt several times since then. It is within the grounds of the Muharraq coast guard station so access is sometimes limited. Generally, however, if you present yourself at the gate on a weekday (Saturday to Wednesday) between 7 am and 2 pm they will let you in.

To reach the fort, turn right at the first set of lights as you come off the causeway exiting the expressway from Manama, then swing around to the left onto the coast road. The Coast Guard base is a short distance down the road and will be immediately in front of you.

### Qal'at Arad (Arad Fort)
The foundations of this fort also date from the 16th century, though much of what is visible today originated during the brief Omani occupation of Bahrain at the beginning of the 19th century. The fort has been beautifully restored and is now used for concerts. Its opening hours are the same as for Qal'at Abu Mahir.

To reach the fort take the causeway from Manama to Muharraq and keep right at the turn for the airport. Turn right at the Muharraq Club Service Station, follow the wall of the sporting club and turn right again and follow the road to the end.

### Muharraq Souk
The Muharraq souk is a lot less modern than the Manama souk and, for that reason, is rather more interesting. The heart of the souk is the area between Shaikh Abdulla Bin Isa Ave and Shaikh Hamad Ave.

### Dhow Trips
Technically you need a permit to take a dhow trip (these are, after all, ocean-going vessels) but if you go down to the wharf at the Muharraq end on the Manama-Muharraq causeway you might be able to strike a deal with a dhow captain.

A more sensible approach would be to get a group of three or more together and contact a tour operator. Tourism Projects Company (☎ 211025) has dhow trips from BD 3 per person. Bahrain Explored (☎ 246266) also arranges dhow trips at prices which vary according to the size of the group, trip duration and day of the week, but start from BD 7 per person.

### Getting There & Around
Three bus routes are based at the Muharraq Bus Terminal. The buses start around 5.30 am and run until the early evening.

Route 4 – Muharraq Bus Terminal, Shaikh Sulman Rd, Maternity Hospital, Bahrain Airport, Arad, Al-Hidd, Medical Centre

Route 6 – Muharraq Bus Terminal, Shaikh Sulman Rd, Bahrain Airport, Maternity Hospital, Ad-Dayr, Samahij

Route 10 – Muharraq Bus Terminal, Shaikh Sulman Rd, Maternity Hospital, Bahrain Airport, Arad, Halat As-Sultah

To get to the airport from Manama by bus you must go to Muharraq first and then change to any of the Muharraq buses. With only one bus an hour on Route Nos 6 and 10 and two an hour on Route No 4, this could be a pretty slow process. The buses stop running in the early evening and are of little use to people catching flights at wacky hours of the morning.

Service taxis also gather at the Muharraq Bus Terminal.

# Kuwait

Life in Kuwait during the last few decades has rarely been dull. As if being a micro-state with Saudi Arabia, Iraq and Iran for neighbours was not enough, there was the sudden rush of money which, in the 1950s, made Kuwait the prototype of what later came to be known as an oil sheikhdom. That was followed by territorial disputes, breakneck industrial development, a roller coaster experiment with parliamentary democracy, social tensions, the nationalisation of the oil industry, a stock market scandal of mind-boggling proportions, the collapse of the oil market, a rash of Iranian-inspired terror bombings and eight nerve-wracking years of Iran and Iraq bleeding each other white just over the horizon. Kuwaitis are often accused of being arrogant, but anyone who weathers all of that over one generation and comes out smiling deserves some points for endurance.

Then came the invasion. Suddenly Kuwait was to be the test case for US President George Bush's 'New World Order'. There was a theory, fairly widespread at the time, that the Gulf crisis was destined to be the great defining moment of the post-cold war world. A couple of years down the line that looks a bit overstated. Returning to Kuwait 10 months after the country's liberation from Iraqi occupation I found it a strangely eerie place. The government seemed obsessed with precisely recreating the appearance the country had prior to the invasion. The result, once again, was the prototypical oil state, but though Kuwait may look the same, it has certainly changed, and it may be a few more years before anyone, Kuwaitis included, is really able to say how.

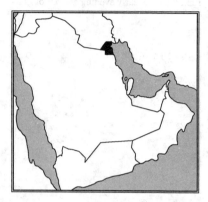

Kuwait is a newcomer to the world scene. The headland now occupied by Kuwait City was settled only some 300 years ago. Prior to that the most important part of what is now the State of Kuwait was the small island of Failaka, which lies just outside the mouth of Kuwait Bay and controls the sea lanes approaching it (a point which, many centuries later, was not lost on the Iraqis, who heavily garrisoned the island). The island also served as a convenient stopping-off place for ancient travellers bound from Mesopotamia to the Indian Ocean and beyond.

Failaka was inhabited during the Bronze Age though it is not entirely clear whether it then belonged to the Bahrain-based Dilmun empire or was a southern outpost of Sumeria. It was the Greeks, however, who put Failaka, which they called Ikaros, on the map.

By 325 BC, Alexander the Great had crossed the Indus River and conquered parts of what is now India. As he prepared to return to Babylon, Alexander ordered Nearchus, a Cretan commander in his army, to build a fleet and return to Mesopotamia by sea, reconnoitring the coast of Persia while Alexander went by land. The fleet was built near

## Facts about the Country

### HISTORY
**A Greek Colony in the Gulf**

By the standards of Bahrain or Oman,

Kuwait

0    25    50 km

present-day Karachi and Nearchus eventually rejoined Alexander in Babylon. By then the young king was considering a campaign to conquer Arabia, probably with an eye toward the wealth of the frankincense producing regions in southern Arabia. Nearchus was sent back to the Gulf, this time with the task of scouting the Gulf's Arabian coastline. He launched several different survey vessels, and his troops are known to have travelled at least as far as Hormuz. But the Arabian campaign was never to be. Alexander died at Babylon only days before he planned to depart for Arabia.

By the time Alexander's empire collapsed, a Greek colony had been established on Failaka. Alexander himself is said to have christened the island Ikaros. Though the island was inhabited, when Nearchus arrived its earlier character was rapidly Hellenised. Ikaros became a centre for trade, fishing and pearling. It was no great metropolis, but it seems to have been reasonably prosperous.

## The Beginnings of Kuwait

Failaka may have been prosperous but throughout most of the Christian era it was not a place of importance. The adjacent areas of the mainland had even less to recommend them and it was not until the 17th century that anything much happened there.

It is unclear both when Kuwait was founded and when the Al-Sabah, Kuwait's ruling family, first arrived there. Official tradition says the family arrived in the area in 1716, though other sources give 1722 or even 'sometime in the 1670s' as the date. What is known is that the Al-Sabah were members of the Utbi tribal federation and that they, and many others, migrated to the Gulf from the Najd region in central Arabia following a period of drought and famine. The Utbis initially went to Basra where they appealed for help to the Ottoman authorities. From Basra they are thought to have wandered south to the headland where Kuwait City now stands.

The word *kuwait* is an Arabic diminutive meaning 'small fort'. The term is thought to refer to a fort or storehouse where the local sheikh kept arms and/or food and livestock at the time of the Utbis' arrival. Kuwait at that time was nothing more than a few tents and the storehouse-cum-fort. The land was arid and any significant agriculture or grazing was negligible. The site did, however, have one clear asset: the bay is one of the best natural harbours on the Arabian side of the Gulf.

The Utbis placed themselves under the protection of the Bani Khalid, then the most powerful tribal confederation in eastern Arabia and the Gulf. They divided among themselves the responsibilities attached to the new settlement: the ancestors of the Al-Sabah family were appointed to handle local law and order and relations with the Bani Khalid. Another family, the Al-Khalifa, was put in charge of the pearl trade, though within a generation they had departed for the better pearling banks of the central Gulf, and by the end of the 18th century, they had conquered Bahrain where they still rule.

In 1752 the Utbis confirmed the right of the Al-Sabah family to rule Kuwait. Today's ruling family takes its name from an ancestor who was confirmed as ruler in that year and reigned until 1756. He spent this brief period taking the first steps to establish Kuwait as a major trading centre.

## Turks, Persians & Britons

The small settlement grew quickly. A Dutch trader who visited Kuwait in 1756 wrote that it had a fleet of some 300, mostly small, boats. The town could also muster 4000 armed men in times of crisis. The mainstay of the economy was pearling. By 1760, when the town's first wall was built, Kuwait's dhow fleet was said to number 800 and camel caravans based there travelled regularly to Baghdad, Riyadh and Damascus.

The great Danish explorer Carsten Neibuhr visited Kuwait, which he called Graine, in 1765 and described it as a town of some 10,000 people, though during the summer, 70% of its inhabitants would disappear, to work the pearl banks or travel with the caravans. According to Neibuhr, in spite of (or maybe because of) the town's prosperity the Utbi and Bani Khalid families still periodically fought over it. Failaka, he said, served as a retreat for noncombatants.

By the early 19th century Kuwait was a thriving trading port. The British traveller W G Palgrave, who visited in 1865, attributed this prosperity to the town's good government.

But trouble was always, quite literally, just over the horizon. It was often unclear whether Kuwait was part of the Ottoman empire or not. Certainly the Ottomans maintained a claim to the emirate, even after it formally became a British protectorate at the end of the 19th century. Official Kuwaiti history is adamant that the Al-Sabah domains were always independent of the Ottomans. In any event, Constantinople's control of the fringes of its empire had always been pretty nominal and never more so than during the 19th century.

International politics in 18th and 19th century Kuwait meant playing the Ottomans against the Persians. It was a game at which the Al-Sabah became remarkably adept. As the years went by, the British were involved as well. The East India Company temporarily moved its Basra office to Kuwait twice in the late 18th century (in 1776 and again in 1793-95) to escape the wars between the Ottomans and Persia. In return, the British drove back the Ottomans when they threatened Kuwait in 1795.

During the second half of the 19th century the Kuwaitis generally got on well with the Ottomans. They skilfully managed to avoid being absorbed into their empire as the Turks sought (less than entirely successfully) to solidify their control of eastern Arabia (then known as Al-Hasa). They did, however, agree to take the title of provincial governors of Al-Hasa.

It was that decision which led to the rise of Shaikh Mubarak Al-Sabah Al-Sabah, commonly known as Mubarak the Great (reigned 1896-1915), the pivotal figure in the history of modern Kuwait. Mubarak was vehemently opposed to accommodating Turkey as outlined in the titles. Deeply suspicious of Turkey and convinced (probably correctly) that Constantinople planned to annex Kuwait, he overthrew and murdered his brother, Shaikh Mohammed, did away with another brother (Jarrah) and installed himself as ruler.

In 1899 Mubarak signed an agreement with Britain modelled on the Exclusive Agreements Britain had signed with the other Gulf rulers over the previous four decades. In exchange for the Royal Navy's protection he promised not to give away territory to, take support from or negotiate with any other foreign power without British consent. The Ottomans continued to claim sovereignty over Kuwait, but they were now in no position to enforce it. Britain's motive for signing the treaty of 1899 was a desire to keep Germany, then the main ally and financial backer of Turkey, out of the Gulf. The Germans had already built a railway line from Constantinople to Baghdad and an extension to Basra and Kuwait was planned. The treaty was London's guarantee that there would never be a railway link from Europe, via Turkey, all the way to the Gulf.

In 1913 the British confirmed Kuwait's independence from the Ottomans by defining the emirate's border with the Ottoman province of Basra. When Iraq became independent in 1932, it reluctantly accepted this border but renounced it after Iraq's monarchy was overthrown in 1958. The Turkish threat faded when Britain occupied Mesopotamia during WW I.

After the palace coup Mubarak's reign was both prosperous and quiet. The population more than tripled (to 35,000 in 1910) and the first schools were opened. Two of Mubarak's four sons went on to become rulers. It is only from these two branches of the royal family that the country's Emirs are now chosen.

The 1920s, however, were a different story. Around the turn of the century Mubarak had played host for several years to the Al-Saud family. They had been driven from their traditional base in Riyadh and had landed up in Kuwait after wandering along the edge of the Empty Quarter desert for a time. It was from Kuwait that the young Abdul Aziz Bin Abdul Rahman Al-Saud set out first to reclaim Riyadh and then to restore the kingdom stretching from the Gulf to the Red Sea which his family had ruled in the late 18th and early 19th centuries.

As he became master of more and more of Arabia, Abdul Aziz never made much secret of his belief that the entire peninsula was, by rights, part of the Saudi kingdom. His years in Kuwait notwithstanding, he eventually turned his attention to the city and unleashed the *ikhwan*, or brotherhood, his much feared army of Bedouin Islamic fundamentalist warriors. Though Abdul Aziz himself was unusually broad-minded the same could not be said of many of his followers, and they took a dark view of what they saw as the loose-living ways of the Kuwaitis.

Kuwait, at that time, had no defensive wall so one was hurriedly erected. The gates along Al-Soor St in modern Kuwait City are all that remain of it today. Hoping to put an end to the Saudi threat to Kuwait, the British, in late 1922 and early 1923, negotiated a formal treaty under which Abdul Aziz recognised Kuwait's independence. His price, however, was two-thirds of what the ruler, Shaikh Ahmed, had always understood to be his land. The British told Shaikh Ahmed that it was a small price to pay to guarantee the country's independence. The attacks, however, did not stop until some years later (the last one took place in 1930) when Abdul Aziz was forced to crush the ikhwan, who had by then become a threat to his own throne.

### The First Oil State

In 1911, the Anglo-Persian Oil Company (the forerunner of today's BP) requested permission from the British government to negotiate a concession agreement with the ruler of Kuwait. The British refused, but did go to the trouble of sending an official of their own to inspect the seepages which had attracted Anglo-Persian's attention in the first place.

With much political manoeuvring, in which the British tried in vain to keep US companies out of the region, it was not until 1934 that an oil concession was granted. The contract went to a joint venture owned 50-50 by Anglo-Persian and the US-based Gulf Oil Company. Together the two companies set up the Kuwait Oil Company (KOC) through which they ran their operations in the emirate.

The first wells were sunk in 1936 and by 1938, it became obvious that the sheikhdom was virtually floating on oil. The outbreak of WW II forced KOC to suspend its operations for several years, but when export operations took off after the war so did Kuwait's economy. Though the state's royalties were slightly lower than those received by Saudi Arabia, Iraq and Iran, the emirate's relatively small population made the revenues huge when calculated on a per capita basis.

The first great rush of oil money came in 1951. In that year Prime Minister Mohammed Mossadiq of Iran nationalised the assets of the Anglo-Iranian Oil Company (as Anglo-Persian was renamed after Persia became Iran in 1935), effectively cutting off the flow of Iranian oil to the company's operations outside the country. Both Anglo-Iranian and its competition rapidly stepped up production elsewhere, including Kuwait,

to take up the slack. Between 1946 and 1956 Kuwait's output rose from 800,000 to a staggering 54 million long tons per year.

Emir Abdullah Al-Salem Al-Sabah (reigned 1950-65) became the first 'oil sheikh'. His reign was not, however, marked by the kind of profligacy with which that term later came to be associated. Kuwait's trading wealth had, up to that point, given it a very high standard of living in local terms and had brought with it some degree of development. Kuwait's geographical position, crammed as it was between Iraqis, Persians, desert nomads, Gulf Arabs and the British had led to the development of an open-minded society rather than a xenophobic one. Moreover, when foreign workers began to flood into the country, the Kuwaiti government went out of its way to see that as many of them as possible were Arabs.

As the country became dramatically wealthy health care, education and the general standard of living improved on a similar scale. In 1949 Kuwait had only four doctors. By 1967 it had 400. The city wall was torn down in 1957 to make way for the rapid, oil-driven growth.

With this flood of money Kuwait was rapidly transformed almost beyond recognition. This, however, was meagre compared to what happened in the '70s. In 1973 Kuwait's oil revenues totalled US$1.7 billion. In 1978 they totalled US$9.2 billion.

Part of these revenues was accounted for by the nationalisation of KOC. In 1974 the government bought 60% of the company. In March 1975, with tension between the Arab world and the West still high in the wake of the 1973-74 oil embargo, Kuwait announced that it was taking over the remaining 40% of the company, though this action was not implemented until December of that year.

### Independence

On 19 June 1961 the treaty with Britain was terminated by mutual consent and Kuwait became an independent state.

In the years leading up to independence, the Al-Sabah family's position in society had been reinforced by the fact that the early oil revenues were paid directly to the ruler. Many, however, still saw Kuwait as little more than a British colony, including the emirate's large population of Egyptian and Palestinian workers, many of whom rioted during the Suez crisis of late 1956, when some of the country's oil pipelines were blown up.

Abdullah was succeeded by Shaikh Sabah Al-Salem Al-Sabah (reigned 1965-77). The current Emir, Shaikh Jaber Al-Ahmed Al-Sabah, served as Finance Minister under Abdullah before becoming Crown Prince and Prime Minister under Sabah.

As Suez had proved, wealth alone could not guarantee stability. The country's labour unions struck in 1967, accusing the government of not giving sufficient support to the Arab and Palestinian cause during that year's Arab-Israeli war. The government sought to placate them first by briefly cutting off the flow of oil to the West during the war and later by taking a prominent role in the Arab summit which took place in Khartoum several months after the war. At Khartoum Kuwait promised huge sums of money to the 'frontline' states confronting Israel and to various Palestinian organisations. When war broke out again in 1973, the government sent Kuwaiti troops to fight along the Suez Canal, partly to blunt the criticism it expected in the National Assembly.

The Kuwaiti parliament has had quite a history. The British first talked the then-ruler, Shaikh Ahmed, into appointing an advisory council in 1921, though he soon dissolved it and returned to ruling alone. A Constituent Assembly, charged with drafting a constitution for the new state, was elected a few months after independence in 1961. The constitution itself was officially promulgated in 1962. Elections for Kuwait's first National Assembly were held later that year and the Assembly first convened in 1963. Though representatives of the country's leading merchant families occupied the bulk of the seats, radicals had a toehold in the body from its inception. The first years of constitutional government were turbulent; leftists in the National Assembly almost immediately began pressing for faster social change and the country had three cabinets between 1963 and 1965.

In August 1976 the cabinet resigned, claiming that the Assembly had made day-to-day governance impossible. The Emir suspended the constitution, dissolved the National Assembly and asked the Crown Prince/Prime Minister of the outgoing government to form a new cabinet, which he did the following day. When new elections were held in 1981, it was only after the electoral laws had been revised in a way which, the government hoped, would guarantee that the radicals won no seats in the new parliament. While this succeeded after a fashion, the Assembly's new conservative majority proved just as troublesome, in its own way, as the radicals had been. Parliament was dissolved again in 1986. The Emir said, at the time, that public arguments over policy were dividing Kuwaitis at a time when the country was coming under threat from Iran during the Iran-Iraq war. Some opposition figures have long contended that the Assembly's real sin was to question the degree to which the Al-Sabah family continued to dominate Kuwait's government.

In December 1989 and January 1990, an extraordinary series of demonstrations took place calling for the restoration of the 1962 constitution and the reconvening of the suspended parliament. The demonstrators challenged the Emir's right to rule without the National Assembly and were met by riot police, tear gas and water cannon. In June of that year, elections were held for a Consultative Council which was supposed to spend four years advising the government on possible constitutional changes prior to the election of a new Assembly. Pro-democracy activists demanded the reconvening of the old Assembly and denounced the Consultative Council as unconstitutional.

### The 1980s: Boom to Slump

During the late 1970s Kuwait's economy seemed to be roaring ahead. The country's stock exchange (the first in the Gulf) was among the top 10 in the world by value and bankers were lining up to buy securities denominated in Kuwaiti dinars.

By the mid-80s everything was different. In the winter of 1985-86, the price of oil collapsed and the economies of all the Gulf states were severely effected. But in Kuwait there were other problems as well. In addition to its regular stock market the country had developed a parallel financial market which, while not strictly legal, was allowed to operate openly and with virtually no regulation. The market, known as the Suq Al-Manakh, operated on a system of postdated cheques which made it virtually impossible for investors to lose money. In 1982, however, panic ensued when some investors got jittery, tried to reclaim their money and found that the dealers were unable to honour the cheques. Within days the entire system collapsed and hundreds of people became bankrupt. The scandal left behind US$90 billion in the worthless postdated cheques and a mess which the Kuwaiti government has been trying to sort out ever since.

Just as the government began to deal with the fallout from the Suq Al-Manakh fiasco, another problem arose. As the Iran-Iraq war, which had begun in 1980, dragged on into its third year, the emirate's location only a few miles from the frontlines made investors nervous. Though some Kuwaiti companies made a lot of money trans-shipping embargoed goods to Iraq the war was, on the whole, a disaster for the country's economy. It did not help matters much that from 1983 Iran sought to punish (officially neutral) Kuwait for its thinly veiled support for Iraq. From 1983 to 1985 the country suffered a string of Iranian-inspired terror-bombings, including highly publicised attacks on the US and French embassies. These attacks scared off foreigners, exacerbated the Sunni-Shiite split in the population and made the government fanatically security-conscious.

### Iraq & Kuwait

Iraq has never really accepted the idea of Kuwait as an independent state: the 1990 invasion was only the latest attempt by Iraq to challenge Kuwait's existence. Minor skirmishes and the occasional major incident have been regular features of Iraqi-Kuwaiti relations since the 1950s. Within hours of Kuwait's gaining independence from Britain in 1961, Iraq reasserted its long-standing claim to the emirate. The Emir called in the British who sent a small force to Kuwait. This proved to be enough to deter the Iraqis in the short term, and the force was replaced three months later by a joint Arab League force.

The most serious of the two countries' many border clashes took place in March 1973 when the Iraqis moved an estimated 3000 troops onto Kuwaiti territory, occupied one Kuwaiti border post and shelled another. After a short time Iraq withdrew under pressure from the Arab League (led by Egypt, which was then preparing for war with Israel and regarded the Iraq-Kuwait border dispute as an unnecessary distraction). Even then, however, Iraq's Foreign Minister went out of his way to assert a claim to Warba and Bubiyan islands.

On the other hand, Iraq had never, even in 1961, attempted to launch an all-out invasion of Kuwait, and by 1990 the Kuwaitis could reasonably claim that Baghdad was in their debt. Throughout the eight-year-long Iran-Iraq war, Kuwait had been a vital lifeline for both sides flowing into Iraq and exports flowing out. Even after the 1983-85 Iranian-sponsored terrorist bombings and a later Iranian decision to shell Kuwaiti territory, the emirate stood by Iraq politically and by contributing enormous sums of money (partly because Kuwait was concerned that an Iranian victory would spill the Islamic revolution into its territory). At the end of May, 1990, the Emir of Kuwait travelled to Baghdad for an Arab summit where, in the traditional Arab manner, he was embraced and kissed by President Saddam Hussein.

Nobody knows exactly when, or why, Saddam decided to invade Kuwait. It is easy to note, in retrospect, that there were signs of trouble. Months before the invasion, for example, the Iraqis had signed a treaty defining once and for all their border with Saudi Arabia. Kuwaiti officials sought a similar treaty and were rebuffed in Baghdad. Some have seen this as the first sign that Saddam was planning to swallow his smaller neighbour. Saddam has never, however, been overly fastidious about international law.

Saddam is known to have badgered the Kuwaitis about money during a closed session of the Baghdad summit. He accused them of waging 'economic warfare' against Iraq by exceeding their OPEC oil production quota which, he claimed, they were doing in an attempt to hold down the price of oil artificially. Both then and after the invasion, the Iraqis also claimed that Kuwait was demanding repayment of the loans Kuwait had extended to Baghdad during the war with Iran, a claim which the Kuwaitis have consistently denied. It had been generally understood at the time the money was transferred to Baghdad that the loans were, in fact, gifts.

The first clear public sign of trouble came on 16 July 1990 when Iraq sent a letter to the Secretary-General of the Arab League accusing Kuwait of exceeding its OPEC quota and of stealing oil from the Iraqi portion of an oil field straddling the border. Iraq's Foreign Minister told an Arab League meeting in Tunisia that 'we are sure some Arab states are involved in a conspiracy against us'. The charge of quota violations was true, Kuwait had long been one of OPEC's most notorious overproducers, but there was nothing new in this and Iraq itself was hardly blameless on that score. Iraq's accusations over the oil field are harder to pin down but ultimately lack substance: the Kuwaiti portion of the disputed Rumailah oil field produced a paltry 25,000 barrels per day.

The day after the Arab League meeting, Saddam repeated his accusations in a speech marking Iraq's Revolution Day and vaguely threatened military action against Kuwait and the United Arab Emirates (UAE). Over the next two weeks the Secretary-General of the Arab League, Saudi Arabia's Foreign Minister and President Hosni Mubarak of Egypt all travelled between Kuwait City and

Baghdad seeking to diffuse the growing crisis Iraq had manufactured.

At the end of July 1990, the Kuwaitis were rapidly discovering that all the money they had lavished on development projects around the region over the previous 30 years had not bought them many allies. In addition, Saddam increasingly appeared determined to pick a fight. In the two weeks leading up to the invasion, the various mediators bent over backwards to offer Iraq a graceful way out of the dispute on five or six occasions. Each time Iraq replied by launching another verbal salvo in the direction of Kuwait. The Iraqis agreed to attend reconciliation talks with the Kuwaitis in Saudi Arabia in late July but then stalled over the ground rules for the talks, and continued to mass troops just north of the border.

When the tanks came crashing over the border at 2 am on 2 August the Kuwaitis never had a chance. The Iraqis were in Kuwait City before dawn and by midday they had reached the Saudi border. The Emir and his cabinet fled to Saudi Arabia.

The United Nations quickly passed a series of resolutions calling on Iraq to withdraw from Kuwait. The Iraqis replied that they had been invited in by a group of Kuwaiti rebels who had overthrown the Emir. The absurdity of this claim was shown up by the failure of the Iraqis to find even one Kuwaiti willing to serve in a quisling government. On 8 August Iraq annexed the emirate.

An emergency summit of the Arab League was held in Cairo on 10 August but Saddam refused to attend. The Iraqis contended that Saudi Arabia's decision a few days earlier asking the USA for troops to defend the Kingdom was at least as significant a threat to the region's security as Iraq's annexation of Kuwait, and a number of the League's members agreed. The League passed a resolution condemning the invasion but was deeply split.

Western countries, led by the USA, began to enforce a UN embargo on trade with Iraq by stopping and searching ships bound for Iraq and Jordan. In the months that followed

US and other forces flooded into Saudi Arabia as the diplomatic standoff over Kuwait deepened. Tens of thousands of refugees, many of them Arabs and Asians who had been working in Kuwait, fled the emirate only to find themselves sweltering in makeshift transit camps on the Iraqi-Jordanian border in the middle of the summer.

The anti-Iraq coalition's forces eventually numbered 425,000 US and 265,000 troops from 27 other countries. They were backed up by an increasingly long list of UN Security Council resolutions calling on Iraq to withdraw from Kuwait. Tales of atrocities were publicised around the world by Amnesty International, Middle East Watch and Kuwaiti exiles. At the end of November, the US and the UK secured a UN resolution authorising the use of force to drive Iraq out of Kuwait if Baghdad did not pull out voluntarily before 15 January 1991.

With less than a week to go before the expiration of the 15 January deadline the US Secretary of State, James Baker, met with Iraqi Foreign Minister Tariq Aziz in Geneva. The talks lasted for nearly six hours but came to nothing. In the final hours before the deadline a number of national leaders, including Mubarak of Egypt and French President François Mitterrand, televised appeals to Saddam to withdraw from Kuwait before it was too late. Yasser Arafat of the PLO rushed to Baghdad to try to broker a deal.

The deadline passed, the Iraqis did not budge, and within hours waves of allied (mostly US) aircraft began a five-week bombing campaign over Iraq and Kuwait.

The ground offensive, when it finally came, lasted only 100 hours and was something of an anti-climax. Iraq's army, which had been touted in the West for the previous six months as one of the most fearsome military machines on earth, simply disintegrated. While there were relatively few casualties on the allied side, controversy has persisted over the number of civilian and military deaths in Iraq and Kuwait. Numbers from 10,000 to 100,000 or more have been offered.

## Liberation & Beyond

When allied forces arrived in Kuwait City on 26 February 1991 they were greeted by jubilant crowds. The city's infrastructure had been almost completely destroyed during the war though many buildings had survived relatively intact (the same could not be said of their contents which had, in many cases, been looted by the Iraqis).

For the first few days anarchy reigned in the liberated city. Some Kuwaitis turned their fury on what was left of the emirate's large Palestinian population. Kuwaiti society seemed split between those who had stayed throughout the occupation and those who had fled. The government declared martial law but the Crown Prince, who also served as martial law administrator, did not return from exile in Saudi Arabia until six days after liberation and it was another 10 days before the Emir himself returned. The royal family was slightly embarrassed by the fact that both the UK and US embassies in Kuwait City were reopened several days before the Crown Prince returned. By the time the Emir returned both British Prime Minister John Major and US Secretary of State James Baker had come and gone.

Amid criticisms that it was moving too slowly, the government set about rebuilding the country, concentrating first on roads and utilities and afterwards on repairing homes and businesses and clearing the country of land mines. Some of the damage inflicted by the retreating Iraqis could only be described as spiteful. As they withdrew from Kuwait, the Iraqis had systematically blown up every oil well in the country and set most of them on fire. For many months thereafter the country was covered in a dense cloud of black smoke from the burning wells, the last of which was extinguished in November 1991, 8½ months after the end of the war.

Even before press censorship was lifted at the end of 1991 a heated debate had begun over the country's political future. In keeping with a promise the Opposition had extracted from the Emir during the occupation, elections for a new National Assembly took place in October 1992. The Opposition

Top: The Kuwait Towers, Kuwait
Bottom: Kuwait National Museum, Kuwait

Top: Mutrah, Muscat, Oman
Bottom: Street in Ruwi, Muscat, Oman

shocked the government by winning over 30 of the new parliament's 50 seats. In keeping with Kuwaiti tradition the Crown Prince was reappointed as Prime Minister. Opposition MPs secured six of the 16 seats in the Cabinet, though the Al-Sabah family retained control of the key defence, foreign affairs and interior ministries. As with past elections the 1992 vote was restricted to the 70,000 or so adult Kuwaiti males holding 'first class' citizenship (those whose ancestors had been resident in Kuwait prior to the 1920s).

By the second anniversary of the invasion Kuwait's government had done an admirable job of erasing many of the physical scars of war and occupation. Its apparent goal is to make Kuwait look exactly as it did before the invasion. Healing the psychological and personal scars is clearly going to take much longer.

## GEOGRAPHY

Kuwait's 17,818 sq km of land are mostly flat and arid with little or no ground water (much of which is brackish, anyway). The desert is generally gravelly. The country is about 185 km from north to south and 208 km from east to west. Its coastline is unexciting and the desert inland is not particularly interesting. The only significant geographic feature is the now infamous Al-Mutla ridge where allied aircraft massacred a column of retreating Iraqi forces in the closing hours of the war.

## CLIMATE

In the summer (April to September) Kuwait is hellishly hot. Its saving grace is that it is nowhere near as humid as Dhahran, Bahrain or Abu Dhabi. The winter months are often pleasant but can get fairly cold, with daytime temperatures hovering around 18°C and nights being genuinely chilly. A good medium-weight jacket and a jumper are essential travelling items for a winter visit to the emirate. Sandstorms occur throughout the year but are particularly common in spring.

## GOVERNMENT

Since the suspension of the National Assembly in 1986, Kuwait has been ruled by Emiri decree with the cabinet, in which the Crown Prince serves as Prime Minister, exercising day-to-day governmental authority. A new 50-member National Assembly was elected in October 1992 and convened later that month.

Voting for the Assembly is restricted to adult, male, 'first class' Kuwaiti citizens. Whether to extend the franchise to all Kuwaitis, and especially to women, is a subject of heated debate in the country.

The ruling family itself picks the Emir from one of two branches of the family. These are known as the Jaber and the Salem branches and refer to two of the four sons of Mubarak the Great who ruled Kuwait from 1896 to 1915. The choice of the Emir alternates between these two branches (though this pattern has been broken once since Mubarak's death). The current Emir, Shaikh Jaber Al-Ahmed Al-Sabah, is from the Jaber branch of the family while the Crown Prince (who is two years younger than the Emir), Shaikh Saad Al-Abdullah Al-Sabah, is from the Salem branch.

Kuwait has maintained a markedly independent foreign policy. For many years it was the only Gulf state to have diplomatic relations with the former Soviet Union and its allies. In the wake of the invasion it has drawn decidedly closer to the West. Since liberation, defence agreements have been signed with the USA, the UK and France.

## ECONOMY

Among the Gulf states, Kuwait's oil reserves are second only to those of Saudi Arabia. Immediately prior to the invasion, production was running at about 1.8 million barrels per day. A large petrochemical industry was built up from the late '60s onward and its reconstruction is high on the government's list of priorities.

Attempts to diversify the economy have met with mixed success. The government sunk a lot of money into agriculture in the '70s, particularly into growing alfalfa and into dairy and poultry farming, but most of the country's food has always been imported and there is no sign of that changing in the short term.

Apart from oil, the country is best known for its investment policies. These sometimes bring unwelcome publicity, as when the London-based Kuwait Investment Office began buying large blocks of stock in British Petroleum (BP). A British court later forced the KIO to sell some of the stock, though there was a certain delicious irony in the government of Kuwait making even a veiled bid for control of one of the oil companies which had originally made it rich. The government has also sought to diversify the country's role as a player in all levels of the oil industry, rather than simply being a producer/refiner of crude oil. It has purchased distribution networks and petrol stations (such as the Q8 chain in the UK) in other parts of the world.

The Fund for Future Generations was established in 1976 as a hedge against the day when oil ran out. For many years 10% of all oil revenues were paid into the fund, the balance of which could not be touched for a minimum of 25 years. By 1988 the fund is thought to have held about US$86 billion. It provided an invaluable source of cash during the occupation when the government used it to support Kuwaitis living in exile and to pay some of the costs of the allied coalition.

In 1961 the government set up the Kuwait Fund for Arab Economic Development, the first such development fund in the Gulf. In the '70s and '80s, Kuwait gave away as much as 10% of its GNP in aid (as against the figure of 0.7% which the UN recommends and which very few developed countries meet).

## POPULATION & PEOPLE

Prior to the invasion, Kuwait's population was 2.2 million, of whom about 616,000 (28%) were Kuwaitis. Most Kuwaitis are Sunni Muslims, and there is a Shiite minority of about a third. Nationalisation of the workforce had been a major topic of discussion

for several years, though only limited progress was made. Immediately after liberation, the government announced that it would never again allow Kuwaitis to become a minority in their own country. This implied a target population of about 1.2 million, but within months there were indications that the occupation had not blunted the Kuwaitis' desire for servants and drivers or made them any more willing than before to do manual labour. As a result, by early 1992 the foreign population of the emirate was said to have crept back ahead of the native population, though no firm figures were available.

## EDUCATION

Kuwait has long provided free education to all Kuwaitis and, before the invasion, to many of the foreigners living in the country. As early as the 1950s Shaikh Abdullah was stressing the importance of education, including women's education (an unusual attitude in the Gulf in those days). The University of Kuwait was founded in 1964; in 1980 more than half its students were women. The government has been trying to channel more young Kuwaitis into the country's eight technical colleges as part of its long-term goal of getting more Kuwaitis into the workforce.

## ARTS

The arts scene in Kuwait is fairly limited. One gallery of the National Museum used to display the works of local painters but this, along with the rest of the museum, was destroyed by the Iraqis. Sadu House (see the Kuwait City section) is a cultural foundation dedicated to preserving Bedouin art traditions, especially weaving. Though it too was damaged by the Iraqis, it looked set to reopen once the restorations were over.

## CULTURE
### Traditional Lifestyle

There is not a lot of this left. Even before the Iraqis arrived the Kuwaitis had managed to eliminate most vestiges of life-before-oil in Kuwait City. Weekend picnics in the desert, which were part of the traditional lifestyle,

Weaver

are clearly out of the question for another year or two until all the mines are cleared.

### Taboos & Avoiding Offence

Kuwait is a lot more relaxed about matters of public conduct than other Gulf countries. Aside from the obviously immodest by Muslim standards (short skirts, halter tops, etc) women can dress as they want and there is never any need for a woman to wear an *abayya* (long, cloak-like black garment), veil or headscarf. During Ramadan, the Muslim month of fasting, you should refrain from eating, drinking or smoking in public. As always you should never photograph people, especially women, without their permission.

Non-Muslims may enter mosques, even during prayer time, as long as proper dress is observed. Women and men should be well covered by wearing long-sleeved clothing; women must also cover their heads. Be quiet in mosques, do not move around unnecessarily and do not take photographs.

### RELIGION

Islam is the state religion and Islamic sharia is identified in the constitution as 'a main source of legislation'. Kuwait's brand of Islam is not as strict as that practised in Saudi Arabia, but the country is not as liberal as Bahrain.

### LANGUAGE

Arabic is the official language but English is very widely understood.

See the Facts about the Region chapter for a glossary of Arabic words and phrases.

# Facts for the Visitor

### VISAS & EMBASSIES

Everyone except nationals of the other Gulf states needs a visa to enter Kuwait. Kuwait requires everyone entering the country to have a sponsor and it does not issue tourist visas. Large hotels can sponsor a visa, which is a fairly straightforward process: you send a telex or fax to the hotel including your passport data (date & place of issue, date of expiration, date of birth, etc), arrival and departure dates, flight numbers and reason for visit (ie, 'business'). The hotels usually prefer a fax copy of the actual passport. The process takes at least three weeks as all visas must be approved by State Security. Most people will receive a single-entry visa valid for one month and for a one-month stay, though business travellers from Western countries which played a large role in the anti-Iraq coalition (the USA, UK, France and Canada, for example) are often given multiple-entry visas valid for one year. These allow the holder to come and go at will, though you can still stay in the country for only one month at a time.

Business travellers visiting a company in Kuwait are sponsored by that particular company, which files various papers with the Ministry of Interior in Kuwait City before the visa can be issued. While it can be picked up at any Kuwaiti diplomatic mission the pick-up point usually has to be specified at the time the papers are filed. You may have to bring a letter supporting your visa to the embassy.

The embassies themselves are of little use to the casual traveller as they only issue visas against instructions from Kuwait. In other words, you cannot simply walk in and apply for a visa.

If your passport contains an Israeli or a South African stamp you will be refused entry to Kuwait.

### Kuwaiti Embassies
Addresses of some Kuwaiti embassies are:

UK
    45/46 Queen's Gate SW7 (☎ (071) 589 4533, 581 2698
USA
    2940 Tilden St NW, Washington DC 20008 (☎ 966-0702)

### Visa Extensions
It is rather difficult to stay in Kuwait for more than one month on a business visa. Even the one-year multiple-entry visas only allow you to remain in the country for a month at a time. People with one-year multiple-entry visas needing to remain in the country for longer than a month have to fly out every 30 days and then come back in (Bahrain is the most common destination). Thus, for business travellers there really is no such thing as an exit/re-entry visa.

### Foreign Embassies in Kuwait
See the Kuwait City section for a list of embassies.

### DOCUMENTS
Health certificates are only necessary if you are arriving from a part of the world with a disease problem. An International Driving License is not usually necessary.

If you want to take pictures in Kuwait you will need a photo permit – see Film & Photography further in this section.

### CUSTOMS
Alcohol is banned in Kuwait and before you get it into your head to smuggle in a bottle you should be aware that it is rare for anyone to get past customs without their baggage being searched. The duty-free allowance for tobacco is 200 cigarettes, 50 cigars and half a kg of loose tobacco.

Bans on pornographic material, guns and ammunition also apply.

### MONEY
#### Currency
Kuwait's post-war currency is still the Kuwaiti dinar (KD) but all of the old banknotes have been demoniterised. The new design is more or less the same but the colours of the bills have changed. You do not have to worry about getting ripped off. Every bank, and most moneychangers, display posters showing the old and new bills and even before this book went to press the old bills were long gone from circulation. Pre-invasion coins are still valid.

The KD is divided into 1000 fils. Notes come in denominations of KD ¼, ½, 1, 5, 10 and 20. Coins are worth 5, 10, 20, 50 or 100 fils. The Kuwaiti dinar is a hard currency and there are no restrictions on taking it into or out of the country (nor are there restrictions on the import or export of foreign currencies).

#### Exchange Rates
| | | |
|---|---|---|
| US$1 | = | KD 0.285 |
| UK£1 | = | KD 0.530 |
| DM1 | = | KD 0.178 |
| FF1 | = | KD 0.048 |
| A$1 | = | KD 0.210 |

#### Costs
Kuwait was never cheap but a lot of prices have doubled since the Iraqi invasion. As the post-liberation euphoria faded in the closing months of 1991 a lot of people began to grumble about the high cost of just about everything in Kuwait. Accommodation prices are absurd. Rooms at the cheapest hotel in Kuwait City start at KD 15, which is about US$52.50. On the other hand, bus and taxi fares are no higher than they used to be and it is still possible to feed yourself reasonably well for only one dinar. A rock-bottom budget would be KD 17.500 per day, but you

are likely to find yourself spending rather more than that.

## Tipping
Generally a tip is not expected except in fancier restaurants. As in the rest of the Gulf the service charge added to your bill in such places goes into the till, not to the waiter or waitress.

## Bargaining
Bargaining is not as common as you might think. If you ask for a discount at, say, a hotel it is likely to be offered but that initial discount probably represents the bottom line. The main exception to this rule is consumer electronics, but I can't think of a more expensive place in the Gulf to buy such things.

## WHEN TO GO
The best time to visit is from mid-October to mid-March, though if you come in summer it is a relief to know that Kuwait is somewhat less humid than the Gulf's other cities (but no less hot).

## WHAT TO BRING
Aside from the usual Gulf necessities of sunglasses, a hat and long-sleeved, loose clothing people visiting in the winter months might want to bring at least a medium-weight jacket and a jumper. These are often necessary at night and could prove useful during the day as well.

## TOURIST OFFICES
There is neither a tourist office nor any semblance of tourist infrastructure in Kuwait. For information on what is happening around town the two English-language newspapers, *Arab Times* and *Kuwait Times*, are your best sources of information.

## BUSINESS HOURS & HOLIDAYS
Shops are open Saturday to Wednesday from 8 or 9 am until about 1 pm and from about 4 pm until 6 or 7 pm. On Thursdays most businesses will only be open in the morning. Government offices work Saturday to Wednesday from 7 am to 1.30 pm but may close at 11.30 or noon on Thursdays. Friday is the weekly holiday and almost nothing is open during the day, though some shops in the centre and in the souk may open in the late afternoon and early evening.

Secular holidays are New Year's Day (1 January), and National Day (25 February). At this writing it was still unclear whether the government intended to make Liberation Day (26 February) a holiday or not. On the first anniversary of liberation, in 1992, there were no official ceremonies. The government announced that this was out of respect for the hundreds of Kuwaitis still being held prisoner in Iraq, implying that the day may be observed in future years.

Religious holidays are tied to the Islamic Hejira calendar. Eid Al-Fitr (the end of Ramadan), Eid Al-Adha (Pilgrimage), Lailat Al-Mi'raj (the Ascension of the Prophet), the Prophet's Birthday and the Islamic New Year are all observed (for dates see the table of holidays page 28).

## CULTURAL EVENTS
There are no particular cultural festivals in Kuwait. Film and theatre festivals are organised on an irregular basis and are advertised in local newspapers. The local papers are also your best source for information on the rare Western theatre company or musical group to pay a visit to Kuwait.

## POST & TELECOMMUNICATIONS
### Postal Rates
Postal rates for letters or postcards weighing up to 20 grams are 25 fils within Kuwait, 50 fils to Arab countries and 150 fils to the rest of the world. For cards or letters weighing 20 to 50 grams postage costs 40 fils domestic, 80 fils in the Arab world and 280 fils everywhere else. Aerogrammes cost 50 fils for delivery in the Arab world and 150 fils to everywhere else. Express service ('Mumtaz Post') is available for an additional 200 fils.

Air parcel service to Arab countries costs 900 fils for the first 500 grams and 250 fils for each additional 500 grams. Surface rates are 850 fils for the first kg, KD 1.150 for one to three kg and KD 1.500 for three to five kg.

Ask at the post office for parcel rates outside the Arab world as they vary significantly from country to country.

### Sending Mail

At this writing, postal service out of Kuwait was pretty bad but it will no doubt improve with time. Until it does, most of Kuwait City's residents were using courier services such as DHL whenever they had something important to send. This was quite efficient but also very expensive and it certainly is not the way to send a letter or a postcard.

### Receiving Mail

Again, things were far from perfect when this book went to press, but they were getting better all the time. The post office no longer offers Poste Restante service so a friend's office or your hotel is probably your best bet. Again, courier services are more reliable than the regular post.

### Telephone

Kuwait's telephone system has been restored (and improved) a lot faster than the postal service. It is now pretty easy to make calls to anywhere in the world, though calls to other Arab countries (eg Egypt) or to Eastern and Central Europe can be quite difficult. See the Kuwait City section for information on government telephone offices.

When calling Kuwait from the outside world the country code is 965, followed by the local seven-digit number. There are no area or city codes.

The USA Direct access code from Kuwait is 800-288. For MCI CallAmerica, Dial 800-624. These services connect you directly to an operator in the USA. You may then make a collect (reverse charges) call or bill the call to a phone company credit card. Unfortunately the service is not yet available to other countries.

Payphones take 50 and 100 fils coins. Two different types of card phone are in use though neither is seen much outside of the telecom offices and post offices, where the relevant cards are sold. Phonecards cost KD 5 or KD 10.

### Fax, Telex & Telegraph

These services are available from the government communications centres, though there are usually long lines there. It's probably easier, but more expensive, to go to a big hotel and send a fax or telex from there.

### TIME

Kuwait is three hours ahead of GMT. When it's noon in Kuwait City, the time elsewhere is:

| City | Time |
| --- | --- |
| Paris, Rome | 10 am |
| London | 9 am |
| New York | 4 am |
| Los Angeles | 1 am |
| Perth, Hong Kong | 5 pm |
| Sydney | 7 pm |
| Auckland | 9 pm |

### ELECTRICITY

Electric voltage in Kuwait is 220 or 240 volts AC. Both the Continental and the British standard prong configurations are in use (though the latter is more common), and neither necessarily indicates what current is coming out of the wall.

## LAUNDRY

Laundromats are unknown in Kuwait. If you don't feel like washing your clothes in your hotel room's sink, your only option is the hotel laundry.

## WEIGHTS & MEASURES

The metric system is in use in Kuwait.

## BOOKS & MAPS

There are not a lot of good books on Kuwait. *The Merchants* by Michael Field (Overlook Press, Woodstock NY, 1985) has a chapter on the Alghanims, arguably Kuwait's most important merchant family. Geoffrey Bibby's *Looking for Dilmun* (Penguin Travel Library, 1972) includes several chapters on the archaeological excavations on Failaka Island and also paints an interesting picture of life in Kuwait in the '50s and '60s.

*The New Arabians* by Peter Mansfield (Ferguson, Chicago, 1981) has a summary on Kuwait's history. Mansfield's *Kuwait: Vanguard of the Gulf* (Hutchinson, London, 1990) is a more general history of Kuwait, though it has a very official feel about it.

The hotel bookshops around Kuwait City stock the usual collection of glossy coffee-table books, and the Ministry of Information publishes several books of facts and figures on the country as well as a rather gruesome collection of photographs of Iraqi atrocities in occupied Kuwait called *The Mother of Crimes Against Kuwait in Pictures*.

See the Facts about the Region chapter for a list of more general books on the Gulf and the Middle East.

## Travel Guides

There are practically no guidebooks to Kuwait. Most of the 'guides' you will see on sale in the emirate are little more than advertising circulars. *The Economist Business Traveller's Guides – Arabian Peninsula* is a bit out of date but contains a lot of useful information on business laws and regulations.

## Maps

The government's drive to reconstruct Kuwait City exactly as it was before the war means that pre-invasion maps are perfectly adequate for finding your way around the city. The *Oxford Map of Kuwait*, identifiable by the night time photo of the Kuwait Towers on the cover, is the best of the locally available maps. Most hotel bookshops have it. A better map, easy to recognise because of its yellow cover, is published by the Ministry of Information and distributed free at Kuwaiti embassies abroad. I've never seen it on sale in Kuwait.

## MEDIA
### Newspapers & Magazines

*Arab Times* and *Kuwait Times* are Kuwait's two English-language newspapers. They are very similar in content. Both provide adequate foreign coverage, largely reprinted from the British newspapers. They also provide the best local news coverage of the Gulf's many English-language rags.

The bookshops in the big hotels are the best places to look for foreign newspapers and magazines. These usually appear about two days late. The *International Herald Tribune*, the main British papers and *Le Monde* are usually available, as are magazines like *Time* and *Newsweek*.

### Radio & TV

In early 1992 the US military's AFRTS (Armed Forces Radio & Television Service) was still broadcasting on several FM and AM frequencies around Kuwait City. One programme carried a mixture of rock and country music while another broadcast US radio newscasts 24 hours a day. At the time nobody seemed to know whether these were going to be a permanent feature of Kuwait's audio landscape or not. The English service of Kuwait Radio was not, at that time, back on the air. The US signals are highly local and you will only be able to pick them up clearly in central Kuwait City.

Channel 2 of Kuwait TV broadcasts programmes in English each day from around 5 pm until midnight.

## FILM & PHOTOGRAPHY

In theory a photography permit is necessary to take pictures of anything in Kuwait. Before the invasion this rule was never enforced so long as one confined oneself to obvious 'tourist' photography (ie the Kuwait Towers or the courtyard of the National Museum). As you might expect people are rather more sensitive about photography now than they used to be.

The problem with the photography permits is that they must be approved personally by the Minister of Information which makes them very difficult to obtain.

Sometimes I have had permits and sometimes I have not, but I have never had any trouble taking pictures in Kuwait, even after the liberation. If you are discreet and do not photograph anything sensitive you should be OK. Also remember that in addition to military areas, the palaces and the airport, all embassies and government buildings are strictly off limits for shutter bugs.

## HEALTH

Health care has been another priority on the government's list of services-to-restore quickly. See the Kuwait City section for more information on how to get medical treatment in Kuwait, and the introductory Facts for the Visitor chapter for a more general discussion of health in the Gulf.

The drinking water in much of the country is not yet dependable and you would be well advised to stick to bottled water.

## WOMEN TRAVELLERS

Harassment of women has been an increasingly serious problem in Kuwait since liberation. A circular sent out by the US embassy in Kuwait City, as this book was being researched, advised women visitors to the emirate to dress conservatively, not to respond to approaches in the street and to avoid eye contact with men. Women should not travel alone at night in unfamiliar neighbourhoods. If you are followed go to a public place, such as the lobby of a hotel. A number of embassies keep records of harassment of their female nationals and if you have any problems you might want to report it to your embassy's consular section. They may not be able to do anything on the spot, but foreign governments seem to be putting pressure on the Kuwaiti administration to crack down on sexual harassment.

## DANGERS & ANNOYANCES

Although post-liberation Kuwait is not as safe a place as it used to be, Kuwait is still a far cry from cities like New York or Jakarta in terms of crime. Muggings and having your pocket picked are not among the things you need to worry about in Kuwait. The things that will scare you are much nastier.

You must be aware, above all, of the lingering danger of mines throughout the country. While Kuwait City and the residential sections of other urban centres like Al-Jahra and Al-Ahmadi are clear of mines much of the desert and, outside of the capital, much of the coastline, are still filled with them. Furthermore, while Kuwait City's beaches are clear there was, in early 1992, a persistent problem with seaborne mines washing up on the beach a couple of times each week. Since this situation changes from month to month as mine clearance proceeds, the best course before venturing outside the city is to contact your embassy, which will certainly be up on the latest information regarding what parts of the country are safe and which aren't.

If you are going north toward the Iraqi border bear in mind that the border is not marked. On several occasions in 1992, foreigners travelling or working in the border zone were arrested by Iraqi troops who claimed that they had strayed into Iraqi territory. In at least one instance such an arrest took place several km inside Kuwait. If you get into this sort of trouble the UN troops who patrol the border zone have no authority to help you. You'll probably be taken to Baghdad and may be put on trial. The bottom line is that for now you should not go any further north than the checkpoint on the Al-Mutla ridge without a very good reason. Most of those arrested by the Iraqis have been ordinance experts working on mine clearance projects.

## WORK

With very few exceptions it is not legal to work in Kuwait on a business visa. A business visa cannot be changed to a residence permit in Kuwait. You have to go back to your country of origin and get a residence visa there. Kuwait is currently trying to cut down on the number of foreign workers in the country so residence permits are going to be hard to come by in the foreseeable future. Coming to Kuwait to look for a job is both illegal and almost certainly a waste of time.

## ACTIVITIES

The problem of land and seaborne mines has pretty well put what used to be a bustling water sports culture in Kuwait into the deep freeze. Mines have also put an end to the desert safaris and wadi bashing.

## ACCOMMODATION

Getting a bed for the night in Kuwait was never cheap but since the war prices have gone up by 100 to 150% at most of the country's hotels. Quality has not followed. The result is that while the five-star places at least provide service for the money they ask there are a number of places (the Kuwait Continental Hotel springs readily to mind) charging five-star prices but offering nothing that approaches a five-star level of service. The bottom end of the market has disappeared and a lot of what's left is grossly overpriced. Standards have remained reasonable – there are no downright filthy hotels in Kuwait. Expect to pay at least KD 18 to KD 20 for a single and KD 23 to KD 25 for a double.

### Flat Rental

Rental is only an option if you are going to live in Kuwait, in which case you are likely to be provided with housing anyway. Small one or two-bedroom flats in the parts of the city where most foreigners live start at around KD 400 per month. Flats are a lot cheaper in other parts of the city, notably the mid-to-outer suburbs such as Hawalli, but many of these neighbourhoods are not particularly safe.

---

### The Water Trade

Kuwait has long been known for its fine natural harbour, but like so many places in the Middle East it is chronically short of water. Today Kuwait has an abundant supply of fresh water and even bottles its own mineral water, but during the first half of this century the rapidly growing town actually imported drinking water from Iraq.

From 1907 until 1950 traders drew fresh water from the Shatt Al-Arab waterway at the head of the Gulf, loaded it onto dhows and shipped it down to Kuwait. The trade peaked in 1947 when it was estimated that 80,000 gallons of water per day were arriving in Kuwait by boat. It was a far cry from the 19th century when Kuwait was small enough that, despite its famously arid landscape, it could still meet its needs from rainwater and the area's few wells.

Not surprisingly, Kuwait invested some of its early oil revenues in a mostly unsuccessful search for ground water.

The seaborne trade in fresh water stopped after Kuwait's first desalination plant was built in 1950. But although desalination capacity now far exceeds the country's demand for fresh water the government still devotes significant sums of money to research into new desalination techniques. Desalination is just about the most expensive way imaginable to acquire fresh water and the technology has not improved over the last 40 years as much as some scientists had hoped. Kuwait's own consumption has risen radically over that period, from 1800 gallons per capita in the '50s to 22,000 gallons per capita in the mid-80s, according to the government's own figures.

Natural resources are precious and, as any Bedouin can tell you, in the desert water is far more valuable than oil. ∎

## FOOD & DRINKS

There is a word for cheap food in Kuwait: biryani. Biryani, not Indian, because while most of Kuwait's cheap restaurants are Indian places many of them rarely seem to have anything other than biryanis on the menu. Anyway, the biryanis are pretty good and usually cost under a dinar. Aside from the Indian places the only cheap eats are Western fast food: burgers, pizza, etc. As you might guess tiny restaurants have not been at the top of anybody's post-war reconstruction priority list so the selection is rather limited.

Cafes, mostly located either in hotels or shopping centres, offer Western-style snacks and sandwiches at reasonable prices and the city is well stocked with good, up-market eateries. As usual, most of the latter are in the big hotels, but I have listed several excellent non-hotel places in the Kuwait City section.

All drinks are nonalcoholic and include soft drinks, mineral water, fruit juice, coffee and tea.

## ENTERTAINMENT

Dining out and going to the movies are about all you can look forward to in Kuwait for some time to come. While a few restaurants in five-star hotels have live music (almost invariably Arabic singers) there are few other forms of public entertainment. There are several cinemas in Kuwait City. They mostly show Indian, Pakistani and Arabic films though the occasional English-language movie turns up as well, almost invariably starring Arnold Schwarzenegger or Sylvester Stallone.

# Getting There & Away

## AIR

Travel agencies in Kuwait operate a comfortable cartel. In early 1992 virtually every airline office and travel agency in the city was displaying a poster from the Kuwait Travel & Tourism Agencies Association announcing that in the interests of improved customer service all of the travel agents in

the country were agreeing (in other words, being ordered) to adhere to KTTAA's unified pricing policy. 'That means no discounts', one clerk said when I asked about the signs. He was less candid when I asked how a price-fixing agreement was supposed to provide 'improved customer service'. Still, as is the case just about everywhere else in the Gulf there are far too many travel agencies in Kuwait and in their desperation for business most of them are willing to bargain down the price of tickets, but don't expect a large discount. Since they are cutting into their fairly slim commissions you can't expect to knock more than 5% off a ticket price and the trade-off for that will be locking yourself into the dates and times on the ticket. The further you are travelling (ie Los Angeles as opposed to Bahrain) the better your chances are of getting some sort of discount. Ask hotel staff or expat acquaintances for advice on finding a competent travel agent.

### To/From the USA

Fares to New York start at KD 338 one-way and KD 437.500 for a two-month return. Individual airlines, especially from what used to be the Eastern Bloc, sometimes have special fares on offer. For example, when I was last in Kuwait, Aeroflot was offering return tickets to New York or Washington via Moscow for only KD 302.

### To/From the UK

Three-month return tickets to London start at KD 303.900 and one-way tickets from KD 264.500. As noted above, you might make a tour of airline offices to check for special offers which could save you KD 100 or more.

### To/From Other Gulf States

Sample one-way and return fares to other cities in the Gulf in Kuwaiti dinars include (all returns require a three-day minimum/14-day maximum stay):

| To | One-Way | Return |
|----|---------|--------|
| Abu Dhabi | 49.900 | 68.800 |
| Bahrain | 26.400 | 38.800 |
| Dhahran | 28.300 | 38.800 |
| Doha | 35.900 | 49.300 |
| Dubai | 49.900 | 68.800 |
| Jeddah | 66.000 | 91.400 |
| Muscat | 69.800 | 96.800 |
| Riyadh | 39.300 | 54.100 |
| Sharjah | 49.900 | 68.800 |

## LAND

Buses operate between Kuwait and Cairo via Aqaba in Jordan and Nuweiba in Egypt. Agents specialising in these tickets (the trip takes about two days) are in the area around the municipal bus terminal. In Cairo there are a number of agents on Talaat Harb St and Tahrir Square advertising bus transport to Kuwait.

## LEAVING KUWAIT
### From Kuwait Airport

Be sure to be at the airport two hours before departure time. Check-in times are sometimes even longer for long-haul flights to Europe, Asia and North America, but for any flight it would be a good idea to double-check the check-in rules in advance. Before you actually get inside the terminal your car may be searched at a checkpoint on the Airport Rd and all baggage is X-rayed at the door of the airport. This can sometimes be a cumbersome process, so allow some extra time for it.

### Departure Tax

There is an airport departure tax of KD 2. If this was not added into the price of your ticket at the time of purchase you can expect it to be collected in cash at the airport. Tickets sold outside Kuwait rarely have the tax added in. Look for 'KWD 2.000' or something similar in the 'tax' box just below the part of the ticket that shows the cities between which you are travelling.

# Getting Around

## BUS & TAXI

Inter-city bus services have not been restored though there is a taxi rank on Al-Hilali St across from the municipal bus terminal. These are not service taxis per se though if a group of people want to go to Al-Jahra, Al-Ahmadi, etc the drivers would probably be willing to make a deal.

## CAR

If you hold a driving license and residence permit from another Gulf country you can drive in Kuwait without any further paperwork. Holders of driving licenses from other countries can usually get a temporary Kuwaiti license (valid for 30 days) issued against their home country driving license. Any car rental company can easily do this for you (all it really involves is filling in a form), and they will cheerfully charge KD 7.500 for the service.

## Car Rental

See the Kuwait City section for information on car rental agencies and costs.

## LOCAL TRANSPORT
### Bus

Ten bus routes are currently operating around Kuwait City, though more of the pre-war services may already have been restored. Fares are usually 150 fils, though some of the longer trips cost 250 fils. If you know where you are going the buses can be a good option, but note that while route numbers are displayed on the buses the names of the destinations are not.

### Taxi

Most Kuwaiti taxis have no meters. Bargaining the fare in advance may save you some grief at the end of the trip but it may also cost you money. Around town, taxis are orange-coloured. See the Kuwait City section for details of the proper fares and more information on the city's taxi system.

# Kuwait City

This is a lovely place to be in: the weather delicious, hot at midday, but too cold to sit in the shade without a *very* warm coat.

So wrote Freya Stark on her arrival in Kuwait in March 1937. Kuwait City, in 1992, was definitely unlovely. The damage done by the war proved to be less drastic than it had originally looked but the once-gleaming streets were still marred by more than a few rubble heaps and burnt-out buildings. Returning for the first time since the war it seemed to me that the National Museum, outwardly sound but inwardly scarred, reflected the country's mood better than any other place in Kuwait.

## Orientation

There are not a lot of street signs in Kuwait City but the place is not very difficult to find your way around. The commercial centre is the area from Kuwait Bay inland to Al-Soor St between the Al-Jahra Gate and Mubarak Al-Kabeer St. The coastal road is commonly called Arabian Gulf St and appears that way on some maps. The few signs on the ground, however, say 'Al-Khalij Al-Arabi St' (same thing, only transliterated, instead of translated, from the Arabic). The National Assembly building, what's left of the National Museum, the Emir's palace (Sief palace) and the Grand Mosque all lie along Arabian Gulf St.

The main shopping and commercial area is Fahd Al-Salim St, which becomes Ahmed Al-Jaber St north of Al-Safat Square, where the commercial centre begins to taper off. The souk is the area off between the Municipal Park and Mubarak Al-Kabir St. Up-market shopping places are clustered along the lower end of Fahd Al-Salim St (near the Sheraton Hotel) and just east of it.

From the centre the city spreads inland becoming ever broader as it goes. The main arteries are a series of numbered Ring Rds and Arabian Gulf St, which continues far down the coast to Al-Salmiya and beyond.

With the exception of Baghdad St, which is now Bush St, none of the major streets in the city have been renamed.

## Information

**Money** Kuwait City has no great central area for banks. You will find them pretty evenly distributed throughout the city. There are a few around Fahd Al-Salim St, a couple near the Science & Natural History Museum on Abdulla Al-Mubarak St and one in the Salhiya Commercial Centre on Mohammed Thunayyan St. People staying in or near the Kuwait International Hotel (formerly the Hilton) should use the National Bank of Kuwait branch in the hotel's upper lobby.

American Express (☎ 2413000, 2413325) is represented in Kuwait by Al-Ghanim Travel from their office on the ground floor of the Salhiya Commercial Centre. They are open Saturday to Wednesday from 8.30 am to 1 pm and 4.30 to 8 pm and are closed Thursday afternoon and all day Friday. American Express card holders can cash personal cheques through a bank in the same shopping complex but be warned that the commissions involved are pretty steep. They do not hold mail for AMEX clients.

**Post** The GPO is on Fahd Al-Salim St near the intersection with Al-Wattiya St. It is open Saturday to Wednesday from 7 am to 7 pm and Thursday from 7.30 am to 3.30 pm. Closed Friday. The GPO has a card-phone booth from which international calls can be made and phonecards are on sale at a nearby window. Poste Restante facilities, which were available before the invasion, had not been restored at the time of writing. Also note that you now have to show some form of identification to get into the post office (a passport is usually sufficient). The Safat Post Office, at the intersection of Abdulla Al-Mubarak and Al-Hilali Sts, is mainly for PO box holders but counter services are offered as well. It is open the same hours as the GPO.

**Telecommunications** The main telephone office is on Abdulla Al-Salim St at the base of the huge and, at last report, half built,

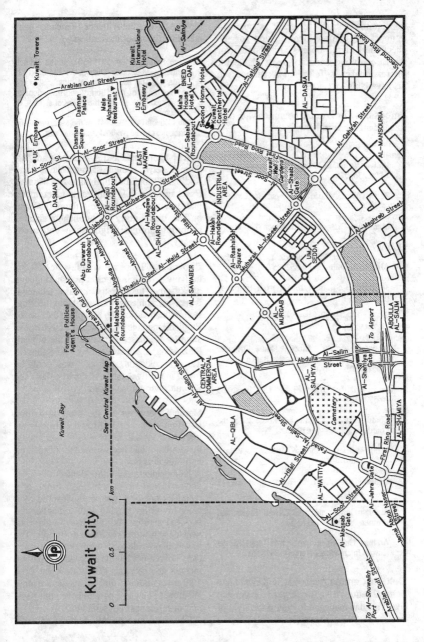

Kuwait City

telecommunications tower. It is open 24 hours a day. Bring identification for the checkpoint at the door. Card phones (for which cards are on sale) are available for international calls. Telex and fax services are also available.

**Embassies** Some of the countries with diplomatic missions in Kuwait are:

Canada
Da'iya District, El-Mutawakil St, Area 4, House 24 (☎ 2563025)
Egypt
Surra District, Tariq Ibn Ziyad St, Block 4 (☎ 5338927)
France
Mansouria District, St 13, Block 1, Villa 24 (☎ 5319850)
Germany
Bahiya District, St 14, Block 1, Villa 13 (off Abdulla Al-Salim St) (☎ 2520857)
India
34 Istiqlal St, near the Iranian Embassy (☎ 2530600)
Italy
Sharq District, Omar Ibn Al-Khattab St, Villa 6 (☎ 2445120)
Netherlands
Jabriah District, St 1, Block 9, House 40A (near the Fifth Ring Rd and opposite Bayan Palace; ☎ 5312650)
Norway
Surra District, Block 3, St 13, House 23 (☎ 5323014)
Oman
Udailia District, St 3, Block 3, House 25 (by the Fourth Ring Rd; ☎ 2561962)
Sweden
Faiha District, Shahba' St, Block 7, Villa 3 (☎ 2523588)
Switzerland
Udailia District, St 32, Block 3, House 12 (☎ 2551872)
UK
Arabian Gulf St, near the Kuwait Towers and Dasman Palace (☎ 2432046)
USA
Arabian Gulf St, entrance from opposite the Kuwait International Hotel (☎ 2424151)

**Cultural Centres** According to Kuwaiti law cultural centres have to charge a membership fee. This has managed to cramp the style of even the French. (Kuwait is the only place in the Gulf where the Alliance Française operates directly out of the embassy.)

Alliance Française (☎ 5319850), at the French embassy, Mansouria District, St 13, Block 1, Villa 24. The KD 10 annual membership fee covers usage of their library and invitations to films, exhibitions and the occasional play or lecture.
British Council (☎ 2533204), in the Mansouria district, next to the Nadi Al-Arabi stadium

**Travel Agencies** Fahd Al-Salim St and Al-Soor St between the Al-Jahra Gate and the Radio & TV building both have lots of small travel agencies. It is pointless to recommend one over another. Despite a theoretical ban on the discounting of published airfares shopping around might save you some money.

**Bookshops** There are very few bookshops in Kuwait which stock English-language books other than textbooks and technical works on subjects like civil engineering. Before the invasion the best place to look for English-language books was the large bookstore on the basement level of the Kuwait Plaza shopping centre on Fahd Al-Salim St. The best selection, such as it was, could be found in the five-star hotels, particularly the Kuwait International Hotel.

**Medical Services** At the time of writing government hospitals provided free treatment to everyone regardless of nationality, though there had been some talk of making non-Kuwaitis pay.

Nonresidents can either contact the hotel doctor if you are in a five-star hotel, or a company doctor if you are sponsored by a company or are staying with someone who is. As a last resort you can always make your way to the nearest hospital or polyclinic. The hospitals provide long-term and emergency care. Polyclinics handle everyday outpatient matters and referrals. They are open from 7.30 am to midnight and the queues are long. Wherever you go be sure to have your passport or residence card with you.

There are also private doctors, and two

private clinics, for whose services you will be expected to pay. Note that private medical practice is quite strictly regulated and the private doctors cannot, among other things, prescribe continuing medication or perform laboratory tests.

## National Museum

What remains of the National Museum is open Saturday to Thursday from 8.30 am to 12.30 pm and 4.30 to 8 pm. The museum compound fronts on Arabian Gulf St but is entered through the gate around the corner from the Sadu House (look for a short road leading to a parking lot). The museum closes one hour earlier on Friday mornings, and is closed all day Saturday. Admission is free but identification (iqama, or residence permit, for residents and passport for visitors) is required.

The museum was once the pride of Kuwait and its centrepiece, the Al-Sabah collection, was one of the most important collections of Islamic art in the world. During the occupation, however, the Iraqis systematically looted the exhibit halls. Having cleaned out the building they smashed everything they could and then set what was left on fire. It does not look too bad from the street, but the scene inside is far from pretty. You can see the results of this handiwork by heading up the ramp opposite the main entrance and turning right. This is where the Al-Sabah collection used to be. Another destroyed section of the building is open on the ground level to the left of the entry gate. This is where the archaeological exhibits were. The Planetarium, which was also torched, is open for inspection.

The plan was to leave those sections of the building in their present state as a monument to the occupation. A hall at the back of the museum complex is being restored and is said to be the future home of those antiquities which the Iraqis eventually returned plus whatever the government manages to build up from scratch.

## Sadu House

Sadu House is a small building near the National Museum on Arabian Gulf St. The house is a combination museum and cultural foundation dedicated to preserving Bedouin arts and crafts, particularly weaving (sadu is the Arabic word for weaving). The museum used to contain an interesting display of Bedouin artwork and everyday items used before the oil era both in Kuwait City and by the desert nomads. There was also a shop which was the best place in Kuwait to buy Bedouin goods. The foundation worked to keep alive the skills of traditional craftspeople (mostly women) and offered courses in weaving and pottery for both Kuwaitis and expatriates. At this writing it had not yet reopened, but it may have done so by the time you read this.

## Old National Assembly Building

This is the distinctive white building with the sloping roof on Arabian Gulf St near the National Museum. The building was designed by Jorn Utzon, the Danish architect who also designed the Sydney Opera House. The two sweeping roofs are supposed to evoke Bedouin tents. It is not open to the public.

In the late '80s, when the first rumblings of what became Kuwait's 1989-90 democracy movement were heard, the government drove home the message that the old parliament was not returning by changing the building's name to the Permanent Chamber of the Council of Ministers. Most maps continued to refer to it as the National Assembly Building but the subject was a sensitive one. The Iraqis badly damaged the interior of the building and its restoration became a government priority after liberation. When the National Assembly was reinstated in 1992, the building once again become the home of Kuwait's parliament.

## Sief Palace

Sief Palace, at the intersection of Mubarak Al-Kabeer and Arabian Gulf Sts north-east of the National Museum, is the seat of the Emir's court. The oldest parts of the building date to the turn of the century, but even from the outside it is obvious that the Iraqis practically demolished the place. When I was last in Kuwait you could see cranes rising up from behind the main gate. The beautiful clock tower managed to survive the war, though there is a gaping hole where the clock itself used to be. The interior of the palace was not open to the public before the invasion so it is unlikely that it will be open when the restoration work is finished.

It would also be a good idea to forget about taking pictures of the palace unless you have a permit. It was considered a sensitive site well before August 1990. Next door, the low-set, very modern building with lots of soldiers around it is the Foreign Ministry. Don't photograph this building either.

### The Grand Mosque

This huge, modern mosque opposite the Sief Palace was opened in 1986. It cost KD 13 million to build and the government says that it can accommodate over 5500 worshippers. The central dome is 26 metres in diameter and 43 metres high.

### The Former Political Agency

About 750 metres along Arabian Gulf St from Sief Palace (moving toward the Kuwait Towers) you will find a modest white house with blue trim. From 1904 until the late '30s this was the Political Agency, the British headquarters in Kuwait. Freya Stark spent most of March 1937 here. She adored Kuwait and lavished praise on her host, Gerald de Gaury, but was less impressed by the building, which she referred to as a 'big ugly box'. Viewed straight on it seems quite small, but from the side its true dimensions are clearer. The widow of the last British Political Agent continued to live here for many years, usually spending her winters in the emirate. The building, which has never been open to the public, was heavily damaged during the Iraqi invasion.

### Kuwait Towers

On Arabian Gulf St beyond the UK Embassy, the towers are rather hard to miss. Designed by a Swedish architectural firm and opened in 1979 they have become the country's main

landmark. The largest of the three towers rises to a height of 187 metres. From a distance they look fine but once you get closer it is obvious that they were not well maintained by the Iraqis and were later damaged in the war. At this writing they were still closed to the public, though that will no doubt change.

Before the invasion the upper globe housed a two-level observation deck. The upper level, at 123 metres, revolved, taking 30 minutes to make a circle. The largest tower's lower globe (at 82 metres) had a restaurant, coffee shop and a private banquet room. The lower globe on the largest tower and the single globe on the middle tower are used to store water. The small tower with no globes is used to light up the other two.

### Tariq Rajab Museum

This museum is at House 16, St 5, Block 12, in the Jabriya district. The house is on a corner two blocks north and one block west of the New English School, near the intersection of the Fifth Ring Motorway and the Fahaheel Expressway. It is open Saturday to Thursday from 9 am to noon and 4 to 7 pm; closed Friday. There is no sign on the building but it is easily identified by its entrance – a carved wooden doorway flanked by two smaller doors on each side. All four of the door panels are worked in gilt metal.

The museum, which is housed in the basement of a large villa, is a private collection which was assembled by Kuwait's first Minister of Antiquities. The focus is on Islamic art. Amazingly, it appears to have survived the occupation and war entirely intact.

Turn left as you enter the exhibit area to reach an excellent display of Arabic manuscripts and calligraphy. The same hall also has a wide selection of ceramics and pottery from various parts of the Islamic world. A small hall between this gallery and the main entrance contains antique clothes and jewellery.

Traditional costumes and jewellery are displayed in the hall to the right of the entrance. The exhibit is particularly interesting because it covers not only Islam's

Arab/Middle Eastern heartland but also much farther flung areas such as the countries of what was Soviet Central Asia (Kazakhstan, Uzbekistan, etc).

### Science & Natural History Museum
On Abdulla Al-Mubarak St, the museum is open Saturday to Thursday from 8.30 am to noon and closed on Fridays and holidays. Admission is free. Though the collection seems to consist largely of stuffed animals there is some variety. The ground floor also contains animal skeletons, including a few dinosaurs, though the Iraqis trashed a transport display which included Kuwait's first municipal bus and one of the first aircraft used by Kuwait Airways. The 1st floor has a display on space exploration and many more stuffed critters.

### Old City Gates
Three of Kuwait City's five gates lie along Al-Soor St (the street which follows the line of the old city wall): Al-Shaab, Al-Shamiya and Al-Jahra. Of the Al-Maqsab Gate, only the foundations remain. These sit in a small green site on Al-Soor St between the Sheraton Hotel and Arabian Gulf St. The fifth gate (Dasman Gate) was near the Dasman Palace by the Kuwait Towers. Despite its ancient appearance the wall, which the gates were part of, was only constructed around 1920. It was built in a hurry as part of the effort to defend the city against the ikhwan, the group of Islamic fundamentalist warriors loyal to Abdul Aziz Bin Abdul Rahman Al-Saud, later the first King of Saudi Arabia. The wall was torn down in 1957.

### Covered Souk
The souk, broadly defined, lies between the Municipal Park and Mubarak Al-Kabeer St from Ahmad Al-Jaber St to Ali Al-Salim St. Moneychangers, gold sellers, electronics merchants, etc tend to group into specific areas. The meat and vegetable market, which opens quite early in the morning and is arguably the most interesting part of the souk, is in the very centre of the souk area. The gold souk is just off Ali Al-Salim St. Parts of the souk weathered the occupation and war pretty well while others, sometimes only a few metres away, were reduced to piles of rubble. Walking through it the effect is spooky, sort of a market-cum-construction site.

### Places to Stay – bottom end & middle
All hotels in Kuwait have air-conditioning and private baths. TVs are also standard as are mini-fridges (at the bottom end, though, there might not be anything in them). Many hotels do not have heating in the rooms and you will certainly notice this in December or January. Most of the country's hotels also hit you for a 15% service charge – where applicable this has been added into the rates quoted. The rates listed here are initial quotes. Since the war, hotel managers seem rather less willing to bargain over rates for short stays than they used to be. You can expect to take KD 2 off the price of a single or KD 3 off a double if you are staying a week or more, but not much beyond that.

Kuwait's cheapest hotel is outside the centre on an unmarked street behind the Kuwait International Hotel. The *Maha House* (☎ 2521218) charges KD 15/20 for singles/doubles. Anywhere else it would be absurdly overpriced, but in Kuwait this passes for value-for-money. Winter travellers should note that its rooms are unheated.

In the centre are several decent places that, again, pass for inexpensive in Kuwait and are a few KD more than the Maha House. The *Phoenicia Hotel* (☎ 2421051), at the corner of Fahd Al-Salim and Al-Hilali Sts, remains one of the better values in town at KD 17/23. It is a bit plush and the baths range from OK to just adequate. The hotel summons vaguely the atmosphere of an Oriental brothel (Shanghai, circa 1935). Further down Fahd Al-Salim St, the overpriced *Carlton Hotel* (☎ 2423171) has reasonably clean but rather tatty rooms for KD 20/27. The bathrooms are a bit creaky, and with two rooms hooked up to each water tank the hot water could be sporadic. The lobby features a weird fountain that looks like a petrified tree growing out of a wading pool.

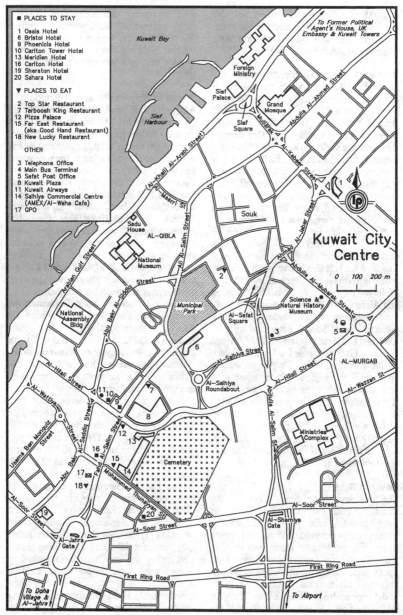

PLACES TO STAY
1 Oasis Hotel
6 Bristol Hotel
9 Phoenicia Hotel
10 Carlton Tower Hotel
13 Meridien Hotel
16 Carlton Hotel
19 Sheraton Hotel
20 Sahara Hotel

PLACES TO EAT
2 Top Star Restaurant
7 Tarboosh King Restaurant
12 Pizza Palace
15 Far East Restaurant
   (aka Good Hand Restaurant)
18 New Lucky Restaurant

OTHER
3 Telephone Office
4 Main Bus Terminal
5 Safat Post Office
8 Kuwait Plaza
11 Kuwait Airways
14 Salhiya Commercial Centre
   (AMEX/Al–Waha Cafe)
17 GPO

Kuwait City Centre

0   100   200 m

To Former Political
Agent's House, UK
Embassy & Kuwait Towers

Kuwait Bay

Foreign Ministry

Sief Palace

Sief Harbour

Grand Mosque

Sief Square

(Al–Khalij Al–Arabi Street)

Al–Maarri St

Souk

Al–Mubarak

Abdulla Al–Ahmad Street

Al–Kabeer Street

Ahmad Al–Jaber Street

Sadu House

AL–QIBLA

National Museum

Street

Municipal Park

Al–Safat Square

Science & Natural History Museum

Abdulla Al–Mubarak Street

National Assembly Bldg

Abu Bakr Al–Siddiq

Al–Salhiya Street

Al–Salhiya Roundabout

Al–Hilali Street

Al–Wazzan St

AL–MURGAB

Al–Hilali Street

Al–Wattiya

Usama Ben Monqiz Street

Abu Bakr Al–Saddiq Street

Fahd Al–Salim Street

Mohammed Thunayan St

Cemetery

Ministries Complex

Al–Soor Street

Al–Shamiya Gate

Al–Soor Street

Al–Jahra Gate

First Ring Road

First Ring Road

To Doha
Village &
Al–Jahra

To Airport

The *Bristol Hotel* (☎ 2439281), at the corner of Fahd Al-Salim and Ali Al-Salim Sts charges KD 18/25, including breakfast. Even before the war it had problems: no hot water, for one. The whole place seems to be falling apart, if slowly. For the moment it is clean enough but very drab. Also note that each bath is shared between two rooms.

The *Sahara hotel* (☎ 2424121), between Mohammed Thunayyan St and Al-Soor St, was once the best value in town but its postwar price increase of approximately 150% makes it a somewhat dubious choice at KD 23/30.

North of Al-Safat Square is the *Oasis Hotel* (☎ 2465489) at the intersection of Ahmad Al-Jaber and Mubarak Al-Kabeer Sts. This is another place whose 100% postwar price increase destroyed whatever claims it once had of being a good value. Singles/doubles are KD 30/37.

If you are going to pay those sort of rates you can do better for your money outside the centre. I would recommend the *Second Home Hotel* (☎ 2532100), just behind the Kuwait Continental at the Al-Dasma roundabout (intersection of Al-Istiqlal St and the First Ring Rd). It's a friendly place though no longer the pre-invasion bargain it once was. Rooms are KD 23.500/27.500 with the usual discounts available for longer stays.

The *Kuwait Continental* (☎ 2527300) is excessively overpriced at KD 34.500/40.250. Some of the troops from UNIKOM (United Nations Iraq-Kuwait Observer Mission – the UN force that monitors the border area) stay here.

### Places to Stay – top end

At this end of the market a pretty good bet is the *Carlton Tower Hotel* (☎ 2452740, fax 2401624) which, at KD 40.250/51.750 including the service charge, is the cheapest place that can arrange a visa. It also boasts a good downtown location on Al-Hilali St just off Fahd Al-Salim St and is a bit cheaper than the other hotels in this category.

Kuwait's five-star hotels operate a price cartel. I once saw an article in *Arab Times* announcing that the general managers of the

big hotels had met to agree on a 20% price rise for the coming season. The *Meridien* and the *Sheraton* are the only five-star hotels in the city centre, of which the former is nicer and has better service. The *Kuwait International Hotel* (formerly the Hilton), opposite the US embassy on Arabian Gulf St in Beneid Al-Gar, is the favourite haunt of journalists and visiting VIPs. All of these hotels charge KD 45/55 for singles/doubles plus the 15% service charge which means you are really looking at KD 51.750/63.250. They will often come down KD 5 to KD 10 if you ask for a 'corporate rate'.

All five-star hotels can arrange visas for business visitors. Generally the hotel will require that you stay with them for at least two nights. The maximum stay on this sort of visa is usually one month.

*Le Meridien Kuwait* (☎ 2455550, telex 44458 MERIHTL KT, fax 2438391), Al-Hilali St, downtown
*Kuwait International Hotel* (☎ 2530000, telex 22039 HILTELS KT, fax 2563797), Arabian Gulf St, Beneid Al-Gar District, opposite the US embassy
*Kuwait Sheraton* (☎ 2422055, telex 22434 SHERA-TON KT, fax 2448032), Fahd Al-Salim St, downtown, near the Al-Jahra Gate

### Places to Eat

**Cheap & Medium-Priced** As always, Indian food is the cheapest. There is an enormous concentration of small Indian/Pakistani restaurants in the area around the bus station – especially on Abdulla Al-Mubarak and Al-Hilali Sts. The menu never varies: chicken or mutton biryani or fried chicken or chilli chicken. Occasionally samosas are available, but don't hold your breath. A meal rarely costs more than KD 1. Among the better places is the *Top Star Restaurant* in the souk. Enter the souk from the south-west end of Al-Safat Square by the big Citizen sign, take the third alley on the left after the sign and head up the stairs.

Along Fahd Al-Salim St the *Tarboosh King Restaurant* has kebabs and decent grilled chicken. Half a chicken with rice and soup costs KD 1.500. Also on Fahd Al-Salim St the *New Lucky Restaurant*, at the small plaza just west of the GPO, is a good bet. The menu consists only of biryanis and fried chicken or fish. A meal costs KD 1 or less.

*Pizza Palace*, at the corner of Al-Hilali and Fahd Al-Salim Sts, has so-so pizza for KD 1 to KD 2.500. Burgers and chicken are also available.

*Al-Waha Cafe*, in the Salhiya Commercial Centre, has mostly Western food (omelettes, burgers, etc) starting from about KD 2. The location, next to a fountain with a sidewalk cafe atmosphere, is not exactly Paris but come July you'll value the fact that it is indoors. Its position, in one of the city's most up-market shopping malls, also makes it a good spot for a coffee break.

The *Far East Restaurant* (a smaller sign calls it the *Good Hand Restaurant*) on Mohammed Thunayyan St near the Salhiya Commercial Centre serves mostly Filipino food. Main dishes, all of which seem to include coconut milk as an ingredient, cost KD 1.750 to KD 2.500.

**Expensive** My highest recommendation in Kuwait is the *Mais Alghanim*, a terrific Lebanese restaurant on Arabian Gulf St, between the Kuwait Towers and the intersection with Al-Soor St. It is in a white prefab building, which also contains the local DHL office. The restaurant is at the end of the building closer to Al-Soor St (the large sign is in Arabic only but there's a smaller one in English by the door). Founded in 1953 it is one of the country's older establishments. Meals cost about KD 3 to KD 4. It is worth going out of your way for. Expect queues for the garden tables in the winter and the indoor (air-conditioned) ones in the summer.

For up-market Indian food try *Mughal Mahal* on Jaber Al-Mubarak St, near the intersection with Al-Hilali St in the Al-Sharq district. Great meals cost KD 4 to KD 5.

If you want to break your budget but don't feel like hotel food try the *New Koreana Restaurant* on the 1st mezzanine floor of the Salhiya Commercial Centre. The menu is mostly Korean though there are some Japanese dishes as well. The food is great and the service magnificent but a meal is likely to set you back KD 8 to KD 10.

Outside the centre try the *Steakhouse* adjacent to the Sultan Centre shopping complex, south of the centre on Arabian Gulf St. A couple of km north of the Sultan Centre the same company runs a complex called *The Sultan Centre Restaurants*, which include a quite good Mexican place that has even managed the trick of making a drinkable nonalcoholic frozen margarita! Plan on spending close to KD 10 per person.

### Entertainment

The city's handful of cinemas finally reopened in January 1992. The main cinemas in Kuwait City are the Al-Firdaus and Al-Hamrah, both at the Al-Maqwa roundabout (intersection of Jaber Al-Mubarak and Hilali Sts). There are usually two shows per night; check *Arab Times* or *Kuwait Times* to see what's on.

### Things to Buy

In terms of antiques, there's very little to buy in Kuwait. Hotel gift shops often have shiny, imported 'Arabian' gift items, but the souvenir trade, never very big in the first place, has hardly been at the top of the government's list of rebuilding priorities. Consumer electronics are widely available but the prices are pretty high. If and when the Sadu House reopens you should see whether they are once again selling Bedouin weavings.

### Getting There & Away

**Air** Kuwait International Airport is 16 km south of the city centre. For some annoying reason currency exchange facilities are only located in the departure area (as opposed to arrivals where they would be rather more useful). Since the war, all carriers are operating out of Terminal 1. There is no word on when the second terminal will once again be functional. Check-in time is officially two hours but some carriers insist on your being there three hours in advance, so you should call the airline to double-check. Security is tight enough that you should not let this slip too much.

Some of the airlines which fly to/from Kuwait are:

Aeroflot
  International Commercial Centre, just off Fahd Al-Salim St near the Phoenicia Hotel (☎ 2428331)
Air France
  Al-Hilali St, near the Meridien hotel (☎ 2430224)
Air India
  Ali Al-Salim St, near the intersection with Fahd Al-Salim St (☎ 2438185)
Air Lanka
  Al-Soor St, near the Al-Jahra Gate (☎ 2424444)
British Airways
  Corner of Fahd Al-Salim and Ali Al-Salim Sts (☎ 2425635)
Czechoslovak Airlines
  Fahd Al-Salim St, near the Al-Jahra Gate (☎ 2433141)
Cyprus Airways
  Al-Soor St, between Mohammed Thunayyan St and the Al-Jahra Gate (☎ 2435685)
EgyptAir
  Fahd Al-Salim St, just west of Al-Safat Square (☎ 2431165)
Gulf Air
  Fahd Al-Salim St, across from the Kuwait Plaza shopping centre (☎ 2450180)
KLM
  Corner of Fahd Al-Salim and Ali Al-Salim Sts (☎ 2424220)
Kuwait Airways
  Kuwait Airways tower, Al-Hilali St (☎ 2451303)
Lufthansa
  Al-Soor St, between Mohammed Thunayyan St and the Al-Jahra Gate (☎ 2422493)
Malev
  Fahd Al-Salim St, near the intersection with Ali Al-Salim St (☎ 2450200)
Olympic
  Fahd Al-Salim St (☎ 2420002)
Saudia
  Al-Hilali St, near the Meridien hotel (☎ 2426310)
Syrian Arab Airlines
  Fahd Al-Salim St between the Phoenicia Hotel and the GPO (☎ 2410484)
ZAS – Airline of Egypt
  Fahd Al-Salim St between the Phoenicia Hotel and the GPO (☎ 2456700)

**Bus** Inter-city bus services – to Al-Ahmadi and Al-Abdaliyah via Al-Jahra – had not yet been restored at this writing. When these

services are resumed they will operate from the main bus terminal, just off Al-Hilali St.

International bus service to Cairo can be booked through any of the small travel agencies around the intersection of Abdulla Al-Mubarak and Al-Hilali Sts.

**Taxi** While there is a taxi rank across the street from the bus station there is no formal service taxi system operating in Kuwait. You could strike a deal with one of the drivers to go to another city but it would be hit-or-miss.

**Car** Renting a car is another thing that has doubled in price since liberation. The major agencies (Avis, Europcar, Budget) all charge KD 14 to KD 16 per day for the smallest cars (usually Daewoos). Al-Mulla is the cheapest of the larger local agencies with cars from KD 6 per day. Al-Mulla has an office on Fahd Al-Salim St and an outlet in the upper lobby of the Kuwait International Hotel. For information on driving license laws see the Facts for the Visitor section.

### Getting Around
**To/From the Airport** Taxis charge a flat KD 4 between the airport and the city. Bus 101 runs between the main bus terminal off Al-Hilali St and the airport every 30 minutes from 5.30 am to 9 pm. The fare is 150 fils.

**Bus** The central terminal for Kuwait's municipal buses is near the intersection of Al-Hilali and Abdulla Al-Mubarak Sts. The bus system is being slowly restored. Though there were once several secondary bus terminals operating in different parts of the city only the Messilah station, on the coast southeast of the centre, is again functioning in any significant way. Buses start running at 5.30 am and go every 12 to 20 minutes until 8 or 9 pm, depending on the route. Fares are usually 150 fils, though some of the longer trips cost 250 fils. Numbers are displayed on the front of buses but destinations are not. The following routes are operating (all routes operate in both directions):

Route 11 – Sharq Bus Terminal (on Dasman Square at the eastern end of the centre), Ahmed Al-Jaber St, Fahd Al-Salim St, Jamal Abdul Nasser St, Al-Sabah Hospital, Al-Azam Hospital

Route 13 – Main Bus Terminal, Fahd Al-Salim St, Jamal Abdul Nasser St, Airport Rd, Old Keefan, New Keefan

Route 14 – Main Bus Terminal, Souk, Mubarak Al-Kabeer St, Cairo St, Bush St (formerly Baghdad St), Hamad Al-Mubarak St, Al-Biljet St, Al-Ta'aoun St, Messilah Bus Terminal

Route 18 – Main Bus Terminal, Souk, Mubarak Al-Kabeer St, Cairo St, Third Ring Rd, Tunis St, Fourth Ring Rd, Canada Dry St, Mohammed Ibn Al-Qassim St, Al-Gaha St, Al-Gahahz St, Jamal Abdul Nasser St, Al-Azam Hospital

Route 23 – Riyadh St, King Faisal St, Al-Waleed Ibn Abdul Malik St, Ibrahim Ibn Al-Adham St, Mahata Khatan

Route 24 – Main Bus Terminal, Souk, Abdulla Al-Mubarak St, Al-Maghreb St, Third Ring Rd, Musa Ibn Al-Museer St, Ibn Khaldoun St, Qutaiyba St, Beirut St, Tunis St, Amman St, Abdel Karim Al-Qatabbi St, Hassan Al-Banna St, Messilah Bus Terminal

Route 29 – Main Bus Terminal, Fahd Al-Salim St, Gamal Abdel Nasser St, Airport Rd, Al-Ghazali St, Al-Farwaniya St, Airport Rd, Sixth Ring Rd, Al-Glibbe St, Al-Hasawi

Route 38 – Main Bus Station, Fahd Al-Salim St, Souk, Mubarak Al-Kabeer St, Al-Hilali St, Jaber Al-Mubarak St, Al-Istiqlal St, Third Ring Rd, Tunis St, Fourth Ring Rd, Fahaheel Rd, Bayan, Shahid Salim Al-Kindi, Mishrif Area, Sabah Al-Salim District, Messilah Bus Terminal

Route 101 – Main Bus Station to/from the Airport (Terminal 1)

Route 102 – Main Bus Terminal, Souk, Mubarak Al-Kabeer St, Al-Istiqlal St, Third Ring Rd, Cairo St, Fahaheel Rd, Mecca St, Al-Dabous, Fahaheel Bus Station

**Taxi** Unfortunately, Kuwait has developed one of those taxi systems where there are no meters and the trick is to know what you ought to pay when you get in. Bargaining in advance may save you some grief at the end of the trip but it will also cost you money. Around town, taxis are orange-coloured. In general, anything within the city centre is about KD 1. Longer trips just outside the centre (eg from the Sheraton to the International Hotel) cost about KD 1.500. If you bargain, or take the taxi from a rank in front of a five-star hotel, expect to pay double this.

You might also try calling Ibrahim Taxi (☎ 2446720). Their service gets good reviews locally and costs about the same as hailing a cab on the street.

Individual drivers also stop to pick up passengers. This is not a free ride as the driver will expect to be paid the equivalent taxi fare for the trip. If you take a lift this way (which unaccompanied women should definitely not do) bear in mind that it is illegal and you could find yourself in trouble if the car is stopped at a checkpoint. You should also negotiate the price with the driver beforehand to avoid any misunderstandings.

# Around Kuwait

### FAILAKA ISLAND

The site of Kuwait's main archaeological site, Failaka is definitely worth the trip once the bomb disposal experts get it cleaned up. Before the invasion Failaka was Kuwait's only inhabited island but its strategic position, controlling the seaborne approaches to Kuwait City, caused the Iraqis to turn it into a heavily fortified base. After liberation it was found, like much of the mainland, to be filled with mines.

At this writing the island was still not open to the public, but once the mines have been cleared the plan is to reopen the island's archaeological sites and restore the ferry link to the mainland.

Failaka, which the Greeks called Ikaros, is the best known, and probably the earliest, Hellenistic settlement in the Gulf. It was also the first part of Kuwait to attract the attention of professional archaeologists who began digging here in early 1958 as documented in Geoffrey Bibby's book *Looking for Dilmun*. Though it is best known as a Hellenistic site Failaka's history goes back to the Bronze Age Dilmun civilisation which was centred in Bahrain. The Greeks arrived in the 4th century BC in the form of a garrison placed here by one of Alexander the Great's admirals. A small settlement existed on the island prior to this, but it was as the Greek town of

Ikaros that the settlement became a real city or at least a large town.

As you enter the site, the road swings around to the left and ends in front of a group of prefabricated buildings. These are the archaeological museum and the on-site administrative offices.

The **mud house** on a small rise between these buildings and the sea contains a display of island life prior to the coming of oil. The display includes glassware, old navigational equipment and models of traditional Gulf sailing vessels.

**Tel Sa'ad**, the most ancient of Failaka's three excavated sites, is the excavation next to the building with the ethnographic display. This was a Bronze Age settlement connected with Dilmun. Its centrepiece is the **Temple of Anzak**, the large open area in the centre of the excavation. Anzak was the chief god of Dilmun. Note the column base in one corner of the temple. Beyond the temple, the area toward the sea may have been a fortification of some sort. The area behind the temple (away from the sea) probably contained houses.

The **inn** is a bit further up the coast (away from the site entrance) and is easy to spot, just look for the small metal lookout tower nearby. Little of the building remains, but the floor plan is clearly visible.

The temple is the centrepiece of Failaka. It, too, is easy to spot from a distance, thanks to the presence of a small sun shelter erected over part of the excavation. It is about 100 metres inland from the inn. This was the heart of the main Hellenistic settlement. The temple, which was probably dedicated to Artemis, lay at the centre of a square fortress that was 200 metres on each side. Two re-erected columns mark the entrance to the temple, which is of the standard Greek two-chamber type. The remains of the altar are also clearly identifiable in front of the temple. Kuwait's most famous archaeological find, the **Ikaros Stele** (which, prior to the Iraqi invasion, was on display in the Kuwait National Museum) was found here. It would have stood to the left of the temple entrance, as one faces the temple from the altar. Sur-rounding the temple is a large excavated area of houses and fortifications. The entire complex dates from 330 to 150 BC.

Ferries to and from Failaka have always operated from a terminal at Ras Al-Ard (also called Ras Salmiya). This had been almost completely rebuilt and should be now operating again. The trip to Failaka takes one hour by regular ferry and 30 minutes by hovercraft.

To reach the site from the ferry terminal on Failaka, turn right as you exit the terminal building. Almost immediately you will see the mud house, the one which contains the ethnographic display, on a low hill to the right beyond a wall. The entrance is a gate in this wall with seals on either side marked Kuwait National Museum.

## AL-AHMADI

Built to house Kuwait's oil industry in the 1940s and '50s, Al-Ahmadi was named for the then-Emir, Shaikh Ahmad. It remains, to a great extent, the private preserve of the Kuwait Oil Company (KOC). As with Dhahran in Saudi Arabia and Awali in Bahrain, the visitor driving through Al-Ahmadi's streets has the vague feeling of being in a suburb somewhere in the south-western USA. Unlike Dhahran (but like Awali) the gates have long since come down and one need not have a reason to be allowed to drive into 'Little America'.

Al-Ahmadi has shops, supermarkets, banks, travel agents, parks, recreational facilities and a stadium. What it does not have is a hotel. There is, however, a guest house for people having business with KOC. The town's two sites of note are the Oil Display Centre on Mid 5th St and a small zoo in the Public Gardens.

The **Oil Display Centre** exhibits are a brief introduction to oil from its formation underground through the prospecting process to extraction, refining, sales and distribution. The display is small but well organised and rather self-congratulatory. The centre is open Saturday to Wednesday from 7 am to 4 pm. Admission is free.

The **zoo** is in an annexe to the Public

Gardens and houses a very small collection of animals, mostly African (zebras, gazelles, etc) and such birds as peacocks. Few of them, aside from camels, are indigenous to Arabia. The zoo is open daily from 7 am to 4 pm. Admission is free.

To reach the town, take the Al-Safr Motorway south out of Kuwait City until you reach the Al-Ahmadi exit. Follow first the blue signs for North Al-Ahmadi, and then the smaller white signs for the Display Centre. After the turn for North Al-Ahmadi go left on Mid 5th St (the first roundabout) to reach the Display Centre. To reach the zoo from there, continue along Mid 5th St and turn left on 7th Ave (the first left past the Display Centre). Take the first right turn (onto Mid 7th St) and follow the road until it ends at the entrance to the Public Gardens.

## AL-JAHRA

Al-Jahra, an industrial and agricultural town approximately 32 km west of Kuwait City, has a name which lives in Kuwait's history as a battle site, though those with memories of the Gulf War will remember it for a much more recent battle.

In 1920 Kuwait's ruler, Shaikh Salem Bin Mubarak, learned that Abdul Aziz Bin Abdul Rahman Al-Saud, the future founder and King of Saudi Arabia, planned to turn his much feared warriors, the ikhwan, loose on Kuwait. Salem decided to make his stand at Al-Jahra. After being routed by the ikhwan in a battle near the city the Kuwaiti forces

retired to Al-Jahra's Red Fort from where they sought to wear down the more numerous Saudis in a war of attrition. In the meantime, a messenger was sent to the British to invoke the 1899 Anglo-Kuwaiti treaty. A relatively minor British show of force in the waters off Al-Jahra was enough to turn the tide of the siege in the Kuwaitis' favour. The victory also established the Al-Sabah more firmly in Kuwait itself. Two years after the battle of Al-Jahra, Abdul Aziz was prevailed upon to open talks with the Al-Sabah which ended in his recognising Kuwait's independence in exchange for a large chunk of its territory.

Al-Jahra's role in the most recent war over Kuwait is somewhat less romantic. In the final hours of the Gulf War, as Iraqi troops began to evacuate Kuwait City, a huge traffic jam developed just outside Al-Jahra, where the main road from Kuwait City turns north toward the Iraqi border. The convoy stalled on the approach to the Al-Mutla ridge, just west of Al-Jahra, where it was caught by a coalition air attack. The convoy was demolished by the allies and the debris pushed off to the side of the road to rust, where at last report they still were – a gruesome collection of the mangled remains of cars, trucks and a few tanks.

The town's only site of the more conventional variety is the **Red Fort**, famed in Kuwaiti history from the 1920 siege. It is a low rectangular mud fort near the highway. The name is thought to derive from the colour of the walls. The fort is built around a large open courtyard with several annexes on its west side. Small signs (in Arabic and English) scattered around the complex identify the functions of the various parts of the complex, though after a while one empty mud-walled room starts to look pretty much like another. All four of the low towers at the fort's corners can be climbed to get a better view.

The annexe in the fort's south-west corner (through the large wooden door with a number 4 above it) was the harem, the Emir's private enclosure. Moving north, the next annexe includes a small mosque. Note the simple, unadorned mihrab (prayer niche) in the south wall.

The fort is on Marzouk Al-Mat'aab St next to a park. Coming from Kuwait City, take the main Al-Jahra exit from the expressway onto Marzouk Al-Mat'aab. The Red Fort is on the right, about 200 metres south of (ie, inland from) the highway, though you can't see it until you are right in front of it. It is open daily, except Fridays and public holidays, from 8 am to 1 pm and 4 to 6 pm, though the closing hours are rather flexible. On two occasions I have arrived around 1.45 pm and found it open. Admission is free but identification is required.

Al-Jahra's main street is Marzouk Al-Mat'aab St from the point beyond the Red Fort where it loops around to the right at an intersection (marked on maps as a traffic circle, though it's not really that big) to its intersection with Da'abal Al-Khazaai St, which runs back to the expressway. The stretch of road in question has a number of small restaurants though most have signs only in Arabic.

## DOHA VILLAGE

On an arm of land jutting out into Kuwait Bay, Doha Village is the site of several small dhow-building yards and a fishing village of squalid shacks. The dhow yard is not particularly interesting. If you are planning a trip to Bahrain, the dhow yard there is far more interesting and easier to get to. The fishers' shacks lie along the road, beyond the concrete walls of the dhow yards. The bus from Kuwait City stops at the end of the concrete wall.

To reach Doha Village, take the Al-Jahra Rd west from Kuwait City and follow the signs for Entertainment City. After taking the turn-off for Entertainment City (ie, when it is rising up in front of you) make the first U-turn and you'll see a small sign for Doha Village. Do not go straight, past Entertainment City, or you'll wind up in Doha Port.

# Oman

Long known as the hermit of the Middle East, the Sultanate of Oman is slowly emerging from its shell. Only a few years ago the Sultanate required even other Gulf Arabs to obtain visas. It is now expecting 50,000 tourists a year by 1995.

Oman is quite different from the other Gulf states. Indeed, occupying the south-eastern corner of the Arabian peninsula it, technically, is not a Gulf country at all. In contrast to the vast desert wasteland of Saudi Arabia or the tiny city-states of the Gulf, Oman is a land of dramatic mountains and long unspoiled beaches. Its capital, Muscat, does not have the nouveau-riche feel that typifies much of the rest of the Gulf. Oman's development since the ascension of Sultan Qaboos Bin Said is all the more striking both because the country's oil reserves are so limited and because under the previous Sultan, Said Bin Taimur, the country was almost hermetically sealed off from the outside world. But Said's xenophobic rule was very much the exception in Omani history. During the 17th, 18th and 19th centuries Oman was an imperial power which vied first with Portugal and later with Britain for influence in the Gulf, the Indian Ocean and along the coasts of India and East Africa.

Tourism is still a new concept for the Omanis and the country has taken a cautious approach to its development. In many ways Oman remains the most traditional country in the Gulf though, at least on the coast, its traditions are often more outward looking than it's given credit for.

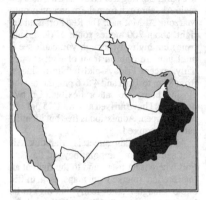

## Facts about the Country

### HISTORY
#### The Land of Frankincense
As in much of the rest of Arabia the earliest known settlements in Oman date from the 3rd millennium BC. Though the harbours of Oman's Batinah coast were on the margins of the trade routes which linked Mesopotamia to the Indus valley they do not appear to have been rich places during the 2nd and 3rd millenniums BC.

It was not until much later, and not along the Batinah coast but in the far south of the country, that Oman became economically important to the ancient world.

Dhofar, Oman's southernmost region, is one of the few places in the world where the trees which produce frankincense will grow. Frankincense is an aromatic gum which is obtained by making incisions in the trunks of trees of certain species of the *boswellia* family. These trees grow only in southern Oman, the Wadi Hadhramaut in Yemen and northern Somalia.

The incense has a natural oil content, which means that it burns well. It also has medicinal qualities. This combination and its relative scarcity made it one of the most sought after substances. (The frankincense and myrrh offered as gifts to the infant Jesus were, at the time, far more valuable than the gold.) Frankincense became crucial to the religious rites of almost every people in the known world. The temples of Egypt, Jerusa-

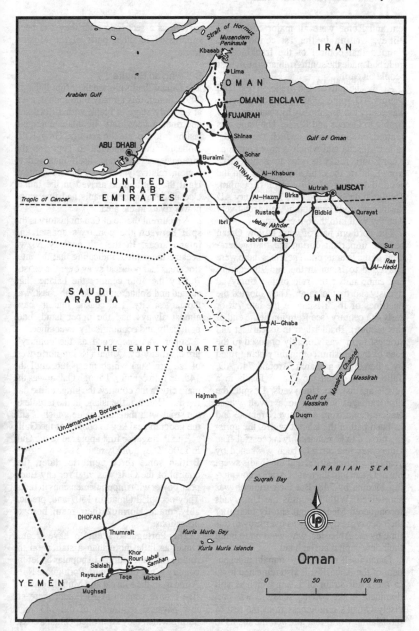

Oman

0        50        100 km

lem and Rome were all major customers. Pliney, writing in the 1st century AD, claimed that control of the frankincense trade had made the south Arabians the richest people on earth.

At the height of the trade in the 2nd century AD, some 3000 tons of frankincense was yearly moving mostly by sea from south Arabia to Greece and Rome. The trade was centred on Sumhuram, which the Greeks called Moscha and which is now known as Khor Rouri. Today its ruins are a short drive from Salalah, the capital of Dhofar and the second-largest city in modern Oman. Though it declined after the 3rd century AD the incense trade kept south Arabia relatively wealthy well into the 6th century.

The northern part of what is now Oman became important during the first generations of the Islamic era. The tribes there were converted to Islam in the mid-7th century and came under the rule of the Umayyad dynasty shortly thereafter. They adopted the doctrines of Ibadi Islam in the late 7th or early 8th century (see Religion at the end of this section). Ibadi Islam in its earliest and strictest form was violently opposed to the idea of the Muslim community being ruled by a hereditary monarch. Around 746 AD, Talib Al-Haqq led the Omani Ibadis in a revolt against the Umayyads. Despite the disadvantages inherent to a revolt whose leaders came from a relatively remote and isolated part of the Islamic world, the uprising proved to be remarkably successful. The Umayyads had already been weakened by years of internal strife, and the Ibadis swept out of Oman into the rest of Arabia, conquering Medina by 748. But their triumph was short-lived. Within months the Umayyads reconquered Medina, but shortly thereafter their decaying dynasty was overthrown, this time by the Abbasids, who went on to build their new capital at Baghdad.

Oman itself managed to remain independent of the Abbasids. It also remained loyal to the Ibadi strain of Islam which is still dominant in the country today. It was precisely Oman's remoteness from the rest of the Islamic world that allowed the Ibadis to

survive as a sect long after they had been suppressed in other parts of the Muslim world.

## Building an Empire
The Omani Ibadis elected their first Imam in 749. Though this already represented, even at an early stage, a break with strict Ibadi doctrine, a hereditary Imamate emerged, lasting into the late 9th century. Though the Abbasids then managed to suppress the Imamate per se, Oman itself managed to remain relatively free of Abbasid control. Until the Portuguese arrived in the Indian Ocean in 1607 the Omanis had few naval power rivals in the area.

A recurrent theme of Omani history is the split between the country's coastal and inland areas. In the 9th century Nizwa became the capital, indicating that the interior areas had political sway over the coasts. But by the 10th century the balance had shifted and Sohar, on the Batinah coast, was the largest city. The coastal regions have almost always had the upper hand, both politically and economically, ever since.

Sohar was succeeded as the country's principal city by Qalhat (18 km north-west of modern Sur) which prospered until the 14th or 15th century. Though Qalhat was the main city in the country, the kings of the day lived in Hormuz, the island in the middle of the strait with the same name which is still the geographical key to control of the Gulf.

The Portuguese first appeared in the Gulf in 1506. They quickly realised, as would the British some three centuries later, that control of the Gulf was vital for any European power with imperial intensions in India. They occupied Oman in 1507 and, predictably, made Hormuz their main base of operations.

The Portuguese seem to have treated Oman as little more than a station on the route to India. Contrary to popular belief the country is not littered with Portuguese forts. Aside from the Muscat and Mutrah forts and five bronze cannon at Al-Hazm, there are few physical reminders of the 143 years during which they controlled Oman's coastline. This dearth of Portuguese ruins strongly implies that Lisbon's interest in the country did not extend much beyond the protection of its supply lines.

It was, however, the Portuguese who first brought Muscat to prominence when, in 1622, they made it their main base in the region after being driven out of Hormuz. They built up and fortified the town but were not able to hold it. In 1650 Imam Sultan Bin Saif expelled the Portuguese from Muscat and Oman. Omani independence is usually dated from this victory, by which reckoning Oman is the oldest independent state in the Arab world.

The recapture of Muscat marked the beginning of a great expansion of Omani power throughout the Gulf and the Indian Ocean. Almost immediately Omani merchants began to build up their influence along the East African coast. Politically, the Ibadi Imamate, though still based in the agricultural area around Jebel Akhdar, controlled much of the country under a new line of Imams descended from the Al-Ya'ribi clan.

Four years before the expulsion of the Portuguese the Imamate, which then controlled other parts of the coast, had signed its first treaty with the British who were then vying with the Portuguese for influence in the area. The Treaty of 1646, signed with the British East India Company, covered trading rights and allowed British merchants to practice their religion. It also established a separate judicial system for British subjects and employees of the company. The Dutch East India Company got similar rights in 1670 but was soon forced out of Oman by the British and the French.

In all this, the Omanis retained their independence, which is a lot more than can be said for much of the rest of the Gulf over the next 300 years. Their growing empire in East Africa, where Omani and British merchants competed in much the same way as the British and the Dutch competed in the Gulf, gave the Omanis an economic power base which none of Arabia's sheikhs could match.

Far from finding themselves under the heel of imperialism, by the end of the 18th century the Omanis were ruling their own far-flung empire. At its peak in the 19th century, Oman controlled both Mombasa and Zanzibar and operated trading posts even further down the African coast. It also controlled portions of what are now India and Pakistan. It was not until the British withdrew from India in 1947 that Oman surrendered its last colonial outpost at Gwadar, in what is now Pakistan, near that country's border with Iran.

In 1749, Ahmed Bin Said, the first ruler of the present dynasty (the Al-Busaid), was elected Imam. In 1786, with maritime trade becoming more and more important to the empire, the capital was formally moved from the interior to Muscat. It was around this time that the Al-Busaid adopted the title of Sultan, which implied temporal authority in a way that the religious title of Imam didn't.

Treaties providing for British protection of the Sultanate were signed in 1798 and 1800. These involved the British government, as opposed to the East India Company, and unlike the treaties Britain signed with the Gulf sheikhs later in the 19th century, they were neither imposed by force nor did they turn Oman into a protectorate. Oman, for one thing, was better able to defend itself than were the Gulf sheikhdoms. For their part the British were concerned mainly with protecting their own supply lines to India which were then being threatened by the French, who had just occupied Egypt.

The treaties marked the beginning of a special relationship between Britain and Oman which continues to this day. They were later supplemented by similar 'peace, friendship and navigation' treaties in 1891, 1939 and 1951.

The Omani empire reached its peak in the mid-19th century under Sultan Said Bin Sultan (reigned 1804-56), who added Dhofar to his realm and pushed the Sultanate's control far down the East African coast. The Sultan commanded an army of 6500 men and a navy which included 15 ships. When he died the empire was divided between two of his sons. One became the Sultan of Zanzibar, whose progeny ruled Said's African colonies well into the 20th century, while the other became known as the Sultan of Muscat and Oman – the coast and interior of today's Sultanate which were then regarded as two separate realms ruled by one monarch.

## Muscat & Oman

The split between Muscat and Oman had been confirmed in the late 18th century when conservative tribes in the interior elected their own Imam. They apparently felt that the Sultan in Muscat had grown too liberal and were certainly dissatisfied with the re-introduction of a hereditary monarchy, which went against strict Ibadi tradition.

In the 19th century it became common for the positions of Imam and Sultan to be held by different men. The Imam of Oman increasingly came to represent the political interests of the interior against those of the coast, though in keeping with strict Ibadi doctrine, the post of Imam was not always filled. Despite his title the Sultan's writ rarely extended very far inland. From 1868 to 1873 one Sultan managed to claim both posts, but this was unusual. The result was that Muscat's control of the interior depended to a great extent on the tribes' opinion of the Sultan of the day.

Following Sultan Said's death, the division of the empire cut Muscat off from some of its most lucrative domains, causing the country to stagnate economically during the late 19th century. The British exacerbated this situation by pressing the Sultan to end the trade in slaves and arms for which Oman had long been known. This left the Sultan a great deal poorer and lack of money made the interior even harder to control. This episode also highlighted the extent of the British influence in the Sultanate. Many of the Sultan's advisors were British and the army (known as the Muscat and Oman levies) was commanded by British officers.

In the early 20th century the imams started holding more and more power in the interior, while the sultans' power decreased.

When Sultan Faisal Bin Turki died in 1913 the interior's tribes refused to recognise his son, Taimur Bin Faisal, as Imam. In 1915,

with the Sultan's control still tenuous and tensions running high, a group of tribes tried to take over Muscat but were pushed back by the British. Things remained unsettled until 1920 when the Sultan and the Imam signed a treaty at Seeb. Under the treaty, the Sultan recognised the Imam as a spiritual leader and allowed him limited temporal jurisdiction over the interior without formally yielding his own claim to sovereignty. For the next 35 years the treaty was the main document governing relations between the rival leaders.

The treaty's weakness was that it avoided the one really important question: namely, who had ultimate authority over the inland areas. In 1938 a new Sultan, Said Bin Taimur, came to power. When he sought to extend his writ into the interior in the early '50s the British backed him, largely because they believed that there might be oil there. To prospect for it, they needed the Sultan to have effective control of the area and Oman's undefined borders with Saudi Arabia and Abu Dhabi to be clearly marked.

The territorial dispute centred on the Buraimi oasis, which now straddles the border between Oman and the United Arab Emirates (UAE) but was then under Saudi control. In 1952 Said, the British and the Imam managed a rare show of unity in ejecting the Saudis from Buraimi. But the Saudis continued to lay claim to the area and, in 1954, Said concluded that the Imam had taken the Saudis' side in the dispute. This brought to a head the entire question of sovereignty and the Treaty of Seeb. Said's forces occupied Ibri, cutting the Imam off from Buraimi. Having been outflanked on the ground the Imam, Ghalib Bin Ali, sought to outflank Said politically by applying to the Arab League for recognition as ruler of an independent state.

In December 1955, Said responded by occupying the Imamate's dual capitals of Nizwa and Rustaq. He then annexed the whole of the interior on the grounds that Ghalib had violated the Seeb treaty. The Arab League was generally sympathetic to Ghalib's membership application (an attitude which was probably more anti-

British than pro-Imamate) but was in no position to help him. The British, by contrast, were very much in a position to help Said, in return for securing oil concessions for British companies.

Ghalib was allowed to go into exile in his home village but his brother, Talib, escaped to Cairo and returned 18 months later to continue the civil war. The revolt was short-lived. With British help the Sultan was back in control within three months, though the Imam and his brother held out from a base near Jebel Akhdar until early 1959.

Said Bin Taimur (reigned 1938-70) was a fascinating figure, 'an arch-reactionary of great personal charm', in the words of the British writer Peter Mansfield. He was opposed to any sort of change and sought to isolate Oman from the modern world. Under his rule, a country which only a century earlier had rivalled the empire builders of Europe became a medieval anachronism.

Said personally issued all visas. He forbade travel inland by residents of the coast and vice versa. He opposed education, which he saw as a threat to his power. Most Omanis were not allowed to leave the country and the few who managed to get out were rarely allowed to return.

One of the positive aspects of Said's rule was that he did manage to clear off Oman's then-large foreign debts and bring some semblance of stability to the country.

What little contact Said had with the outside world came through his British advisors and Muscat's trading families. Some of the traders were foreign and some were Omani but all had roots in the society going back several generations. Said allowed them to establish commercial empires in Muscat based on hugely lucrative monopolies for the import of the few goods which he, grudgingly, regarded as crucial to his survival. In exchange, the trading families tacitly agreed to stay out of politics and not to import anything which Said felt smacked of progress or the West (eg eyeglasses, radios, books). That one of the most prominent of these trading firms still bears the distinctly un-Omani name of W J Towell & Company

testifies that Oman was not always an economic backwater sealed off from the outside world. (W J Towell & Co was founded in the 1860s by an American adventurer who later sold out to his Scottish assistant who in turn sold the company to his Indian-born assistant.)

Through customs receipts, the merchants also provided Said with most of the country's income of about UK£50,000 per year, a sum which had changed little since the turn of century. A few merchants were getting rich, but trade had stagnated in the country as a whole and most of the population relied on agriculture or fishing (both concentrated on the north coast) for their livelihood.

## Sultan Qaboos

In 1958 Said boarded himself up in his palace at Salalah, which he rarely left thereafter. The formation of a nationalist rebel group, the Dhofar Liberation Front, in 1962 did little to change this. The DLF's battle against the state, known as the Dhofar rebellion, began in 1965 and was far more serious than Said's earlier clashes with the Imamate. Over time (and, after 1967, under South Yemeni influence) the DLF moved from a pan-Arabist toward a more doctrinaire Marxist ideology. In 1966 a dissident group of Dhofari soldiers almost succeeded in assassinating Said.

The combination of the ever-escalating rebellion and Said's refusal to spend any of the money which he had begun to receive from oil exports in 1967 soon began to try even London's patience. In July 1970 Said was overthrown by his only son, Qaboos, in a bloodless palace coup. The British denied any involvement in or advance knowledge of the coup, but this is hard to believe as British officers effectively commanded the army at the time. Said spent the rest of his life living in exile in a London hotel.

Sultan Qaboos Bin Said was only 30 years old when he came to power. He had been educated abroad, including a stint at Sandhurst, the British military academy. Returning to Oman in 1964 he spent most of the next six years under house arrest in

Salalah. On assuming power, Qaboos flew to Muscat where he promptly repealed his father's oppressive social restrictions, surrounded himself with foreign – mostly British – advisors and began to modernise Oman's semi-feudal economy.

There was a certain urgency in Qaboos' programme to bring the country into the 20th century. Oman's oil revenues were and still are small and its resources limited. Qaboos saw the need to move quickly if the oil wealth was to have any significant effect on his people's lives. He pushed localisation of the workforce much harder than the rulers of the other Gulf countries. Oman, he knew, needed foreign aid and know-how, but it could hardly afford the luxury of the armies of foreign labourers who had built the infrastructure of places like Kuwait.

Despite Qaboos' seeming desire to make a clean break with the past, the Dhofar rebellion continued unabated. In 1973, the Sultan asked Iran for help in quelling the rebellion. As the rebels were receiving aid from Marxist South Yemen, the Shah of Iran, who was in the process of grinding down his own country's communist party, was only too happy to oblige. Qaboos also received assistance from several hundred British troops, including elite SAS units. By 1976 the rebels, never very great in number to begin with, had been reduced to a few bands operating out of South Yemen. The rebellion only ended, however, when Oman and South Yemen established diplomatic relations in 1982 and the Aden government cut off its assistance to the rebels.

In foreign affairs Qaboos has carved out a reputation for himself as a maverick. In spite of Oman's past military ties with the Shah, he has managed to maintain friendly relations with post-revolutionary Iran. Oman was also one of only two Arab countries (the other was Sudan) which refused to break diplomatic ties with Egypt after it signed a peace treaty with Israel in 1979.

In developing his country, the Sultan has shown an acute desire to preserve as much as possible of Oman's traditional character. Old port-cities like Muscat and Mutrah have

been modernised without being bulldozed out of existence. The construction of modern housing and office blocks around Greater Muscat has been confined to areas like Qurm or Ruwi, which had few, if any, inhabitants 25 years ago. This pattern has also been reflected in many provincial cities. One of the reasons why Oman has been so slow and cautious in opening up to tourism is this wish to preserve much of the country's traditional culture.

## GEOGRAPHY

Oman has the most diverse geography of the Arab Gulf states. It is approximately 300,000 sq km in area, although this is a rough estimate since the portion of the border running through the Empty Quarter desert is undefined. It occupies the south-eastern corner of the Arabian peninsula and boasts some 1700 km of coastline. Oman's territory also includes the Musandem peninsula which overlooks the Strait of Hormuz. The Musandem peninsula is separated from the rest of the country by the east coast areas of the UAE, though Oman controls a tiny enclave of territory entirely surrounded by the UAE. Oman also includes a number of islands, the most important of which is Massirah.

Much of the country's population is concentrated in the strip of land along the coast of the Gulf of Oman, though the largest city, after the capital, is Salalah in the far south on the Arabian Sea coast. The northern coastal strip is isolated from the rest of Arabia by the Hajar mountains on the other side of which are the seemingly endless sands of the Empty Quarter. The highest peak in the country is Jebel Akhdar (the 'green mountain') at 3075 metres.

The mountainous areas of the interior and the Musandem peninsula are strikingly beautiful and fiercely rugged while the southern coast is tropical in appearance. The northern coastal strip, known as the Batinah coast, becomes progressively more barren as one moves south along it from the UAE border toward Sur.

## CLIMATE

Oman's varied geography makes for a wide range of climatic conditions. Coconuts are grown in the southern coastal areas while the highlands around Jebel Akhdar produce roses and grapes.

Muscat is hot and very humid from mid-March until October and pleasantly warm from October to March. In the Salalah area, humid weather with temperatures approaching 30°C is common even in December. The Salalah area gets drenched by the monsoon rains every year from June to September.

## FLORA & FAUNA

Oman has one of the most rigorously green governments. The Sultanate has a fascinating array of animals ranging from various sorts of molluscs (several new varieties of sea shells have been discovered on Oman's beaches) to a herd of rare Arabian oryx, bred for release into the wild on a special farm owned by the Sultan. An area has also been set aside around Ras Al-Hadd, the easternmost tip of the Arabian peninsula, as a protected breeding ground for the giant sea turtles which live in the Indian Ocean and come ashore there each year to lay their eggs.

The same sort of attention has also been accorded the country's plant life. The Sultan's horticultural activities even led to a new species of flower being named after him in early 1990.

The government runs a scheme for protecting coastal areas and there are a number of nature preserves, known as National Protected Areas, scattered around the country.

## GOVERNMENT

The government is very much a one-person show. The Sultan is the ultimate authority. National Day, for example is celebrated each year on the Sultan's birthday (18 November) and not on the anniversary of his assumption of power (23 July). The Sultan is also Prime Minister, Foreign Minister and Defence Minister (lower-ranking ministers of state run the latter two ministries on a day-to-day basis). Day-to-day governing is carried out through a Cabinet appointed by the Sultan.

The Sultan married in 1976 but later divorced. He has no children and no designated heir. Speculation about the succession is not, however, one of Muscat's favourite parlour games. In Oman this simply is not done.

There's an oft-quoted remark by the Sultan to the effect that the country is not yet ready for Western-style parliamentary democracy and that no purpose would be served by setting up a sham parliament. The implication is that, over time, the country will move toward a less personalised system of government. In January 1992, an elected Consultative Council, or *majlis ash-shura*, convened for the first time, replacing an appointed State Consultative Council which had existed since 1981. Though a far cry from a Western parliament, the Council is widely seen as a first step toward broader participation in government. It mainly comments on draft laws and such other topics as the Sultan chooses to put in front of it.

## ECONOMY

In 1970, when development in much of the rest of the Gulf was already well under way, Oman still had only five km of surfaced road (between Muscat and Mutrah). There were only three primary schools in the country and no secondary schools. There was one hospital which was run by US missionaries. Today, Oman has a modern system of roads, housing and health care to rival that of any other Gulf state.

Though the economy is essentially oil-based, Oman's oil production is relatively modest by Gulf standards. Agriculture in the inland areas and fishing on the coast continue to be important sources of income for much of the population.

The government has been more successful than any other in the region at 'localising' its economy, that is, replacing foreigners with Omanis wherever possible. It is far more common to see Omanis in service positions or doing manual jobs than it is to see other Gulf Arabs doing similar jobs.

## POPULATION & PEOPLE

Oman's population is estimated to be about 1.1 million, concentrated in Muscat and along the Batinah coast. While Omanis are Arabs, the country's long trading history has led to a great deal of mingling and intermarriage of Omani Arabs with other ethnic groups. There has been an Indian merchant community in Muscat for at least 200 years and, in the north, it is also common to find people who are at least partly of Persian or Baluchi ancestry.

## EDUCATION

Free primary and secondary education are one of the mainstays of Oman's modernisation programme. Sultan Qaboos University on the outskirts of Muscat is the country's main post-secondary institution. The government has also been working hard in recent years to eradicate illiteracy, which remains high among older people living in the interior.

## ARTS

Oman has devoted a great deal of effort to preserving its traditional arts, dance, music and culture. While it is possible that you may come across traditional dancing simply while driving down a road (as I once did), the best place to observe such things is usually at one of the many museums scattered around greater Muscat. There are no regular programmes of, for example, folk dancing, though occasional performances are announced in the local press, usually timed to coincide with some sort of official cultural exchange programme.

For information on Omani craftwork see the Things to Buy section in this chapter.

## CULTURE

Oman's seemingly omnipresent Ministry of Culture & National Heritage is charged with both protecting the country's environment and preserving its traditions and lifestyle. The ministry is central to the Sultan's goal of building a genuinely Omani, as opposed to tribal, identity.

## Traditional Lifestyle

Despite the modern appearance of Muscat's Qurm, Ruwi and Medinat Qaboos districts, much of the country, including parts of the capital area, remains intensely traditional. Every spring the Sultan spends several weeks driving around the country on a 'meet the people tour'. This is covered extensively on Omani TV. A few minutes viewing one of the reports will show you the extent to which the day-to-day life of the average Omani living in a town in the interior or a fishing village on the coast are close to what they would have been centuries ago. Omanis seem to be adept at assimilating what they want or need of modern life, enjoying its benefits without letting the new technology adversely affect their own lives and values.

## Taboos & Avoiding Offence

Many Omanis, even in Muscat, still live in very traditional circumstances, and they're generous and welcoming to foreigners. However, as Oman has only been open to the outside world just over 20 years, a degree of sensitivity is required. Taking photographs anywhere in Oman is a sensitive matter and taking pictures of women is almost always out of bounds. In rural areas it is important to dress modestly. The taboos are no different from those which apply in other Gulf states (see the Facts about the Region chapter).

Also note that outsiders are definitely not welcome in the Lewara quarter of Mutrah, where many of the capital's Shiite Muslims live. There are usually a couple of people sitting in the gateway which leads from the Mutrah corniche into the Lewara quarter and their manner tends to be polite but firm.

Non-Muslims are not permitted to enter mosques in Oman.

## RELIGION

Most Omanis follow the Ibadi sect of Islam. The Ibadis are one of the Muslim world's few remaining Kharijite sects, and are a product of Islam's earliest fundamentalist movement. In 657 Ali, the fourth Caliph and the Prophet's cousin and son-in-law, agreed to peace talks with his main rival for the leadership of the Muslim community.

The Kharijis ('seceders') were originally followers of Ali but broke with him on the principle that by agreeing to discuss the leadership question he had compromised on a matter of faith. This compromise, they held, rendered him unworthy of both their loyalty and the leadership itself.

Various Khariji sects developed over the next 200 years, all generally adhering to the principle that the Muslims should follow the adult male who was best able to lead the community while upholding the law. If the leader failed to uphold the law he could be replaced almost instantly. Most Kharijis also rejected out of hand the idea that any person could have an hereditary claim on the leadership. The various Khariji sects differed largely in their interpretation of the term 'upholding the law' and how strictly pure the leader had to be to remain worthy of the community's loyalty. The leader, or imam, was to be chosen by the community as a whole. The Ibadis were among the more moderate of the Khariji sects.

The Ibadis are one of the few Khariji sects which has survived into the 20th century. They take their name from Abdullah Bin Ibad Al-Murri Al-Tamimi, a theologian who was probably from Najd, in modern Saudi Arabia, but who did most of his important teaching while living in Basra (in today's southern Iraq) during the late 7th century. His teachings seem to have caught on in Oman partly because they touched the right political chords at a time when the Omani tribes were rebelling against the Damascus-based Umayyad caliphate. Ibadism came to thrive on the edges of the Muslim world – the only other place where a really strong Ibadi dynasty was ever established was western Algeria in the 8th century.

A hereditary Ibadi Imamate emerged in Oman from the mid-8th to the late 9th century, when it was suppressed by the Abbasid empire which had replaced the Umayyads as the predominant power in the Muslim world. This adoption of a system of hereditary rule is one of the elements which

distinguishes Ibadism from the more strict (and now defunct) Khariji sects, though Ibadis still retain the broad Khariji rejection of any embellishment of the basic pattern of worship laid down by the Prophet.

In one form or another the Imamate continued in the remoter parts of Oman's interior until well into the 20th century (see the history section of this chapter).

## LANGUAGE

Arabic is the official language though English is widely spoken in business circles. In the northern coastal areas you can also find traders and sailors who also speak Farsi and/or Urdu.

See the Facts about the Region chapter for a glossary of Arabic words and phrases.

# Facts for the Visitor

## VISAS & EMBASSIES
### No Objection Certificate (NOC)

Unless you are a citizen of another Gulf country you need a visa to enter Oman, but before you obtain one you must first get a No Objection Certificate (NOC). This is an official piece of paper stating that neither your Omani sponsor nor the government has any objection to your plans to visit the country. Once the NOC is issued you will be informed of its number and your airline will get a telex from the immigration department quoting this number and authorising them to board you for your flight to Muscat. Without this telex you almost certainly will not be allowed to board the plane. Having made it to Muscat and stood in the usually huge line at the NOC window, you will be given a small slip of paper which you take to passport control and trade for a visa.

If your passport shows any evidence of travel to Israel you will be denied entry to Oman.

### Obtaining an NOC

A few five-star hotels can set up an NOC in about a week for either businesspeople or tourists. It is nearly impossible to pick up this sort of NOC anywhere except at Seeb International Airport in Muscat. If you want to come in by bus from Dubai you can either book through a travel agent in the UAE, who will arrange the visa, or try to get a visa through an Omani embassy.

Unaccompanied women do not appear to have trouble obtaining NOCs. Occupations are a different matter. Omani officialdom is obsessed with security. I've heard stories of people being turned down because they were civil servants or once worked as security guards at an embassy. A journalist might or might not get the visa depending on how effective the hotel is at convincing the immigration department that you really are coming just for a holiday. Certainly a journalist planning to do any work in the country ought to go through the Ministry of Information instead. People of Palestinian origin are also likely to encounter problems obtaining an NOC.

### Visas from Omani Embassies

There are mixed reports about how easy it is to get a visa through an embassy. Western capitals seem to be the best bet. It takes about a week and visas are usually valid for a three-week stay. You need four photographs and a list of all the countries you have visited in the past year. If you want to take the bus into the country from Dubai this is pretty much your only option as hotel-issued visas usually have to be picked up at the airport. If you do plan to enter the country by land, however, you should also make this clear to the people at the embassy, or else they may stamp your visa 'Not valid for entry by road'.

### Hotel-Sponsored Visas

If you want to get a visa through a hotel it is pretty straightforward. Telex or fax the hotel (telex and fax numbers are listed in the Muscat section for those hotels which can sponsor tourists), make a reservation and send them a copy of the first page (the part with your photo and personal data) of your passport. You might also have to provide a list of countries visited in the last year and

you may be asked to mail four photos to the hotel, so try not to do all this at the last minute. Be sure to give the hotel your exact arrival details and a contact number so that they can let you know when the NOC is ready. Obviously the hotel is going to charge you for this service, though the cost is likely to be pretty nominal compared to what you are going to pay for the room. The hotel will usually require a three-night minimum stay. The trick of moving to a cheaper hotel – common in the UAE – is not a good idea. It is illegal and the odds on your getting caught are pretty high.

Bear in mind that tourism is still very new and tightly controlled in Oman. The authorities make no secret of the fact that they are not much interested in you visiting unless you are prepared to fork over US$ 100 or more per night.

### Omani Embassies

Following is a list of some Omani embassies abroad:

Austria
　　Waehringerstrasse 2-4, 1090 Vienna (☎ 222-316452)
Bahrain
　　Diplomatic Area, Al-Fatih Highway (near the National Museum), Manama (☎ 293663)
France
　　50 Ave de Lena, 75116 Paris (☎ (1) 47230163)
Germany
　　Lindenallee 11, D-5300 Bonn-2 (☎ 22-8357031)
Kuwait
　　Udailia, St 3, Block 3, House 25, by the Fourth Ring Rd (☎ 2561962)
The Netherlands
　　Koninginnegracht 27, 2514 AB Den Haag (☎ 70-3615800)
Qatar
　　Ibn Al-Qassin St, Al-Hilal District, Doha (☎ 670774)
Saudi Arabia
　　Al-Raed District, Riyadh (☎ (1) 4823120)
UK
　　44B Montpelier Square, London SW7 1JJ (☎ (071) 5845332/3)
USA
　　2342 Massachusetts Ave, NW, Washington DC, 20000 (☎ (202) 3871980/1)
　　866 United Nations Plaza, Suite 540, New York NY (☎ (212) 3553505)

## Visa Extensions

In theory these are available to tourists and businesspeople through their hotel/sponsor but you are going to have to come up with a good reason why you need it. If you have come in on a tourist visa issued by an Omani embassy you will have to go to the Immigration and Passports Directorate in Muscat.

Exit/Re-entry visas are not available for tourists and are not necessary for resident expatriates.

## Foreign Embassies in Oman

See the Muscat section for a list of embassies in the capital.

## DOCUMENTS
### Site Permit

A permit from the Ministry of Culture & National Heritage in Muscat is needed to visit most archaeological sites, old forts, etc. They are issued without fuss at the ministry, which is in the same building as the Natural History Museum in the Ministries Area of Medinat Qaboos. Sometimes the permits also need to be signed by the provincial governor. I was once turned away from a fort because the door attendant would not honour the permit until it had also been signed by the provincial governor. If that happens to you, just ask directions to the governor's office and get the extra signature.

### Road Permit

A Road Permit is necessary for crossing borders by land. At the time of writing it was only possible to drive into the UAE as the border with Yemen was closed. They are easily obtained in three to five days through your sponsor. The only problem is that permits are not issued to single women. That means that unmarried female travellers, even expatriates, cannot drive to Dubai for the weekend. More importantly, it also means that they cannot ride up to Dubai with their married friends in their car, let alone catch a ride with a single male friend. This is the only such travel restriction on single and/or unaccompanied women in the Sultanate.

## CUSTOMS

Non-Muslims can bring in one bottle of booze. There are no unusual regulations regarding things like cameras, computers or cassette players.

## MONEY

Banking hours are Saturday to Wednesday from 8 am to noon and Thursday from 8 to 11 am. Moneychangers keep the same hours and usually also open from around 4 to 7 pm. Some of the moneychangers, particularly the ones in and around the Mutrah souk, are also open for an hour or two on Friday afternoon from 4.30 or 5 pm.

### Currency

The Omani riyal (OR) is divided into 1000 baisa (also spelled baizas). Notes come in denominations of 100 and 200 baisa, and OR 1, 5, 10, 20 and 50. Coins are 5, 10, 25, 50, and 100 baisa. The notes have both English and Arabic script but the numbers on the coins appear only in Arabian characters. The riyal is a convertible currency and there are no restrictions on its import or export. Foreign currency can also be taken into or out of the country freely.

### Exchange Rates

| US$1 | = | OR 0.385 |
|------|---|----------|
| UK£1 | = | OR 0.585 |
| DM1  | = | OR 0.240 |
| FF1  | = | OR 0.071 |
| A$1  | = | OR 0.264 |

### Costs

It is possible to travel cheaply in Oman, on a budget of OR 10 per day in Muscat and OR 15 outside the capital, where cheap hotels are much rarer. A bus ticket from Muscat to any provincial city in the north of the country costs only a few riyals and a bus ticket to Salalah is only OR 10 one-way. Decent accommodation can be found in Muscat for under OR 10 and you can fill your stomach for 500 baisa or less at one of the country's innumerable cheap Indian restaurants.

Oman does not have middle-range hotels

and restaurants, so once you leave the low-budget category you are likely to see costs head for the stratosphere fairly rapidly. Even staying in a relatively modest hotel and eating in medium-priced restaurants you could easily see costs hit OR 40 per day.

### Tipping

Tipping is not expected in cheaper places while more expensive restaurants tend to include a service charge (though this often goes to the restaurant not the waiting staff).

### Bargaining

Most prices are fixed in Oman. This applies to restaurants, hotels and taxis (ie, the first price you hear is likely to be the only price on offer). The only things you can expect to dicker over will be souvenirs in the souk. Even in the souk, however, bargaining can be a frustrating experience. Shopkeepers tend to be inclined to offer a small discount from the marked price but not much else. The price of a souvenir turban is not likely to move by more than a few hundred baisa. Even if you are spending OR 100 on old silver jewellery or daggers you are likely to find that the shopkeeper offers an initial discount of 10 to 15% off the marked price and then refuses to budge.

### Consumer Taxes

A 5% municipality tax is applied to all hotel and restaurant bills.

### WHEN TO GO

Mid-October to February or mid-March is the best time to visit. The monsoon season in the south is from June to September, and while you probably do not want to be in Salalah during the rains it is definitely worth a visit in October when everything in Dhofar is still lush and green.

### WHAT TO BRING

Sunglasses and a hat are the first essentials, plus a good sunscreen for anyone who burns easily, especially in the southern part of the country. These, and anything else you might need, are all easily available in Muscat. See the introductory Facts for the Visitor chapter for more general notes on essentials for any Gulf trip.

### TOURIST OFFICES

There are no tourist offices in Oman. See the Muscat section for information on tour companies and programmes offered by the various large hotels.

### BUSINESS HOURS & HOLIDAYS

Businesses are open daily from 8 am to 1 pm and 4 to 7 or 7.30 pm except Friday. Most businesses are also closed on Thursday afternoons. Many of the shops in Muscat's Mutrah souk are open during the early evening hours on Friday. Banks are open Saturday to Wednesday from 8 am to noon (11 am on Thursday). The moneychangers in and around the Mutrah souk keep more or less the same hours as other businesses. Government offices are open from 7.30 or 8 am until 2 pm from Saturday to Wednesday and until 1 pm on Thursday.

Secular holidays observed in Oman are New Year's Day (January 1), National Day (November 18) and the Sultan's Birthday (November 19).

The Islamic holidays of Eid Al-Fitr, Eid Al-Adha, the Islamic New Year and the Prophet's Birthday are all observed (for the dates see the table of holidays page 28).

### CULTURAL EVENTS

The National Day festival features all sorts of highly visible official celebrations. Observance of the two Muslim Eids is a bit more traditional, often marked with spontaneous dancing in the streets, even in Muscat.

### POST & TELECOMMUNICATIONS

#### Postal Rates

Sending a postcard costs 30 baisa inside Oman, 50 baisa to other Gulf and Arab countries and 150 baisa to the rest of the world. Postage for letters weighing 20 grams or less is 50 baisa inside Oman, 80 baisa to other Gulf countries and 100 baisa to the rest of the Arab world. Postage on letters to everywhere else is 200 baisa for the first 10 grams, 350

baisa for 20 grams and OR 1 for anything between 20 and 50 grams.

Parcel rates for up to one kg are OR 1 within Oman. Elsewhere surface/air rates are: Gulf countries OR 2/3, other Arab countries OR 3/3, rest of world OR 4/6.

### Sending Mail

Post offices are open weekdays from 7.30 am until 2 pm. They close at 11 am on Thursday and are closed all day Friday.

### Receiving Mail

You can use the Poste Restante service at the GPO in Ruwi or the branch post office in Muscat to receive mail. Have your mail addressed to: Your Name, Poste Restante, Ruwi Central Post Office, Ruwi, Sultanate of Oman, or to the Muscat Post Office, Muscat, Sultanate of Oman. American Express clients can also receive mail through the AMEX office in the capital. See the Muscat section for details.

### Telephone

Surprisingly there is no central public telephone exchange in the Muscat area (particularly surprising since there is one in Salalah). Your best bet for phoning home is to go to a hotel and call from there. The same goes for sending faxes and telexes. This is not cheap, but at least it works. Overall the telephone system is excellent and you should have little trouble making international calls.

When calling Oman from the outside world the country code is 968, followed by the local six-digit number. There are no area or city codes.

### TIME

Omani time is GMT plus four hours. When it's noon in Muscat, the time elsewhere is:

| City | Time |
| --- | --- |
| Paris, Rome | 9 am |
| London | 8 am |
| New York | 3 am |
| Los Angeles | 12 midnight |
| Perth, Hong Kong | 4 pm |
| Sydney | 6 pm |
| Auckland | 8 pm |

### ELECTRICITY

The electricity voltage in Oman is 220/240 volts AC with British-style three-pin plugs.

### LAUNDRY

There are no launderettes. If you are not a wash-it-in-the-sink sort of person it's fairly easy to get your laundry done through even the cheapest hotels, though it might take 48 hours. A moderately sized load will cost OR 1 or OR 2.

## WEIGHTS & MEASURES

Oman uses the metric system. In the souks silver jewellery is often sold according to weight, measured in Tolas. Tolas are sometimes called 'Thallers' after the Maria Theresia Dollar, an 18th century Austrian coin which became the model for Arabia's common currency of the 19th and early 20th century. One Tola is equal to 11.75 grams.

## BOOKS & MAPS
### People & Society

Oman has been thoroughly covered by a variety of travellers. *Travels in Oman – On the track of the early explorers* by Philip Ward (Oleander, Cambridge & New York, 1987) combines a modern travel narrative with the best of the 18th, 19th and early 20th century travellers' accounts of the country. *Sultan in Oman* by James Morris is a travelling journalist's account of a visit to Oman in the 1950s, though you should be aware that it is banned in the country.

Some of the action in Wilfred Thesiger's classic *Arabian Sands* (originally published in 1959, now available in a paperback edition from Penguin) takes place in and around Salalah, which Thesiger visited at the end of one of his journeys into the Empty Quarter. The final section of the book is an account of a trip around Oman's northern interior.

### History

There are few good history books devoted specifically to Oman. Michael Field's *The Merchants* (Overlook Press, Woodstock NY, 1985) has a fascinating chapter on the growth of modern Oman built around the story of W J Towell & Co, one of Oman's biggest family-owned trading companies. *The Arabs* by Peter Mansfield (Pelican, 2nd edition published 1985) has a brief but useful chapter on Oman.

### Travel Guides

*Oman – A MEED Practical Guide* is comprehensive but in need of a new edition. *The Economist Business Traveller's Guides – Arabian Peninsula* is a very useful how-to-do-business-with-the-Arabs sort of book.

The *APEX Explorer's Guide to Oman* (Apex Publishing, Muscat) is absolutely indispensable for anyone planning a spot of wadi bashing. In addition to detailed route descriptions and invaluable driving tips it also features a section on taking photographs in the desert and notes on what to see if you feel like dropping OR 300 on a tour of Muscat by helicopter. If you plan to do any shopping for antique jewellery *Oman Silver* by Ruth Hawley (Longman) might be a good investment. Most of Muscat's hotels have it in their bookshops and most of the shopkeepers in Muscat's silver souk also have well-thumbed copies. Both of these titles are widely available in Muscat.

### Bookshops

The only two places to look for books, newspapers, etc are in the bookstalls at the Muscat and Salalah Holiday Inn hotels. Elsewhere there simply are no foreign-language bookshops. The hotels stock publications like the *APEX Explorer's Guide to Oman* and coffee-table books on Oman and the other Gulf states. If you want good foreign-language novels then bring them with you. Books in Oman are quite expensive – a paperback novel that sells for US$ 4.95 in the USA will cost OR 6 or more in Muscat.

### Maps

The best map is the Bartholomew *Map of the Sultanate of Oman*. It has a light blue cover with a picture of the Seeb Clocktower on one side and palm trees on the other. Unfortunately it is pretty hard to find, and it's even harder to get hold of a copy in English. Its inset maps of Salalah and the various districts of Greater Muscat are excellent and the road map of the country as a whole is by far the most up-to-date one. The Oxford *Map of Oman*, available in most hotel bookshops in Muscat, is not quite as good but you can navigate well enough with it.

The Bartholomew *Map of the Arabian Gulf* is OK on northern Oman. The larger

Bartholomew *Map of the Arabian Peninsula* makes a nice wall-hanging but the scale is too large for it to be of much use as a road map.

## MEDIA
### Newspapers & Magazines
The *Times of Oman* and the *Oman Observer* are the local English-language newspapers. Foreign newspapers and magazines are available only in the bookshops in Muscat's five-star hotels and are usually about three days old. Outside of Muscat you can forget about finding foreign papers except, maybe, at the Salalah Holiday Inn.

*Oman Today* is a magazine-cum-handbook published every two months and widely available throughout the Sultanate for 500 baisa. Each issue has a comprehensive listing of clubs, activities, restaurants and entertainment, including visiting musical or theatrical acts. It is mainly aimed at the expat community. A less thorough listing of activities in Oman can be found in *What's On*, a monthly publication based in the UAE and available in the Sultanate.

### Radio & TV
Omani TV broadcasts a daily newscast in English at 8 pm and shows English-language movies two or three nights a week (usually around 11 pm).

The Sultanate of Oman FM Service is the local English-language radio station. It broadcasts on 90.4 FM every day from 7 am to 9 pm with news bulletins at 7.30 am, 2.30 and 6.30 pm. The fare is mostly classical music interspersed with light entertainment.

The main source of information for the expat community is the seemingly omnipresent BBC World Service. *Oman Today* lists the frequencies on which one can pick up the BBC in Oman.

## FILM & PHOTOGRAPHY
Oman is a very security-conscious place. An Omani police officer's idea of what is security related may differ significantly from yours. Don't photograph anything even vaguely military (though forts still in use by the police are generally OK if, like the three forts in Muscat and Mutrah, they are also recognised tourist attractions). Do not photograph people, especially women, without asking their permission first. Tourism is still very new to Oman so exercise caution, tact and discretion at all times.

## HEALTH
Since his ascension to power Sultan Qaboos has made improving health care and hygienic standards in Oman one of his main priorities. The result today is one of the most squeaky-clean countries you could ever hope to visit. Even the smallest restaurants in the souk are usually held to quite high standards of cleanliness. The tap water is drinkable throughout the country and no special vaccines are necessary, though a cholera jab would be a logical precaution if you are planning extensive travel off the beaten track in the interior and gamma globulin is always a good idea. Malaria, virtually endemic only 30 years ago, now occurs only very rarely in Oman and almost exclusively in the south. See the introductory Facts for the Visitor chapter for more information on prudent health precautions in the Gulf states.

## WOMEN TRAVELLERS
Oman is one of the easiest countries in the Gulf for women to travel in. Still, the usual advice for the region applies: avoid wearing clothing which is overly tight or revealing. Trousers are OK as long as they are loosely cut, though some expatriate women prefer long dresses. There is no need for a foreign woman to wear a headscarf, though in rural areas you will certainly gain respect by doing so. Shorts are always a bad idea outside the big hotels and especially in any traditional area such as the Mutrah souk. The interior is more conservative than the coast, which does not mean that you must dress particularly conservatively, but that an extra measure of tact is in order.

## DANGERS & ANNOYANCES
Oman is a very orderly society and harassment, of both women and men, is far less of

a problem here than in some of the other Gulf states. In general you should find it a reasonably open and easy place to travel so long as you dress properly and avoid doing anything which the police might construe as spying.

## WORK

One of the quickest ways to make yourself unpopular with the authorities is to start looking for work while visiting the country on a tourist visa. The rules on imported labour are still pretty strict. If you want to work in Oman you should go back home and apply for a job from there.

Assuming that you do have a contract and a job, your company will usually send you the NOC number before you fly out and you'll get a short-term visa at the airport. This will later be modified by your sponsor into a residence visa. Exit/Re-entry visas are not necessary for expatriates, who usually receive two-year multiple-entry visas.

## ACTIVITIES

The variety of terrain in Oman makes weekend mountain and desert motoring particularly worthwhile. The *APEX Explorer's Guide to Oman* is essential reading for anyone planning to see the country by 4WD.

Water sports are becoming the recreational mainstay of some of the five-star hotels. The main ones in Muscat all either have a beach of their own or have arranged to use somebody else's, and sport small fleets of sailboats, windsurfers, peddle boats, etc. Several have diving gear available for guests to rent.

All of the big hotels also have health clubs which you can join. The Al-Bustan Palace boasts the fanciest and most expensive of these with an annual fee of OR 235 for singles and OR 350 for couples. The cheapest health club is at the Ruwi Novotel where a year's membership will set you back only OR 80 (couples OR 100).

*Oman Today* has complete listings of the various clubs, societies and ethnic cultural associations in Oman.

## HIGHLIGHTS

If you are in Oman for only one day between planes or on a quick business trip, you must absolutely not miss the Mutrah souk. This is undoubtedly one of the best traditional markets left anywhere in Arabia. Those with a little more time, and a desire to learn more about Oman's history, should take in the Sultan's Armed Forces Museum in the capital's Bait Al-Falaj district.

Outside Muscat try to see the old fortress and the market in Nizwa. Sur, with its fortress and dhow-building yard, is the most interesting northern coastal town after Muscat.

## ACCOMMODATION
### Camping

There are no formal camping grounds in Oman. Camping in the mountains or the desert is more a matter of finding a good spot and setting up shop. Be careful, however, not to intrude on land that may belong to someone and be sure not to choose a camp site which might cause problems. Do not, for example, camp in the shadow of a village, especially if you plan to drink. This might offend the locals and you could, unwittingly, be on someone's land.

There are also certain practical and safety related aspects of camping in the desert which you should be aware of. The first is to always have more than one vehicle if at all possible and never to leave the city without letting someone know where you are going and when you plan to return. Anyone planning an overnight trip of this sort should pick up *Staying Alive in the Desert* by K E M Melville (Roger Lascelles, London, 2nd edition 1981).

### Hotels

Muscat has a range of hotels to suit most budgets, all of which are quite clean. Outside of the capital most hotels are still fairly clean but you will find your choice of accommodation severely limited. Most of Oman's main provincial towns have a single government-run hotel and, occasionally, a less fancy privately owned hotel. Even Salalah, the largest city in the country after Muscat, has only three hotels. In Muscat you can spend anything from OR 5 to OR 70 on a single room but in Salalah the price range is OR 15.700 to OR 34.500.

## FOOD

Eating cheaply in Oman almost always means eating Indian. There is little in the way of traditional cuisine. Muscat and Salalah are full of small Indian restaurants where the food is good, if not too varied. Often the menu is little more than whatever curry the cook decided to make on the day, but it is usually pretty good.

Muscat also has a number of up-market Indian and Lebanese restaurants and the usual collection of Western-style fast-food establishments, especially fried chicken places. The big hotels offer the usual selection of international fare.

## DRINKS

Small restaurants are likely to offer you a choice of little more than Pepsi or water. Larger restaurants will have a wider variety of soft drinks as well as fruit juice, sometimes freshly squeezed. Alcohol is available only in larger hotels and expensive restaurants.

## ENTERTAINMENT

There is a disco at the Muscat Inter-Continental Hotel and most of the other large hotels have lounge acts of some sort in their bars. *Oman Today* and the UAE-based *What's On* magazine are your best sources for this sort of information.

## THINGS TO BUY

Oman is unquestionably the best place in the Gulf to go souvenir shopping.

### Daggers

The country's most distinctive product is the *khanjar*, also spelled *khanja*, the curved dagger worn by Omani men on important occasions and in rural areas still sometimes worn every day. Traditionally the handles of these daggers were made from rhino horn

though today they are almost always made from either plastic or wood.

If a shopkeeper tells you that the handle of the dagger he is trying to sell you is made from rhino horn consider three things. First, virtually every country in the world strictly prohibits the import of anything containing rhino horn. Second, do you really want to help promote the illegal slaughter in East Africa of an endangered species? And third, is it real rhino horn, anyway? The fact is that if the shopkeeper is asking less than OR 700 for the dagger it is *not* made from rhino horn. Even if you did find one of these for sale, and you were willing to smuggle it back home, before forking over a couple of thousand dollars ask yourself this question: do you know enough about these things to be sure that it really *is* rhino horn?

Khanjas with plastic or wood handles (the only ones you are likely to see anyway) go for anywhere from OR 40 to OR 200 depending on the extent and quality of the decoration on the dagger, scabbard and belt.

If you really want to make your passage through airport security a nightmare you can explore the selection of guns and swords that are also on sale in many silver shops.

### Jewellery

Silver jewellery is easier to pack than a khanja, tends to be more affordable and is less likely to freak out the people running the X-ray at the airport. Traditional jewellery ranges from small silver boxes designed to hold kohl (traditionally used as makeup by both men and women) to huge belts or chestpieces. It is often very intricately designed. Thin layers of gold or bronze, coloured glass and old coins are all used to decorate the basic silverwork. Silver jewellery is almost always sold according to weight, measured in tolas (see Weights & Measures earlier in this section).

Shopkeepers looking for a sale are apt to make great claims for the age of their wares. Bear in mind, however, that most of this stuff was made as wedding jewellery. As it was (and still is) considered an insult for a bride to be given used jewellery to wear on her wedding day the tradition has long been that a woman's jewellery is melted down and sold for its weight after her death. For this reason very little of the jewellery you will see on sale in the souks of Muscat and Nizwa is more than 50 to 60 years old. Kohl boxes are usually the cheapest silver pieces available at OR 8 to OR 15 and from there the sky is the limit. Much of what is available is worn and battered so try to go shopping when you have a few hours to look closely at the various offerings. You could get one or two really nice pieces for OR 30 to OR 50.

You will also see Maria Theresia dollars, or Thallers, as they are commonly known, on sale in many jewellery shops. Along with the Indian rupee these were the common currency of the Gulf for much of the 19th and early 20th centuries. Regardless of when they were minted all Maria Theresia dollars bear the date 1780 (presumably the date on the original which the 19th century Arabian silversmiths used as a model). As with the jewellery, you can safely assume that the ones you'll see on sale are nowhere near that old. They contain about 20 grams of solid silver and sell for about OR 3 a piece.

### Clothing
Other things to buy include caftans. The turbans worn by virtually every Omani man also make good presents, generally costing about OR 10.

# Getting There & Away

### AIR
There are no bucket shops in Muscat, though you might save 10% or so by shopping around. If you are headed east it is often possible to get discounts on flights to Bangkok. Travel agents are usually willing to discount the regular fares quoted below if you are willing to lock yourself into particular travel dates.

### To/From the USA
Return fares to the eastern USA from Muscat

generally cost OR 500 to OR 600 depending on the season and how badly the agent wants to sell the ticket. The high season is mid-June to mid-October and about 10 days either side of Christmas.

### To/From the UK
Although you might think that flights to London would be fairly cheap because of the sheer number of British expats in Oman, this is not the case. At about OR 500 for a return ticket, it is almost the same price as flying to New York and more expensive than a low-season return to Sydney. (Look at a map and try to figure *that* one out.) One-way fares are about OR 360. If you want to fly to London at Christmas time it would be wise to book very early, say, in August or September.

### To/From Australia
Low-season (February to August) return fares to Sydney on Gulf Air are OR 480. The high-season (September to January) fare is OR 530.

### To/From Other Gulf States
A sample of one-way and cheap return fares from Muscat to other Gulf cities, with the minimum and maximum stay requirements follows:

| To | One-Way | Return | Min/Max |
|----|---------|--------|---------|
| Abu Dhabi | OR 47 | OR 49 | 3/7 days |
| Bahrain | OR 81 | OR 85 | 3/7 days |
| Dhahran | OR 79 | OR 111 | 3/14 days |
| Doha | OR 69 | OR 72 | 3/7 days |
| Dubai | OR 44 | OR 46 | 3/7 days |
| Jeddah | OR 127 | OR 176 | 3/14 days |
| Kuwait | OR 91 | OR 127 | 3/14 days |
| Riyadh | OR 91 | OR 127 | 3/14 days |
| Sharjah | OR 44 | OR 46 | 3/7 days |

### LAND
Leaving by land means leaving to the UAE as the border with Yemen is not open to travellers. For overland travel to the UAE in your own vehicle you will need to obtain a Road Permit (see Documents earlier in this section). Note, however, that road permits are not issued to single women. If you travel

by bus the permit is usually secured by the bus company after you show them that you have a UAE visa (or an Omani visa if you are coming from Dubai). Road permits have to be obtained via your sponsor. If your visa is sponsored by a hotel and you plan to drive in, the hotel will usually need an extra three to five days for processing the visa to obtain the road permit.

## SEA

At present there are no scheduled seaborne passenger services to or from Oman, though cruise ships occasionally call at Muscat.

## LEAVING OMAN

Departure formalities at Muscat's Seeb International Airport are fairly straight-forward. The airport is efficient and the staff are not overstretched, so things tend to move along smoothly. You should appear at the airport at least an hour in advance of departure time. Bear in mind that it takes a good 30 minutes by taxi and an hour by bus to reach the airport from Mutrah.

## Departure Tax

There is a tax of OR 3 for all departing international passengers at Seeb airport in Muscat.

# Getting Around

## AIR
## Local Air Services

Oman Aviation flies once per day to Salalah for OR 32 one-way, OR 64 return. A discount return fare of OR 48 is available on weekends (there is an extra flight in each direction on Wednesday and Friday). Muscat to Sur is OR 14 one-way, OR 28 return. There are also flights to Khasab in Musandem and to Massirah Island, though the odds on your getting permission to visit either of these places are very slim.

## BUS
## Service & Reservations

Inter-city buses are operated by the Oman National Transport Company (ONAT) which has daily services to most of the main provincial towns.

The main bus station is on Al-Jaame St in Ruwi, Muscat; tickets are sold in an office at the main terminal. Outside Muscat the stations tend to be little more than roadside lay-bys and tickets are available either at a nearby shop or from the bus driver. Complete timetables for all routes are posted at the Ruwi terminal. In provincial towns there is usually a small signboard with the timetables for the routes from that town posted at the stop. Tickets for all inter-city services are available in advance, at least in Muscat, but reservations are accepted only for the express services to Salalah. It is generally a good idea to book seats to Salalah a day or two in advance.

## Costs

With the exception of Salalah none of the main inter-city routes costs more than OR 4 each way. The fare to Salalah is OR 10 one-way, OR 18 return. See the Muscat section for more detailed information on costs and the frequency of ONAT's services.

## TAXI

Service taxis out of Muscat are difficult to find and slow to fill. From the provinces back into Muscat they are a marginally better bet. The fact is that ONAT's buses have largely replaced the service-taxi system. The buses are a lot more comfortable than a service taxi anyway.

## CAR
## Road Rules

Seat belt use is mandatory for passengers in the front seat of cars. The fine for not wearing one is OR 10. Traffic laws are enforced fairly strictly especially in Muscat. People may drive fast but you will see little of the reckless lunacy that passes for driving in much of the rest of the Gulf.

### Rental

Renting a car in the Sultanate is fairly easy but it is not cheap. Most foreign driver's licenses are accepted for people on business or tourist visas. Resident expats must obtain an Omani license. This can usually be issued against a foreign driving license without any further test being administered.

Rates for compact cars start at about OR 10 to OR 14 per day plus OR 2 to OR 3 per day for insurance. You can plan on spending about OR 90 to OR 100 net to rent a car for a week. Rentals usually include 150 free km per day but beyond that you will probably be paying 100 baisa per km. This adds up pretty quickly considering how spread out the capital is, let alone driving anywhere else.

### HITCHING

While Omanis thumb rides all the time, especially in rural areas, it is not a common practice for foreigners. On the other hand it is not illegal. I've met people who have happily spent days thumbing their way around Dhofar. However, you might attract the unwelcome attentions of the police by doing so.

### LOCAL TRANSPORT
#### To/From the Airport

There are two bus routes from Muscat to Seeb airport. The express bus from Salalah also stops at the airport. There are no buses to/from Salalah Airport. The taxi fare between Salalah airport and the town centre is about OR 1 but is negotiable.

### Bus & Taxi

Only Muscat has a local bus system and Salalah is the only provincial city with enough local taxis to be worth mentioning. See the sections on those two cities for details of services and fares.

# Muscat

Muscat is a port the like of which cannot be found in the whole world where there is business and good things that cannot be found elsewhere.

So wrote the great Arab navigator Ahmed Bin Majid Al-Najdi in 1490 AD. Five centuries later Muscat still enchants visitors in a way that no other city in the Gulf can even begin to. Maybe this is because Muscat does not have that slightly artificial feel which typifies so much of the rest of the region.

### History

Muscat's history dates from at least the 1st century AD and it was probably mentioned by Ptolemy. But while it was settled at this time it was neither large nor important. Even well into the Islamic era it was eclipsed by Sohar and Hormuz which, lying in the midst of the strait of the same name, was by far the most important port in the area for many centuries.

Muscat first gained importance during the 14th and 15th centuries. It was little more than a small trading post, albeit an important one. Muscat was an outpost of the powerful kings of Hormuz and, eventually, it became their entrepôt. It was in this role that, inevitably, it attracted the attentions of the Portuguese who conquered the town during the 16th century.

It was not, however, until 1622, after they themselves had been driven out of Hormuz, that the Portuguese made Muscat their main stronghold in the area. It was around this time that the town walls (a refurbished version of which still stand) were built. But by then Lisbon's era in the Gulf was drawing to a close. Muscat was Portugal's last stronghold in the region and Omani reconquest of the town in 1650 effectively ended the Portuguese era in the Gulf.

Since the mid-18th century Muscat has been the seat of the Al-Busaid dynasty, the current ruling family of Oman. Since then it has seen the growth and, later, the partition of a maritime empire which once controlled much of the coast of East Africa.

Despite the splendour of this history, the Omani capital languished in an almost medieval torpor for most of this century. During the 1960s, as the economies of the other Gulf states roared ahead, life in what was then known as Muscat and Oman seemed to slip further and further behind.

All of that changed in the wake of the 1970 palace coup which brought Sultan Qaboos Bin Said to power. The advantage which Muscat gained from a late start was the opportunity to learn from the mistakes of others. The result is a capital which has retained much of its traditional architecture and beauty, while making great strides toward modernisation in a remarkably short span of time.

## Orientation

You will sometimes hear Muscat referred to as the 'three cities' or the 'capital region'. Greater Muscat covers a huge area from Seeb airport in the west to the Sultan's palace in the east. Moreover, the various districts of the city do not mesh seamlessly into one another. On the contrary, they are often sep-

arated by low hills and ridges which serve, to a certain extent, to compartmentalise the capital's various districts.

The 'three cities' are Muscat, Mutrah and Ruwi. Muscat is the old port area. It is the site of the Sultan's palace and a fascinating place to wander around but it has few shops and, except for the old city walls, there is not much to see. The real attraction is the traditional feel of the place. Mutrah, three km north-west of Muscat, is the main trading and residential port area. Its long, sweeping corniche is one of the most beautiful spots in Arabia, and its souk one of the best. Behind the corniche is a labyrinth of streets and alleys into which few tourists ever venture.

A few km inland from Muscat and Mutrah lies Ruwi. A generation ago this was an undeveloped valley; today it is the capital's modern commercial district. The Ruwi valley actually includes the districts of both Ruwi and Bait Al-Falaj (which derives its name from the fort that now houses the Sultan's Armed Forces Museum and was once virtually the only building in the valley). Part of this area is also formally known as *Mutrah Al-Tijari*, or Commercial Mutrah, though I have never heard anyone

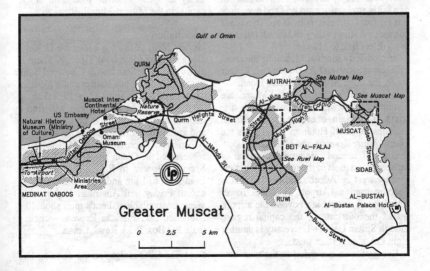

Greater Muscat

Gulf of Oman

QURM

MUTRAH — See Mutrah Map

Al-Mina St.

See Muscat Map

Muscat Inter-Continental Hotel

Nature Reserve

Mutrah Corniche

US Embassy

Qurm Heights Street

Ruwi Street

Mutrah High St.

MUSCAT

Natural History Museum (Ministry of Culture)

Qaboos Street

Oman Museum

Al-Nahda St.

BEIT AL-FALAJ

See Ruwi Map

Sidab Street

SIDAB

To Airport

Ministries Area

MEDINAT QABOOS

RUWI

AL-BUSTAN

Al-Bustan Palace Hotel

Al-Bustan Street

0    2.5    5 km

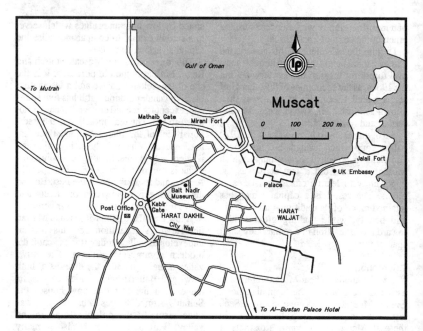

use that name. In general the whole area is referred to simply as Ruwi. Ruwi is laid out as a fairly straightforward grid and even now it is far from completely built up. Two roads connect the Ruwi valley to Mutrah but there is no direct link to Muscat.

Immediately south of Muscat lie the small villages of Sidab and Al-Bustan and, further south, the huge Al-Bustan Palace Hotel.

Along the coast to the west of Mutrah are a number of new, mostly residential, districts. The main ones are Qurm, which includes the Gulf Hotel and overlooks the Qurm Nature Reserve, and Medinat Qaboos, the site of several ministries, a couple of museums and most of the foreign embassies. Further west is 'Adeeba and beyond that is Seeb International Airport. The Clock Tower roundabout, several km beyond the airport, marks the outskirts of the capital region, though Sultan Qaboos University is another eight km or so further west.

Except for an excursion to the museums and embassies of Medinat Qaboos you are likely to spend most of your time in the capital in the Muscat-Mutrah-Ruwi area.

### Information

**Money** Most of the big banks are in Ruwi along Markaz Mutrah Al-Tijari St. There is also a branch of Standard & Chartered Bank next to the Ruwi bus station and a plethora of moneychangers (plus a few banks) along Souk Ruwi St. In Mutrah you will find a number of moneychangers on the Corniche and around the entrance to the souk.

American Express (☎ 708035, 708470) is represented in Oman by Zubair Travel & Services Bureau in Ruwi. They are open from 8 am to 1 pm and 4 to 6 pm every day except Friday. All American Express services are available. Client's mail should be addressed to: American Express – client's mail, PO Box 3833, Ruwi, Oman.

**Post** The GPO is right on the dividing line

between Ruwi and Bait Al-Falaj at the northern end of Markaz Mutrah Al-Tijari St. It is open Saturday to Wednesday from 7.30 am to 1.30 pm and 4 to 6 pm. On Thursdays and holidays they keep a shorter 8 to 11 am schedule. There is a Philatelic Department on the upper floor.

**Telecommunications** There is no telephone office in Greater Muscat. To make an international call either arm yourself with a kg or so of coins and head for a payphone, or go to the business centre in one of the big hotels and phone from there; bring lots of money because this option will not be cheap.

**Foreign Embassies** Embassies are open from Saturday to Wednesday. Some Arab embassies are open on Thursday mornings as well.

Germany
  Near the Al-Nahdha Hospital on Al-Nahdha Rd in Ruwi (☎ 702164)
Netherlands
  Ruwi St, Ruwi, near the Novotel Hotel (☎ 705410)
New Zealand (consulate)
  At the Ruwi end of Mutrah High St near the Mutrah Hotel (☎ 795726)
UAE
  Medinat Qaboos Diplomatic Area to the sea side of Sultan Qaboos St, beyond the Al-Khwair roundabout (☎ 602869)
UK
  In Muscat, between the Sultan's palace and the Jalali fort. The British handle emergencies for Australian and Canadian citizens (☎ 738501)
USA
  Medinat Qaboos Diplomatic Area to the sea side of Sultan Qaboos St, beyond the Al-Khwair roundabout (☎ 698989)

**Travel Agencies** The capital's greatest concentration of travel agents is in and around Markaz Mutrah Al-Tijari St in Ruwi. Your best bet is to ask for advice from locals or at the reception desk of a big hotel.

**Bookshops** The selection is not great and the prices are very high but the bookshops in the five-star hotels are your best bet.

**Medical Services** Since you are almost certainly in the country under the sponsorship of a hotel, call the hotel doctor if you get sick. You may or may not be charged for a consultation with the hotel doctor. Expatriates usually have some sort of medical plan through their company and this would be the place you should go first if visiting an expat.

Should you need hospitalisation this will probably be free, though if things get really serious you are likely to find yourself on the first plane headed home.

**Emergencies** Dial 999 for the police, an ambulance or to report a fire.

### Things to See
**Jalali, Mirani & Mutrah Forts** All three forts took on more or less their present form in the 1580s during the Portuguese occupation of Muscat. Of the three, the Portuguese built only Mutrah fort from scratch, though their alterations to the other two were so extensive that the forts can be said to be of Portuguese rather than Arab construction.

All of the forts are still used by the police and/or military and are closed to the public, though Mutrah fort has, occasionally, been opened to foreign tour groups with special permission. It's OK to photograph the forts.

### Things to See – Medinat Qaboos
**Oman Museum** The Oman Museum is in the Ministries Area; look for a small, white building next to the much larger, brown Ministry of Information building. It's open Saturday to Wednesday from 8 am to 2 pm, and Saturday and Tuesday evenings from 5 to 9 pm; closed Thursday and Friday. Admission is free. A free guidebook in English and French is on offer, but it is little more than a condensation of the signs on the walls.

The museum is small but well organised. It covers a lot of ground in only a few rooms and is well worth the trek to Medinat Qaboos.

Displays on the ground floor cover the history, geography and geology of Oman. The 1st floor has a small display on Islam, consisting mostly of manuscripts, a fair to

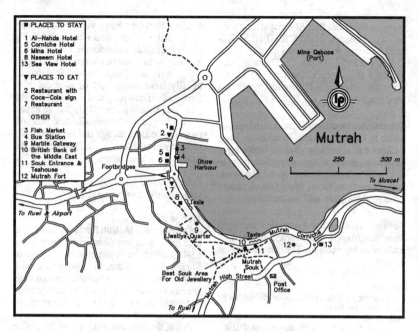

**PLACES TO STAY**
1 Al–Nahda Hotel
5 Corniche Hotel
6 Mina Hotel
8 Naseem Hotel
13 Sea View Hotel

**PLACES TO EAT**
2 Restaurant with Coca–Cola sign
7 Restaurant

**OTHER**
3 Fish Market
4 Bus Station
9 Marble Gateway
10 British Bank of the Middle East
11 Souk Entrance & Teahouse
12 Mutrah Fort

Mina Qaboos (Port)

Mutrah

0    250    500 m

To Muscat

Dhow Harbour

Footbridges

To Ruwi & Airport

Taxis

Liwatiya Quarter

Taxis—Mutrah Corniche

Best Souk Area For Old Jewellery

Mutrah Souk

Mutrah High Street

Post Office

To Ruwi

middling display of Omani arts and crafts and an excellent room on architecture in the Sultanate.

**Children's Museum** This museum, near the Foreign Ministry off Sultan Qaboos St (it's well signposted), is open Sunday to Thursday from 8 am to 2 pm and Monday and Thursday from 4 to 8 pm. It is closed on Friday and Saturday; admission is free. The museum is a practical, science-oriented place with lots of hands-on displays. You do not have to be a child to have fun here.

**Natural History Museum** This is a place you should definitely try to visit before heading out of the capital. The museum is on Sultan Qaboos St in the Ministries Area, across from the ice skating rink. The English portion of its sign is in quite small lettering – look for a silhouette of a lynx above the Arabic script. It is open Saturday to Wednesday from 8 am to 2 pm. Adjacent to the

museum is the Ministry of Culture & Natural Heritage, which is where you must go to obtain permits for visits to forts and archaeological sites throughout the country. These are usually issued on the spot but you will have to show identification.

The first hall to the right as you enter the museum contains a brief description of Oman's geography, geology and flora and fauna. To the left, the main gallery has lots of stuffed specimens of the fauna. Everything is labelled in both English and Arabic.

**Things to See – Mutrah**

**Mutrah Fish Market** The fish market is at the northern end of the Mutrah Corniche near the Mina and Corniche hotels. In addition to fish, meat is also sold here and you will sometimes find shell merchants. The best time to come is early in the morning. The market usually opens around 6.30 am.

**Mutrah Souk** The Mutrah souk is without a

doubt the most interesting souk in the Arab Gulf states. Be sure to stop for a drink at the teahouse on the left-hand side of the main entrance. Most visitors head immediately for the eight or 10 shops specialising in antique silver jewellery. To reach these turn up the first alley on your right (more or less opposite the teahouse) after entering the souk through the main gateway on the Mutrah corniche. You will go up a slight incline, passing through a portion of the cloth souk, before reaching the small group of shops selling antique silver. As with any good Arab souk, however, the best thing to do is simply to wander at will. The Mutrah souk is not really very big and you are in no danger of getting lost, though there may be moments when it does not look that way.

## Things to See – Ruwi

**Sultan's Armed Forces Museum** This museum is open Sunday, Monday and Wednesday from 8.30 am to 1 pm. Admission is 500 baisa. You are usually required to go through the museum with a guide (even if the two of you do not share a common language) and photography is strictly prohibited.

The museum, run by the Omani army, is in the Bait Al-Falaj fort, which is one of the oldest buildings in Muscat. It's quite well presented and the lower floor is definitely worth a visit.

The fort itself is the building which gives its name to the Bait Al-Falaj district. It was originally built in the late 18th or early 19th century as a royal summer home.

The museum is divided into sections on: Pre-Islamic Oman, Oman & Islam, the Portuguese in Oman, the Al-Ya'aribah (Al-Ya'ribi) Dynasty, the Al-Busaidi (Al-Busaid) Dynasty, the establishment of the armed forces and the 'incident at Jebel Akhdar and Dhorfur (Dhofar) mutiny' (the insurrections which the current Sultan had to put down during his early years on the throne).

The ground floor's exhibits provide an excellent outline of Omani history. The exhibits on the upper level are more specifically military in nature.

**Ruwi Souk** The Ruwi souk is a good place for shopping, but it is not exactly a tourist attraction. Like the rest of Ruwi it is a modern creation. Those in search of gold jewellery should try Souk Ruwi St.

**The Clock Tower** During the day, little distinguishes Ruwi's clock tower, just off Al-Jaame St, from the dozens of other such structures around the Gulf. You have to stop by after dark for the full effect. The base of the tower on the side facing Al-Jaame St is made up entirely of TV screens and once the sun goes down they blare out Oman TV's signal to any and all passers-by with the loudspeakers strategically positioned around the adjacent square. It's reminiscent of George Orwell's *1984*.

## Activities

Pick up a copy of *Oman Today* for information on Muscat's various sporting clubs and societies. Health clubs and water-sports centres open to the travellers are all attached to the big hotels. The offerings are fairly standard: windsurfing, water skiing, etc.

## Organised Tours

Sunny Day Tours (☎ 592992) is the main tour operator in the country with a large selection of day trips around Muscat and the north of the country and overnight desert camping safaris. The Oman National Transportation Company (ONAT) (☎ 590046, extension 59) also runs tours around the capital and to the main towns in the northern part of the country. The day tours of Muscat cost OR 4.500 while out-of-town trips cost OR 10 to OR 12. Sample itineraries include Nizwa, Bahla and Jabrin or Sohar, Al-Suwadi and Barka.

## Places to Stay – bottom end

Most of Muscat's cheap hotels are on the Mutrah Corniche. The best value-for-money is the *Al-Nahda Hotel* (☎ 714196) at the northern end of the Corniche, near the

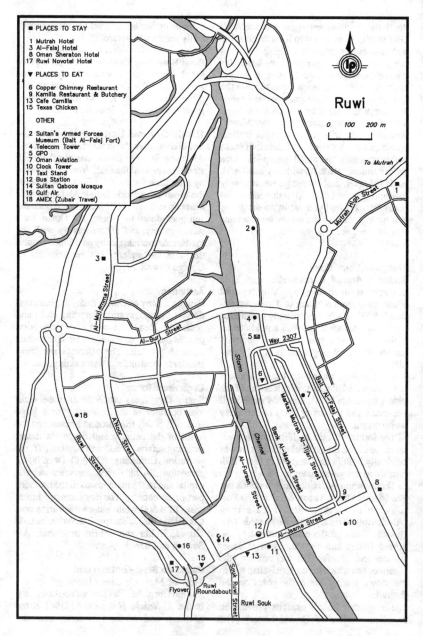

PLACES TO STAY
1 Mutrah Hotel
3 Al-Falaj Hotel
8 Oman Sheraton Hotel
17 Ruwi Novotel Hotel

▼ PLACES TO EAT
6 Copper Chimney Restaurant
9 Kamila Restaurant & Butchery
13 Cafe Camilla
15 Texas Chicken

OTHER
2 Sultan's Armed Forces
  Museum (Bait Al-Falaj Fort)
4 Telecom Tower
5 GPO
7 Oman Aviation
10 Clock Tower
11 Taxi Stand
12 Bus Station
14 Sultan Qaboos Mosque
16 Gulf Air
18 AMEX (Zubair Travel)

Ruwi

0    100    200 m

To Mutrah

Mutrah High Street

Al-Moj Jamma Street

Al-Buri Street

Way 2307

Storm

Channel

Bait Al-Falaj Street

Markaz Mutrah Al-Tijari Street

Bank Al-Markazi Street

Al-Noor Street

Ruwi Street

Al-Fursan Street

Al-Jaame Street

Souk Ruwi Street

Ruwi Roundabout

Flyover

Ruwi Souk

entrance to Mina Qaboos. Singles/doubles are OR 7/11 which is pretty hard to beat. The rooms are small but clean. Moving down the Corniche the next stop is the *Corniche Hotel* (☎ 714707) which is pretty good if you can get one of the rooms on the sea side. The rooms at the back of the hotel are rather cramped and have uncomfortably small bathrooms. Rooms are OR 10.500/14.700. The service is rather slow, though. A much better bet, at the same price, is the nearby *Naseem Hotel* (☎ 712418). At the far end of the Corniche the cheapest place is the *Sea View Hotel* (☎ 714555) at OR 5.500/10.500. Again, it's a great deal if you can get a room overlooking the water (and provided you do not mind sharing the bath with one other room).

The *Mina Hotel* (☎ 711828) is a bit more up-market than the other Mutrah hotels at OR 11.200/14.000. It's the only hotel with a restaurant that serves alcohol.

The *Mutrah Hotel* (☎ 798401) is at the Ruwi end of Mutrah High St. Rooms are OR 13.650/19.950. Nearby, the *Oman Hotel*, up an alleyway across Mutrah High St from the Mutrah Hotel, has big, bare, grubby rooms for OR 5/7.

### Places to Stay – middle

The capital's two medium-priced hotels are both in greater Ruwi. The *Al-Falaj Hotel* (☎ 702311, telex 3229 HOTEL ON, fax 795853) on Al-Mujamma St in Bait Al-Falaj is the oldest in the city. At OR 31.625/38.825 (including tax and service) it is the cheapest place that can sponsor visas. The *Ruwi Novotel* (☎ 704244) on Ruwi St in Ruwi is a bit cheaper at OR 27.300/33.600 net, but they do not arrange visas.

### Places to Stay – top end

Muscat's top-end hotels can all sponsor tourist or business visas. The prices quoted here include 15% tax and service charge.

The *Al-Bustan Palace* (☎ 740200, telex 5477 BUSHTL ON, fax 799600) is a long way from anything else in the capital region, but it's worth the drive just for a look at the massive atrium lobby. Nestled away in its

own cove south of Muscat, the hotel was built in the early '80s as the venue for a Gulf Cooperation Council summit meeting. The hotel is a small resort with an emphasis on water sports. Singles/doubles start at OR 69/74.750. If you want to live like an emir you can always stay in the Grand Deluxe Suite for a mere OR 506.

In Ruwi the *Oman Sheraton* (☎ 799899, telex 3352 SHERATON ON, fax 795791) is somewhat more modest. Rooms start at a mere OR 49.400/54.400.

In Medinat Qaboos the *Muscat Inter-Continental Hotel* (☎ 600500, telex 5491 IHC MCT ON, fax 600012) is another self-contained mini-resort with its own beach but it's not as grand as the Al-Bustan Palace. Rooms start from OR 50.600/56.350 (more if you want a sea view).

### Places to Eat

**Cheap & Medium-Priced** Of the several small restaurants at the northern end of the Mutrah Corniche, the best is the place with the green *Restaurant* sign near the roundabout opposite the Mina Hotel. It is fairly spartan, and sometimes water is the only drink available, but the biryanis are quite good and cost only 500 baisa per helping. Stand-up snacks are available from the kiosk at the bus station on the Mutrah Corniche. Further north, the restaurant next to the Al-Nahda Hotel (which is missing its sign so that only a Coca-Cola billboard is showing) has decent shawarma but the sit-down food in the restaurant is not very good.

The only restaurant in Mutrah that serves alcohol is *Albahr* (which is Arabic for the sea, not a misspelling of the English word bar), the restaurant at the Corniche Hotel. They won't serve booze, however, unless you order a meal. The view of Mutrah is great and the Indian food is excellent. Meals cost about OR 3, plus drinks.

There are several good bets in Ruwi, such as the *Kamilia Restaurant & Butchery* just off Al-Jaame St. The fare here includes biryanis at OR 1.800 including soup and salad. Chinese main dishes cost OR 1.200 to OR 1.500. Outdoor tables are available during the winter. The view of the parking lot is hardly romantic but the breeze is nice. A cafe serving shawarma and an ice cream shop, both also run by Kamilia, are part of the same complex.

Across Al-Jaame St from the Ruwi bus station *Cafe Camilia* is a good spot for a quick snack with sandwiches and shawarma for 200 baisa.

Ruwi is also the place to go for Western fast food. There is a *Pizza Hut* off Bait Al-Falaj St, beyond the Sheraton Hotel and the clock tower. *Texas Chicken* at the corner of A'Noor and Al-Jaame Sts has good chicken as does the *Penguin Restaurant* in the O C Centre at the Ruwi Roundabout.

**Expensive** The food in *The Atrium*, the coffee shop in the Al-Bustan Palace Hotel, is not stunning but it provides one with a good excuse to visit the hotel. On the other hand, even coffee and a sandwich here is likely to cost OR 3 to OR 4. In the afternoons they offer a British-style High Tea for OR 2.500.

*La Mama* in the Oman Sheraton has Italian/Mexican cuisine at normal big hotel prices, which means OR 8 to OR 10 for a meal. The food is OK but the portions are small; try the nachos.

The *Copper Chimney Restaurant*, just off Markaz Mutrah Al-Tijari St near the GPO in Ruwi, has excellent Indian food in a very nice setting. Dinner is fairly expensive at OR 5 to OR 7 but they often have a lunch buffet for OR 2.200, which is highly recommended. Not as good but still worth a look is the *Cooper Chimney Chinese Restaurant*, on the floor immediately above the main Cooper Chimney restaurant.

### Entertainment
Muscat is rather thin when it comes to entertainment. There is a disco at the Muscat Inter-Continental and many of the big hotels have lounge acts of some sort in their bars.

### Things to Buy
The best place to shop is the Mutrah souk. See the Things to Buy heading in the Facts for the Visitor section for details of the souk's shopping possibilities.

### Getting There & Away
**Air** Seeb International Airport is 37 km from Muscat or Mutrah. The departure tax is OR 3. For airport flight information call 519223 or 519456. Some of the airlines flying out of Muscat are:

Air India
 Markaz Mutrah Al-Tijari St, Ruwi (☎ 708639)
Air Lanka
 Mezoon Travel, Al-Burj St, Bait Al-Falaj (☎ 796680)
British Airways
 Al-Jaame St (access from Markaz Mutrah Al-Tijari St), Ruwi (☎ 702244)
EgyptAir
 Al-Burj St, Bait Al-Falaj (☎ 796134)
Gulf Air
 Ruwi St, near the Ruwi Roundabout (☎ 703555)
KLM
 Markaz Mutrah Al-Tijari St, Ruwi (☎ 708989)
Kuwait Airways
 Bahwan Travel Agencies, Markaz Mutrah Al-Tijari St, Ruwi (☎ 707119)
Lufthansa
 Al-Burj St, Bait Al-Falaj (☎ 708986)
Middle East Airlines (MEA)
 Mezoon Travel, Al-Burj St, Bait Al-Falaj (☎ 796680)
Oman Aviation (also handles Air Tanzania)
 Just off Markaz Mutrah Al-Tijari St, Ruwi (☎ 707222)
Royal Jordanian
 Mezoon Travel, Al-Burj St, Bait Al-Falaj (☎ 796680)
Swissair
 Bank Al-Markazi St, Ruwi (☎ 701813, 703303)
Thai Airways International
 Bahwan Travel Agencies, Markaz Mutrah Al-Tijari St, Ruwi (☎ 705934)
UTA
 Bahwan Travel Agencies, Markaz Mutrah Al-Tijari St, Ruwi (☎ 704318)

**Bus** The Ruwi bus station is the main depot for inter-city buses in the Sultanate. The buses to Salalah are luxury air-conditioned models of a rather higher standard than those on most of the other inter-city routes. They depart daily at 7 am, 6 and 7 pm (12 to 13 hours, OR 10 one-way, OR 18 return). During Ramadan the 7 pm bus departs an hour later and during the mid-June to mid-September monsoon season the morning bus leaves at 6 am.

Other inter-city routes include: Rustaq (one daily, three hours, OR 1.500), Sohar (five daily, four hours, OR 2.200), Buraimi (three daily, six hours, OR 3.600) and Nizwa (eight daily, three hours, OR 1.600).

The only international bus service is to Dubai. Buses leave twice a day, at 7.30 am and 2.30 pm, from the Ruwi bus station. During Ramadan the late bus leaves at 5.30 pm. The trip takes six hours. In Dubai the buses come and go from Airline Centre on Al-Maktoum Rd in Deira, Dubai. The fare is OR 9 one-way, OR 16 return.

**Taxi** There are inter-city service taxis in Oman but they're hard to find in the capital. The main service-taxi stand (for trips to Nizwa and other points north and west of Muscat) is at the Clock Tower Roundabout *beyond* Seeb airport. That's an awfully long way to go in search of a service taxi. Short of trekking out beyond Seeb, the best place to try for service taxi rides is the stand across the street from the Ruwi bus station.

**Car** There are several rental agencies in the area around the Ruwi Roundabout as well as the usual desks in big hotels and at the airport.

### Getting Around

**To/From the Airport** Bus Nos 23 and 24 leave for the airport from the Mutrah bus terminal at 20 and 50 minutes past the hour from 6.20 am to 9.50 pm every day. The route also passes the Ruwi bus station and the Qurm Roundabout. The fare is 200 baisa. Taxis to the airport cost OR 5 from anywhere in the capital area if taken privately, 500 baisa if shared. If you are really interested, the express bus from Salalah also stops at the airport on its way into Muscat so, in theory, you could use it to connect to/from the south.

**Bus** ONAT's system of local buses covers greater Muscat fairly thoroughly. Most fares are either 100 or 200 baisa, depending on the distance travelled. Destinations are displayed on the front of the buses in Arabic and English, but the bus numbers are only in Arabian numerals. The main bus station is on Al-Jaame St in Ruwi (the same place that the inter-city buses leave from) and there is a secondary station by the roundabout next to the Mina Hotel in Mutrah. Bus Nos 8, 23 and 24 run between the Mutrah and Ruwi stations three or four times an hour for 200 baisa. Bus No 28 makes the long trek to Sultan Qaboos University (beyond the airport) for 300 baisa.

**Taxi** As in so many other Middle Eastern countries, a pernicious fare system operates in Muscat. If you bargain you will inevitably pay two or three times what you ought to, but the only way to pay the proper fare is to know it before you get into the cab and not to raise the subject of money at all – just hand the driver the proper sum at your destination.

Regular taxis also function as local service taxis, usually travelling from ranks in various parts of the city. Local service taxis also come disguised as pick-up trucks and mini-vans. There is one rank on the Mutrah Corniche, and another in Ruwi opposite the bus station. Drivers usually stand by their vehicle shouting the destination or cruise around the neighbourhood looking for the last couple of passengers when they are almost full.

A taxi between Mutrah and Ruwi costs OR 1 in either direction if you take it all to yourself ('engaged'), or 200 baisa if shared. Mutrah to Qurm is OR 3 engaged or 300 baisa shared, and Ruwi to Qurm OR 2 engaged or 300 baisa shared.

# Northern Oman

## SOHAR

Sohar is one of those places where history casts a shadow over modern reality. A thousand years ago it occupied three times its present area and was the largest town in the country. Sohar today is something of a dis-

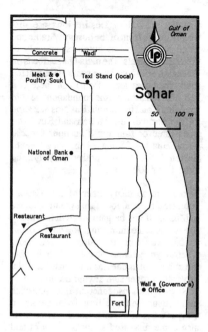

Salalah. The main reason you are likely to stop here is to get petrol on the way south. If you are travelling by bus, the southbound Salalah Express stops here for about an hour for meals. The resthouse has 10 tolerable rooms for OR 6/10 a single/double. The fare in the restaurant is chicken or the curry-of-the-day served on an ample pile of rice for OR 1.

## SUR

Sur (Sour) has a lot going for it, starting with a nearly ideal location. It is a fairly quiet place but has great beaches and several interesting things to see. Sur is only 150 km down the coast from Muscat as the crow flies, though by road it is a bit over twice that distance.

The **fortress** (permits from Muscat required) is on the outskirts of town on the road from Muscat and Ibra. The highlight of the town itself is the **dhow builder's yard** on the coast just beyond the town. A nearby ferry will carry you across the narrow sound to **Ayega**, a small village where many of the dhow builders live. The two-storey sand-coloured building near the Ayega ferry landing is the house reserved for the Sultan whenever he comes to visit. The ferry crossing is free and takes about two minutes.

Cheap beds can be found in the town centre at the *Sour Hotel* (☎ 440090). Singles/doubles are OR 10/15, all with bath. The rooms are sparsely furnished but adequate. If you think you may be using the air-conditioner make sure it works before you take the room. The *Arabian Sea Restaurant* on the ground floor of the same building is a good enough place to eat. Several similar small restaurants are in the area near the hotel. Four km from the centre the *Sur Resort Beach Hotel* (☎ 442031) is an up-market place with rooms at OR 20/25. It has a decent, if unexciting, restaurant and coffee shop.

Service taxis for Muscat (OR 4) and Ibra (OR 2.500) tout for passengers in the parking lot around the corner from the Sour Hotel. Buses for Muscat (OR 2.500, daily at 6 and 7 am, four hours) leave from the lay-by in front of the Al-Shath Restaurant.

appointment; it is only worth the trip if you are not pressed for time. It is a popular stopping-place for people on their way to/from Buraimi and the UAE. Visiting its only real site, the impressive looking **fort**, requires, as always, a permit from Muscat.

To reach the fort (coming from Muscat), turn right when you arrive at the roundabout with a rotating globe atop an open pyramid. Continue on this road. The fort will be on the right. The *Sohar Hotel* (840058) is about seven km beyond the globe-roundabout (through another roundabout) and on the left. Coming from Muscat, continue north about three km along the highway beyond the turn for Sohar and it's on your left. There are a few small Indian restaurants in town just up the coast from the fort. The hotel also has a small restaurant.

## AL-GHABA

Al-Ghaba is not much more than a crossroads 342 km south of Muscat on the road to

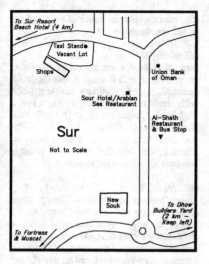

To Sur Resort Beach Hotel (4 km)

Taxi Stand● Vacant Lot

Shops

Union Bank of Oman

Sour Hotel/Arabian Sea Restaurant

Al–Shath Restaurant & Bus Stop ▼

**Sur**

Not to Scale

New Souk

To Dhow Builders Yard (2 km – Keep left)

To Fortress & Muscat

## AL-HAZM

The town of Al-Hazm is little more than a fort surrounded by a few houses off the road from Muscat to Rustaq, but it is well worth the stop.

To visit the **fort**, which does not appear to be actively used by the local police but remains under their jurisdiction, you will need a permit from the Ministry of Culture & National Heritage (obtained at the Natural History Museum in Muscat). You will probably also be given a (non-English speaking) police officer as a guide when you visit the fort.

Before you enter take a look at the *falaj* (irrigation canal) which flows underneath the fort. It is still in use, irrigating the gardens surrounding the fort.

Entering the fort itself note the carved doors. The inscription on the left-hand door dates its construction to 1162 AH (circa 1750 AD). The inscription on the right identifies Imam Sultan Bin Saif II, a member of the Al-Ya'ribi dynasty who reigned from 1706 to 1719, as the fort's builder.

As you enter the fort move around to your right to see the well, which is about 25 metres deep. At the end of the corridor beyond the well is a room with a huge stone pillar in its centre.

When you get to the centre of the fort you will again encounter the falaj. An inscription to the right of it dates this part of the fort to 918 AH (1512 AD). The Imam's tomb is just beyond the hole in the wall.

There used to be a small mosque in a room upstairs and to the right. The room is easily identified by its mihrab, or prayer niche. Another flight of stairs nearby leads to a room which may once have been used as a Koranic school. Nearby, another doorway leads to a room directly above the main gate. Note the holes through which callers were scrutinised. The holes were also used for pouring hot oil onto the heads of unwelcome visitors. If you keep climbing up through the bastions you will pass a set of antique cannon and cannon balls bearing the crest of the Portuguese monarchy. These cannon and the Muscat forts are virtually the only physical remnants of Oman's century and a half of Portuguese rule. Keep going all the way to the top of the tower for a good view of the surrounding countryside.

Al-Hazm is 20 km north of Rustaq. Turn off at a sign for 'Al Hazm Fort' and follow the road for 1.5 km. It is impossible to miss.

## RUSTAQ

Some 175 km west of Muscat Rustaq (Rostaq) is best known today for its imposing **fort**, though for a time in the middle ages it was Oman's capital.

A permit from Muscat is necessary to enter the fort. To enter the fort you go up a ramp, pass through a second gate once inside the fort (note the niche above the light bulb at this second gate – it is from here that the hot oil would have poured down on any attacking army) and then go up a flight of stairs and through an archway. At this point the first door on your left leads to the fort's prison. Inside, a low and narrow hole in one wall leads to what was once the women's section of the prison. Having made your way back out of the prison area go straight and then look down to the left to see the spring which rises inside the fort. This natural supply of fresh water would have left the fort's defenders particularly well positioned to withstand a siege. A nearby staircase leads down to a washing basin.

Upstairs, over the second door on the left, at the top of the stairs, you'll see slits for archers to shoot from. Once upstairs (moving anti-clockwise around the court) the first room was for the guards while the second leads to a windowless 'final punishment' prison. The third room was another guard room, from where there's a good view of the surrounding date palms and mountains. The fourth room was a Koranic school, one room of which contained a small mosque. Just off this room is a well with a stone-cut basin for the ablutions Muslims must perform before prayer. At the back of the school complex another staircase leads up to the lower of two roofs. Turn right, then go straight to reach the library. The small room to the right of the library was reserved for the Imam. The closet-sized room next to this was the prayer room of the Imam's wife. A storeroom (which looks a lot like the library in its present state) at the rear of the roof level includes the entrance to an underground passage. Local legend has it that this used to connect Rustaq with the fort at Al-Hazm.

One of the fort's turrets is sometimes open to visitors. Try to get the guide to take you up it. The view is worth the climb.

There is a small souk near the entrance to the fort. It is good for shopping though in size and variety it is only a pale shadow of Nizwa or Muscat. The best time to visit is early morning, especially on Fridays.

Rustaq's only other site is a small, very new-looking, white mosque on the edge of town next to which is a natural spring. There are no hotels in Rustaq though the town has a few small restaurants.

### Getting There & Away

There is one bus a day to Muscat from Rustaq. The bus originates in the town but you can probably get the driver to let you off on the main road opposite the fort if you're coming from Muscat. To return to Muscat you might be able to flag down the bus, but it's probably better to walk into town and get on the bus there.

### A'THOWARAH

Near Al-Nakhal, a few km off the road connecting Birka with Rustaq, A'Thowarah is a beautiful, green, roadside stopping place with picnic tables. A spring emerges into a wadi here to form a stream and a small oasis. It is a perfect place for a stroll or a picnic. Put your hand into the stream close to the point where it rises from the rocks – the water is surprisingly warm even in winter.

### NIZWA

Only 45 years ago Wilfred Thesiger was forced to keep well clear of Nizwa. As the seat of the Imams who then ruled much of the country's interior it had a reputation for ferocious conservatism. Thesiger's Bedouin companions were convinced he would have little chance of emerging from the town alive. Today, visitors need have no such worries; Nizwa has rapidly emerged as one of Oman's major tourist centres. It is probably the country's most popular destination after Muscat.

Most tourists visit Nizwa on day trips from Muscat, 172 km away, and spend only an hour or two in the town. By public bus Nizwa is a fairly easy day trip from the capital. Those with time to spare, however, should pause for a day or so to get the real feel of the place. In addition to its aesthetic charms Nizwa is also the centre for Oman's jewellery and craft industries. Most of the khanjas you see on sale in Muscat's Mutrah souk are manufactured here. Prowl the back alleys of the souk and you may even find a group of Indians or Pakistanis hard at the work of dagger-making under the watchful eye of an Omani craftsman.

### Orientation & Information

Nizwa's main visual landmark is the large, blue-domed mosque which is on your left if you enter the town from the direction of Muscat. The old souk is the area immediately behind the mosque, though the lot just in front of it may also have some merchants

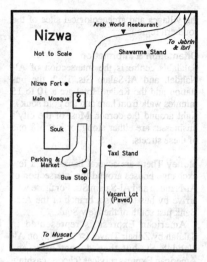

Nizwa
Not to Scale

- Arab World Restaurant
- To Jabrin & Ibri
- Shawarma Stand
- Nizwa Fort
- Main Mosque
- Souk
- Taxi Stand
- Parking & Market
- Bus Stop
- Vacant Lot (Paved)
- To Muscat

selling goods off the back of trucks. Past the mosque the main street swings around to the right into the town's modern business area. The taxi stand and bus stop are both by the parking lot in front of the mosque.

## Things to See

Visually, **Nizwa Fort** is hardly the most impressive set of battlements in Oman but it has an impressive history. The fort was built in the mid-17th century by Sultan Bin Saif, the first Imam of the Al-Ya'ribi dynasty. For the next 300 years it was the primary seat of the Imamate, serving as a combination palace, seat of government and prison.

The town's other great attraction is its **souk**. The atmosphere in the souk is great, though its popularity with package tours is beginning to show. Most people visiting with groups have only an hour or so to spend here, so the merchants are often not interested in serious bargaining – there will always be another group along later. The result is that Nizwa-made jewellery and khanjas actually cost more here than they do in Muscat.

## Places to Stay & Eat

The *Nizwa Motel* (☎ 410500) is on the

Muscat road, 4.5 km from the centre. It's on the left if you are coming from the capital. The food in the restaurant is OK.

For a quick snack in town there's the shawarma stand at the small shop on the right-hand side of the main street (coming from Muscat), under the Pepsi sign. For full meals try the *Arab World Restaurant & Cafeteria*, which is across the street and under a larger Pepsi sign.

## Getting There & Away

ONAT operates eight buses per day between Nizwa and Muscat (three hours, OR 1.600). Service taxis are also available to Muscat (OR 2), Ibri (OR 2) and Rusallah (OR 1.500)

## JABRIN

Jabrin (Jibreen) is another stop on the Old Forts Route through Oman's interior. It is just over 50 km from Nizwa on the Ibri road and is pretty easy to visit from Muscat in one day, even using pubic transport (provided you get an early start). If you are stretching the trip out overnight you should plan to stay in Nizwa as there is no hotel in Jabrin.

To reach the fort from Nizwa follow the Ibri road for 44.5 km then turn right at a sign for Jabrin. After another four km the pavement ends at a small roundabout. Turn right, go 300 metres, and you will reach the fort.

Despite its imposing battlements, the fort was originally built as a palace. Its construction was ordered in the mid to late 17th century by Imam Bal'arab Bin Sultan Al-Ya'ribi, who is also buried there. The design was only later modified to fortify the building.

You will need a permit from Muscat to enter the fort. Many of the rooms inside the fort are labelled, most of them in English. Jabrin is worth visiting if only for the restoration job. It is a much more dramatic place than Nizwa and its restored state gives one some sense of what it looked like in its prime. Various household items and furnishings are on display throughout the fort. Since everything is reasonably well marked the best way to see the fort's interior is simply to wander through it, preferably heading up whenever possible to end your tour with the view from the roof.

## BURAIMI

The long-disputed Buraimi oasis straddles the border between Oman and Abu Dhabi in the UAE. Both the Omani and the Emirati sides of the oasis are covered in this book's UAE chapter. This is because the Omani portion of the oasis is effectively in a customs union with Abu Dhabi.

Approaching the oasis from the Omani side requires a Road Permit (see the Oman Facts for the Visitor section), and involves passing through Omani customs and immigration. Once through this checkpoint you can pass freely between the Omani town of Buraimi and the city of Al-Ain, in the UAE. You can also continue up the road to anywhere else in the UAE. Approaching the oasis from the UAE side does not involve a customs check or require any documentation beyond that ordinarily required to enter the UAE.

# Southern Oman

## SALALAH

Oman's second city, the capital of the country's Southern Region and the birth-place of Sultan Qaboos, Salalah is a striking change from Muscat. It is so positioned as to catch the Indian summer monsoon (virtually the only corner of Arabia which does so) and, as a result, it is cool, wet and green from mid-June to mid-September just as the rest of Arabia is going through the worst of the summer heat.

Salalah is also the capital of the province of Dhofar, which has a population of about 300,000.

Though Salalah has a small museum the real attraction of the area is its temperate climate, the striking mountain scenery just after the monsoon and the beautiful beaches of white sand which stretch for miles along the coast. It is also a good base for exploring the villages and archaeological sites of the southern region.

### Orientation & Information

Salalah's centre is the intersection of Al-Nahdah and Al-Salam Sts. Both the bus station and the Redan Hotel are a 10 to 15 minutes walk from here and the gold souk is right around the corner. Most of the city's businesses are either along, or just off, one of these streets.

**Money** There are several banks and a few exchange houses around the intersection of Al-Nahdah and Al-Salam Sts. For those who arrive by bus there is a branch of the Arab Bank just south of the New Souk.

American Express is represented in Salalah by Zubair Travel (☎ 291145) on Al-Nahdah St, but they do not offer any American Express services (cheque cashing, client's mail, etc).

**Post & Telecommunications** The GPO is on Al-Nahdah St, next to the telephone company's administrative centre (the place with the big antenna), though you have to exit Al-Nahdah St and enter the building from the back. It is open Saturday to Wednesday from 7.30 am to 1.30 pm and Thursday from 9 to 11 am. Closed Friday.

The telephone office is at the intersection of Al-Nahdah St and Al-Muntazah St. It's open every day from 7.30 am to 12.30 am. Telex facilities are also available.

### Museum

Salalah's museum is in the Cultural Centre on A'Robat Rd (access is from the back side, via Al-Nahdah St). There is no English lettering on the building, but it is the huge white place, the second building west of the intersection of A'Robat Rd and Al-Nahdah St. When you enter the main door the museum is to your left. The doors on the right lead to a theatre. The museum is open Saturday to Wednesday from 8 am to 2 pm. Admission is free.

Going into the museum from the Cultural Centre's main lobby you will find yourself

PLACES TO EAT
8 Abu Salah Trad Est Restaurant
10 Chopsticks (Chinese Restaurant)
12 Antco Bakery

OTHER
1 Cultural Centre (Museum)
2 Dhofar Governor's Office
3 GPO
4 Al-Zahra Al-Omania Centre (Gulf Air/
   Oman Aviation/Haffa House Hotel)
5 ONAT Bus Station
6 Redan Hotel
7 Oman Cinema
9 Al-Ghafri & Sons Bus Stop
11 Zubair Travel (AMEX/Avis Rent-a-Car)
13 Oman United Exchange Company
14 Telephone Office

INDIAN OCEAN

Salalah

0      0.5      1 km

in one large room containing stones with inscriptions in the ancient script known as South Arabian. There are also displays of pottery, weapons, seashells, traditional costumes and tools and a large exhibit of jewellery. Most of the exhibits are labelled in Arabic only.

### New Souk

There is nothing special about this souk. Meat, fish, fruit, vegetables and, occasionally, livestock are on sale. It is also the home of the bus station and a few modern shops, most of which sell textiles.

### Al-Balid

The old city of Al-Balid, site of the ancient city of Zafar, lies about two km east of the centre on the coast, just west of the Holiday Inn. There is a fence around the site and, in theory, you need a permit to enter, but there are so many holes in the fence and places where it has simply been torn down that this is hardly a problem. I was taken there permitless by a government guide.

There is not much to see. The site is heavily overgrown and is likely to impress only serious students of archaeology. Near the mound which dominates the site are the remains of a large building said to have been a mosque.

## Places to Stay

There are three hotels in Salalah and none of them are cheap.

The cheapest of the three is the *Redan Hotel* (☎ 292266) on Al-Salam St in the centre. Singles/doubles are OR 15.700/20. The location is good and the rooms are large and clean. The *Haffa House* (☎ 295444) in the Al-Zahra Al-Omania Centre at the Clock Tower Roundabout just outside the centre charges OR 25.300/28.750. This is a large but rather dull place. On the coast, just beyond Al-Balid, the *Salalah Holiday Inn* (☎ 235333) charges OR 34.5000/43.125. For that price it offers the compensations of a pool, private beach and health club.

## Places to Eat

At the bottom of the price scale you would be hard-pressed to do better than the *Antco Bakery* on Al-Nahdah St. They offer reasonably cheap Chinese food with a few Indian dishes on the menu as well. It is pretty easy to fill up here for OR 1. The *Al-Manzar Restaurant* on Al-Salam St has a broad selection of Indian and Chinese dishes. Meals go for OR 2.500 to OR 3, but it is nothing to write home about. For a quick snack, *Abu Salah Trad Est*, near the main intersection, is a small Indian place offering sandwiches, coffee and tea. Cheap but more substantial Indian meals are available at the *Gareez Restaurant* on Al-Salam St next to the Redan Hotel.

*Chopsticks*, a Chinese restaurant, is a bit more up-market but for anything much fancier you'll probably have to head for the Holiday Inn. The Holiday Inn has a couple of restaurants all of which serve the basic hotel menu of European dishes (steaks, sandwiches, pasta, omelettes, etc) and Oriental, usually Lebanese, food.

## Entertainment

What social life there is in Salalah centres on the Holiday Inn. For the latest information get a copy of *Oman Today* or just stop by the hotel when you are in town. Outsiders can join the hotel's health club on a monthly basis. You are not supposed to use the hotel pool unless you are staying there though this appears to be flexible when business is slow. If, for example, you buy lunch or a couple of drinks at the poolside bar they may have no objection to your taking a dip though you should check beforehand. The Holiday Inn has a nightclub with live entertainment, usually a Filipino singer and a belly dancer, and a disco on weekends.

## Getting There & Away

**Air** Salalah's small airport is served by Oman Aviation and their flights to Muscat (the only destination) are operated jointly with Gulf Air. Both airlines have offices in the Al-Zahra Al-Omania Centre by the Clock Tower Roundabout. Gulf Air (☎ 293131) is on the ground floor and Oman Aviation (☎ 295747) is on the 1st floor.

**Bus** Buses leave the ONAT office in the New Souk for Muscat every day at 7 am, 6 and 7 pm (12 to 13 hours, OR 10 one-way, OR 18 return). During Ramadan the 7 pm bus departs an hour later and during the mid-June to mid-September monsoon season the afternoon buses leave at 5 and 6 pm.

Al-Ghafri & Sons also run a bus to the Ruwi station in Muscat every day at 5 pm. Departures are from their office on Al-Salam St. At OR 8 one-way and OR 15 return, the fare is a bit cheaper than ONAT, and you'll arrive in Muscat at 5 am.

## Getting Around

There is no local bus system in Salalah. Surprisingly, there is also no service-taxi stand in Salalah for either local or city travel. Neither do private taxis spend a lot of time cruising around looking for fares. If you need a taxi the best place to look is at the New Souk or near the main intersection where the drivers tend to hang around waiting to be hired. There is also a taxi rank at the Holiday Inn. Anywhere in the city (including to and from the Holiday Inn) the fare should be from 500 baisa to OR 1.

There is a car-rental desk at the Holiday Inn and an Avis office at Al-Zubair Travel (☎ 291145) on Al-Nahdah St. The rates are the same as in Muscat.

## AROUND SALALAH

There are very good beaches all along the road to Mughsail once you're about five km out of Salalah. The road runs along the beach which is open to the public, including women (though women should not wear bikinis). The water is generally calm but the wind can sometimes kick up a lot of sand.

Your only option to visit the area around Salalah is to rent a car. There is no bus service among the towns on the southern coast and overnight camping on the beach is not allowed. You should not have too much trouble hitching rides, though they are often for only a few km at a time. It's too hot and humid to cycle most of the time, and there is nowhere to hire a bike unless you bring one along.

### Khor Rouri

Centuries ago Khor Rouri was an important port holding down the southern end of the frankincense route. It was then known as Sumhuram. From the small bay, boats and rafts took the frankincense to Qana, 640 km down the coast in what is today Yemen, on the first stage of its journey to the bazaars of Damascus and the temples of Rome. Today, little remains of the city except the ruins of a palace-cum-fort sitting atop a mound of rather nondescript looking rubble, though the view out over the ocean is nice.

A permit is needed to visit the site, but there are enough holes in the fence that you should not have any trouble getting in if the attendant is nowhere to be found. The site is in slightly better condition than Al-Balid and individual rooms among the ruins are easier to make out, though it would take an archaeologist to find out what any given room was used for. The steel cage near the left-centre of the fort (as you face the sea) marks the site of an old well. Nearby (down and to the right, still facing the sea) you can see inscriptions on some of the stones.

To reach the site take the road from Salalah toward Mirbaat (Mirbat) and turn at the Khor Rouri sign. The site is 3.5 km off the main Mirbaat road along a dirt track. Keep right at the fork and you will see the

---

### Ubar

In early 1992 a group of US explorers announced that they had found the remains of Ubar, one of the great lost cities of Arabia. According to legend Ubar was a sort of an Arabian cross between Atlantis and Sodom and Gomorrah. Scholars are fairly certain that the place *did* exist, that it came to control the frankincense trade and that, as a result, it grew incredibly wealthy. That is about all that is known for sure. The Koran says that God destroyed Ubar, causing it to sink beneath the sands, because the people were decadent and turned away from religion.

Predictably some scholars have disputed the expedition's claim to have found Ubar, and at the time of writing the site, inland from Salalah and off the main road running from Salalah to Thumrait, was still not open to the public. But this will probably change soon. It would be worth asking about trips to Ubar both at the tour agencies based in Muscat and at the Salalah Holiday Inn. ■

Tree from which frankincense is extracted

mound and the fence on your right just before you reach the ocean.

The nearby village of **Taqa** is also worth a stop. It is one of the few places where the sewn boats which were common to the region in the early years of Islam are still made and used.

### Jabal Samhan

Jabal Samhan is a high plateau 41 km by road east of Salalah. It's worth the diversion (on a clear day) for the striking views over the surrounding countryside especially during the green months of the late summer. To reach it, turn at the sign saying 'Tawi Attair 18 km' and follow the road to the end, up a steep incline.

### Ayn Razat

Ayn Razat is a spring rising in a landscaped garden approximately 25 km east of Salalah. It makes a pleasant stop for half an hour or so if you are making a tour of the sites east of Salalah. To reach Ayn Razat head east out of Salalah and follow the signs. From the roundabout where Ayn Razat is signposted it is another 10.5 km.

### Mughsail

About 30 km west of Salalah along the coastal road this is the best place in the area to go for long, unspoiled beaches.

### Thumrait

There is not much to the town of Thumrait, 80 km inland from Salalah on the road to Muscat, but the contrasts in scenery make it worth the drive if you have the time and a car. The first half of the drive is spent climbing to and through the mountain plateau overlooking Salalah. The second half of the route takes you along the plateau itself and finally into the desert area behind it. The plateau is strikingly green in the late summer and early autumn right after the monsoon season but rapidly reverts to desert once the rains are over.

# Musandem Peninsula

Separated from Oman by the east coast of the UAE, the Musandem peninsula is a closed military zone. Although the Oman Aviation timetable lists flights to Khasab, the only town in the area, I have never met anyone who has been there. I have twice requested permission to go there but was turned down. However, things may have changed and you can try enquiring at the Ministry of Culture office which issues site permits or ask tour operators.

The other Omani territory, an enclave near the UAE's Fujairah, is a tiny area – a few sq km of semi-desert grazing land – and if it were not for a sign on the road saying it's part of Oman you would not know the difference. There are no customs controls, just a sign saying you've crossed the border. However, your UAE car insurance is not valid once you cross into the enclave.

Top: Dhow building yard, Sur, Oman
Bottom: Omani women, Nizwa, Oman

Oasis at A'Thowara, Oman

# Qatar

In Albert Hourani's book *A History of the Arab Peoples*, Qatar ranks a grand total of two references (Bahrain has seven, Kuwait 17). Arthur Goldschmidt's *A Concise History of the Middle East* mentions the country only once – its listing in a population table. The index to John Bagot Glubb's *A Short History of the Arab Peoples* does not list Qatar at all and, to add insult to injury, Glubb did not even bother to mark the place on the book's maps.

Qatar has always had a way of falling off the outside world's radar screens. Most foreign maps of Arabia drawn prior to the 19th century do not show the Qatar peninsula. The British writer Peter Mansfield once remarked that even quiz show champions were likely to have trouble finding the place. I would only add that if few Westerners can locate Qatar even fewer can pronounce it correctly. The stress is on the first syllable. The first vowel is short, the second one silent: 'QaT-r'.

Though the country opened its doors to tourists in 1989 its remoteness and the continuing ban on alcohol have all served to keep it off the agendas of even the more intrepid travellers. It's really not all that bad. Give Qatar a chance... you may be surprised.

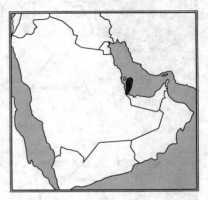

landscape was little more inviting then than it is now.

Qatar is the only significant place in the Gulf to have no Portuguese ruins of any sort. Since the Portuguese conquered, or at least attacked, just about everywhere else in the Gulf this strongly implies that 16th century Qatar was either uninhabited or very nearly so. Qatar is not mentioned in any substantial way by the various European travellers who reached the Gulf between the 16th and early 18th centuries.

For most of its recorded (ie, recent) history Qatar has been dominated by the Al-Thani family who arrived in the mid-18th century and became the peninsula's rulers about 100 years later. The Al-Thani family is a branch of the Tamim tribe and are thought to have arrived in Qatar from southern Najd in central Arabia. Originally they were nomadic Bedouins, but the area's sparse vegetation led them to settle in the peninsula's coastal areas where they became fishers and pearl divers.

By the mid-18th century Qatar was already well established as a pearling centre. Activity was then centred on Zubara, in the north-west, which was under the control of

## Facts about the Country

### HISTORY
#### Beginnings

Archaeological digs have shown that the Qatar peninsula was inhabited during the Stone Age when the region's climate was milder than it is today. But the archaeologists have found little evidence of habitation between the most ancient of times and the modern era. Qatar does have its share of ancient grave mounds but there are no known sites connecting it to the Bahrain-based Dilmun empire. Apparently the

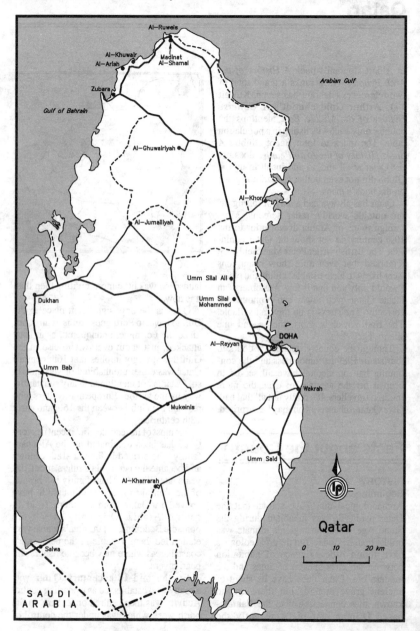

Qatar

0    10    20 km

the Al-Khalifa family (who are now the rulers of Bahrain). Since that time, and even into the present day, tension between the Al-Khalifa and the Al-Thani has been a constant feature of Qatar's history. The Al-Thani fought several long battles with the Al-Khalifa for control of the peninsula, and did not get full control of Zubara until 1937. In the 1950s, the first archaeologists to survey Qatar hesitated when it came time to visit Zubara for fear that the Emir would accuse them of being Bahraini spies! Today Zubara is firmly under Qatari control and the principal territorial dispute between the two countries concerns the Hawar Islands, which lie just off Qatar's western coast.

Doha was never a trading port of the importance of Kuwait or Manama. Throughout the 19th and early 20th centuries Qatar remained shockingly poor, even by pre-oil Gulf standards. Seemingly bleak and remote places like Zubara were so hotly contested precisely because they controlled access to the one thing which provided enough money to feed the local populace: the pearl beds.

## The Rise of the Al-Thani

Qatar's first Al-Thani Emir was Shaikh Mohammed Bin Thani who took effective control of most of the peninsula from the Al-Khalifa and established his capital at Al-Bida, today's Doha, in the mid-19th century. To strengthen his position vis-à-vis the other tribes in the area, he signed a treaty with Britain in 1867. At the time he was almost certainly seeking British protection from the Al-Khalifa.

Shaikh Mohammed died later that year and was succeeded by his son, Jasim (sometimes also spelled Qasim). From the 1870s onward Jasim, who reigned until his death in 1913, became a master at maintaining his own independence by playing the British off against the Turks.

In 1872 he signed a treaty with the Turks allowing them to place a garrison in Doha, though he never allowed it to grow very large and, reportedly, refused to take any money from Constantinople. The presence of Turkish troops did, however, provide Jasim

with a certain amount of cachet locally. As the nominal representative of the Ottoman sultan, Jasim was a powerful figure in eastern Arabia during the late 19th and early 20th centuries, exercising significant influence, though not quite sovereignty, over the region's tribes.

But being the Turk's man also had its drawbacks. The Ottomans maintained only a small presence in the region while the British, who were the dominant power in the Gulf, were on the ground in force. Though in practical terms Qatar was independent, this state of affairs also meant that it was, in a sense, surrounded by hostile forces. Over the years the small Turkish garrison in Doha began to seem more destabilising than reassuring. In 1893, Jasim fought a small battle against the Turks but when he died, on the eve of WW I, the Turks were still in Doha.

Jasim's successor, Sheikh Abdullah, oversaw the withdrawal of the Ottoman garrison in 1915 after Turkey entered WW I on the side of Germany. The British almost certainly had a hand in this withdrawal, and, in 1916, they signed an Exclusive Agreement with Abdullah modelled on the agreements they already had in place around the Gulf. According to the agreements, Britain undertook to protect the local ruler in exchange for a promise that the ruler would not have any dealings with other foreign powers without British permission. The 1916 agreement was extended and modified by another treaty signed in 1934.

Abdullah's expulsion of the Turks was a combination of necessity and prudence. With Britain and Turkey on opposite sides in the war, and the British controlling the rest of the Gulf, switching alliances seemed like a wise move. On a local level, Abdullah also had to worry about Abdul Aziz Abdul Rahman Al-Saud, the founder and future king of Saudi Arabia, who was then in the process of conquering most of eastern Arabia. The Turks were in no position to help Qatar in the event of a Saudi attack, even assuming they wanted to do so. Qatar's 1916 agreement with Britain only obliged the Royal Navy to defend the Emirate from an attack by sea, but the commitment to Abdullah and his line which the treaty embodied almost certainly caused Abdul Aziz to decide against invading Qatar.

## Oil

Even before the collapse, around 1930, of the pearl market, life in Qatar was rough. With poverty, hunger, malnutrition and disease all widespread, the Emir welcomed the oil prospectors who first arrived in the early 1930s. In 1935, he granted a concession to Petroleum Development (Qatar), or PDQ, the forerunner of today's state-run Qatar Petroleum Corporation (QPC). PDQ was a subsidiary of the Iraq Petroleum Company which, in turn, was owned by a collection of US, British and French oil interests.

The prospectors struck oil in 1939 but because of WW II, production did not begin for another 10 years. It was only then, in 1949, that the British finally posted a political agent to Doha. Until that time the country had been covered by the political agent based in Bahrain.

At that point things began to move very quickly. The new British agent was followed, a few years later, by a financial advisor sent to help the Emir deal with the unprecedented sums of money he suddenly found himself holding. Even then, the Qataris were shrewd enough to maintain some balance. As he and his father had done in politics prior to WW I, Abdullah carefully balanced the sources of the advice he received. An Egyptian named Hassan Kamil was hired to offer the Emir additional financial advice, and he stayed on as advisor to subsequent emirs for several decades.

Abdullah abdicated on account of his advancing age in 1949. He was succeeded by his son, Ali (reigned 1949-60) who presided over the first stages of Qatar's oil boom. The quantity of oil produced in Qatar was not in itself huge but the country's tiny population made it instantly wealthy on a per capita basis. Much of the early revenue was devoted to establishing the basics of modern life: Qatar's first school opened in 1952 and health-care facilities were immediately upgraded, though a full-scale hospital did not open until 1959.

At this time a key figure in government was the man who is now Emir, Khalifa Bin Hamad Al-Thani. Shaikh Ali had little interest in the day-to-day business of government with the result that by the mid-50s, Khalifa (Ali's nephew) was, to a great extent, running the country. At the beginning of the '60s Ali abdicated in favour of his son, Ahmed, but the new Emir was as uninterested in the government as his predecessor had been. By all reports, Ahmed spent most of his reign pursuing *la dolce vita* abroad and when he was at home seemed more interested in falconing than affairs of state. With Ahmed's ascension, Khalifa became Deputy Ruler and Prime Minister.

Between local politics and the development of the country Khalifa, was very active. As quiet as Qatar usually is, it was not entirely spared from the turmoil which swept the Arab world during the '60s, including a general strike in 1963. With time, however, the ever-increasing flow of oil money seemed to blunt many people's political ambitions. Attempts by some Qataris to form leftist political groups in the '70s never gained significant support, and the country has been stable ever since.

## Independence

When the British announced that they would leave the region by the end of 1971, Qatar entered talks with Bahrain and the Trucial States (now the UAE) on forming a confederation. When Bahrain pulled out of the talks because it did not think that the governmental formulas gave it sufficient weight, Qatar followed Bahrain almost immediately.

It was somehow indicative of his style of government that Shaikh Ahmed proclaimed Qatar's independence, on 1 September 1971, in Geneva rather than Doha. At that point his demise probably became inevitable. Khalifa took power in a palace coup on 22 February 1972. It seems that the real impetus for Ahmed's ouster lay with a broad circle of male members of the ruling family and in the end, Ahmed's mistake was to lose their confidence. After his overthrow, Ahmed went into exile in Dubai.

Khalifa was well prepared to take over. By the time of the coup he had been Qatar's de facto ruler for more than 15 years and had already at one time or another run the departments of foreign affairs, oil & finance, and education & culture. He had also headed both the police force and the secret police. One of his first moves as Emir was to crack down on the extravagant ways of certain members of the royal family.

The years since Khalifa's palace coup have been marked by political stability. As was the case throughout the Gulf, the dramatic rise in oil prices after 1974 gave the government more than enough money to build one of the world's great all-encompassing welfare states.

Still, Qatar has been affected by the political turbulences of its neighbours. Like the other small states of the Gulf, Qatar viewed Iran's 1979 revolution with great alarm. In 1983 the government announced that it had discovered a cache of hidden weapons and foiled a plot to overthrow it. The Hawar Islands dispute with Bahrain has been another consistent, if low-level, cause of tension.

Since independence, Qatar has retained its close defence ties with Britain and has increased defence cooperation with both the USA and France. US and Canadian troops were stationed in Doha during the Gulf War.

Qatar's foreign policy has tended to closely follow the lead of Saudi Arabia, though in recent years Doha has ruffled some feathers (including those of Riyadh) by seeking closer ties with Iran. In 1991, the Qataris and Iranians signed an agreement under which Iran will supply Qatar with fresh water via an undersea pipeline, a project which has been met by reservations by some of Doha's Gulf Cooperation Council (GCC) neighbours.

## GEOGRAPHY

The Qatar peninsula, which is shaped a bit like a thumb, juts northward into the Gulf from the east coast of the Arabian peninsula.

It is about 160 km long and 55 to 80 km wide. The country's total area (including a number of small islands) is 11,437 sq km. The desert tends to be flat (the highest elevation in the country is only about 40 metres above sea level) and gravelly. There is virtually no natural vegetation.

## CLIMATE

Summers (May to September) in Qatar are ferociously hot, with temperatures often hitting 45°C and sometimes approaching 50°C. The summer weather also tends to be terribly humid. The winter months are much milder with pleasant, cool evenings. Sandstorms are common throughout the year, especially in the spring.

## FLORA & FAUNA

Qatari fauna is limited to birds such as the hubura and bat and animals that are pretty hard to spot, such as the sand cats. The Emir is said to have a private herd of Arabian oryx though neither these nor much of anything else are to be seen roaming freely. You will, of course, see camels but not a lot of them. Qatar's lack of natural vegetation has meant that it never acquired a large population of Bedouins and, thus, no large herds of camels, at least by Arabian standards.

## GOVERNMENT

Qatar is ruled by an emir: Shaikh Khalifa Bin Hamad Al-Thani. Shaikh Khalifa's son, Hamad, is Crown Prince and Minister of Defence. The Emir can appoint and dismiss Cabinet ministers at will, though turnover in the Cabinet doesn't often occur. Laws are announced in Emiri decrees. Though he is, in theory, an absolute monarch the Emir must always retain the support and confidence of the other members of the ruling family. Retaining this support requires not only good government but ongoing and wide-ranging consultation with the Cabinet, other members of the ruling family and representatives of the country's larger merchant families.

Much of this consultation is informal though some of it takes place at the regular *majlis* (court) which the Emir and other members of the ruling family hold. Any member of the public (usually the men) can address the Emir or some other senior figure during these sessions about any issue. Regular, formalised consultation also takes place through an Advisory Council whose 30 members are appointed by the Emir. The Council can comment on proposed laws though it can neither change the proposals nor propose new laws on its own.

Qatar has one of the most all-embracing welfare state systems in the world. Qataris are entitled to free education and health care and free or nearly free housing. The prices of food, electricity and water are heavily subsidised.

## ECONOMY

Qatar has an oil-based economy, though in the future, natural gas is likely to be at least as important as oil. The country's oil may well run out in another decade or so but the North Field is one of the largest natural gas fields in the world and can probably produce for a century or more. The government has tried to diversify the economy but, as elsewhere in the Gulf, this has met with only limited success. Steel, fertilisers and petrochemicals are the country's main non-oil products. Most of Qatar's industry is based at Umm Said, south of Doha. Qatar is a member of OPEC.

## POPULATION & PEOPLE

About 400,000 people live in Qatar, of whom about 25% are Qataris. This makes it the smallest country in the Arab world by population. It is also the only Gulf country where there are more foreigners than citizens. Most Qataris are of Najdi (central Arabian) ancestry, though there are also a number of families of Persian descent.

The foreign population represents a mix of people from Asia, the Indian subcontinent and the Arab world (Egyptians, Palestinians, Syrians, Jordanians, Lebanese). Britons make up the largest contingent among the country's Western expatriate population.

## EDUCATION

The country's first school opened only in 1952 but progress since then has been fast. The University of Qatar opened in 1977 but before 1977 hundreds of Qataris were sent to Egypt, Lebanon and the West to further their educations. All education, including university, is free for Qataris. Foreign children living in Qatar usually attend international schools which teach a particular national curriculum.

## ARTS & CULTURE

### National Theatre

Qatar's National Theatre (☎ 831333) is on the Corniche in the Ministry of Information building. The 500-seat auditorium is used for the performance of Arabic plays and also serves as the venue for visiting foreign companies. Depending on the event, tickets are QR 25 to QR 50 and can be obtained from the box office. To find out what's on enquire at a big hotel or stop by the theatre.

### Art Gallery

The Al-Sadd Art Gallery (☎ 427333) features shows by both Qatari and foreign artists. It is open Saturday to Thursday from 8 am to noon and from 4 to 6 pm.

### Traditional Dancing

On Friday afternoons during the summer (May to September) various troops performing traditional dances can be seen around Doha and Al-Khor. Montazah Park, just beyond the C Ring Rd in Doha, is a good place to go on an early summer evening to see traditional dancing. Shows usually start around 5 pm.

### Taboos & Avoiding Offence

Qatar is more liberal than Saudi Arabia but a far cry from Bahrain or Dubai. Qataris are quite accustomed to the presence of large numbers of foreigners with different habits in their midst, and virtually everyone in the country has travelled abroad at one time or another. Still, Qatar is a very conservative place by Western standards and the usual

Traditional Dancing

social taboos that exist in the Gulf certainly apply here as much as anywhere else.

Dress conservatively and do not wear shorts in public except at the beach or at a hotel's swimming pool. Women should always cover their shoulders and avoid clothing that is overly tight or revealing.

If you are offered coffee or tea in someone's home or at a business meeting – it would be unusual if you weren't – it is considered very impolite to refuse.

### RELIGION

Most Qataris adhere to the austere Wahhabi sect of Islam which also dominates in Saudi Arabia. Qatari Wahhabism, however, is less strict than the Saudi variety. For example, alcohol, which is strictly prohibited in Saudi Arabia, is available to non-Muslims in Qatar, though it is not sold publicly in hotels the way it is in Bahrain or the UAE.

### LANGUAGE

It may cross your mind in Doha that Urdu, the Pakistani language, would be more useful here than Arabic. In fact many of the thousands of Pakistanis in Qatar have been living here for a very long time and they tend to speak good Arabic. In Doha, as is the case in every other capital city in the Gulf, you

should have no trouble getting around in English.

See the Facts about the Region chapter for a glossary of Arabic words and phrases.

## Facts for the Visitor

### VISAS & EMBASSIES

Nationals of GCC countries and British passport holders with right of abode in the UK do not need a visa to enter Qatar. The following information applies to everyone else.

Tourist visas are available to people of any nationality (except Israelis) and regardless of their occupation (ie, no problems for writers, journalists, etc). You will be denied entry if your passport contains an Israeli stamp.

While visas are now fairly easy to obtain, they are issued in a manner which guarantees that a stay in Qatar is not likely to be cheap.

### Hotel-Sponsored Visas

To obtain a Qatari visa, you need a sponsor who is responsible for your actions while you are in the country. The only way to obtain a tourist visa is to organise a hotel to sponsor you. This is a fairly straightforward process but you will be required to stay in the hotel sponsoring you for as long as you are in the country. It is possible to transfer your sponsorship from one hotel to another but you'll still be staying in the top-level hotels. Trying to get a cheap hotel to assume responsibility for you once you are already in Doha is probably a losing venture. Trying to get a cheapie to sponsor you in the first place is a complete waste of time.

Having decided to spend some money, here's what you do. Contact the reservations department of one of the big hotels (telex and fax numbers for hotels which will sponsor tourist visas are listed in the Doha section) with your passport details, reason for visit (business, tourism, etc) your arrival and departure dates and flight information. The last item is important as you will be picking your visa up at the airport. It usually takes between four days and a week to process visa requests.

The hotel should send back a telex or fax acknowledging your reservation and quoting your visa number. If the acknowledgement you receive does not include the visa number you should contact the hotel again and ask for it. If you don't have a proper visa number (ie, one matching the list that the airline has received from Qatari immigration), you may not be allowed to board the plane. Gulf Air is particularly strict on this score. This system makes it impossible to enter the country overland or by sea.

At Doha airport, head for the window where visa forms are distributed. Once you have your form just get in line for passport control, the immigration officer does the rest.

Tourist visas are valid for 14 days and cost QR 105. Seven-day business visas cost QR 120. The hotel or company sponsoring you may have paid this fee in advance. If you are sponsored by a hotel the visa fee will probably be added to your bill along with a service charge. If the visa fee has not been prepaid then you will have to pay it yourself at the airport. There is a bank next to the visa desk.

A final note: you might want to change money at the bank near the visa pick-up window (before passport control). The bank in the arrivals area beyond customs never seems to be open.

### Transit Visas

It is possible to obtain a 72-hour transit visa on arrival at Doha airport if you are holding an onward ticket. You are likely to find, however, that the airlines are extremely reluctant to board passengers whose tickets show an overnight transit in Qatar but who do not have a tourist visa.

### Qatari Embassies

In regards to visa matters, Qatari embassies are of little use to the traveller. For tourists and business travellers all visa formalities are handled in Doha, including picking up the visa itself, as outlined in the previous section.

Addresses of some Qatari embassies abroad include:

Iran
     Bozorgrah-é Afrigha, 4 Kheyabun-é Gol Azin (☎ 221555)
UK
     30 Collingham Gardens SW5 (☎ (071) 3706871)
USA
     600 New Hampshire Ave NW, Washington 20037 (☎ 3380111)

### Visa Extensions

Tourist visas can easily be extended for an additional 14 days and business visas for seven days. Renewing a tourist visa costs QR 200. Visa renewal is handled by the hotel or company acting as your sponsor.

### Exit/Re-Entry Visas

These are necessary for resident foreigners who want to leave the country and return later and must be obtained by the sponsor. Tourists or business people need a new visa each time they enter the country.

### Foreign Embassies in Qatar

See the Doha section for the addresses of embassies in Qatar.

### CUSTOMS

Arriving at Doha airport you are apt to find visa pick-up and customs fairly fast and efficient and passport control quite slow. This is mainly because the passport control officers are left with the job of filling out the several forms required to process each visa.

You are not allowed to import alcohol into Qatar, and, in my experience, booze is the main thing that the customs officers are on the lookout for. Books and photographs in your possession may also come in for careful scrutiny, though I have never had any problems in this respect. Pork products are also prohibited. There is no limit on the number of cigarettes and cigars or the amount of loose tobacco you can bring in.

### MONEY
### Currency

The Qatari riyal (QR) is divided into 100

dirhams, which are also commonly referred to as *halalas*. Notes come in QR 1, 5, 10, 50, 100 and 500 denominations. Coins are 25 and 50 dirhams. The Qatari riyal is fully convertible so there is no black market and there are no exchange controls. Many shops will also accept Saudi riyals.

## Exchange Rates

| | | |
|---|---|---|
| US$1 | = | QR 3.64 |
| UK£1 | = | QR 5.50 |
| FF1 | = | QR 0.67 |
| DM1 | = | QR 2.27 |
| A$1 | = | QR 2.50 |

### Costs

On an absolutely rock-bottom budget, that is staying in the youth hostel, eating in the cheapest restaurants and walking almost everywhere, you might be able to live in Doha on QR 35 a day. You will not be able to do this, however, as the cheapest hotel that sponsors visas (the Oasis) charges about QR 300 per night, though you could probably get a discount on that rate. So even if you still walked a lot and ate cheaply it would be hard not to spend QR 300 or more per day.

### Tipping

A service charge is usually added to restaurant bills in Qatar but this rarely goes to the waiting staff. Local custom does not require that you leave a tip after a meal though it would certainly be appreciated.

### Bargaining

The sort of traditional shops where serious bargaining usually takes place in the Gulf are becoming fewer and further between in Qatar. Small discounts are sometimes offered to customers in modern clothing stores and you can almost always negotiate a bit off the price of electronic goods, rental cars and hotel room, but the price of everything else is usually fixed.

### Consumer Taxes

Aside from a 5% hotel tax (which the cheapest places appear to ignore) there are no consumer taxes in Qatar.

## WHEN TO GO

Because the heat is so fierce in the summer and sandstorms are so common in the spring and winter, the best time to visit Doha is in November or late February and early March. This is the period during which you are most likely to get bearable temperatures with a minimum of wind.

## WHAT TO BRING

A hat and sunglasses are absolutely essential during the summer and a light windbreaker is a good idea in the winter. Visitors during the winter months should also bring a light sweater for the evenings.

## BUSINESS HOURS & HOLIDAYS

Shops and offices are open from around 8 am until noon and may reopen in the late afternoon from 4 or 5 until 7 pm. Some of the modern Western-style shopping malls stay open until 9 or 10 pm. Friday is the weekly holiday and many businesses also close early on Thursday. Embassies and government offices are closed all day Thursday.

The Islamic holidays of Eid Al-Fitr (the end of Ramadan), Eid Al-Adha (Pilgrimage) and the Islamic New Year are all observed (see the table of holidays page 28).

Qatar's National Day is on 3 September. Embassies and government offices are closed but most private businesses stay open.

## POST & TELECOMMUNICATIONS
### Postal Rates

It costs QR 1 to send a postcard to Europe and QR 1.50 to North America, Asia or Australia. To Arab countries, the rate is 50 dirhams and to other Gulf states, 25 dirhams. Local postcard postage is 15 dirhams.

Postage for letters (per 10 grams) is: Europe, QR 1.50; USA & Australasia, QR 2; Arab countries, 75 dirhams; Gulf countries, 50 dirhams; and locally 25 dirhams.

Parcel rates vary from country to country. Parcel postage is by the kg, and after the first kg the rate generally goes down a bit. Sample

rates for sending a one kg parcel by air/sea are: Australia QR 63/40, New Zealand QR 67/41, USA QR 53/41, Canada QR 54/40, UK QR 47/38, France QR 57/50, Germany QR 46/50.

### Sending Mail
Most hotels sell stamps and there are several post offices around Doha, including one in The Centre, the capital's main shopping mall.

### Receiving Mail
Poste Restante is available through any post office in Qatar. You need to fill out an application form and produce proof of identity.

### Telephone
The telephone system in Qatar is excellent and direct-dialling overseas calls rarely takes more than one attempt. Phonecards worth QR 50 and QR 100 can be purchased at the Main Telecommunications Centre in Doha though as yet there are few card phones outside the Telecommunications Centre itself.

When calling Qatar from abroad the country code is 974. There are no area or city codes.

### Fax, Telex & Telegraph
These services are available through the Main Telecommunications Centre in Doha or through the business centre of any big hotel. As with the telephones the service is very good.

### TIME
Qatar is three hours ahead of GMT. The clocks do not change during the summer. When it's noon in Doha, the time elsewhere is:

| City | Time |
| --- | --- |
| Paris, Rome | 10 am |
| London | 9 am |
| New York | 4 am |
| Los Angeles | 1 am |
| Perth, Hong Kong | 5 pm |
| Sydney | 7 pm |
| Auckland | 9 pm |

### ELECTRICITY
The electric voltage is 230 volts AC. Qatar uses British-style sockets.

### LAUNDRY
The closest thing to a laundromat in Qatar is the kiosk at The Centre shopping mall, through which the Ramada Hotel accepts outside laundry. This service is not cheap. Most of the small hotels in the souk also offer laundry service for guests.

### WEIGHTS & MEASURES
Qatar uses the metric system.

### BOOKS & MAPS
The literature on Qatar is a bit thin. One of the few books on the market which focuses entirely on Qatar is Helga Graham's *Arabian Time Machine* (Heinemann, London, 1978). Subtitled 'Self-Portrait of an Oil State' the book is a collection of interviews with Qataris about their life and traditions both before and after the oil boom and about how Qatari society has coped with its sudden wealth.

Peter Mansfield's *The New Arabians* (Ferguson, Chicago, 1981) has a fairly short chapter on Qatari history. A better bet might be *The Merchants* by Michael Field (Overlook Press, Woodstock NY, 1985) which has lots of good general information on the Gulf in pre-oil days. It also has a chapter devoted to the Darwish family, one of Qatar's more prominent merchant clans.

'The Day Before Tomorrow', the Qatar chapter in Jonathan Raban's *Arabia Through the Looking Glass* (Picador, London, 1981), is probably the best section of this wonderful book. During a short visit in 1979, Raban managed to speak to a particularly interesting cross-section of people: Qatar's leading playwright, a local TV producer and a Jordanian officer working for the Qatari army in addition to the usual collection of somewhat jaded Western expats.

See the introductory Facts for the Visitor chapter for a more general list of books on the Gulf and the Middle East.

### Travel Guides
*Qatar – A MEED Practical Guide* is badly in need of updating but is still a useful book for anyone planning to live in Qatar. *The Economist Business Traveller's Guides – Arabian Peninsula* is a useful how-to-do-business-with-the-Arabs sort of book.

### Bookshops
Doha has hardly any foreign-language bookshops and, unusually, even the newsstands of five-star hotels do not provide their usual, if expensive, selection of foreign-language novels. Try the bookshop in The Centre on Salwa Rd.

### Maps
Most of the available maps of Doha leave much to be desired. The Oxford map is hopelessly out of date and on too small a scale while the *Business & Tourist Map of Doha City* (QR 20, most bookshops) has too many drawings of buildings and too few streets, especially around the city centre. The *Tourist Map of Doha*, published by Gulf Air and available free at most big hotels, is an improvement on either of the above. The best map available is the one compiled by Doha's municipal government, but you have to go down to the municipality to get one.

## MEDIA
### Newspapers & Magazines
The *Gulf Daily News* is the local English-language newspaper. The best place to find foreign newspapers and magazines (which usually arrive a day or two after publication) is at The Centre, the shopping complex on Salwa Rd.

### Radio & TV
Qatar TV's second channel (channel 37, UHF) broadcasts programmes in English from late afternoon until about midnight seven days a week. With a good antenna you can usually also pick up the English stations broadcasting from Abu Dhabi, Saudi Arabia, Dubai and Bahrain. They all show a selection of British and US entertainment programmes, movies and documentaries. In addition, you can see CNN on Channel 55, Bahrain TV's English-language frequency from about 11 pm each night until 6 pm the following day. Another frequency out of Bahrain shows BBC World Service Television 24 hours a day.

Qatar FM broadcasts programmes in English from early morning until late evening, with an eclectic musical selection.

## FILM & PHOTOGRAPHY
Film is easy to find in hotels and shopping centres all over town, though getting anything other than colour prints developed can be a hassle. There are no restrictions on taking pictures aside from the usual ban on military sites (including the airport) and the courtesy and caution which are always required when taking pictures of people in the Gulf.

## HEALTH
Unless you are arriving from an area where cholera, yellow fever or some similar disease is endemic, vaccination certificates are not required for entry into Qatar.

Like other Gulf countries the standard of health and health care in Qatar is very high. There is no need to take malaria prophylactics nor do you need any shots beyond the usual regimen that any traveller should have (mainly DPT or a tetanus booster and gamma globulin).

If you do get sick, hospital care is free in Qatar.

## WOMEN TRAVELLERS

Though most Qataris follow the Wahhabi sect of Islam, the country does not have the sort of restrictions on women and their movements for which Saudi Arabia (the heartland of Wahhabism) is known and there is no local equivalent of Saudi Arabia's religious police, the *matawwa*. Still, one must accommodate oneself to the local style of life. Women wearing very tight or revealing clothing will attract leers and comments in public places. A woman should always travel in the back seat when taking a taxi. Women should also avoid making eye contact with men whom they do not know as this is often misinterpreted as a come-on. Single women may also find that they are unwelcome in the cheapest tier of hotels and restaurants. The Doha youth hostel, to cite one example, is only open to men.

## DANGERS & ANNOYANCES

The main thing to watch out for in Doha is the driving. Much of the city's traffic system is defined by a series of roundabouts. There are often no lights to control entry to these roundabouts with the result that, when traffic is heavy, people have to force their way into a moving stream of vehicles. When traffic is light the situation is worse; many drivers simply sail straight into the roundabout without slowing down at all.

## WORK

Qatar is not the sort of place where you can expect to pick up a few months of casual work waiting tables or teaching English. To obtain a work visa one usually has to have a job, and a signed contract, in hand before arriving in Qatar. It is possible, however, to arrive in the country on a tourist visa, look for a job and then have one's employer pick up the sponsorship and convert the tourist visa into a residence visa. This is usually an option only for people with specialised professional skills.

## ACTIVITIES

Although there are several sporting clubs in and around Doha where members can play squash, racquetball, tennis, etc, they are of little use to tourists as none of them offer day memberships. For the visitor the best options are the health clubs at the big hotels. These tend to be scaled-down versions of the bigger clubs though some, notably the one at the Sheraton, are pretty big in their own right. You can usually use the club if you are staying in the hotel. Nonguests can often use hotel swimming pools for a small fee.

## ACCOMMODATION

### Hostel

For men only there is a youth hostel on the outskirts of Doha.

### Hotels

There are no hotels outside of Doha which, considering the size of the country, is not really a problem. You could easily start in Doha, drive first to the UAE border then north to the tip of the peninsula and back down to Doha again all in a morning.

It is fairly easy to find good hotels for under QR 100, and QR 200 will buy you splendid accommodation, but the visa and sponsorship rules are such that you probably won't be staying in any of these places. The Oasis is the cheapest hotel that sponsors tourist visas and a single there costs about QR 285 per night, including the service charge (though you can almost certainly arrange some sort of discount). On the other hand the facilities at all of these places are quite good.

## FOOD

Qatar does not have an indigenous cuisine worth mentioning. Outside of the restaurants at the big hotels (which offer fairly predictable fare) Doha itself is filled with the usual collection of Western fast-food places and small Indian and Pakistani restaurants offering little more than curries and biryani dishes. At the Pakistani restaurants you can usually eat for about QR 10 while Western fast food is a bit more expensive. Meals at the big hotels cost at least QR 50 and usually closer to QR 100 during the frequent 'theme' nights held in the hotel restaurants.

### Self-Catering

The best place for do-it-yourself shoppers is the huge supermarket in the complex known as The Centre, on Salwa Rd near the Ramada hotel. Unless you have cooking facilities this is not likely to save you a lot of money over the cheaper Indian restaurants.

### DRINKS

Fruit juice and soft drinks are about all that you will find in the average Qatari restaurant. The cheaper the restaurant the slimmer your selection is likely to be. In the cheapest places in the souk nothing more than tap water, which is OK for drinking, may be available.

As for alcohol, you can't bring it in and you can't buy it in hotels but some non-Muslim foreigners are allowed to have it. Non-Muslims living in the country who have a monthly income above a certain level are given a permit allowing them to purchase a certain amount of alcohol each month. The purpose of this system is to allow Western and well-to-do expats to have alcohol while keeping it out of the hands of Asian and subcontinental expats. It is illegal for a non-Muslim to offer or serve alcohol to Muslims.

### THINGS TO BUY

You are not likely to find much in the way of Arabian souvenirs in Doha. If you are flush with money there are a couple of stores in the centre and in the large hotels specialising in Persian carpets. Much of the Arabian stuff you will see (eg incense burners) is actually made in Pakistan.

# Getting There & Away

### AIR
### To/From Europe & North America

Flying to Doha from North America is absurdly expensive. Going the other way tends to be cheaper but you are still looking at US$ 1000 or so. There is daily service between Doha and the UK, both direct and via Bahrain, and most of the major West European airlines fly to Doha between one and three times a week. Fares on all of these routes change constantly. Your best bet for finding a good fare out of Qatar is to ask friends and acquaintances whether they know a good travel agent or to trudge around to eight or 10 of them yourself.

### To/From Other Gulf States

Flying around the Gulf is never cheap and Qatar is no exception to this rule. Following are samples of the cheapest one-way and return fares with minimum and maximum stay requirements:

| To | One-Way | Return | Min/Max |
| --- | --- | --- | --- |
| Abu Dhabi | QR 330 | QR 350 | 3/7 days |
| Bahrain | QR 240 | QR 250 | 3/7 days |
| Dhahran | QR 250 | QR 340 | 3/14 days |
| Dubai | QR 430 | QR 450 | 3/7 days |
| Jeddah | QR 780 | QR 1090 | 3/14 days |
| Muscat | QR 730 | QR 760 | 3/7 days |
| Riyadh | QR 400 | QR 550 | 3/14 days |

There are several other fare categories, the general rule being that the longer you stay the more expensive it gets.

### LAND

There are no buses or taxis to Saudi Arabia or the UAE. In theory, one can drive one's car, but this is really only a viable option for those holding residence visas. Tourist and business visas have to be picked up at the airport and it is not possible to arrange to get them either at a Qatari embassy or at the frontier.

## SEA

At the time of writing there were no scheduled passenger sea services to or from Qatar, though plans were in place to start a jetfoil service between Bahrain and Dubai via Doha.

## LEAVING QATAR

You must arrive at Doha airport at least 45 minutes prior to the scheduled departure time of your flight though in my experience an hour or more would be a better bet. Long-haul flights to Europe sometimes have a two-hour check-in time, so it would be a good idea to double-check with your airline in advance. Check-in procedures tend to be slow and inefficient and if there is the slightest confusion about whether your visa for your destination is in order you can expect even more delays. Once you have checked in, passport control and security tend to move smoothly. There is no departure tax.

Remember to reconfirm your flight at least 72 hours before departure; Gulf Air is especially picky on this score.

# Getting Around

Qatar does not have a bus or service-taxi system, so regular taxis and renting a car are your only options for getting around the country. Though the taxis have meters you should probably negotiate the fare in advance for any trip outside the city. You can rent a car for about QR 100 per day.

## CAR
### Road Rules

Driving in Qatar is on the right side of the road and the visitor is well advised to be on his or her toes, particularly when negotiating Doha's lethal system of roundabouts. I'm not sure whether right turns are, in fact, legal at red lights but everybody makes them and if you find yourself blocking someone who wants to do so you are likely to be subjected to a fierce blast of the horn.

## Rental

You can rent a car on most foreign driving licenses. Licenses from other GCC countries are accepted only from GCC nationals and from foreigners who can show a residence visa from the country whose license they are presenting. See the Doha section for more details.

## HITCHING

Driving north out of Doha you will sometimes see men, almost always Qataris, trying to thumb lifts. I have never seen a foreigner hitching in Qatar and such a sight would almost certainly attract the attention of the local police.

## WALKING

In this climate, walking outdoors for more than a couple of hundred metres is not really an option for much of the year. You can walk around Doha but be prepared for people to give you lots of funny looks and for every taxi driver to slow down on the assumption that you are searching for a lift.

# Doha

Around the Gulf, Doha has earned the unenviable reputation of being the dullest place on earth. You will be hard-pressed to find anyone who'll claim the place is exciting. That said, there's nothing *wrong* with Doha; the bay is pleasant and there are enough interesting sites around town to keep a traveller occupied for a day or two.

## Orientation

Like some cities in the Gulf, modern Doha is laid out in honour of the private car. To the extent that there is a city centre it is probably the string of large buildings along the Corniche between the Qatar National Bank and the Emir's Office. The area inland from the waterfront includes the GPO, Doha Fort, the Ethnographic Museum and what pass, in Qatar, for cheap hotels. The main business district is further inland beyond which lie the

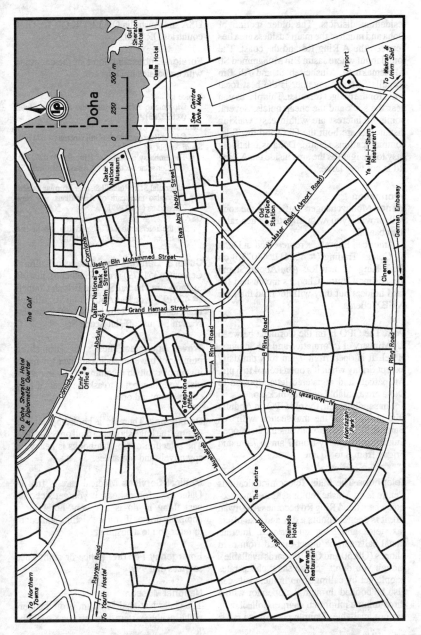

residential districts. The older section of Doha and much of the main business area lies between the A Ring Rd and the coast. The roundabout where Jasim Bin Mohammed St, Al-Asmakh St, Musheireb St and Ali Bin Abdulla St come together is the best focal point for the budget traveller. This places you near the souk and the cheap hotels. Several points of interest are within easy walking distance as are both the GPO and the Telecommunications Centre. Doha is relatively easy to navigate as the area inside the A Ring Rd is not very large.

## Information
**Money** Moneychangers' offices in the souk will provide you with slightly better rates than banks.

American Express is represented in Doha by Contas Trading (☎ 422411, 440770) on the B Ring Rd near Ras Abu Aboud St and the Airline Centre. Cheques are cashed for card holders but they will not hold mail for AMEX clients.

**Post** The GPO is on the Corniche between the Ministry of Information and the Sheraton Hotel. It is open from 7 am to 8 pm daily except Friday when it's open from 4 to 6 pm. All parcels and registered letters posted to Doha are available here for pick-up.

For sending mail, the old GPO on Abdulla Bin Jasim St, at the intersection with Al-Bareed St, is more convenient. It is open Sunday to Thursday from 7 am to 7 pm and Friday from 8 to 10 am.

**Telephone** The Main Telecommunications Centre is on Musheireb St near the intersection where the A Ring Rd becomes Al-Diwan Rd. It is open 24 hours a day and also offers fax, telex and telegram services. International calls can be direct-dialled from card phones (QR 50 and QR 100 cards available), though you don't get the same cheap rates people get by calling from home. Calls can also be booked through the operator with a three-minute minimum charge. Collect calls are not available. Sample per minute rates:

USA and Australia QR 13; UK QR 10; Gulf countries QR 3.60.

**Foreign Embassies** Some of the countries with embassies in Doha are:

France
    Diplomatic Area, beyond the Sheraton Hotel (☎ 832283)
Germany
    C Ring Rd, opposite the Gulf cinema (☎ 671100)
Saudi Arabia
    The embassy is on the C Ring Rd (☎ 427144). The Consular Section is on Ali Bin Abi Talib St.
UK
    Al-Istiqlal St in Rumailiah, near Murmar Palace. They also take care of Australians and New Zealanders (☎ 421991)
USA
    At the intersection of Ahmed Bin Ali St and Al-Jazira Al-Arabiya St (☎ 864701)

**Cultural Centres** The American Cultural Center (☎ 351279) is on Muaither St, just off Suhaim Bin Hamad St. The British Council (☎ 426193) is on Ras Abu Ayoub St. Alliance Française (☎ 417548) has its office on Ibn Naeem St, just off Ibn Seena St.

**Travel Agencies** There's an astonishing number of travel agencies all over town and it is impossible to recommend any in particular. Your best bet is to ask the locals if they can recommend one.

**Bookshops** There is a bookshop in The Centre, the huge shopping mall on Salwa Rd. The selection of English books is heavy on spy novels and romances.

**Medical Services** Medical care is free in Qatar even for visitors. If you get sick, the best thing to do is ask your hotel (or a company doctor if you are visiting someone) to refer you to a hospital.

**Emergency** For fire, police or ambulance services dial 999.

## National Museum
The Qatar National Museum is on the Corniche at the eastern end of town near the

intersection with Al-Muthaf St. The museum is open Sunday to Thursday from 9 am to noon and 3 to 6 pm (4 to 7 pm in the summer). It is closed Friday mornings and all day Saturday. Admission is QR 2.

Before entering, take a moment to look at the building. Most of the complex which the museum now occupies once served as a palace for Shaikh Abdulla Bin Mohammed, Qatar's ruler from 1913 to 1951.

Once inside, turn right to reach the aquarium (stuffed fish on the upper level, live ones in the basement) and the artificial lagoon with its display of dhows.

The geology and archaeology exhibits are in the building on the far side of the courtyard, opposite the main entrance. The archaeology display, which occupies most of the ground floor, includes the usual collection of arrowheads, potsherds, flint, etc. The section on seafaring and traditional celestial navigation methods is particularly interesting. The lower level of this building is a jumbled collection of displays on desert life, Islam and astronomy as well as an exhibit on the oil industry. Each room is quite well laid out but there appears to be no pattern to the floor as a whole.

The courtyard is surrounded by a series of rooms displaying artefacts showing the traditional lifestyle of the Qatari people as well as crafts.

### Ethnographic Museum

Located in the parking lot off Al-Najada St, between Al-Asmakh and Grand Hamad Sts, the museum is open Sunday to Thursday from 9 am to noon and 3 to 6 pm and Friday from 3 to 6 pm. It is closed Saturday. Admission is free.

The museum is in a traditional Qatari house from the early 20th century, which has been restored and provides a look at what life in Qatar was like before the oil era. Signs explain the function of the various rooms in the house and their importance in the life of the family.

Of particular interest is the building's wind tower. In addition to being one of the better preserved wind towers in the Gulf, it is one of Qatar's few remaining examples of this form of traditional Gulf architecture. When inside the museum be sure to spend a few minutes sitting under the wind tower to appreciate the ingenuity involved in designing this pre-electricity form of air-conditioning.

### Doha Fort

The Doha Fort is at the corner of Jasim Bin Mohammed and Al-Qalaa Sts (enter from the Jasim Bin Mohammed St side). Officially, the fort is open Sunday to Thursday from 9 am to noon and 3 to 6 pm and Friday from 3 to 6 pm, but the hours seem pretty erratic. Admission is free.

The interior of the fort consists of a large, paved courtyard with a fountain and a black Bedouin tent. The displays run the gamut from model dhows to paintings of Qatari life. The rooms surrounding the courtyard contain wire fish-traps, woven mats, stone carvings, etc. The roof provides a nice view of the courtyard.

### Old Police Station

This tiny fort-like building at the corner of Al-Matar Rd and Al-Waab St, between the B and C Ring Rds, was once a police post on the outskirts of Doha but is now little more than a curiosity within the city's urban sprawl. The small whitewashed building (on the left if you are coming from the centre) is easy to miss. You can't go in, but a peek through the windows confirms that you're not missing much... the interior is empty.

### Zoo

Doha's zoo, on the Dukhan Rd west of the city, is far from the centre of town . It is open from 1 to 5 pm daily except Saturday. The general public is admitted only on Thursday, Friday and Sunday. Monday and Wednesday are for families and Tuesday for women and children under nine. Admission is QR 5 for adults, QR 2 for children under nine.

### Organised Tours

Only the Doha Sheraton (not the Gulf Sheraton) offers tours and you have to be staying

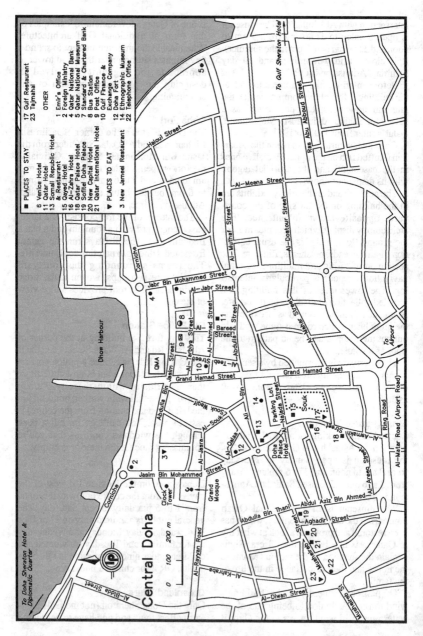

Central Doha

0   100   200 m

To Doha Sheraton Hotel &
Diplomatic Quarter

To Gulf Sheraton Hotel

To Gulf Sheraton Hotel

To Airport

■ PLACES TO STAY

6   Venice Hotel
11  Qatar Hotel
13  Somali Republic Hotel
    & Restaurant
15  Qayed Hotel
16  Al-Zahra Hotel
18  Qatar Palace Hotel
19  Sofitel Doha Palace
20  New Capital Hotel
21  Qatar International Hotel

▼ PLACES TO EAT

3   New Jameel Restaurant

17  Gulf Restaurant
23  Tajmahal

OTHER

1   Emir's Office
2   Foreign Ministry
4   Qatar National Bank
5   Qatar National Museum
7   Standard & Chartered Bank
8   Post Office
9   Bus Station
10  Gulf Finance &
    Exchange Company
12  Doha Fort
14  Ethnographic Museum
22  Telephone Office

there to sign up. A few other travel companies are operating around town but they are geared to groups and are not really set up to deal with individual travellers. Try Tourist Travel (☎ 421832, 421324), or ask at the numerous travel agencies.

## Places to Stay – bottom end & middle

Doha's *Youth Hostel* (☎ 867180), which is only open to men, is at the corner of Al-Luqta and Maha Sts, near the roundabout dominated by the Passports & Immigration Department. It is a long way west of town and if you do not have a car the only way to get there is by taxi. Getting a taxi back into the centre from the hostel is not going to be easy. The hostel itself is a decent place with six-bed dorms at QR 10 per night. The sign is only in Arabic, but you'll recognise the IYHF-style logo on the building.

For those on a really tight budget, the cheapest place in town is the *Somali Republic Restaurant & Hotel* (☎ 321422) on Ali Bin Abdulla St. Singles/doubles are QR 50/80, none with bath. The rooms are clean and have air-conditioning. Another real cheapie is the *Qayed Hotel* (☎ 425396) on Al-Asmakh St, near the corner of Al-Najada St. Rooms are QR 60/80, all with bath. It's a tolerable enough place where the all-important air-conditioning tends to be a bit noisy but works. The *Al-Zahra Hotel* (☎ 321503) nearby offers rather spartan rooms at QR 70/100, all including equally spartan toilets. A little further down the street, and several steps up in terms of both price and quality, is the *Qatar Palace Hotel* (☎ 421515). Rooms are QR 160/200 plus a 15% tax and service charge, but they will readily discount to QR 120/160 net.

At the intersection of Al-Muthaf and Al-Meena Sts, the *Venice Hotel* (☎ 413793) is good value at QR 80 for singles or doubles without bath. There are also some rooms which share a bathroom with only one other room. These cost QR 80/100.

At its discounted rate the *New Capital Hotel* (☎ 445445), on Musheireb St between Aghadir St and the Telecommunications Centre, is one of the better deals in town.

They charge QR 230/260 but when things are slow (ie, most of the time) they may discount that rate to QR 125/150. This is the cheapest place in town for those who crave a swimming pool. Next door, the *Qatar International Hotel* (☎ 321761) is very clean and modern but not quite as good as the New Capital. The *Qatar Hotel* (☎ 413171) on Al-Ahmed St has rooms for QR 100/140, regardless of whether or not they have a private bath. You might be able to bargain QR 10 to QR 15 off the starting price. A few singles, all with private baths, are available. The rooms are reasonable enough, though you can do better for less money at the Qayed.

## Places to Stay – top end

These are the places which can arrange your visa. All of these hotels add 17% in taxes and service to the quoted prices. As elsewhere in Doha, the glut of hotel space means that most will readily offer discounts.

At the very top of the scale lies the *Doha Sheraton* (☎ 833833, telex 5000 DOSHER DH, fax 832323), built for 1984's Gulf Summit (an event which it also hosted in 1990). Dominating the north side of Doha Bay the hotel, constructed as a flat-top pyramid, has become the country's main architectural landmark. The lobby is enormous and has a small, but well-laid out, display of 17th and 18th century Islamic antiquities. Singles/doubles are QR 480/580 and there's a pool and health club. If you can't afford to stay here at least drop by and take in the sweeping view of Doha and the bay from the rooftop restaurant.

Not to be confused with the Doha Sheraton is the *Gulf Sheraton Hotel* (☎ 432432, telex 4250 GLFHTL DH, fax 418784) on Ras Abu Aboud St at the eastern end of the city. This used to be simply the Gulf Hotel, which is how most people still refer to it. Rooms are QR 350/450. Next door the *Oasis Hotel* (☎ 424424, telex 4214 OASIS DH, fax 327096) attracts business travellers on a budget and is the cheapest hotel in Qatar that sponsors visas for tourists. Rooms are QR 245/295. Fans of Jonathan Raban should note that he stayed at the Oasis while researching his book on Arabia.

Downtown the *Hotel Sofitel Doha Palace* (☎ 435222, telex 5151 SOFTEL DH, fax 439186) on Abdul Aziz Bin Ahmed St asks QR 300/400 for rooms.

Further out, at the intersection of Salwa Rd and the C Ring Rd, the *Ramada Renaissance Hotel* (☎ 417417, telex 4664 DH, fax 410941) has rooms from QR 310/350. The occupancy rate here is clearly low – I was once upgraded from a regular room to a suite because, the clerk said, I was a 'regular customer'. I had stayed in the hotel only once before, two years earlier!

### Places to Eat
**Cheap** The best cheap fare is Indian/Pakistani. Try the *Gulf Restaurant* on Al-Asmakh St between the Qayed Hotel and the Qatar Palace Hotel (same side of street as Qayed). They specialise in curries (chicken, mutton or fish) for QR 4 to QR 5. The menu also features freshly baked bread which arrives at your table still warm.

*Tajmahal*, on Musheireb St across from the Telecommunications Centre, is a nice Indian restaurant with starters at QR 2 to QR 6 and main dishes at QR 7 to QR 12. There are several smaller Indian places around the parking lot below the restaurant. In the same neighbourhood, *Arsh Bilqees Restaurant*, on Masafi St behind the Sofitel Hotel, is also worth a try. They have a selection of biryanis, mutton, chicken, etc for QR 10 to QR 15.

*New Jameel Restaurant*, at the western end of Abdulla Bin Jasim St, has fresh juice, fairly simple food (a plate of rice with mutton for QR 6) and ice cream.

Affordable Western-style meals (QR 10 to QR 30) can be eaten at the cafe in The Centre on Salwa Rd. Ice cream freaks will be glad to know that there is a *Baskin-Robbins* next to the cafe.

**Expensive** I highly recommended *Ya Mal-i-Sham*, a Lebanese restaurant on Al-Matar Rd, directly opposite the main entrance to the airport (the pink neon sign is hard to miss). Mezzas and soups cost about QR 5 and main

courses are QR 15 to QR 25. The fare is the usual Lebanese mix of chicken, kebabs, mixed grill and pigeon plus good Gulf fish.

The best food in Doha is to be found at the *Caravan Restaurant*, opposite the Ramada Hotel at the intersection of Salwa Rd and the C Ring Rd. The restaurant is built around a huge all-you-can-eat (30 or more main courses) buffet of Chinese, Thai, Japanese, Filipino and Indian dishes for QR 35. Most of the dishes are also available à la carte, but that will cost you at least QR 30 so you might as well take the buffet.

Spending more than about QR 50 on dinner means eating in a hotel. The Doha Sheraton and Ramada hotels are reputed to have the best food in town with the formal restaurant at the top of the Sheraton topping the list. Lunch or dinner in one of the big hotels will run QR 60 and up. The Ramada's coffee shop is generally accounted to be one of the best eateries in town. They run a series of 'speciality' nights (Indian, Far Eastern, etc) with very large buffets.

### Entertainment
There are a couple of cinemas in town but they show only Pakistani and Indian films. Once in a blue moon the British Council may bring a travelling theatre company through town. Doha, however, is the kind of place where going out means dinner out and that's about it. Some of the big hotels offer light entertainment (ie, live background music) with their theme-night dinners.

Arabic plays and the occasional foreign troop can be seen at the National Theatre on the Corniche. The Ministry of Information has an art gallery in Doha and sponsors displays of traditional dancing in summer. (See the Arts & Culture heading in the Facts about the Country section.)

### Getting There & Away
**Air** Some of the airlines flying in and out of Doha are:

Air India
    Airline Centre, Ras Abu Aboud St (☎ 418423, 418424)

British Airways
    Airline Centre, Ras Abu Aboud St (☎ 321434, 321435)
EgyptAir
    Trans Orient Travel, Al-Matar Rd, near the airport (☎ 458331)
Gulf Air
    Al-Matar Rd, near the airport entrance (☎ 455444)
KLM
    Airline Centre, Ras Abu Aboud St (☎ 321208, 321209)
Kuwait Airways
    Airline Centre, Ras Abu Aboud St (☎ 328381)
Lufthansa
    Next to the Emir's Office, off Jasim Bin Mohammed St (☎ 418666)
PIA (Pakistan International Airlines)
    Airline Centre, Ras Abu Aboud St (☎ 426290, 426291)
Royal Jordanian
    Airline Centre, Ras Abu Aboud St (☎ 431431)
Saudia
    Ras Abu Aboud St, opposite the Airline Centre (☎ 430077)

**Bus** There are no international bus services, and the domestic services seem to be a bit theoretical. The parking lot across from the Old GPO on Al-Bareed St is allegedly the bus station, but I've never seen a bus there. A small white shed in the parking lot marked 'Public Transport Office' is, I suppose, the ticket office, but I've never found that open either. Nor are there any service taxis which is quite unusual in the Middle East.

**Car Rental** Avis, Budget, and Europcar's rates start at around QR 150 per day for a small car including insurance and unlimited mileage. You might be able to bargain this down to about QR 100. The rental desks at the airport are often closed but arrangements can be made in most medium-sized hotels and in all of the big ones. In town, cheaper rates are sometimes available from Al-Muftah Rent-A-Car (☎ 328100, 426649) on Musheireb St, across from the telephone office. They are open Saturday to Thursday from 7 am to noon and 3 to 6.30 pm.

**Getting Around**
**To/From the Airport** A taxi between the airport and the centre will cost QR 10 to QR 15.

**Taxis** There are lots of taxis in the city so you should not have too much trouble finding one. Flag drops are QR 2 and the meter adds 10 dirhams every 200 metres (rates are higher at night).

# Around Qatar

### WAKRAH
Sixteen km south of Doha on the Umm Said road, Wakrah is little more than a lay-by with a small **museum** and some good beaches just south of the town.

The museum, however, keeps somewhat unpredictable hours and on the three occasions that I tried to visit, it was closed. Behind the museum are the ruins of what is thought to be a palace.

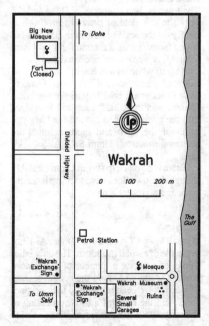

Wakrah

## UMM SILAL MOHAMMED

The attraction of Umm Silal Mohammed, the first town north of Doha, is its **fort**. The town appears to the left of the road about 25 km north of Doha. The turn is marked by a small white sign in Arabic which is immediately followed by a big yellow sign, also in Arabic, with a big red arrow pointing left. This road takes you to a roundabout.

Take the first right out of the roundabout and drive straight through the town for 1.4 km to reach the fort. It's on the left. The fort is open when someone is around to unlock the door (mornings are your best bet). Just beyond the main fort there is a tower, this one without a gate blocking access, though there's really nothing to see.

Taking another right turn immediately after turning out of the roundabout and following this road for a km will bring you to some old, ruined mud-brick fortifications.

## UMM SILAL ALI

The town is 37.5 km north of Doha and the only site is a field of **grave mounds**. It is hardly on the scale one finds in Bahrain but if you haven't seen a mound field yet Umm Silal Ali is worth a quick diversion.

A small white sign in English to the left of the road points toward the town. Coming from Doha you'll have to pass the sign, do a U-turn, backtrack half a km and turn right into the town. A small mound field lies just north of the town and more mounds are scattered in among Umm Silal Ali's buildings.

There is no place to stay in Umm Silal Ali, though the town does have two small restaurants and a grocery store.

## AL-KHOR

A small town 67 km north of Doha, Al-Khor is the site of a small **museum**. The only other things of note are a number of old **watchtowers** scattered around the centre, several of which have been restored to their original form, and the ruins of a **mosque** dating to the early 1950s. An Arabic inscription inside

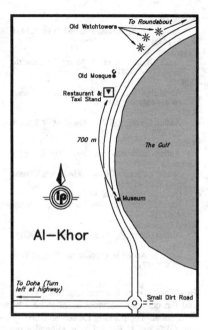

the mosque says that it was built in Ramadan 1372 AH (1953 AD). The view of the ocean is splendid and the setting is quite peaceful. If you have the time, Al-Khor is a pleasant day trip out of Doha.

There's no place to stay in Al-Khor, but the *Ain Helaitan Restaurant & Coffeeshop*, on the corniche between the ruined mosque and the museum, is a good place for a snack. The Turkish coffee (QR 2) is excellent.

Coming from Doha, the turn for Al-Khor is 16 km north of Umm Silal Ali. It is not very well marked. Look for the 'Al-Khor Exchange' sign. To reach the museum follow the main road into town until you reach a roundabout near the coastline. Turn left and proceed along the coast for about 650 metres. The museum is the white building on the right. The ruined mosque is another 700 metres along the coast on the landward side of the road, but if you're driving you'll have to go a km or so past it before you can make a U-turn.

## ZUBARA

Near Qatar's north-western coast, 105 km north of Doha, Zubara's **fort** was built in 1938 as a border police post. The fort, a small four-bastion structure around a courtyard, was used by the military until well into the 1980s. Today well-to-do Qataris occasionally travel up here on falconing expeditions, but that's about it.

Nothing you'll see around here even hints at the place's history. Until about 100 years ago, Zubara was the main settlement in Qatar. For almost 200 years it was controlled by the Al-Khalifa, Bahrain's ruling family, but hotly contested between them and Qatar's Al-Thani family. The fort you see today was built shortly after the Al-Thanis wrested the place from Bahraini control once and for all.

Several of the rooms around the fort's courtyard have displays of items, mostly potsherds, found at or near the fort. You can also climb one of the towers for a rather bleak view of the surrounding desert.

Two km beyond the fort are the ruins of some much older coastal fortifications. A rough dirt road to the ruins starts at the rusty gate next to the fort – the attendant will open it for you –and leads down the hill and to the right. Low brick fortification walls and the

excavated remains of a city are clearly visible but there are no explanatory signs of any sort.

To reach Zubara, turn left at the police post 68 km north of Doha (there's a small white sign in English) and follow the road. You can't miss the fort. On a clear day you'll see it from a distance of almost seven km and there's absolutely *nothing* around it.

## AL-RUWEIS

The Qatar peninsula's northernmost point offers little to the traveller. There are a few small grocery stores and restaurants and a causeway out to the fishing village on **Ras Abu Amran** island but that's about it.

If you've got a car, a couple of hours to kill and it's not too hot, try the drive between Al-Ruweis and the Zubara fort. The road passes several abandoned coastal villages, most notably **Al-Khuwair** and **Al-Arish**. The roads/tracks to these places shown on the *Oxford Map of Qatar* are mostly nonexistent, but you can easily spot the abandoned villages from the main road and you shouldn't need a 4WD for the short trek across the desert to reach them. The towns were abandoned in the 1970s. The shells of houses and shops clustered around a ruined central mosque can be a bit spooky.

# Saudi Arabia

Arabia has intrigued travellers for centuries. Vast and mostly arid, it is the cradle of the Islamic religion, the Arab race and the Arabic language – a language considered holy by Muslims.

Today's Saudi Arabia retains that mystique, in part because it is so incredibly difficult to visit. The Kingdom has an abundance of places to go and things to see, from the spectacular ruins of Madain Salah in the north-west, to the forests and traditional architecture of the south-western Asir region and the vast date groves of the Eastern Province's Al-Hasa oasis.

Seeing many of these places involves a fair amount of effort and paperwork; the climate is often harsh and the social regulations which govern life in the Kingdom strike the average visitor as more than a bit Draconian. Still, Saudi Arabia offers the traveller the rare opportunity of exploring a country where tradition and modernity are still working out their accommodation with one another.

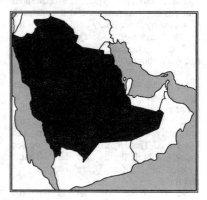

# Facts about the Country

## HISTORY
### Traders' Crossroads
Leaving aside the vast desert wilderness of the Empty Quarter, Saudi Arabia, historically, socially and geographically, can be divided into three regions. The eastern and western coasts of the country, along the Gulf and the Red Sea respectively, were important stations along the trade routes of antiquity. Until modern times the third region, the deserts of north-central Arabia, was a remote and rarely visited area of Bedouin camel-herders and, in the oases, small farming settlements.

Until the 18th century the history of what is now Saudi Arabia is largely the history of the coastal regions. In the Gulf this history goes as far back as any yet recorded. Parts of what is now eastern Saudi Arabia were first settled in the 4th or 5th millennium BC by migrants from what is now southern Iraq. These people were known as the Ubaid culture. The geography of the Gulf was quite different then and throughout Arabia the climate was far less harsh than it is today. Archaeologists have shown that many of the ancient sites now lying on the coast of the Gulf were once islands. Other sites which are now surrounded by large expanses of desert were once coastal regions or sat on the shores of lakes. Some sites, such as Tarut Island, have been inhabited almost continuously since Neolithic times.

The Ubaids were in contact with the Bahrain-based Dilmun empire, which appears to have controlled a large portion of the Saudi coast – the tell on which Tarut Fort sits has yielded Dilmun era pottery. Though apparently ruled from Bahrain during this period, the Eastern Province does not contain the large number of grave mounds for which Bahrain is known.

Civilisation appears to have come to the western part of the Arabian peninsula somewhat later. Cave paintings have been found in north-central Arabia but the earliest major site in the west of the peninsula is Al-Fao, a city on the edge of the Empty Quarter which was an important stop on the caravan route from Yemen to the Mediterranean. Al-Fao reached its peak between about 200 BC and 400 AD. Finds from the excavations at Al-Fao can now be seen in the museum at Riyadh's King Saud University.

The best known of the western Arabian kingdoms was that of the Nabataeans. Their empire, centred on Petra (now in southern Jordan) stood astride the main frankincense route from Yemen's Wadi Hadhramaut to Damascus. Madain Salah, north of modern Medina, was the empire's second most important city. By levying a 25% toll on all goods passing through their territory, the Nabataeans became extremely rich. The empire thrived in the 1st century BC, at one point stretching as far north as Damascus, but declined in the 1st century AD when the Romans began transporting the frankincense by ship.

The Romans appear to have taken a political interest in Arabia only once. In 25 BC Aelius Gallus, a Roman general, led a force of some 13,000 men south through what is now western Saudi Arabia in an attempt to conquer the frankincense producing regions of Wadi Hadhramaut and Dhofar, in modern Yemen and Oman, respectively. His army rolled through what is now Medina and later conquered Najran but had to turn back at Marib (now in Yemen) because of thirst.

## The Coming of Islam

The decline of the frankincense trade after the 3rd century AD moved Arabia to the margins of the ancient world.

The Gulf, the Arabian side of which lay on the edge of Persia's Sassanian empire, retained some importance as a trade route between Mesopotamia and India. A large Christian community grew up there during the 4th and 5th centuries, and there were bishops based in the town of Darin on Tarut Island, and in Qatif on the mainland. There may also have been bishoprics in the Al-Hasa oasis and near Jubail. Though Christianity seems to have been the largest religion in the area by the late 5th century, the strong Persian influence in the region has led some scholars to believe that Zoroastrianism was also widespread.

Central Arabia, the area now known as Najd, was populated largely by pagan nomadic tribes. Most of these nomads worshipped spirits which they believed were embodied in animals or things around them (rocks, trees, etc), though some Christian communities existed in the oasis villages as did a few monasteries. In the western part of the peninsula, now known as the Hejaz, there were large Jewish communities, particularly at Yathrib (today's Medina). The Kaaba at Mecca was an important centre of pagan pilgrimage, its focus then, as now, being the black stone, thought to be a meteorite, lodged in one corner of the structure. The Kaaba itself was then filled with idols which were later cast out by Mohammed.

With the exception of a few trading centres along the Gulf and a few oasis settlements along the caravan routes in the west, Arabia at the dawn of Islam was an isolated and dangerous wilderness ruled by a multitude of local warlords. Though two large Christian empires, the Ethiopian and the Byzantine, lay nearby monotheism had not taken root very deeply. Life in the Gulf revolved around pearl diving and fishing. In the Hejaz the most important settlements were Yathrib, which was mostly agricultural, and Mecca, which lived off a combination of trade and pagan pilgrimage.

According to tradition Mohammed was born in Mecca sometime around the year 570. In the year 610 he began to receive what he believed to be revelations from God, conveyed to him through the archangel Gabriel. Thus began Mohammed's ministry, which was to continue until his death, at Medina, in 632. By the time of the Prophet's death the religion he founded had swept all others before it throughout the Hejaz. For a more detailed discussion of Islam and the life of the Prophet see under Religion in the Facts about the Region chapter.

## The Centre Shifts

After Mohammed's death many of the tribes which had allied themselves to him militarily, and became at least nominally Muslim in the process, did not consider themselves to be under any obligation to his successors. The first of Mohammed's successors as leader of the Muslim community, Abu Bakr, declared this to be apostasy and set out to force the tribes back to Islam. This process took most of the next year but left the Muslims, by 633, in control of most of Arabia. It also laid the groundwork for the conquests which followed. Over the next century the Muslim armies of Arabia swept out to conquer much of what we now know as the Middle East and North Africa. Within a few generations the Muslim world stretched from the Pyrenees in Europe to China. In the process, however, the new religion's Arabian birthplace soon lost much of its political, though not spiritual, importance.

By the middle of the 7th century, Islam's political centre of gravity had shifted outside the peninsula – first to Damascus, later to Baghdad and Cairo – never to return. Mecca and Medina retained their importance as spiritual centres, but increasingly their political importance lay only in the prestige that a Muslim ruler could acquire by controlling them. Most of the rest of the peninsula returned to its traditional ways, a constant tug of war between the Bedouin camel-nomads of the desert and the residents of the towns and villages which dotted the coasts, the caravan routes and the oases.

From 961 Mecca came under the rule of the Sherifs, descendants of Mohammed through his grandson Hassan. For 300 years the Sherifs ruled the city independently while the rest of the Hejaz was controlled by the Shiite Fatimid dynasty of Egypt. The Fatimids were succeeded, in 1169, by another Cairo-based dynasty, the Ayyubids (Saladin and his descendants), who controlled the region from 1169 to 1229. In 1250, however, the Ayyubids were overthrown by their own class of slave-soldiers, the Mamluks. In 1269 the Mamluk Sultan

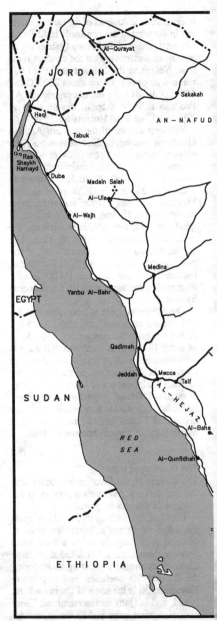

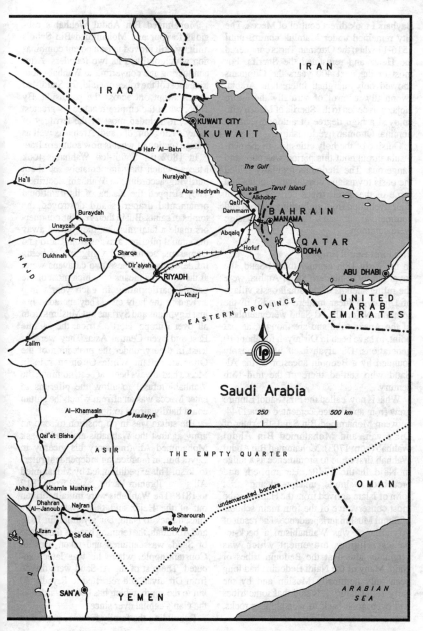

Baybars I took direct control of Mecca. The city remained under Mamluk control until 1516-17 when the Ottoman Turks conquered the Hejaz and reinstated the Sherifs. For most of the next 400 years the Ottomans showed only marginal interest in Arabia. Eventually, control of virtually the entire Hejaz was ceded to the Sherifs of Mecca who enjoyed a high degree of autonomy under nominal Ottoman overlordship.

Outside of the holy cities life in the peninsula throughout this period was poor and dangerous. The Bedouins regularly raided the oasis towns and coastal settlements and some of the desert tribes derived much of their livelihood from ambushing pilgrim and commercial caravans. Famine and disease were common.

### The First Saudi Empire

In the early 18th century the Al-Saud, the royal family of modern Saudi Arabia, were the ruling sheikhs of the small oasis village of Dir'aiyah (near modern Riyadh) in the southern Najd. The Al-Saud were members of the Aneza tribe and are thought, at that point, to have been in Dir'aiyah for about 10 generations. Dir'aiyah itself was probably founded by a Bedouin ancestor of the Al-Saud who settled there in the mid-15th century.

What is now called the First Saudi Empire grew from an alliance, cemented circa 1744, between Mohammed Bin Saud, the ruler of Dir'aiyah, and Mohammed Bin Abdul Wahhab (born 1703). Mohammed Bin Abdul Wahhab first came to prominence as a judge in Najd in the 1740s. He applied, and preached, a simple, unadorned and strict form of Islam derived from the Hanbalis, the most conservative of the four main schools of Sunni Muslim jurisprudence. The result of this alliance was Wahhabism, a back-to-basics religious movement which was originally aimed at the Bedouin tribes of Najd. Many of the Najdi Bedouins had long been only nominally Muslim and by the early 18th century it is said that some tribes had even gone back to worshipping rocks, trees or the tombs of local saints.

Mohammed Bin Abdul Wahhab's religious fervour and Mohammed Bin Saud's military skill proved to be a potent combination which outlived its two founders. After conquering and converting to Wahhabi doctrine most of the tribes of Najd, the Saudi-led forces swept out across the peninsula. By 1806, when the empire reached its greatest extent, it included most of the territory of today's Kingdom of Saudi Arabia as well as a large section of what is now southern Iraq.

In 1802 the Saudi-led Wahhabis took Mecca, which they immediately set about purifying according to Wahhabi doctrines. They stripped the Kaaba of its traditional ornamental draperies and destroyed the tombs of saints. But in their zeal the conquerors made a fatal mistake: they turned away the annual pilgrim caravans from Cairo and Damascus, accusing the pilgrims of being infidel idolaters. These two caravans were, at the time, the means by which most of the people participating in each year's hajj arrived in the holy city. They included not just Egyptians and Syrians but Muslims from all over Europe, North Africa, the Middle East and even Central Asia. They were, at least in theory, under the protection of the Ottoman sultan. While Ottoman rule in Mecca had always been, at best, nominal, the Wahhabi refusal to allow the pilgrims to enter Mecca was an affront which the sultan could hardly afford to ignore.

The sultan was in no position to send an army against the Wahhabis and had to ask Mohammed Ali (in theory his viceroy in Egypt but, in practice, an independent ruler) to do so. This expedition, led by Mohammed Ali's son, Ibrahim Pasha, lasted from 1812 to 1818. The Wahhabis were initially driven out of the Hejaz and then systematically chased back to Najd. Dir'aiyah fell in 1818 and Abdullah, the reigning head of the House of Saud, was captured and taken back to Constantinople, where he was later executed. The rest of the Al-Saud were driven from Dir'aiyah and retreated to Riyadh, 30 km to the south, which has been regarded as the clan's capital ever since.

Rebuilding the family fortunes proved to

be a slow process. In 1843 Faisal Bin Saud, then the head of the family, managed to drive the Ottoman-Egyptian forces out of Najd and restore Saudi rule over Dir'aiyah. But when Faisal died in 1867 his sons squabbled over the succession. With the Al-Saud divided internally the Ottomans sought to gain control of Najd by offering their support to the rival Al-Rashid family. The Al-Rashid set themselves up in Ha'il, 640 km north of Riyadh. In 1891 Mohammed Bin Rashid drove the Al-Saud from Riyadh and became the undisputed ruler of Najd until his death in 1897.

## The Rise of Abdul Aziz

After their expulsion from Riyadh some of the Al-Saud family wound up in prison in Ha'il while others retreated to the desert and the edges of the Empty Quarter. Part of this second group eventually migrated to Kuwait where the ruling sheikh took them in.

It was in Kuwait that the next head of the family came of age. Abdul Aziz Bin Abdul Rahman Al-Saud was a remarkable man. He combined deep personal piety with an intuitive grasp of military strategy and diplomacy which bordered on genius. In later years he would be known throughout the Arab world as The Lion of Najd and to the world at large as Ibn Saud, King of Arabia.

In 1902 Abdul Aziz set out to restore the family fortunes, and almost immediately succeeded in recapturing Riyadh from the Al-Rashids in a swift night-time attack with a force of about 30 men. He rapidly took control of the rest of southern Najd before pausing to consolidate his power.

Alarmed by the loss of Riyadh the head of the Al-Rashid family, usually referred to as Ibn Rashid, appealed to the Ottomans for help, claiming that Abdul Aziz was getting support from the British. This was not true though Ibn Rashid may well have believed it. By 1905 Ibn Rashid had been reinforced by more than 5000 Turkish troops. These, however, proved undisciplined. Abdul Aziz simply avoided them – letting them fester in the sun and cause trouble in Ha'il while he

turned his attentions elsewhere. By 1906 the Saudis were consistently winning their skirmishes with the Al-Rashid and gaining ever more tribal support. They soon moved out of Najd toward the Gulf and, in 1912-13, drove an Ottoman garrison out the Al-Hasa oasis. From there, however, Abdul Aziz could go no further: the Gulf sheikhdoms were under British protection and the British had made it clear that they were not willing to see their clients overthrown.

When WW I broke out Ibn Rashid declared his support for the Ottomans, a move which led Abdul Aziz to seek British help for the first time. In December 1914 he signed a treaty with the British ceding them a measure of control over his foreign policy in exchange for an annual subsidy and their recognition of his sovereignty over Najd.

Throughout his conquest of the peninsula Abdul Aziz's fighters were drawn mostly from the *ikhwan* (brotherhood), a society of Bedouin warriors which he founded in 1912. The ikhwan were nomads who had been resettled in oasis farming villages. This made them easy to round up as a fighting force, and easy to drill in the Wahhabi religious doctrines. Eventually, there would be 100 ikhwan colonies. The ikhwan's zeal was supplemented by Abdul Aziz's diplomacy, which was built around alliances with the tribes he conquered. Usually Abdul Aziz would marry a daughter of his conquered rival. After a fairly brief period the bride was usually returned to her family loaded with gifts. The children these unions produced became links binding together the Al-Saud and the other family.

In 1930, Abdul Aziz had to suppress the brotherhood for fear of losing his own throne after many of his former warriors came to believe Abdul Aziz, through his rather modest contact with foreigners (mostly the British), had opened Arabia to too many outside influences. By that time the ikhwan had also angered the British by raiding across the border into Iraq, Kuwait and Trans-Jordan. They ignored Abdul Aziz's orders to stop this practice, thus putting him in a difficult position.

### Britain, Turkey & the Hejaz

Though Ottoman forces, under Ibrahim Pasha, had driven the Saudis out of the Hejaz in the early 19th century, Ottoman prestige there never quite recovered. Throughout the 18th and 19th centuries the Ottoman empire was in decline, losing territory either in Europe or to Europeans almost every year. With so many problems in Greece, the Balkans and North Africa, the Hejaz was never at the top of Constantinople's agenda.

The loss, during the 19th century, of virtually all of the empire's European provinces changed the nature of the Ottoman state. For the first time in several centuries an Ottoman sultan found himself ruling an empire which was overwhelmingly eastern and Islamic. If, however, the sultan was going to stress his realm's Islamic identity (and around the end of the 19th century a conscious decision to this effect was taken in Constantinople) then day-to-day control of the Hejaz, and especially of the holy cities, was essential.

In 1900 Sultan Abdul Hamid II (reigned 1876-1909) announced that a railway would be built from Damascus to Medina with a later extension to Mecca. The ostensible purpose of the project was to make it easier for pilgrims to reach the holy cities, but trains are equally good at carrying troops and Abdul Hamid's real motive for the project was to bring the Hejaz back under firm Ottoman control. The Hejaz Railway line to Medina began operation in 1908.

With the outbreak of WW I in 1914 the Turkish army officers who were the power behind the throne in the Ottoman empire prevailed on Sultan Mohammed V to declare a *jihad*, or holy war, calling on Muslims everywhere to rise up against Britain, France and Russia. This alarmed the British, who vastly overestimated the sultan's virtually nonexistent influence over India's large Muslim population. To counter him they negotiated an alliance with Hussein Bin Ali, the Grand Sherif of Mecca. In 1916 Sherif Hussein agreed to lead an Arab revolt against the Turks in exchange for a British promise to make him King of the Arabs after the war – a promise which the British did not keep.

### A New Kingdom

Throughout WW I and during the years immediately following it Abdul Aziz concentrated his energies on finishing off Al-Rashid rule in the northern Najd, and on conquering Asir, the small kingdom lying between the Hejaz and the Yemen, and the remaining portions of what is now Saudi Arabia's Eastern Province. It was only then that he turned his attention to the Hejaz. In 1924, with Abdul Aziz's forces already in control of Taif and threatening Mecca, Sherif Hussein abdicated as King of the Hejaz. He went into exile in Cyprus where he died in 1931. On the same day (16 October) that Hussein departed from Jeddah the first of the ikhwan entered Mecca unopposed, wearing pilgrim garb and carrying no weapons. Abdul Aziz himself did not enter the holy city until early December. He, too, arrived dressed as a pilgrim.

Abdul Aziz set about conquering Medina and the rest of the Hejaz while laying siege to Jeddah. He also bent over backwards to show the rest of the Muslim world that he was a fit custodian of the holy cities, largely by ending the practice of fleecing pilgrims. Jeddah surrendered in December 1925. The following month Abdul Aziz formally assumed the title of King of the Hejaz in addition to his title as the Sultan of Najd. In 1932 he combined the two crowns and renamed the country the Kingdom of Saudi Arabia.

The Al-Saud were once again the rulers of Arabia, but their Kingdom was still desperately poor. It has been estimated that in the 1920s the country's total revenue was just over UK£200,000 per year, almost a third of which came from Abdul Aziz's British subsidy. Finances had always been a problem. Arabia was far from rich and tradition required that Abdul Aziz, as the ruler, share whatever wealth came into his possession while also lavishing gifts on both allies and conquered rivals. Thus when the oil prospectors first came calling Abdul Aziz thought they were wasting their time looking for oil in his country, but he was in no position to turn down the money they offered.

In 1920 Frank Holmes, a New Zealander who had served with the British army, was the first to approach Abdul Aziz about an oil concession. Holmes' Eastern & General Syndicate was granted a concession in 1923 but the company failed to find sufficient backing for exploration and the concession lapsed after two years.

After oil was discovered in commercial quantities in Bahrain in 1932, the companies showed renewed interest in Saudi Arabia. Abdul Aziz's own interest in oil had also revived. The Kingdom's financial crisis in the early '30s was severe. The market for pearls collapsed around 1930 when the Japanese discovered how to culture them and the Great Depression led to a drop in demand for Saudi Arabia's other export product, dates. The Kingdom's only other significant source of income was the pilgrimage to Mecca which, like the date market, had been badly hit by the Depression. The total number of pilgrims dropped from about 100,000 per year in the early 20th century to only 20,000 in 1933.

Thus in May 1933 Abdul Aziz granted an oil concession to Standard Oil of California (SOCAL), which paid him a much needed cash advance of UK£50,000 against future royalties. Drilling began in 1935 but oil was not found in commercial quantities until 1938. By then SOCAL had sold half its interest in the concession to the Texas Oil Company (now Texaco). In 1944 SOCAL and Texaco formed the Arabian American Oil Company, or ARAMCO, to run their operations in the Kingdom. In 1948 ARAMCO sold some of its shares to Standard Oil of New Jersey (now Exxon) and Socony Vacuum (Mobil). ARAMCO was phenomenally successful (it is said never to have failed to make a profit) and for many years was the largest US firm operating outside the USA.

Though oil was discovered in Saudi Arabia in 1938, WW II forced production to shut down almost immediately. After the war, however, things took off and by 1950 the Kingdom's royalties were running at about US$1 million per week which, at the time, was an unbelievable sum of money for Abdul Aziz.

By 1960 81% of the Saudi government's revenues came from oil. This was reinforced over the years by the government's rising stake in the oil industry. Saudi Arabia started its relationship with the oil companies on the basis of a royalty agreement but in 1950 Abdul Aziz demanded and got 50-50 profit sharing with ARAMCO. In late 1972 the Kingdom took a 25% stake in the oil company and its assets. That share was increased to 60% in 1974 and 100% in 1980.

### After Abdul Aziz

Abdul Aziz died in 1953 and was succeeded by his son Saud who immediately embarked on a reign of profligacy. With his garish palaces and habit of riding around the desert in a Rolls Royce tossing gold coins to the Bedouins, Saud soon became the embodiment of tasteless excess. His habits were particularly destructive because the country was still largely the King's personal fief. Oil revenues were paid directly to the monarch. There was no distinction between the King's private funds and the state treasury. Although Abdul Aziz had set up a Council of Ministers shortly before his death, there was still no real system of government in the modern sense of the term. Under King Saud this system was not proving very workable.

In March 1958 the family forced Saud to surrender his powers, but not the crown, to his younger brother Prince Faisal, then the Foreign Minister. Faisal immediately began to modernise the country's administration and set about trying to get the Kingdom's finances back in order. Thanks to Saud, the government was now in debt to ARAMCO.

But the idea of Saud as a figurehead did not fit with the conception that he, and many others, had of the Saudi monarchy. In December 1960 Saud regained his powers with the help of the Kingdom's small clique of Western-educated technocrats. This group threw its support behind Saud on the understanding that, in return, he would institute some form of representative government. Faisal resigned as Prime Minister. Saud, though in declining health, returned to his free-spending ways.

From late 1962 Saudi Arabia found itself involved in a bloody proxy war against Egypt, with the two countries supporting opposite sides in Yemen's civil war. There was general agreement within the royal family that a republican government in Yemen posed a threat to the Saudi monarchy, but the family also increasingly came to believe that Saud, with his poor health and lack of financial sense, was incapable of dealing with the situation. On 3 November 1964, after a long internal struggle, the family forced Saud to abdicate. He went into exile, living mostly in Athens until his death in 1969.

## King Faisal

One of Faisal's first acts as king was the final abolition of slavery in Saudi Arabia. It was a sign of things to come. Over the 11 years of his reign the Kingdom was to move a long way toward becoming a modern country.

An essential first step in this was ending the costly Egyptian-Saudi proxy battles being fought in Yemen. In 1965 Faisal invited Egyptian President Gamal Abdel Nasser to Jeddah for talks on the conflict. Both sides eventually agreed to suspend aid to their respective clients and pull out their troops (which, in Egypt's case, numbered more than 50,000), but the agreement collapsed in a climate of mutual mistrust. It was only Egypt's defeat in the 1967 Arab-Israeli war that brought the Saudi-Egyptian war in Yemen to an end (though the Yemeni civil war itself continued until April 1970).

However, relations between the two countries did not really begin to improve until after Nasser's death in 1970. Faisal's relations with Nasser's successor, Anwar Sadat, were much better and when the 1973 Arab-Israeli war broke out the Riyadh-Cairo axis was an important political element before, during and after the conflict.

The wealth which came Saudi Arabia's way in the '60s brought with it increased political clout. The Kingdom participated in the brief attempt by Arab states to cut the flow of oil to the USA and Britain during the 1967 war, and while the oil weapon proved ineffective then, the Arab world's oil producers learned a number of lessons which proved useful later. The West, in contrast, seems to have drawn precisely the wrong conclusions, coming to believe itself immune from the threat of an embargo.

In the run-up to the 1973 war the USA was given ample warning that the situation, both politically and economically, would be different from 1967. Faisal said repeatedly that if the USA continued to support Israel it could not expect an endless flow of cheap Arab petroleum. The warnings were ignored and when Arab states, led by the staunchly pro-Western Saudis, announced the embargo in October 1973, no one was more shocked than the Americans. The embargo covered only the USA and the Netherlands, the European country which the Arabs judged to be most vocally pro-Israel. Its effect was largely psychological (at the time the USA imported less than 10% of its oil from Saudi Arabia), but if the goal was to get the West's attention it certainly succeeded. By the time the sanctions were lifted less than a year later, the Arab Gulf states in general, and Saudi Arabia in particular, had found their way onto the West's psychological map of the world. The press coverage was far from favourable, but the Arabs were no longer being ignored.

The price of oil increased fourfold and Faisal, who controlled 30% of OPEC's overall production and 35% of the non-Communist world's proven, exploitable reserves, immediately became a force to be reckoned with on the world stage.

If Abdul Aziz had been astonished by the money oil earned him in the '50s, the sums it now brought to his son were truly staggering. Between 1973 and 1978 Saudi Arabia's annual oil revenues went from US$4.35 billion to US$36 billion. Amid the flood of money, however, Faisal and his Oil Minister, Ahmed Zaki Yamani, emerged as OPEC's main voice for moderation and price stability. They both realised that pulverising the economies of the West was not in their interest. The West not only bought the oil but it

Top: Zubara fort, Zubara, Qatar
Bottom: Dhows at the Qatar National Museum, Doha, Qatar

Top: Tombs at Madain Salah, Saudi Arabia
Bottom: Najran fort, Najran, Saudi Arabia

was also where much of Saudi Arabia's substantial financial surplus was invested.

## The Boom

A building boom began in Saudi Arabia as money was poured into utility and infrastructure projects and the construction from scratch of a petrochemical industry.

Faisal, however, did not live to see it. In 1975 he was assassinated by a nephew, who was said to have been deranged. The motive for the killing was never fully explained and has provided grist for the region's conspiracy theorists ever since. He was succeeded by his half-brother, Khalid, with another half-brother, Fahd, as Crown Prince.

It is difficult today to appreciate the extent to which Saudi Arabia was modernised during King Khalid's reign (1975-82). Most accounts of Riyadh and Jeddah in the late '70s describe the cities in terms of huge construction sites. The physical growth of these cities was staggering. For example, in the early '70s Riyadh's old airport, which today appears to be fairly close to the centre, was well outside the city. People visiting Riyadh or Jeddah after an absence of only a few years often found the cities changed beyond recognition.

The accomplishments of this period were genuinely astonishing, though the result today is a certain degree of overcapacity.

In the late '70s everyone seemed to be making easy money; some Saudis, however, were troubled by the outside influences which were now flooding into the Kingdom. The royal family has always walked a fine line between those of their subjects who want Saudi Arabia to join the modern world and those who fear any contact with modernity. The country's Islamic identity has never been a subject of debate. Rather, the tension has always been between those, including most of the senior members of the royal family, who believe that modernisation and Islam are generally compatible and those who reject this idea.

This tension in Saudi society became clear in November 1979 when some 300 radicals seized control of the Grand Mosque in Mecca. Booming their demands out through the mosque's public address system, the group, mostly Saudis though some foreigners were also involved, criticised the royal family and Kingdom's modernisation. The zealots may have assumed that the populace would rally to their call, but this did not happen. It took government troops 10 days to retake the mosque, an operation in which over 250 people died, including 117 of the radicals. Another 63 people were captured when the mosque was retaken. Six weeks later they were executed.

At about the same time riots broke out in and around Qatif, a predominantly Shiite town in the Eastern Province. These were related to long-standing grievances among the country's Shiite minority, and the timing was connected to the Shiite holiday of *ashoora*, the public observance of which had long been banned in the Kingdom. Saudi National Guard forces suppressed the disturbances, killing at least 12 people and arresting hundreds more.

## King Fahd

King Khalid died in June 1982 and his half-brother, Fahd, became the fourth of Abdul Aziz's sons to rule Saudi Arabia. Fahd was well prepared for the job. Khalid's health had long been poor and for much of his reign Fahd, then Crown Prince, had been the country's ruler in all but name.

The seizure of the Grand Mosque, the riots in Qatif and the Iranian revolution had all given the monarchy a scare. The threat from Iran in particular, which was openly hostile to King Fahd and the Al-Saud family, led Fahd to deepen his country's defence ties with the USA, Britain and France.

Relations with Iran, always tense since the 1979 Islamic revolution, reached a new low in 1987. In July of that year, as the hajj reached its climax, demonstrations broke out in Mecca. The details are hotly disputed but it is fairly clear that some of the 150,000 Iranian pilgrims then in Mecca had arrived with the intention of staging demonstrations against the USA and Israel. The Saudis have long demanded that the hajj be kept free of politics. This stance is in keeping with Wahhabi doctrine but is anathema to the Iranians. The demonstrations in front of the Grand Mosque degenerated into a stampede. The Iranians later accused Saudi authorities of firing on the crowd; the Saudis denied this and, in response, produced a small mountain of weapons they said had been confiscated from Iranian pilgrims during the 1986 and 1987 pilgrimages. At least 400 pilgrims, most of them Iranians, were dead by the time the square in front of the mosque was cleared, and for several years thereafter the Iranians boycotted the pilgrimage.

In the wake of Iraq's invasion of Kuwait in 1990, Saudi Arabia worried that it might be Baghdad's next target and asked the USA to send troops to defend the Kingdom. Saudi Arabia eventually found itself playing host to over 500,000 foreign (mostly US, British and French) troops. Once the war was over and the troops had gone home, the one clear legacy of the crisis was the demand for political change. In November 1990, apparently in response to criticism that he had not consulted widely enough before inviting foreign troops, King Fahd announced that plans were underway for a Consultative Council, or *majlis ash-shura*. In March 1992 the King announced that the Council would be appointed before the end of the year and outlined its duties. Like similar councils in some of the other Gulf states it is to be a consultative body without any actual legislative authority. In many ways its creation simply codifies and formalises the wide-ranging system of consultation which has always existed in Arabian society.

## GEOGRAPHY

Saudi Arabia is about 2.2 million sq km in area, most of it desert. In geological terms the Arabian peninsula is an extension of north-eastern Africa.

Western Saudi Arabia is dominated by a mountain chain running the entire length of the country and generally becoming higher and broader as one moves south towards Yemen. The Kingdom's tourist resorts are in this area: Taif, in the mountains above

Mecca, and the forests of the Asir region. The scenery throughout the Asir region is particularly striking, with evergreen forests overlooking desert wadis. In many places the mountains drop sharply to the Red Sea coastal strip. To the east, however, they gradually turn into a series of low hills before merging into the deserts of the central Arabian plateau.

About half of Saudi Arabia is taken up by the Rub' Al-Khali, or Empty Quarter. This is the largest sand desert in the world, an area about the size of France. The region is so fierce that even the Bedouins, who call it simply the Sands, are reluctant to venture into it. North of the Empty Quarter the great deserts of central Arabia stretch into Iraq. This is the region known to earlier generations of Westerners as Arabia Deserta. Much of it is a gravel desert, sometimes with a thin covering of sand or a bit of scrub growth. The extreme north-west of the Kingdom contains Arabia's second great sand desert, the Nafud.

The Eastern Province is a low-lying area which contains a number of *sabkhas* (salt flats). The desert here tends to be thin and crusty and because of the low elevations the air often seems particularly thick and damp. The main geographical feature of the east is the gigantic Al-Hasa oasis, centred on the town of Hofuf, with its miles upon miles of date palms.

## CLIMATE

Summers in the Kingdom are unbelievably hot. Daytime temperatures rise to 45°C or more from mid-April until October throughout the Kingdom, with high humidity in the coastal regions. In the summer it gets to 38°C or so overnight on the Red Sea coast. In places like Jizan, on the coast, this weather continues well into November. Even in December or January it can be uncomfortably hot.

In the dead of winter (December-January) temperatures in the main cities will drop into the teens during the day and even hit single digits in some places, particularly in the central deserts, overnight. In the coastal areas it rains regularly, less often in Riyadh.

## FLORA & FAUNA

A drive across Saudi Arabia's deserts will provide you with wonderful opportunities for viewing desert scrub growth and tamarind trees. In the forested areas of Asir there are various sorts of evergreens.

Aside from camels you are not likely to see much wildlife. The desert is full of nocturnal creatures such as hedgehogs and sand cats, and there are wild monkeys in the forest of the Asir region.

### Asir National Park

Saudi Arabia's only national park sprawls over a large portion of the south-western Asir region. See the Abha entry for complete details of the park and its facilities.

## GOVERNMENT

In theory Saudi Arabia's king is an absolute monarch, but in practice the system is not quite that simple. Abdul Aziz, the founder of the present Saudi dynasty, was a traditional Arab tribal leader. He acquired power and territory through conquest but maintained them through diplomacy. The system of government in the Kingdom today is a blend of this traditional system and modern ideas of administration. Thus, while much of the country's day-to-day life is supervised by a system of extremely bureaucratic ministries, every Saudi citizen also retains the right to take any grievance, be it a lost camel or a complex commercial dispute, directly to the King.

Important decisions are rarely taken by the king alone. Before acting he usually consults the Cabinet, senior members of the royal family and the country's religious and business establishments.

King Fahd's announcement, in early 1992, that a Consultative Council was to be created, aimed to formalise and modernise this traditional system of give-and-take between the ruler and the various elements of Saudi society. The Council's members are appointed by the King. About the time the Council was announced, King Fahd told a newspaper that elective democracy was not an appropriate system of government for

Date Picking

Saudi Arabia or the other Gulf states. The Council can comment on proposed laws and recommend changes but does not have any legislative authority.

After King Fahd, the next person in line for the throne is his half-brother, Prince Abdullah, who heads the National Guard. In theory the succession passes down the line of King Abdul Aziz's sons with the family collectively deciding which prince is best suited to take charge. In 1992 King Fahd announced plans to formalise this system through an electoral college of the 400 sons and grandsons of Abdul Aziz.

Saudi Arabia has no constitution. King Fahd and his predecessors have often said that the Koran is the only constitution which the country needs. Much of the legal system is based on a straight application of Islamic *sharia* law as interpreted by the Hanbali school of Islamic jurisprudence, the most conservative of Sunni Islam's four main legal schools.

## ECONOMY

Prior to the discovery of oil, the peninsula's

economy revolved around the hajj in the west, date farming and pearling in the east and tribal raiding in the centre.

After WW II oil quickly replaced these traditional pursuits as the main source of income. In the early '70s Saudi Arabia embarked on a long-term diversification programme. Economic development schemes focused on heavy industry, petrochemicals and agriculture. Today the Kingdom churns out huge amounts of steel and cement, boasts one of the world's largest petrochemical industries and is a net exporter of wheat.

All of this costs money (wheat does not grow in the desert without very expensive human assistance), and money in Saudi Arabia usually means oil. The Kingdom has long had to strike a balance between deriving most of its income from oil and oil-related industries and its long-standing commitment to price stability in the world oil market. This has led to some enormous adjustments in its output over the years. In 1979 the country was pumping about eight million barrels of oil per day (bpd). In 1983 the figure dropped to five million bpd but in early 1992 it was back up to 8.5 million bpd and plans were in the works to expand capacity to 10 million bpd.

The result of all this is that when the bottom drops out of the oil market, as happened in 1986 when oil fell below $10 per barrel, spending plans have to be radically redefined. Similarly, if the oil price heads for the stratosphere, as happened in 1973-74 and again in 1979-80, impossible projects suddenly become possible. In either case the resulting shock waves are felt throughout the economy.

This is not simply a question of how much money the government can channel into infrastructure and agriculture projects each year. Much of the diversification drive of the '70s and '80s created industries related to oil, whether directly or indirectly. Many of the country's private businesses are service companies whose main clients are either the government, the government-owned oil and petrochemical industries or their employees. To a greater extent than most Saudis like to

admit, the national economy still fluctuates with the oil price.

## POPULATION & PEOPLE

Because of its size and its history Saudi Arabia is a much less ethnically homogeneous place than is generally thought. The central Najd region was cut off from most of the rest of the world for many centuries and the population there is quite homogeneous. Pure- blooded Najdis often have long faces and sharply defined features. The Hejaz, on the other hand, presents one of the most mixed populations imaginable. For 14 centuries Muslims have been arriving in the Hejaz from all over the world and until earlier this century many of them stayed on. Hejazis may be as dark- skinned as sub-Saharan Africans or as pale as someone from northern Europe. As people have become more mobile this diversity increasingly applies to Saudis as a whole. One even encounters a handful of Saudis with distinctly Chinese features. Natives of the Gulf area fall somewhere between these extremes. The communities of what is now eastern Saudi Arabia were not, until recently, as cosmopolitan as the traditional trading centres of Bahrain or Sharjah, though they did have some contact with Iran and India in the century or so before the discovery of oil. Saudis of the south-western Asir region are distinctly Yemeni in appearance and dress.

The expatriate population is quite varied. Every medium-size or larger city has huge contingents of Egyptians, Indians, Pakistanis and Filipinos. In Riyadh and Jeddah there are significant communities of almost every Western, Arab and Asian nationality.

Exactly how many people live in Saudi Arabia is unclear. The government says there are 15 million Saudi citizens, but most private estimates put the figure closer to 12 million, of whom about seven million are thought to be Saudis.

## EDUCATION

The growth of the Saudi educational system over the last two generations has been as striking as the development of the country itself, though at times it has been far from smooth. Virtually every innovation had to be fought for by reformers.

Educating women was even more problematic – the first girls' school was opened in 1956 by the wife of the future King Faisal. Even then it had to be disguised as an orphanage. In September 1963 the news that a girls' school was shortly to open in Buraydah touched off riots there. From these difficult beginnings there has grown a system of free primary and secondary education for all Saudi citizens. By 1985 there were nearly two million children (including almost 800,000 girls) in the Kingdom's primary and secondary schools. There are around 100,000 students in Saudi Arabia's seven universities. Saudi education is strictly segregated at all levels (in some university courses male professors lecture their female students through video systems) and foreign children are not allowed to attend Saudi schools.

Most of the larger foreign communities in the Kingdom (Indian, Pakistani, etc) run schools following their own systems. Children of Western expatriates usually attend American or British-system international schools, or are educated at boarding schools in other countries.

## CULTURE

Possibly the most enduring Western myth about Saudi Arabia is the belief that all Saudis are incredibly rich. It is true that few, if any, Saudis are destitute but there is a great deal of distance between those two extremes.

### Bedouins

The Kingdom has a fairly large population of nomads. They are known as Bedouins, or Bedu, in common parlance, and as camel-nomads in anthropological terms. Because many of them wander freely across international borders in search of forage for their animals, nobody knows how large this population is. They are extremely adaptable. Water may now be carried in plastic containers instead of animal skins and Bedouin families may take radios with them across

the desert, but their essential way of life has hardly changed since the time of the Prophet.

You will see Bedouins everywhere in the Kingdom. Even in Riyadh it is not unusual to see a Bedouin man driving a small Japanese-built pick-up truck, from the back of which his camel is serenely observing the world. Aside from that sort of encounter, the only time you are likely to meet Bedouins is if you happen upon one of their encampments while driving in the desert. Should this happen, it is important that you approach the situation with tact and discretion. Although most Bedouins are hospitable there are some who want nothing to do with foreigners. Do not go marching up to a Bedouin camp uninvited. If the residents want to invite you in for coffee or tea it will be obvious, regardless of any language barrier which may exist. If you are invited into someone's tent follow the guidelines outlined under Taboos & Avoiding Offence, both in this section and in the Facts about the Region chapter. Within reason foreigners' faux pas usually provoke amusement, not anger, among Bedouin hosts.

### Taboos & Avoiding Offence

Saudi Arabia is still one of the most insular societies on earth and a certain degree of tact and discretion is called for, even in big cities.

Dress conservatively. Shorts in public are absolutely out of the question. Women should always cover their shoulders and should not wear clothing that is overly tight or revealing. Take things offered to you with the right, not the left, hand and avoid showing the soles of your feet to people.

Do not attempt to photograph people without their permission. Men should not photograph Saudi women or even ask permission to photograph them, and foreign women should think twice before doing so. Do not take pictures of, or attempt to enter, mosques, as this is strictly forbidden.

When offered coffee or tea in someone's home or at a business meeting, it is considered very impolite to refuse.

Life under Saudi Arabia's strict brand of Islam takes some getting used to. Alcohol and pork are illegal, and so are theatres and cinemas. Women are not allowed to drive and must be accompanied by their husband or a male relative to travel by bus or train (Saudia Airlines domestic services are exempt from this rule). At prayer time all shops must close and even TV programmes are interrupted. The only exceptions are the restaurants in the big hotels. What follows are some notes on a few of the trickier aspects of day-to-day life. See under Women Travellers in the Facts for the Visitor section for information directed specifically at female visitors and residents.

**Alcohol** Booze is illegal in Saudi Arabia which is not to say that it does not exist. Illegal alcohol comes in two varieties: imported and homemade. The former is alcohol (usually whisky) which has either been smuggled in or procured through one of the embassies.

Homemade firewater comes in several varieties. The most common, and the most potent, is *siddiki* (Arabic for 'my friend'), sid for short. This is a very pure distilled spirit, frequently 96 to 98% alcohol when it comes out of the still, at which point it is almost always cut 50-50 with water. *Don't drink it straight.* Even after it has been diluted sid is still very potent. If properly made it has very few impurities so it hits you a lot harder than regular booze. The most common mixer is 7-Up. If improperly made, sid can make you blind or even kill you.

Homemade wine and beer are also common, and almost anyone can tell you how to take the local nonalcoholic beer or grape juice and ferment it.

Only a fool would try to bring alcohol into the country or to move the stuff around. If you get caught, plan on spending a minimum of three months or so in prison. This is flexible and depends a lot on both the nature of your offence and on how badly your sponsor wants to get you out. As with drugs in Western countries, possession is one thing while dealing is another thing entirely. Flogging is also part of the standard punishment, though this is rarely applied to Westerners.

When released from prison you will be deported and blacklisted.

**The Religious Police** Formally known as the Committee for the Propagation of Virtue and the Prevention of Vice, the *matawwa*, or religious police, have a fearsome reputation as a squad of moral vigilantes out to enforce Islamic orthodoxy as they understand it. This is not exactly true. The system of recruiting and training matawwa has become a bit more formal over the years. The religious police are part of the complex system of give-and-take involving liberals and conservatives through which the Al-Saud maintain order in the country.

Matawwa activity tends to come in waves. The clearest sign that one of these waves is sweeping over a city is a shopping centre in which almost every door carries a notice asking women not to enter the premises. For their part, men should bear in mind that Saudi law makes the five daily prayers mandatory for all Muslims. If you are a Muslim, or if the matawwa *think* you are a Muslim, you may be ordered into the nearest mosque on pain of arrest. They have also been known to stop couples in public and demand proof of marriage.

The best way to deal with the matawwa is to steer clear of them. However, if you do find yourself facing an angry-looking religious policeman the first thing to do is to keep calm. The second thing to do is be polite but firm. Above all, do not turn the situation into a confrontation. Afterwards report the incident to your embassy. In recent years most Western embassies have taken to keeping a log of matawwa activity directed against their nationals. These things tend to go in cycles and after enough Saudis and enough embassies have complained to the government the authorities crack down on the matawwa in a given area.

**Ramadan** Ramadan, the month during which Muslims fast from dawn until dusk, is marked throughout the Muslim world but nowhere with as much fervour as in Saudi Arabia. Do not make the mistake of thinking that a Ramadan visit to a place like Egypt has prepared you for Ramadan in the Kingdom. As is the case everywhere in the Muslim world, life in the Kingdom moves more slowly during Ramadan, at least during the day. Non-Muslims must always remember, however, that in Saudi Arabia public observance of the fast is *mandatory*. This is applied very broadly. In an office where there are no Muslim staff, for example, everyone must still forego their morning coffee on the off-chance that a Muslim might enter the room (people in such situations often clear out a desk drawer and keep the coffee cup in there). If you are caught smoking, drinking or eating in public you can be sent to prison, usually until Ramadan is over. That extends to smoking while riding in a car.

## RELIGION
### Islam
Most Saudis are Sunni Muslims who follow the Wahhabi sect of Islam. The country also has a Shiite minority who constitute between five and 10% of the population. Most of the Shiites live in the Eastern Province, where they may account for as much as a third of the population, though there are also small Shiite communities in the Asir region, near the Yemeni border.

No non-Muslim may hold Saudi nationality and the public profession of all other faiths is banned. Non-Muslims may not enter mosques in Saudi Arabia. Non-Muslims are also barred from the area surrounding Mecca (about 25 km from the city in all directions) and may visit only the outskirts of Medina. Although it is not clear what the penalties are for violating, or attempting to violate, these bans are, my advice is to drop any idea of testing the Saudis on this one.

See the Facts about the Region chapter for a more general discussion of Islam.

**Wahhabism** Wahhabism takes its name from Mohammed Bin Abdul Wahhab (1703-92), a preacher and judge from the central Najd. He began to preach in the 1740s in response to what he saw as an ever-increas-

ing lack of respect for Islam among the Bedouin tribes of central Arabia. By the mid-18th century many of the Bedouin tribes were only nominally Muslim and a few are said to have returned to pagan religious practices. Abdul Wahhab preached a return to Islam's origins and traditions as interpreted by the Hanbali school of Islamic jurisprudence. This meant strict adherence to the Koran and the Hadith (accounts of the Prophet's words and actions) as interpreted by Islam's leading scholars.

Wahhabism is a rather austere form of Islam. It frowns on tobacco as well as alcohol and pork, and well into this century tobacco smoking was illegal in what is now central Saudi Arabia. Wahhabis reject such concepts as sainthood and forbid the observance of holidays such as the Prophet's birthday, which most other Muslims celebrate. Even the term Wahhabi makes strict followers of the sect uncomfortable because it appears to exalt Mohammed Bin Abdul Wahhab. Strict Wahhabis prefer the term *muwahidin*, which translates as unitarian, because they profess only the unity of God.

## LANGUAGE
Arabic is the official language of Saudi Arabia. English is the universal language of commerce in the Kingdom and you should have no trouble getting by with it in all of the main cities and towns.

# Facts for the Visitor

## VISAS & EMBASSIES
Visas are very, very difficult to obtain. Saudi Arabia has a well-deserved reputation as one of the hardest places in the world to visit. All persons entering the Kingdom must have a Saudi sponsor – in effect, someone who will vouch for your conduct during your stay in the country. Tourist visas are not available and hotels are unable to sponsor business travellers. Your options consist of visitor's, residence or transit visas and, for Muslims, hajj and umrah visas. Once you are in the

country your sponsor has sole control over everything affecting your visa. Only a Saudi can apply for an entry visa, a visa extension, an exit visa or an exit/re-entry visa. If you need to extend your stay in the country you will have to do it through your sponsor.

From the first of Ramadan each year Saudi embassies in Muslim countries issue only hajj visas until the hajj is over about three months later. There's no longer a ban on issuing visas to people whose passport contains an Israeli stamp, but this could cause you problems with some border guards who may not be aware of the new regulations.

A final note: all official business in Saudi Arabia is conducted according to the Muslim Hejira calendar. Any Gregorian date you see on a document is there solely for the foreign community's convenience. The Hejira calendar is 11 days shorter than the Western calendar, though this can vary by a day either way. A visa valid for a stay of one month is valid for a Hejira month, not a Gregorian month. This means, for example, that if you have a one-month visa and you stay for a month according to the Western calendar you will have overstayed your visa by a day or two – and you will be in trouble.

### Visitor Visas

To obtain a visitor visa (ie, a business visa) you will need a formal invitation telex from the company or Saudi individual sponsoring you. This really means that you need to have your visa number. An 'invitation' is essentially an acknowledgement that your sponsor has obtained a visa on your behalf and that authorisation to issue this visa has been sent to the Saudi embassy in a particular city. At that point all you have to do is appear at the embassy bearing your visa number. If you do not have a visa number do not bother going to the embassy. Visas are filed by number, not name. No number, no visa. If you show up with the number in the morning, you can usually pick up your visa the same afternoon. Visitor visas can be picked up at any Saudi diplomatic mission, though the pick-up site has to be specified when the visa application is filed by the sponsor in the Kingdom.

### Residence Visas

In addition to all the paperwork which your sponsor will have to file in the Kingdom, to obtain a residence visa you have to produce copies of your employment contract and academic or professional qualifications. Then you have to fill out, and have translated into Arabic, several lengthy forms detailing your own and your family's background. You will also have to submit the results of an extremely comprehensive medical examination (the embassy will provide the form for your doctor to fill out), including a blood test which shows you to be HIV negative. It usually takes a couple of months to pull all of this paperwork together at both ends. Eventually your sponsor should inform you of your visa number, against which you can collect an entry visa. This will be converted into a residence visa once you arrive in the country. At that point you will almost certainly have to surrender your passport to your employer and you will be issued with an *iqama*, or residence permit. Residence visas are issued only in your home country or in a country in which you have permanent residence.

### Transit Visas

Transit visas are the only remotely easy option for entry into the Kingdom. Their validity ranges from 24 hours to seven days, depending on the manner in which you are transiting the country. In all cases they must be obtained in advance.

**Airport Transit Visas** The 24 and 48-hour transit visas are for people passing through Saudi airports. These are issued by Saudi embassies after you have shown them your airline tickets and convinced the people at the embassy that when it came to purchasing these tickets you had absolutely no choice other than an overnight transit in Saudi Arabia. If, for example, you are flying Saudia Airlines from Cairo to Nairobi via Jeddah the embassy is going to want to know why you can't take a nonstop EgyptAir or Kenya Airways flight. There is a fairly good chance that your request for a transit visa will be turned down so before buying a plane ticket you should consider carefully whether you really want to run the risk of being trapped in the transit lounge at Riyadh, Jeddah or Dhahran airport for a day or two. If you do get this sort of transit visa you will have to surrender your passport to the immigration authorities at the airport and collect it again on the way out.

**Road Transit Visas** Road transit visas are fairly straightforward. People driving between Jordan and either Kuwait or Yemen are usually issued three-day transit visas. As a general rule these are only issued at the Saudi embassies in Amman (Jordan), Kuwait City and Sana'a (Yemen). You have to go to the embassy with your carnet and proof that you already have a visa for the country at the other end of the road. People driving between Jordan and Bahrain or the UAE often get seven-day transit visas. If you are coming from Oman you will have to pick up the transit visa in Abu Dhabi.

In theory it is possible to hitch a ride on any of these routes, though in practice you probably will not get a transit visa unless you are already attached to a vehicle. So your best bet is to link up with a driver in, say, Amman and apply with that person for the transit visa.

Transit visas for travel between Kuwait and Jordan usually restrict the traveller to transiting the TAPLINE (Trans-Arabian Pipeline) service road. If you have this sort of visa you should banish any thought of getting off the TAPLINE road and heading down to Riyadh for a few days. In the unlikely event that you make it to Riyadh (or Jeddah, or anywhere else) and back to the TAPLINE road without getting caught at one of the numerous checkpoints, you are almost certain to be spotted when trying to leave the country.

**Hajj & Umrah Visas**
For hajj visas there is a quota system of one visa for every 1000 Muslims in a country's population. Exactly how this system is administered varies from country to country

though, as a rule, it is fairly difficult to get a hajj visa outside of your home country.

Umrah visas are issued to any Muslim requesting one. To obtain the visa, you must apply either in your home country or in a country where you hold permanent residence. All you need is to show a round-trip plane ticket to Jeddah. If you are not from a Muslim country or do not have an obviously Muslim name, you will be asked to provide any official document that lists Islam as your religion. Converts to Islam must provide a certificate from the mosque where they went through their conversion ceremony.

Umrah visas are valid for one week and only for travel to Jeddah, Mecca and Medina and on the roads connecting them to one another. If you are travelling by road, they allow you to travel on the road between the holy cities and the border.

**Saudi Embassies**
Some of Saudi Arabia's embassies overseas include:

Australia
    12 Culgoa Circuit, O'Malley, Canberra 2606 ACT (☎ (06) 2862099)
Bahrain
    Al-Jufayr, Manama near the Great Mosque, behind the Al-Hamra Building (☎ 727223)
Iran
    59 Kheyabun-é Bokharest (☎ 624294)
Jordan
    1st Circle, Jebel Amman (☎ 641076)
Qatar
    The main embassy is on the C Ring Rd in Doha (☎ 427144). The Consular Section is on Ali Bin Abi Talib St.
Syria
    Al-Jala'a Ave, Abu Roumaneh (☎ 334914)
UAE
    Karamah St near the intersection with Dalma St, Abu Dhabi (☎ 465700)
UK
    30 Belgrave Square SWIX (☎ (071) 235 0303)
USA
    601 New Hampshire Ave NW, Washington DC, 20037 (☎ (202) 342-3800)

**Visa Extensions**
These must be obtained by your sponsor.

### Exit/Re-Entry Visas

People in the Kingdom on a visitor visa do not need an exit visa to leave the country. Foreigners holding residence permits need exit/re-entry visas to leave and re-enter the Kingdom. A final exit visa is issued to people leaving at the end of a work contract. Both types of visa must be obtained on your behalf by your sponsor.

Generally, exit/re-entry visas for people employed in the Kingdom are good for a single trip and allow you to stay out of the country for two months. Dependents and people whose sponsors submit proof that they need to stay away for more than two months for work-related reasons can get six month exit/re-entry visas. A multiple exit/re-entry visa, usually valid for six months, is issued to workers only in special cases where the sponsor specifically requests it and can show that a need for such a visa exists. They are also sometimes issued to children of people working in the Kingdom where the child is attending school in Bahrain or the UAE.

As with other visas the dates on exit/re-entry visas refer to Hejira, not Gregorian, months. If you have a six month exit/re-entry visa its validity is about a week shorter than it looks according to a Western calendar. On a two month exit/re-entry visa the difference will be one to three days. Do not expect a lot of flexibility from immigration officials at the airport on this score, even if you are only a day late in re-entering the country.

### Foreign Embassies in Saudi Arabia

See the Riyadh and Jeddah sections for listings of embassies and consulates in the country.

## DOCUMENTS

### Travel Letters

Technically, foreigners living in the Kingdom need to have the permission of their sponsor to travel outside of the city in which they reside. In practice this is only enforced for travel between provinces. This permission takes the form of a letter from your sponsor approving your travel plans.

This is handled by a company or a ministry's Government Affairs department which also handles all visa-related paperwork. The maximum validity of a travel letter is one Hejira month.

Foreigners on a visitor visa can travel anywhere in the Kingdom, except Mecca and Medina for non-Muslims, with only their passport. The problem you may encounter is that a lot of the people who ought to be aware of this fact aren't. While researching this book I always had trouble purchasing domestic air tickets because the Saudia counter staff would insist on seeing my nonexistent travel letter. However, the security people at the airport always knew the rules so I never had any trouble actually getting onto a plane. For the same reason people on a visitor visa who make overland trips should expect delays at checkpoints around the country. The guards at the checkpoint often do not know the rules and insist on seeing a travel letter. Don't worry about this. Usually the guards will take your passport to their officer and you will be on your way within five to 10 minutes. Similarly, you can expect a worried look from clerks at small hotels, youth hostels and any hotel outside of a big city when they find out that you have a passport but no travel letter. It is highly unlikely, however, that you will be turned away from a hotel because of this.

### Site Permits

To visit virtually any fort, ruin or archaeological site in the Kingdom you must first obtain a permit. The only exceptions are Dir'aiyah and the Najran fort. Permits for all sites except those in the area between Dammam and Jubail are issued by the Department of Antiquities office at the Riyadh Museum. Permits for all Eastern Province sites except those in and around the Al-Hasa oasis are issued at the Regional Museum of Archaeology & Ethnography in Dammam.

In Riyadh you have to file the application one morning and return a day or two later to collect the permit. In Dammam they can often issue permits the same day provided you arrive before 10 am. Resident foreigners will have to bring along their iqama and, if the site involves a trip to a province other than the one where they live, a travel letter will also be required. People in the country on a visitor visa require only a passport.

Once you get to the place you plan to visit it is often necessary to take the permit to the local branch of the antiquities office. Most of the Kingdom's archaeological sites do not have permanent attendants so this is often the only way to get the gate unlocked. In some places, notably Al-Hasa, you may also have to trek around to a couple of offices to get the permit validated before anyone will open up the site for you. As government officials stop work around 1.30 or 2 pm you have to get an early start.

Note that some Eastern Province sites and the South Dhahran archaeological sites, are in military areas. To visit these you will need a guide arranged by the antiquities authority in charge of permits in that area. This can be complicated and probably ruled out for a lone sightseer.

## CUSTOMS

It is standard procedure for Saudi customs officers to search every bag thoroughly, but the searches are rarely malicious.

The import of anything containing alcohol or pork is strictly forbidden. Customs officers also pay close attention to any books, magazines or photographs you are carrying. Videotapes are often held at the airport for a day or two for screening by censors. Anything deemed pornographic (which, in Saudi Arabia, could include vacation photos of your family and friends at the beach) or politically sensitive may be confiscated.

## MONEY
### Changing Money

Banking hours are generally 8.30 am to noon from Saturday to Thursday. These hours can vary locally by half an hour or so in either direction. Moneychangers are among some of the Kingdom's larger banking operations and often offer slightly better rates than banks, though if you are only changing a few

hundred dollars you are unlikely to notice the difference.

Two of the Kingdom's largest financial houses, the Al-Rajhi Banking & Investment Corporation and the Al-Rajhi Commercial Establishment for Exchange will change only Visa travellers' cheques, not American Express or Thomas Cook. Some banks will not change travellers' cheques at all, some will only change brands they sell. Changing cash is never a problem.

There is not much of a pattern to this, though a few things can be stated with certainty: first, if you are carrying AMEX travellers' cheques head for the nearest branch of the Saudi British Bank as they will always change them. Second, always have with you the original purchase receipt for the cheques, whatever brand they may happen to be, because without it few banks will exchange them. Third, try not to get stranded in the boondocks without money. As you move away from the Jeddah-Riyadh-Dhahran corridor changing money tends to become an increasingly frustrating and time-consuming experience.

### Currency

The Saudi riyal (SR) is divided into 100 halalas. It is a hard currency, and there are no restrictions on taking either riyals or foreign currency into or out of the country. Notes come in SR 1, 5, 10, 50, 100 and 500 denominations. All of the notes except for the SR 500 have King Fahd's picture on the front (the SR 500 note shows King Abdul Aziz), though some older money with King Faisal's picture is still in circulation. The King Faisal-era notes are larger than the current ones and are differently coloured but they are still valid. Coins come in 5, 10, 25 and 50 halala and SR 1 denominations.

### Exchange Rates

The riyal is pegged to the US dollar, so while the US$/SR rate rarely moves by more than a halala or so either side of SR 3.75, the rates against other Western currencies change constantly.

| US$1 | = | SR 3.75 |
|------|---|---------|
| UK£1 | = | SR 5.70 |
| FF1  | = | SR 0.69 |
| DM1  | = | SR 2.36 |
| A$1  | = | SR 2.59 |

## Costs

Saudi Arabia is not a cheap place, but it is possible to travel there relatively cheaply if you put your mind to it. Filling your stomach for SR 15 or less is never a problem. Beds are not quite so cheap, generally bottoming out at SR 55 to SR 90 in hotels. Youth hostels charge only SR 8 per night but can be difficult to reach. It is possible to cross the peninsula for less than SR 200, which is not bad considering that it's about 1600 km by road.

Travelling around the Kingdom can be done on about SR 50 a day, though SR 100 is a more realistic low-budget estimate.

## Tipping

Tips are not generally expected by waiters in Saudi restaurants. The service charge added to your bill is not an automatic tip but goes straight into the till. Most waiters in the Kingdom, even in expensive hotel restaurants, are paid very small salaries and a few extra riyals would certainly be appreciated.

Foreign drivers of the white limousine taxis generally expect a small tip while the Saudis who drive most of the Kingdom's yellow cabs usually do not.

## Bargaining

In Saudi Arabia the price of almost anything is negotiable up to a point. Travel agents, though not the airlines, are almost always willing to knock a few riyals off the initial price they quote you for a ticket. Hotels too will usually offer some sort of discount on the room rate if you ask. You can assume that food prices, in both supermarkets and restaurants, are fixed but most consumer goods are, to some extent, bargainable. Bargaining, however, frequently means asking for a discount and being offered it. After that initial offer the price may not go any lower. In a

Bedouin market or the souks of Najran and Hofuf, more serious bargaining often takes place but the lengthy haggling sessions which are part of the West's mythology of Arabia are largely a thing of the past.

## WHEN TO GO

The best time to visit Saudi Arabia is between November and February when the climate over much of the country is at its mildest. During these months it can be fairly cold at night in desert areas like Riyadh though the weather in Jeddah tends to be wonderful. Sandstorms are, however, always a possibility and there is no way to predict their occurrence.

The Asir mountains are at their best a bit earlier and a bit later than the rest of the country – during the main winter months they are often locked in fog which makes driving dangerous and robs you of the views which are the area's main attraction. Try to visit Taif and Abha in September-October or March-April. During the summer all of the hotels in the mountain areas tend to be booked solid.

If possible, stay away from the Kingdom during Ramadan. If you don't like crowds it would also be a good idea to avoid Jeddah for two or three weeks either side of the hajj.

## WHAT TO BRING

Sunglasses and a hat are absolutely essential. Your clothing should be long and loose. The sun is very intense and people tend to burn quickly in Saudi Arabia so it is a good idea to bring along a thin, long-sleeved garment of some sort, in addition to your sunscreen, especially in July and August.

For the winter months, particularly in desert areas such as Riyadh, Medina and Ha'il, you will want a jumper and a light to medium-weight jacket. The climate in Asir in the winter can be genuinely foul, and warm clothing will definitely be in order.

## TOURIST INFORMATION

Even though Saudi Arabia does not issue tourist visas, tourist information does exist. There is a small but growing tourist industry catering to Saudis, Gulf Arabs (the only people who can get into the Kingdom without a visa) and resident expatriates. This industry exists mostly in and around Abha and Al-Baha and, to a lesser extent, Hofuf. Its services consist of weekend packages, sometimes including tours, run by the larger hotels. Look for ads in the *Arab News* and *Saudi Gazette* announcing promotions at the various hotels and consult the city headings in this chapter for further information.

## BUSINESS HOURS & HOLIDAYS
Banks and shops in Saudi Arabia are open from 8 or 8.30 am until 1 or 1.30 pm from Saturday to Wednesday. Many shops, but not banks, reopen in the afternoon from about 4 to 7 pm, though big shopping centres, particularly in Jeddah and Alkhobar, may stay open until 10 pm. Few businesses are open on Thursday afternoons and almost everything is shut up tightly on Friday.

At prayer time *everything* closes; even Saudia airlines stops answering its telephone numbers for reservations. The only exceptions are the coffee shops in five-star hotels. The length of the prayer break can be anything from 20 to 45 minutes. If you are already inside a restaurant and eating, the staff may let you hang around and finish your meal, or they may throw you out. This usually depends on whether or not the religious police have recently been active in the area. In any event, if they do let you stay in the restaurant they are unlikely to let you leave before the place officially reopens.

Wahhabism is so strict on matters of observance that no holidays other than Eid Al-Fitr and Eid Al-Adha are observed in the Kingdom (for the dates see the table of holidays page 28).

Saudi National Day is 23 September though it is not widely observed.

Much of the country, and virtually the entire government, also tends to shut down for two to three weeks at hajj time each year. People tend to be more preoccupied with the pilgrimage and its logistics the further west you get. In the Eastern Province there is little change in the rhythms of life, whereas in Jeddah, and especially Mecca and Medina, the hajj tends to consume everyone's time for several weeks both before and after the actual week of the pilgrimage.

## CULTURAL EVENTS
The Kingdom's only cultural and folkloric festival, the Jinadriyah National Festival, takes place every year at a special site about 45 km north-east of central Riyadh. See the Riyadh entry for more details.

Some of the larger Western companies occasionally manage to bring in classical musical groups, though you will have to be pretty well connected to the expat grapevine to hear about these.

## POST & TELECOMMUNICATIONS
### Postal Rates
Airmail postage for letters sent to addresses outside the Arab world is SR 1.50 for the first 10 grams and SR 1 for each additional 10 grams. Within Saudi Arabia, to other GCC countries (the countries covered by this book) and to Iraq postage is 50 halalas for the first 20 grams and 50 halalas for each additional 10 grams. It is 75 halalas for the first 10 grams to the rest of the Arab world. Postcard postage is SR 1 outside the Arab world and 50 halalas inside the Kingdom and to other Arab countries.

Small packets (up to one kg) sent by air to destinations outside the Arab world cost SR 6 for the first 100 grams and SR 3.50 for each additional 100 grams. Surface mail rates are SR 3/1.50. The rate for small packets sent by air to addresses inside the Kingdom or in other Arab countries is SR 3/1.75. For surface mail the rates are SR 1.50/0.75.

Up to five kg of printed matter can be sent by airmail for SR 4.50 for the first 100 grams, SR 2.50 for each additional 100 grams. By surface mail the cost is SR 2/0.75. Domestically and to Arab countries the rates are SR 2/1.25 airmail, SR 1/0.50 surface.

Registering a package or letter costs SR 3 internationally and SR 2 inside the Arab world.

## Sending Mail

The lines in Saudi post offices tend to be rather long, especially at the end of the month when many foreign workers are sending their salaries home to their families. Other than that the system is fairly straightforward.

## Receiving Mail

This can be a problem. There is no door-to-door postal service in Saudi Arabia and mail is delivered only to post office boxes. There are no poste-restante facilities and American Express does not hold mail. The best approach is to find a sympathetic friend who will let you get mail through his or her company. Resident expats usually get their mail through their sponsoring company. If you are in the country on a visitor visa your sponsor's address is probably your best bet.

## Telephone

Saudi Arabia has an excellent telecommunications system. Almost every town has a telephone office through which international calls can be made. Some of the telephone offices also offer fax, telex and/or telegraph service. Long-distance calls can also be made from payphones but this requires a lot of SR 1 coins – the payphones are surprisingly antiquated in comparison with the high-tech standards of the rest of the phone system. Moreover, they constantly beep throughout the call, which can get pretty annoying.

USA Direct service is available from pretty much everywhere in the Kingdom except Jizan. The access code is 1-800-100.

The country code for calls to Saudi Arabia is 966. This is followed by an area code for the individual city and the local seven-digit number. The dialling-out code for international calls is 00 followed by the country code, area code and number. To make a long-distance call within the Kingdom dial 0 followed by the area code and number.

## Fax, Telex & Telegraph

In addition to the telephone centres, you can send faxes or telexes from the business centre in the big hotels. This will not be cheap but the service is reasonably efficient.

## TIME

Time in Saudi Arabia is GMT plus three hours. Clocks are not changed for summer time. When it's noon in the Kingdom, the time elsewhere is:

| City | Time |
| --- | --- |
| Paris, Rome | 10 am |
| London | 9 am |
| New York | 4 am |
| Los Angeles | 1 am |
| Perth, Hong Kong | 5 pm |
| Sydney | 7 pm |
| Auckland | 9 pm |

## ELECTRICITY

Both 220 and 110 volts AC are found in various places in the Kingdom, though the latter is the more common of the two.

## LAUNDRY

There are no laundromats in Saudi Arabia. You can either do your washing in the hotel sink or send it to the hotel laundry.

## WEIGHTS & MEASURES

The metric system is used in Saudi Arabia.

## BOOKS & MAPS

### People & Society

C M Doughty's *Travels in Arabia Deserta* (Dover Books, 1888) is the grand-daddy of modern Arabian travel literature. If you don't feel like ploughing through its 1400 pages, Penguin publishes an abridged version. Doughty's writing inspired, among others, T E Lawrence whose *Seven Pillars of Wisdom* (1926, Penguin paperback) is both a classic of modern literature and an extraordinarily self-serving account of the Arab revolt in Hejaz and Trans-Jordan during WW I. *Revolt in the Desert*, also by Lawrence, is a shortened version of Seven Pillars. The troika of 20th century Arabian travel classics is completed by Wilfred Thesiger's *Arabian Sands* (1959, Penguin paperback) in which he recounts his two journeys across the Empty Quarter in the late 1940s. *Fool's Paradise* by Dale Walker (Vintage Books, New York, 1988) is an interesting description of travel in modern Saudi Arabia.

*The Merchants* by Michael Field (Overlook Press, Woodstock NY, 1985) includes an interesting chapter on the Alirezas, one of the Hejaz's most prominent merchant families. In a similar vein you might also want to look for *At the Drop of a Veil* by Marianne Alireza (Houghton Mifflin, Boston, 1971), a Californian who married into the Jeddah-based merchant family in the 1940s.

*The Kingdom of Saudi Arabia* is a Ministry of Information-sponsored coffee-table book packed with wonderful photographs.

### History

The best work on modern Saudi Arabia is Robert Lacey's *The Kingdom* (Avon, New York, 1981). *The House of Saud* by David Holden & Richard Johns (Pan, London & Sydney, 1981) focuses on the royal family and is also interesting. Peter Mansfield's *The New Arabians* (Ferguson, Chicago, 1981) contains a shorter and slightly more propagandist history of the country.

### Travel Guides

There are very few travel guides to Saudi Arabia on the market. Berlitz publishes a pocket guide to the country, though this is often outdated and of rather limited use. *The Economist Business Traveller's Guides – Arabian Peninsula* is the best among the many how-to-do-business-with-the-Arabs sort of books on the market.

### Bookshops

The selection of English-language books available in the Kingdom tends to be rather thin. Hotel bookshops and a few bookshops in the Kingdom's larger cities tend to stock mostly spy novels, a bit of pulp fiction and a few classics, often Dickens and Hemingway.

### Maps

The best maps of Saudi Arabia are those drawn by Zaki Mohammed Ali Farsi, commonly known as the Farsi Maps. They are available at most bookshops and hotels in the Kingdom for about SR 20 each. The series includes city maps of Riyadh, Jeddah, the Eastern Province (Dammam/Alkhobar), Abha & Khamis, Taif, Mecca and Medina. There is also a road map covering the entire country. The Riyadh, Jeddah and Mecca city maps and the national map are also available in the form of 'A to Z' atlases, each of which is about the size of a phone book. Most of the other professionally drawn maps of the country, including both the Bartholomew and Oxford maps, are hopelessly out of date.

## MEDIA

### Newspapers & Magazines

The *Arab News*, *Saudi Gazette* and *Riyadh Daily* are the country's English-language newspapers. *Arab News* is the largest and most widely read and is particularly interesting for its 'Islam in Perspective' column in which a leading Saudi religious scholar answers readers' questions about Islamic beliefs and practices. All of these papers tend to have fairly good foreign news coverage.

Major foreign newspapers and magazines are widely available in the Kingdom's main cities, usually at the big hotels and the large,

Western-style supermarkets. Periodicals usually appear two or three days after publication, by which time they have received a very thorough going-over by Saudi censors. Scantily clad women are made modest with black-magic marker. Advertisements for alcoholic beverages and articles which are regarded as politically sensitive (which includes almost anything dealing with Saudi Arabia) are ripped out of each and every copy on sale. Before buying a foreign publication you might want to flip through it quickly to see how much has been removed.

### Radio & TV

Channel 2 of Saudi Arabian TV broadcasts exclusively in English, except for a French-language newscast every night at 8 pm. The programmes are a mixture of old and heavily edited American shows and locally made documentaries and talk shows. The news in English is broadcast every night at 9 pm.

In the Eastern Province your TV choices are wider. Channel 3 is ARAMCO's television station. It tends to be a more up-to-date version of Channel 2 (ie, American programmes from about two years ago instead of 10 years ago). They also broadcast a lot of American sports. Viewers in the Dammam-Alkhobar area can also usually pick up the English-language stations from Bahrain (one channel carrying CNN during the day and entertainment programmes in the evening, and an all-news channel carrying BBC World Service TV 24 hours a day), Qatar and, if the weather is good, Abu Dhabi.

Radio broadcasts in any language other than Arabic are rarer. In the Eastern Province Radio Bahrain (98.5 FM) comes in fairly clearly. ARAMCO also has a station that broadcasts mostly country & western music. Everywhere else in the country you will have to stick to short-wave frequencies.

### FILM & PHOTOGRAPHY

What used to be the rule of thumb for Eastern bloc travel is still a good guide in the Kingdom: never point your camera at anything you might feel inclined to bomb, blow up or shoot at during a war.

In Saudi Arabia this always extends to mosques and includes archaeological sites, though in the latter case it is not enforced with any degree of uniformity. You should never go wandering through a souk or a Bedouin market with a camera around your neck. Keep it out of sight in a bag and ask permission before you start snapping.

Film is easy to find in the Kingdom's main cities, but check that it has not passed its expiry date. There are numerous shops specialising in one or two-hour photo processing, but most of these places can only handle colour prints. Slides or B&W film tend to take a lot longer, sometimes a week or more, and the results are often less than satisfactory.

### HEALTH

The standard of health care in Saudi Arabia is very high and almost any ailment can be treated inside the country. Many diseases which were once endemic, such as malaria, are now virtually unknown in the Kingdom. Though a cholera shot and a gamma globulin booster might not be a bad idea if you are planning to spend a lot of time far off the beaten track, there are no special precautions which need to be taken before visiting Saudi Arabia.

Health care in the Kingdom is organised through one's sponsor. Saudi law requires that employers provide comprehensive health coverage for all of their employees, and if you are working in the Kingdom your company will probably have a standing relationship with a particular hospital or clinic to which you will be referred for treatment. Visitors in need of medical attention should contact their sponsor. At a pinch, most big hotels have a doctor on call.

There are occasional outbreaks of diseases, such as meningitis, because of the extremely crowded conditions at the hajj. It is something which you should be aware of but should not worry about.

The quality of drinking water varies greatly in the Kingdom. Even in Riyadh and Jeddah it may be necessary to obtain 'sweet water' for drinking and cooking from a central source. This varies even from neighbourhood to neighbourhood within a given city. On the whole you should probably stick to bottled water.

See the Facts about the Region chapter for a more general discussion of health in the Gulf.

## WOMEN TRAVELLERS

Men and women are strictly segregated in Saudi society and the trend over the last few years has been toward increasingly rigorous enforcement of this rule.

Restaurants usually have a family section where women, whether accompanied or not, must sit. Restaurants which do not have a family section often will not serve women, and there has been a trend in recent years to bar women entirely from some smaller shops and fast-food outlets. This varies from place to place and enforcement is generally much tighter when a particular city is experiencing a lot of matawwa activity. It does, however, work both ways. Some shops specialising in women's clothing are off limits to men. Museums and some shops have special women-only hours and banks catering only to female customers are becoming increasingly common.

Municipal buses have separate sections for women – at the back, screened off from the rest of the bus. Unaccompanied women cannot travel by inter-city bus or train and some taxi companies will not give them rides. A woman leaving the country usually has to be accompanied to the airport by her husband even if he is not travelling. Unmarried female expatriates are usually driven to the airport by a company representative carrying a letter authorising their departure. Domestic travel by air requires a letter from one's sponsor for female expatriates. No special documents are necessary for women in the country on a visitor visa but unaccompanied female visitors are still unusual enough that you can expect delays at the airport security checkpoints.

An unaccompanied woman cannot check into a hotel without a letter from her sponsor,

and it would probably also be a good idea for the sponsor to contact the hotel in advance.

The dress regulations for women are not nearly as fearsome as has sometimes been portrayed. Skirts above the knee and tight pants are out, but it is not necessary for a foreign woman to wear the *abayya* (a long, black cloak-like garment) and a floor-length skirt, though in places where the matawwa are particularly active it might be a good idea. In the main cities (Riyadh, Jeddah and Dhahran/Alkhobar) and in smaller places which either have, or see a lot of, foreigners (Jubail, Yanbu, Taif, Abha, Hofuf) there is no need for foreign women to cover their heads, let alone wear a veil. In more remote or conservative areas (Jizan, Ha'il, Najran) it is advisable for foreign women to cover their heads. The only place where I have ever heard of foreign women having to wear veils is Buraydah.

Women who are, or appear to be, of Arab descent are likely to be held to far tighter standards of dress than Western or Asian women, especially outside of the main cities.

Reports of sexual harassment vary widely but leers and obscene comments, usually in Arabic, seem to be fairly common. Women in closed public spaces, like aeroplanes, should expect rather a lot of this sort of thing. Though men will stare they are less likely to touch. The general atmosphere of harassment is less intense than in places like Egypt, Tunisia or Morocco. This works both ways as for every Saudi man who looks on you as a sex object there is another who is genuinely alarmed by the thought of even being in the same room with you.

In general it is best to remain stoical in the face of comments and to shout at, not punch, anyone who gropes you. The social opprobrium that comes from having touched a woman in public is one of your most effective weapons in these situations.

## DANGERS & ANNOYANCES

Saudi Arabia is a very safe country and street crime is almost unknown. The main thing that you will have to worry about is the rather frightening way that people drive. As a rule the driving gets crazier as one moves further west in the country.

Men, particularly younger men, should be prepared for a certain amount of sexual harassment from other men. It is not uncommon to be propositioned in a restaurant or followed around by someone.

## ACTIVITIES

Desert drives, or wadi bashing, are popular throughout the country and it is usually fairly easy to find someone in the local expat community who can give you advice on where to go for a picnic in the desert. Water sports are less common, largely because most Western beach wear is considered unacceptable in the Kingdom.

### Language Courses

It is possible to study Arabic while living or working in the Kingdom, but you have to look hard for courses. The few schools which offer Arabic classes often have to scrape around to get enough students. See the Riyadh and Jeddah headings for listings.

### HIGHLIGHTS

Visitors to Riyadh should not miss the museum and, if at all possible, should find a few hours for a trip to Dir'aiyah. In Jeddah the main attractions are the old city and its souks, particularly the Souk Al-Alawi. People with an extra few days should head either south-west for Abha and the Asir National Park or north-west for a look at the spectacular ruins of Madain Salah. In the Eastern Province try to visit the ARAMCO exhibit in Dhahran.

## ACCOMMODATION

Places to stay range from youth hostels to five-star hotels. No matter how cheap the hotel you can count on it having air-conditioning, although a few of the cheaper places in the mountains have ceiling fans.

Saudi law requires the presentation of proper documents to check in at any hotel or hostel. For visitors this means a passport. Expatriates will require their iqama and a travel letter from their sponsor. Small hotels

and youth hostels often will ask you to go out and make a photocopy of these documents if you did not arrive with xeroxes in hand. People with a visitor visa will need xeroxes of the first page of the passport and of the entry visa. Expatriates should have a copy of the page of the iqama that has the photograph on it and a copy of the travel letter. Large hotels will do this for you. Women travelling alone need a letter from their sponsor to check into any hotel, and it is usually a good idea for the sponsor to contact the hotel in advance to double-check the arrangements.

### Camping

The only formal camping grounds in Saudi Arabia are those in the Asir National Park. Sites in the park are allocated on a first come, first served basis. Camping in the desert is also popular. This should never be attempted alone or without proper equipment. The best idea is to look for travelling companions who are already experienced desert campers and accompany them.

### Hostels

Saudi Arabia's youth hostels (*bayt ash-shabab* in Arabic) are a treat. They are almost always spotless, rarely crowded and are among the best in the world. In a number of the Kingdom's hostels a single or double room with a private bath is standard. Stays are limited to three nights at any particular hostel, though the management tends to be flexible about this. Unfortunately, the hostels are often located at the local stadiums and are miles from anywhere. It is not always possible to get from the airport or bus station to the hostel by public transportation.

Saudi Arabia is an IYHF member and hostel cards are always required. Foreigners can purchase cards for SR 30 per year. This can be done at any hostel but the process is a lot smoother in Riyadh, Dammam and Jeddah than anywhere else. In addition to the fee you will need two passport-sized photographs, a copy of your passport or iqama and, for residents, a letter from your employer. The Saudi Arabian Youth Hostels Federation Handbook is available for free at all of the bigger hostels and many of the smaller ones. It contains complete listings of the Kingdom's 19 hostels and their facilities.

## Hotels

Hotels usually bottom out at about SR 50 for a single without bath and around SR 70 for rooms with private bath. What you get for this price varies wildly. Always look at the room before saying yes. Bargaining over the price is usually, though not always, an option. A lot will depend on how full the hotel is at the time. The rule of thumb seems to be that the more the room costs the better your chances are of getting a discount. In any event you should always have a clear understanding with the management of what the room rate is before you say yes.

The major international hotel chains are amply represented in the Kingdom. Singles/doubles in four and five-star hotels cost between SR 200/300 and SR 350/450. Some big hotels, the Abha Inter-Continental for example, have quite good weekend packages on Wednesday and Thursday nights.

## FOOD

Eating cheaply in Saudi Arabia usually means eating either Western-style fast food or Indian food served in rather dingy surroundings. Outside the main cities grilled chicken and *foul* (a fava beans dish) are the most common cheap dishes. For a quick, and very cheap, meal try shawarma. They usually cost SR 3 each and two of them and a drink can keep you going for most of the afternoon.

For more up-market dining, every big city has a selection of moderately priced Oriental restaurants. Filipino and Thai food are the cheapest whereas Chinese food tends to be the most expensive. This is because there are many more low-paid Filipino and Thai workers than Chinese in the Kingdom. Thus, Chinese food has largely become an up-market business catering to well-off Saudis and expats. The bigger cities also have a selection of up-market Lebanese, Indian and Western eateries.

Traditional coffee houses, in which every-one drinks tea, not coffee, are becoming rarer. There are a few in Jeddah and in some of the provincial cities but most have yielded to Western-style cafes situated in shopping malls.

## DRINKS

The selection consists of soft drinks, mineral water and fruit juice. Saudi 'Champagne', which you will sometimes see on menus and which can generally be ordered by name, is a mixture of apple juice and Perrier.

## ENTERTAINMENT

Almost every form of public entertainment is banned in Saudi Arabia. This includes cinemas, theatres and even lounge singers in hotel restaurants. The exceptions are sporting events and a big folkloric festival near Riyadh each year. Soccer and camel racing are the most popular. Unless you read Arabic it is very difficult to keep up with the soccer scene in the Kingdom because the English-language newspapers tend to ignore it. The games are played at the local stadiums and tickets tend to be fairly cheap (around SR 10), though you'll need to have some Arab friends to know when the matches are scheduled to take place. Camel races take place throughout the winter months. The best place to see them is in Riyadh, where there is a large camel track just outside the city centre.

## THINGS TO BUY

Among the best buys in the Kingdom is silver Bedouin jewellery. Although this is a Yemeni speciality, you can find a really good selection in the souks of Abha, Khamis Mushayt and Najran. Bedouin jewellery is wonderful and one should take one's time shopping around for good pieces. Expect to pay anywhere from SR 100 to SR 700, depending on size and the intricacy of the work, for pieces in good condition.

Gold jewellery is also good to buy as the work can be quite striking and the pieces are relatively inexpensive.

If you have a lot of space in your luggage woven Bedouin bags make great souvenirs. Prices, after bargaining, range from SR 50 to

SR 1000, again depending on the size and the quality of the work. The best place to look for weavings is the Hofuf souk or the weekly camel market in Nuraiyah, though you should be aware that as more and more foreigners are now visiting the Hofuf souk the merchants there have taken to importing mass-produced weavings from Syria to keep up with demand.

Most of the other Arabian souvenirs you will see in shops around the Kingdom – incense burners, for example – come from somewhere else, usually Pakistan.

# Getting There & Away

## AIR

A return plane ticket from the USA to Saudi Arabia is likely to cost over US$1000, even if purchased from a bucket shop. From Europe it is not a lot cheaper. Flying out of Saudi Arabia to North America, Europe and the Far East is usually much cheaper. Fares fluctuate wildly, and cheap fares are usually available only through travel agents, not the airlines.

Youth/student fares are often available for international travel out of the Kingdom but they are rarely, if ever, the cheapest way to fly. Don't count on the travel agent to tell you this. If you ask for a youth fare (the cut-off age is usually 26) without mentioning other options, most of the Kingdom's travel agents will simply quote a price and will not point out the cheaper fares, if they exist.

## LAND

### To/From Bahrain

There are five buses per day between Bahrain and Dammam/Alkhobar. The trip takes about three hours and costs SR 40. See the Dammam section for more details.

### To/From Egypt

There are daily bus services from Riyadh, Jeddah and Dammam to Cairo via Aqaba, Jordan. From Riyadh the trip to Cairo takes 36 to 40 hours and costs SR 400. Jeddah-

Cairo costs SR 345 and takes about 36 hours. From Dammam the trip takes about 48 hours and costs SR 480. All of these prices include the ferry crossing between Jordan and Egypt.

From Cairo, all the buses to Saudi Arabia leave from the Alexandria Bank building on Kasr El-Nil St. One-way tickets are E£220 to Riyadh, E£200 to Jeddah and E£270 to Dammam. These can be obtained from Marrakech Travel (☎ 3546046) at the corner of Tahrir St and Tahrir Square in Cairo.

See the Riyadh, Jeddah and Dammam sections for more details.

### To/From Jordan & Syria

If you want to go to Amman or Damascus by bus from Riyadh your only option for the moment is to buy a ticket to Aqaba (on one of the Cairo-bound buses) and change there to Jordan's JETT buses.

From Jeddah, SAPTCO, the Saudi Public Transport Company, has direct services several times a week to both Amman (20 hours, SR 225) and Damascus (30 hours, SR 250). You can also travel to Jordan and Syria on the Istanbul-bound buses run by the Turkish companies. They offer slightly cheaper fares than SAPTCO to Amman, but not to Damascus.

From Dammam SAPTCO has a service to Damascus (SR 250) and Amman (SR 250) three times per week. The trip takes about two days.

See the Riyadh, Jeddah and Dammam sections for more details.

### To/From Turkey

Service between Riyadh and Istanbul is a lot less frequent than it used to be. At the time of writing only SAPTCO was operating services between Riyadh and Turkey. The fare is SR 550 to Istanbul, SR 500 to Ankara. SAPTCO says it takes only 48 hours to get from Riyadh to Istanbul, but I would recommend that you take that claim with a very large pinch of salt. Several Turkish bus companies offer service three times a week from Jeddah to Istanbul for SR 300 and claim a rather more believable journey time of 72 hours. The buses travel via Ankara (60 hours,

SR 275). See the Riyadh and Jeddah sections for more details.

## To/From the UAE

SAPTCO runs buses between Dammam and Abu Dhabi (six to nine hours, SR 240) three times per week. See the Dammam section for more details.

## SEA
## To/From Egypt

The car ferry connecting Jeddah with Suez is the main seaborne route in and out of the country. The trip takes about 36 hours if the boat travels directly between Suez and Jeddah and about three days if it stops in Aqaba, Jordan. Unfortunately you cannot always count on being accurately informed of the route the boat is taking. The food on these boats is pretty dreadful so you might want to bring your own (enough to last for the longer trip). The trip is very long and very dull, and the heat and humidity on the Red Sea can become fierce. See the Getting There & Away section in Jeddah for details.

## To/From Jordan

Boat service to Aqaba, at the south-west corner of Jordan, is less frequent than service to Suez. You might be better advised to take the bus. The shipping agencies along Al-Mina'a St in Jeddah which sell tickets to Egypt and Sudan also sell tickets to Aqaba. See the Jeddah section for more details.

## To/From Sudan

Regular passenger shipping services operate between Jeddah and Port Sudan. If you try this be sure that your visa allows it – many Sudanese visas issued to foreigners now come stamped 'By Air Only', and Sudanese customs officials are not flexible in such matters. Once in Port Sudan you will have to register with the security police and obtain a travel permit to continue on to Khartoum or anywhere else. This process usually takes at least several days. For details see the Jeddah Getting There & Away section.

## LEAVING SAUDI ARABIA

Departing from the Kingdom through Riyadh, Jeddah, Dhahran or Medina airports is fairly straightforward. You should be at the airport two hours before the scheduled departure time. Flights to India, Pakistan and Egypt tend to be filled with workers who are taking home small mountains of electronic goods and presents. Check-in procedures for these routes tend to be very slow, mostly because of the time needed to figure out everybody's excess luggage bills, so it might be a good idea to arrive even earlier.

On flights to London and New York at Christmas time, and to Cairo year-round, Saudia and EgyptAir often require that passengers obtain their boarding passes three days in advance, presumably to prevent overbooking. Check with the airline to see whether this rule is still in force. In any event always reconfirm your flight.

### Departure Tax

There is no departure tax for international flights leaving Saudi Arabia.

# Getting Around

## AIR

All domestic air services in the Kingdom are operated by Saudia (Saudi Arabian Airlines), which is quite reliable. The most frequent and efficient service is on the Jeddah-Riyadh-Dhahran corridor.

Because of the size of the country air travel is the main mode of transport. Considering the distances involved, Saudia's domestic services, though no great bargain, are reasonably priced. There are, however, a few quirks in the system. There are no flights, for example, between Abha, Jizan and Najran, the three main towns in the south-west. Flying between these cities involves backtracking to Jeddah which is both expensive and time-consuming.

Following is a table of fares between the Kingdom's main cities. All of the fares shown are one-way economy class and are

**Airfares**

| | Riyadh | Jeddah | Dhahran | Medina | Ha'il | Taif | Abha | Jizan | Najran |
|---|---|---|---|---|---|---|---|---|---|
| Riyadh | | 240 | 120 | 210 | 170 | 210 | 240 | 280 | 240 |
| Jeddah | 240 | | 360 | 110 | 210 | 90 | 160 | 170 | 210 |
| Dhahran | 120 | 360 | | 330 | 290 | 330 | 360 | 400 | 360 |
| Medina | 210 | 110 | 330 | | 120 | 140 | 270 | 280 | 320 |
| Ha'il | 170 | 210 | 290 | 120 | | 380 | *370 | 450 | 410 |
| Taif | 210 | 90 | 330 | 140 | 380 | | 120 | *260 | *300 |
| Abha | 240 | 160 | 360 | 270 | *370 | 120 | | *330 | *370 |
| Jizan | 280 | 170 | 400 | 280 | 450 | *260 | *33 | | *380 |
| Najran | 240 | 210 | 360 | 320 | 410 | *300 | *370 | *380 | |

quoted in Saudi riyals. Round-trip fares are double the one-way fare. A '*' next to the fare indicates that there is no direct connection and that you will have to change planes in Jeddah.

## BUS

Getting around by bus is probably your best bet if you are not pressed for time and do not have a car. Bus fares are one-half to two-thirds of the equivalent airfare. In Asir, where there are few flights between the main towns and flying often requires going back to Jeddah, the bus will probably be just as quick and the fare may be only about 20% of what a flight would cost. The view is also likely to be a lot better.

Buses are operated by SAPTCO, which has comfortable, air-conditioned buses that usually run on time. On longer routes the buses have an on-board toilet and in all cases the buses make rest stops every couple of hours.

You can buy bus tickets only on the day of departure or one day in advance. There are no seat reservations but when you purchase a ticket your name will be added to a passenger list for the specific bus you request. This ensures that the buses do not get overbooked. When purchasing tickets you will also have to show identification and, for residents, a travel letter.

Women are not allowed to ride inter-city buses unless they are accompanied by their husband or a male relative.

## TRAIN

Saudi Arabia has the only stretch of railway track in the entire Arabian peninsula – one line from Riyadh to Dammam, via Hofuf and Abqaiq. Trains leave twice a day in each direction every day except Thursday. The schedule is:

**From Riyadh**

| | | |
|---|---|---|
| departs Riyadh | 7.51 am | 4.20 pm |
| departs Hofuf | 10.25 am | 6.55 pm |
| departs Abqaiq | 11.08 am | 7.38 pm |
| arrives Dammam | 11.51 am | 8.21 pm |

**From Dammam**

| | | |
|---|---|---|
| departs Dammam | 7.30 am | 4 pm |
| departs Abqaiq | 8.15 am | 4.45 pm |
| departs Hofuf | 9 am | 5.30 pm |
| arrives Riyadh | 11.30 am | 8 pm |

## Classes

Saudi trains have both 1st and 2nd-class carriages. There is also a restaurant car. Sandwiches, coffee, tea and soft drinks can be purchased from vendors in the passenger section.

## Reservations

The trains are not very crowded but it still pays to buy your ticket a day or so in advance, or in the morning for the afternoon train. The process of scrutinising people's IDs both when tickets are purchased and when going through security before boarding can be a bit slow. Also note that the ticket windows in the stations close at prayer time, meaning you'll have to get the ticket early if departure and prayer times coincide.

## Costs

At SR 60 one-way, a 1st-class train ticket between Riyadh and Dammam costs the same as the bus and delivers a much more comfortable ride. At SR 40 one-way, a 2nd-class ticket is the cheapest way to travel between Riyadh and the Eastern Province.

## TAXI

Service taxis usually cluster around the bus station in each city and cover most of the destinations the buses go to at the same prices. They leave when full, which could mean anything from five to 11 passengers, depending on the size of the vehicle.

## CAR & MOTORBIKE

Despite its large public transport system, Saudi Arabia remains a country which glorifies the private car to an extent rivalled only by the USA. It is possible to get around in a Saudi city without your own wheels but it's a real pain in the neck, especially in Riyadh. Even if you save money by taking buses between cities there is a lot to be said for renting a car at each destination.

Motorcycles are a fairly rare sight on Saudi roads.

## Road Rules

Saudi Arabia's most famous rule of the road is the one which says that women are not allowed to drive. Aside from that, however, there is nothing particularly surprising. Driving is on the right side of the road. Right turns are allowed at red lights unless specifically forbidden. Indeed, if you don't plan to turn right, get over into one of the left lanes or someone is likely to come up behind you and lean on his horn until you move. The speed limit is usually 120 km per hour on open highways, and 50 or 60 km per hour in towns. While citations for speeding are rare, be aware that they also involve a night in jail.

## Rental

If you are in the country on a visitor visa you can rent a car on a driving license from most Western countries. Licenses from other GCC countries are only accepted from GCC nationals and people who can show that they live in the country that issued the license.

Rental rates are government controlled with insurance and the collision-damage waiver mandatory. In addition, all companies seem to rent the same line of cars so there's not much point in shopping around. If you are going to be taking the car to different parts of the country it is a good idea to stick to the larger agencies. If you get into trouble or decide to drop the car off early, a company with offices around the Kingdom can prove much more useful than a small, local agency.

Rates start at SR 110 for a Toyota Corolla or similar. That includes insurance and 100 free km per day. Additional km are 40 halalas each. A discount of 20, 25 or 30% on this price is almost always available for the asking, and since it has usually been agreed on among the rental companies shopping around for discounts is about as pointless as shopping around for rates.

Motorcycles and 4WD vehicles are difficult, if not impossible, to rent.

## Purchase

Expats usually buy cars from other expats, if only to save time on the paperwork. Company cars are still a fairly standard perk for most foreigners in the Kingdom, language teachers excepted.

## BICYCLE

Bicycles, like motorcycles, are a rare sight in the Kingdom.

## HITCHING

Hitching is common in the Kingdom among less well-off Saudis and among Indians, Pakistanis, Filipinos, etc. It is rare enough among Westerners that anyone trying it would be likely to attract the unwelcome attention of the first policeman who happened by. In the Hejaz and Asir regions, hitchers are usually expected to pay the equivalent of the bus fare along the same route.

## WALKING

Saudi Arabia is a car-oriented society. Distances within cities are long and walking can be considered downright weird. I was once questioned by the police for taking a stroll around the neighbourhood where I was living at the time. In any case the heat makes walking any significant distance a chore during most of the year.

## BOAT

There are no domestic boat services along either the Gulf or the Red Sea coasts.

## LOCAL TRANSPORT

### To/From the Airport

Getting to the airport in a Saudi city is not always straightforward. In Riyadh there are no buses, only very expensive taxis. In Jeddah only one of the airport's two terminals is served by bus. In Dhahran buses run to the airport frequently, though when the new Dhahran airport opens this may not be the case. See the individual city entries for more information.

### Bus

Full-scale municipal bus systems operate in Riyadh, Jeddah and the Dammam-Alkhobar area of the Eastern Province. Smaller scale local services operate in cities like Taif and Abha. Local fares are always SR 2. Riyadh and Jeddah also have confusing mini-van systems which operate more or less along the main SAPTCO bus routes. These also charge SR 2 per trip.

### Taxi

Taxis in the Kingdom's main cities have no meters, and because things are so spread out the rides tend to get fairly expensive.

## TOURS

A few of the big hotels in Abha and Hofuf organise city tours and the Medina Sheraton runs a very popular weekend tour to Madain

Salah and the Hejaz Railway. See the relevant city sections for more details.

# Riyadh

Riyadh (Riyad, Riad, Ar-Riyadh) rises from the desert like a high-tech oasis of glass, steel and concrete. There are freeways, office towers, housing which stretches off beyond the horizon, big hotels, bigger hospitals and the biggest airport in the world – none of which was here 25 years ago.

While Riyadh, and the nearby oasis town of Dir'aiyah, are the ancestral home of the Al-Saud family, it is only in the last generation that Riyadh has become the centre of government in the Kingdom. Though technically Saudi Arabia's capital since the nation's establishment in 1932, it was eclipsed by Jeddah until quite recently. The ministries, embassies and just about everything else were headquartered in Jeddah well into the 1970s.

## History

Riyadh became the Al-Saud's capital after 1818 when the family was driven out of Dir'aiyah by soldiers loyal to the Ottoman sultan. The village was not part of the family's ancestral territory but it had fallen under their control in the mid-18th century, as the First Saudi Empire was being built. After making Riyadh their capital, the Al-Saud spent most of the 19th century using it as a base for a seemingly endless series of tribal wars, most notably with the Al-Rashid clan, whose base was the northern city of Ha'il. In 1891 the Al-Saud were forced to abandon the city to the Al-Rashid and wandered for a time along the edges of the Empty Quarter before migrating north to seek refuge in Kuwait.

It was from Kuwait that the young Abdul Aziz launched his now famous raid on the family capital, beginning the string of conquests which would eventually restore the Al-Saud as masters of most of the Arabian peninsula. Between Abdul Aziz's conquest

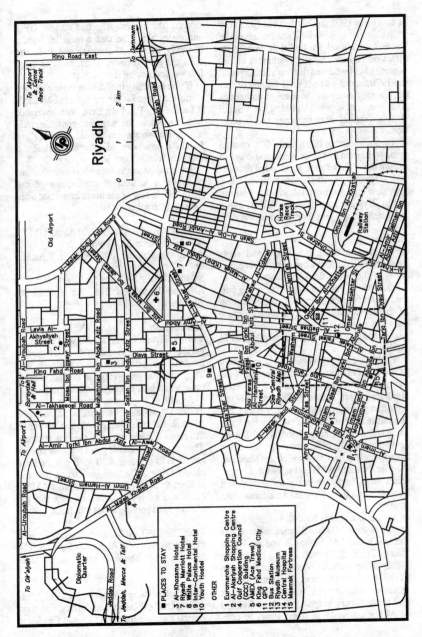

# Riyadh

To Airport & Camel Race Track

Ring Road East

To Dammam

Old Airport

Makkah Road

Salah Al-Din Al-Ayubi Road

Al-Malek (King) Abdul Aziz Road

Al-Ma'ther Street

Al-Malek Abdul Aziz Road

Horse Race Track

Railway Station

Omar Ibn Al-Khattab

Omar Al-Mokhtar St.

Al-Amir Ibn Al-Salman Ibn Abdul Aziz

Al-Dhahran St.

Al-Jamiah Street

Al-Amir Abdul

Al-Amir Amin

Al-Bathaa Street

Al-Amir Mohammad Ibn Abdul Aziz Road

Layla Al-Akhyaliyah Street

Moss Ibn Nosayr Street

Olaya Street

Al-Urubah Road

King Fahd Road

To Buraydah & Hail

Al-Takhassosi Road

Al-Amir Soltan Ibn Abdul Aziz Street

Al-Amir Torki Ibn Abdul Aziz

Al-Awal Road

Al-Ihsa Street

Abu Feras Street

Al-Amir Faisal Ibn Torki Ibn Abdul Aziz Street

Al-Ahsa Street

See Central Riyadh Map

Al-Washem Street

Al-Amir Al-Darei

Faisal Street

Al-Imam Turki Ibn Abdul

Al-Malek Said Street

Amro Ibn Al-As Street

Al-Imam Faisal

King Abdul Aziz Road

Al-Imam Torki Ibn Abdul

Al-Imam Mohammed

To Airport

Al-Urubah Road

Umm Al-Hamm Street

Makkah Road

Al-Malek Khalid Road

Diplomatic Quarter

To Dir'aiyah

To Jeddah, Mecca & Taif

Jeddah Road

0   1   2 km

**PLACES TO STAY**

3   Al-Khozama Hotel
7   Riyadh Marriott Hotel
8   White Palace Hotel
9   Inter-Continental Hotel
10  Youth Hostel

**OTHER**

1   Euromarche Shopping Centre
2   Al-Akariyeh Shopping Centre
4   Gulf Cooperation Council (GCC) Building
5   AMEX (Ace Travel)
6   King Fahd Medical City
11  GPO
12  Bus Station
13  Riyadh Museum
14  Central Hospital
15  Masmak Fortress

of the city in 1902 and his death in 1953 very little changed in Riyadh. Even the advent of Saudi Arabia's oil era had little immediate effect on Riyadh. Most government affairs continued to be carried out from Jeddah until the 1970s and it was not until the end of that decade that many of the foreign embassies finally moved to what had long been Saudi Arabia's capital more on paper than in practice.

Throughout the 1950s and '60s, change came to Riyadh in a slow, measured way but during the '70s the pace accelerated dramatically. Even by Gulf standards Riyadh is a very new city – almost nothing that you can see in Riyadh today predates WW II and a great deal of it is less than 20 years old.

### Orientation

In addition to being brand-new and spotlessly clean Riyadh is a big, spread-out mess. Most of the street signs are written only in Arabic, and if you can read Arabic you will find that most of the city, with the exception of the Al-Bathaa district, is actually quite easy to navigate. Unfortunately, most of the usable maps of the city are available only in Arabic.

The first thing you should do is get a copy of the Farsi map and learn the names of the main districts. Because most of the road signs are only in Arabic directions in Riyadh are often given in relation to landmarks, but this entire system relies on your having some knowledge of the main districts. Al-Bathaa is the central, older portion of town immediately adjacent to which are Masmak, Al-Murabba and Al-Wazarat. North of these areas lies Olaya, the main residential and business area for the capital's business community.

To the extent that Riyadh has any centre at all it is the Al-Bathaa district, more or less the area around Al-Bathaa St and Al-Malek (King) Faisal St, which is also called Al-Wazir St, between Al-Washem and Tariq Ibn Ziyad Sts. However, from Al-Bathaa the city spreads out for about 10 km in all directions and almost everything within about five km of Al-Bathaa could, in some sense, be con-

sidered 'the centre'. The bus station, GPO and everything else that a traveller needs, however, are in Al-Bathaa, and it is the cheapest part of town. Thus, most of what follows focuses on that district.

If you are using the Farsi map note that on some editions of it the positions of Makkah Rd and King Fahd Rd have been reversed. Makkah Rd is the one that runs approximately east-west, past the old airport. King Fahd Rd runs perpendicular to Makkah Rd and parallel to Olaya St.

Informal names for streets are much more common here than in other parts of the Kingdom. A few of the more important ones include (formal name first):

Al-Malek Abdul Aziz St: Old Airport Rd
Al-Malek Faisal St: Al-Wazir St
Al-Amir Soltan Ibn Abdul Aziz St: Tallateen St
Salah Al-Din Al-Ayoubi St: Sitteen St
Al-Imam Faisal Ibn Torki Ibn Abdulla St: Al-Khazan St

### Information

**Money** Riyadh has no shortage of banks. A good place to look is along Olaya St between the Al-Khozama Hotel and Makkah Rd. They all change money, as do the various moneychangers in Olaya and Al-Bathaa.

American Express is represented by Ace Travel (☎ 4648812) on Olaya St, between Makkah Rd and Jaber Al-Ahmed Al-Sabah St (about 4.5 km north of the bus station). They are open Saturday to Thursday from 9 am to 1.30 pm and 4.30 to 8 pm, and are closed Friday. Cheques are cashed for card holders through a nearby bank. Lost AMEX cards can be replaced in one day, but the client's mail service is not available.

**Post** The GPO, on King Abdul Aziz St, near the intersection with Al-Bathaa St, is open 24 hours a day. There is no poste restante service.

**Telephone** There are several sets of international call cabins around the city. The most central ones are by the Al-Foutah Garden at the intersection of Al-Dhahirah and Al-Imam Faisal Ibn Torki Ibn Abdulla Sts. There are also call cabins on Jareer St, near the intersection with Salah Al-Din Al-Ayoubi St. The telephone code for Riyadh is 01.

**Foreign Embassies** All of the following embassies are in the Diplomatic Quarter. All street signs in the Diplomatic Quarter are in Arabic and you'll be hard-pressed to find anyone, including diplomats living there, who knows the street names. The best idea is to call the embassy you want to visit and ask for directions, for which it helps to be good with national flags. Maps are of little help as they usually show the plots which each country has been assigned, regardless of whether the embassy is actually located there (for example, all maps show the Mexican embassy in the Diplomatic Quarter when, in fact, it is in an office building near the old airport). Allow time to get lost. If you're getting about by taxi it might also be a good idea to have the cab wait for you. It can often be nearly impossible to find a taxi in the Diplomatic Quarter. Telephone numbers of the embassies are:

| | |
|---|---|
| Australia | (☎ 4887788) |
| Belgium | (☎ 4882888) |
| Canada | (☎ 4882288) |
| Denmark | (☎ 4880101) |
| Finland | (☎ 4881515) |
| France | (☎ 4881255) |
| Germany | (☎ 4880700) |
| Ireland | (☎ 4882300) |
| Italy | (☎ 4881212) |
| Jordan | (☎ 4880071) |
| Kuwait | (☎ 4883500) |
| Netherlands | (☎ 4880011) |
| New Zealand | (☎ 4887988) |
| Norway | (☎ 4881904) |
| Sweden | (☎ 4883100) |
| Switzerland | (☎ 4881291) |
| UK | (☎ 4880077) |
| USA | (☎ 4883800) |
| Yemen | (☎ 4881757) |

Embassies outside of the Diplomatic Quarter include:

**Egypt**
For visas go to the Consulate, Ja'far Ibn Abi Taleb St, Al-Sulaymaniya District, near the Indian School (☎ 4653131)

**India**
Old Airport Rd, behind the Ministry of Petroleum & Minerals (☎ 4777006)

**Pakistan**
Al-Malaz District, Farazdaq St, near the Obaid hospital (☎ 4768080)

**UAE**
Al-Aziziyah District, Prince Torki Ibn Abdul Aziz Al-Awal St (☎ 4826803)

**Cultural Centres** Some of the cultural centres in Riyadh include:

Alliance Française (☎ 4766436), Al-Dhobbat, just behind the Hyatt Regency Hotel
British Council (☎ 4621818), Level Two, Tower B of the Al-Musa Building, on Olaya St, opposite the King Fahd library

**Bookshops** The best selection of English, French and German books is at the Jarir Bookstore branch in the Al-Akariyah Centre (ground level) on Mosa Ibn Nosayr St in Olaya. There is a small library at the US Embassy.

**Medical Services** Embassies can usually steer their nationals toward doctors in emergencies. Expats will have a company doctor.

**Emergency** Dial 999 for the police, 997 for an ambulance, 998 to report a fire.

**Site Permits** Permits for visits to all forts and archaeological sites in the country, except for those in the Eastern Province, can be obtained at the Riyadh Museum. Permits for sites in the Eastern Province are issued at the museum in Dammam (except for sites in Hofuf, permits for which must be obtained here). The only exceptions to this rule are Dir'aiyah and the Najran Fort, for which permits are not required. For permits, which are issued free, bring your passport. The office which issues permits is at the back of the museum compound. Enter from a side street at the green sign marked Ministry of

Education, General Department of Antiquities & Museums.

## Riyadh Museum

Start your tour of Riyadh at the museum (☎ 4020303), in the Department of Antiquities office on Al-Imam Abdul Aziz Ibn Mohammed St in the Umm Seleem district, near the central hospital. It's open Saturday to Wednesday from 8 am to 2 pm and admission is free.

After you enter through the main gate the **Ethnographic Hall** is immediately to your right. Its centrepiece is a large model of the Masmak Fortress. The rest of the display includes carved and painted doors from Qassim (the region immediately north of Riyadh) and Qatif (a largely Shiite town in the Eastern Province which was once the major port on the Arab side of the Gulf). Also on display are clothes, musical instruments, weapons, cooking utensils, several beautiful woven bags and some jewellery.

The **main hall** is straight on from the main gate. The displays are well laid out with signs in both English and Arabic. The introductory display contains some items from archaeological digs in the Eastern Province. Turn right and follow the displays around the main hall, moving from the Stone Age to early Islam. The galleries are particularly thorough on geography and archaeology. The last room of the exhibit has an interesting display on Islamic architecture.

## Masmak Fortress

This was the citadel in the heart of Old Riyadh and the residence of the Al-Rashid garrison that Abdul Aziz and his small band overcame in 1902 to regain control of the city. During the raid one of the future king's companions heaved a spear at the door with such force that the head is still lodged in the doorway. The fort is built of dried mud.

The fortress is open Saturday to Wednesday from 7.30 am to 1.30 pm. Permits, issued at the museum, are required for admission.

Once inside you will find a nicely reconstructed traditional diwan on the ground floor. An open courtyard at the rear of this

level has a well which still works, and is surrounded by six interestingly painted doors. If you want to see the empty rooms behind them the attendant can usually be persuaded to unlock one of the doors.

On the upper level, head for the main room on the side of the building nearest to the street where you entered. Note the beautiful carved gypsum walls and the three columns supporting the wooden roof.

Main doorway, Murabba Palace

## Murabba Palace

This combination fortress and palace was built by King Abdul Aziz in 1946. Permits are required here and it's open Saturday to Wednesday from 8 am to 2 pm.

The lower level consists of a courtyard with a date palm growing in its centre and surrounded by a number of closed rooms.

The upper level has a display of traditional clothes and crafts. Note the enormous camel saddle in the room immediately to your left at the top of the stairs. Another part of this level is the hall which was Abdul Aziz's formal reception area for guests. It contains mostly chairs and carpets though some old rifles are also on display.

## King Faisal Centre for Research & Islamic Studies

The King Faisal Centre has a gallery of manuscripts and Islamic art in its complex behind the Al-Khozama Hotel in Olaya. The Centre usually has an exhibit focusing on some aspect of Islamic art or culture, though not always. Admission to the exhibits is free. The upper floor of the hall houses a small permanent exhibition on the treatment and preservation of old books and manuscripts.

## King Saud University Museum

King Saud University, on the western edge of Riyadh near the Diplomatic Quarter, has a small museum displaying finds from the university's archaeological digs at Al-Fao and Rabdhah. The museum is open from Saturday to Wednesday mornings, but to visit it you must first make an appointment through the university's public relations office (☎ 4678135). They usually require only a day to arrange a visit for one or two people, but larger groups will require several days' notice.

The museum is worth the effort. Many of the displays are labelled only in Arabic but this is unlikely to be a problem as a member of the museum staff is almost certain to be assigned to guide you around.

Al-Fao, on the edge of the Empty Quarter near modern Sulayyil, is a pre-Islamic site which reached its peak between 300 BC and 300 AD. The beautiful miniature bronze statues discovered there and displayed in the museum show both Egyptian and Nabataean influences. Rabdhah, about 100 km east of Medina, was a station on the Zubayda Pilgrims road which linked Mecca and Medina with Persia and Iraq.

## The Main Covered Souk

The souk has been a victim of Riyadh's rush into the 20th century. Small portions of it remain, however, particularly immediately east of Al-Bathaa St for a few blocks either side of Abu Ayoub Al-Ansari St. Ask for Souk Al-Bathaa.

## Al-Foutah Garden

There isn't much greenery in central Riyadh so Al-Foutah Garden, though not exactly lush, is a welcome change.

## Al-Thumairi Gate

On Al-Malek Faisal St, opposite the Middle East Hotel, this is an impressive restoration of one of the nine gates which used to lead into the city before the wall was torn down in 1950. Across the street, near the hotel, are some reconstructed bits of the city wall itself.

## Language Classes

The Centre of Languages and Scientific Services (☎ 4567380) offers Arabic classes. In early 1992, the Al-Imam Islamic University, on the road to the airport, announced that it would offer Arabic classes to expatriates.

The German embassy regularly organises language courses. Contact the embassy (☎ 4880700) for information.

## Festivals

Saudi Arabia's one, big, institutionalised cultural occasion is the Jinadriyah National Festival. It is organised every year by the National Guard and takes place at a special site 45 km north-east of central Riyadh. The festival includes traditional dancing, art and craft shows, camel racing, lectures and poetry readings. It usually lasts one or two weeks and takes place in February. Note that since Ramadan will coincide with part, or all, of February from 1993 until about 1998, the festival may be moved to another time during those years.

## Places to Stay – bottom end

The *Youth Hostel* (☎ 4055552) is on Shabab Al-Ghansani St, a side street between Al-Malek Fahd Rd and the junction of Al-Amir Sa'ad Ibn Abdul Aziz St and Abu Feras Al-Hamdani St in the Al-Namodhajiyah District. Beds are SR 8. The hostel is not on any bus route nor within walking distance of the bus station (count on paying SR 18 for a cab).

The cheap hotels are all clustered in the vicinity of the bus station. The prices quoted here include the service charges, where

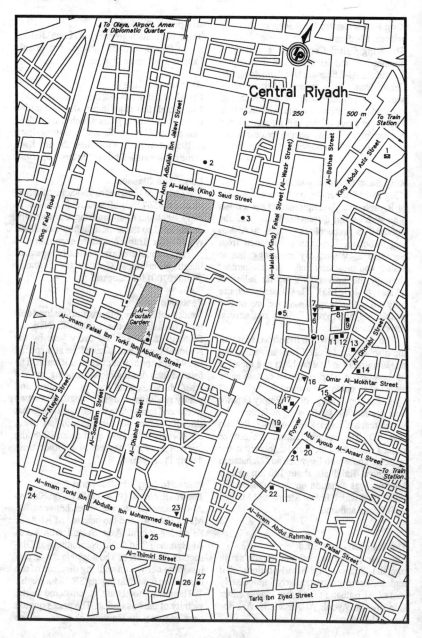

**Central Riyadh**

0        250        500 m

■ PLACES TO STAY

| 8 | Al-Bathaa Hotel |
| 9 | Safari Hotel |
| 11 | Mamora Hotel |
| 12 | Asia Hotel |
| 13 | Abalkhail Hotel |
| 14 | Riyadh Hotel |
| 15 | Ghazi Hotel |
| 17 | Al-Haramain Hotel |
| 18 | Al-Medina Hotel |
| 19 | Al-Rawdah Hotel |
| 20 | Cairo Hotel |
| 22 | Al-Jazeera Hotel |
| 26 | Middle East Hotel |

▼ PLACES TO EAT

| 6 | Gad Snack Bar |
| 7 | Farah Snack Bar |
| 16 | Bofiya Snack Bar |
| 23 | Geneva Snack Bar |

OTHER

| 1 | GPO |
| 2 | Murabba Palace |
| 3 | Water Tower |
| 4 | Telephone Office |
| 5 | Saudi British Bank |
| 10 | Bus Station |
| 21 | Al-Mudifar Exchange |
| 24 | Saudi British Bank |
| 25 | Masmak Fortress |
| 27 | Al-Thumairi Gate |

applicable. In most cases it should be possible to bargain SR 10 to SR 15 off the quoted price. All these hotels have air-conditioning.

The *Middle East Hotel* (☎ 4111994) on Al-Malek Faisal St is a bit out of the way but certainly the cheapest place in town after the youth hostel. Singles/doubles are SR 45/70, none with private bath but including breakfast. The rooms are very small and a bit cramped and the toilet is nothing to write home about. Still, the price is hard to beat.

The *Cairo Hotel* (☎ 4014045) on Abu Ayoub Al-Ansari St, just off Al-Bathaa St, is drab but clean though some of the rooms are windowless. Rooms are SR 65/100 with bath. All rooms have a fridge and telephone,

but the windowless ones are rather cell-like and those with windows are not a lot better. The *Sageer Hotel* (☎ 4052871), in an alley opposite the Cairo Hotel, offers rooms of a similar standard with bath for SR 85/100. To reach the hotel, follow the sign with Arabic writing and a red arrow into the alley then take the first right. There is another sign in English down the alley. Further down Al-Bathaa St, *Al-Jazeera Hotel* (☎ 4121107) has good rooms at SR 70/110.

A particularly good bet is the *Abalkhail Hotel* (☎ 4056660), two short blocks off Al-Bathaa St behind the Asia Hotel. The large, clean rooms are good value at SR 80/120 so long as you get the ones with attached bath (some are without bath for the same price). Nearby on Omar Al-Mokhtar St, the *Riyadh Hotel* (☎ 4020007) charges the same price.

West of Al-Bathaa St there are several good-value hotels along Al-Imam Faisal Ibn Torki Ibn Abdulla St (Al-Khazan St). The *Al-Rawdah Hotel* (☎ 4122278) and *Al-Medina Hotel* (☎ 4032255) are across the street from each other about a block from the intersection with Al-Bathaa St. Both charge SR 55/83 for rooms without bath and SR 66/99 with bath. *Hotel Alrajehi* (☎ 4123557), up an alley behind the Al-Rawdah Hotel, is a bit more up-market at SR 80/140 for rooms with bath.

On Al-Bathaa St, the *Al-Haramain Hotel* (☎ 4011616) has clean rooms with TV for SR 77/116 with bath, SR 66/99 without. Further along Al-Bathaa St, on the opposite side of the Al-Haramain Hotel, the *Mamora Hotel* (☎ 4013493) has OK rooms at SR 70/100, all with Turkish toilets.

**Places to Stay – middle**

The *Asia Hotel* (☎ 4035127), off Al-Bathaa St next to the Mamora Hotel, is one of the cheaper mid-range hotels in the city at SR 83/127 for singles/doubles, all with bath, TV and a well-stocked minifridge. Another good value is the *Safari Hotel* (☎ 4055533), on a side street off Al-Bathaa St. Singles/doubles are SR 120/180 though you might be able to talk them down to SR 80/120. The *Al-Bathaa Hotel* (☎ 4052000) looms over the street of the same name. The rooms, also with TV and fridge, are quite large and cost SR 150/195. Nearby, the *Al-Oroba Hotel* (☎ 4025553) is very nice but no great bargain at SR 165/214.50. The *Ghazi Hotel* (☎ 4022287), on Al-Ghorabi St just off Al-Bathaa St, has good rooms, a nice atmosphere and a slightly weird decor at SR 110/165.

Outside the centre the *White Palace Hotel* (☎ 4787800) on Al-Malek Abdul Aziz St (Old Airport Rd) has a good location and is very good value at SR 130/170.

### Places to Stay – top end

All of the rates quoted include the service charge. A discount is usually available for the asking, though how big the discount is will depend on how busy they are.

*Hotel Al-Khozama* (☎ 4654650, fax 4648576), Olaya St, in Olaya, near the intersection with Al-Amir Soltan Ibn Abdul Aziz St (commonly called Tallateen St). Consistently ranked as one of the best hotels in town and widely reputed to have the best hotel food around. Singles/doubles cost SR 322/420.

*Hotel Inter-Continental Riyadh* (☎ 4655000, fax 4657833) Al-Ma'ther St. SR 345/448.50.

*Hyatt Regency Riyadh* (☎ 4791234, fax 4775373) Al-Malek Abdul Aziz St (Old Airport Rd). SR 345/448.50.

*Minhal Holiday Inn* (☎ 4782500, fax 4772819), at the airport end of Al-Malek Abdul Aziz St, is a bit cheaper than other hotels in this category at SR 287.50/373.75.

*Riyadh Marriott Hotel* (☎ 4779300, fax 4779089) Al-Ma'ther St, near Makkah Rd. SR 345/448.50.

### Places to Eat

**Cheap & Medium-Priced** The area around the bus station is packed with small coffee shops, shawarma stands and restaurants, the latter mostly being of the chicken-and-kebab variety. A meal, usually consisting of a half or whole chicken and a huge pile of rice, costs between SR 10 and SR 15. Try the *Bofiya Snack Bar* on Al-Bathaa St for good, quick snacks (shawarma, etc). The sign is in Arabic but look for the orange and yellow stripes. Another good place for shawarma, pastries and something that resembles pizza is *Farah*, on Al-Bathaa St just across from the Al-Bathaa Hotel. Look for a sign in Arabic with red and white lettering and a picture of a hamburger. *Gad* is a similar place nearby; there's also a rather larger and swisher version of it in Olaya just off Al-Amir Soltan Ibn Abdul Aziz St, near the King Faisal Centre. Another good spot for burgers, shawarma and coffee is *Geneva*, on Al-Imam Torki Ibn Abdulla Ibn Mohammed St. A notch further up the scale is the open buffet at the *Al-Sheikh Restaurant* in the Al-Bathaa Hotel.

Al-Amir Soltan Ibn Abdul Aziz St (Tallateen St) in Olaya is a good place to look for affordable food of all types. There is a very good *Thai Restaurant* on Olaya St, near the Ace Travel office. Riyadh also seems to have more Western fast-food eateries than any other city in the Kingdom.

**Expensive** One of the better bets is *Da Pino*, an Italian restaurant in the Al-Khozama Centre next to the Al-Khozama Hotel on Olaya St in Olaya. Main dishes are SR 30 to SR 40 and you can count on paying SR 75 for a meal. On the hotel circuit, the Friday brunch at the *Hyatt Regency Hotel* on Al-Malek Abdul Aziz St is among the best in the Kingdom, though the *Riyadh Intercontinental* has a better spread. The Al-Khozama Hotel on Olaya St has, overall, the best food in town. Try the *Caravan Stop Restaurant* just off the lobby.

### Entertainment

Riyadh's nightlife is notoriously thin, even by Saudi standards. Even the souks do not stay open as late as they do in Jeddah or Alkhobar. Your only option, if you don't know anyone in Riyadh, is to dine out.

### Things to Buy

Spices and the occasional items of weaving can be found if you wander deep into the Souk Al-Bathaa. There is a shop selling expensive Arabian antiques in the shopping plaza attached to the Al-Khozama Hotel. Otherwise Riyadh is not a good place to shop for anything other than electronics. These you can find at either the Al-Akariyah Shopping Centre on Mosa Ibn Nosayr St in Olaya or the strip of shops along Olaya St near the intersection with Makkah Rd.

## Getting There & Away

**Air** King Khalid International Airport (the airport code is RUH) is a long way from the city – nearly 40 km from Al-Bathaa. There are four commercial terminals and a royal terminal. Of the four commercial terminals No 1 is not in use, No 2 is for domestic flights, No 3 for Saudia international flights and No 4 for foreign airlines.

Riyadh is Saudia's base of operations and there are frequent flights to just about everywhere in the Kingdom. Sample one-way economy-class fares include: Jeddah SR 240, Dhahran SR 120, Gassim (Buraydah) SR 110, Ha'il SR 170, Taif SR 210, Abha and Najran SR 240, Jizan SR 280. See the fare table in the Facts for the Visitor section for more details.

Some of the airlines serving Riyadh are:

Air France
  Al-Malek Abdul Aziz St (☎ 4769666)
Biman Bangladesh Airlines
  Ace Travel, Olaya St (same office as American Express) (☎ 4623376)
British Airways
  King Faisal Centre (behind the Al-Khozama Hotel, between Olaya St and Makkah Rd), street level (☎ 4645550)
EgyptAir
  Salah Al-Din Al-Ayoubi St (☎ 4784004)
Emirates
  Olaya St, between Al-Amir Soltan Ibn Abdul Aziz St and King Fahd Rd (☎ 4655485)
Ethiopian Airlines
  Al-Malek Abdul Aziz St (☎ 4782140)
Garuda
  Mosa Ibn Nosayr St, across from the Al-Akariyah Centre, Olaya (☎ 4655898)
Kuwait Airways
  King Faisal Centre (behind the Al-Khozama Hotel, between Olaya St and Makkah Rd), 1st floor (☎ 4631218)
Lufthansa
  King Faisal Centre (behind the Al-Khozama Hotel, between Olaya St and Makkah Rd), street level (☎ 4632004)

MEA (Middle East Airlines)
  King Faisal Centre (behind the Al-Khozama Hotel, between Olaya St and Makkah Rd), street level (☎ 4656600)
Olympic
  King Faisal Centre (behind the Al-Khozama Hotel, between Olaya St and Makkah Rd), 1st floor (☎ 4644596)
PIA (Pakistan International Airlines)
  Makkah Rd, near the intersection with Olaya St (☎ 4659600)
Royal Jordanian
  At the corner of Al-Amir Soltan Ibn Abdul Aziz St and King Fahd Rd (☎ 4625697)
Saudia
  The main reservations offices are at the intersection of Al-Ma'ther St and Al-Malek Abdul Aziz St and at the old airport (☎ 4772222)
Swissair
  Al-Malek Abdul Aziz St (☎ 4766444)
Syrian Arab Airlines
  King Faisal Centre (behind the Al-Khozama Hotel, between Olaya St and Makkah Rd), street level (☎ 4632610)
Turkish Airlines
  Olaya St, between Al-Amir Soltan Ibn Abdul Aziz St and King Fahd Rd (☎ 4631600)

**Domestic Buses** The bus station just off Al-Bathaa St is SAPTCO's inter-city depot. You'll need identification to buy a ticket and the lines tend to be long. Unaccompanied women are not allowed to travel by bus.

Services include: Jeddah (13 hours, SR 130) via Taif (10 hours, SR 100) at 10 am, noon, 5, 8.30, 9.30 and 11 pm. These buses go around Mecca and are OK for non-Muslims. A few years ago the same buses went through Mecca, forcing non-Muslims to change at Taif. If you are a non-Muslim bound for Jeddah it would be prudent to double-check that the routing has not changed again.

Other routes include: Dammam (five hours, SR 60) at 9.30 am, 2, 5, and 10.30 pm; Hofuf (3½ hours, SR 45) at 10 am and 6 pm. To Buraydah (SR 60) some buses take the old road, a 7½ hour trip through the desert, while others go straight up the new highway making the journey in about four hours. Fast buses leave at 9.15 am, 5.30 and 9.30 pm, continuing to Medina (12 hours, SR 140). Slow buses to Buraydah leave at 11.30 am (via Shagra, SR 30) and 2.30 pm (via Al-

Zulfi, SR 45). Change at Buraydah for Ha'il. Buses for Khamis Mushayt (12 hours, SR 125) leave at 9 am, 2 pm (two buses), 4 and 8.30 pm. Local buses connect Khamis Mushayt to Abha, Jizan and Najran.

For Muslims only, buses leave for Mecca (12 hours, SR 115) at 10.30 am, 5.30 and 8 pm.

**International Buses** There are a number of agents for international passenger and freight services clustered around the bus station. In general, the buses headed for Turkey via Jordan and Syria are between the SAPTCO station and Al-Bathaa St while the buses to Egypt are on the far side of the station as you approach it from Al-Bathaa St. The prices are generally the same to a given destination no matter who you go with, but some shopping around might be in order to see who is offering the best discount this week. All the buses to a given destination usually leave in a convoy.

SAPTCO runs international as well as domestic services, information on which is available from the information desk in the main terminal. SAPTCO buses to Istanbul cost SR 550, SR 500 to Ankara. The route goes via Amman and Damascus but SAPTCO will not sell tickets to those destinations. SAPTCO also has daily buses to Cairo.

Egyptian companies send their bus convoys off to Cairo every Sunday, Tuesday and Thursday morning at 9 am. Lunch in Buraydah is almost always included and some companies throw in other free meals as well. For more information see the Getting There & Away section for Saudi Arabia.

**Service Taxi** These also leave from the SAPTCO station and are probably a better bet than the bus if you are headed north. In the early morning (before 8 am) taxis for Buraydah usually fill up fairly quickly. The fare is SR 60. It's more difficult to get a service taxi to the Eastern Province and Jeddah. The drivers are unlikely to take non-Muslims, especially if they have already filled some of the seats with Muslims,

because it would mean taking the long detour around Mecca.

**Train** The railway station is on Al-Amir (Prince) Abdul Aziz Ibn Abdullah Ibn Torki St, 2.5 km east of the bus station. Trains leave daily, except Thursday, and the journey to Dammam takes about four hours. See the Getting Around section for a complete time-table. The ticket office is open from 6 am to 10 pm. Women are not allowed to travel by train without a male escort.

To reach the station from Al-Bathaa go up Omar Ibn Al-Khattab St, following the 'Railway Station' signs.

**Car Rental** As prices are fixed by the government, the best place for car hire is at the airport where you can see which company has a car of the size you want. Expect to pay SR 110 per day, including insurance, for the smallest cars available (usually Toyota Corollas) from all the companies. With whatever discount they are offering at the time that should drop to SR 90 to SR 100. Most big hotels also have a car-hire desk. There is a Budget Rent-A-Car office on Olaya St near the Al-Khozama Hotel.

**Getting Around**
**To/From the Airport** SAPTCO has cancelled its bus service to King Khaled airport. The buses and minibuses marked 'Airport' go to the old airport via Al-Malek Abdul Aziz St. Your only option is taxis. Both yellow taxis and white limos have meters, and the trip to the airport could cost anything from SR 30 to SR 70, depending on where you catch the cab. From the airport the white limos have a set tariff of SR 55 to most districts in the city though a few of the areas closer to the airport are only SR 45. The yellow cabs have a rank separate from the limos at each terminal. They tend to insist on the same fares as the limos, and if the drivers will not bargain you might as well take one of the limos, which are almost always more comfortable and their drivers often have a better idea where they are going.

**Bus** SAPTCO buses and minibuses cover most of the city. Fares on either are SR 2. There is no route map. Both the buses and the minibuses have their routes posted in the front window, though on the latter this may be only in Arabic. The small and packed minibuses follow more or less the same route as the buses, and the route numbers are applicable in either direction.

Sorting out these routes is difficult because SAPTCO's timetables tend to use old unofficial names and to be inconsistent about these names. Here are some of their main Riyadh routes (using the actual names of the main streets the routes follow):

No 1 – Al-Sulaymaniya, Al-Malek Abdul Aziz St, Al-Bathaa St, Qataybah Ibn Moslem St, Al-Amir Abdullah Ibn Abdul Rahman Ibn Faisal St, Al-Amir Mohammed Ibn Abdul Rahman Rd

No 2 – Al-Uraijah St, Solaiman Ibn Moshrif St, Al-Imam Torki Ibn Abdullah Ibn Mohammed St, Al-Imam Abdul Aziz Ibn Mohammed Ibn Saud St, Al-Imam Faisal Ibn Torki Ibn Abdullah St, Abu Ayoub Al-Ansari St, Al-Amir Salman Ibn Abdul Aziz St

No 3 – Salah Al-Din Al-Ayoubi St, Al-Jami'ah St, Al-Malek Abdul Aziz St, Al-Bathaa St

No 4 – Al-Badia'h St, Al-Imam Mohammed Ibn Saud Ibn Meqren St, Al-Atayef St, Tariq Ibn Ziyad St, Al-Imam Abdul Rahman Ibn Faisal St, Al-Unoze St

No 5 – Al-Foutah Garden, Al-Sowailim St, Salam St, Al-Amir Abdullah Ibn Abdul Rahman Ibn Faisal St, Dirab Rd, Al-Shafa District; returns to centre via Al-A'sha St, Al-Frayyan St, Al-Dhahirah St

No 6 – Al-Hizam, Amro Ibn Al-A'as St, Al-Malek Saud St, Khaled Ibn Lo'ay St, Al-Malek Faisal St, Al-Bathaa St, Ammar Ibn Yasir St, Al-Kharj Rd, Al-Aziziyah; returns via Al-Bathaa St, Al-Malek Abdul Aziz St instead of Al-Malek Faisal St, Khaled Ibn Lo'ay St, Al-Malek Saud St

No 7 – Al-Bathaa St, Al-Malek Faisal St, Al-Malek Saud St, Al-Nasiriyah St, Al-Ma'ther St, Al-Jawhrah Bint Ibn Maamar St, Al-Malek Khaled Rd, Umm Al-Hamam St, Al-Uroubah Rd, Diplomatic Quarter

No 7A – Al-Bathaa St, Al-Malek Faisal St, Al-Malek Saud St, Al-Nasiriyah St, Al-Ma'ther St, Al-Jawhrah Bint Ibn Maamar St, Al-Malek Khaled Rd, Umm Al-Hamam St, Al-Uroubah Rd, King Saud University

No 8 – Al-Bathaa St, Al-Washem St, Al-Malek Saud St, Al-Nasiriyah St, Al-Takhassosi St

No 9 – Al-Bathaa St, Al-Amir Abdul Aziz Ibn Moad'ad Ibn Jalawi St, Al-Ma'ther St, Olaya St, Mosa Ibn Nosayr St, Al-Sulaymaniyah

No 9A – Al-Bathaa St, Al-Amir Abdul Aziz Ibn Moad'ad Ibn Jalawi St, Al-Ma'ther St, Olaya St

No 10 – Al-Roudah, Makkah Rd, Al-Ihsa St, Omar Ibn Abdul Aziz St, Salah Al-Din Al-Ayoubi St, Al-Jami'ah St, Al-Malek Abdul Aziz St, Al-Malek Faisal St (returning via Al-Bathaa St)

No 11 – Al-Sulaymaniyah, Al-Malek Abdul Aziz St, Al-Bathaa St, Manfuha Al-'Am St, Itaiygah District

No 12 – Al-Rabwah, Omar Ibn Abdul Aziz Rd, Fatimah Al-Zahra' St, Jareer St, Salah Al-Din Al-Ayoubi St, Al-Dhahran St, Omar Ibn Al-Khattab St, Al-Malek Abdul Aziz St, Al-Malek Faisal St, Al-Imam Torki Ibn Abdullah Al-Mohammed St, Al-Shaikh Abdul Latif Ibn Ibrahim St, Manfuha Al-'Am St, Manfuha District, Hallat Abdullah Station; returns via Al-Bathaa St instead of Al-Malek Faisal St

No 12B – Al-Rabwah, Omar Ibn Abdul Aziz Rd, Fatimah Al-Zahra' St, Jareer St, Salah Al-Din Al-Ayoubi St, Al-Dhahran St, Omar Ibn Al-Khattab St, Al-Malek Abdul Aziz St, Al-Bathaa St, Al-Imam Faisal Ibn Torki Ibn Abdullah St; returns via Al-Malek Faisal St instead of Al-Bathaa St

No 14 – Al-Garradiyah Bus Station, Al-Medina Al-Monawarrah Rd, Al-Rayes St, Tariq Ibn Ziyad St, Al-Bathaa St, Omar Al-Mokhtar St, Al-Dhahran St, Omar Ibn Al-Khattab St, Ali Ibn Abi Taleb St, Al-Amir Abdul Mohsin Ibn Abdul Aziz St and vice versa via Al-Dhahran St

No 15 – Ka'b Ibn Zohayr St, Abdul Malek Ibn Hisham St, Al-Swaidi St, Al-Amir Abdullah Ibn Abdul Rahman Ibn Faisal St, Salam St, Al-Sowailim St, Al-Imam Torki Ibn Abdullah Ibn Mohammed St

No 16 – Al-Bathaa St, Al-Imam Faisal Ibn Torki Ibn Abdullah St, Al-Imam Abdul Aziz Ibn Mohammed St, Al-Imam Torki Ibn Abdullah Ibn Mohammed St, Uhod St, Al-Uraijah St, Solaiman Ibn Moshrif St, Al-Badia'h St, Mo'awyah Ibn Abi Sufyan St, Al-Dakhal Al-Mahdoud St; returns only via Al-Badia'h St, Al-Imam Torki Ibn Abdullah Ibn Mohammed St

No 17 – Al-Bathaa St, Tariq Ibn Ziyad St, Al-Amir Salman Ibn Abdul Aziz St, Al-Kharj Rd, 2nd Industrial City

No 19 – Al-Sulaymaniyah, Al-Amir Mamdouh Ibn Abdul Aziz St, Al-Malek Abdul Aziz St, Al-Malek Faisal District, Olaya St

No 110 – Al-Bathaa St, Al-Malek Abdul Aziz St, Omar Ibn Al-Khattab St, Al-Dhahran St, Salah Al-Din Al-Ayoubi St, Al-Naseem

**Taxi** There are two kinds of taxis: white and yellow cabs. In both cases a flag-drop is SR

5. After that the yellow cabs are cheaper. Most yellow cabs are driven by Saudis, with the driver usually being the owner. The meter ticks over in 50 halala increments. The white ones are driven by non-Saudis, usually Filipinos or Egyptians, and tend to be better maintained. Their meters work in 70 halala increments. The drivers in the white cabs are more likely to speak English.

## AROUND RIYADH
### Dir'aiyah

Riyadh's most interesting site is outside the city. On the capital's northern outskirts, about 30 km from Al-Bathaa, lie the ruins of Dir'aiyah, the first capital of the Al-Saud clan and the Kingdom's most popular and easily accessible archaeological site (no permits required).

*Dir'aiyah*, by Stevie Wilberding & Isabel K Cutler, contains some excellent photographs, a good historical essay on the city and three 30 to 60-minute walking tours of the site. The book is available in most local bookshops for about SR 20.

The site was settled in 1446 by an ancestor of the present royal family but reached its peak in the late 18th and early 19th centuries during the First Saudi Empire, in particular under King Saud the Great (ruled 1803-14). It didn't last long. The Ottoman sultan sent an army to the Hejaz in the early 19th century to recapture the holy cities and crush Saudi power in the peninsula. In 1818 they reached Dir'aiyah which surrendered after a six-month siege. King Abdullah, Saud's son and successor, surrendered and was eventually executed. Dir'aiyah was razed and what was left of the Al-Saud and their followers moved to Riyadh. Reconstruction of Dir'aiyah's ruins began in 1981.

The site is open during daylight hours and admission is free. Still photography is permitted but no videos.

Entering through the main gate the office on the left has a small display of clothes, weapons and handicrafts. A larger visitor's centre is planned. The **Palace of Salwa** is the impressive building towering up behind the office. Across the street from the office

is the restored **Mosque of Mohammed Ibn Abdul Wahhab**, the founder of Wahhabism. To reach the main area of the ruins continue straight past the office and turn left around the wall which will eventually appear in front of you. This is the **Palace of Fahd**.

To reach Dir'aiyah from Riyadh, leave the city centre following the signs for the airport. Once you're on the expressway to the airport look for signs for Dir'aiyah. Follow these until you reach a big, red Freeway Ends sign, and exit there. Follow this road to a T-junction and turn left. After about 500 metres you'll see the ruins to your left. Turn left at the first crossroads; from here a couple of small white signs will point you to the ruins.

# Najd (Central Region)

## BURAYDAH

Buraydah has an unenviable reputation as the least hospitable city in Saudi Arabia. The only major town of the Qassim region, it lies 330 km north of Riyadh on the road to Ha'il. It is the only place in the Kingdom where all foreign women are required to be veiled.

Geographically, the desert plains running north from Qassim are also the Kingdom's agricultural heartland, though Ha'il is more important than Buraydah as an agricultural centre. It is a place most people pass through as there's not much to see and do. However, if you do stop here, take a walk through the residential areas two or three blocks on either side of Khobib St, between the communications tower and the Riyad Bank building. A few examples of interesting traditional Najdi mud-brick houses are still around to be seen. Foreigners are still a slightly unusual sight here so try not to draw too much attention to yourself.

### Orientation & Information

Buraydah's main road is Khobib St, also known as Commercial St, which runs north-south through the city. At the northern outskirts of town it becomes the Medina Rd. There appear to be no street signs in either

Arabic or English, and the Arabic signboards only give the names of the cross streets. The main intersections are at First St and, farther north, the intersection dominated by the Riyad Bank building.

Coming from Riyadh the service-taxi station is a one-storey brown building on the east side of Khobib St at the last set of traffic lights before the communications tower, which is clearly visible atop a small hill on your left. The bus station is across the street and halfway up the hill, near the tower.

You can change money at the Saudi American Bank on Khobib St, just north of the bus station. There's also an office of the Al-Rajhi Banking & Investment Corporation a few hundred metres further north. The telephone code for Buraydah is 06.

## Places to Stay

Buraydah has an excellent and easy to reach *Youth Hostel* (☎ 3233926). It is at the Sporting City, 12 km north of the town centre. From the bus station take bus No 2 (every 30 minutes, SR 2) all the way to the end of the line. It's about a 30-minute ride. The bus stops at a T-junction near the sports complex. Turn left, then follow the complex's wall around to the right to reach the gate. Beds are SR 8 per night.

The *Al-Gassim Hotel* (☎ 3241858) is the only place to stay in the town itself. Singles/doubles cost SR 110/165. It's on the west side of Khobib St, one long block beyond the Riyad Bank building. The rooms are quite clean and big. The Turkish toilets are also clean. The *Al-Dubaikhy Hotel* (☎ 3248733), 10 km north of the centre on the Medina Rd, is slightly cheaper at SR 83/121 for rooms with bath, SR 72/110 without. The rooms are simple but clean and some have a fridge and TV. This place, however, is not a good idea if you do not have a car – taxis demand SR 20 for the trip from town and once the driver has left you are likely to find that getting back into the centre is a bit of a problem.

The upper end of the local market is the *Al-Salman Hotel* (☎ 3240373), with rooms at SR 287.50/372.60 including the service charge. To reach it follow Khobib St almost to the big, golf-ball-like water tower, turn right (there's a sign in Arabic) and follow the road through four traffic lights. You'll see the hotel. Alternatively, you can call from the bus station and they will send a car to get you.

## Places to Eat

Khobib St has a number of small restaurants between the bus station and the Riyad Bank building. The fare is mostly Turkish but there are some Indian/Pakistani places as well. On the west side of Khobib St, near the Riyad Bank intersection, try *Restaurant* (that's all it says in Arabic too), a chicken-and-kebab place. To find it, look for the large blue sign with Arabic writing. The word 'restaurant' appears in English in smaller letters. Half a chicken, a huge pile of rice and salad costs SR 10. The *Gülüm Restaurant*, two blocks north of the bus station on Khobib St, has very good hummus. A meal of kebab, bread, hummus and salad costs SR 10. The restaurant is on the same side of the street as the bus station. The teahouses around the bus station seem to be one of the city's main social centres.

## Getting There & Away

Saudia flies to Buraydah (which its timetables list as Gassim) several times a day from Riyadh (SR 110 one-way, economy class) and once or twice a day to/from Jeddah (SR 230). Direct flights also operate to Dhahran (SR 230), Medina (SR 140) Arar (SR 190), Gurayat (SR 280), Jouf (SR 160) and Tabuk (SR 260).

SAPTCO runs five buses a day to Riyadh. The trip takes four hours by the new road and 7½ hours by the old road and costs SR 60. They also have one bus to Ha'il (four hours, SR 40) and two to Medina (eight hours, SR 80).

Service taxis go to the same destinations as the buses at the same prices but fill very slowly, particularly in the direction of Ha'il. Local taxis cluster near the bus station.

## HA'IL

Ha'il (pronounced Hay-El), 640 km northwest of Riyadh, was formerly the seat of the

Al-Rashid family, the Al-Saud clan's most formidable rivals. It is now the centre of the Kingdom's vast agricultural programme, and most of Saudi Arabia's wheat crop comes from the area around Ha'il.

## Orientation & Information

Ha'il's main street, the one coming from Riyadh and Buraydah, runs north-south and centres on Commercial District Square by the Al-Bank Al-Saudi Al-Hollandi building. Old Ha'il is roughly east of this street and the newer areas are west of it, except for the Al-Qashalah Fortress. There's another square bearing the same name north-east of the one just described. This second square looks more like a parking lot and is dominated by the fruit and vegetable souk. You are unlikely to get the two mixed up. The bus station is at the Al-Qashalah Fortress, three blocks south of Commercial District Square. The telephone code for Ha'il is 06.

To change money, head for Al-Bank Al-Saudi Al-Hollandi or the offices of the Riyad Bank and Saudi French Bank nearby. Ha'il's post office is in the small cream building at the first set of lights north of Commercial District Square. Local and international-call cabins are also available here. The Ha'il GPO is well south of the centre on the Medina Rd. The Saudia office is next to the Al-Bank Al-Saudi Al-Hollandi building.

Before doing any sightseeing your permit, which must be obtained in Riyadh, has to be validated at the Antiquities Section of the Ministry of Education office in town (ask for *maktab al-athaar*). The office is on the 1st floor and is open from about 8 am until 1 pm from Saturday to Wednesday. These are also more or less the hours during which you can visit the sites. The staff are quite friendly and will probably insist on accompanying you to the sites. Ask permission before you start taking pictures at the forts, even if you have a permit.

## Al-Qashalah Fortress

This mud fortress is impressive but somewhat younger than it looks. It was built in the 1930s and was used mostly as a barracks for

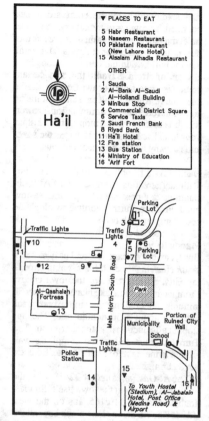

Abdul Aziz's troops in Ha'il. As Ha'il had traditionally been the seat of the rival Al-Rashid clan, the King may have thought it prudent to build a new garrison for his troops rather than take over the quarters of the Al-Rashid sheikhs whom he had only recently conquered. (It was typical of Abdul Aziz's approach to rivals that, having conquered, he would try to co-opt them rather than dispossess them.)

The entrance is through the south gate by the bus station. Inside there's a large courtyard which has been cut in half by a wall to create a separate area for the King's police and soldiers. The entire courtyard is surrounded by a two-storey gallery, the lower half of which is whitewashed, as are a few of the pillars on the upper lever. The small square building in the courtyard contains a display of artefacts from Ha'il and the surrounding desert region. On the east side of the courtyard is a small mosque. A foundation stone dates the mosque's construction to 1362 AH (1943 AD). To reach the mosque, turn right once you enter the courtyard then pass through another gate, also to your right.

### 'Airif Fort

Built about 200 years ago, 'Airif Fort was a combination observation post and stronghold. From the nearby fragments of Ha'il's wall it appears to have been sited just outside the city proper. It also appears to be the fort sketched by Lady Anne Blunt when she and her husband Wilfred visited Ha'il in 1889. After climbing up the hill and going through the main gate into the fort, look to your right for an open hall filled with low pillars. A niche in the south wall identifies it as a small mosque, partially open to the sky.

### Barazan Square

Two restored towers in this square adjacent to Ha'il's central mosque are all that remains of another of Ha'il's palaces.

### Outside Ha'il

About 25 km south-east of the city, **Jebel Yathrib** is the site of rock inscriptions dating from the 5th and 6th centuries BC. **Jubha**, 100 km north-west of Ha'il, has prehistoric rock paintings. As with the sites in Ha'il, you will need a permit from Riyadh which must be validated in Ha'il. Someone from the Antiquities office in Ha'il will accompany you to the sites but you will probably be expected to provide transport (4WD recommended).

### Places to Stay

The *Youth Hostel* (☎ 5331485) is at the stadium, a 20 to 30-minute walk south of the bus station. Beds are SR 8. The hostel entrance is on the side of the complex, not the main road. Alternatively, walk into town from the bus station (about 10 minutes) and catch a minibus from the parking lot in front of the Al-Bank Al-Saudi Al-Hollandi building. These leave when they are full so be prepared to wait. The fare is SR 2.

The *Ha'il Hotel* (☎ 5320180) is on King Khalid St but there are no street signs anywhere in the vicinity. The hotel is a lot better than it looks from the street. Singles/doubles with bath cost SR 132/171, though they will readily discount that to 120/155. To reach the hotel walk west from Commercial District Square and turn left at the first set of traffic lights. The hotel will then be on your right.

The *Al-Jabalain Hotel* (☎ 5323100) is south of the city centre beyond the youth hostel. There is no sign in English but for sheer size the place is pretty hard to miss. The prices, including the 10% service charge, are the same as at the Ha'il Hotel. If you have a car, the Al-Jabalain is definitely the better value of the two.

### Places to Eat

Ha'il has few eating spots. For Western food try the *Habr* hamburger place on the corner of Commercial District Square. The *Naseem Restaurant* is on the first side street south of Commercial District Square, near the Riyad Bank office. There is no sign in English but it is pretty hard to miss. Look for a large blue and white sign with lettering in Arabic and Hindi and a picture of a chef holding a chicken. Half a chicken and a pile of rice costs SR 10. The same menu, but in slightly less chaotic surroundings, is found at the *Alsalam Alhadis Restaurant* south of Commercial District Square, on the main north-south road and almost directly across the road from the Ministry of Education office. For more up-market dining there is a restaurant at the Al-Jabalain Hotel.

### Getting There & Away

Ha'il's small airport is south-west of the centre. There are two flights a day to/from Riyadh (SR 170 one-way, economy class), daily service to Jeddah (SR 210) and one or two flights a week to Dhahran (SR 290),

Medina (SR 120), Arar (SR 120), Jouf (SR 90), Rafah (SR 90) and Tabuk (SR 190).

SAPTCO runs one bus a day to Buraydah (four hours, SR 40) at 8 am and one to Medina (6½ hours, SR 60) at 9 am. Southbound the bus is by far your best bet, but if you want to take a chance with service taxis they wait to fill up in the parking lot behind the Habbr restaurant on Commercial District Square.

For getting around locally without waiting for the mini-vans in Commercial District Square to fill up, there are usually taxis with meters in front of the Saudia office.

# Jeddah

The white town hung between the blazing sky and its reflection in the mirage which swept and rolled over the wide lagoon.
**T E Lawrence**, *Seven Pillars of Wisdom*

Once a modest port living mostly off the pilgrim trade, Jeddah (Jiddah, Jidda) has evolved into one of the Arab world's most important commercial centres. Jeddah has also managed the feat, rare in today's Arabia, of building around, rather than over, its history. One of its nicest aspects is that a surprising amount of Lawrence's white mirage has survived into our era.

But while historical Jeddah still exists it is dwarfed by the modern metropolis. Within its walls Jeddah occupied about one sq km of land. Today it is approximately one thousand times that size.

It has been called the 'Paris of Arabia' and if this title seems a bit overstated, it is difficult to deny Jeddah its place as the most interesting and friendly of the Kingdom's big cities. However, it's an extremely hot and humid place.

## History

Jeddah has long served as Mecca's outlet to the sea. Mecca was a thriving commercial centre long before the coming of the Prophet. It was an important stop on the caravan route from Yemen to Egypt and Syria and a local centre of pilgrimage for the tribes from the surrounding deserts. The spread of Islam made the holy city a religious centre for people from the four corners of the earth, many of whom arrived by sea, and Islam soon transformed Jeddah into a thriving metropolis in its own right. Until well into this century pilgrims in their hundreds of thousands would land each year at Jeddah and make the two-day overland journey to Mecca.

Jeddah is in the Hejaz, or Western Province. The entire Hejaz came under nominal Turkish control in the 16th century, though the local rulers retained a great deal of autonomy. The first foreign consuls arrived during the first half of the 19th century.

After the Wahhabis, under Abdul Aziz, took control of the city in 1925, the foreign presence (which had increased notably during WW I) began to expand even further. Foreign representatives to the new king's court were posted to Jeddah, rather than to the official capital, Riyadh, because of the latter's relative inaccessibility. Diplomatically, this was easily finessed as Najd and the Hejaz were, technically, two separate states which simply happened to have the same king until 1932. After that it was more a matter of convenience. The embassies stayed in Jeddah until the early 1980s, and as late as the mid-70s a sizeable chunk of the Saudi bureaucracy was headquartered here rather than in the official capital. Today, the city's forte is commerce, though it still remains the principal port of entry for the more than two million pilgrims who make their way to the holy cities each year.

## Orientation

Everything centres on Al-Balad, the strip of buildings on the coast between the old foreign ministry building and the bus station, and on the old city which lies directly inland from them. The old city is the area bounded by Al-Malek Abdel Aziz St, Makkah Al-Mukarramah Rd and Ba'najah St. The modern strip of buildings lies between Al-

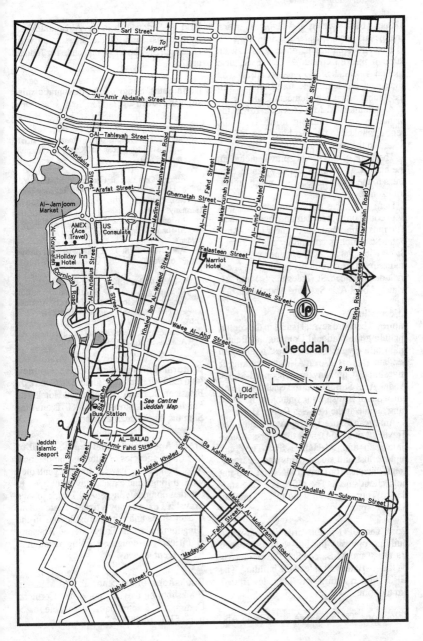

Malek Abdel Aziz St and Ha'il St, which changes its name to Ba'ashan St in this area.

The street cutting a north-south swath through the old city is Al-Dahab St, also spelled Al-Zahab St. Both names are used on signs and are legitimate transliterations of the Arabic name, which means Gold St).

Al-Madinah Al-Munawwarah Rd is the principal street running north from the centre, flanked to the east by Al-Amir Fahd St and to the west by Al-Andalus St.

The bulk of the urban sprawl, including the airport, is north of the city centre. The areas to the south and east are mostly industrial zones.

Here too, there are a number of streets with commonly used, but unofficial, names. The most important one to know is Al-Amir Fahd St, which is commonly called Sitteen St or King Fahd St. The names of several main streets are commonly anglicised. These include Falasteen St (Palestine St) and Al-Malek Abdel Aziz St (King Abdul Aziz St).

## Information

**Money** There are several banks in the centre, including the National Commercial Bank's main office which is the tallest building in Jeddah. There is also an Al-Rajhi Banking & Investment Company branch on Al-Malek Abdel Aziz St opposite the Shaheen Hotel, and a Saudi British Bank branch in the shopping arcade at the Red Sea Palace Hotel.

American Express is represented by Ace Travel (☎ 6651254), near the intersection of Falasteen and Al-Hamra Sts. They can replace lost and stolen cards and cash personal cheques for card holders but will not hold client's mail. The office is open Saturday to Thursday from 9 am to 1.30 pm and 4.30 to 8 pm.

**Post** The GPO is the large red-and-white building opposite the bus station, between Ba'ashan and Al-Bareed Sts. The entrance is on the Al-Bareed St side of the building. The GPO is open Saturday to Thursday from 7 am to 9 pm.

**Telephone** The telephone office is on Abo

Bakr Al-Seddeeq St in the Al-Sharafeyyah district, just south of the intersection with Falasteen St. The telephone code for Jeddah is 02.

**Consulates** Some of the diplomatic missions in Jeddah are:

Egypt
    Behind the Al-Mousadiyah Centre in the Al-Andalus District, near the King Fahd hospital (☎ 6605025)
France
    Adham Commercial Centre, Al-Madinah Al-Munawwarah Rd, near the Hyatt Regency Hotel (☎ 6510082)
Germany
    Al-Iman St in the Al-Hamra District, behind the Al-Hamra hospital (☎ 6653344)
Jordan
    Wadi Al-Kharj St in the Al-Azizeyyah district (☎ 6607630)
UK
    Off Al-Andalus St, near the Al-Bilad Hotel, in the Al-Shate'e district. The British also handle diplomatic matters for citizens of Canada, Australia and New Zealand in Jeddah (☎ 6641811)
USA
    Falasteen St, near the intersection with Al-Andalus St, Ruwais district (☎ 6670080)

**Cultural Centres** The British Council (☎ 6723336) is in the Middle East Centre on Falasteen St, next to the Marriott Hotel. The Saudi French Centre (☎ 6827860) is on A'taa St in the Al-Salamah district.

**Travel Agencies** Central Jeddah is full of tiny travel agencies of dubious competence. Most companies have a travel agent they work through and expats may be obliged to use that company. In general I stick to Ace Travel if I have to buy a ticket. There are no bucket shops and current regulations in the Kingdom make it unlikely that you'll get any significant discount by going through a travel agent anyway.

**Bookshops** In the centre the Al-Mamoun Bookshop, on the 1st floor of the Corniche Commercial Centre, has a reasonable selection of English books.

**Emergency** Dial 999 for the police, 997 for an ambulance, 998 to report a fire.

**Dangers & Annoyances** Jeddah is notorious for having the craziest driving habits in the Kingdom. Riding or driving through the city can be a pretty nerve-wracking experience.

## Walking Tour & Old City Walls

Most of Jeddah's sites lie along the course of the old city walls, which were torn down in the late 1940s. The walls ran along Al-Malek Abdel Aziz St, Makkah Al-Mukarramah Rd and Ba'najah St. A circuit of these streets should take under an hour on foot.

Along the route are the three reconstructed old city gates, which are all that remains of the wall. They are the North City gate on Maydan Al-Bayal; Bab Makkah at the intersection of Makkah Al-Mukarramah Rd and Ba'najah St; and Bab Sharif on Ba'najah St near a hospital and now opening onto a large parking lot.

Near the North City Gate are several good examples of traditional Jeddah architecture in various states of preservation.

The old city is now a protected urban area. Buildings there cannot be torn down unless they are dilapidated beyond repair, in which case they must be replaced with something of a similar size and architectural style. Many of the older houses within the old city walls are constructed not of stone but of coral quarried from reefs in the Red Sea.

## The Shorbatly House

Just east of the North City Gate, this house is one of the few examples of the city's traditional architecture which has been restored to its original state.

## Municipality Museum

The museum is in the restored traditional house opposite the National Commercial Bank's headquarters building. There is no sign in English but the house is impossible to miss. The museum is open in the mornings from Saturday to Thursday. Admission is free, but a permit from the Jeddah Municipality (☎ 6695566, 6607671) is required. Having obtained the permit you will be expected to make an appointment with the museum's curator.

The house is the only surviving building of the British Legation in Jeddah during WW I. T E Lawrence stayed at the Legation when he visited in 1917, though there is no way of knowing whether he actually stayed in this particular house as the Legation then included several other buildings as well.

The photographic display in the entrance hall includes aerial photographs of Jeddah in 1948, 1964 and 1988 that dramatically illustrate the city's growth.

The rest of the house is a combination of exhibits (silver, old weapons, etc) and rooms done up in traditional style. It is very ornate, with lots of Egyptian and Syrian furniture with mosaic inlay work and presumably reflects the way in which Jeddah's wealthier citizens would have lived until only a generation ago.

## The Naseef House

Along the old city's main thoroughfare, Souk Al-Alawi, stands one of the city's most famous houses. The Naseefs are one of Jeddah's old-line merchant clans. In the 19th and early 20th centuries their family home was one of the most important houses in Jeddah. The tree in front of the house was, as recently as the 1920s, the only tree in all of Jeddah and thus an indicator of the family's wealth and importance. After conquering the city in 1925 King Abdul Aziz expropriated the house for his own use until a palace could be built.

To find it, look for a large stone doorway set slightly back from, and raised a few steps above, the level of the street at the turn for the Al-Alawi Traditional Restaurant.

## Al-Shafee Mosque

The Al-Shafee mosque, near the centre of Al-Balad, is one of the oldest in the city. The easiest way to reach it is to enter the souk near Bab Makkah. You'll pass through a covered section of the cloth souk followed, on the right, by a small park. When the street swings around to the left, keep going straight on the broad, straight pedestrian street (not the narrower one where the road bends). You should see the minaret, which is white with brown trim and a green dome, on the right-hand side of the street. The entrance, for Muslims only, is through the carved wooden gate and the doors on the right.

## The Corniche Sculptures

There are quite a few major sculptures and dozens of smaller ones along the Corniche, between the area around the port and the Obhur hotel in the ritzy Obhur Creek district further north. Among the subjects are a pair of hands, a dhow and what appears to be three gigantic feathers.

## The Souk

The souk, one of the better ones left in the Kingdom, starts on the inland side of Al-Malek Abdel Aziz St within the confines of the old city walls. It twists back into the old city, sometimes for a block or two, and in places all the way back to Bab Makkah. The souk has suffered something of a loss of character since large sections of it were paved over and, in places, fitted with bizarre green and white columns, but it remains a great place to spend hours strolling and browsing. The Souk Al-Alawi area is particularly good and has retained much of its traditional flavour.

## Language Courses

The Saudi French Centre (☎ 6827860) offers six-week courses in both spoken and written Arabic. The Centre is on A'taa St in the Al-Salamah district. Arabic classes are also offered by the Daalah Language Centre (☎ 6604929) on Falasteen St.

## Organised Tours

The Red Sea Palace (☎ 6428555) has one-hour city tours every Friday for SR 15.

## Places to Stay – bottom end

The Youth Hostel (☎ 6886632) is located at the stadium, 12 km east of the city centre on the Mecca Expressway. Beds are SR 8 per night. The hostel is behind the green buildings of the Sporting City. There is no access by bus. The easiest way to reach it by car is to take exit No 8 from the expressway, *not* the stadium exit which is further on. The sign says 'Local Traffic'. The exit numbers are small and are in the upper right-hand corner of the directional signs.

In the following hotels, except for the Shaheen, all rooms have a TV, fridge and telephone. Service charges, where applicable, are included.

In the centre, Jeddah boasts one of the Kingdom's best budget hotels. The *Shaheen Hotel* (☎ 6426582) is in an alley between Al-Malek Abdel Aziz St and the Corniche Commercial Centre. Singles/doubles are SR 47/65, dorm beds (three or four to a room) cost SR 27 per person. Breakfast is included. It's a clean place with friendly management. The clientele often consists of Nigerians on their way to or from Mecca. Be warned that the water sometimes disappears for a day or two at a time and one side of the building has no water at all.

The *New Arafat Hotel* (☎ 6484852) is on Al-Malek Abdel Aziz St in the same building as Fahad Travel, beside a large building with a Riyad Bank sign. The rooms are a bit bare but the hotel is good value at SR 77/116 for rooms with bath and SR 66/99 without. The hotel's name on the sign is only in Arabic but look for a big sign running down the corner of the building saying Hotel in English.

The *Al-Nahda Saudi Hotel* (☎ 6471158) on Mina'a St has small but clean rooms for SR 88/132 with bath, SR 77/110 without.

Ba'najah St is a good place for moderately priced beds. The best is the *Al-Almen Hotel* (6483953), near the intersection with Al-Dahab St. It's very clean with large, airy singles/doubles/triples at SR 88/132/154 with bath and SR 77/115/125 without – recommended. Opposite the Al-Almen the *Tysir Hotel* (☎ 6471777) has only doubles at SR 100 with bath and SR 83 without. Toward the Corniche, near the undefined point where Al-Malek Abdel Aziz St becomes Ba'najah St, is the *Middle East Hotel* (☎ 6483330). The rooms are tiny but modern and well kept.

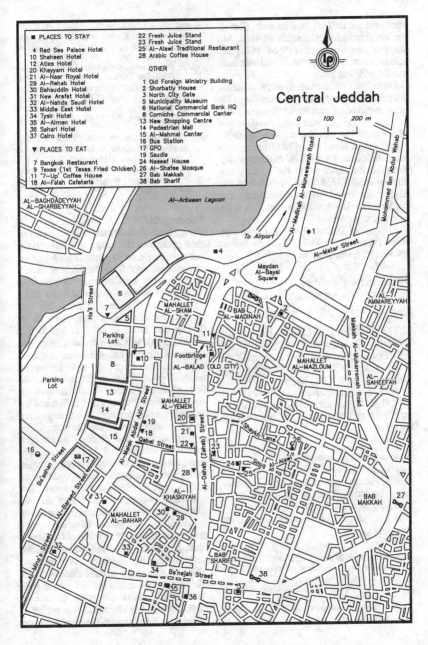

PLACES TO STAY

4 Red Sea Palace Hotel
10 Shaheen Hotel
12 Atlas Hotel
20 Khayyam Hotel
21 Al-Nasr Royal Hotel
29 Al-Rehab Hotel
30 Bahauddin Hotel
31 New Arafat Hotel
32 Al-Nahda Saudi Hotel
33 Middle East Hotel
34 Tysir Hotel
35 Al-Almen Hotel
36 Sahari Hotel
37 Cairo Hotel

PLACES TO EAT

7 Bangkok Restaurant
9 Texas (1st Texas Fried Chicken)
11 '7-Up' Coffee House
18 Al-Falah Cafeteria

22 Fresh Juice Stand
23 Fresh Juice Stand
25 Al-Alawi Traditional Restaurant
28 Arabic Coffee House

OTHER

1 Old Foreign Ministry Building
2 Shorbatly House
3 North City Gate
5 Municipality Museum
6 National Commercial Bank HQ
8 Corniche Commercial Center
13 New Shopping Centre
14 Pedestrian Mall
15 Al-Mahmal Center
16 Bus Station
17 GPO
19 Saudia
24 Naseef House
26 Al-Shafee Mosque
27 Bab Makkah
38 Bab Sharif

Central Jeddah

0     100     200 m

They cost SR 88/132, all with bath. East of the intersection of Ba'najah St with Al-Dahab St, the *Cairo Hotel* (☎ 6478115) has bare but clean rooms for SR 77/115 with bath and SR 66/99 without.

On Al-Dahab St, the *Atlas Hotel* (☎ 6438520) is a clean, modern place. The rooms are a bit small but some of them have balconies. They cost SR 88/132, all with bath, and there are triples at SR 154. Nearby, at 59 Al-Dahab St, the *Khayyam Hotel* (☎ 6437049) has good, small rooms at SR 88/132. Next door the *Bard Al-Din Hotel* (☎ 6440871) only has doubles at SR 132. Also on Al-Dahab St, the *Al-Andalus Hotel* (☎ 6476565) only has doubles for SR 93, all with bath. It's a bit drab and run-down.

Just off Al-Dahab St is the *Bahauddin Hotel* (☎ 6477811) which is good value at SR 88/132 for singles/doubles.

### Places to Stay – middle

Jeddah's middle range is a bit thin, but there are a few good value hotels on or near Al-Dahab St.

The *Al-Rehab Hotel* (6479636), just off Al-Dahab St, is excellent value at SR 100/150 for singles/doubles. On Al-Dahab St the *Al-Nasr Royal Hotel* (☎ 6473329) has very nice rooms at SR 132/170.50.

A bit more expensive is the *Sahari Hotel* (☎ 6477744), just south of the intersection of Al-Dahab and Ba'najah Sts. Rooms are SR 165/214.50.

### Places to Stay – top end

Jeddah has the usual selection of top-flight hotels, though most of them are a long way from the centre. You can usually get a discount on these rates simply by asking for it. The rates quoted here include the service charge.

*Alfau Holiday Inn* (☎ 6611000, fax 6606326), on the Corniche just south of its intersection with Falasteen St. Singles/doubles are SR 322/420.

*Alhamra Sofitel* (☎ 6602000, fax 6604145), Falasteen St, between Al-Madinah Al-Munawwarah Rd and the US Consulate General. Singles/doubles are SR 320/420.

*Hyatt Regency Jeddah* (☎ 6521234, fax 6516260), Al-Madinah Al-Munawwarah Rd, a short distance south of the Falasteen St intersection. Singles/doubles are SR 379.50/448.50.

*Jeddah Inter-Continental Hotel* (☎ 6611800, fax 6611145), just south of the Holiday Inn on the Corniche. Singles/doubles are SR 379.50/494.50

*Jeddah Marriott* (☎ 6714000, fax 6715990), Falasteen St west of the intersection with Al-Madinah Al-Munawwarah Rd. Singles/doubles are SR 368/477.

*Red Sea Palace Hotel* (☎ 6428555, fax 6422395), Al-Malek Abdel Aziz St, between the National Commercial Bank headquarters building and Maydan Al-Bayal. This is the only top-flight hotel in the city centre. It is also a bit cheaper than the others at SR 299/391 for singles/doubles.

### Places to Eat

**Cheap & Medium-Priced** There are a lot of cheap places in the centre offering mostly fast food. *Texas*, on Al-Malek Abdel Aziz St, around the corner from the Shaheen Hotel, and opposite the Corniche Commercial Centre, has both shawarma and the traditional burgers, fries and fried chicken fast-food menu. Shawarma cost SR 3, burgers SR 7 or SR 8, half a chicken SR 12. In the Corniche Commercial Centre the *American Corner* has the usual fast-food menu and also serves US-style submarine sandwiches. *Al-Falah*, a cafeteria near the Saudia office Al-Malek Abdel Aziz St, has a similar menu including good coffee and ice cream. There are a couple of Filipino places on the ground floor of the Corniche Commercial Centre, one offering hamburger, potato and salad for SR 5. The small *cafeteria* in the Al-Faisaleyyah Centre, between the National Commercial Bank headquarters building and the Red Sea Palace hotel, has reasonable burgers. Level four of the Al-Mahmal Centre has a collection of medium to cheap fast-food places covering a wide range of cuisines. Try *Tarboosh* for Arabic food, *Silk Rd* for Chinese food or *Texas* for burgers and fried chicken. There are two places specialising in roasted chicken on Al-Malek Abdel Aziz St, a block from the New Arafat Hotel. Both are good. Capuccino addicts should head for the *House of Coffee*, where the coffee is worth the extra riyal over the cafeteria prices. They have downtown cafes in the Al-Mahmal Centre and in the building on Al-Malek Abdel Aziz St that also houses the main Saudia office. Al-Dahab St has two open-air traditional *coffee houses*, where men sit on high couches, smoke water pipes and drink tea, not coffee.

Outside the centre, there's a *Pizza Hut* off Al-Andalus St, south of the Falasteen St intersection.

**Expensive** I can highly recommend the *Al-Alawi Traditional Restaurant*, just off Souq Al-Alawi St in the old city. The 'traditional' food is Moroccan, not Saudi, but it's a great place with a nice garden. Main dishes are SR 30 to SR 40 but you can get out for much less by sticking to the appetisers. Try the Hariri soup (a thick beef and vegetable soup) for SR 5. Avoid the Perrier which is absurdly overpriced at SR 12 for a small bottle.

*Da Pino Pizzeria*, in the Red Sea Palace Hotel on Al-Malek Abdel Aziz St, is quite good. Meals cost from SR 50 to SR 80. Seafood, both Lebanese and Western, is the speciality at the *Dolphin Restaurant* on the Corniche near the intersection with Falasteen St. Meals start at SR 75 but they're worth it. The *Gulf Royal Chinese Restaurant* has excellent, if pricey, food. Meals cost SR 50 and up. They have one restaurant in the Al-Mahmal Centre and one in the shopping mall on Falasteen St next to the Marriott hotel. Another place for good Oriental food is the *Bangkok Restaurant*, on the 2nd floor of the Corniche Markets building overlooking Ha'il St and the Corniche Commercial Centre's parking lot.

## Things to Buy

Jeddah is not Saudi Arabia's best spot for antiques and traditional souvenirs but it is a good place to look for almost everything else. The old city's gold souk is particularly good. The supermarket in the Jamjoom Centre on Falasteen St has a small area featuring a good selection of craft items and silver jewellery, most of which is new though there are also a few old pieces on display. The Airport Souk, at the old airport, is reputed to

be a good place to shop for almost anything from antiques to housewares.

## Getting There & Away

**Air** The King Abdul Aziz International airport is about 30 km north of the city on Al-Madinah Al-Munawwarah Rd. Saudia flights, both domestic and international, leave from the south terminal. Foreign airlines use the north terminal. The only way to get from the north to the south terminal, or vice versa, is by taxi. This will cost you about SR 20.

The big, tent-like structure at the northern end of the airport is a special hajj terminal used by pilgrims en route to Mecca. It deals with the huge number of pilgrims who flock to Saudi Arabia each year. (In the final weeks before hajj a planeload of pilgrims lands at the airport every few minutes in addition to the regular commercial services.)

Jeddah is Saudia's second hub, after Riyadh, and you can fly directly from here to pretty much anywhere in the Kingdom. There are usually 10 to 15 flights per day to Riyadh (SR 240 one-way, economy class), five or six to Dhahran (SR 360) and at least one per day to Abha (SR 160), Gassim/Buraydah (SR 230), Jizan (SR 170), Ha'il (SR 210), Medina (SR 110), Najran (SR 210), Tabuk (SR 240) and Yanbu (SR 90).

International fares vary significantly from month to month. Here's a sample of cheap one-way and return fares, with minimum and maximum stay requirements:

| To | One-Way | Return | Min/Max |
|----|---------|--------|---------|
| Abu Dhabi | SR 1019 | SR 1412 | 3/14 days |
| Athens | SR 1837 | SR 1949 | 10/35 days |
| Bahrain | SR 695 | SR 962 | 3/14 days |
| Cairo | SR 1082 | SR 1288 | 0/60 days |
| Damascus | SR 1167 | SR 1557 | 0/60 days |
| Doha | SR 813 | SR 1128 | 3/14 days |
| Dubai | SR 1090 | SR 1509 | 3/14 days |
| Kuwait | SR 979 | SR 1357 | 3/14 days |
| London | SR 3415 | SR 3619 | 10/35 days |
| Muscat | SR 1455 | SR 2017 | 3/14 days |
| New York | SR4002 | SR 4672 | 7/30 days |
| Rome | SR 2727 | SR 2891 | 10/45 days |

Some of the airlines flying out of Jeddah include:

Air Algérie
  Adham Commercial Centre, Al-Madinah Al-Munawwarah Rd, near the Hyatt Regency Hotel (☎ 6515232)
Air France
  Intersection of Al-Madinah Al-Munawwarah Rd and Abdallah Ibn Zayd St, near the Hyatt Regency Hotel (☎ 6512000)
Air India
  City Centre building, Al-Madinah Al-Munawwarah Rd, north of the intersection with Falasteen St (☎ 6652111)
Austrian Airlines
  Al-Amoudi Centre (1st floor), Al-Madinah Al-Munawwarah Rd, just north of the intersection with Falasteen St (☎ 6602356)
British Airways
  Al-Amoudi Centre on Al-Madinah Al-Munawwarah Rd (☎ 6693464)
Cyprus Airways
  Al-Amoudi Centre on Al-Madinah Al-Munawwarah Rd, north of the intersection with Falasteen St (☎ 6513541)
EgyptAir
  Intersection of Al-Madinah Al-Munawwarah Rd and Al-Malek Khaled St in the Al-Sharafeyyah district (☎ 6441515)
Emirates
  City Centre building on Al-Madinah Al-Munawwarah Rd, north of the intersection with Falasteen St (☎ 6659405)
Ethiopian Airlines
  Adham Commercial Centre, Al-Madinah Al-Munawwarah Rd, near the Hyatt Regency Hotel (☎ 6512365)
Garuda Indonesia
  City Centre building on Al-Madinah Al-Munawwarah Rd, north of the intersection with Falasteen St (☎ 6695388)
Gulf Air
  Abo Bakr Al-Seddeeq St near the intersection with Abdallah Ibn Zayd St, near the Hyatt Regency Hotel (☎ 6517756)
KLM
  Falasteen St, between Al-Andalus St and the Jamjoom Market (☎ 6670888)
Korean Air
  City Centre building on Al-Madinah Al-Munawwarah Rd, north of the intersection with Falasteen St (☎ 6657107)
Kuwait Airways
  Al-Amoudi Centre on Al-Madinah Al-Munawwarah Rd, just north of the intersection with Falasteen St (☎ 6694111)

Lufthansa
  City Centre building, 1st floor, Al-Madinah Al-Munawwarah Rd, north of the intersection with Falasteen St (☎ 6650000)
Libyan Arab Airways
  Al-Malek Abdel Aziz St between the Red Sea Palace hotel and the National Commercial Bank headquarters building (☎ 6441200)
Olympic
  Adham Commercial Centre, Al-Madinah Al-Munawwarah Rd, near the Hyatt Regency Hotel (☎ 6511280)
PIA (Pakistan International Airlines)
  Al-Malek Abdel Aziz St between the Red Sea Palace Hotel and Maydan Al-Bayal (☎ 6422642)
Royal Jordanian
  Intersection of Al-Madinah Al-Munawwarah Rd and Abdallah Ibn Zayd St, near the Hyatt Regency Hotel (☎ 6514949)
Swissair
  Intersection of Abo Bakr Al-Seddeeq St and Abdallah Ibn Zayd St, near the Hyatt Regency Hotel (☎ 6514000)
Tunis Air
  Adham Commercial Centre, Al-Madinah Al-Munawwarah Rd, near the Hyatt Regency Hotel (☎ 6530881)
Turkish Airlines
  City Centre building on Al-Madinah Al-Munawwarah Rd, north of the intersection with Falasteen St (☎ 6600127)

**Domestic Buses** The SAPTCO bus station (☎ 6481131) is on Ba'ashan St. Thanks to a change in routings none of the eastbound inter-city buses go through Mecca anymore and, therefore, they are all open to non-Muslims, but non-Muslim passengers would be well advised to double-check – it changed once so, presumably, it could change back. Also, there is no computerised reservation system so only a portion of the seats on each bus can be sold in Jeddah. This could be a problem for the overnight services to Riyadh and the Eastern Province. However, if the clerk says he has tickets only to Taif, don't let that worry you as you can probably pick up a seat onward to Riyadh in Taif (where the eastbound buses make a 30 to 45-minute stopover).

The more accurate timetable is the one inside the station above the main ticket desk, not the one outside the building.

Eastbound there are five buses daily, at 8

am, noon, 3.30, 6 and 9 pm; they go to Taif (2½ hours, SR 30) and continue on to Riyadh (13 hours, SR 130), Hofuf (16 hours, SR 175) and Dammam (19 hours, SR 190).

Southbound, buses for Jizan (11 hours, SR 90) with continuing service to Al-Towal (12 hours, SR 100) leave every two hours from 8 am until 10 pm with a final run at 11 pm. Buses for Abha (10 hours, SR 90) and Khamis Mushayt (11 hours, SR 120) leave at 7 and 10 am and at 4 pm.

There are two buses per day to Yanbu (five hours, SR 60), at 10 am and 6 pm.

For Muslims only, buses go to Mecca (one hour, SR 15) 16 times a day, roughly once every hour from 6.30 am. The last run of the day is at 11.15 pm. There are nine buses per day to Medina (six hours, SR 50) at two-hour intervals from 7.30 am until 11.30 pm.

**International Buses** SAPTCO's international services depart from the same terminal as their domestic ones. There is a daily bus to Cairo (36 hours, SR 345, including the ferry crossing) at 4.30 pm. Buses to Amman (20 hours, SR 225) leave every Tuesday, Wednesday and Saturday at 10 am. To Damascus (30 hours, SR 250), they leave every Monday, Tuesday and Thursday at 10 am. The trips to Egypt, Syria and Jordan include free meals at designated rest stops.

International services are also offered by several Turkish bus companies operating from a small station next door to SAPTCO. The companies are Has, Oztur and Tur and they send their buses off in a convoy every Tuesday, Wednesday and Sunday afternoon between 2 and 3 pm. The route is Istanbul (three days, SR 300) via Amman (20 hours, SR 200), Damascus (30 hours, SR 250) and Ankara (60 hours, SR 275). All companies charge the same fare but some may be willing to offer a discount, so ask around. These buses take the coastal road north via Yanbu but, again, non-Muslims ought to double-check that the bus isn't going through Mecca or Medina before putting down their money.

**Service Taxi** These come in two varieties:

taxis, which take about five passengers, and trucks which take seven to nine passengers. (The trucks are called 'GMCs', which is the most common make of the vehicle). As with all service taxis they leave when full. The fares are a few riyals less than the equivalent bus fare but, as service taxis are not as commonly used in Saudi Arabia as they are in other Arab countries, they take a long time to fill up. In addition most of the drivers will be headed east via Mecca which means that non-Muslims cannot go along. The service-taxi stand is on Al-Mina'a St across from the Red Sea Shipping Company's office. Fares are: Mecca, SR 10/8 by taxi/GMC; Medina, SR 51/40; Taif SR 21/17; Riyadh, SR 125/101; Ha'il, SR 97/78; Al-Kharj, SR 135/109; and Dhahran, SR 175/151.

**Boat** You can travel by sea from the Jeddah Islamic Port to Suez (Egypt) and Port Sudan. Before the Gulf War it was also possible to travel to Aqaba (Jordan) by boat, but this service had not been resumed at this writing. It is quite an experience: one of the boats on the Suez run is a converted Danish cruise liner whose lounges still have signs identifying them as the 'Mermaid Pub' and the 'Viking Bar.' The portrait of King Fahd in the 1st-class lounge hangs near a large map of Copenhagen's Tivoli amusement park.

All of the boat services are somewhat irregular with sailings at intervals of six or eight days rather than on a regular weekly basis, but you can count on three or four sailings a month for each boat.

The most popular route is to/from Suez, and it's no great bargain. Fares start at SR 250 in deck class and run to SR 500 in 1st class. The trip to Suez takes about 36 hours direct, about three days if the boats again start travelling via Aqaba. Be sure you know what route the boat is taking – I was once assured that I was on a direct boat only to find myself on the long, three-day trip! The journey to Port Sudan takes eight or nine hours and costs around SR 400 in 1st class, SR 350 in 2nd class and SR 300 on the deck.

Some shopping around is probably a good idea as the fares can vary greatly from one company to another. Most of the shipping companies have offices along Al-Mina'a St but since each company is pushing its own boat your best bet is a visit to Azco Travel (☎ 6474000), also on Al-Mina'a St near the intersection by the flyover. They offer the same prices as the individual shipping companies but can book any of the boats on the Suez and Port Sudan routes, making it a fairly easy matter to compare prices and sailing dates.

For boats to Jeddah from Egypt see Marrakech Travel (☎ 3546046) at the corner of Tahrir St and Tahrir Square, or Yara Tours & Shipping (☎ 3925393) on Mohamed Sabry Abualam St (off Talaat Harb Square), both in Cairo. The latter has slightly lower prices in 1st class.

**Car Rental** The airport is your best bet. The rental agencies are clustered in the arrivals areas and it is fairly easy to shop around, though the rates are pretty much the same at all the counters. In the city the easiest thing is to head for one of the big hotels. Try the Budget Rent-A-Car office in the shopping arcade adjacent to the Red Sea Palace Hotel.

## Getting Around

**To/From the Airport** Bus No 20 runs to the south terminal (all Saudia flights, both domestic and international) from Maydan Al-Bayal. The fare is SR 3. To get to the north (foreign carriers) terminal you will have to take a taxi from the south terminal (about SR 20). A taxi to either terminal from the centre costs about SR 50 on the meter. Coming into the centre from the airport, there are set tariffs. The yellow cabs charge SR 50 and the white limos charge SR 70.

**Bus** It's best to stick to the orange and white SAPTCO buses for getting around town. Minibuses also prowl the streets of Jeddah but they have no markings to indicate where they are going. SAPTCO's buses have their routes clearly displayed in English on a sign in the front windscreen. Bus trips anywhere in the city are SR 2, the sole exception being the airport which costs SR 3. Thrifty Tickets

(three trips for SR 5) can be purchased at the SAPTCO inter-city terminal. You can sometimes also get a local route map at the inter-city terminal, but make sure it's up to date. Local buses start running around 5 am and continue until around midnight.

The main bus routes around the city are:

Route 3 – Follows the Makkah Rd, from Bab Makkah to Kilo 20

Route 3A – Bab Makkah, Makkah Al-Mukarramah Rd to Kilo 7, Ben Ladin St as far as the Ring Rd Expressway; returns via same route

Route 4 – Bab Makkah, Makkah Al-Mukarramah Rd, Al-Jame'ah St, Abdallah Al-Sulayman St to the gate of the University Hospital, Abdallah Al-Sulayman St (in the other direction), Ali Al-Murtadi St; returns via same route

Route 4A – Bab Makkah, Makkah Al-Mukarramah Rd, Al-Malek Khaled St, Ba Khashab St, Al-Jame'ah St, Abdallah Al-Sulayman St, Quwaizah District; returns via same route

Route 5 – Maydan Al-Bayal, Al-Malek Abdel Aziz St, Ba'najah St, Al-Zahab St, Al-Malek Khaled St, Al-Televizyoun St, Al-Mahjar St, Industrial City (returns via same route until Ba'najah St where the bus turns east to follow Ba'najah St, Makkah Al-Mukarramah Rd route back to Maydan Al-Bayal)

Route 6 – Safeway Supermarket (Al-Andalus District), Abd Al-Rahman Shubokshi St, Mohammed Ibn Abdul Aziz St, Ha'il St, Turky Ibn Abdul Aziz St, Al-Mustashfa Al-'Aam St, Al-Iman St, Al-Hamra'a St, Ha'il St, Falasteen St, Al-Andalus St, Al-Maadi St, Ha'il St, Binzert St, Al-Madinah Al-Munawwarah Rd, Maydan Al-Bayal (returns from Maydan Al-Bayal via: Al-Malek Abdel Aziz St, Ba'najah St, Makkah Al-Mukarramah Rd, Al-Madinah Al-Munawwarah Rd, Al-Madares St, Ha'il St)

Route 7 – Maydan Al-Bayal, Al-Malek Abdel Aziz St, Ba'najah St, Makkah Al-Mukarramah Rd, Al-Madinah Al-Munawwarah Rd, Hera'a St, Al-Kournaish Rd as far as the Al-Bilad Hotel; returns via same route

Route 7A – Saudia City, Al-Amir Abdallah St, Al-Madinah Al-Munawwarah Rd, Maydan Al-Bayal (returns to Al-Madinah Al-Munawwarah Rd from Maydan Al-Bayal via Al-Malek Abdel Aziz St, Ba'najah St, Makkah Al-Mukarramah Rd)

Route 7B – Maydan Al-Bayal, Al-Malek Abdel Aziz St, Ba'najah St, Makkah Al-Mukarramah Rd, Al-Madinah Al-Munawwarah Rd, Al-Amir Abdallah St, Ahmed Al-Moujahed St, Sari St, Mustafa Menkabou St, Quraysh St, Al-Amir Sultan St as far as Hera'a St; returns via same route

Routes 8 & 8A – SAPTCO Garage (Al-Amir Met'ab St), Sawt Al-Hegaz St, Al-Amir Majed St (8A takes a detour here to the Vegetable Market via Abdallah Sharbatly and Umm Al-Qura Sts returning by the same route to Al-Amir Majed St), Al-Amir Abdallah St, Al-Makarounah St, Falasteen St, Al-Amir Fahd St, Makkah Al-Mukarramah Rd, Al-Madinah Al-Munawwarah Rd, Al-Madares St, Maydan Al-Bayal and vice versa (returns to Makkah Al-Mukarramah Rd via Al-Malek Abdel Aziz and Ba'najah Sts)

Route 9 – Al-Badawi (northern end of Al-Amir Fahd St), Al-Amir Fahd St, Al-Malek Khaled St, Al-Madinah Al-Munawwarah Rd, Maydan Al-Bayal, Al-Malek Abdel Aziz St, Ba'najah St, Makkah Al-Mukarramah Rd, Al-Malek Khaled St (returns to Al-Badawi on Al-Amir Fahd St

Route 10A – Al-Manara Souk, Al-Sahafa St, Al-Tadaamun St, Al-Amir Met'ab St, Falasteen St, Khaled Ibn Al-Waleed St, Mohammed Ibn Abdul Wahaab St, Maydan Al-Bayal, Al-Madinah Al-Munawwarah Rd to Al-Madares St where the bus makes a U-turn and returns to Maydan Al-Bayal, Al-Malek Abdel Aziz St, Ba'najah St, Makkah Al-Mukarramah Rd, Al-Matar Rd, Al-Amir Fahd St, Al-Malek Khaled St, Al-Tawbah St, Falasteen St and back to Al-Manara Souk by the outbound route

Route 11 – Maydan Al-Bayal, Al-Malek Abdel Aziz St, Ba'najah St, Makkah Al-Mukarramah Rd, Al-Matar Rd, Al-Malek Khaled St, Al-Amir Fahd St, Falasteen St, U-turn, back south on Al-Amir Fahd St to Bani Malek St, Bani Malek St as far as the Civil Aviation Presidency where the bus takes another U-turn and returns to Al-Amir Fahd St (returns to Maydan Al-Bayal via Al-Amir Fahd St, Al-Malek Khaled St, Al-Madinah Al-Munawwarah Rd)

Route 12 – Maydan Al-Bayal, Al-Malek Abdel Aziz St, Ba'najah St, Makkah Al-Mukarramah Rd, Al-Iskan St, Industrial City and; returns via same route

Route 17 – Maydan Al-Bayal, Al-Malek Abdel Aziz St, Ba'najah St, Al-Zahab St, Petromin; returns via same route

Route 20 – To and from the airport (south terminal) from Maydan Al-Bayal via Al-Madinah Al-Munawwarah Rd

**Taxi** Both yellow cabs and white limousines have meters, though you might have to remind the driver to turn it on. Both types charge Sr 5 for a flag drop. The fare then increases in 50 halala increments in the yellow cabs and 70 halala increments in the limos.

# The Hejaz (Western Region)

## MECCA

Muslims refer to Mecca (Makkah) as *al-mukarramah*, which translates roughly as 'the Revered'. It was here that the Prophet Mohammed was born in the 6th century AD, here that he began his preaching career and it was to Mecca that he returned for a final pilgrimage shortly before his death in 632.

Mecca and the holy sites in its immediate vicinity are strictly off limits to non-Muslims. There are checkpoints on the roads approaching the city and non-Muslims are strongly advised not to try getting past these. The most famous non-Muslim who managed to visit Mecca was Richard Burton, the great British explorer who disguised himself as an Afghan Muslim and participated in the hajj in 1853.

Mecca is Islam's holiest city. All devout Muslims attempt a hajj to Mecca at least once in their lifetime. With an area of some 26 sq km, Mecca is in the Sirat Mountains, 70 km east of Jeddah. The city centres on the the Grand Mosque and the sacred Zamzam well inside it. The Kaaba, which all Muslims face when they pray, is in the mosque's central courtyard. According to tradition, the Kaaba was built by Abraham and his son Ishmael as a replica of God's house in heaven.

As a non-Muslim I could not visit Mecca. However, the religious and scholarly literature on the holy sites is ample and easily available throughout the Kingdom. Muslims seeking practical information on hotels and restaurants in Mecca may want to consult the *Makkah Al-Mukarramah City & Hajj Guide*, part of the Farsi Maps series of 'A to Z' guides to Saudi cities.

## TAIF

Taif (Tai'if, Al-Taif), nestled in the mountains above Mecca, is the summer capital of Saudi Arabia. During the summer months it is noticeably cooler than Jeddah and a great deal less humid. The town's main attractions

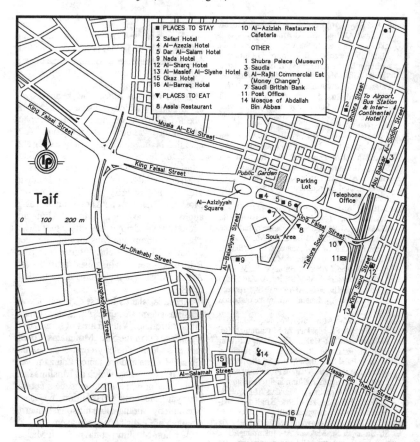

Taif

0    100    200 m

PLACES TO STAY
2 Safari Hotel
4 Al–Azezia Hotel
5 Dar Al–Salam Hotel
9 Nada Hotel
12 Al–Sharq Hotel
13 Al–Maslef Al–Slyahe Hotel
15 Okaz Hotel
16 Al–Barraq Hotel

▼ PLACES TO EAT
8 Assla Restaurant

10 Al–Azizlah Restaurant
   Cafeteria

OTHER

1 Shubra Palace (Museum)
3 Saudia
6 Al–Rajhi Commercial Est
  (Money Changer)
7 Saudi British Bank
11 Post Office
14 Mosque of Abdallah
   Bin Abbas

are its weather, its scenery and its relaxed atmosphere.

### History

The town is quite important historically. Traditionally, it has been the military gateway to Mecca and many an army has positioned troops here over the centuries. In 1802 the warriors of the First Saudi Empire massacred the entire male population of the town. Taif was also the site of one of the key early battles of the Arab revolt against Ottoman rule during WW I. The seizure of the town in 1916 by forces loyal to Sherif Hussein was

one of the events which eventually convinced the British that Hussein's embryonic Kingdom of the Arabs would be worth their backing.

In 1924, however, an army under the command of the Sherif's son, Ali, contributed to a far less glorious chapter of the town's history. Knowing that an attack by Abdul Aziz's forces was imminent, Ali and his army slunk away under cover of darkness. The ikhwan army, which entered the city after the Hashemites had left it undefended, killed at least 300 people. The second Wahhabi massacre at Taif was deeply embarrassing to Abdul Aziz though it ultimately worked to his political advantage. Word of the deaths in Taif spread rapidly to Mecca and Jeddah and led, a month later, to Sherif Hussein's abdication under pressure from Mecca's scholars and Jeddah's merchants.

In recent years Taif has also become something of a minor diplomatic centre. In 1988, it hosted peace talks involving the USSR, the Afghan government and the Mujahideen rebels. The following year, the town was the site of a lengthy peace conference that sought to bring an end to Lebanon's civil war, and from August 1990 until March 1991 Taif was the seat of Kuwait's government-in-exile.

### Orientation & Information

Taif centres on a nameless square formed by the intersection of King Faisal and Shubra Sts. It looks like a square because of the large parking lot across from the Saudi telephone office. Most of the budget hotels are a bit east of this intersection and cheap restaurants are all over the central area. The bus station and airport are some distance north of the centre.

For changing money there are a number of banks around the main intersection. There is a post office just off the south side of the intersection, opposite the Saudi Telephone building, though the GPO is north of town, near the bus station. The telephone office, from which only international calls can be made, is in the small white building next to the much larger PTT office building on the north-west side of the main intersection. For long-distance calls inside Saudi Arabia you'll have to use the payphones at the front (change is available at the desk in the telephone office) or go to the GPO where there are still more payphones. The telephone code for Taif is 02.

The Saudia office is on Abu Bakker Al-Siddiq St about 200 metres north of the main intersection.

### Abdallah Bin Abbas Mosque

Taif's central mosque, though a bit fortress-like at first glance, is a good example of simple, refined Islamic architecture. Note the interesting minaret which is earth-coloured with brown and white trim and a white dome. If you look just below the four long windows on the minaret's mid-section you will see several balconies which give a nice effect.

### Tailors' Souk

One of the few surviving bits of traditional Taif can be found just off the main square, at the intersection of Shubra and King Faisal Sts around the corner from the post office. Next to a Turkish restaurant and several small grocery stores is an old archway of sand-coloured stone. There are two small mock pillars just above the archway and, above them, a circular frieze design. The short alleyway beyond this arch, part of the tailors' souk, is a quick trip into Old Taif. At one time much of the city (and many other Middle Eastern cities) consisted of small, alley-like streets of this kind making up the various souks.

### Shubra Palace

This beautifully restored traditional house doubles as the city's museum. It is open only on Thursdays from 9 am to 7 pm, though even these hours are erratic. The collection includes a women's camel saddle covered in shrouds and two stills for making rose water. King Abdul Aziz used to stay here when he visited Taif in his later years.

### Around Taif

The small village of Al-Hada, 20 km south of Taif, is also worth visiting if you are interested in seeing a rural Saudi/Hejazi village.

### Organised Tours

The Inter-Continental Hotel sometimes offers weekend tours of the surrounding mountain areas. The four day, three night Frankincense Route tour, roughly following part of the old Yemen-to-Damascus caravan route, starts at the Inter-Continental and continues down to Al-Baha and Abha.

## Places to Stay

Taif is a very crowded city on summer weekends (ie, from Wednesday afternoon until Friday afternoon). From May to September reservations are strongly recommended.

## Places to Stay – bottom end & middle

The *Youth Hostel* (☎ 7253400) is at the King Fahd Sporting City, 22.5 km north of the centre. From the bus station go north (away from the centre) and turn left at the sign for the Sporting City. The No 10 bus runs from the centre to the hostel via the bus station and stops about 100 metres from the gate. Note that bus routes in Taif change frequently. Ask the driver or the clerk at the bus station before boarding to make sure that the bus is, in fact, going to the Sporting City. Look for a small, blue Youth Hostel sign by the wall of the complex. Beds are SR 8. The hostel is infinitely superior to any of the hotels listed under this heading and is far more likely to have space at weekends.

All of the rooms at the following hotels have air-conditioning, except for the Dar Al-Salam which has ceiling fans. The Dar Al-Salam Hotel is also the only one where not all the rooms have a TV, telephone and fridge. Service charges, where applicable, have been included in the prices. Summer rates are usually for the period from 1 June to 30 September.

The *Dar Al-Salam Hotel* (☎ 7360124) on King Faisal St, just west of the main intersection, is the only real cheapie in town. Singles/doubles are SR 39/61 (SR 51/79 in summer). The rooms are small and spartan but some have balconies.

On King Saud St, the *Al-Sharq Hotel* (☎ 7323651) has exceedingly clean rooms and friendly management. The prices are SR 88/132 with bath and SR 77/110 without. Summer rates are SR 97/145 with bath, SR 85/121 without. Further along King Saud St the *Al-Masief Al-Siyahe Hotel* (☎ 7324786) is also very clean but a bit drab. Rooms are SR 99/110 with bath and SR 66/88 without (SR 115.50/170.50 and SR 99/148.50, respectively, in summer). A bit further down on the same street and up the price scale is

the *Al-Barraq Hotel* (☎ 7360610) at SR 165/ 214.50 (SR 209/264 in summer), where all rooms have attached baths. The *Okaz Hotel* (☎ 7328051) on Al-Salamah St, near the Abdallah Bin Abbas mosque, is a reasonably good deal at SR 77/115 for rooms with bath, SR 66/99 without. Summer rates are SR 100/150 with bath, SR 86/29 without.

Probably the best of Taif's slightly more expensive hotels is the *Nada Hotel* (☎ 7324177), just off Al-Baladiyah St. The rooms are very nice and quite a good deal at SR 100/150 (SR 150/200 in summer). Other hotels in this price category include the *Al-Azezia Hotel* (☎ 7321666) on Al-Aziziyyah Square. Rooms are SR 150/ 200 (SR 175/225 in summer) but that seems to be very negotiable (off season they offered me a suite at the single rate).

The *Safari Hotel* (☎ 7367800) on Shubra St, about 300 metres from the main intersection, is another good bet. The hotel has big, airy rooms, all with bath, for SR 110/165 (130/195 in summer).

## Places to Stay – top end

People with money tend to converge on the *Inter-Continental Hotel* (☎ 7328333, fax 7361844), 13 km north of Taif's centre, or on the *Al-Hada Sheraton* (☎ 7541400, fax 7544831), 20 km south of Taif overlooking the village of Al-Hada. Both charge SR 368/ 478 (SR 441.50/574 in summer) a single/ double. Neither can be reached by public transport.

## Places to Eat

The number of small Turkish restaurants in the centre of Taif is quite astonishing. Try the *Assia Restaurant*, a friendly place on King Faisal St with good kofta and kebabs. The portions are huge and meals cost SR 10 to SR 15. The *Al-Aziziah Restaurant Cafeteria*, further east on King Faisal St, is another good bet. It's a lot bigger and nicer inside than it looks from the street. The prices are about the same as those at the Assia. There are a lot of small restaurants along King Saud St between the Al-Sharq and the Al-Barraq hotels.

The Al-Azezia Hotel has a restaurant/ coffee shop which is worth trying, especially if you want quieter surroundings than the Assia. There is also a small *cafe* adjacent to the bus station. For more up-market dining the two large hotels are your only option. Neither is great though the breakfast buffet at the Inter-Continental is a good deal at SR 25.

If you are staying at or headed for the youth hostel, eat in town. There is no place to eat within three km of the hostel.

### Getting There & Away

**Air** The airport is 25 km north of the town. Daily flights operate to Riyadh (SR 210) and Dhahran (SR 330). Direct flights are also available to Jeddah (SR 90), Abha (SR 120), Medina (SR 140) and Tabuk (SR 330).

**Bus** The SAPTCO bus station (☎ 7369924) is on Al-Matar Rd, 2.5 km north of the main intersection. There are seven buses daily to Riyadh (10 hours, SR 100; with connections to Hofuf and Dammam). Departures are at 1.30 and 10.30 am (there are two buses at 10.30, one via the old road, which takes several hours more) and 2.30, 6.30, 9.30 and 11.30 pm. There are two daily buses to Abha (10 hours, SR 90) at 10.30 am and 1.30 pm. The Abha buses go via Al-Baha (2½ hours, SR 30) and continue on to Khamis Mushayt. Another bus to Khamis Mushayt via Bisha leaves at noon. There are seven Jeddah-bound buses for non-Muslims each day (2½ hours, SR 30), at 2.15, 3.30, 5.45, 6.45 and 8.15 am and 7.15 and 9.15 pm.

For Muslims only there are six buses per day to Mecca (1½ hours, SR 15) at 1.15 and 7 am and at 1, 3.30, 5.15 and 7 pm. The buses at 1.15 am and 1, 3.30 and 5.15 pm continue on to Jeddah.

Note that the timetable on the wall of the station is years out of date. Up-to-date printed schedules are sometimes available.

**Service Taxi** Service taxis are on the north side of the parking lot at the main intersection. A few of them are headed for Riyadh or Abha but most travel between Taif and Jeddah via Mecca, which makes them off limits to non-Muslims. If you can fill a taxi with non-Muslims the driver probably won't object to going around Mecca, but he might ask for a few riyals more. The fares are fluid but usually about the same as the comparable bus fare.

**Car** If you are driving up to Taif from Jeddah there are two options: the Taif Escarpment Rd (also called the Al-Hada Rd) and the truck route. The Escarpment Rd is spectacular but, because of the way people drive, it can be a pretty hair-raising experience. Personally, I prefer the truck route, which is longer, slower and less scenic but a lot easier on the nerves. In any case, the Escarpment Rd is closed every year from October to May. To reach the Escarpment Rd from Jeddah you go either straight through Mecca or around Mecca to the south on the non-Muslims road. For the truck route, leave the Mecca Expressway at the non-Muslims exit and turn left toward Shumaisi at the top of the overpass (instead of turning right for the main non-Muslims road around Mecca). If you take the main road around Mecca and find the Escarpment Rd closed, there is no way for non-Muslims to join the truck route from the east side of Mecca – you'll have to go all the way back around Mecca and start again.

**Car Rental** If you need to hire a car, take a cab to the Inter-Continental Hotel north of town and hire one there. It might also be possible to hire a car through the Al-Azezia Hotel in town. Another possibility would be Marhaba Rent-A-Car (☎ 7323204) on King Saud St.

### Getting Around

**Bus** Local buses cost SR 2 per trip. No route map is available and the routes keep changing, but it is usually at least possible to get from the bus station to the youth hostel. At this writing Bus No 10 ran from the main intersection to the Sports City (youth hostel) via the bus station, but ask the driver first in case things have changed. There is no regular bus to the airport though SAPTCO sometimes puts on a special airport-to-centre route during the Muslim holidays and on summer weekends.

## MEDINA

Medina (Medinah, Al-Madinah) is Islam's holiest city after Mecca and was the first community to accept the Prophet's message wholeheartedly. Like Mecca, it is off limits to non-Muslims though its *haram*, or forbidden area, is much smaller. The word *medina* in Arabic means 'city', and the name is a shortening of *medinat an-nabi*, or 'city of the Prophet.' Pious Muslims refer to Medina as *al-munawwarah*, or 'the Radiant'.

Mohammed fled to the city, which was then called Yathrib, from Mecca in 622 and lived the remaining years of his life there. The city's centrepiece is the Prophet's Mosque where Mohammed is buried. This mosque was originally the house in which Mohammed lived, though it has been enlarged many times over the centuries and is now said to cover an area greater than the entire town did in Mohammed's lifetime.

Medina is a 390-km drive from Jeddah and 920-km cross-desert trek from Riyadh. The outskirts of the city, which include the airport and the Medina Sheraton hotel, are open to non-Muslims. You should not, however, come to Medina with the idea that you can see anything of the holy sites just because the haram is smaller. Everything of religious or historical significance lies within the forbidden zone. At the Sheraton you are still a good five km away from the Prophet's mosque. At best you may catch distant glimpses of the holy sites. From the Sheraton you have a clear view of the Al-Qeblatain mosque, built on the site where Mohammed and his companions are said to have camped for the night before entering Yathrib in 622.

The only hotel in the city which is open to non-Muslims is the *Medina Sheraton* (☎ (04) 8230240, fax 8251628). It is a decent place though the food is not all that great. The Sheraton is also the only place in Medina where non-Muslims can eat. They charge about SR 350/450 a single/double, though

during the pilgrimage season and the two Muslim holidays the rates can double or triple. The hotel runs a popular weekend package tour to the ruins of Madain Salah and the Hejaz Railway. See the Madain Salah entry for more details.

### Getting There & Away

The airport, which is open to non-Muslims, is Saudi Arabia's smallest one with international service. From Medina, Saudia flies nonstop to Cairo (three times a week), Damascus (once a week) and Istanbul (once a week). No foreign airlines operate scheduled flights to Medina.

Domestic destinations include several flights per day to Riyadh (SR 210 one-way, economy class) and Jeddah (SR 110). Direct flights also operate to Abha (SR 270), Arar (SR 210), Dhahran (SR 330), Gassim/Buraydah (SR 140), Ha'il (SR 120), Tabuk (SR 160), Taif (SR 140) and Wedjh (SR 110).

## MADAIN SALAH

Doughty called it 'that fabulous Medáin Sálih, which I was come from far countries to seek in Arabia'. More than a century later this windswept plain remains one of the most compelling places in the Kingdom. Though an excellent paved road now runs as far as the site's gate, getting here still involves some effort. Don't think twice – you'll be glad you came.

### History

The origin of the name Madain Salah (Medin Saleh, Mada'in Salih) is uncertain, though it may be associated with the Midianites of the Old Testament. Their empire is known to have included some of what is now northwestern Saudi Arabia. The site we know today as Madain Salah may have been inhabited as long ago as the 1st millennium BC by the Minaeans. It is known to have been inhabited by the Thamudites and the Lihyanites later on. Another source for the name may be the Koranic story of Salih, which would make Madain Salah the 'City of Salih', one of the pre-Mohammedian prophets recognised by Islam. The details of the

Madain Salah

story of Salih vary but the outline is as follows:

Sometime around the year 2000 BC God sent Salih as a Prophet to the people of what we now know as north-western Arabia. Salih preached monotheism in a city where some 47 gods were worshipped. The people demanded a quite specific sign of Salih's lone God as proof of his existence: a red-coloured, pregnant camel was to emerge from a specific rock outside the town on a specific day and at a specific time. When a red, pregnant camel did, in fact, emerge from the appointed rock on the appointed day and at the appointed time, the local pagan priesthood was enraged. They declared that anyone believing in the sign would be punished, and one of the town's richer citizens hired several men to kill the miraculous camel. The camel's unborn calf, however, survived the attack and returned to the cleft in the rock from which its mother had emerged. A ridge near Al-Ula is still known today as the Mount of the Camel. Salih then announced that the killers of the camel had three days to live. On the third day God caused an earthquake to destroy the town and all its inhabitants as punishment for their having doubted Him and His prophet.

Historically the city which God punished was almost certainly the one we now know as Al-Ula or, more likely, a village near present day Al-Ula, 22 km from Madain Salah. Al-Ula's main period of settlement, around 700 BC under the Lihyanites, is much later than the period associated with the story, but the similarity of the name of the prophet in the story and the site now called

Madain Salah may be the source of the confusion. To this day many Saudis refuse to visit Madain Salih because they believe the area to be cursed by God.

Today, Madain Salah has a much simpler claim to fame. It is by far the best known and most spectacular archaeological site in the Kingdom. During its heyday Madain Salah was an important stop on the caravan routes between the Hadhramaut and Syria. The tombs for which it is now known were mostly carved between 100 BC and 100 AD, when it was ruled by the Nabataeans in whose empire it was second in importance only to Petra in present-day Jordan.

Though inscriptions indicate that the site had been occupied for hundreds, possibly thousands, of years prior to their arrival, the Nabataeans first appeared in Madain Salah around 100 BC, about 200 years after they had replaced the Edomites as the rulers of Petra. At its greatest extent the Nabataean empire stretched south to the borders of Yemen, north to Damascus and west to Gaza. On the basis of archaeological evidence found further south from Madain Salah, the Nabataeans were predominantly farmers, as opposed to traders, raiders or herders. They became rich from selling water and protection to the incense and spice caravans which had to pass through their territory. At the time frankincense was the most valuable commodity in the world and most of the frankincense caravans had to pass through the Nabataean empire. (Early Christians would have been far more impressed, in the Christmas story, by the wise men's gifts of frankincense and myrrh than by the gold.) For allowing the caravans to pass the Nabataeans charged a toll of 25%.

However, the city's heyday was brief – the latest dated tomb in Madain Salah was built in 76 AD. The city and the Nabataeans went into decline in the 1st century AD when the Romans began to load the frankincense onto ships and take it to Egypt by sea. The site, however, remained occupied even after its splendour faded. Other less expensive commodities continued to move along the caravan routes making the area too valuable to abandon. In later centuries the pilgrim road from Damascus to Mecca passed through Madain Salah.

Doughty, in the 1880s, appears to have been the first European to see the tombs, in which he reported there were still bones. He describes his visit in excruciating detail in Chapter IV, Volume I of *Travels in Arabia Deserta*.

## Touring the Site

Madain Salah's tombs are less spectacular than those at Petra but they're better preserved. This is largely due to the fact that the local stone here is much harder than that found at Petra and has thus weathered centuries of wind and rain rather better. Still, in places it has eroded in some pretty bizarre forms resembling anything from a multicoloured layered cake to melted and refrozen ice cream.

From the entrance the easiest way to approach the site is to follow the track which extends from the main gate. You don't need a 4WD for any of what follows, though in much of the rest of the site it would be necessary. You do not want to do this on foot, even if the weather is good. Following this track, which is quite well defined, twist around past the **first tomb** on the right. A short distance beyond this you will glimpse **Qasr Farid**, the largest tomb at the site and the one on all the posters, over a rise to the

right. To reach it follow the track straight for a short distance and then turn around the low rise over which you saw the tomb.

Back on the main track and a bit further on is a fenced-in area surrounding what is thought to have been Madain Salah's main residential district. This is closed to visitors. The **main tomb area** is to the right of this, occupying both sides of a large outcrop of rock. While on the near side of the main tomb area, if you step back and look up you'll distinguish a tomb which was abandoned in the early stages of construction and would, if completed, have been the largest in Madain Salah. Only the step facade was cut, but it dramatically proves the theory that the Madain Salah and Petra tombs were carved from the top down.

On the side of the main tomb area away from the main gate is the **Diwan**, a 'meeting room' carved into a hillside to shield it from the wind. Next to this is a narrow passageway between two rock faces reminiscent of Petra's famous entryway, the Siq, though on a much smaller scale. As you pass through this mini-Siq note the small altars carved into the cliff face and the channels which brought water down into several small basins. Once through, climb the hill to your right for a good view over the site.

The **railway station** is on the edge of the main Madain Salah site. It was part of the Hejaz Railway, of *Lawrence of Arabia* fame (though Lawrence never operated this far south), and is in the process of being restored by the government. The station itself has already been restored and now houses the remains of one of the pre-WW I engines which plied the route between Damascus and Medina during the line's short lifetime (1908-1917). If you look carefully while driving from the station back toward the site gate you can clearly distinguish the railway's gradient. Near the station is a small **Turkish fort**, the same one in which Doughty stayed for several weeks after arriving from Damascus. The presence here of the fort, which was an overnight resting place on the Pilgrim road from Damascus to Mecca, explains why a railway station was built here seemingly in the middle of nowhere. The railway town, which includes the station and the other buildings around it in various states of repair, was built in 1907.

## Getting There & Away

Madain Salah is just off the main road from Medina to Al-Ula. Look for a sign pointing to the 'Antiquities'. It is a right turn if you are coming from Medina. Permits for the site must be obtained in Riyadh and can take anything from a day to a week. In addition to the names and passport or iqama numbers of the people in the party, you will also need the registration papers for your vehicle if you are driving yourself. Your permit, and possibly your vehicle papers, will be checked at the site entrance and you may be given a local cop as an escort.

All this can be avoided by booking the Medina Sheraton's Madain Salah tour. It includes arrival at the hotel on a Wednesday and a slide presentation on Madain Salah and Petra the same evening. The trip to the site, with a guide from the hotel, starts around 6.30 am Thursday and gets you back to the hotel in the early evening. Friday is at leisure. The tour costs SR 700 per person on a double occupancy basis (SR 750 for singles). The price includes the trip to the site, two nights at the hotel, all meals from dinner Wednesday to lunch Friday and airport transfers. The tour is for groups of 10 or more but single people can tack themselves onto groups that are already going. The tours only operate when there are enough people to go on them. The hotel usually needs three weeks to arrange the tour so the best bet for singles is to contact the hotel (☎ (04) 8230240, fax 8251628; ask for the sales department) at least a month before you'd like to go. I highly recommend it.

# Asir (The South-West)

The dramatic mountains of the Asir range are on the edge of the same geological fault line which emerges further to the south-west as Africa's Great Rift Valley. The mountain chain includes Jebel Sawdah, the 2910-metre peak near Abha which is the highest point in Saudi Arabia. Large sections of both the mountain range and the coastal plain have been incorporated into the Asir National Park.

One of the earliest accounts of the region is the record of the march southwards by Aelius Gallus, a Roman general who set out, in 25 BC, to conquer the frankincense-producing regions of Hadhramaut and Dhofar, in present-day Yemen and Oman, respectively. He led his troops south along the main caravan route which passed through the Asir range and continued east of it. The fact that he did not pass through Mecca is one of the strongest pieces of evidence for the theory that the main caravan road of the time did not pass through the future holy city, though it did go through Yathrib (modern Medina). Aelius Gallus conquered Najran but never made it to the frankincense regions. His troops had to turn back at Marib (in present-day Yemen) because of thirst.

Asir was an independent kingdom until it was conquered by Abdul Aziz in 1922, but it had long had close ties with Yemen. The Saudi-Yemeni war of the mid-30s revolved, in part, around Yemeni claims to Asir, claims which were revived by Yemen's Republican government after the country's monarchy was overthrown in 1962. Despite these recurring arguments, Saudi control of the region has never been in serious doubt since the '20s.

The region's architecture has a distinctly Yemeni look about it. The most distinctive feature of the houses are the shingles sticking out from their sides. These are designed to deflect rain away from the mud walls of the house.

South from Taif the road into the Asir mountains rises steadily and the scenery becomes ever more dramatic. Every village seems to have its ruined watchtower and those traditional mud houses become increasingly common as one moves south. Another common sight are wild monkeys which can often be seen along the main roads throughout Asir. Allow yourself time to stop and explore this fascinating place.

## AL-BAHA

Al-Baha, 220 km south of Taif and 340 km north of Abha, is the secondary tourist hub of the Asir region. The area's attraction has mainly been that it is a lot less developed than Abha. While accommodation is not a problem in Al-Baha, transport sometimes is. If you are making a tour of Asir by bus it might be a good idea to give Al-Baha a miss. The scenery is a bit spread out, and you'll have seen a lot from the bus anyway. Without your own car there's not much point in stopping here. Keep going to Abha, where you would be well advised to hire a car.

### Orientation & Information

The town is little more than a crossroads where the Taif to Abha road joins the east-west road which runs to the youth hostel and the airport. What few services there are in Al-Baha are all along the small built-up section of these two thoroughfares. Both the Post Office and the Saudia office are on the east-west road, just east of the junction with the Taif-Abha road. The bus station is on the Taif-Abha road, a few hundred metres north of the junction with the east-west road. The telephone code for Al-Baha is 07.

### Things to See

The main attraction is the surrounding countryside, for which Al-Baha serves as a jumping-off point. The best way to see the area is in your own car and very much at leisure. Near town, the **Raghdan Forest** is a nice spot with some good views.

### Places to Stay & Eat

Getting to the *Youth Hostel* (☎ 7254384) can be a problem. It is at the Sporting City, about 30 km east of the centre, and it has been known to turn away foreigners. This is the only place in the Kingdom where I have heard of this happening. You can't get to the place without your own car. Assuming you have wheels, turn east (left if you are coming from Taif) on the east-west road at Al-Baha's

main intersection and follow the signs for the airport. It is impossible to miss the Sporting City. Beds are SR 8.

The only cheap hotel in town is the *Al-Baha Hotel* (☎ 7251007), on the east-west road east of the junction with the Taif-Abha road (ie moving toward the airport). Singles/doubles with bath are SR 66/99 (from June to September SR 85/128) including the service charge. All rooms have ceiling fans. The hotel has no heating and it can get quite chilly in winter.

The *Raghdan Houas* (☎ 7253091), across the street from the Al-Baha Hotel and between it and the intersection, has big, bare rooms for SR 100 per person per night. They didn't seem too keen, however, on renting out rooms for periods of less than a month.

The only hotel on the Taif-Abha road is the *Al-Zulfan Hotel* (☎ 7251053). Rooms are SR 220/275 (SR 275/374 in summer). The four-star *Al-Baha Palace* (☎ 7252000, fax 7254724) is on a hill west of the centre and it has good views. Rooms are SR 230/299; SR 276/356.50 in summer. Both hotels have restaurants.

Cheap food in Al-Baha is Turkish food. In the centre the *Istanbul Servet Restaurant*, on the Taif-Abha road, roughly across the street from the Al-Zulfan Hotel, has good salads and kofta. There is also a good, cheap Turkish restaurant attached to the Al-Baha Hotel. Meals at either place cost about SR 13 to SR 15.

### Getting There & Away

Al-Baha's small airport is about 30 km east of the main road junction. There is a daily flight to Riyadh (SR 250 one-way, economy class). Saudia also operates scheduled flights from Al-Baha to Jeddah (SR 100), Dhahran (SR 370) and Bisha (SR 90).

There are two SAPTCO buses a day to Abha, at 2 and 5 pm (SR 60, seven hours), and three to Taif, at 9.30 am, 2 and 5 pm (SR 30, 2½ hours). The bus station is on the Taif-Abha road, a short distance north of the intersection with the east-west road. If you are coming from Taif, it is on the left. Local and service taxis queue up in the parking lot next to the bus stop.

## ABHA

If Saudi Arabia ever opens up to tourism, Abha, the capital of the south-western province of Asir, is likely to be one of the main attractions. The relatively cool weather, forested hills and striking mountain scenery have made it a very popular weekend resort. Like Taif, it is very crowded on summer weekends and reservations are strongly recommended.

You'll need to have a car in Abha as taxis are hard to find and local buses do not serve the main areas of the Asir National Park.

### Orientation

The town centre is small and rather dull. The main streets are King Khalid and King Abdul Aziz Sts, and their intersection is Abha's nominal centre. (King Khaled St is called Al-Bahar St between King Abdul Aziz and King Faisal Sts). These names come from the Farsi maps. On the ground you will find few, if any, street signs. Drivers are likely to find the streets of the town quite crowded. Your best bet to get anywhere is to head out to the Ring Rd and go around. Six main roads feed into the Ring Rd. Clockwise, starting from the north, these are respectively the roads to Taif/Al-Baha, the industrial city of Khamis Mushayt (via the airport and the youth hostel), a road leading to the plains below the city, a road down the escarpment to Jizan and the Tihama coastal plain, and two roads leading up into the mountains.

### Information

**Tourist Office** There is no tourist office in Asir. The few bits of tourist information come from the Inter-Continental Hotel which offers packages including tours of the Asir National Park, Najran and the Red Sea. See Organised Tours later in this section.

**Money** Several banks are in the area around the main intersection. There are also a couple of banks at the intersection of King Abdul Aziz and Prince Abdullah Sts.

**Post & Telecommunications** The post office and telephone office are side by side on King Abdul Aziz St, near the intersection with Prince Abdullah St. The telephone code for Abha is 07.

### Shada Palace

Abha's only in-town site is the Shada Palace. It was built in 1927 as an office/residence for King Abdul Aziz's governors in the region. After falling into disuse it was restored and reopened as a museum in 1987. The Palace is the large, traditional tower immediately behind the large police station on King Faisal St, across from the bus station. It is open Saturday to Thursday from 9 am to 1 pm and 4 to 7 pm. Admission is free; children under 12 are not allowed inside.

The ground floor of the palace has an exhibit of regional handicrafts and traditional household goods. A brightly painted staircase leads to restored sitting rooms and men's and women's quarters on the upper two floors. The displays here include old money, weapons, silver jewellery and weavings. The roof is also open to the public but the walls are fairly high so you won't be able to see much. In earlier days the high walls afforded the privacy necessary for the women of the family to sit on the roof on cool summer evenings.

### Asir National Park Visitors' Centre

The Asir National Park Visitors' Centre sits imposingly on the southern edge of the Ring Rd. It is not a tourist office but rather an introduction to the Asir National Park. It is open daily only in summer, from 4 to 8 pm, and only for families. If you want to see it in the winter, or you are male and have no women and/or children along, you must first obtain a permit from the park headquarters on the Qara'a road, 1.8 km from the junction with the Ring Rd.

The most interesting exhibit is the scale model of the park near the entrance. Follow the stairs upwards for brief lessons in the geography, flora, fauna and culture of the area. Beyond the final room is an observation deck with a striking view of the valley below.

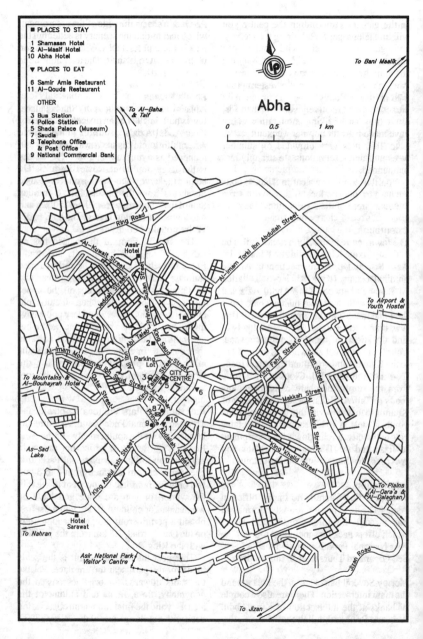

■ PLACES TO STAY

1  Shamaan Hotel
2  Al-Masif Hotel
10  Abha Hotel

▼ PLACES TO EAT

6  Samir Amis Restaurant
11  Al-Qouds Restaurant

OTHER

3  Bus Station
4  Police Station
5  Shada Palace (Museum)
7  Saudia
8  Telephone Office
   & Post Office
9  National Commercial Bank

Abha

0        0.5        1 km

To Bani Maalik
To Al-Baha & Talf
To Airport & Youth Hostel
To Mountains & Al-Bouhayrah Hotel
To Plains (Al-Qara'a & Al-Dalaghan)
To Nahran
To Jizan

Ring Road
Al-Kuwait Street
Assir Hotel
Jeddah Street
Sultan Street
Prince Abi Taleb Street
Al Ibn Abi Taleb Street
King Saud Street
Al-Imam Torki Ibn Abdullah Street
Al-Imam Mohammed Ibn Saud Street
Qatar Street
King Fahd Street
Jizan Street
Parking Lot
CITY CENTRE
King Talab Street
Al-Behar St
Makkah Street
Al-Andalus Street
King Abdul Aziz Street
King Khalid Street
As-Sad Lake
Hotel Sarawat
Al-Abdiah Street
Asir National Park Visitor's Centre
Jizan Road

In the gardens surrounding the centre you will find telescopes for admiring the scenery, and a garden where Asir's wild monkeys can sometimes be seen. An old ruined building sits atop the hill behind the centre.

## Asir National Park

The park covers some 450,000 hectares of land from the Red Sea coast to the desert areas east of the mountains. The parts easily accessible to visitors amount to a number of non-contiguous mini-parks. Each of these includes a camping ground/picnic area. The camp sites are a series of small clearings where you can park a vehicle, with trees and/or rocks separating the sites. They are allocated free of charge on a first come, first served basis. You have to bring your own tent and facilities are virtually nonexistent. The park is divided into two main parts: the mountains to the north-west of the city and the plains to the south-east. Technically the park area extends all the way down to the coast, though there are no signs or other obvious marks of this once you are out on the road to Jizan. If you are pressed for time stick to the mountains. They are a lot more interesting.

The two main camping ground areas in the mountains are **Al- Soudah**, a few km beyond the Inter- Continental Hotel, and the remote **Al- Sahab** area. Al-Soudah, which is near the summit of Saudi Arabia's highest mountain (Jebel Sawdah, 2910 metres), is the most spectacular part of the park. Three main roads loop up into the mountains and connect with one another through many smaller roads. Try a drive up the **Nahran road** to the Jebel Nahran microwave relay station. When you reach the gate at the top turn around and go back; this route has a number of good viewing spots.

The main park areas to the south-east of Abha are **Al-Dalaghan** (Dalgan), 26 km from Abha, and, further down the same road, **Al-Qara'a** (Qara), for which the road is named. Both areas consist of a large area of rounded boulders and small evergreen trees, which look rather like a giant's rock garden. The main difference between them is that

Al-Qara'a sits on the edge of the escarpment, which means that the scenery is better but the weather less predictable. Wild monkeys can often be seen in both areas.

### Organised Tours

For the moment the Inter-Continental Hotel more or less has a monopoly on organised tourism in Abha. They offer several two and three-night packages, some of which include excursions to Najran and/or the Red Sea. In addition to staying in the hotel, these usually require a group of at least 10 adults. On weekend days, when there are a few single guests in the hotel, they also offer a one-day tour of the Abha region for SR 90 (not including lunch – that's another SR 30). Contact the hotel (☎ 2247777, fax 2244113) for more information.

### Places to Stay

For a resort there are remarkably few places to stay in Abha. This may be partly because most people who come here do not mind spending a lot of money and partly because the Inter-Continental Hotel is so huge.

The *Youth Hostel* (☎ 2270503) is at the Sporting City, 20 km west of Abha off the Abha-Khamis road. Beds are SR 8 but there is no bus service.

Every place except the youth hostel has higher rates in the summer (May to September), during which it would be a bad idea to arrive in Abha on a Wednesday or Thursday without a reservation.

Probably the best value for money in Abha, after the hostel, is the *Al-Masif Hotel* (☎ 2242651), 500 metres north of the main intersection. Singles/doubles are SR 90/180; SR 150/280 in summer. The only hotel in the centre is the *Abha Hotel* (☎ 2248775), where rooms cost SR 110/165 (SR 143/240 in summer).

The *Assir Hotel* (☎ 2244374), on the Taif road one km north of the centre, charges SR 50/72 (SR 66/99 in summer). All rooms have private baths. A bit closer to town, the *Shamasan Hotel* (☎ 2251808) charges SR 90/130 (SR 143/195 in summer). On the Ring Rd the *Hotel Sarawat* (☎ 2247717), with good views over the town, charges SR 200/260 (SR 270/360 in summer).

Up in the mountains the *Inter-Continental* (☎ 2247777, fax 2244113) has a fairly standard five-star rate of SR 345/449 (SR 414/541 in summer) including the service charge. Their weekend B&B package includes two nights accommodation with breakfast for SR 400/600 in the winter, SR 500/720 in the summer, and is available every Wednesday, Thursday and Friday night. In the low season this is a pretty good deal, and if you are going to splurge once in the Kingdom, the Abha Inter-Continental is a pretty good place to do it. The hotel is said to have been originally designed as a palace for a Saudi prince. Whatever your budget, it is worth dropping by for a cup of coffee and an opportunity to marvel at its sheer scale. The lobby is enormous and the coffee shop alone is larger than a lot of the hotels listed in this book.

The hotel also has a shop selling Bedouin jewellery. The selection is very good and the prices, though high, are not outrageous.

To reach the hotel, take the Al-Soudah road for about 22.5 km from its junction with the Ring Rd. The hotel will be on your left.

### Places to Eat
There are a few restaurants scattered around the centre but there's not much choice as they all seem to be chicken-and-kebab places. On the other hand, they are cheap. Meals cost SR 10 to SR 15. Try the *Samir Amis Restaurant* on King Abdul Aziz St across the street from the supermarket complex – it's the one with a lot of chickens being roasted outside. If you start up King Khalid St from the National Commercial Bank you'll find several other small places. One good bet is *Al-Qouds*, across the street from the post office.

### Getting There & Away
**Air** The airport is 25 km from town. To get there, take the Abha-Khamis road to the turnoff just beyond the turn for the Sporting City. Saudia's Abha ticket office is near the post office on King Abdul Aziz St. There are several flights each day to Jeddah (SR 160, one-way, economy class) and Riyadh (SR

240). One of the Riyadh flights continues on to Dhahran (SR 360). Direct services also operate between Abha and Medina (SR 270), Taif (SR 120), Tabuk (SR 400) and Sharurah (SR 160).

**Bus** The SAPTCO station is in the big parking lot on King Faisal St, a couple of blocks north of the intersection of King Khalid and King Abdul Aziz Sts. The ticket office is the small trailer across from the police station. It tends to be open only just before a bus leaves. There is one bus per day to Jizan (SR 25, four hours) at 10 am and one at 9 pm from Khamis Mushayt. Buses for Taif (SR 90, 10 hours) leave daily at 8 am and noon. Buses to Riyadh, Jeddah and Najran leave from Khamis Mushayt. Local Bus No 21 runs between Abha and Khamis Mushayt for SR 2.

### Getting Around
Here you are a bit stuck as there do not seem to be a lot of taxis, and none of the bus routes serve the main areas of the park. The usual car rental rates for Saudi Arabia apply and you can rent a car at the airport or go to one of the small agents in the centre.

## KHAMIS MUSHAYT
Khamis Mushayt (Khamis, for short) is 26 km east of Abha. Its main industry appears to be the giant King Khalid air base. Khamis is usually spoken of as Abha's twin city, though it is a bit difficult to see what the two places have in common. Its only interest for the traveller lies in the fact that more than half of SAPTCO's buses to/from the Abha-Khamis area operate from the Khamis terminal which is open more regular hours than the Abha terminal.

Khamis' small, modern souk, bus terminal and Saudia office are all clustered around two central squares, between which stands the *Al-Azizia Hotel* (☎ 07-2220900). Singles/doubles are SR 132/214.50 (SR 170.50/214.50 in summer), including the service charge. The souk is reputed to be a good place to shop for silver jewellery, but if

Top: View of Abha, Saudi Arabia
Bottom: Tarut fort, Tarut Island, Saudi Arabia

Top: Closing shop at prayer time, Buraydah, Saudi Arabia
Bottom: Traditional Yemeni-style house, Najran, Saudi Arabia

you are headed for Najran, wait until you get there as the selection is much better.

Buses leave from the SAPTCO terminal in front of the Al-Azizia Hotel. The bus to Jizan (four hours, SR 25) leaves daily at 9 pm. Buses to Riyadh (12 hours, SR 125) leave at 10 am, 1, 4, 6.30 and 8.30 pm. Buses to Najran (4½ hours, SR 30) depart at 10 am and 5.30 pm and to Jeddah (11 hours, SR 90) at 9.30 am, 5 and 7.30 pm.

## HABALAH

The deserted village of Habalah (Habella), about 60 km from the centre of Abha, is one of the most dramatic sites in the Asir National Park. A traditional farming village, Habalah appears to hang from a 300-metre-high cliff face above terraced fields and a broad valley. The village was settled about 350 years ago by Kahtani tribes who were said to have been fleeing from the Ottomans. Habalah, like many other villages in Asir, grew coffee, fruits and vegetables and raised sheep, chickens and goats. It was inhabited until about 1980. If you look carefully along the rim of the cliff above the village you can still see the iron posts to which ropes were tied to lower people and goods to the village. Several parking lots on top of the cliff overlook Habalah, though the one furthest to the left as you arrive at the site is the only one with a view of the village. This parking lot also has a restaurant overlooking the village and the valley.

To reach Habalah take the Qara'a road from Abha past Al-Dalaghan. Three km beyond the Al-Dalaghan turn, the road ends in a T-junction. Turn left and follow the road to the village of Wadiain where you will see a sign pointing toward Al-Habla Park. Follow the sign and keep left when the road forks at a junction with two small blue signs, one of which has an arrow pointing left. After about two km the road forks again; keep left and you'll reach the parking lot overlooking the village.

## ABHA TO NAJRAN

The first third or so of the 280-km drive from Abha to Najran is along twisting roads

descending toward the desert plains. You will see lots of fascinating old, new and newly restored architecture. The village of **Qarn Waqsha**, about 90 km south of Abha, is worth a brief stop for a look at its splendid ruined fort and watchtower, situated on a hill rising from the middle of the village. The village has many traditional houses.

**Dhahran Al-Janoub** (Zahran Al-Janoub), 165 km south of Abha and 112 km north-west of Najran, is a convenient stopping place if you need a rest or decide to break the trip. It too has its share of traditional architecture. The *Al-Aren Hotel* (☎ (07) 2550388) in the centre of town, along the Abha-Najran road, has singles/doubles for SR 88/132. It's on the left if you are coming from Abha.

There are five checkpoints between Abha and Najran and you can expect increasingly close scrutiny as you move south. The situation along the border with Yemen always seems to be tense and foreigners moving about are subject to special scrutiny. Be sure you have your iqama and a travel letter, or your passport if you are in the Kingdom on a visitor visa. You can also expect to be asked to produce the car's papers at some or all of the checkpoints – the *istimara* (registration) if you own the car, or a xerox of the document if it's a company cars. If you're driving a rented car the rental agreement usually suffices, but be sure that you have a xerox of the actual registration before heading off to the south.

## NAJRAN

Najran (Nejran) is one of the most fascinating and least visited places in the Kingdom. Set near the Yemeni border, in an oasis which sprawls some 20 km along the Wadi Najran, the site has been inhabited for about 4000 years. Najran was the last major stop on the frankincense route before the road split into eastern and western branches 60 km to the north at Bir Hima. It has remained an important desert trading centre to this day. Najran has long been reputed to be the main base for the lucrative smuggling traffic between Saudi Arabia and Yemen. Yemen's cultural influence is stronger here than anywhere else in the Kingdom. This is obvious in both the local architecture and the attitude of the people toward outsiders. Najranis are extremely outgoing and deeply conservative at the same time. The most obvious place to see this seeming contradiction at work is in the souk, where fully veiled women run shops alongside men and serve male customers – an unusual sight in the Kingdom.

### History

Najran was already an important city during the 1st millennium BC when the Sabeans swept over much of this corner of Arabia. Its main period of prosperity came during the 1st and 2nd centuries BC when it was known as Al-Ukhdood. The Roman general, Aelius Gallus, captured Al-Ukhdood in 24 BC during his unsuccessful expedition to the Wadi Hadhramaut.

The next major conquest of the city was by the Himyarites who arrived around the year 250 AD. Najran was still part of Himyar when its inhabitants were converted to Christianity in the 5th century. Christianity gave way to Islam in 630-31 (10 AH) though the Christian community remained fairly numerous for a time. Within a generation, however, the town's Christians were expelled from the country in line with a saying of the Prophet that 'there shall not remain two religions in the land of Arabia'.

In later centuries Najran's inland location made it of interest to the Turks. The Yam, the leading tribe of the region, controlled Najran through an alliance with the Turks in the 16th century, in exchange for which they were given the right to levy tribute from the area's other tribes. By the mid-17th century, however, they had switched their allegiance to the Zaidi imams of Yemen. Later, Najran was part of the First Saudi Empire in the late 18th and early 19th centuries. After the empire fell it spent a century as a border area disputed between the independent kingdoms of Asir and Yemen. Saudi troops finally took control of the city in 1934. Shortly thereafter the Imam of Yemen ceded Najran to King Abdul Aziz as part of the treaty ending the 1934 Saudi-Yemeni war.

### Orientation & Information

Najran is an easy place to find your way around. Driving in from Abha, you hit a T-junction; this is the only road leading to Najran and everyone calls it the Main Rd. Turning left at the junction takes you to Najran airport and the Empty Quarter and turning right leads you into Faisaliah, a modern business district just before Najran. Most of the shops and businesses, the youth hostel, the two hotels, Saudia, the telephone office, the post office and the bus station are all along, or a short distance off, the Main Rd in Faisaliah. Except for the bus station all of them are on the right-hand side of the road if you are coming from Abha or the airport. Continuing on Main Rd you reach Najran's centre, where the fort and the souk are located.

If you need to change money in the centre, there are a couple of banks on the Main Rd, near the traffic lights where you turn to reach the fort. The distance along the Main Rd from the junction with the Abha road to the turn for the fort is 13 km. The airport is 35 km from the fort, and 22 km from the Abha road junction. The telephone code for Najran is 07.

### Najran Fort

Though the well in the fort's inner courtyard is said to date from pre-Islamic times, the present fort was begun in 1942 as a royal residence. It was built to be a self-sustaining complex, with its own stock pens, storage rooms for food, guards quarters and even a radio station. This insistence on self-sufficiency may indicate that Najran's new Saudi rulers had less than complete faith in the Imam of Yemen's renunciation of his claim to Najran and his ceding of the oasis to Saudi Arabia. The fort fell out of everyday use in 1967, when the Saudi-Yemeni relations became, if not stable, then at least somewhat predictable.

During its relatively brief, 25-year history, the fort's various governors managed to expand it dramatically. It was always a big place. Even today, with all of the later additions removed, the complex still includes about 60 rooms, including the livestock pens. Most of these remain bare though their carved doors and shutters have survived or been recreated and are some of the most colourful examples of this traditional Arabian art form to be seen in the Kingdom. A few rooms now house displays. Be sure to see the coffee room on the 2nd floor of the **Prince's House**, the large building right in front of you as you pass through the main gate into the fort. Turning right from the main gate and then right again you will come to a doorway with a modern sign in Arabic beside it. This leads to a small exhibit of local silverwork, leather goods, weapons, clothes, tools and pottery.

The fort is more or less in the centre of town. From Abha, follow the Main Rd until you see the fort beyond the houses to your right, then turn right at the first set of traffic lights. It is open daily from 8 am to 5 pm. Admission is free and you don't need a permit to get in.

## Museum

Najran boasts one of the Kingdom's newest and best museums. It is open Saturday to Wednesday from 8.30 am to 2 pm. Admission is free; photography is prohibited. The museum is several km off the Main Rd and sits in front of the archaeological site of Al-Ukhdood, which was inhabited from about 500 BC through the 10th century AD.

Entering the museum you start the tour of the exhibit halls by moving to your right. The first part has information on the age of the earth and the formation of wadis and deserts. Other exhibits outline archaeological finds in and around Najran and sketch the importance of Al-Ukhdood which was mentioned in the Koran.

The second part of the gallery is an ethnographic display with examples of local crafts, desert life, water and irrigation and tools. There are also a number of photographs taken in Najran by Harry St John Philby in 1936.

To reach the museum, turn off the Main Rd at the sign for Al-Jurbah. Go 3.3 km and turn left at the traffic lights. (At the time of writing this involved crossing the wadi on a dirt track, but a bridge was under construction.) The museum is on the right after 1.8 km.

## Places to Stay & Eat

Najran's *Youth Hostel* (☎ 5225019) is one of the smaller ones in the Kingdom but is a clean and friendly place, about nine km from the fort. As you pass through Faisaliah watch out for the Najran Municipality on your right. Some distance past this the Main Rd swings around to the left while a smaller street continues on straight. Keep going straight on the smaller road. Take the first right and then take the second right from the street onto which you turned. The hostel will be on your right after less than 200 metres. It's across the street from a school.

Aside from the youth hostel there are two hotels in Najran, both just off the Main Rd, approximately 10 km from the fort and three km from the junction with the Abha road. Coming from Abha, the *Okhdood Hotel* (☎ 5222614) is the first one you'll pass. They have rooms for SR 132/170.50, including the service charge. The *Najran Hotel* (☎ 5221750), about one km closer to the centre, is a slightly better value at SR 88/132.

Fill your stomach at *Cindy's*, a restaurant on the Main Rd near the turn for the youth hostel and within easy walking distance of it. The fried chicken is good and they also serve Filipino food. Meals cost about SR 12.

## Things to Buy

Najran is famous for its silver jewellery. A lot of mostly elderly women have small shops in the souk area behind the fort with stocks of silver jewellery for sale, though it may not always be out on display. You can also buy brightly painted incense burners locally made from clay for SR 5 to SR 10.

## Getting There & Away

The Saudia office is on the Main Rd a little bit toward the centre from the turn for the Najran Hotel. There are daily flights to Riyadh (SR 240 one-way, economy class) and Jeddah (SR 210). Direct flights also operate from Najran to Dhahran (SR 360) and Shararah (SR 90).

The bus station is on the Main Rd, 1.7 km from the turn for Abha. Buses for Riyadh (SR 120, 12 hours) leave daily at 9 am and 8 pm. To Khamis Mushayt (SR 30, 4½ hours) buses leave at 10 am and 6.15 pm. To reach Abha change to a local bus at Khamis.

There are not a lot of service taxis in Najran though a few can be found in the parking lot opposite the traffic lights in the centre, where you turn to reach the fort.

## SHARURAH

The town of Shararah lies deep in the Empty Quarter, about 330 km east of Najran. A generation ago Shararah and other settlements like it were hopelessly remote wells known only to a handful of Bedouins. Today, you can reach it in a few hours from Najran. The desert scenery on the drive out to Shararah is spectacular and includes a long drive of about 100 km through what can only be described as a canyon of sand dunes rising to heights of 100 metres or more on each side of the road. The photograph on the 'Road in the Empty Quarter' poster sold throughout Saudi Arabia was taken on the Najran-Shararah road near the western entrance to the sand canyon.

The road is modern and fast and there is a surprising amount of traffic on it. Still, this is not a trip to be undertaken lightly. You absolutely *must* leave the eastern outskirts of Najran with a full tank of petrol as well as some food, water and a spare tyre in proper condition. Make all the routine checks that one should make on any car before embarking on a long journey. There is a petrol station about halfway to Shararah and you should make a point of stopping there to top up, check the radiator, etc. Don't do this trip alone; tell someone that you are doing it; and, most importantly, don't get off the road. These last three points ought to be obvious but you would be surprised how many people do not take these basic precautions.

There is nothing to see in Shararah itself. Desert buffs can drive the 55 km beyond Shararah to **Wuday'ah** where the road trails

off into an endless plain of red sand stretching toward Saudi Arabia's undefined border with Yemen.

If you do not want to drive yourself the only other way to get to Shararah is to fly. Saudia has nonstop flights to Shararah from Abha (SR 160 one-way, economy class), Jizan (SR 160) and Najran (SR 90). One-stop service is available from Jeddah (SR 280) and Riyadh (SR 240). On most routes there are two or three flights per week.

## JIZAN

Even in November the heat and humidity of Jizan (Gizan) can make the place almost unlivable. There is little of interest in Jizan except for its old souk. Like Najran, Jizan only came under Saudi control in the mid-1930s, following the war with Yemen.

### Orientation & Information

The heart of the town is one long street which does not appear to have a name. It begins at a huge roundabout on the town's outskirts where the road from Abha, the Airport Rd, the road to the Sports City and several other streets all converge. From there it runs straight down to the Corniche and the port, with one other intersection near the Al-Jazeera Restaurant, about 200 metres from the Corniche. The Corniche has three levels, of which the one furthest from the coast is the main traffic artery.

The bus station is just off the main road, between the first and second levels of the Corniche. The post office is on a fairly busy street a short distance south of, and parallel to, the main road. The souk is between these two streets. The phone office is just off the big roundabout while a number of banks can be found at the end of the main road near the Corniche. The airport is about five km northeast of the centre. The telephone code for Jizan is 07.

### Things to See

The **fort** overlooking the town is Jizan's most interesting site, but because of the adjacent communications tower it has been classified as a sensitive site, which means the military may still be using it. It is not open to the public and photography is forbidden.

The **old souk** is a treat. It is one of the most traditional souks left in the Kingdom. To reach it, face the sea and turn left onto the Corniche from the main street. Go left again at the small roundabout between the Saudi Cairo Bank and the Port Authority building. At the first set of lights turn left yet again. If you have a car you can park in the lot which will appear on your right after about 250 metres.

The **animal market** at the base of the artificial hill behind the fort is worth a look. It's also a good spot to shop for pottery.

### Places to Stay

The *Youth Hostel* (☎ 3221646) is at the Sports City, just over eight km from the Corniche. Beds are SR 8. From the main roundabout take the road that leaves the roundabout between the Abha road and the phone office and follow it for seven km. If you are coming from Abha or Jeddah take the last road you come to before having gone all the way around the traffic circle.

The only other options are the four-star *Al-Hayat Gizan Hotel* (☎ 3221055, fax 3171774) on the Corniche south of the centre. Singles/doubles are SR 230/300, including 15% service charge. In town, just north of the main road between the roundabout and the Corniche, the *Gizan Sahari Hotel* (☎ 3221686) has rooms with bath for SR 110/165, without bath for SR 88/132. The hotel has no sign in English.

### Places to Eat

At the *Cost Pearl Brosted Cafateriea* (sic), on the main road near the junction with the Corniche, a serving of rice with chicken, meat or vegetables costs less than SR 10. Across the street the *Al-Jazeera Modern Restaurant* has a good traditional coffee house on its upper level, with open sides, ceiling fans, hookahs and a TV set roaring out the soccer match of the evening.

### Getting There & Away

There are several flights a day to both Jeddah

(SR 170 one-way, economy class) and Riyadh (SR 280), with regular services also operating to Dhahran (SR 400) and Sharurah (SR 160). To reach the Saudia office turn right onto the first Corniche from the main road and go right at the first set of traffic lights.

The bus station is between the first and second Corniches and a bit to the left as you face the sea. Look for a SAPTCO trailer in a parking lot surrounded by a fence. There are seven buses a day to Jeddah (11 hours, SR 90) at two-hour intervals from 8 am until 10 pm, but with no 2 pm bus. Buses to Abha and Khamis Mushayt (four hours, SR 25) leave at 10 am and 4 pm. Change at Khamis for Riyadh.

# The Eastern Province

For centuries the main settlements in what is now the Eastern Province of Saudi Arabia had been the oasis towns of Qatif and Hofuf and their respective entrepôts at Darin, on Tarut Island, and Uqayr. With the exception of Hofuf, all of these towns are now provincial backwaters.

On the other hand, the growth of the Dhahran area over the past two generations has been as spectacular as that of Riyadh and Jeddah, though if you arrive from either of those cities this may not be immediately evident. The Dhahran-Dammam-Alkhobar area, usually appearing on larger maps as a single dot marked 'Dhahran', is neither huge and new, like Riyadh, nor is it a modern city grown from the core of an ancient port, like Jeddah. Prior to the discovery of oil less than 60 years ago, Dammam and Alkhobar were tiny fishing and pearling villages and Dhahran did not exist.

The Dhahran area is smaller than Riyadh or Jeddah and has a reputation for being a relatively relaxed place. Foreigners became a common sight in the Eastern Province long before they gained similar acceptance elsewhere in the Kingdom. Outside of Greater Dhahran the provincial towns of the Eastern

Province are much like those of any other region of Saudi Arabia though, again, the attitude is more relaxed than in the country's central regions.

Although Dammam is the capital of the Eastern Province, a lot of the services of interest to the traveller (American Express, bookshops with an English-language selection and virtually all of the airline offices, for example) are in Alkhobar. There are two foreign consulates in the Eastern Province, the UK in Alkhobar and the US in Dhahran.

## DAMMAM

The capital, Dammam, is the longest settled and largest town of the Dhahran-Dammam-Alkhobar group. It is a bit run-down compared to Alkhobar but a lot cheaper.

### Orientation & Information

Downtown Dammam is roughly the area bounded by King Abdul Aziz St to the north, King Khaled St to the south, 9th St to the east and 18th St to the west. The centre is the area around the intersection of 11th St, which appears on some maps and street signs as Dhahran St, and King Saud St.

There are banks and moneychangers at the intersection of 11th and King Saud Sts. The main post office is at the corner of 9th St and Al-Amir Mansour St. There do not appear to be any call cabins in Dammam but there is a complex of payphones on 9th St with an office which provides change. More international payphones can be found at the intersection of King Saud and 11th Sts. The telephone code for Dammam is 03. Note that if you are trying to locate someone at ARAMCO, the oil company has its own, very efficient, directory assistance service; ring 8720115.

In emergencies, dial 999 for the police, 997 for an ambulance and 998 to report a fire.

### The Regional Museum of Archaeology & Ethnography

The museum (☎ 8266056) is at the railroad crossing on 1st St near the Dammam Tower. It's on the 4th floor and is open Saturday to Wednesday from 7.30 am to 2.30 pm. Don't

be put off by the dumpy street-level lobby. Admission is free. The collection includes Stone Age tools, pottery (mainly Hellenistic and early Islamic) and examples of Bedouin crafts and traditional dress. Unfortunately many of the explanatory texts are only in Arabic, though most of the items in the display cases are labelled in English too.

The museum is also the place to pick up permits for visiting the Eastern Province's main archaeological sites of Qatif, Tarut Island, Thaj and Al-Hina. The only exception are the sites in the Hofuf area, for which permits must be obtained in Riyadh. A passport or iqama is required for permits, which can usually be processed the same day.

### Places to Stay – bottom end & middle

The *Youth Hostel* (☎ 8575358) is at the Sports Centre on the Dammam-Alkhobar expressway. Beds are SR 8 per night. Take bus No 1 from either city and get off midway between the two cities at the buildings in front of the stadium (not the green buildings nearby, and not at the big stadium on the edge of Dammam).

The *Al-Jaber Hotel* (☎ 8322283), on 11th St between King Saud and King Khaled Sts, is a reasonable value with simple, clean rooms with TVs at SR 66/99 with bath, SR 55/82.50 without. The *Al-Haramain Hotel* (☎ 8325426) is just off King Saud St, west of the intersection with 11th St. Rooms are SR 77/115. Most of the rooms have private baths though some of the doubles do not (the price is the same). The place is a bit bare, but reasonably clean. The *Gulf Flower Hotel* (☎ 8262170), on 9th St across from the main post office, has rooms at SR 88/110, all with bath, TV and telephone. The *Safari Hotel* (☎ 8272777) on 11th St is a decent mid-range place at SR 120/155. Also in the centre, but slightly more expensive, is the *Balhamar Hotel* (☎ 8320063), just off King Saud St up an alley next to the Al-Danah Shopping Centre. Rooms there cost SR 138/182.

A good medium-priced option, though it is a bit out of the centre, is the *Dammam Hotel* (☎ 8329000), a set of prefabricated buildings behind the Dammam Oberoi that

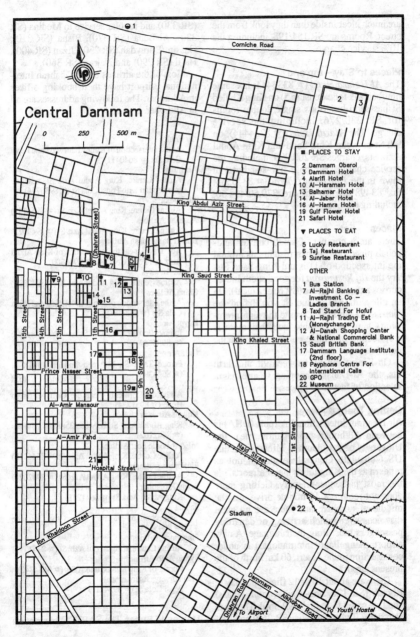

Central Dammam

0    250    500 m

Corniche Road

King Abdul Aziz Street

King Saud Street

King Khaled Street

Prince Nasser Street

Al—Amir Mansour

Al—Amir Fahd

Hospital Street

Ibn Khaldoon Street

Najd Street

Stadium

Dammam – Alkhobar Road

Dhahran Road

To Airport

To Youth Hostel

(Dhahran Street)

15th Street
14th Street
13th Street
11th Street
9th Street
1st Street

■ PLACES TO STAY
2  Dammam Oberoi
3  Dammam Hotel
4  Alariti Hotel
10  Al—Haramain Hotel
13  Balhamar Hotel
14  Al—Jaber Hotel
16  Al—Hamra Hotel
19  Gulf Flower Hotel
21  Safari Hotel

▼ PLACES TO EAT
5  Lucky Restaurant
6  Taj Restaurant
9  Sunrise Restaurant

OTHER
1  Bus Station
7  Al—Rajhi Banking &
   Investment Co —
   Ladies Branch
8  Taxi Stand For Hofuf
11  Al—Rajhi Trading Est
   (Moneychanger)
12  Al—Danah Shopping Center
   & National Commercial Bank
15  Saudi British Bank
17  Dammam Language Institute
   (2nd floor)
18  Payphone Centre For
   International Calls
20  GPO
22  Museum

are much nicer inside than they look from the street. Rooms are SR 154/198, including the 10% service charge.

## Places to Stay – top end

The *Al-Hamra Hotel* (☎ 8333444, fax same number; ask for extension 5) on King Khaled St has semi-luxurious single/double rooms for SR 230/276, including the service charge. The *Alarifi Hotel* (☎ 8334444), on 9th St between King Saud and King Abdul Aziz Sts, charges SR 200/299, including the service charge. The only five-star hotel in town is the *Dammam Oberoi* (☎ 8345555, fax 8349872). Rooms are 379.50/494.50, including service.

## Places to Eat

There are a number of small chicken-and-kebab places and Indian restaurants around the intersection of 11th and King Saud Sts. Try the *Taj Restaurant* for good south Indian curries and great prices (SR 6 for a meal). On an alley off King Saud St you'll find the *Sunrise Restaurant*. Despite the sign promising Chinese and Arabic food, their menu is a collection of simple curries and biryanis, but it's adequate.

On King Saud St, between 9th and 11th Sts, the Al-Danah Shopping Centre has a selection of fast-food places.

## Getting There & Away

**Air** Dhahran International Airport (DHA) is between Alkhobar and Dhahran, near the University of Petroleum & Minerals and the US Consulate General. Although not as modern as the Kingdom's major airports, it's the most passenger-friendly. Getting there does not require a 45-minute drive into the middle of nowhere and there are no great distances over which arriving or departing passengers must drag their luggage. A new airport (King Fahd International) is under construction in the desert, 60 km north of the present airport.

There are about 10 or 12 flights per day to Riyadh (SR 120, one-way, economy class) and five or six to Jeddah (SR 360). There are also daily flights to Abha (SR 360) and Taif

(SR 330) and regular service to Medina (SR 330), Al-Baha (SR 370), Bisha (SR 310), Gassim/Buraydah (SR 230), Jizan (SR 400), Ha'il (SR 290) and Najran (SR 360).

Most of the airlines using Dhahran International Airport have their booking offices in Alkhobar. The following addresses are all in Alkhobar.

Air France
    At the intersection of King Abdul Aziz and Pepsi
    Cola Sts (☎ 8640411)
Air India
    Airline Centre, King Abdul Aziz St, near the
    intersection with Pepsi Cola St (☎ 8980744)
Air Lanka
    Airline Centre, King Abdul Aziz St (☎ 8951153)
Austrian Airlines
    Airline Centre, King Abdul Aziz St (☎ 8949025)
Biman Bangladesh Airlines
    Ace Travel, near the intersection of King Abdul
    Aziz and Pepsi Cola Sts (☎ 8946300)
British Airways
    Airline Centre, King Abdul Aziz St (☎ 8942024)
China Airlines
    At the intersection of King Abdul Aziz and Pepsi
    Cola Sts (☎ 8981060)
Egypt Air
    Intersection of Dhahran St and the Corniche
    (☎ 8985252)
Gulf Air
    Prince Talal St, between 2nd and 3rd Sts,
    (☎ 8644390)
KLM
    Alkhobar Corniche, near the Gulf Meridien
    Hotel (☎ 8951234)
Kuwait Airways
    King Abdul Aziz St, between 25th and 26th Sts
    (☎ 8642102)
MEA (Middle East Airlines)
    Airline Centre, King Abdul Aziz St (☎ 8646118)
Philippine Airlines
    Airline Centre, King Abdul Aziz St (☎ 8942021)
Royal Jordanian
    King Abdul Aziz St (☎ 8641231)
Saudia
    Intersection of Dhahran St and the Corniche
    (☎ 8943333)
Singapore Airlines
    Airline Centre, King Abdul Aziz St (☎ 8951515)
Syrian Arab Airlines
    Corner of King Khaled and A Sts (☎ 8644342)
Thai Airways International
    Pepsi Cola St (☎ 8954111)

**Domestic Buses** The SAPTCO bus station

is a few blocks north of the centre at the intersection of 11th St and the Corniche.

The services to Qatif and Safwa are classified as local and leave from the same part of the station as the routes to Alkhobar and the airport. Bus No 9 goes to Qatif via Saihat and Jarudiyah. Route No 10A goes from Saihat to Qatif, Safwa and Umm Al-Sahik. Route No 10B is Saihat-Anak-Qatif. Route No 11 follows the same route as 10B and then continues on to Tarut Island. The fare for any of these trips is SR 2.

There are inter-city buses to Hofuf (2½ hours, SR 20) daily at 7.30, 9.30 and 11.30 am, and at 1.30, 3.30, 5.30 and 7.30 pm. All Hofuf buses travel via Abqaiq (1½ hours, SR 13). To Riyadh (five hours, SR 60), there are buses at 7.30 and 11.30 am, 3 and 5 pm. There is one bus daily to Jeddah (19 hours, SR 190) via Taif (16 hours, SR 160). The bus departs at 2 pm and goes around Mecca, so it's OK for non-Muslims. For buses to Mecca (SR 175) or to Jeddah and Taif at other times of the day, change in Riyadh. There is also a 10 am bus to Hafr Al-Batn (about five hours, SR 65), continuing along the TAPLINE road to Al-Qurayat (17 hours, SR 195).

**International Buses** The Saudi-Bahraini Transport Company's buses to Bahrain (three hours, SR 40 one-way, SR 70 return) leave every day at 8 and 11 am and at 2, 5 and 8.30 pm. All the Bahrain buses go via Alkhobar. Buses leave Bahrain for Saudi Arabia at 8.30 am, noon, and 3, 6 and 8.30 pm. There are fewer buses during Ramadan and more during Eid Al-Fitr and Eid Al-Adha. Tickets are available at the SAPTCO station.

SAPTCO's other international services from the Eastern Province include: Cairo (SR 480), daily; Damascus (SR 250) on Sunday, Tuesday and Thursday at 2 pm; Amman (SR 250) on Saturday, Tuesday and Thursday at 9.30 am, and Abu Dhabi (SR 240) on Tuesday, Wednesday and Thursday at noon. The trip to Egypt, Jordan or Syria takes about two days. Abu Dhabi should be six to nine hours, depending on how long it takes the bus to clear customs.

**Train** The train station is south-east of the city centre, near the Dammam-Alkhobar Expressway and a housing development. Trains leave daily except Thursday at 7.30 am and 4 pm for Riyadh (four hours, SR 60/40 in 1st/2nd class) via Abqaiq (30 minutes, SR 10/6) and Hofuf (1½ hours, SR 20/15). See the Facts for the Visitor section for a complete timetable.

**Service Taxi** You'll find a few service taxis at the SAPTCO station and at the intersection of King Saud and 11th Sts, but there's not much traffic and the wait for a cab to fill up is likely to be pretty long. The fare is SR 25 to Hofuf.

**Car Rental** There are a number of car rental agencies in the area around the intersection of 11th and King Saud Sts.

**Getting Around**
**To/From the Airport** Buses run from the bus station to the airport approximately every 30 minutes for SR 2. A taxi between the airport and Dammam costs about SR 40.

**Bus** Local buses are based at the SAPTCO station. All fares are SR 2. Routes and route numbers are posted in the front window of each bus. Virtually all local services are to Alkhobar, but along different routes. The main routes are: No 1 along the Dammam-Alkhobar expressway via the Industrial Area; No 3 via Thuqba, the airport and Dhahran/King Fahd University of Petroleum & Minerals (UPM); No 5 via the Coast Rd and No 6 via the Tubaishi Industrial Area.

**Taxi** There is the usual choice of yellow cabs and slightly more expensive white limos. Contrary to what some of the taxi drivers, particularly at the train station, may tell you there are no set fares from the train station or the airport into Dammam or Alkhobar. The drivers are supposed to use the meter.

**ALKHOBAR**
Alkhobar (Al-Khubar, Khobar) is the newest of the three cities that make up Greater

Dhahran. The first recorded settlement was in 1923. It grew rapidly because of its proximity to the early ARAMCO camps at Dhahran, particularly after the oil company engineers built a pier at Alkhobar to take the early oil shipments over to Bahrain for processing.

## Orientation

Khobar (the 'Al' is frequently dropped in common usage) is a fairly compact grid. The central business area is bounded by Pepsi Cola St (officially 28th St, but universally referred to by its nickname) to the north, Dhahran St to the south, the Gulf to the east and King Abdul Aziz St to the west. The Corniche is officially Prince Turky St but you'll be hard-pressed to find anyone who calls it anything other than the Corniche.

## Information

**Money** There are a number of banks and exchange houses along King Khaled St and on the side streets just off it, between 1st and 3rd Sts.

American Express (☎ 8953862) is represented in the Eastern Province by Kanoo Travel. Their office for AMEX business is at the corner of King Khaled and 1st Sts and is open Saturday to Thursday from 8.30 am to 12.30 pm and from 3.30 to 7.30 pm.

**Post & Telecommunications** The Khobar post office is just off Dhahran St near the intersection with the Corniche. The telephone office is on Prince Talal St between 4th and 5th Sts. Look for a small parking lot with the SAPTCO office on the corner at the 5th St side of the square. The telephone office is the small brown building in the parking lot. It is open daily from 8 am to 11.30 pm. The telephone code for Alkhobar is 03.

**Consulates** The UK has a consular officer who works out of the British Trade Office (☎ 8570595) in the Al-Bustan compound, near the Al-Aswaq supermarket.

**Travel Agencies** The two main clusters of travel agencies are around the intersection of Pepsi Cola and King Abdul Aziz Sts and on King Khaled St between Dhahran and 4th Sts.

**Bookshops** Khobar is a better place than Dammam to look for books, but the selection is still pretty thin. The best selection is at the International Book Shop at the intersection of Pepsi Cola and King Fahed Sts. There is a smaller branch with a smaller selection of the same store in the Khobar souk at the corner of A St and Prince Mohammed St.

## King Fahd Causeway

Khobar's main attraction is the King Fahd Causeway, a 25-km long engineering marvel linking Saudi Arabia to Bahrain. Customs takes place on an artificial island halfway along. Restaurants (awful on the Saudi side, tolerable on the Bahraini side) and spectacular views can be found in the twin towers on the island.

## Things to Buy

The Arab Heritage on Prince Saad St, just off Pepsi Cola St near the bottling plant, is widely reputed to be the best place in the Kingdom to shop for Arab artwork, traditional clothing and crafts. However, it is *very* expensive. A lot cheaper and a good bit tackier is Souvenir Store for Antiques on Prince Nasser St, two blocks south of Pepsi Cola St. Their items supposedly come from all over Arabia, the Middle East and the Indian subcontinent, but beware of the salespeople. I once caught them out trying to palm off Thai pillowcases as Bedouin work from Medina.

The Al-Harmain Store, on King Khaled St between 2nd and 3rd Sts, has a small but interesting selection of old silver jewellery and a few weavings and coffee pots. They also sell authentic tourist-rip-off papyrus from Egypt (that stuff turns up in the most amazing places).

## Places to Stay

Bus No 1, which runs between the Alkhobar and Dammam bus stations, stops near the

*Youth Hostel*. See the Dammam listing for more details.

The closest thing to an inexpensive hotel in Khobar is the *Safari Hotel* (8951001), at the corner of Prince Sultan and 1st Sts. Singles/doubles are SR 95/140. Next door, the *Al-Iqbal Hotel* (☎ 8943538) has rooms for SR 130/170. Nearby, at the intersection of Prince Mansour and 4th Sts, the *Al-Kadisiyah Hotel* (☎ 8641255) has large rooms with rather dowdy decor at SR 125/175.

If you're looking for luxury but trying to avoid five-star prices the best options are the *Al-Nimran Hotel* (☎ 8645861, fax 8947876) on Pepsi Cola St, and the *Park Hotel* (☎ 8950005, fax 8987271) on the Corniche, one block from the intersection with Dhahran St. Rooms at either place are SR 230/300.

The top end of the local market is represented by the *Gulf Meridien* (☎ 8646000, fax 8981651), on the Corniche near the intersection with Pepsi Cola St, and the *Algosaibi Hotel* (☎ 8942466, fax 8947533), on Prince Abdullah Ben Jalawi St behind the Pepsi Cola bottling plant.

Last but not least, the *Dhahran International Hotel* (☎ 8918555, fax 8918559), adjacent to the airport, is where the world's TV correspondents were set up during the Gulf War. The proximity to the airport allowed the camerapeople to get dramatic shots of warplanes taking off. The hotel was the backdrop for broadcasts by American TV reporters.

All three of the big hotels charge SR 345/449, including service, for singles/doubles.

### Places to Eat

The area bounded by Dhahran St, 4th St, the Gulf and Prince Bandar St is filled with good, cheap restaurants. Most are of the Indian/Pakistani and South-East Asian variety. *Phuket Restaurant*, on King Faisal St one block north of Dhahran St, has good Thai meals for SR 20 to SR 25. There are a number of similar places in the same area.

The *Turkey Cock* on Pepsi Cola St, across from the Pepsi plant, is one of the Eastern Province's best kept secrets with excellent set meals for SR 15 (main dish, salad, rice). For more expensive eating try the coffee shop at the *Gulf Meridien*. The breakfast buffet there is very popular.

The restaurant on the King Fahd Causeway to Bahrain is not very good, but on a clear day the views can make up for a lot of bad food and worse service. The upper level is only for families. The lower level has both a cafeteria and a slightly fancier restaurant with table service.

### Getting There & Away

The bus station is on Prince Talal St between 4th and 5th Sts. Look for a small parking lot with a SAPTCO office (☎ 8949687) on the corner at the 5th St side of the square. There are no domestic inter-city services from Khobar. For inter-city routes take a bus to the Dammam terminal, all departures are from there. Bus No 8 runs from the Khobar terminal to the airport via Dhahran St and 20th St. See the Dammam entry for other local bus route listings, including the different Dammam-Khobar routes.

Buses to Bahrain leave daily at 8.45 and 11.45 am and at 2.45, 5.45 and 9.45 pm. Tickets are available from the SAPTCO office for SR 40 one-way, SR 70 return.

A taxi between Khobar and the airport should cost about SR 40.

### DHAHRAN

Apart from the ARAMCO visitor centre, which has the best museum in the Kingdom, there is little that is either of interest or accessible in Dhahran. Aside from the airport, Dhahran consists of the ARAMCO compound, which is a small city in itself, the US Consulate General (☎ 8913200) near the airport, and the University of Petroleum & Minerals. Admission to any of these requires identification showing that you live, work, study or have business there.

The **ARAMCO Exhibit** is open Saturday to Wednesday from 8 am to 6.30 pm, Thursday from 9 am to noon and 3 to 6.30 pm and Friday from 3 to 6.30 pm. Thursdays and

Fridays are for families only; admission is free.

The centre is a comprehensive layperson's guide to the oil industry with a minimum of pro-Big Oil preaching and an emphasis on explaining the technical side of the industry. It's also fun, especially for kids, with lots of buttons to push, user-participation displays and quizzes.

As you enter the building go straight ahead and up the stairs; a display there outlines the exhibits and suggests different itineraries for seeing them depending on how much time you have to spend. You could easily spend two or three hours at the exhibit. About two-thirds of the space is taken up by displays on how oil is formed, found, extracted and refined. There is a short history of ARAMCO itself and a fascinating display on Arab science and technology covering timekeeping, astronomy and alchemy.

## QATIF

Qatif (Qateef), 13 km north of Dammam, is one of the centres of the Eastern Province's large Shiite community. It was first settled around 3500 BC and in the centuries prior to the discovery of oil it was the main settlement on this part of the Gulf coast. Some early European maps of the region identify the Gulf as the 'Sea of Elcatif', testifying to the town's relative size and importance in the 17th and 18th centuries.

While there are a couple of interesting things to see in Qatif, there is no place to stay. Qatif and nearby Tarut Island make an interesting day trip from Dammam.

### Things to See

Both of Qatif's protected sites lie in the town centre. To enter both sites, permits from the museum in Dammam are necessary.

The **Al-Shamasi House** was built by Mohammed Al-Shamasi around 1910 and remained occupied until the mid-1980s. It is now an archaeological zone and has been restored by the government as an example of typical Eastern Province architecture. The inscriptions and wall decorations are especially interesting. On the upper floor is a

*khalwa*, or prayer room. The old storerooms on the ground floor were used mainly to store dates.

The fortified quarter of Old Qatif, **Al-Qalah**, was partly inhabited until the mid-1970s. The first fort on the site was built as long ago as the 3rd century BC, reportedly by a local potentate named 'Andshir Ben Babek, though the oldest building still standing is a 14th century AD mosque. Much of what can be seen today consists of two and three-storey houses jammed together along narrow alleyways and covered streets. Some of these are as much as 400 years old, though most are of much more recent construction. At one time, Al-Qalah housed some 30,000 people, sheltered behind walls nine metres high and two metres thick and surrounded by 11 circular guard towers.

Once in the centre you will easily recognise Al-Qalah by the fence and the big blue Department of Antiquities signs which mark archaeological sites. If you're coming from Dammam, get to King Abdul Aziz St in the town centre (following the Tarut directions, below) and take the second street on the right (the first is only a small alley) beyond the Al-Bank Al-Saudi Al-Hollandi branch. Al-Qalah will be on the left. If you're pressed for time, however, head for Tarut, which is much more interesting. The Al-Shamasi House is a short distance from Al-Qalah.

## TARUT ISLAND

For centuries the small island of Tarut has been one of the most important ports and military strongholds on the Arabian side of the Gulf. Parts of the island, particularly the town of Darin, have been inhabited since prehistoric times. In the early years of this century the island served as the entrepôt for Qatif, which was then one of the major towns of eastern Arabia. Today Tarut is connected to the mainland by a causeway.

### Tarut Fort

Tarut Fort is one of Saudi Arabia's most photographed ruins. It is a very big, and relatively well preserved and restored, bastion which has survived from a much larger structure built by the Portuguese in the 16th century. The nearby houses cover the tell, below which the rest of the fort and earlier ruins lie. Visits to the fort require a permit from the Dammam museum.

The site itself was first settled during the Stone Age and became important during the 3rd millennium BC when it was part of the Bahrain-based Dilmun empire. There is little to be seen of the remains of this era except a stairway inside the fort. The lighter coloured portions of this stairway are thought to be about 5000 years old and are the only surviving bit of some earlier structure. The stairway is the basis of a theory that the fort is built on top of the site of a 3rd millennium BC city, though more excavations would be needed to prove this.

Near the centre of the ruins you can see the remains of a well which has been dry for many years. The fort also overlooks a natural spring which is still used by local women as a bathing pool, but the government has constructed a building around it.

### Qasr Darin

Qasr Darin is a site so exposed and so thoroughly ruined that you do not need a permit to see it. Though it is in much worse shape than Tarut Fort, Qasr Darin is, in fact, much the younger of the two. It was built in 1875 by Abdul Wahab Pasha to guard the main seaborne approaches to the island at the height of the pearl trade. As at Tarut Fort, what is now visible only hints at the original extent of the building which at one time covered over 8300 sq metres.

### Getting There & Away

Tarut is connected to the mainland town of Qatif by a causeway. To reach Tarut take the Jubail expressway north and exit at the sign for Anak and Qatif. Follow the road for 4.8 km through the village of Al-Jesh and turn left at a sign for 'Qateef'. Go straight for 2.5 km and keep right, ignoring the directional sign for Tarut, when the road forks. From the fork go another 2.5 km and turn right at the petrol station, which has three huge stone cars on pillars acting as sun shades. Keep

going straight for six km, during which you will cross the causeway onto the island, and then turn right at an intersection-cum-roundabout. Follow a narrow road through Tarut town for about one km and you will see Tarut Fort on the right. To reach Qasr Darin continue on the same road for two km until it swings around to the right. At that point just keep hugging the coastline for another six km and you'll see the ruins on the right, near the pier.

### JUBAIL

Jubail was little more than a fishing village until the mid-70s when the government decided to turn it into one of the Kingdom's two showpiece industrial cities – the other is Yanbu, on the Red Sea coast. The earliest oil exploration operations in Saudi Arabia were based in Jubail, which was the original base for CASOC (California Arabian Standard Oil company – the precursor of ARAMCO). The company moved its headquarters to Dhahran only after drilling began.

Jubail town is about 90 km north of Dammam. It is dwarfed by the industrial city, officially referred to as Madinat Al-Jubail Al-Sinaiyah,which has been built a few km to the north. The industrial city is a complex of petrochemical plants, an iron works and a host of smaller 'satellite' companies, most of which are support firms supplying the major industries. Many of these firms were lured to the area with the promise of, among other things, almost nonexistent rents so long as they set up shop on government-owned and administered tracts of land. The project is overseen by the Royal Commission for Jubail & Yanbu, and Jubail is often referred to simply as the Royal Commission.

The Saudis are exceedingly and justifiably proud of the developments at Jubail, though it is not exactly a hot spot for tourists. The only thing to see in the industrial city is the **Visitor Centre** at the Royal Commission's headquarters. This is open Saturday to Wednesday from 7 am to noon and 1 to 4 pm. You must, however, have an appointment to visit the centre, which is arranged through the Royal Commission's public relations office (☎ 3414427). The display covers the history of the Royal Commission and the construction of Jubail.

To reach the Royal Commission building take the first Jubail exit off the highway from Dammam and follow the signs. It's pretty easy to find.

### Places to Stay & Eat

Jubail has only two hotels and neither is cheap. In town the *Sharq Hotel* (☎ 3611155) on Jeddah St charges SR 132/165 for singles/doubles. In the industrial city the *Holiday Inn* (☎ 3417000) charges SR 345/448.50, including the 15% service charge. The telephone code for Jubail is 03.

The main drag, Jeddah St, has a collection of small Indian restaurants, roasted-chicken shops and fast-food outlets. For some variety you might try *Jabal Lebnan*, just off Jeddah St; look for the sign pointing to a 'Lebanon Restaurant'. It's not the best Lebanese food I've ever had but it beats having lunch at Kentucky Fried Chicken. Main dishes cost SR 10 to SR 15, mezza are SR 10 and under.

### The Jubail Church

Despite what you may hear, the ruins commonly known as the Jubail Church do exist. People in the Saudi archaeology bureaucracy acknowledge the site's existence, but they do not like to talk about it and will not issue permits for visits to the site. The official reason is that the site is still being excavated.

Even without a permit you can still get a pretty good view of the site from outside the fence. The site itself is fairly easy to find and, if you are in the area anyway, it is worth the diversion.

To reach the church from Dammam, drive almost all the way to Jubail and leave the expressway at the exit for ARAMCO and Jubail North. Turn left under the bridge and left again to get back on the expressway as though you were headed back toward Dammam. About one km past the point where you got back on the expressway (1.5 km from the left turn after passing under the bridge) turn right, off the highway, at the first building. Look for a sign with a triangular C-C-C logo. Turn right in front of this building and follow its wall around to your left. Follow a good, wide dirt road that runs between two rows of trees. After about one km the road goes up and over two large sets of pipes and then crosses a service road. Follow the track over an area of sand and rocks, keeping to the right when it forks. After a few hundred metres you will see a large fence ahead of you and to the right. Keep going straight and after another few hundred metres two more fences will become visible in front of you. The church is enclosed by the one straight ahead; you should be able to see its walls from a distance. The total distance from the place where you leave the road to the fence is 1.8 km. You do not need a 4WD.

The ruins are strikingly well preserved. They were unearthed in 1986 by a group of people on a desert picnic who were digging out one of their vehicles after it got stuck in the sand.

The ruins probably date from the 4th century which would make them older than any church now existing in Europe. Little is known about this particular church but it was probably connected to one of the five Nestorian bishoprics which existed in this part of the Gulf in the 4th century.

The main building consists of one large room, though foundation lines on the floor indicate that there were probably originally three rooms in this space. Three smaller chambers connect to the east side of this main room. The walls of the smaller chambers are still standing and beside the doorways the marks where four stone crosses were affixed to the wall are still clearly visible. These crosses were in place when the church was unearthed but went missing sometime in late 1986 or early 1987. Of the three smaller chambers, the central one contains two sets of well-preserved half-columns. The large number of seashells scattered around the area indicate that the church sat on the coast in its time. In the south-east corner of the enclosure which includes the church you can see a second, smaller set of ruins. These may have been cells for monks attached to the church.

### HOFUF

The Al-Hasa oasis, centred on the town of Hofuf, is one of the largest in the world. A hundred years ago a large part of Europe's dates came from here and it is still one of the world's leading areas for date production. The oasis seems to go on and on and, if you have time and a car, exploring the small villages scattered through this large, lush area can be a pleasant way to spend an afternoon or two.

## Orientation & Information

There is not much to Hofuf itself. The centre is very compact. King Abdul Aziz St is the main commercial street and intersects with Al-Khudod St to form a central square containing the bus station and bounded by a mosque and the large, white Riyad Bank building. Both of the centre's hotels are an easy walk from this intersection.

There are several banks around the main intersection and an Al-Rajhi branch on King Abdul Aziz St just south of the main intersection.

The telephone office is north of the centre at the intersection of the Dammam Rd (officially Prince Abdullah Ben Jalawi St) and Hajer Palace Rd. It is open daily from 7.30 am until midnight. The telephone code for Hofuf is 03.

The Saudia office (☎ 5863333) is on Al-Khudod St just off the main intersection.

## Qasr Ibrahim

Seeing Qasr Ibrahim, Hofuf's fort, involves more than the usual number of hassles. Not only do you need a site permit which has to be issued in Riyadh, but once you arrive in Hofuf your permit must be validated by both the local antiquities office and the head of the local education department. Both are several km from the centre behind the big prison on the road to the youth hostel. Both are only open in the morning from Saturday to Wednesday.

First, take the permit to the Antiquities Office. After they have examined it you will be sent over to the Education Department, 600 metres down the road. Head for the manager's office on the 3rd floor and be prepared for an interrogation. While everyone at the Antiquities Office is very friendly, the people at the Education Department are decidedly suspicious of foreigners who want to have a look at the local antiquities. I was grilled by the man in charge for about 15

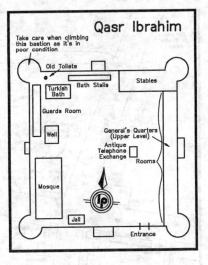

minutes before he would sign my permit. Once the permit is signed, you must take it back to the Antiquities Office where you will be provided with an escort for your trip to Qasr Ibrahim. Since your escort will be planning to head home at about 1 pm you would be well advised to start this whole process before 9 am. It probably won't take that long but you never know.

However, Qasr Ibrahim is worth the hassle even if you cannot get an English-speaking guide from the Antiquities office. It is very

Qasr Ibrahim

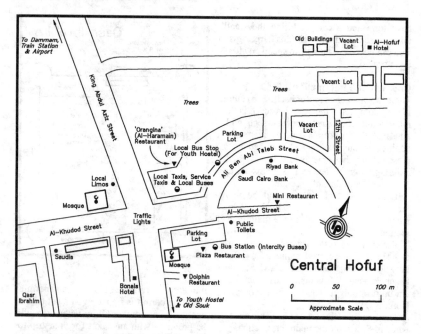

well preserved. The fort is on Al-Khudod St, a short walk from Hofuf's main intersection, and the entrance is on the back side.

Qasr Ibrahim is almost entirely of Turkish construction. The mosque inside the walls is the oldest part of the complex, having been built circa 1566 (974 AH). The first fort on this site was built just over a century later in 1688-89 (1100 AH). The present fort dates from the beginning of the 19th century, and a Turkish garrison continued to occupy it until Abdul Aziz conquered Hofuf in 1913.

Inside the fort take a look at the jail, next to the mosque, and the underground cells inside it. The Turkish bath near the north-west corner of the compound was used during Abdul Aziz's time to store dates, the smell of which still lingers inside. Near the bath you can see a small excavated area showing the underground system which was used for heating water. In the courtyard there is an old telephone exchange which also dates from Abdul Aziz's time. The stairs

along the eastern wall lead to what were the commanding officer's quarters. These are usually closed.

## Souk

Hofuf's real treat is the souk. It's just off King Abdul Aziz St, about 300 metres south of the main intersection. This is one of the few places in the country where handmade Arabian coffee pots, as opposed to mass-produced ones imported from Pakistan, can still be found. Several shops also have good collections of Bedouin weavings and a few have old silver jewellery. Prices vary greatly according to size and quality. The best place to look for souvenirs is at the northern end of the souk, the one closer to the main intersection. As more and more foreigners have begun to shop in Hofuf's souk the shopkeepers have met the rising demand for Bedouin weavings by importing them from Syria. Saudi-made weavings tend to have darker colours than Syrian ones. Ask before you buy.

You will also find a few shops selling weavings near Qasr Ibrahim.

## Places to Stay

The *Youth Hostel* (☎ 5800692) is at the stadium. It's a long way out and is not served by public transportation. Beds are SR 8. To reach the hostel take Bus No 2 (SR 2, sporadic service) from the bus station to the large T-junction by the prison (the white building on the left with a guard tower). There is a stadium behind it but that's not the one. Turn right at the junction and follow the road for half a km until it forks. Keep left at the fork and follow the road for another 2.5 km. A cab from the bus station costs SR 12 to SR 15.

In town the *Bonais Hotel* (☎ 5827700) is on King Abdul Aziz St near the bus station. Singles/doubles are SR 99/148, most with bath but some without for the same price. The *Al-Hofuf Hotel* (☎ 5877082) is on 13th St, a five-minute walk from the bus station. It's a friendly, middle-range, place with rooms at SR 132/198, all with bath. With advance notice they can put together weekend package tours of the area for groups of eight or more. To reach the Al-Hofuf Hotel from the bus station, leave the square by the road in front of the Riyad Bank. Turn left on 12th St, then right on 13th St.

## Places to Eat

Hofuf is a bit short on restaurants but there is a very good small place across the main intersection from the bus station. A meal of chicken, rice and salad costs SR 12. It's called the *Al-Haramain Restaurant* but the sign is written only in Arabic. Look for the Orangina sign and a large Lipton tea ad. Near the SAPTCO station the *Plaza Restaurant* has good, cheap Indian food. A meal of chicken or mutton curry with rice costs only SR 7. The *Dolphin Restaurant*, just off King Abdul Aziz St, is a good place to look for fresh juice and Arabic sweets.

## Getting There & Away

At this writing Saudia was operating daily flights from Hofuf to Riyadh (SR 120 one-way, economy class) with continuing service to Jeddah (SR 360) twice a week. It is probably safe to assume that the frequency of service to Hofuf will increase once the new Dhahran Airport opens. The new airport is about an hour further from Hofuf by car than the present one.

The bus station (☎ 5873687) is at the intersection of King Abdul Aziz and Al-Khudod Sts. Buses run to Dammam (2½ hours, SR 20) via Abqaiq (one hour, SR 13) daily at 7 and 10 am, noon, and at 2.30, 4, 6 and 8 pm. To Riyadh (3½ hours, SR 45), there are buses daily at 7.30 am and 3 pm. Service taxis congregate in the parking lot across the street from the bus station. International buses to Egypt, Syria, Jordan and Turkey leave from the whitewashed building with red, yellow and blue stripes, on Hajer Palace Rd near the train station.

The train station is a long way from the town centre. To reach it, head north on the Dammam Rd and turn west onto Hajer Palace Rd at the telephone office. Once you are on Hajer Palace Rd the station is beyond the second set of traffic lights. Trains leave daily except Thursday for Riyadh at 9 am and 5.30 pm (SR 45 1st class, SR 30 2nd class) and for Dammam (via Abqaiq) at 10.25 am and 6.55 pm (1½ hours, SR 20 1st class, SR 15 2nd class).

## Getting Around

Both yellow taxis and white limos have ranks at the main intersection. The local bus system can also get you to some of the further-flung corners of the oasis.

## KAILABIYAH

The village of Kailabiyah, about 12 km north-east of Hofuf, is the site of the **Juwafia Mosque**, Saudi Arabia's holiest after Mecca and Medina. According to Islamic tradition, the mosque was built in the year 632 AD (10 AH) during the last months of the Prophet's life. Tradition also says that it was on this site that Mohammed led the communal Friday prayer for only the second time outside of Medina. The original mosque is long gone. What is visible today is a fragment of a later mosque, a relatively small piece of what was once the wall facing Mecca. All you'll see is a bit of stonework vaulting. Some minor restoration work has been done to the vaulting, and carpeting has been added so that it can be used as a prayer area. It is set in the middle of a very nice park. If you have a car the mosque is well worth the 17-km drive from Hofuf.

To reach the mosque from Hofuf's main intersection start along Ali Ben Abi Taleb St, passing the Riyad Bank on your left. Turn right at the first set of traffic lights, near a fire station, and continue straight until you reach a T-junction. Turn left at the T-junction and follow the road; you'll pass a sign for the northern villages and, further on, a sign for Holailah. About 600 metres past this sign the road splits into three; keep left, following the sign for Battiliyah (the sign also says Kailabiyah but only in Arabic). After 4.2 km you'll come to a set of traffic lights. Turn left; a small green sign in Arabic points the way to Kailabiyah. This takes you into the village. You will pass a new mosque on the right. Just beyond this is a small grocery store with a Pepsi sign in Arabic. Once you pass this store take the second turn on the right (the first turn is only a small street.) Follow the road until you see a turn marked by a small blue sign and a small white sign, both in Arabic. Turn here. Follow this road 4.25 km until it ends in a parking lot. You will see a small, white building on the left and a blue gate which leads to the mosque and park.

## AROUND THE EASTERN PROVINCE
### Bedouin Market
The Eastern Province's most interesting day trip is the Bedouin Market which takes place every Friday morning in the village of Nuraiyah, about 250 km north of Dammam. The market is something of a local legend and draws Bedouins from as far away as Qatar and Abu Dhabi. From Alkhobar or Dammam take the Jubail Expressway to the Abu Hadriyah turn-off. From Abu Hadriyah follow the signs to Nuraiyah. Once in Nuraiyah head for the new mosque, which is on your left as you enter town, and follow the crowd. Get an early start as the market usually disappears by 10 am. Many combine a visit to the market with an overnight camping trip to Thaj (see below). Nuraiyah is the best spot in the Kingdom for purchasing Bedouin art such as rugs, bridles and saddlebags for camels.

### Fortresses
The ruined fortresses of **Thaj** and **Al-Hina** lie about 100 km out in the desert west of Dammam and are a short distance off the old road to Nuraiyah. You need to obtain permits from the Dammam museum; also ask there for directions to the sites.

Thaj is much the more interesting of the two sites. The city, though large, had only a single period of occupation lasting about 400 years. Its brief peak was reached sometime between 300 and 100 BC and the site is known to have been in ruins by the 6th century AD. The city, now surrounded by desert, then stood on the edge of a lake.

# The United Arab Emirates

If you can only visit one country in the Gulf, the United Arab Emirates is probably your best choice. It has the most relaxed entry regulations of any of the countries covered by this book and offers a lot of things to see over a wide variety of terrain, all contained in a relatively small area. The UAE also has the best tourist infrastructure of any of the Gulf states.

The UAE is a union of seven sovereign sheikhdoms which was formed in 1971 when the British withdrew from the Gulf. Despite their small size, each emirate has its own, distinct features. The capital, Abu Dhabi, is one of the most modern cities on earth, where almost nothing is more than 25 years old. Dubai is unquestionably the most vibrant city in the Gulf and has one of the best cityscapes in the region. In the emirates north of Dubai – Sharjah, Ajman, Umm Al-Qaiwain and Ras Al-Khaimah – life moves at a slower pace but each emirate is quite different from its neighbours. The Hajar Mountains provide a particularly dramatic backdrop for both Ras Al-Khaimah, the northernmost of the Gulf coast emirates, and Fujairah, which overlooks the Gulf of Oman on the country's east coast. Both are becoming popular winter destinations for tourists from northern Europe.

Travel agencies in Europe are pushing the UAE as a land of contrasts: mountains, beaches, deserts and oases, camel racing, Bedouin markets and the legendary duty-free shopping of Dubai. All this in a compact geographical tour package with good hotels and no-fuss visas. You can even touch toe and go shopping in Oman for a few hours to boot. The brochures trumpet the 'Arabian Experience' and are clearly aimed at up-market tourists in search of an exotic but comfortable destination where few of their friends have been – the sort of people who would have gone to Morocco or Tunisia 30 years ago.

You can have this type of holiday or you

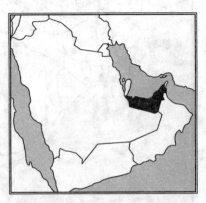

can have a fine time in the UAE without booking a package tour. It is one of the best places in the Gulf for the independent traveller, and with over 100,000 tourists already making the trip each year, you should see it soon before mass tourism in the UAE really hits its stride.

# Facts about the Country

### HISTORY
### Early Settlement
Less is known about the early history of the area that is now the UAE than about other areas of the Gulf. Although the first archaeological digs in the country took place over 30 years ago, the Emirates have never received the sort of sustained attention that has been lavished on the ancient sites of Bahrain and Kuwait.

It is certain, though, that this part of Arabia, like much of the rest of the Gulf, has been settled for many centuries. A few pot-sherds from the 4th millennium BC have been found around Jebel Hafit in the Al-Ain area. The earliest significant settlements,

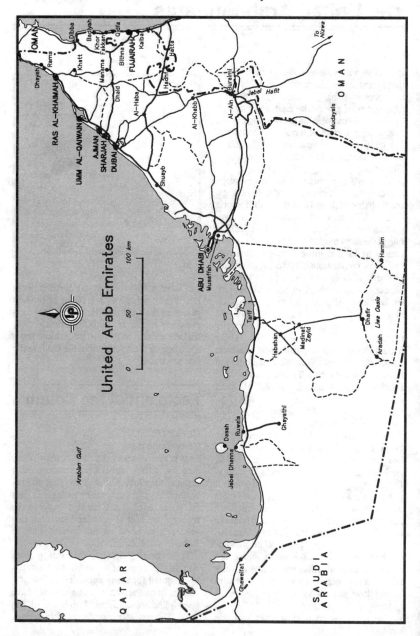

both inland and on the coast, are from the Bronze Age and show that during the 3rd millennium BC, the Gulf had a much more temperate climate than it does today. Around this period, a distinct culture arose near modern Abu Dhabi. This culture, called Umm An-Nar after the small island where it was first discovered, thrived for only a few hundred years and little is known about it. What can be said is that the people of Umm An-Nar were probably fishers and that they were not part of the Bahrain- based Dilmun empire which was then the rising power of the central and northern Gulf. It also seems fairly certain that the Umm An-Nar culture extended well into the interior and down the coast of what is now Oman. Digs near Al-Ain, on the border with Oman, show evidence of an agricultural-based society existing in the area, contemporary to the Umm An-Nar society though the exact relationship between these oasis and coastal communities is still unclear. There were also settlements at Badiyah (near Fujairah) and at Rams (near Ras Al-Khaimah) during the second half of the 3rd millennium BC.

The Greeks were the next major cultural influence to appear in the area. Ruins showing strong Hellenistic influences have been found at Meleiha, about 50 km from Sharjah, and at Al-Dour in the emirate of Umm Al-Qaiwain.

### Battle Site & Caravan Route

By the early centuries of the Christian era the climate in the Gulf was far less hospitable than it had been during the Bronze Age. In the centuries leading up to the coming of Islam, people of the lower Gulf and its inland areas gained much of their livelihood from their location on the main trade routes. Ruins from this era can be seen at the village of Shimal, near Ras Al-Khaimah, in the form of a set of 4th century AD fortifications on a hilltop overlooking the sea.

The region next appears in history in 635, at the dawn of the Islamic era, when Dibba (on the northern coast of Fujairah) was the site of the battle which traditionally marks the completion of the Islamic conquest of the Arabian peninsula.

During the Middle Ages most of what is now the UAE was part of the Kingdom of Hormuz which controlled the entrance to, and most of the trade in, the Gulf. The first known reference to the area by a European is a manuscript written in 1498 by the Portuguese explorer, Vasco de Gama, which records his rather sketchy observations of Khor Fakkan, Dibba and Ras Al-Khaimah. By 1515, the Portuguese had occupied Julfar (near today's city of Ras Al-Khaimah) and built a customs house through which they taxed the Gulf's flourishing trade with India and the Far East. Later, they also built a fort. Except for a brief interlude in the early 1620s when Julfar revolted, the Portuguese stayed on in the town until 1633. At that point, having lost control of Hormuz, they were forced to abandon the area in the face of attacks by hostile tribes from the land and the British and Dutch from the sea.

After the departure of the Portuguese, the lower Gulf was taken over by the Al-Ya'ribi Imams of Oman before passing into Persia's sphere of influence in the mid-18th century.

### The Qawasim & the Bani Yas

The rise of British naval power in the Gulf in the mid-18th century coincided with the rise of two important tribal confederations along the coast of the lower Gulf. These were the Qawasim and the Bani Yas, the ancestors of the rulers of four of the seven emirates which today make up the UAE.

The Qawasim, whose descendants now rule Sharjah and Ras Al-Khaimah, were a seafaring clan based in Ras Al-Khaimah and their influence extended, at times, to the Persian side of the Gulf. Their main rivals for local power were the Al-Busaids who are now the ruling family of Oman. In 1798, the Al-Busaids signed a treaty with the British. From Britain's point of view, the main purpose of this agreement was to keep the French out of Oman and away from India. The Qawasim felt that the British had just allied themselves with their enemies and that made the British ships fair game for their raids. The Qawasim hostility towards the British was exacerbated by the influence of the strict and somewhat xenophobic doctrines of Wahhabi Islam. The British East India Company, which owned most of the ships in question, looked on the Qawasim's activities as simple piracy, and the government in London tended to agree.

The British dubbed the area the Pirate Coast and launched their own raids against the Qawasim in 1805, 1809 and 1811 but following every skirmish, the situation along the coast returned to 'normal' the moment they left. In 1819, the British decided to resolve the situation by mounting a full-scale invasion of Qawasim territory. A large fleet was dispatched from Bombay and, in 1820, it destroyed or captured every Qawasim ship it could find and occupied the Qawasim forts at Ras Al-Khaimah and Linagh, in Persia. The Royal Navy then imposed a General Treaty of Peace on nine Arab sheikhdoms in the area and installed a garrison in the region.

The treaty still allowed the sheikhs to attack each other – which they continued to do with entirely too much gusto for British taste. Thus, in 1835, the British imposed the Maritime Truce. This was modified several times (notably in 1839 when the British forced the sheikhs to ban slavery) until, in 1853, the truce became the Treaty of Peace in Perpetuity. Under this latest treaty, the British assumed responsibility for arbitrating disputes among the sheikhs. The Europeans then took to calling the area the Trucial Coast, a name it retained until 1971.

Throughout this period the main power among the Bedouin tribes of the interior was the Bani Yas tribal confederation, the ancestors of the ruling families of modern Abu Dhabi and Dubai. The Bani Yas were originally based in Liwa, an oasis on the edge of the Empty Quarter desert but moved to Abu Dhabi island, off the Gulf coast, in 1793. They engaged in the traditional Bedouin activities of camel herding, small-scale agriculture in the Liwa and Buraimi oases, tribal raiding and extracting protection money from merchant caravans passing through their territory. After the British outlawed slavery on the coast, the Bani Yas also took over the slave trade. Buraimi became eastern Arabia's main slave market, a position which it retained until the 1950s. The Bani Yas divided into two main branches in the early 19th century when Dubai split from Abu Dhabi.

## The Trucial Coast

In 1892, the British extended their power over the coast through a series of Exclusive Agreements under which the sheikhs accepted formal British protection and, in exchange, promised to have no dealings with any other foreign power without British permission. The British had insisted on the agreements after rival powers, particularly the French and the Russians, had begun to show interest in the Gulf. London regarded control of the area as essential for the protection of Britain's empire in India.

So long as the Russians and the French were kept out of the region and the lines of communication to India remained secure, the British did not much care what happened in the Gulf. The area became a backwater. Throughout the late 19th and early 20th centuries, the sheikhdoms were all tiny enclaves of fishers, pearl divers and Bedouins. The area's few merchants were mostly Indian or Persian.

For most of this period, Sharjah was the most populous and powerful of the emirates. As the century drew to a close, Sharjah lost influence to Abu Dhabi which, from 1855 until 1909, was ruled by the forceful Shaikh Zayed Bin Mohammed, usually referred to today as Zayed the Great. The power of any individual ruler depended very much on the force of their personality. Following Zayed's death, however, Abu Dhabi went into decline as his family fought over the succession.

The next emirate to rise to prominence was Dubai, under the leadership of the Al-Maktoum family. Even during the period of Zayed the Great's rule, Sharjah had remained the area's main trading centre. But Sharjah's rulers in the early years of this century were both weak and xenophobic. At the turn of the century, a large group of traders left Linagh, on the Persian coast, apparently after changes to the tax regulations. They chose to settle in Dubai instead of Sharjah and, in 1903, arranged for the main Indian-based British steamship line to drop Linagh in favour of Dubai as its main port of call in the lower Gulf. The opening of regular sea links with India and the northern Gulf marked the beginning of Dubai's growth as a trading power.

In the years immediately before and after WW I, the British connection kept Abdul Aziz Bin Abdul Rahman Al-Saud, the future king of Saudi Arabia, from conquering the sheikhdoms of the Trucial Coast. Even so, the British presence remained very low-key. Until 1932, when Imperial Airways (the predecessor of British Airways) built a rest house in Sharjah for passengers and crew on its flights to India, there were no permanent British facilities in what is now the UAE. A permanent British political agent was not appointed anywhere on the Trucial Coast until WW II.

However, it was the prospect of oil that changed the way the British ran their affairs on the Trucial Coast. The actual territories of the various sheikhs had never been properly defined. Abu Dhabi and Dubai even went to war over their competing claims in 1945-47. (Neither side shed much blood but Dubai lost some territory.)

Before oil concessions could be granted, there was an immediate need to determine the boundaries between the sheikhdoms. Each of the local rulers claimed enormous swaths of territory and was willing to concede nothing to his neighbours. Eventually, the borders of the seven emirates which now make up the UAE were drawn up by the British. This, incredibly, involved a British diplomat spending months riding on a camel around in the mountains and desert asking village heads, tribal leaders and groups of Bedouins which shaikh they owed allegiance to. Even that failed to settle all of the competing claims. As part of an ongoing and only partially successful attempt to modernise the governments of the Trucial Coast, and in the hope of settling the rival territorial claims

amicably, the British set up the Trucial States Council in 1951. This was a cabinet consisting of the rulers of the sheikhdoms and the direct predecessor of today's UAE Supreme Council. It met twice a year under the aegis of the British Political Agent in Dubai.

Meanwhile, Dubai was cementing its reputation as the region's busiest trading centre. In 1939, Shaikh Rashid Bin Saeed Al-Maktoum became the regent for his ailing father, Shaikh Saeed. (Rashid only formally succeeded to the leadership when his father died in 1958.) He quickly moved to bolster the emirate's position as the lower Gulf's main entrepôt. At about the same time, the rulers of Sharjah made the near-fatal mistake of allowing their harbour to silt up. This was even more costly for them than it might otherwise have been because, in nearby Dubai, Rashid was improving facilities along Dubai's waterfront, known as the Creek.

## The Oil Era

There is a certain irony in Abu Dhabi's present status as the UAE's richest member; in the decades prior to the discovery of oil, Abu Dhabi was the poorest of the Trucial Coast sheikhdoms. During the early years of the 20th century, particularly the two decades following the death of Zayed the Great, it had also been one of the most violent. With the ascension of Shaikh Shakhbut Bin Sultan in 1928, some stability returned to the emirate but the decline of the pearling industry a few years later left Shaikh Shakhbut the ruler of a land that was destitute and shockingly bleak, even by Arabian standards.

In 1939, hoping to break the cycle of poverty, Shaikh Shakhbut granted a concession to the British-owned Iraq Petroleum Company. It would, however, be another two decades before Abu Dhabi received any oil revenues. In the meantime, the region's territorial controversies continued to preoccupy the Shaikh.

In October 1949, Saudi Arabia formally laid claim to the Buraimi oasis on the grounds that it had been part of the First Saudi Empire in the late 18th century. It ignored the fact that for over a century the oasis had been divided between Abu Dhabi and Oman. In fact, the dispute was about oil which geologists from ARAMCO (the oil concessionaire in Saudi Arabia) suspected lay beneath the oasis. The key to the dispute was the fact that Saudi Arabia's borders were undefined. If it could be proven that Buraimi was in Saudi Arabia, it would also be in ARAMCO's concession area.

In 1952, the Saudis occupied part of Buraimi, allegedly after offering Shaikh Zayed Bin Sultan (now the ruler of Abu Dhabi but then the governor of the oasis) a large bribe to recognise the Saudi claim. Three years and several arbitration attempts later, Zayed and the Trucial Oman Scouts (who were commanded by British officers) drove the Saudis out of the oasis. The current UAE-Oman border running through the oasis was settled in 1966 though Saudi Arabia did not drop its claim to Buraimi until 1974, and then only in exchange for a percentage of the oil revenues from Abu Dhabi's portion of the oasis.

Meanwhile, still desperate for oil, Shaikh Shakhbut had given another concession, this time for offshore exploration, to an Anglo-French consortium in 1953. Five years later, it was this group of prospectors which first struck oil – 20 years after the Shaikh had first hoped to solve his financial problems through the oil companies. It soon became apparent that Abu Dhabi's reserves were enormous. Exports began in 1962 and, with a population at the time of only 15,000, the emirate was obviously on its way to becoming very rich. Later, under Shaikh Zayed, the emirate set up the Abu Dhabi National Petroleum Company (ADNOC) through which it nationalised the concession agreements during the 1970s.

Oil money firmly established Abu Dhabi as the leader among the Trucial Coast sheikhdoms. Dubai was already becoming a relatively wealthy trading centre in the early '60s and, in 1966, was found to have oil of its own. The other sheikhs, however, were not so lucky, and all of them inevitably began to look to Abu Dhabi for subsidies.

The problem was that Shaikh Shakhbut, having waited so long for the oil money to begin coming in, proved to be completely incapable of handling his newly found wealth. In the early and mid '60s his rule became increasingly erratic. Shakhbut had little understanding of modern banks and did not trust them. He became increasingly suspicious of all foreigners and is said once to have told oil company representatives that he was the one with the upper hand because they needed the money more than he did. In 1966, the British engineered Shakhbut's deposition by Shaikh Zayed, Shakhbut's brother who was also the long-time governor of Abu Dhabi's portion of the Buraimi oasis. After spending several years abroad, Shakhbut eventually retired to Al-Ain, the main town within Abu Dhabi's portion of Buraimi.

### The Federation

Britain's 1968 announcement that it would leave the Gulf in 1971 came as a shock to most of the ruling sheikhs. Within a few weeks, the British began work on forming a single state consisting of Bahrain, Qatar and the Trucial Coast. Plans for such a grouping, which was to be known as the Federation of Arab Amirates, were announced in February 1968. The federation came into existence on 30 March of that year but it collapsed almost immediately, largely because of the area's numerous boundary disputes.

The British decided to try again and negotiations dragged on for the next three years. Bahrain eventually pulled out of the talks, claiming that the proposed formulas did not give it enough standing within the federation. Qatar followed suit, on the theory that if Bahrain was going to be an independent state, so would Qatar be. Finally, in July 1971, a provisional constitution for a new federation, to be known as the United Arab Emirates, was announced. The emirs had agreed to a formula under which Abu Dhabi and Dubai (in that order) would carry the most weight in the federation but which would leave each emir largely autonomous.

The new country came into existence on 2 December 1971. The provisional constitution was supposed to be in place for only five years but it was formally extended in 1976 and has remained in force ever since.

At the time many outsiders dismissed the UAE as a loosely assembled, artificial and largely British creation. While there was some truth in this charge, it was also true that the emirs of the smaller and poorer sheikhdoms knew that their territories had no hope of surviving as independent states. Umm Al-Qaiwain, for example, at the time probably had a population of only 5000. Ras Al-Khaimah initially decided not to be part of the federation but after only three months its ruler changed his mind and joined the UAE.

Since independence, the UAE has been one of the most stable and untroubled countries in the Arab world. Although the Trucial Oman Scouts were used to suppress an attempted coup in Sharjah a few weeks after independence, the country has remained remarkably calm since then.

This does not mean that political life in the UAE has been devoid of controversy. Border disputes among the emirates continued throughout the '70s, and the degree to which 'integration' among the seven sheikhdoms should be pursued has been a subject of constant debate.

When his first five-year term as President of the UAE expired in 1976, Shaikh Zayed threatened to resign if the other six emirs did not settle their outstanding border disputes and give up their private armies. Nobody dared to call his bluff. In 1979, Shaikh Zayed and Shaikh Rashid of Dubai sealed a formal compromise under which each gave a little ground on his respective vision of the country. The result was a much stronger federation in which Dubai remained a bastion of free trade while Abu Dhabi imposed a tighter federal structure on the other emirates. In practice, this meant the 'federalising' of the welfare-state system, the police, the legal system and the telecommunications network. Rashid, who was already Vice-President, also agreed to take the title of Prime Minister

as a symbol of his commitment to the federation.

The collapse of oil prices in the mid to late '80s hit the country unevenly. Abu Dhabi remained very rich but was forced to scale back its subsidies to the smaller emirates. Dubai weathered the financial storm fairly well but Sharjah, which had only recently begun oil production and was in the midst of a building boom, wound up deeply in debt. In 1987, the brother of Sharjah's ruler used this debt as an excuse to attempt a palace coup. The ruler, Shaikh Sultan Bin Mohammed Al-Qasimi, was in the UK at the time but he quickly flew to Dubai where he enlisted the help of the ruling Al-Maktoum family. The Al-Maktoums threatened to use force if necessary to restore Shaikh Sultan to power. The coup leader, Shaikh Abdul Aziz Bin Mohammed, eventually backed down under pressure from the Supreme Council. At the Council's suggestion, Sultan appointed Abdul Aziz as Crown Prince as a gesture of reconciliation. In February 1990, apparently feeling that enough face-saving time had elapsed, Sultan sacked Abdul Aziz. Sultan's son, Ahmed, was named as the new Crown Prince a few months later.

In 1990-91, the UAE contributed troops to the anti-Iraq coalition and foreign soldiers and sailors were based there during the months prior to the liberation of Kuwait. The result was a strengthening of the country's already strong ties with the West, though this has not prevented the UAE in general, and Dubai in particular, from maintaining good relations with Iran.

In the summer of 1991, Abu Dhabi found itself on the receiving end of a lot of unwelcome publicity when Western financial regulators, led by the Bank of England, closed down the scandal-ridden Bank of Credit & Commerce International (BCCI), of which Abu Dhabi was the major shareholder. BCCI was a bank regulator's nightmare. It had over 430 branches in 73 countries, was registered in Luxembourg through holding companies in the Cayman Islands, funded mostly by Abu Dhabi and managed from London by Pakistanis. In the

UAE, where BCCI's retail operations had made it one of the largest local banks, the collapse posed a delicate political problem. While negotiating over BCCI's future with the Bank of England and other Western regulatory and legal authorities, Abu Dhabi moved to protect the bank's local customers by buying up all of its branches in the UAE and reconstituting them as the Union National Bank.

## GEOGRAPHY

The UAE is about 83,600 sq km in area. The Emirate of Abu Dhabi represents over 85% of this total. The smallest of the emirates by area is Ajman, with only about 250 sq km of land.

The coastal areas, particularly along the Gulf, are marked by salt flats. Much of the inland area of the UAE is a nearly featureless desert running to the edges of the Empty Quarter. This desert, which is mostly part of Abu Dhabi, is marked by a few oases, such as Liwa and Buraimi, but on the whole it is among the bleakest areas of the Arabian peninsula.

The coastal lands immediately north-east of Abu Dhabi are much the same as the desert to the south and west of the city but further north along the coast the land slowly becomes greener until, when one reaches Ras Al-Khaimah, the landscape is quite hospitable. The northern end of the Hajar mountain chain runs through the UAE and ends in the Omani enclave of Musandem on the southern side of the Strait of Hormuz. These northern sections of the UAE – the inland areas around Ras Al-Khaimah and the east coast of the country from Fujairah to Dibba – are green and inviting with striking mountain scenery.

## CLIMATE

The further south you travel in the Gulf the hotter and more humid the summer. From May to September, daytime temperatures in the low 40s°C are common in Abu Dhabi and Dubai. In the east coast cities of Fujairah and Khor Fakkan, the climate is not quite so bad

and the mountains above Ras Al-Khaimah also provide some relief.

In the winter months all of the emirates enjoy very good weather, though it can get very windy in Abu Dhabi, Dubai and Sharjah. In the desert areas around Al-Ain, it can get very cold on winter nights with temperatures sometimes dropping into the single digits. Winter days in the inland deserts can be pleasantly brisk, with temperatures in the mid-teens.

## FLORA & FAUNA

The varied terrain of the UAE makes for an equally wide variety of plants and animals, though few of these are visible to the casual observer. Outside of the mountain areas around Fujairah and Ras Al-Khaimah, much of the vegetation you are likely to see is not indigenous but rather part of the local government's 'greenery' programme. The Abu Dhabi Emirate is particularly keen on establishing parks and planting trees.

The desert south and west of Abu Dhabi city is particularly bleak and featureless and only a naturalist with some experience of desert flora and fauna could find much to enthuse over. The Buraimi oasis is quite another story. Its natural groves of date palms have been supplemented by acres and acres of grass and trees planted in municipal parks around the UAE portion of the oasis (noticeably less money has been spent on the Omani side). There are grassland plains outside of Al-Ain running toward the natural green slopes of Jebel Hafit.

The UAE's fauna includes the Arabian leopard and the ibex but you are unlikely to see them. You could get lucky, of course, but your glimpse of wildlife is not likely to extend beyond camels and wild goats. In the spring and the autumn, flocks of birds migrating between Central Asia and East Africa can sometimes be seen in the northern emirates.

## GOVERNMENT

The UAE consists of seven emirates: Abu Dhabi, Dubai, Sharjah, Ajman, Umm Al-Qaiwain, Ras Al-Khaimah and Fujairah.

Though there is a Federal Government over which one of the emirs presides (in practice this is always Shaikh Zayed of Abu Dhabi), each of the rulers is completely sovereign in his own emirate. Each emirate is named after its principle town.

The degree of power which the seven emirs should cede to the Federal Government has been one of the hottest topics of debate in government circles since the founding of the country in 1971. Over the years, Abu Dhabi has been the strongest advocate of closer integration while Dubai has fought hardest to preserve as much of its independence as possible.

Politics in the Gulf tend to be rather opaque but in this case the relative interests of the various emirs are fairly clear. Abu Dhabi is the largest and wealthiest emirate with the biggest population. It is, therefore, the most dominant member of the federation and is likely to remain so for some time. Further integration of the seven emirates is obviously in Abu Dhabi's interest. Dubai is a reasonably wealthy emirate with an equally obvious interest in upholding its free-trade market. Sharjah and Ras Al-Khaimah both have relatively small oil revenues but they, and the other emirates, are dependent on subsidies from Abu Dhabi though the extent of this dependence varies widely. The smaller emirates wish to strike a balance between integration which reduces the prerogatives of the individual emirs and independence which leaves them in a potentially precarious financial position.

The forum where these issues are discussed is the Supreme Council, the highest body in the country. The Council comprises the seven emirs and it tends to meet informally. On an official level, its main duty is to elect one of the emirs to a five-year term as the country's President. In 1991, Shaikh Zayed of Abu Dhabi was elected to his fifth term as President. Shaikh Maktoum, the ruler of Dubai, is the country's Vice-President and Prime Minister.

There is also a Cabinet and the posts are distributed among the emirates. Most of the Federal Government's money comes from Abu Dhabi and Dubai. They each contribute a portion of their oil revenues and so get to hold most of the important Cabinet posts.

The Cabinet and Supreme Council are advised, but cannot be overruled, by the Federation National Council. This is a 40-member consultative body whose members are appointed by the respective emirs. Abu Dhabi and Dubai hold almost half of the Council's seats. All the Council's members come from leading merchant families.

## ECONOMY

The seven emirates are quite diverse economically. Of the seven, only Abu Dhabi is an oil state in the same sense as Qatar and Kuwait. It is the third-largest oil producer in the Gulf after Saudi Arabia and Kuwait. Like the other big Gulf producers, it has diversified into petrochemicals and other oil-related industries. Abu Dhabi is also a generous donor of development aid. Most of this is channelled to poor Arab countries through the Abu Dhabi Fund for Arab Economic Development which was established in 1971.

Dubai is the second-richest emirate. Its income from oil is now about one-quarter of that received by Abu Dhabi but in the decades before Abu Dhabi became oil-rich, Dubai had already established itself as the main trading (and smuggling) port in the region. The discovery of oil in the mid-60s boosted the economic modernisation programme implemented by Dubai's ruler, Shaikh Rashid Bin Saeed Al-Maktoum. Today, in addition to oil and being one of the Gulf's main business centres, Dubai is also the home of a huge dry-dock complex, one of the Middle East's busiest airports and a large free-trade zone at Jebel Ali.

Sharjah, once the most prosperous of all the emirates, has spent most of this century living in the shadow of Dubai. It has received a modest income from oil since the early '70s but found itself deeply in debt after the oil price collapse of the mid-80s. Oil revenue was used to build a large airport which is remarkably busy despite its proximity to Dubai. Both the airport and Sharjah's seaport facilities derive much of their income from cargo though in recent years Sharjah airport has also become the main port of entry for tourists visiting the UAE.

Ras Al-Khaimah, the northernmost emirate on the country's Gulf coast, derives its income from oil. Ras Al-Khaimah has also invested heavily in tourism in recent years and it is now a stop on most package tours of the UAE. Fujairah, the only emirate without a coastline on the Gulf, has also entered the tourist market though it is primarily a cargo port. Fujairah, Ajman and Umm Al-Qaiwain all receive substantial subsidies from the Federal Government.

## POPULATION & PEOPLE

There are estimated to be just over two million people living in the UAE, of whom about 25% (500,000) are UAE citizens (or 'Nationals').

The Emiratis themselves come from a number of different backgrounds. All of the northern emirates have substantial communities of people from Persian, Indian or Baluchi ancestry. Whether or not these people are actually UAE citizens depends on how long ago they or their ancestors came to the area and how they have earned a living since then. Abu Dhabi is probably the most purely Arab of the emirates, because until the discovery of oil, its main population centres were in the isolated areas of Al-Ain and Liwa, both oases deep in the desert.

## EDUCATION

As in all of the Gulf states, universal education is a relatively new concept but it has made great strides in the last 20 to 30 years. As recently as 1952, there were no schools in any of the emirates except for a handful of traditional mosque schools where boys learned the Koran by rote. The first modern school was opened in 1953 in Sharjah. Primary education is now compulsory in the UAE and secondary education is very widespread. The government has traditionally been willing to pay the cost of overseas study for UAE citizens.

The United Arab Emirates University in Al-Ain, the first and only university in the country, opened in 1977. It now has 8000 students and two-thirds of them are women.

## ARTS

There is a government-run art gallery at the Cultural Foundation in Abu Dhabi and a government-run Women Craft Centre but traditional art, on the whole, is confined to the country's museums.

## CULTURE
### Taboos & Avoiding Offence

The UAE is probably the most liberal country in the Gulf but it is still a very conservative place by Western standards. Women should not wear overly tight or revealing clothing (eg miniskirts, short shorts, bikini tops, etc) and men should not walk around bare-chested in public. Women may want to stick to one-piece bathing suits at the beach, though bikinis are probably OK around the pool at big hotels. Conservative dress is particularly in order in rural areas. This means long, loose clothing. Short sleeves are OK, even for women, but sleeveless clothes (especially on women) may cause offence in more traditional areas.

The same social etiquette exists in the UAE as elsewhere in the Gulf. Do not photograph people in general, and women in particular, without their permission and always avoid pointing your camera at anything even remotely military (this includes all airports).

Though alcohol is legal everywhere in the country except Sharjah you should never, ever drive while you're drunk. If you are caught doing so, there will be, at the very least, a steep fine to pay and you may wind up spending a month or more in jail.

## RELIGION

Most Emiratis are Sunni Muslims subscribing to the Maliki or Hanbali schools of Islamic law. Many of the latter are Wahhabis, though UAE Wahhabis are not nearly as strict and puritanical as the Saudi Wahhabis. There are also smaller communities of Ibadi and Shiite Muslims; for more details on

Wahhabi and Ibadi Islam see the Religion sections in the Saudi Arabia and Oman chapters. The Shiites are probably descended from merchants and workers who crossed to the Trucial Coast from Persia in the late 19th or early 20th century.

## LANGUAGE

Arabic is the official language of the UAE but English is very widely understood. In Dubai, you could also get by using the Persian language, Farsi. Urdu can be reasonably useful in Abu Dhabi and Dubai because of the large number of Pakistani expatriates.

# Facts for the Visitor

### VISAS & EMBASSIES

Citizens of other Arab Gulf (GCC) countries and British nationals with the right of abode in the UK do not need visas to enter the UAE. GCC nationals can stay pretty much as long as they want. Britons can stay for a month and can renew their entrance stamp for another two months.

If your passport shows any evidence of travel to Israel or South Africa you will be denied entry to the UAE.

For everyone else, the most common way to enter the UAE is on a 15-day transit visa. These cannot be extended or renewed. To get one you need a sponsor – a UAE national who takes responsibility for you and your actions and who undertakes to make sure that you leave when your visa expires.

Larger hotels can sponsor transit visas for businesspeople and tourists. Some hotels will also, on request, set up a 30-day visit visa. These have the double advantage of allowing you to stay in the country longer and can also be renewed. If your visa has been arranged by a friend through their company this is probably what you will get.

Both visit and transit visas are almost always deposited at the airport for you to pick up on arrival. You go to a desk in the arrivals area and pick up a form which you then take to passport control. If you are entering the country on a transit visa you will leave passport control carrying a copy of this form. Do not lose it, as you have to give it back on the way out. The system is the same for visit visas except that you will not have the form when you leave passport control.

You can also pick up visas at the port in Sharjah if you are arriving by boat from Iran.

Transit visas cost Dh 120 and visit visas Dh 60, though most hotels will charge you Dh 170 for arranging either one.

Note that if you are a naturalised citizen of a Western country or if you are a Westerner of Arab (especially Lebanese, Palestinian or Iraqi) origin, visa approval could take a long time so apply early. You're also better off applying through one of the larger hotels.

### Hotel-Sponsored Visas

To get a visa you ring up one of the big hotels and organise for them to sponsor you. The hotel will usually require you to stay one to three nights. Once you have the visa, however, you are free to go anywhere in the country or to move to a cheaper hotel though if you are moving downmarket, it would be wise not to advertise it. When you make your reservation the hotel will need a fax of the first page of your passport (the one with your photograph) along with the purpose of your visit (tourism is OK) and your flight arrival data. Be sure to get the hotel to fax you back a copy of the visa when it is ready or the airline may not let you travel.

Processing the visa can take anywhere from two days to three weeks. Generally, the biggest and most expensive hotels in Dubai are the fastest while smaller hotels anywhere, and big hotels in out-of-the-way places like Fujairah, take the longest. If you are planning to get your visa through a hotel, try to enter the country through the airports of Abu Dhabi, Dubai or Sharjah.

While there are a lot of cheap hotels which claim to sponsor visas, many of them provide rather questionable service and my advice is that you enter the country through one of the more expensive places. Smaller hotels will claim that they can set up visas and then start asking you about a personal guarantor. This means someone living in the UAE who can officially take responsibility for you. If you do have a friend who can take official responsibility for you, he or she can probably arrange a visa through his/her company, thus sparing you the dubious services of cheap hotels. If you do not have a personal guarantor, then you are probably wasting time and energy with the cheap hotel in question.

A lot of the cheap hotels can also string you along forever without producing a visa. It makes far more sense to splash out and stay at a good hotel and get the visa organised right the first time.

### UAE Embassies

With the advent of the transit/visit visa procedure, UAE embassies tend to only issue residence visas. Some of the UAE embassies addresses include:

Iran
  Kheyabun-é Vali-yé Asr, Kheyabun-é, Shahid Sartip Vahid Dastgerdi (☎ 221333, 295029)
UK
  30 Princes Gate, SWJ (☎ (071) 581 1281/4113)
USA
  600 New Hampshire Ave NW, Washington DC 20037 (☎ 338 6500)

### Visa Extensions

Transit visas cannot be extended, though people have been known to stay in the UAE for a year or more simply by flying out to Bahrain or Doha every other weekend and picking up a new visa on their return. Visit visas must be extended through the sponsor. If you entered on a visit visa sponsored by a hotel and have spent most or all of the visa's one-month validity in that hotel, this should not be a problem.

### Foreign Embassies in the UAE

See the Abu Dhabi and Dubai sections for the addresses of embassies and consulates in those cities.

### CUSTOMS

Arriving in the UAE is a treat. Dubai, in particular, has a reputation for its fast pro-

cessing of arrivals – I once made it from the aeroplane to the street in 16 minutes!

Duty-free allowances vary from emirate to emirate. Passengers arriving at Abu Dhabi can carry 200 cigarettes, 50 cigars or 250 grams of loose tobacco. In Dubai, the allowance is 100 cigarettes or 200 cigars or one kg of tobacco. Sharjah has no restriction on the amount of tobacco products visitors can import.

The rule on alcohol is that you can't take it into Sharjah. As for Abu Dhabi and Dubai, the rules are subject to change but non-Muslims can usually take in one bottle. You would be well advised, however, to double-check this. The alcohol regulations have changed several times in recent years.

### MONEY
#### Currency

The UAE dirham (Dh) is divided into 100 fils. You will also hear the currency occasionally referred to as rupees, especially by Indians and elderly people. When Britain controlled India, the rupee was the official currency in what is now the UAE and from 1948 until independence in 1971, a currency known as the 'Gulf rupee' was legal tender throughout the area.

Notes come in denominations of Dh 5, 10, 50, 100, 200 and 500. Coins are Dh 1, 50 fils and 25 fils.

#### Exchange Rates

The Dirham is fully convertible. Exchange rates are as follows:

| | | |
|---|---|---|
| US$1 | = | Dh 3.67 |
| UK£1 | = | Dh 5.55 |
| FF1 | = | Dh 0.67 |
| DM1 | = | Dh 2.29 |
| A$1 | = | Dh 2.51 |

If you are changing more than US$250 it might pay to do a little shopping around. Moneychangers sometimes have better rates than banks, but some of them either will not take travellers' cheques or will take only one type. It also pays to take a close look at the commissions being charged, especially in Dubai.

## Costs

The UAE is not a low-budget country such as Egypt or Thailand but it is possible to keep costs under reasonable control. Decent hotels can be found for Dh 100 to Dh 150 (less in Dubai). Eating for Dh 10 to Dh 15 is rarely a problem though if your taste runs to alcohol the bill is going to be a lot higher. Getting around is cheap in service taxis which are usually the only way to travel between the emirates.

Plan on spending Dh 150/200 per day for budget/mid-range travel.

## Tipping

Tips are not generally expected in the UAE, though since most waiters receive extremely low salaries they would certainly be appreciated. The service charge added to your bill usually goes to the restaurant, not the waiter.

## Bargaining

Most hotels will offer a discount if you ask for it, but the prices of meals, service taxis, consumer goods, etc are almost always fixed.

## WHEN TO GO

The main tourist season in the UAE is November to February. If you are planning to visit the archaeological sites it would be a good idea to travel in this period. From March to October the climate is often extremely hot and humid. A trip in high summer (July/August) would probably leave you doing very little except running between air-conditioned hotels.

## WHAT TO BRING

A good hat, sunglasses and sun block cream are essential for anyone planning even a short desert expedition and are a good idea if you are staying in the cities.

## TOURIST OFFICES

There are no tourist offices in the UAE though tourist information such as maps, tour company brochures and the occasional glossy pamphlet are often available at the big hotels that cater to tour groups, particularly in Sharjah. See the respective city listings for more information on organised tours.

## BUSINESS HOURS & HOLIDAYS

Government offices start work at 7 or 7.30 am and finish at 1 or 1.30 pm from Saturday to Wednesday. On Thursday everyone goes home around noon. Banks, private companies and shops open from 8 or 9 am until 1 or 1.30 pm and reopen in the afternoon from 4 to 7 or 8 pm from Saturday to Wednesday. Shops may or may not be open on Thursday afternoon. The larger shopping centres and supermarkets in Abu Dhabi and Dubai will stay open until 9 or 10 pm every night. Everything is closed during the day on Friday though some shops may open on Friday evenings.

This is all subject to some local variation. In Ras Al-Khaimah, for example, all shops are required to close for about half an hour at prayer time.

Religious holidays are tied to the Islamic Hejira calendar. Eid Al-Fitr (the end of Ramadan), Eid Al-Adha (Pilgrimage), Lailat Al-Mi'raj (the Ascension of the Prophet), the Prophet's Birthday and the Islamic New Year are all observed (see the table of holidays page 28).

Secular holidays observed in the UAE are New Year's Day (1 January) and National Day (2 December though the celebrations often last to 3 December). Each emirate may also observe its own holidays. In Abu Dhabi, for example, 6 August is a holiday marking the accession of Shaikh Zayed.

## POST & TELECOMMUNICATIONS
### Postal Rates

Letters are charged per 10 grams. To Europe, the rate is Dh 2 per 10 grams; USA and Australia, Dh 2.50; Indian subcontinent, Dh 1.75; Arab countries, Dh 1; Gulf countries, 50 fils. Postcard rates are Dh 1.50 to Europe, Dh 2 to the USA and Australia, Dh 1.45 to Asia, 75 fils to Arab countries and 45 fils within the Gulf.

Parcel postage is priced by the quarter kg. Sending a half kg/one kg package to Australia costs Dh 65.85/85.45; USA, Dh 47.70/70.90; UK, Dh 62.20/70.40. To other Gulf countries the rates range from Dh 20 to Dh 27 depending on the destination.

### Sending Mail

The UAE's postal system is very modern and the post offices are among the most efficient in the Gulf. They also have the shortest queuing lines. Mail generally takes about a week to Europe or the USA and eight to 10 days to Australia.

### Receiving Mail

Poste-restante facilities are not available in the UAE. The American Express offices in Abu Dhabi and Dubai will hold mail for AMEX clients (ie, card holders and people with AMEX travellers' cheques), and this is probably the best way to receive mail while you are visiting the UAE. If you are checking into a five-star hotel the reception desk will usually hold letters and small packages for two or three days prior to your arrival. Be sure to mark these 'Guest in Hotel' and, if necessary, 'Hold for Arrival'.

### Telephone

The UAE has a splendid telecommunications system and you can connect up with just about anywhere in the world from even the remotest areas. Coin-operated phones take Dh 1, 50 and 25 fils coins but card phones are increasingly common throughout the country – they turn up in some fairly odd corners of the desert. The state telecom monopoly is ETISALAT and they, too, seem to have offices just about everywhere.

To call the UAE from abroad, the country code is 971, followed by the city code and the local number. See the individual city entries for local city codes.

The direct-dial rates from the UAE to Australia are Dh 11.50 per minute peak and Dh 7.20 off peak, to the USA (excluding Alaska and Hawaii), Dh 7.50/4.86; Canada, Dh 11.25/7.20; UK, Dh 6.67/4.28; France and Germany, Dh 12/7.83.

The off-peak rates are from 9 pm (7 pm to other Gulf countries) to 7 am every day and all day on Fridays and holidays.

There are Home Country Direct services to the USA and France. MCI Call-America allows you to make either a collect (reverse charges) call or use an MCI credit card when calling the USA. The access code is 800-1-0001. The access number for France Direct is 800-1-9971.

There are a few quirks, however, in the system. Many payphones, for example, have been programmed so that you can't dial through to the operator. You also cannot use payphones to place collect calls or to call into the MCI system. If you have trouble getting through to MCI, don't expect much help from ETISALAT staff – most of them do not know about this service.

### Fax, Telex & Telegraph

Most ETISALAT offices are also equipped to send and receive fax, telex and telegraph messages. They may ask for your local address and contact number before they'll send a fax, and the service is fairly good.

### TIME

The UAE is four hours ahead of GMT. The

Top: Inside the new souk, Sharjah, UAE
Left: Abra captain, Dubai, UAE
Right: The waterfront, Dubai, UAE

Top: Three men enjoying a cup of tea atop Jebel Hafit, UAE
Bottom: View from Dhayah, near Ras Al-Khaimah, UAE

time does not change during the summer. When it's noon in the UAE, the time elsewhere is:

| City | Time |
| --- | --- |
| Paris, Rome | 9 am |
| London | 8 am |
| New York | 3 am |
| Los Angeles | 12 midnight |
| Perth, Hong Kong | 4 pm |
| Sydney | 6 pm |
| Auckland | 8 pm |

## ELECTRICITY

The electric voltage is 240 volts AC in Abu Dhabi and 220 volts AC in the northern emirates. British-style three-pin outlets are in use.

## LAUNDRY

There are few laundromats in the UAE cities, so either wash your clothes in your hotel sink, send them to the hotel laundry or wear them for another day while trying to make up your mind.

## WEIGHTS & MEASURES

The UAE uses the metric system.

## BOOKS & MAPS

### People, Society & History

Books about the UAE's history are hard to find. *The New Arabians* by Peter Mansfield (Ferguson, Chicago, 1981) has a short chapter on the UAE's history. *The Merchants* by Michael Field (Overlook Press, Woodstock NY, 1985) gives a brief sketch on the rise of Dubai as a trading centre.

*Looking for Dilmun* by Geoffrey Bibby (Penguin Travel Library, 1972) includes an interesting account of the early archaeological work at Umm An-Nar and in Buraimi and gives some idea of life in Abu Dhabi just before and after the beginning of the oil boom. For a more intimate view of life on the Trucial Coast before oil was discovered, read Wilfred Thesiger's classic *Arabian Sands* (published in 1959, now available in paperback from Penguin). The young Shaikh Zayed appears in Thesiger's account of his

1948 visits to Liwa, Abu Dhabi, Buraimi, Dubai and Sharjah.

Jonathan Raban's *Arabia Through the Looking Glass* (Picador, London, 1981) has lengthy sections on Abu Dhabi, Dubai and Al-Ain and is well worth reading.

The locally based publishing company, Motivate, publishes a series of glossy picture books on the various emirates.

See the Facts about the Region chapter for a list of more general books on the Gulf and the Middle East.

### Travel Guides

*UAE – A MEED Practical Guide* is the most comprehensive guide to the country but it's geared mainly to resident expats. If you decide to spend the Dh 150 or so that it costs, make sure you buy the third edition (published in 1990) which has a white cover with a blurb for Emirates Airlines. The guide covers almost every conceivable element of day-to-day expat life in the country (eg doctors, dentists, vets, schools, etc).

Of more use to travellers are *Off Road in the Emirates*, by Dariush Zandi, and *The Green Guide to the Emirates* by Marycke Jongbloed, both published by Motivate Publishing and widely available for about Dh 25 to Dh 40. The first, as the name implies, is aimed at the 4WD set. The advertising blurb for the second touts 'an environmentally friendly guide to little-known places of beauty and interest in the United Arab Emirates.'

*The Economist Business Traveller's Guides – Arabian Peninsula* is the best among the many how-to-do-business-with-the-Arabs sort of books on the market.

### Bookshops

Good foreign-language bookshops are hard to find in the UAE. Some of the bigger hotels, notably the Dubai Inter-Continental, have average selections in their bookshops and there are a couple of good bookshops in Abu Dhabi. On the whole, however, the pickings tend to be rather thin.

## Maps

Geoprojects publishes a map of the entire country which is probably the best of the available road maps. The Bartholomew map of the Gulf is too out of date to be of much use to drivers.

The situation with individual city maps varies greatly. There are no good maps of Abu Dhabi. The badly outdated Abu Dhabi inset map on the Geoprojects map of the UAE is about as good as they come. In Dubai, by contrast, there are lots of good maps. The best is the yellow-covered *Dubai Town Map and Street Guide* which is available at most hotels for about Dh 20. The best of the many bad maps on Sharjah is the *Sharjah City Tourist Map*, available free at most of Sharjah's bigger hotels. The tourist map distributed free by all the hotels in Al-Ain and Buraimi is not very good but it is the only one available.

In Ajman, the souvenir kiosk at the museum sells an excellent map of the town for Dh 20. Your best bet for getting around Ras Al-Khaimah and Fujairah are the inset maps on the Geoprojects UAE map.

## MEDIA

### Newspapers & Magazines

*Gulf News* and *Khaleej Times*, both based in Dubai, are the UAE's two English-language newspapers. Both cost Dh 2 and carry pretty much the same international news. Local news in both papers consist largely of 'business' stories which are little more than advertisements masquerading as news. They also tend to have fairly comprehensive coverage of the Indian and Pakistani political and entertainment scenes.

*What's On* is a monthly magazine catering mostly to the expat community. It's a pretty good source of information about what's new at the UAE's hotels, bars, clubs and discos. There are also usually interesting articles on things to see and do in the UAE and Oman, a list of clubs and societies and a quota of advertising masquerading as news. The magazine costs Dh 8, though you will often find it is free in five-star hotels.

## Radio & TV

Abu Dhabi and Dubai each have an English-language TV channel in addition to their Arabic broadcasts, though outside the two main cities the quality of reception is decidedly mixed. You can watch Omani TV (mostly Arabic with the occasional English movie) in Al-Ain. Qatar TV's English channel's reception is OK in Abu Dhabi when the weather is good.

Abu Dhabi and Dubai also have English-language FM radio stations, both of which mix current pop music (mornings) with documentaries (afternoons) and speciality music programmes such as classical or country & western music (evenings).

## FILM & PHOTOGRAPHY

Aside from the usual provisos about anything military-related and the photographing of women, there is no problem with taking photographs in the UAE.

Getting colour prints developed is never a problem – one-hour services are advertised by photo developers on nearly every street in the country. Developing slides or B&W film is much more difficult and you might want to wait and do this somewhere else.

## HEALTH

The standard of health care is quite high throughout the UAE. Should you get sick consult either the hotel doctor, if you are in a big hotel, or your embassy or consulate. Unlike some other places in the Gulf health care in the UAE is neither free nor extremely cheap. Some travel insurance would be very much in order.

No particular shots are necessary for travel in the UAE, though all of the usual travel vaccinations (gamma globulin, etc) should be up to date. An International Health Certificate is required only from travellers arriving from an infected area.

The tap water in Abu Dhabi and Dubai is safe to drink but it often tastes horrible and is heavily chlorinated. Most residents stick to bottled water.

See the introductory Facts for the Visitor

chapter for a more complete discussion of health for travellers to the Gulf.

## WOMEN TRAVELLERS

In general, the UAE is probably the easiest country in the Gulf for women to travel in. Aside from the country's rather rough youth hostels, checking into hotels is not a problem though unaccompanied women might want to think twice about taking a room in some of the cheaper places in Dubai.

This is not to say that all of the usual problems that accompany travel in the Middle East will not arise in the UAE as well: unwanted male visitors knocking on your hotel room door at night, lewd looks and comments in the street, etc. Apply common sense and retain your self-confidence whatever happens.

See the introductory Facts for the Visitor chapter for more details on problems faced by women travelling in the Gulf.

## DANGERS & ANNOYANCES

The UAE, like much of the rest of the Gulf, has a road system built around traffic circles, or roundabouts. People have a tendency to zoom into these at frightening speeds and to try to turn out of them from inside lanes, paying little attention to other cars. Eternal vigilance is the price of avoiding fender-benders. This problem exists throughout the country but is particularly acute in Dubai and Sharjah.

Another problem in Dubai is traffic congestion, particularly on the two bridges crossing the Creek. You would be well advised to get an early start for any daytime trip that involves a bridge crossing. As for the Creek itself, don't go swimming or water-skiing in it. The Creek is splendidly scenic but it is also very dirty, a situation made worse by the fact that very little of it is cleaned by the tides in the Gulf.

## WORK

The UAE is not the place to look for work. Since 1984, the government has applied what is known as the Six Months Rule. This states that if you enter the country on a visit

or transit visa you must leave for six months before you can return on a residence visa. Exceptions to this are rare.

## ACTIVITIES

### Water Sports

Water sports are popular throughout the UAE, and the tourist industry is increasingly pushing the country as a winter 'sea & sun' destination. Most water-sports facilities are tied either to a big hotel or a private club, and thus are not generally accessible to budget travellers. If your life depends on a spot of jet-skiing then you should be prepared to stay in a four or five-star hotel when visiting the UAE.

### Golf

Dubai boasts the only real golf course (with grass) in the Gulf. If you want to play here you should be prepared to pay handsomely for the privilege. See the Dubai section for more details.

### Desert Safaris

You can book a desert safari trip through one of the bigger tour companies in Dubai or Sharjah (see the entries for those cities for details of tour companies and their offerings). An organised desert safari with lunch and/or dinner costs Dh 125 to Dh 185. Overnight desert trips cost about Dh 350.

Unless you have some experience in driving in the desert, do not attempt this activity on your own. Either pick up copies of *Off Road in the Emirates* by Dariush Zandi and *Staying Alive in the Desert* by K E M Melville (Roger Lascelles, London, 2nd edition 1981) before setting out or, if you meet any local residents, you may be able to join them on a wadi-bashing trip.

### Clubs

Abu Dhabi, Dubai and, to a lesser extent, Al-Ain all have a broad range of clubs and societies. For up to date listings of these pick up a copy of the latest issue of *What's On*.

## HIGHLIGHTS

Every visitor to Dubai should find time for

an *abra* ride on the Creek. Abras are the small motorboats which ferry people across the Creek and they can be hired quite cheaply for longer tours of the waterway.

If you have the time to go outside of Abu Dhabi and Dubai, Al-Ain and the Buraimi oasis are well worth a weekend visit. The east coast, particularly the area around Fujairah, has some of the most striking scenery in the country. A good weekend trip would be to drive over the mountains from Dubai or Sharjah to Fujairah, up the coast from Fujairah to Dibba, and then back across the mountains to Dubai/Sharjah.

## ACCOMMODATION
### Camping
There are no camping grounds adjacent to the UAE's cities but camping in the desert is quite common.

### Hostels
There are three youth hostels in the UAE – in Dubai, Sharjah and Fujairah. The Dubai hostel charges Dh 10 per night. Beds in the Sharjah and Fujairah hostels are Dh 15 per night. The Dubai hostel is pretty grim but the ones in Sharjah and Fujairah are OK. In all cases, IYHF cards are required and a working knowledge of Arabic would be useful.

### Hotels
Most of the country's cheap hotels are in and around the Dubai souk. These bottom out at around Dh 50 to Dh 60 for a single and Dh 80 to Dh 100 for a double. There are a few cheaper places but they always seem to be full. The cheapest places that provide reliable visa service cost from Dh 200/300 for singles/doubles.

In Dubai, the five-star hotels cost anything upwards of Dh 625/725. Top hotels in Abu Dhabi are a bit cheaper, starting from around Dh 450/525.

## FOOD
Eating cheap in the UAE means eating either in small Indian/Pakistani restaurants which often seem to have only biryani dishes on the menu, or in Western-style fast-food joints. You can also find relatively cheap Lebanese food. In Dubai and, to a lesser extent, Abu Dhabi, cheap Oriental food is also fairly easy to come by. Abu Dhabi and Dubai both have a wide selection of small cafes and snack shops.

At the top end of the market almost any kind of food can be found in Abu Dhabi and Dubai. In the smaller emirates, top-end food means eating at the big hotels.

## DRINKS
Nonalcoholic drinks such as soft drinks, fruit juices and mineral water are available throughout the country. Alcohol can only be sold in restaurants and bars attached to hotels (in practice, three-star hotels or better). The selection is what you would expect to find in any well-stocked bar. The prices are pretty outrageous – expect to pay as much as Dh 20 for a pint of beer.

Non-Muslim expatriates must obtain an alcohol license (with the permission of their sponsor) to purchase booze for consumption at home. These licenses, which are not available in Sharjah, allow the holder to purchase a maximum of Dh 750 worth of liquor each month.

## ENTERTAINMENT
### Theatre
Western theatre companies regularly visit the UAE, usually under the sponsorship of some international company. These theatre performances almost always take place in one of the five-star hotels. Watch the local English-language press and look for flyers in the lobbies of the big hotels for details.

### Cinemas
Most cinemas in the UAE show Indian and Pakistani films. There are usually several such places in each of the main cities.

### Discos
If you want to dance the night away Dubai is the place to be. While there are discos and bars with dance floors in most of the larger hotels in Abu Dhabi, Fujairah, Al-Ain and

Ras Al-Khaimah, Dubai is clearly the centre of the UAE's nightlife. Pancho Villa's, a Tex-Mex restaurant in Dubai's Astoria Hotel, has a good dance floor, often featuring live rock-and-roll. More conventional discos can be found in most of the five-star hotels in the city.

### Camel Racing

The main spectator sport in the UAE is camel racing. This takes place in various spots around the country during the winter. Ras Al-Khaimah is one of the best places to see camel races, partly because the racing schedule there is relatively predictable and partly because the track is well laid out for viewing. See the Ras Al-Khaimah entry for further details.

### THINGS TO BUY

If you are looking for old Arabian souvenirs the UAE may be disappointing in this respect. There are a few shops in Al-Ain, Abu Dhabi and Dubai which deal in Bedouin jewellery, most of which comes from Oman. If you are travelling on to either Oman or Saudi Arabia, this sort of jewellery is much cheaper in those countries and the selection tends to be better.

The real fame of the UAE, however, is its reputation as the world's largest duty-free shop. If it can be plugged into the wall you can buy it here. Although Dubai and Sharjah are the cheapest places in the Middle East to buy this type of goods, the selection tends to be a bit limited. Going from shop to shop, you will soon notice that they all stock the same three or four varieties of goods (say, VCRs) at pretty much the same prices. You will also discover that the shop assistants are not very knowledgeable about their stock so it helps to have a good idea of what you want before setting off on a shopping expedition. It is also a good idea and it is accepted practice in the UAE to plug your new gadget in at the shop to make sure that it works properly.

### Carpets

Dubai and Sharjah are among the best places outside of Iran to buy Persian carpets. They are certainly the cheapest places outside of Iran to buy Iranian caviar! Buying carpets without getting ripped off takes skill and patience. Do not feel embarrassed or obliged to buy just because the shop attendant has unrolled 40 carpets for you; this is part of the ritual. The best way to get a good price is to visit several stores, ask a lot of questions and bargain hard over a long period of time (preferably two or three visits).

# Getting There & Away

### AIR

Dubai and Abu Dhabi are the country's main international airports, though an increasing number of carriers serve Sharjah as well. There are also small international airports at Ras Al-Khaimah and Fujairah. Abu Dhabi, Dubai and Sharjah all have enormous duty-free shopping complexes that attempt to outdo one another through spectacular promotions. The last time I visited Abu Dhabi was raffling off holiday homes in Spain while, in Dubai, the duty-free shop was giving away expensive cars at the rate of about two per week.

Flying to Europe or the USA tends to be a bit less expensive out of Dubai than from Abu Dhabi, though it is not cheap from either city. As is the case in other Gulf states, airfares in the UAE are fairly strictly regulated and there are no bucket shops.

There is no direct air service between the UAE and North America, though near-daily service is available from Abu Dhabi and Dubai to major European cities such as London, Paris, Frankfurt, Rome and Athens. Within the Middle East, there are frequent services to most of the other Gulf capitals and to Cairo but rather fewer flights to Amman, Damascus and the big cities of North Africa. Dubai probably has the best air links to Iran and Pakistan of any city in the world. All the major cities of the Indian subcontinent can be reached quite easily from the UAE.

See the Abu Dhabi and Dubai sections for sample airfares to other cities in the Gulf, Europe and the USA.

## LAND

There is a daily bus service between Dubai and Muscat. See the Dubai section for details. There are also regular buses between Dammam in Saudi Arabia and the UAE. Tickets to Dammam are sold by Al-Ghaith General Transport (☎ 342882) through their office in the Abu Dhabi central bus station.

## SEA

There are passenger services between Sharjah and Iran. The trip takes 12 hours and costs Dh 180 in 1st class, Dh 170 in 2nd class and Dh 140 in 3rd class. There is also a Dh 20 port tax. For more details contact Oasis Freight Co (☎ 596325) in Sharjah.

Make sure that the hotel organising your visa deposits it at Sharjah port for pick up.

## TOURS

Several major tour companies, including British Airways Holidays, Thomas Cook and Kuoni, offer package holidays in Dubai. The programmes are either 'sea & sun' holidays or a combination of 'sea & sun' with a desert safari and sightseeing outside of Dubai. They all use the beach hotels on the outskirts of Dubai as their base (the facilities are wonderful, but you may end up wishing that you were closer to town). If you really want to travel to the Gulf in high summer this can be quite cheap – as little as UK£450 for a one-week holiday including return airfare from London. Tours are usually most expensive during December, when you should figure on paying about 25% more than in summer.

## LEAVING THE UAE

Leaving the UAE is fairly straightforward. Check-in times at the various airports are officially one hour though it is often a good idea to arrive earlier. The airports in general, and Dubai airport in particular, can get pretty chaotic when flights are overbooked. It also pays to arrive early so you can have time to browse through the duty-free shops.

There is no airport departure tax. If you leave by boat, there's a Dh 20 port tax.

# Getting Around

## AIR & BUS

At the time of writing, there were no air or bus services between the emirates.

## TAXI

If you do not have your own car, the only way to travel between the emirates is by service taxi. Service taxis in the UAE usually carry seven passengers (though there are a few five and nine-passenger taxis) and leave whenever they are full. In Abu Dhabi and Dubai, the local governments operate large taxi depots. Everywhere else, the service-taxi station is usually little more than a vacant patch of ground where the drivers wait for their cars to fill up.

Service taxis can be a bit cramped but they are cheap and a great way to meet people. The main problem is often that, aside from the busy Abu Dhabi-Dubai route, they do not fill up very quickly. Between Abu Dhabi and Dubai there are also minibuses which carry 14 people and charge a few dirhams less than the service taxis. Some sample one-way service-taxi fares (in either direction) are:

| From | To | Fare |
| --- | --- | --- |
| Abu Dhabi | Dubai | Dh 25 |
| Abu Dhabi | Al-Ain | Dh 25 |
| Dubai | Al-Ain | Dh 30 |
| Dubai | Sharjah | Dh 4 |
| Dubai | Ras Al-Khaimah | Dh 15 |
| Dubai | Fujairah | Dh 25 |
| Ras Al-Khaimah | Fujairah | Dh 25 |
| Fujairah | Khor Fakkan | Dh 5 |
| Fujairah | Dibba | Dh 15 |

Bear in mind that taxis may not be running between all cities at all times. A lot depends on where the drivers feel like taking passengers on any given day. You can, of course, get a taxi to take you almost anywhere if you are willing to pay for all of the seats in it.

## CAR

The UAE is one of those countries where having your own wheels can often mean the difference between having fun and spending much of your time planning transportation from here to there.

As noted in the Dangers & Annoyances section, the driving in the UAE can sometimes be a bit reckless, particularly around the country's numerous traffic circles. Many people also try to avoid driving between cities at night whenever possible.

As for licenses, most foreign driving licenses are accepted in the UAE so long as you are either a citizen or a resident of the country that issued the license. Car rental companies will issue you a temporary UAE license against your home license when you rent a car. This applies only to people in the country on either a visit or transit visas. If you live in the UAE, you will need to get a permanent UAE license.

### Road Rules

Driving in the UAE is fairly straightforward. Right turns are not permitted at red lights. The speed limit is 60 km per hour in town and 100 km per hour on the highways. All accidents, no matter how small, must be reported to the police.

### Rental

Small cars start at about Dh 140 per day with another Dh 20 to Dh 30 for insurance. The first 100 or 150 km per day are usually free with additional km costing 40 or 50 fils each. If you rent a car for more than three days you will usually be given unlimited mileage. I have not found the smaller rental agencies to be any cheaper than the big ones, and if you are driving all over the country, it can be reassuring to be able to contact a local office of a bigger agency if something goes wrong.

### HITCHING

Hitching is not illegal but it is not very common either. A foreigner with his (I would

not recommend that women try this) thumb out might get lifts because the drivers were curious, or they might be passed by on the theory that something so strange had to be a bit suspicious.

## LOCAL TRANSPORT
### To/From the Airport

In Abu Dhabi, bus No 901 runs from the main bus terminal to the airport around the clock. It departs every 20 minutes (every 30 minutes between midnight and 6 am). The fare is Dh 3.

Abu Dhabi airport is quite a way out of the city and a taxi cost Dh 45.

In Dubai, bus No 4 goes to the airport from the Deira bus station about every half hour for Dh 1. A taxi to or from the airport costs Dh 30 from anywhere in the city.

### Bus

Only Abu Dhabi, Al-Ain and Dubai have municipal bus systems and these are of varying usefulness. Unfortunately, Abu Dhabi's bus system is almost incomprehensible. Dubai's buses are good for getting from one side of town to the other or getting out to Jebel Ali.

### Taxi

Taxis in Abu Dhabi and Al-Ain have meters but those in Dubai and the other emirates do not. In these cities you should negotiate the fare in advance. See the individual city entries for more information.

## TOURS

There are several companies in Dubai, Sharjah and Ras Al-Khaimah offering half and full-day tours of the various emirates and desert safaris. See the relevant city entries for more details.

# Abu Dhabi

In the 1950s, visitors to Abu Dhabi remarked on the place's remoteness and its bleak appearance. What was then a small fishing village is now a sprawling city covering virtually all of Abu Dhabi island. Everything is modern, sleek and shiny.

## History

Abu Dhabi town was founded in 1761, but the ruling Al-Nahyan family did not move to the coast from their base at Liwa until 1793, when a freshwater well was discovered. Al-Husn Palace, also known as the White Fort, was built over this well when the ruler moved up from the desert.

The town expanded rapidly during the heyday of the pearl trade in the late 19th century. Abu Dhabi was never a major pearling or trading centre like Bahrain or Zubara, but it was prosperous by the rather limited standards of the time. Under Zayed the Great, who ruled the emirate from 1855 to 1909, Abu Dhabi became the most powerful of the Trucial Coast sheikhdoms.

The collapse of the pearling industry in the 1930s decimated Abu Dhabi and the town soon sank into squalor. In a desperate attempt to salvage the emirate, Shaikh Shakhbut (reigned 1928-66) granted oil concessions in the late '30s, but until the oil money began coming in in 1962, the town remained little more than a fishing village.

It is difficult today to imagine what Abu Dhabi looked like only 35 years ago. When Geoffrey Bibby, the archaeologist, first arrived in early 1958 he saw from the window of his aeroplane only the fort and a few huts along a stretch of white sand. The airport at which he landed consisted of 'two rows of black-painted oil-drums marking the approach to a stretch of salt flat'. Al-Ain was a five-day journey across the desert by camel.

It is sadly ironic that after waiting two decades for oil to rescue his impoverished emirate, Shaikh Shakhbut proved unable to handle the flood of money which came his way in the '60s. In 1966, the British eased him out in favour of his brother, Shaikh Zayed, who has ruled ever since and has been the President of the UAE federation since independence in 1971. Abu Dhabi is by far the richest and the most politically important of the seven emirates.

## Orientation

The city of Abu Dhabi sits at the head of a T-shaped island. It is not a compact place, and distances here tend to be bigger than they look (especially once you start trying to get around on foot!). The airport is on the mainland about 30 km from the centre.

The main business district is the area bounded by Shaikh Khalifa Bin Zayed and Istigal Sts to the north, Zayed the Second St to the south, Khalid Bin Al-Waleed St to the west, and As-Salam St to the east. The GPO and the telephone office are just outside this area. The main terminal for buses and service taxis is further to the south. The side of the Corniche facing inland is dominated by big office buildings. The main residential areas are all south of the centre.

The word Shaikh is usually abbreviated to SH on street signs. Some of the streets also have names which are in more common use than their official ones. These include:

Shaikh Rashid Bin Saeed Al-Maktoum St – more commonly called Airport Rd or, sometimes, Old Airport Rd, though it runs to both the old and new airports.

Bani Yaas St – generally extends all the way to the Corniche, well past the point where it officially becomes Umm Al-Nar St.

Zayed the Second St – often called Electra St.

Hazaa Bin Zayed St – commonly known as Defence St.

You are likely to discover, however, that a lot of people who have lived in Abu Dhabi for a long time haven't the foggiest idea what the streets are called – officially or unofficially. That goes triple for the taxi drivers! Directions still tend to come in the form of: 'It's the pink building on the left after you pass the such-and-such supermarket near whatever and across from...'

## Information

**Tourist Office** There is no tourist office in

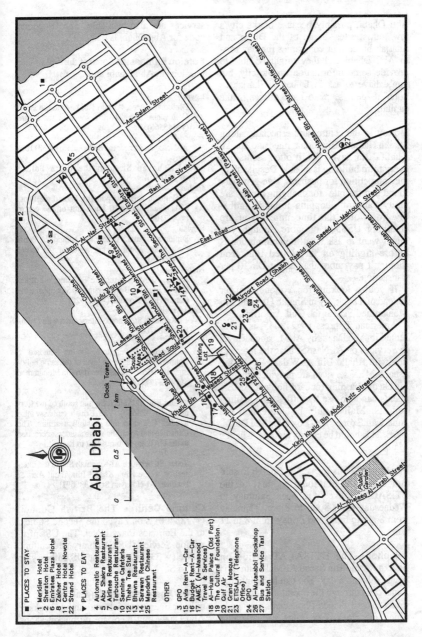

**Abu Dhabi**

**PLACES TO STAY**
1 Meridien Hotel
2 Sheraton Hotel
6 Emirates Plaza Hotel
8 Zakher Hotel
11 Centre Hotel Novotel
22 Strand Hotel

**PLACES TO EAT**
4 Automatic Restaurant
5 Abu Shakra Restaurant
7 Airlines Restaurant
9 Tarbouche Restaurant
10 Semiramis Cafeteria
12 Thaba Tea Stall
13 Bhavna Restaurant
14 Sarawan Restaurant
25 Mandarin Chinese
   Restaurant

**OTHER**
3 GPO
15 Avis Rent-A-Car
16 Budget Rent-A-Car
17 AMEX (Al-Masaood
   Travel & Services)
18 Al-Husn Palace (Old Fort)
19 The Cultural Foundation
20 Gulf Air
21 Grand Mosque
23 ETISALAT (Telephone
   Office)
24 GPO
26 Al-Mutanabbi Bookshop
27 Bus and Service Taxi
   Station

Abu Dhabi, possibly because of the city's few tourist sites. Some of the Dubai and Sharjah-based tour companies run day trips to Abu Dhabi and they might be able to provide some information on the city, but you'd have to ask in Dubai or Sharjah as none of them seem to have offices in the capital.

**Money** In the centre, and especially along Shaikh Hamdan Bin Mohammed and Shaikh Khalifa Bin Zayed Sts, it often seems like every third building is a bank. Despite all of the competition for business, I've generally found that the rates for changing money are pretty standard. Shopping around is probably not worth the time unless you are changing US$500 or more, though you might want to ask what the commission is before signing on the dotted line. You shouldn't pay more than about Dh 10 per transaction.

If you're looking for a moneychanger instead of a bank, try in Shaikh Hamdan Bin Mohammed St near the Gulf Air office.

American Express (☎ 213045) is represented in Abu Dhabi by Al-Masaood Travel & Services on Al-Nasr St near the intersection with Khalid Bin Al-Waleed St. All the usual AMEX services are provided, including cheque cashing for card-holders. AMEX clients can also use the office as a mailing address. Mail should be addressed: c/o American Express, PO Box 806, Abu Dhabi, UAE, and should be clearly marked 'Client's Mail'.

**Post** The GPO is located on Shaikh Rashid Bin Saeed Al-Maktoum St next to the ETISALAT office. It is open Saturday to Wednesday from 8 am to 8 pm, Thursday from 8 am to 6 pm and Friday from 8 to 11 am.

**Telephone** The ETISALAT office on Shaikh Rashid Bin Saeed Al-Maktoum St is open 24 hours a day. You can book international calls through the operator or dial them direct on card phones. Phonecards are on sale round the clock. Fax, telex and telegram

services are also available. The telephone code for Abu Dhabi is 02.

**Foreign Embassies** Some of the diplomatic missions in Abu Dhabi are:

Egypt
    Diplomatic Area, Airport Rd, beyond the Pepsi Cola plant, about 10 km south of the centre (☎ 445566)
France
    Al-Nahayan St, near the Batin Palace (☎ 331100)
Germany
    Al-Nahayan St, near the Batin Palace (☎ 331630)
Jordan
    Diplomatic Area, Airport Rd, behind the Pepsi Cola plant, about 10 km south of the centre (☎ 447100)
Kuwait
    Diplomatic Area, Airport Rd, behind the Pepsi Cola plant, about 10 km south of the centre (☎ 446888)
Netherlands
    Al-Ain Al-Ahlia Insurance Building, 6th floor, Shaikh Hamdan Bin Mohammed St, opposite the Centre Hotel Novotel (☎ 321920)
Saudi Arabia
    Al-Karamah St, near the intersection with Dalma St (☎ 465700)
Sweden
    Al-Masaood Tower (look for the Standard & Chartered Bank at street level of the same building), 10th floor, Shaikh Hamdan Bin Mohammed St (☎ 337772)
UK
    Khalid Bin Al-Waleed St, just south of the Corniche (☎ 326600). The British embassy also handles Canadian and Australian affairs. The Canadian and Australian ambassadors accredited to the UAE are both resident in Kuwait.
USA
    Sudan St, between Al-Karamah St and the intersection where King Khalid Bin Abdul Aziz St becomes Al-Nahayan St (☎ 336691)

**Cultural Centres** The British Council (☎ 788400) is on Zayed the Second St, next to the Emirates Plaza Hotel. The US Information Service (USIS) library and cultural centre (☎ 336567) is at the US embassy on Sudan St.

**Travel Agencies** Travel agents may be the only businesses which outnumber banks in Abu Dhabi, but there are no bucket shops.

Most travel agencies are tiny operations specialising in one service (eg cargo) or one destination (eg Bangladesh). If you need to buy a ticket I would advise going to the big travel agencies, like American Express, whose staff are likely to be a bit more experienced.

**Bookshops** It is hard to find bookshops with a good selection of English-language books. For paperbacks, try the Al-Mutanabbi Bookshop on Zayed the First St.

**Medical Services** Most hospitals will take walk-in patients for consultations and/or treatment. Your embassy can probably provide you with a list of doctors who speak your language.

**Emergency** For the police, dial 999, ambulance 998, fire 997. If you've got problems with the water, ring 722443, for electrical problems, it's 770444.

**Dangers & Annoyances** Abu Dhabi is generally a pretty safe city. What passes for 'low life' can usually be found in the vicinity of the Strand Hotel on Shaikh Rashid Bin Saeed Al-Maktoum St, but it's pretty tame by Western standards.

If you are driving, beware of the taxis which zoom wildly through the traffic. Few of the drivers appear to know what brake lights on the car ahead of them look like and none seem to know how to use directional signals. I try to avoid driving at night in Abu Dhabi whenever possible, even though that means getting into one of those crazy taxis – a real *Catch-22* situation!

### The Cultural Foundation
This large, faceless building on Zayed the First St is more interesting inside than its outward appearance would indicate. It is mainly a library with an attached research and documentation centre, but there are sometimes interesting exhibits on local history, Islamic art, old manuscripts, etc. The gallery area is also sometimes used to show the works of foreign artists. Unfortunately,

the signs on the displays are only in Arabic. The foundation is open Sunday to Wednesday from 7.30 am to 1.30 pm and 4 to 10 pm, Thursday from 7.30 am to noon and 4 to 9 pm; closed Friday. Admission is free.

### Al-Husn Palace
Al-Husn Palace is commonly known as the Old Fort or the White Fort. It is one of the few buildings in Abu Dhabi that's more than 25 years old and its whitewashed walls are just as eye-catching amid today's skyscrapers as they would have been against a backdrop of reed and mud-brick huts 50 or 100 years ago.

The first fort on the site was built over the city's freshwater well at the beginning of the 19th century by Shakhbut Bin Dhiyab, who is considered to be the first Shaikh of the Al-Nahyan dynasty. The present fort was built in the late 19th century by Shaikh Zayed the Great. It is the oldest building in Abu Dhabi. It has been restored and is today used by the Cultural Foundation as a documents centre. The courtyard is worth a look. The fort is open Sunday to Wednesday from 7.30 am to 1.30 pm and Thursday from 7.30 am to noon. Admission is free.

### Women Craft Centre
This is a government-run operation where traditional weavings and other crafts are displayed and sold. The centre is about five km south of central Abu Dhabi on the Airport Rd. It's well signposted.

### Places to Stay
The closest thing to a cheap hotel that you are going to find in Abu Dhabi is the *Strand Hotel* (☎ 335100). It's a pretty grim place, though the rooms are clean, the staff are helpful and it's well located on Shaikh Rashid Bin Saeed Al-Maktoum St across from the ETISALAT office. Singles/doubles are Dh 150/200.

A little bit better are the *Zakher Hotel* (☎ 341940) on Bani Yaas St at Dh 195/265 and the *Emirates Plaza Hotel* (☎ 722000) on Zayed the Second St at Dh 200/250.

Further up-market are the hotels that

arrange visas. These include the *Centre Hotel Novotel* (☎ 333555, fax 343633) on Shaikh Hamdan Bin Mohammed St. Rooms are Dh 350/450. Beach lovers might want to try the *Khalidia Palace Hotel* (☎ 662470) at the west end of the Corniche, where rooms cost Dh 300/400.

The very top end is represented by the usual collection of international chains:

Abu Dhabi Hilton (☎ 661900, fax 669696) at the west end of the Corniche. Singles/doubles cost Dh 475/570 plus a 15% service charge.
Abu Dhabi Inter-Continental (☎ 666888, fax 669153), just south of the western end of the Corniche. Singles/doubles cost Dh 450/530 plus 15%.
Le Meridien Abu Dhabi (☎ 776666, fax 727221) at the east end of the city centre. Singles/doubles cost Dh 450/520 plus 15%.
Sheraton Abu Dhabi (☎ 773333, fax 725149), at the east end of the Corniche. Singles/doubles cost Dh 550/650 plus 15%.

## Places to Eat
### Cheap & Medium-Priced
If you are completely skint look for shawarma. There's a good place on Shaikh Rashid Bin Saeed Al-Maktoum St next to the Strand Hotel, and there are lots of small shawarma stands in the souk. Shawarma usually go for Dh 2.50 or Dh 3 each. Another place for cheap food is the *Thaha Tea Stall* on Zayed the Second St. They have hot tea for 50 fils a glass as well as a selection of sodas and snacks (fried bananas for 50 fils). There are a number of other small restaurants and tea shops on Zayed the Second St between Shaikh Rashid Bin Saeed Al-Maktoum St and East Rd.

For cheap Indian food head for the *Airlines Restaurant* on Bani Yaas St. They offer a Friday buffet for Dh 15 and 'full meal' Tandoori specials during the week (a whole tandoori chicken, bread, soup and salad) for Dh 15. Cheap vegetarian Indian food can be found at the *Bhavna Restaurant* on Zayed the Second St.

A place you should definitely try is *Tarbouche* on Shaikh Hamdan Bin Mohammed St. The word 'Tandoori' appears in big letters in the window, but the fare on offer is almost entirely Lebanese. Appetisers and main dishes cost Dh 6 to Dh 22 (most of the mezza are Dh 6 to Dh 8) and the freshly baked Arabic bread is served hot at your table. The food here is excellent and the staff (they all appear to be one family with pictures of the brothers and cousins in America adorning the walls) are very friendly. Cheaper Lebanese fare in less fun surroundings can be found at the *Automatic Restaurant* near the intersection of Shaikh Hamdan Bin Mohammed St and As-Salam St.

Traditional Arabic kebab and kofta meals are available at *Abu Shakra* on the corner of Shaikh Hamdan Bin Mohammed St and As-Salam St. Full meals cost Dh 17 to Dh 20. A cheaper place with the same sort of food is the *Sarawan Restaurant* on Zayed the Second St. Shawarma and Arabic food can also be found at the *Sannine Cafeteria* on Shaikh Hamdan Bin Mohammed St.

**Expensive** Abu Dhabi has a number of expensive hotel restaurants. Rather bland, but wildly expensive, Mexican food is on offer at *El Sombrero* at the Sheraton Hotel. Count on spending Dh 100 or more per person (though it might be worth the trip just for the nachos). The *Meridien Hotel* seems to be trying to find out how many restaurants it can cram into one hotel, the result is an enormous selection of all types of food, provided you are willing to splash out the money.

For up-market Chinese food, try the *Mandarin Restaurant* on Zayed the First St.

## Entertainment
There's not much happening in Abu Dhabi; most people looking for entertainment spend their weekends elsewhere. Abu Dhabi is probably not as boring as its reputation but it does not have Dubai's energy nor its nightclub scene. Many of the restaurants and bars at the big hotels have live entertainment of typical hotel lounge variety.

## Getting There & Away
**Air** Following is a sample of one-way and excursion return fares from Abu Dhabi with

the minimum and maximum stay requirements:

| To | One-Way | Return | Min/Max |
|----|---------|--------|---------|
| Bahrain | Dh 470 | Dh 500 | 3/7 days |
| Dhahran | Dh 470 | Dh 650 | 3/14 days |
| Doha | Dh 350 | Dh 360 | 3/7 days |
| Jeddah | Dh 1020 | Dh 1410 | 3/14 days |
| Kuwait | Dh 740 | Dh 1036 | 3/14 days |
| London | Dh 2900 | Dh 4140 | 10/90 days |
| Muscat | Dh 500 | Dh 520 | 3/7 days |
| New York | Dh 3620 | Dh 4180 | 14/90 days |
| Riyadh | Dh 610 | Dh 860 | 3/14 days |

Abu Dhabi International airport (AUH) is on the mainland, about 30 km from the centre. You should be at the airport about 90 minutes before departure for short-haul flights (ie, within the Gulf) and two hours before departure for flights to Europe and Asia.

Following is a list of office addresses for some of the airlines flying to Abu Dhabi:

Aeroflot
    Bani Yaas St, just south of the intersection with Shaikh Hamdan Bin Mohammed St (☎ 775477)
Air France
    Al-Nasr St, near American Express (☎ 215810)
Air India
    Shaikh Hamdan Bin Mohammed St, near the intersection with East Rd (☎ 329373)
British Airways
    Corner of Khalifa Bin Zayed and Leewa Sts (☎ 341328)
EgyptAir
    Al-Istiqal St, just west of Shaikh Rashid Bin Saeed Al-Maktoum St (☎ 344777)
Gulf Air
    Corner of Shaikh Rashid Bin Saeed Al-Maktoum St (Airport Rd) and Shaikh Hamdan Bin Mohammed St (☎ 332600 or, 24 hours at the airport, 757083)
KLM
    Al-Masaood Tower, 9th floor (look for the Standard & Chartered Bank office at street level), Shaikh Hamdan Bin Mohammed St (☎ 323280)
Lufthansa
    Al-Masaood Tower, 2nd floor (look for the Standard & Chartered Bank office at street level), Shaikh Hamdan Bin Mohammed St (☎ 213200)
MEA (Middle East Airlines)
    Corner of Khalifa Bin Zayed and Leewa Sts (☎ 339000)
Royal Air Maroc
    Corner of Bani Yaas and Shaikh Hamdan Bin Mohammed Sts (☎ 774950)
Royal Jordanian
    Corner of Khalifa Bin Zayed and Leewa Sts (☎ 321832)
Saudia
    Bani Yaas St, just south of the intersection with Shaikh Hamdan Bin Mohammed St (☎ 773400)
Singapore Airlines
    Corner of Khalifa Bin Zayed and Leewa Sts (☎ 339532)
Swissair
    Leewa St (☎ 343430)

**Bus** The main bus terminal is on East Rd, south of the centre. Inter-city service is only available within the Abu Dhabi emirate. To get to Dubai, you have to take a taxi. Buses run to Al-Ain every 30 minutes from 6 am to 9 pm (2½ hours, Dh 10) and to Ruweis (3 hours, Dh 10) daily at 7 am and 1 and 6 pm.

**Service Taxi** Service taxis and minibuses leave from a station adjacent to the main bus terminal on East Rd. Minibuses carrying 14 passengers charge Dh 20 per person to Dubai. Taxis, carrying five to seven people, charge Dh 30. Taxis also regularly go to Al-Ain (Dh 25) and occasionally to Fujairah and Ras Al-Khaimah (both Dh 50).

**Car** Car rental rates start at about Dh 140 to Dh 150 per day plus insurance. There are a number of rental places downtown, though if you are planning to travel widely around the UAE by rented car it is probably best to stick to one of the larger agencies.

## Getting Around
**To/From the Airport** Bus No 901 runs from the main bus terminal to the airport around the clock, departing every 20 minutes (every 30 minutes between midnight and 6 am). The fare is Dh 3.

**Bus** Local bus fares are Dh 1 or Dh 4, depending on the distance. The system is quite extensive, but there are no bus maps or published timetables nor are the bus numbers posted at the stops. It might be difficult to figure it out.

**Taxi** Taxis are equipped with meters. A flag

drop is Dh 2 and the meters turn over at 50 fils a click. The fares add up slowly, making taxis a reasonably affordable way to get around. Your main problem is likely to be that most of the drivers speak neither Arabic nor English. Urdu speakers, however, shouldn't have any trouble.

## AL-AIN & BURAIMI

The Buraimi oasis straddles the border between Abu Dhabi and Oman. There are a number of settlements in both parts of the oasis, but in the UAE the entire area is referred to by the name of the main town in Abu Dhabi's section: Al-Ain (pronounced so that it rhymes with 'main'). Buraimi technically refers to the entire oasis but is also used when referring to the Omani section.

In the days before the oil boom, the oasis was a five-day overland journey by camel from Abu Dhabi. Today, the trip takes about two hours on a tree-lined freeway. Once in the oasis, you can cross freely between the UAE and Oman – people driving up from Muscat pass through customs before reaching the Omani town of Buraimi – and it is this fact that makes the oasis so appealing.

Al-Ain is the birthplace of Shaikh Zayed, the ruler of Abu Dhabi, and he has lavished money on it. The Omani side of the oasis has not undergone the same treatment. Buraimi is comfortable but still very much a provincial town. The resulting contrasts make Al-Ain/Buraimi one of the most interesting places in either country to visit. (To visit Buraimi from Muscat you will need a Road Permit; see the Oman chapter for details.)

There is a lot to see in both Al-Ain and Buraimi and the area is a popular weekend destination from both Abu Dhabi and Dubai, from which it is roughly equidistant.

## Note

If you have rented a car in the UAE, your insurance will not cover accidents occurring on Omani territory. If you are driving a car that you rented in Oman, you probably will not be allowed to take it through the Buraimi customs post. Also, use of seat belts in mandatory in Oman and this is strictly enforced.

The Royal Oman Police can and will hit you for a hefty fine – about Dh 100 or OR 10 payable on the spot – for violating this law.

## History

The Buraimi oasis is probably the longest inhabited part of what is now the UAE. The country's oldest known artefacts are potsherds from the 4th millennium BC which were found near Jebel Hafit, a short distance from the oasis. Digs near Al-Ain have also turned up a Bronze Age (3rd millennium BC) culture which may have had ties to the Umm An-Nar civilisation that then existed on the Gulf coast near modern Abu Dhabi.

As Arabia's climate became warmer, oases such as Buraimi became increasingly important. The population of Buraimi is known to have increased significantly during the 2nd and 3rd centuries AD, apparently as a result of migration to the oasis by tribes from the surrounding desert. By the 10th century Al-Ain, which was then called Tawwan, was a trading centre along one of Arabia's many caravan routes, a status which it retained into our era.

In the 18th century, the ancestors of today's Saudi Arabian royal family incorporated the oasis into what is now called the First Saudi Empire, a short-lived kingdom which covered even more of Arabia than the present Saudi state. The legacy of this period was Wahhabism, the puritanical strain of Islam practised in Saudi Arabia which, in a somewhat milder form, remains a strong influence in the Al-Ain/Buraimi area to this day.

Abu Dhabi's ruling Al-Nahyan family first moved to the oasis sometime in the 19th century, well after the founding of Abu Dhabi town. Since the early years of the 20th century, the family has ruled the oasis jointly with the Omanis, first with the imams who controlled the interior of Oman and, in the '50s, with the Muscat-based Omani sultans. The 18th century Saudi presence in Buraimi, however, led the Saudi government to claim the entire oasis for its kingdom in 1949. The Saudi claim was prompted by ARAMCO, the Saudi-based oil company, which wanted to drill for oil in the oasis.

In 1952 the Saudis occupied part of Buraimi. The question of sovereignty eventually went to an international arbitration panel in Geneva. When the talks collapsed in 1955, the British and the Al-Nahyan family took matters into their own hands. A Bedouin force, led by Shaikh Zayed who was then the governor of Abu Dhabi's portion of the oasis, along with the Trucial Oman Scouts, who were commanded by British officers, drove the Saudis out of Buraimi. The dispute continued on a lesser level for several more years. The current Abu Dhabi-Oman border was demarcated in 1966. Saudi Arabia formally dropped its claim to the area in 1974.

### Orientation

The Al-Ain/Buraimi area can be very confusing, at least at first. All of the streets in Al-Ain look pretty much the same and most of them do not appear to have names. The streets in Buraimi don't appear to have names either, but there are fewer of them. The two cities straddle the UAE-Oman border and everyone can flow freely back and forth between the two countries without a customs check. The Omani customs post is about 13 km down the road to Muscat.

Basically, Al-Ain wraps around an arm of Omani territory with most of Al-Ain's business district lying just south of the border. To get to Dubai or to some of Al-Ain's suburbs from the centre you drive through Oman for about four km before emerging back into the UAE. The advantage of all this for the budget traveller is that it allows you to stay at the one cheapish hotel in the area which is just across the Omani border. It's also an easy way to see a little of Oman without hassling with visas. Most of the area's services, however, are in Al-Ain which is much larger and more modern than Buraimi.

In Al-Ain, the service taxi station behind the Grand Mosque is very much at the centre of things, but distances in both Al-Ain and Buraimi are large. You could, in theory, walk from the bus or taxi station in Al-Ain to the one semi-cheap hotel which is just over the

Omani border, but with any luggage at all it would be a hell of a hike, especially when it is hot, which is most of the time. The three big hotels are only accessible by car or taxi. Some of the interesting sites, like the Hili Gardens and Jebel Hafit, also require your own transportation.

### Information

There is no tourist office in either city but it's fairly easy to find most of the things worth seeing in Al-Ain by following the big purple road signs. Buraimi has no tourist signs but the market and both of the old forts are adjacent to the main road which runs across Omani territory.

**Money** There are lots of banks in Al-Ain near the Clock Tower Roundabout and the GPO. In Oman you'll see several banks on the main road. Both UAE dirhams and Omani riyals are accepted on both sides of the border at a standard rate of OR 1 = Dh 10.

**Post & Telecommunications** Al-Ain's GPO and telephone office are side by side at the Clock Tower Roundabout. The GPO is open Saturday to Wednesday from 8 am to 8 pm, Thursday from 8 am to 6 pm and Friday from 8 to 11 am. The ETISALAT office is open every day from 7 am to midnight. Buraimi's post office is open only in the morning, and its sign is only in Arabic, but it's more-or-less across the street from the Yameen Restaurant.

The phone systems of the two cities are separate. Thus, if you're in the Hotel Al-Buraimi and want to ring someone 200 metres away in Al-Ain, it's an international call and will be billed as such. Do not be deceived by the fact that the payphones in the two cities look the same. Apparently, ETISALAT and Oman Telecom buy their payphones from the same supplier but they don't accept the same coins.

The UAE telephone code for Al-Ain is 03. There are no telephone area codes in Oman.

**Emergency** In Al-Ain, the phone number for the police is 999, ambulance, 998 and the

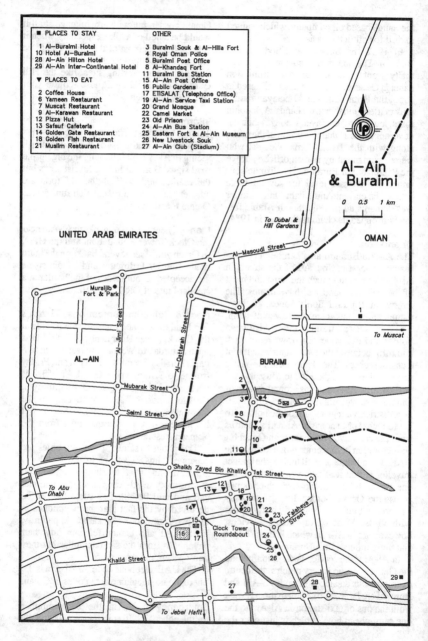

PLACES TO STAY
1 Al–Buraimi Hotel
10 Hotel Al–Buraimi
28 Al–Ain Hilton Hotel
29 Al–Ain Inter–Continental Hotel

▼ PLACES TO EAT
2 Coffee House
6 Yameen Restaurant
7 Muscat Restaurant
9 Al–Karawan Restaurant
12 Pizza Hut
13 Safsuf Cafeteria
14 Golden Gate Restaurant
18 Golden Fish Restaurant
21 Muslim Restaurant

OTHER
3 Buraimi Souk & Al–Hilla Fort
4 Royal Oman Police
5 Buraimi Post Office
8 Al–Khandaq Fort
11 Buraimi Bus Station
15 Al–Ain Post Office
16 Public Gardens
17 ETISALAT (Telephone Office)
19 Al–Ain Service Taxi Station
20 Grand Mosque
22 Camel Market
23 Old Prison
24 Al–Ain Bus Station
25 Eastern Fort & Al–Ain Museum
26 New Livestock Souk
27 Al–Ain Club (Stadium)

Al–Ain
& Buraimi

0    0.5    1 km

To Dubai &
Hili Gardens

UNITED ARAB EMIRATES

OMAN

Al–Masoudi Street

Muraijib
Fort & Park

AL–AIN

BURAIMI

1

To Muscat

Mubarak Street

Selmi Street

Al–Jimi Street

Al–Qattarah Street

2
3
8
7
9
11
10
4
5
6

Shaikh Zayed Bin Khalifa 1st Street

To Abu
Dhabi

13  12
18
19  21
20  22  23
14
15
16  17

Clock Tower
Roundabout

Al–Falaheys
Street

24
25
26

Khalid Street

27

28

29

To Jebel Hafit

fire department, 997. In Oman dial 999 for the police, an ambulance or to report a fire.

## Eastern Fort & the Al-Ain Museum

The museum and fort are in the same compound, south-east of the flyover near the Grand Mosque. The museum is open Sunday to Wednesday mornings from 8 am to 1 pm, Thursday from 8 am to noon and Friday from 9 to 11.30 am. It reopens every afternoon from 3.30 to 5.30 pm (4.30 to 6.30 pm from May to October) and is closed all day Saturday. Museum admission is 50 fils (if somebody is at the door to collect it).

As you enter the museum, take a look at the Bedouin diwan set up to the left of the manager's office. It's a display of what the reception area of a traditional Bedouin tent or home looks like. This particular room is also used to welcome visiting VIPs (which may be why it always looks like it only lacks hot coals for the coffee to be served).

Moving to the right, the first gallery has an interesting display of old 1960s photographs of Al-Ain and Abu Dhabi. It's striking to see how quickly the area has developed.

Around to the left, the next gallery has reconstructions of everyday life in the pre-oil days. Note how most of the figures are dressed more like Omanis than like Gulf Arabs (ie, wearing turbans instead of the gutra and agal headdress). The opposite wall has a large display of weapons.

The third gallery has more weapons, musical instruments and some stuffed examples of the local desert birds. The wall back near the entrance houses a display of some of the decorations Shaikh Zayed has received over the years. The collection is rather eclectic, including both the Order of Isabel the Catholic, bestowed on the Shaikh by King Juan Carlos I of Spain, and a bullet 'from the Palestinian Commando Lyla Khalid'.

The other two galleries house a chronological display on the region's archaeology.

The **Eastern Fort**, next to the museum, is not open to the public, but you can have a look at it from the compound. It was built in 1910 by Shaikh Sultan Bin Zayed Al-

Nahyan and was the birthplace of his son, Shaikh Zayed, the present ruler of Abu Dhabi.

## Livestock Souk

You can see the entrance to the livestock market from the museum/fort parking lot. It's quite a big market and an interesting place to wander around, and an excellent spot to go shopping for sheep and goats (a live sheep costs about Dh 120). The souk attracts Bedouins and townspeople from all over the southern UAE and northern Oman.

The best time to be there is early in the morning (before 9 am) when the trading is at its heaviest.

## The Old Prison

The prison is the fort-like building between the Al-Falaheya St Roundabout and the flyover. It is open rather erratic hours because the people living around the prison courtyard occasionally decide they don't want any visitors and shut the gate. If you get into the courtyard, it is usually possible to climb to the roof of the prison tower for a view out over the oasis and the camel market.

## The Camel Market

Al-Ain's camel market is immediately behind the prison. It's quite a small market but worth visiting for local colour. It is open from early morning until about noon every day, and the best time to visit is as early in the day as possible, before the heat intensifies both the dust and the smell.

## Buraimi Souk & Al-Hilla Fort

Buraimi's souk is bigger than it looks from the road. It's a very practical place selling fruit, vegetables, meat and household goods. You will not find many souvenirs but it's well worth a visit for the atmosphere. The change from the pseudo-modern surroundings of the Al-Ain livestock souk is quite striking. The Al-Hilla Fort, immediately behind the souk, is not open to the public nor is it very old.

### Al-Khandaq Fort

This Omani fort is not open to the public either, but the restoration work in progress in early 1992 suggests that it might soon be open. The fort, much larger than Al-Hilla, is said to be about 400 years old. If you're coming from the centre of Al-Ain you'll see it about 200 metres off the road to your left, about 750 metres past the border.

### Muraijib Fort & Park

This small fort is on Al-Jimi St, several km north-west of Al-Ain's centre. The restored remains of the fortifications are scattered within a beautifully landscaped garden. The garden is open from 4 to 10 pm daily (10 am to 10 pm Fridays and holidays). Admission is Dh 1 but this is not strictly enforced.

Also not strictly enforced is the sign at the entrance, warning in Arabic that no men are allowed in the park. The day I was there nobody was around to collect the admission fee and the only other visitor in the park was also male.

### Jebel Hafit

The views from the top of this mountain are well worth the effort. The summit is about 30 km by road from the centre of Al-Ain (a taxi should make the journey for about Dh 40 round trip).

From the Clock Tower Roundabout head south toward the Al-Ain Club, crossing the bridge. Follow the signs for Ain Al-Fayda and later on Al-Wagan. The final turn-off (a left if you are coming from the centre) is about 15 km from the centre and is well marked.

### Ayn Al-Fayda

Ayn Al-Fayda is a resort area south of the oasis beyond the Jebel Hafit turn-off. The *ayn*, or spring, is at the foot of the far side of the mountain. The area is being developed by the government as a resort.

### Hili Gardens

This combination public park and archaeological site is about eight km north of the centre of Al-Ain, off the Dubai Rd. The site

Ruins at Hili

is open daily from 4 to 11 pm (holidays from 11 am to 11 pm). Admission is Dh 1.

The main attraction is the **Round Structure** which is about 100 metres straight on from the park entrance. It is a 3rd millennium BC tomb, possibly connected to the Umm An-Nar culture, discovered by a group of Danish archaeologists in 1962 and restored in the late '60s.

To reach Hili from the centre, take the Dubai Rd (through Oman) and follow the signs for Hili and Dubai until the purple 'tourist' signs appear.

### Hili Fun City & Ice Rink

The amusement park and skating rink are a few km down the road from Hili gardens. They are open weekdays from 4 to 10 pm, Friday and holidays from 9 am to 10 pm. Both places are closed Saturday and Sunday. Tuesday and Wednesday are for women and small children only. Admission is Dh 25.

## Zoo

Al-Ain's zoo, one of the better ones in the Gulf, is south of town. It is open daily fom 7 am to 5.30 pm. Admission is Dh 2. It has indigenous species including Arabian oryx and gazelle, saluki dogs and bustards. It also has kangaroos, pigmy hippos, vultures, etc.

## Places to Stay

Al-Ain and Buraimi do not have a huge selection of accommodation. There are four hotels in the two towns and only one of them remotely qualifies as cheap. This is the *Hotel Al-Buraimi* (☎ 650492). It's a good place, sitting almost smack on the border, and will be on your right if you enter Oman from the centre of Al-Ain. Singles/doubles are Dh 105/130 or OR 10.500/13.500. This place should not be confused with the *Al-Buraimi Hotel* (☎ 652010), which you can find easily enough by following the blue-and-white signs strategically positioned throughout the Omani part of the oasis. Singles/doubles are Dh 218/261 (OR 23/28) plus 15% tax and service charge. They also have a weekend package of accommodation for one night with three meals included at Dh 500 (OR 52.640) for two people.

Back in the UAE, your choices are the *Al-Ain Hilton* (☎ 686666) at Dh 350/400 plus 15%; and the *Al-Ain Inter-Continental* (☎ 686686) at Dh 320/420 plus 15%. Both hotels have weekend specials on Thursdays and Fridays with rooms at Dh 200/250 plus 15% (though the Hilton only offers doubles for this package).

Remember that when calling the Buraimi hotels from Al-Ain you must first dial 00-968, and when calling Al-Ain from Buraimi it's 00-971-3 then the number. In both cases you will be charged for an international call.

## Places to Eat

**Al-Ain** The best area for cheap eateries is near the Grand Mosque and the Clock Tower Roundabout. The *Muslim Restaurant*, just north of the flyover, offers the usual fare of rice with mutton, chicken or fish for Dh 7. There are a number of cheap to medium-priced places on the nameless street one block north of the Clock Tower and parallel to the border. Try the *Golden Fish* restaurant for fish. Next door, the *Al-Ramla Restaurant* has cheap biryanis and curry chicken.

For more up-market eating, there is the *Golden Gate Restaurant* (west of the Golden Fish and on the same side of the street) which serves Chinese and Filipino food. Main dishes are Dh 15 to Dh 30.

For alcohol and more expensive fare, you have to head for the hotels. *Paco's*, at the Hilton, has surprisingly good Mexican food with main dishes at about Dh 30 apiece. The *Inter-Continental* has a Thai-run fish restaurant with a very wide selection. Prices are by the kg. The *Horse & Jockey Club Pub* at the Inter-Continental has a good evening special: a full meal from their carvery (meat, vegetables, potatoes) including dessert and a drink for Dh 28.

**Buraimi** Buraimi has fewer eating places than Al-Ain. You will probably find your options limited to the standard cheap fare of a helping of biryani rice with fish, chicken or mutton for about Dh 10/OR 1. Try the *Al-Karawan Restaurant* and the *Muscat Restaurant*, both opposite the turn for the Al-Khandaq fort. On Buraimi's main commercial street, the *Yameen Restaurant* has more of the same.

## Entertainment

Paco's at the Hilton, and the Pub at the Inter-Continental, have singers and the Inter-Continental has a disco. There's also a full range of sports facilities at both hotels.

## Getting There & Away

**Bus** Buses run from Al-Ain to Abu Dhabi every 30 minutes from 6 am to 9.30 pm (2½ hours, Dh 10) from the station behind the Al-Ain Cooperative Society's supermarket.

Oman's bus company, ONAT, has three buses a day to and from the Ruwi station in Muscat. The buses leave from a parking lot across from the Hotel Al-Buraimi at 7 am and 1 and 3 pm. The trip to Muscat takes six hours and costs OR 3.600. Tickets can be purchased from the driver. To take this bus you will need an Omani visa which allows you to enter the country by land. Expatriates resident in Oman will need a Road Permit. The Omani customs post is about 13 km from the border.

**Service Taxi** Al-Ain's taxi station is in the big parking lot behind the Grand Mosque. Taxis take four to seven passengers to Dubai (Dh 30) and Abu Dhabi (Dh 25). The trip takes about two hours to either city. You can also occasionally find cabs from Al-Ain to Fujairah (Dh 50) but you should not count on this. A few service taxis going to the same destinations can also be found around the bus station.

**Car** If you want to rent a car, head for the rental desks at the Hilton or the Inter-Continental. There are also several rental agencies in Al-Ain near the Clock Tower Roundabout.

### Getting Around

**Bus** Al-Ain has a thorough but, like Abu Dhabi, nearly incomprehensible municipal bus system. Fares are Dh 1. If you know where you're going, you might be able to find out which is the right bus by asking around at the station. Note that Hindi (not English or Arabic) seems to be the main language spoken there.

**Taxis** The Al-Ain taxis have meters; use them to avoid arguments over the fare with the Omani cab drivers who don't use meters.

Al-Ain taxis charge Dh 2 for a flag drop and 50 fils for each additional km. If you want to go somewhere like Jebel Hafit, however, you'll have to arrange it in advance with the driver. Count on paying about Dh 40 for the trip to Jebel Hafit and back.

# Dubai

In all the Gulf, there is no place quite like Dubai. Dubai's wealth is founded on trade, not oil. It is one of the last bastions of any-thing-goes capitalism; sort of an Arab version of Hong Kong. What opium was to the growth of Hong Kong in late 19th century, gold was to Dubai in the 1960s. Oil, when it was discovered in 1966, merely contributed to trade profits and speeded up modernisation.

The trade passing through Dubai is now for the most part legal. The city remains first and foremost a trading port and most of the local government's activity is directed toward protecting Dubai's status as the Gulf's leading entrepôt. Among the seven emirates which make up the UAE, Dubai has fought the hardest to preserve its independence and to minimise the power of the country's Federal institutions.

There isn't actually a lot to see in Dubai, but in all of the Gulf, you will not find a more easy-going place. Spend a few days wandering through the souks and along the waterfront to take in the city's atmosphere. True, there is almost nothing 'old' in Dubai, but it is the one place in the Gulf where that hardly seems to matter.

### History

Dubai's history really begins in the 1830s when the city broke away from Abu Dhabi. At that time, neighbouring Sharjah was the main trading centre on the Trucial Coast, and for the rest of the 19th century Dubai was simply another sleepy pearling village with a small merchant community.

Things began to change around the turn of the century when Linagh, in what is now Iran, lost its status as a free port. The ruling Al-Maktoum family made a concerted effort to lure Linagh's disillusioned traders to Dubai and also managed to convince some of Sharjah's merchants to relocate. The Al-Maktoums, probably with the assistance of the newly arrived Persian traders, prevailed on a British steamship line to switch its main port of call in the lower Gulf from Linagh to Dubai. When this was accomplished in 1903, it gave Dubai regular links with both British India and the ports of the central and northern Gulf (Bahrain, Kuwait, Bushire and Basra). The town's prosperity quickly grew.

The next key event in Dubai's growth occurred in 1939 when Shaikh Rashid Bin Saeed Al-Maktoum took over as regent for his father, Shaikh Saeed. Sharjah's leadership had, by then, been relatively weak and xenophobic for some years. The entire region was also suffering from the collapse of the pearling industry which, Rashid concluded, was probably never going to revive. With that in mind, Rashid set out to turn Dubai into the region's main trading centre. As Sharjah's harbour silted up, Rashid improved the facilities along the Creek, Dubai's waterfront.

The emirate came to specialise in the 're-export trade'; its merchants imported goods which they then sold to other ports rather than peddling them at home. In practice, this usually meant smuggling in general, and smuggling gold to India in particular. During the 1950s, Shaikh Rashid became one of the earliest beneficiaries of Kuwait's Fund for Arab Economic Development which loaned him money to dredge the Creek and build a new breakwater near its mouth. The project was completed in 1963, and gold smuggling took off like a rocket.

A building boom had begun along the Creek before the discovery of oil near Dubai in 1966, and even after oil revenues began coming in, trade remained the foundation of the city's wealth. Gold-smuggling peaked in 1970, when 259 tons of gold flowed through the emirate.

In the early '70s the Indian government began to crack down on the gold smugglers, but before this occurred Dubai's merchants had already laid the foundations of today's enormous re-export trade in consumer goods bound for the rest of the Arabian peninsula and the Indian subcontinent. This is not to say that Dubai's days as a smuggler's paradise are over. The trade now supposedly focuses on Iran: the dhows take VCRs and Levis jeans to Iranian ports and return laden with caviar and carpets. As was the case with gold, all of these goods leave Dubai perfectly legally; it's the countries at the *other* end of the trade that look on it as smuggling.

Dubai's trade and oil-fuelled building boom eventually provided it with one of the busiest airports in the Middle East, a large dry-dock complex and, at Jebel Ali, what is said to be the largest artificial port in the world. Dubai even boasts the only golf course in the Gulf with real grass (at other golf courses, players carry a small square of astroturf around a series of grassless fairways). By the early '90s, the Dubai Desert Classic had become a well-established stop on the annual pro golf tour.

The man who was the driving force behind all of this, Shaikh Rashid, died in 1990 after a long illness and was succeeded as Emir by his son, Shaikh Maktoum. For several years prior to Rashid's death, Maktoum had been regent for his father in all but name, and the new Emir is expected to continue his father's policies.

## Orientation

Dubai is really two towns: Deira to the east, and Dubai to the west. They are separated by the Creek (*al-khor* in Arabic), an inlet of the Gulf. The Dubai side is sometimes referred to as Bur Dubai when someone wants to make it clear that he or she means the Dubai side as opposed to the entire city. Deira, however, is the city centre. Activity in Deira focuses on Beniyas Rd, which runs along the Creek, Beniyas Square (which, until recently, was called Nasr Square and is still generally known by that name) and the area along Al-Maktoum Rd, Al-Maktoum Hospital Rd, and Naif Rd. The Deira souk, where most of the cheap hotels are located, is most of the area west of Beniyas Square and south of Naif Rd. The cheap hotels are concentrated around Al-Sabkha Rd and in the area of Al-Buteen and Suq Deira Sts.

On the Dubai side, the souk is the whole area along the Creek from Al-Ghubaiba St east to the Ruler's office and inland as far as Khalid Ibn Al-Waleed Rd.

There are four ways of getting from one side of the Creek to the other. The Shindagha Tunnel runs under the Creek at the northern end, near its mouth. The Al-Maktoum Bridge, on the southern edge of the centre, is the main traffic artery across the waterway.

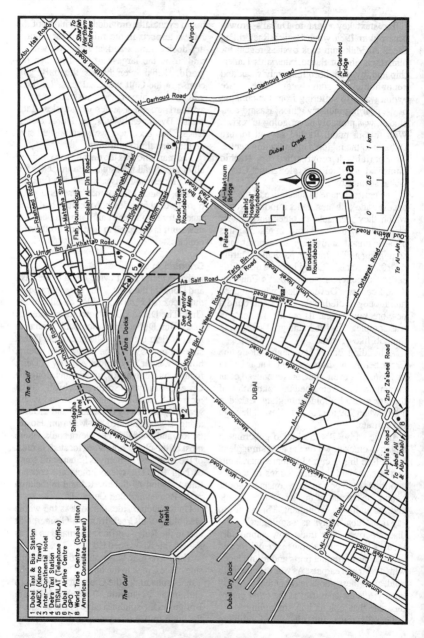

1 Dubai Taxi & Bus Station
2 AMEX (Kanoo Travel)
3 Inter-Continental Hotel
4 Deira Taxi Station
5 ETISALAT (Telephone Office)
6 Dubai Airline Centre
7 GPO
8 World Trade Centre (Dubai Hilton/
   American Consulate—General)

Further south, the Al-Garhoud Bridge is used mostly by traffic trying to bypass the centre. The final method of crossing the Creek is by abra, the small, open water taxis which crisscross the waterway throughout the day.

## Information

**Tourist Office** There is no tourist office in Dubai, though you might be able to get some information from the tour operators listed here and in the Sharjah section.

**Money** There is no shortage of banks and exchange houses in Dubai. In central Deira, especially along Beniyas Rd and on Beniyas Square, every other building seems to contain a bank or a moneychanger. Shopping around is worth it if you are changing more than a few hundred US dollars.

American Express (☎ 524400) is represented in Dubai by Kanoo Travel. Their office is on the Dubai side of the Creek, on Khalid Ibn Al-Waleed St, near the intersection with St 14. They are open Saturday to Thursday from 8.30 am to 1 pm and from 4 to 7 pm. Cheques are cashed for card-holders and mail is held for American Express clients. Address mail to: c/o American Express, Client's Mail, PO Box 290, Dubai, UAE.

**Post** The GPO is on the Dubai side, on Za'abeel Rd. It is open Saturday to Wednesday from 8 am to 11.30 pm. Thursday from 8 am to 10 pm and Friday from 8 am to noon. It has a Philatelic Bureau.

The Deira Post Office, on Al-Sabkha Rd near the intersection with Beniyas Rd, is much smaller. It is open Saturday to Wednesday from 8 am to 8 pm, and Thursday from 8 am to 5.45 pm; closed Friday.

**Telephone** The ETISALAT office at the corner of Beniyas and Umer Ibn Al-Khattab Rds is open 24 hours a day. In addition to telephones, the office has fax, telex and telegram facilities.

**Consulates** A number of countries have consulates in Dubai. Addresses for some of the Western diplomatic missions include:

France
Arbift Building, 10th floor, Beniyas Rd, between the Chamber of Commerce building and the ETISALAT office (☎ 232442)
Germany
Sharaf Building, 6th floor, Mankhool Rd (☎ 523352)
UK
Al-Seef Rd, on the Dubai side of the Creek, near the Dhow Restaurant (☎ 521070)
USA
World Trade Centre, 21st floor, on the Dubai side of the Creek (☎ 371115)

**Travel Agencies** There are lots of travel agencies on Al-Maktoum Rd and around the western end of Beniyas Square. Staff turnover at these places is so high that it is impossible to recommend one or two in particular. If you need to buy a ticket, shop around for prices.

**Bookshops** Try the Al-Ghurair Centre at the corner of Umer Ibn Al-Khattab and Al-Rigga Rds, or the bookshops in the big hotels.

**Emergency** To contact the police or an ambulance call 999; to report a fire, 997. For water problems, call 376666; electricity, 222111.

**Dangers & Annoyances** On the whole Dubai is a very safe city but you should exercise the same sort of caution with your personal belongings as you would at home.

The tendency for drivers to zoom through traffic circles and execute turns across several lanes of traffic seems particularly pronounced in Dubai. Drivers should keep their wits about them at all times.

Finally, do not swim or water-ski in the Creek. The tides in the Gulf are not strong enough to flush the Creek out on a regular basis so it is not a clean waterway.

## The Creek

The obvious place to start your tour of Dubai is at the waterfront. The best idea is to hire an abra for an hour or so. For around Dh 30 (for the whole boat, not per person) the captain should take you up to the Al-Maktoum Bridge, down to the mouth of the Creek and back to the dock where you started. This takes 45 to 60 minutes and is the perfect way to see a great trading port.

Also take some time to walk along the cargo docks on the Deira side of the Creek, between the abra dock and the Carlton Tower Hotel. Dhows bound for every port from Kuwait to Karachi to Aden dock here to load and unload cargo.

### Dubai Museum

Dubai's museum occupies the Al-Fahaidi fort on the Dubai side of the Creek, next to the Ruler's Office. It is open from 8 am to 8 pm daily except on Friday when it's from 2 to 8 pm. Admission is Dh 2.

Al-Fahaidi fort was built in the early 19th century – its construction dates range from 1800 to about 1840. The fort is considered to be the oldest building in Dubai. For many years it was both the residence of Dubai's rulers and the seat of government. The fort's current career as a museum began in 1971.

The entryway has a display of aerial photographs showing the growth of Dubai over the years. It is interesting to note that Deira has always been the more heavily settled side of the Creek.

To the left of the photographs, a doorway leads to a display of traditional clothing, crafts, jewellery and activities.

Entering the fort's courtyard, you'll see on the left a big tank which was used to carry fresh water on pearling boats. Several small boats and a barasti house with a wind tower are also in the courtyard. Throughout much of the Gulf, barasti, or reed, houses were common until the 1950s. This was because they were relatively easy to build and maintain since, unlike mud-brick houses, they do not require water. The circulation of air through the reeds also made barasti houses much cooler than mud-brick structures during the summer. On the far side of the courtyard, a small building contains a complete grave from the Qusais archaeological site. A gallery to the right has more finds

from Qusais (950-550 BC) and Jumeirah (5th and 8th centuries AD) on display.

Coming across the Creek by abra, to get to the museum walk inland from the dock for about 100 metres, keeping left when you can't exactly go straight, until you hit a street with cars (instead of only pedestrians). This is Ali Ibn Abi Talib Rd. Turn left and follow it past the big mosque. You'll see the Ruler's Office on your left and the fort on the right.

### The Ruler's Office

This is the white building, decorated with mock wind towers, fronting onto the Creek. Near it are a few old buildings with wind towers.

### Shaikh Saeed's House

The house of Shaikh Saeed, the grandfather of Dubai's present ruler, has been restored as a museum of pre-oil times. It sits beside the Creek on the Dubai side, near Port Rashid. The 30-room house was built in the late 19th century and for many years, it served as a communal residence for the Al-Maktoum family. This is in keeping with the Arabian tradition of having several generations living in separate apartments within the same house or compound. Shaikh Saeed lived here until his death in 1958. The house was reopened as a museum in 1986 but has since been closed for renovations. When it reopens, it will probably keep hours similar to those of the museum.

The house is built of coral quarried from the Gulf and then covered with lime and plaster. Until recently this was a common building method along both the Gulf and Red Sea coasts of Arabia. In Shaikh Saeed's era, the entrance on Al-Khor St, the one used by visitors today, was the house's back door. The main entrance, opening onto the large, central courtyard, faced the sea. (The Port Rashid complex, which now occupies almost 1.5 km between the house and the open sea, is mostly on reclaimed land.

### Souks

Not much of the old covered souks remain on either side of the Creek. The **Deira**

**Covered Souk**, in the area immediately behind the Shatt Al-Arab Hotel, off Al-Sabkha Rd, specialises mostly in textiles. There is also a small covered souk area on the Dubai side of the Creek near the abra dock.

Deira's **Gold Souk** is on and around Sikkat Al-Khail St between Suq Deira and Old Baladiya Sts. The best place to look for Dubai's famous consumer electronics is around Beniyas Square, near the intersection of Al-Sabkha and Al-Maktoum Hospital Rds, and in the specialist shops which dot the bigger shopping centres. In particular, you might want to try the Al-Ghurair Centre at the intersection of Umer Ibn Al-Khattab and Al-Rigga Rds.

## Activities

Many activities, such as sailing and water sports, are usually organised through clubs. *What's On* is a good source of information for these clubs and other leisure activities in Dubai.

**Golf** The Emirates Golf Club, on the road to Jebel Ali, is the pride of Dubai. It is very exclusive and very expensive. There are only 1600 (very expensive) memberships available but a few of the big hotels have arrangements whereby their guests can use the course. Greens fees are Dh 240.

**Camel Racing** Races take place early on Friday mornings during winter and spring, at the track south of the centre off the 2nd Za'abeel Rd on the Dubai side. Admission is free but try to get there by 8 am.

## Organised Tours

Both Emirates Holidays (☎ 220218) and Gulf Ventures (☎ 271500) offer half-day tours of Dubai for Dh 60. Emirates Holidays also offers a half-day tour of Sharjah and Ajman for Dh 55, full-day tours to Abu Dhabi, Al-Ain, Ras Al-Khaimah, Hatta and the East Coast for Dh 95 each and dhow cruises for Dh 125 (including dinner). Both companies offer all-day desert safaris (about Dh 180) and barbecue dinners in the desert

(about Dh 150). Emirates Holidays has an overnight camping trip in the desert every Thursday for Dh 350.

Net Lines (☎ 664433) offers a wide selection of cruises along the Creek and into the Gulf. Prices start at Dh 50 for a two-hour Sunset Cruise. There are also breakfast, lunch and dinner cruises, and six-hour Friday 'leisure cruises'. Prices for these run from Dh 95 to Dh 190.

See the Sharjah entry for the information on other tour companies.

## Places to Stay

Dubai's hotels are scattered over a wide area, but the cheapies are concentrated in the Deira souk, particularly along Al-Sabkha Rd and in the side streets off Suq Deira St. Absolute rock bottom for singles/doubles is Dh 40/60, but the handful of places in this category are generally filled by quasi-permanent residents. Mid-range hotels are everywhere, though there are a few good ones around Beniyas Square. Four and five-star hotels line the Creek and dot the outskirts of the emirate.

The Deira souk is a great place to stay because of its central location, though anything overlooking Al-Sabkha Rd is likely to be quite noisy. If your budget can manage it, something on or around Beniyas Square will put you right in the heart of the city.

## Places to Stay – bottom end

Dubai's *Youth Hostel* (☎ 665078) is on Qusais Rd on the eastern outskirts of the city next to the Al-Ahli club. To get there from central Deira take the main Rd for Sharjah (Al-Ittihad Rd) and turn right onto Qusais Rd. The Al-Ahli Club is the place on the left with a stadium, the hostel is the next gate down the road. The hostel is only open to men. Beds are Dh 10 per night in cramped, grubby four-bed dorms. It is a pretty makeshift affair and if you've got the car necessary to get out here I'd recommend staying in the Sharjah hostel instead. It's worth the extra 10 minutes in the car and the extra Dh 5 out of pocket.

All of the following hotels claim that they

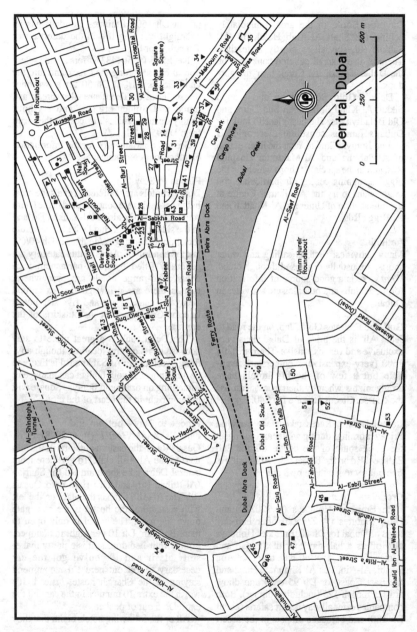

| ■ PLACES TO STAY | | 53 | Copper Chimney Hotel |
|---|---|---|---|
| 4 | Al-Hashmi Hotel | | |
| 5 | Hotel Delhi Darbar | ▼ PLACES TO EAT | |
| 6 | Hariri Hotel | | |
| 8 | Imperial Palace Hotel | 2 | Najaf Restaurant |
| 9 | Al-Zekra Hotel & Restaurant | 7 | Bab-U-Sabkha Restaurant |
| 10 | Saeed Hotel | 21 | Gulf Restaurant & Cafeteria |
| 11 | Stars Hotel | 31 | Stars Night Restaurant |
| 12 | Metro Hotel | 33 | Golden Fork Restaurant |
| 13 | Al-Ikhlas Hotel | 34 | Blue Wing Restaurant |
| 14 | Al-Khayam Hotel | 37 | Cafe Mozart |
| 15 | Al-Najah Hotel | 40 | Popeye Restaurant |
| 16 | Red Sea Hotel | 41 | Pizza Corner |
| 18 | Sina Hotel | 52 | Bhavna Restaurant |
| 19 | Shatt Al-Arab Hotel | | |
| 22 | Avon Hotel | OTHER | |
| 23 | Dubai Orient Hotel | | |
| 24 | Mirage Hotel | | |
| 25 | Victoria Hotel | 1 | Mosque |
| 26 | Royal Prince Hotel | 3 | Police Station (Old Fort) |
| 28 | Phoenicia Hotel | 17 | Several Small Exchange Kiosks |
| 29 | Rex Hotel | 20 | Deira Bus Station |
| 30 | Swiss Hotel | 27 | British Bank of the Middle East |
| 35 | Dubai Inter-Continental Hotel | 32 | Emirates Airlines |
| 36 | Safari Palace Hotel | 42 | Deira Post Office |
| 38 | Carlton Tower Hotel | 44 | Shaikh Saeed's House |
| 39 | Riviera Hotel | 45 | Plaza Cinema |
| 43 | Al-Khaleej Hotel | 46 | Dubai Bus & Taxi Station |
| 47 | Ambassador Hotel | 49 | Ruler's Office |
| 48 | Astoria Hotel | 50 | Dubai Museum |
| 51 | Regent Palace Hotel | | |

can arrange visas, though my experience has been that you're far better off coming in via a more up-market place and sleeping cheap later on.

The best value in Dubai is the *Mirage Hotel* (☎ 271666, fax 272293), in an alley just off Al-Sabkha Rd. The rooms are tiny, the walls are covered with bathroom tiles and you have to share a toilet with three or four other rooms, but the atmosphere is friendly and at Dh 70/120 for singles/doubles you won't beat the combination of price and cleanliness. I highly recommend it.

Other good cheapies which claim to be able to arrange visas are: the *Stars Hotel* (☎ 235000, fax 282659), a friendly Yemeni-run place with a good location in the souk on Al-Buteen St. Rooms are Dh 50/100, all without bath. Nearby, the *Red Sea Hotel*

(☎ 222281, fax 281961), at the intersection of Al-Buteen and Suq Deira Sts, asks Dh 60/80 for similar rooms. The *Imperial Palace Hotel* (☎ 211344, fax 534713) on Naif South St is a bit more expensive, but the rooms are an excellent value at Dh 100/140.

Cheapies which do not purport to arrange visas include the *Al-Ikhlas Hotel* (☎ 235885) on Sikkat Al-Khail St. They only have doubles, which go for Dh 120. Off Sikkat Al-Khail St, behind the Al-Ikhlas, the *Metro Hotel* (☎ 234040) has rooms at Dh 100/120. The *Suls Burg Hotel*, near the Al-Khayam Hotel on Suq Deira St, is a bit rough. Rooms are Dh 70/120, none with bath, but you can do better for this price. The *Al-Najah Hotel* (☎ 228931), at the corner of Suq Deira and Al-Buteen Sts, has tiny rooms for Dh 60/100, each of which shares a bath with another room. The *Al-Sorour Hotel* (☎ 229203), in an alleyway off Al-Buteen St, charges Dh 100/150.

On Al-Sabkha Rd, near the intersection with Naif Rd, the *Saeed Hotel* (☎ 212142) is usually full. If you can get in it costs Dh 80/120. Nearby, also on Al-Sabkha Rd, the *Al-Zekra Hotel & Restaurant* (☎ 274687) charges Dh 100 for rooms, all of them doubles with baths. It looks better inside than it does from the street. The clientele seems to consist mostly of Gulf Arab families. If you really want to be in the thick of things, take a look at the *Shatt Al-Arab Hotel* (☎ 221092) overlooking the bus station at the intersection of Al-Sabkha Rd and Deira St. Rooms are Dh 40/60, none with private baths. Many of the guests look like permanent residents and the place is often full. It's pretty grimy but it has character.

The *Rex Hotel* (☎ 212834) has a great location on Beniyas Square. The rooms cost Dh 100/140, and some are without private bath. Just off Beniyas Square the *Shirazi Hotel* (☎ 216464) is not one of the friendlier places in town, but rooms cost Dh 100/130.

The *Al-Hashemi Hotel* (☎ 233333) on St 9 between the police station and the Naif souk has rooms at Dh 90/120, all with bath. It's very clean if a bit sterile.

### Places to Stay – middle
Even in this price category many of the hotels either won't arrange visas or seem very reluctant when asked. Service charges, where applicable, have been included in the prices.

The *Ritz Hotel* (☎ 236151, fax 238860) is a friendly place with a good spot in the Al-Dallal Building on Beniyas Rd. It bills itself as 'the best hotel in the city for families' and operates with a few preconceptions about Western guests. When I walked in to ask about the rates, the clerk immediately announced that there was no bar! Singles/doubles are Dh 150/173. The *Hotel Delhi Darbar* (☎ 235656, fax 238823) on Naif Rd is, as its name implies, an Indian-oriented place. At Dh 150/200 for large, spotless rooms, it is one of the better deals in this price

range. The *Sina Hotel* (☎ 237323, fax 270606) is in an alley inside the Deira covered souk. The rooms are small but adequate and cost Dh 150/225.

Near the intersection of Suq Deira and Sikkat Al-Khail Sts, the *Al-Khayam Hotel* (☎ 226211) charges Dh 120/150 for rooms, all with private baths. On Suq Deira St, *Dreams Hotel* (☎ 274268) charges Dh 125/155 for small rooms which share their baths with one or two other rooms. The *Asia Hotel* (☎ 215737) on Al-Buteen St, just off Suq Deira St, has only doubles at Dh 200.

The *Dubai Orient Hotel* (☎ 282233), at the intersection of Al-Sabkha Rd and Al-Soor St, has only doubles for Dh 150, all with odd-smelling baths. Next door, the *Avon Hotel* (☎ 258877) charges Dh 172.50/264.50. Across the street is the *Royal Prince Hotel* (☎ 239991), a relatively new place where the rooms are a very good value at Dh 140/180.

The *Hariri Hotel* (☎ 277888) is on St 5, off Naif South St. Rooms cost Dh 150/200. The *Swiss Hotel* (☎ 212181), on Al-Mussalla Rd, is a quite friendly place. Rates are Dh 184/241.50 but they will readily discount those figures.

On Al-Khor St, near the mouth of the Creek, the *Al-Jazeera Hotel* (☎ 225299) has only doubles for Dh 150.

### Places to Stay – top end
**Deira** Unless otherwise noted, all of the hotels in this category will arrange visas. Rates are negotiable, and the service charge is already included in the prices listed here.

One of the better top-end values in the city is the *Al-Khaleej Hotel* (☎ 211144, fax 237140) between Beniyas Square and Al-Sabkha Rd. Singles/doubles are 276/391. Nearby, the *Safari Palace Hotel* (☎ 232155, fax 232155), on St 18 immediately behind Beniyas Rd, is much cheaper at Dh 185/262.50. The *Phoenicia Hotel* (☎ 227191, fax 221629) has a prime location on Beniyas Square. At Dh 207/299 the rates are OK by local standards for their rather ostentatious rooms.

Along Beniyas Rd the *Carlton Tower*

(☎ 227111, fax 228249) is a good top-end place at Dh 367.50/472.50. Next door, the *Riviera Hotel* has similar prices but is less plush and does not serve alcohol.

The *Victoria Hotel* (☎ 272626), in an alley off Al-Sabkha Rd, is a decent if dull place at Dh 200/250, but it won't arrange visas.

There are more expensive five-star hotels (usually the quickest at arranging visas) in Dubai. Discounts from the rates quoted are almost always available. They include:

*Al-Khaleej Palace* (☎ 231000, telex 48388 KHPAL EM, fax 211293) Al-Maktoum Rd. Singles/doubles cost Dh 624/732.
*Dubai Inter-Continental Hotel* (☎ 227171, telex 45779, fax 284777) Beniyas Rd. Singles/doubles cost Dh 780/900.
*Hyatt Regency Dubai* (☎ 221234, telex 47555 HYATT EM, fax 211868) off Al-Khaleej Rd. Singles/doubles cost Dh 708/828.
*Sheraton Dubai* (☎ 281111, telex 46710, fax 213468) Beniyas Rd. Singles/doubles cost Dh 828/948.

**Dubai** The hotels on the Dubai side of the Creek are mostly middle to upper end. Unless it's for business reasons, it is a bit hard to see why one would want to stay on the Dubai side. Deira is a lot more fun. There are no cheap hotels on the Dubai side.

The *Copper Chimney Hotel* (☎ 524005, fax 513181) is near the intersection of Khalid Ibn Al-Waleed Rd and Al-Hisn St. The hotel is on the 6th floor of an office building. Singles/doubles are Dh 130/150 with bath. Singles without bath are Dh 66. The rooms are cramped but well kept and the communal bathrooms are cleaner than the private ones. They claim they can arrange visas if you stay at least three days. Just off Khalid Ibn Al-Waleed St, the *Harbour Hotel* (☎ 511223, fax 511248) is the only other cheapish place in Bur Dubai at Dh 150/200. They can arrange visas.

The main advantage of the *Regent Palace Hotel* (☎ 535555) is its location next to the museum and near the Ruler's Office. Rooms are Dh 200/250 but they do not sponsor visas.

The *Palm Beach Hotel* (☎ 525550, fax 528320) on Khalid Ibn Al-Waleed St has

rooms at Dh 210/312. They said they need two to three weeks to arrange visas which is not usually a good sign. On the same street the *Dubai Marine Hotel* (☎ 520900, fax 521035) charges Dh 354/414.

Top-end places which can sponsor visas include the *Ambassador Hotel* (☎ 531000, fax 534751), with singles/doubles for Dh 253/402.50. It's on Al-Falah Rd near the museum. The *Astoria Hotel* (☎ 434000, fax 535665) is on Al-Nahdha St. They charge Dh 299/414.

**Elsewhere** If you come to Dubai on a package tour you will probably stay at either the *Jebel Ali Hotel* (☎ 35252, fax 35543), a five-star place 50 km west of the centre and adjacent to the Jebel Ali Port, or at the *Chicago Beach Hotel* (☎ 480000, telex 47490 CHBTL) which is about midway between the centre and Jebel Ali. Both are beach resort hotels.

### Places to Eat
**Cheap & Medium-Priced** A good place for an affordable meal is the *Blue Wing*, on Al-Maktoum Rd between the Inter-Continental Hotel and Beniyas Square. Their menu features various Filipino main dishes for Dh 10 to Dh 15, including soup. Meal-sized soups are Dh 8 to Dh 15 and there is also a selection of Arabic and European dishes. A few doors down, toward Beniyas Square, the *Golden Fork* has an odd combination of Oriental dishes and Western fast food. The Western food is cheaper. Two pieces of chicken, French fries, bread and a soda cost Dh 7 – a hard price to beat.

On Beniyas Square, the *Nakhuda Restaurant*, between the Phoenicia Hotel and the Rex Hotel, offers full meals of roast lamb or chicken with salad and soup for Dh 10. On the other side of Beniyas Square, *Stars Night* has an Indian/Arabic menu with main dishes at Dh 12 to Dh 20, including soup and salad. The food is OK but not great.

Across Beniyas Rd from the abra station, *Pizza Corner* is a good medium-priced place with pizzas and burgers. For a quick and cheap meal out on Beniyas Rd, *Cafeteria*

*Al-Abra* has good shawarma and samosas along with fruit juice and soda. The cafe is at the intersection of Al-Sabkha and Beniyas Rds, next to the Abra dock. It's a good place to relax while watching the abras come and go. A bit further up the road, *Popeye* has shawarma, burgers and other snacks. A full meal can easily be had for Dh 10 or less.

If you're looking for something a bit more formal, *Pillars*, the coffee shop in the Phoenicia Hotel on Beniyas Square, has a Dh 25 buffet lunch.

When it comes to coffee, my highest recommendation goes to *Cafe Mozart*, which recreates the atmosphere, food, coffee and service of a Viennese coffee house, right down to the change purse carried by the waitress. The pastries and croissants cost about Dh 2.50 each and are good. The coffee and cappuccino are excellent.

In the cheap hotels area of Deira there are many cheap restaurants, most of them serving Indian and Pakistani food though many of these places will have menus consisting only of biryanis. Naif South St has particularly good pickings. Try *Bab-U-Sabkha* for good, cheap Pakistani food. Another good subcontinental eatery is the *Gulf Restaurant & Cafeteria*, at the intersection of Al-Sabkha Rd and Deira St. Lots of chicken, lamb or fish on a pile of rice costs Dh 12.

On the Dubai side of the Creek, try *Bhavna*, an Indian vegetarian restaurant on Al-Faheidi Rd, next to the Dubai Museum.

### Places to Eat – top end

All of Dubai's best expensive restaurants are attached to the big hotels. *Pancho Villa's*, a Tex-Mex restaurant in the Astoria Hotel on the Dubai side of the Creek, is one of the Gulf's best known restaurants (their bumper stickers can be seen far and wide). Appetisers cost Dh 15 to Dh 20, main dishes Dh 30 to Dh 35.

In the Inter-Continental Hotel, *The Pub* is about as good an imitation of the real thing as you'll find in the Gulf. They serve a varied menu of sandwiches and 'traditional pub food' (shepherd's pie, roast beef, etc). Meals cost Dh 30 to Dh 50. The best Italian food in Dubai is at *Villa Veduta*, an outlandishly expensive restaurant, also in the Inter-Continental. Count on paying no less than Dh 75 per person, lots more if you want Italian wine with your meal. For a somewhat cheaper Italian meal, try *Da Pino* in the Al-Khaleej Hotel.

*Miyako*, in the Hyatt Regency Hotel, serves quite good Japanese food. This could well cost you Dh 100 or more.

### Entertainment

Dubai's cinemas all specialise in Indian and Pakistani films. After-hours social life centres around expensive restaurants and bars and discos in the big hotels. A night out on the town is not going to be cheap. If you're drinking, plan on spending well over Dh 150 and even nondrinkers could easily go through half that in cover charges and overpriced glasses of Pepsi.

The entertainment scene in the big hotels is constantly changing. The best way to keep up is with a copy of *What's On*. Almost everything: country & western, rock, deafening disco or a quiet piano bar is available somewhere. The problem is that with the exception of a few perennials (like Pancho Villa's) the hotels keep changing the motifs in their restaurant/clubs in an attempt to keep everything up-to-date. If you have the time and money to explore it could all be rather interesting.

### Things to Buy

High-priced boutiques filled with the latest of everything can be found in the Al-Ghurair Centre (among other places) at the intersection of Umar Ibn Al-Khattab and Al-Rigga Rds. If you are looking for cheap electronics try the area at the Al-Sabkha Rd end of Beniyas Square. The gold souk is further west, along Sikkat Al-Khail St.

Persian carpets are said to be cheaper at the Sharjah souk. Carpet shoppers in Dubai should try the Deira and Al-Mansoor towers on Beniyas square, both of which have lots of small carpet boutiques.

Haggle hard anywhere in the souk and

when buying anything (I have even haggled over exchange rates with moneychangers) but don't expect the prices of things like electronic goods to come down by more than 10 to 15%. Antiques and crafts may come down a bit more.

## Getting There & Away

**Air** You can fly to almost anywhere from Dubai. The emirate's long-standing reputation as the travel hub of the Gulf was built on a combination of easy landing rights for transiting aircraft and a very big and cheap duty-free shop at the airport. Outside the Middle East, the words most often associated with Dubai are probably 'duty free'. The airport PR staff have turned statistics about the duty-free store into a small cottage industry. My particular favourite: in 1988 Iranian travellers bought 1.5 million bananas in the Dubai AP duty-free store. Bananas were said to be virtually unobtainable in Iran back then.

Sample one-way and return fares from Dubai to other cities (with minimum and maximum stay requirements) include:

| To | One-Way | Return | Min/Max |
|---|---|---|---|
| Bahrain | Dh 550 | Dh 580 | 3/7 days |
| Dhahran | Dh 570 | Dh 790 | 3/14 days |
| Doha | Dh 430 | Dh 450 | 3/7 days |
| Jeddah | Dh 1090 | Dh 1520 | 3/14 days |
| Kuwait | Dh 730 | Dh 1020 | 3/14 days |
| London | Dh 2560 | Dh 3720 | 10/90 days |
| Muscat | Dh 460 | Dh 480 | 3/7 days |
| New York | Dh 3300 | Dh 4180 | 14/90 days |
| Riyadh | Dh 680 | Dh 940 | 3/14 days |
| Sydney | Dh 2400 | Dh 3500 | 0/180 days |

Following is a far from complete list of the carriers, large and small, which fly to and from Dubai International Airport (DXB). Some of the carriers with offices listed in town also have desks at Airline Centre, a type of shopping mall for air travel, on Al-Maktoum Rd in Deira. For general airport information call 245777 or 245555.

Aeroflot
Khalid Ibn Al-Waleed St, Dubai (☎ 524483)

Air France
Al-Maktoum Rd, Deira, just east of the Khaleej Palace Hotel (☎ 222522)
Air India
Al-Maktoum Rd, Deira, just west of the Clock Tower Roundabout (☎ 276787)
Air Lanka
Airline Centre, Al-Maktoum Rd, Deira (☎ 223423)
Alitalia
Al-Maktoum Rd, Deira, across from the Dubai Electricity Company (☎ 284656)
Al-Yemda, Yemen Airways
Al-Maktoum Rd, Deira, just east of the Khaleej Palace Hotel (☎ 284093)
Biman Bangladesh Airlines
Airline Centre, Al-Maktoum Rd, Deira (☎ 226241)
British Airways
Airline Centre, Al-Maktoum Rd, Deira (☎ 213312)
Balkan, Bulgarian Airways
Al-Maktoum Rd, Deira, just east of the Khaleej Palace Hotel (☎ 223250)
Cathay Pacific
Pearl Building, 11th floor, Street 18, Deira (near Beniyas Square) (☎ 283126)
Cyprus Airways
Al-Maktoum Rd, Deira, across from the Dubai Electricity Company (☎ 214455)
EgyptAir
Al-Maktoum Rd, Deira, just west of the Clock Tower Roundabout (☎ 236551)
Emirates
Deira Tower, Beniyas Square, Deira. The main reservations office is at Airline Centre on Al-Maktoum Rd, Deira (☎ 215544)
Gulf Air
Al-Maktoum Rd, Deira, across from the Khaleej Palace Hotel (☎ 285141)
Iran Air
Airline Centre, Al-Maktoum Rd, Deira (☎ 226230)
KLM
Al-Maktoum Rd, Deira, across from the Khaleej Palace Hotel (☎ 225281)
Kuwait Airways
Pearl Building, Deira, (near Beniyas Square, enter from Beniyas Rd side of the building) (☎ 281106)
LOT, Polish Airlines
Al-Maktoum Rd, Deira, across from the Dubai Electricity Company (☎ 214455)
Lufthansa
Pearl Building, 1st floor, St 18, Deira (near Beniyas Square) (☎ 221191)
Malev, Hungarian Airlines
Al-Maktoum Rd, Deira, just east of the Khaleej Palace Hotel (☎ 224159)

MEA (Middle East Airlines)
Airline Centre, Al-Maktoum Rd, Deira (☎ 237175)
Olympic
Al-Maktoum Rd, Deira, across from the Dubai Electricity Company (☎ 214761)
PIA (Pakistan International Airlines)
Al-Maktoum Rd, Deira, just west of the Clock Tower Roundabout (☎ 222154)
Royal Brunei
Airline Centre, Al-Maktoum Rd, Deira (☎ 239456)
Royal Jordanian
Pearl Building, Deira, (near Beniyas Square, enter the building from the Beniyas Rd side) (☎ 232855)
Saudia
Rd 14, just off Beniyas Square, Deira (☎ 236455)
Singapore Airlines
Pearl Building, 2nd floor, St 18, Deira (near Beniyas Square) (☎ 232300)
Swissair
Airline Centre, Al-Maktoum Rd, Deira (☎ 283151)
Turkish Airlines
Al-Maktoum Rd, Deira, just east of the Khaleej Palace Hotel (☎ 215970)

**Bus** Inter-city buses only operate within the Dubai emirate. To go to another emirate, you have to take a service taxi. The inter-city buses leave from the Dubai Bus & Taxi Station on Al-Ghubaiba Rd on the Dubai side of the Creek, next to the Plaza cinema. There are six buses each day to Hatta (Dh 7).

There is also a twice-daily bus service to Muscat, Oman. The buses depart from the parking lot of the Airline Centre on Al-Maktoum Rd, Deira, at 7.30 am and 5.30 pm and travel to the Ruwi bus station in Muscat. The trip takes about six hours and costs Dh 85 one-way, Dh 150 return. For information, call 228151, extension 231. Tickets are sold through the Biman Bangladesh Airlines desk at Airline Centre.

**Service Taxi** There are two service-taxi stations in Dubai, one on either side of the Creek. The Deira Taxi Station is near the intersection of Umer Ibn Al-Khattab and Al-Rigga Rds. The taxis leave when full (five to seven passengers depending on the vehicle). Fares (per person) are: Sharjah Dh 4, Ajman Dh 5, Umm Al-Qaiwain Dh 7, Ras Al-

Khaimah Dh 15, Fujairah, Dh 25. Change at Fujairah for Khor Fakkan. The station also has a local taxi rank.

Service Taxis for Abu Dhabi and Al-Ain leave from the Dubai Taxi & Bus Station on Al-Ghubaiba Rd, on the Dubai side of the Creek, next to the Plaza Cinema. It's Dh 30 per person to Abu Dhabi or Al-Ain in a service taxi. Minibuses to Abu Dhabi cost only Dh 20 pr person and carry 14 passengers. There are also service taxis from here to Jebel Ali for Dh 7.

**Car** There are a number of small rental agencies in town but they do not appear to be any cheaper than the larger, better-established companies with offices in the big hotels. The service at the Europcar desk in the lobby of the Inter-Continental Hotel has been consistently good.

### Getting Around

**To/From the Airport** From the Deira bus station, bus No 4 goes to the airport about every half hour for Dh 1. A taxi to or from the airport costs Dh 30 from anywhere in the city.

**Bus** Local buses operate out of the Deira Bus Station near the intersection of Deira St and Al-Sabkha Rd, and from the Dubai Taxi & Bus Station on Al-Ghubaiba Rd (the station on the Dubai side is the main terminal). Numbers and routes are posted on the buses in English as well as Arabic. Bus No 5 runs between the two stations about every 20 minutes from 6.25 am to 8.50 pm. The fare is Dh 1.50.

From the Dubai-side station bus No 12 goes to the World Trade Centre (Dh 1) and No 90 to Jebel Ali (Dh 4.50).

**Taxi** The taxis have no meters and fares should be negotiated in advance with the drivers. Expect to pay Dh 10 to Dh 20 for trips around the centre. Expensive fixed-price cabs also operate from some of the bigger hotels.

**Abra** Abras leave constantly from early

morning until about midnight. On the Deira side of the Creek the dock is at the intersection of Al-Sabkha and Beniyas Rds. On the Dubai side the dock is in front of a shop called Captain's Stores. The abra captains will let you know when the next one is leaving. They leave when full but it never takes more than five minutes for one of them to fill up. The fare is 25 fils which is collected once you are out on the water.

# The Northern Emirates

## SHARJAH

The third-largest of the seven emirates, Sharjah *(Ash-Sharqa* in Arabic) is a place that too many visitors to the UAE either miss entirely or pass through too quickly. Sharjah has some of the most interesting architecture in the country and its souk offers shopping to rival that of Dubai.

Sharjah has long been seen as Dubai's poor cousin though, in fact, Dubai's ascendance in terms of wealth and political power is relatively recent. During the first half of the 19th century, Sharjah was the most important port on the Arabian side of the lower Gulf, and during the latter half of the century its rulers vied with those of Abu Dhabi for the area's leading political role.

Even after Dubai began to take off as a trading centre, Sharjah remained the more developed of the two in terms of infrastructure. It was in Sharjah that the British chose to set up their main military base in this part of the Gulf and it was here that Imperial Airways developed the Trucial Coast's first international airport.

In recent years, Sharjah has taken the lead in the development of the UAE's tourist industry, and the emirate is now the main point of entry for people arriving on package tours.

## Orientation

Sharjah's business district is the area between the Corniche and Al-Zahra Rd, from the Central Market to Shaikh Moham-

med Bin Saqr Al-Qasimi Rd (or Mohammed Saqr St). This is not a huge area and it's pretty easy to get around. During the day, however, it is a dreadful place for driving because the streets are both narrow and crowded. Downtown Sharjah's main street is Al-Arouba Rd.

There is a secondary business district stretching back towards Dubai along King Faisal Rd. Metropolitan Dubai and Metropolitan Sharjah almost adjoin. Sharjah, however, remains distinctly different from Dubai, and not only because it bans alcohol!

The *Sharjah Tourist City Map*, available free at most of the bigger hotels and at some of the larger travel agencies (like SNTTA), is the best map of Sharjah. A few of the hotels also give away a totally worthless white-coloured *Sharjah Tourist Map* which shows just enough to get you totally confused if you make the mistake of trying to use it.

## Information

**Money** In Boorj Ave, just about every building houses a bank. Moneychangers can be found on the small streets immediately to the east and west of it.

**Post** The GPO is on Government House Square. It is open Friday to Wednesday from 8 am to 8 pm and on Thursday from 8 am to 6 pm.

**Telephone** ETISALAT's office is on Al-Soor Rd (which some of the street signs identify as Al-Mina St and others as Port or Harbour Rd), at the corner of Kuwait Square (officially renamed Al-Safat Square). It is open 24 hours a day. In addition to telephones, telex and fax services are also available. The telephone code for Sharjah is 06.

**Travel Agencies** The Sharjah National Tourist and Transport Company (SNTTA, ☎ 351411) handles all travel-related matters. Their office is on Al-Arouba Rd. Bbecause Sharjah airport handles most of the charter flights coming into the UAE, this has not led to a thriving local bucket-shop industry.

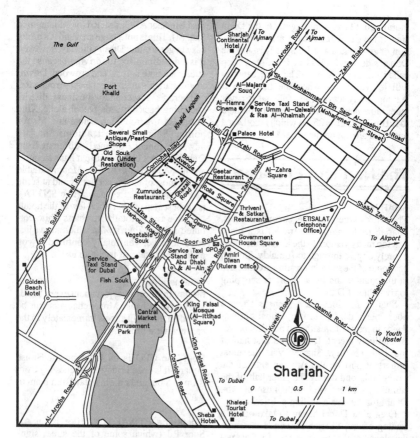

## Rolla Square

Sharjah's main square lies just inland from the intersection of Boorj Ave and Al-Arouba Rd. On holidays and other ceremonial occasions it is used for big, formal parades. The rest of the time it is a public park.

## The Ruler's Office (Amiri Diwan)

This building, on Government House Square, is the seat of Sharjah's government.

## Old Souk

When I visited the Old Souk, which is roughly in the area near the Corniche and

immediately west of Boorj Ave, it was swarming with workers as part of a large-scale restoration project. A few of the shops – antique dealers with wares mostly from India – were still open.

Large sections of the old souk fell to pieces during the 1970s and 1980s. While the restoration was undoubtedly necessary, it did not seem to encompass the entire souk area.

## Central Market

From certain angles, the Central Market (also called the new souk or the Sharjah souk) looks like a set of monster-size oil barrels which have tipped over and had wind towers glued to their sides. Once inside, however, the design works. A lot of people can circulate comfortably and stay reasonably cool in here. There are hundreds of shops and stalls selling just about everything imaginable. The prices are pretty good and, in many cases, a bit cheaper than what things cost in Dubai. The Central Market is reputed to be the best place in the UAE to shop for Persian carpets.

### King Faisal Mosque

Sharjah's central mosque is the largest mosque in the UAE. It is said to be able to accommodate 3000 worshippers. The mosque dominates Al-Ittihad Square next to the Sharjah souk.

### Amusement Park

A pocket-sized Disneyland sits on an island in the Khalid Lagoon. The park is open Sunday to Thursday from 3.30 to 10.30 pm and Friday from 9.30 am to 10.30 pm; closed Saturday. Mondays are reserved for women and children only. Admission is Dh 5.

### Old Watchtower

Old and much restored watchtowers dot the landscape of Sharjah. One worth noting for its location is the lone watchtower which stands guard over a small patch of the coastline at the corner of Khan Rd and Shaikh Sultan Al-Awal Rd.

### Organised Tours

The main tour operators based in Sharjah are SNTTA Emirates Tours(☎ 548296) and Orient Tours (☎ 549333). Both offer half-day tours of Dubai (Dh 55) and Sharjah & Ajman (Dh 50). Full-day trips are available to Abu Dhabi, Al-Ain, Ras Al-Khaimah and to the east coast (Dh 95 per tour). Orient Tours has half-day desert safaris for Dh 125. A full-day desert trip with either company costs Dh 170. Overnight desert trips cost about Dh 350 and all-day mountain-driving trips, Dh 170. SNTTA also has a dinner cruise aboard a dhow (Dh 125) and a '1001

Nights Evening' (ie, a Lebanese dinner and a belly dancing show) for Dh 165.

These tours are offered only once or twice a week, so it is best to call and get the schedule in advance. Brochures for both agencies can be found in the lobbies of most of Sharjah's (and a few of Dubai's) larger hotels.

### Places to Stay – bottom end

Sharjah's *Youth Hostel* (☎ 373342, ext 37) is at the Sharjah Sports Club on Al-Qasmia Rd, about 3.7 km from the GPO. Beds cost Dh 15 per night and IYHF cards are required. The hostel has about 30 beds in four-bed dorms, and you are likely to have a room to yourself. The hostel, however, is only open for men. Residents in the hostel can generally use the Sports Club's swimming pool and bowling alley.

There are only two other semi-cheap hotels in town, both on King Faisal Rd. The *Khaleej Tourist Hotel* (☎ 597888) charges Dh 95/126 for singles/doubles. It is simple but clean and has unbelievably small bathrooms (some with Turkish toilets). Across the street the *Sheba Hotel* (☎ 522522) is a much better value at Dh 95/130, with better rooms and larger baths.

### Places to Stay – middle

The cheapest hotel in the centre is the *Palace Hotel* (☎ 353555) at the intersection of Al-Arouba Rd and Al-Khalij Al-Arabi St. Rooms are Dh 105/175. (All the hotel signs are also in Chinese because the Air China flight crews stay here.) A bit outside the centre is the *Federal Hotel* (☎ 354106) on King Faisal St. Singles/doubles are Dh 126/157.50.

There are two mid-range hotels opposite each other on Shaikh Sultan Al-Awal Rd, north of the centre. The *Sharjah Beach Hotel* (☎ 358311, fax 525422) charges Dh 150/200 for B&B and the *Summerland Apartments* (☎ 354321), Dh 150/180. They are both under the same management and guests at the Summerland Apartments can use the Beach Hotel's private beach. The Beach Hotel can arrange visas for tourists.

Another moderately priced hotel is the *Coral Beach Hotel* (☎ 221011) on the Corniche, just inside Sharjah on the way to Ajman. Rooms are Dh 126/189 and they can sometimes arrange tourist visas.

### Places to Stay – top end
All of the following hotels can arrange visas. Expect to pay a 15% tax and service charge over and above the quoted rates at any of these places.

Sharjah's top hotel is the *Sharjah Continental Hotel* (☎ 371111, fax 524090) at the Corniche end of Shaikh Mohammed Saqr Al-Qasimi St. Rooms cost Dh 400/500. The remaining top-end places are all outside the city centre along Shaikh Sultan Al-Awal Rd. The *Sharjah Grand Hotel* (☎ 356557, fax 372861) charges Dh 300/400. The *Sharjah Carlton Hotel* (☎ 523711, fax 374962) asks Dh 250/350. Further down the road, the *Golden Beach Motel* (☎ 371331) is under the same management as the Carlton. It has the same fax number and charges Dh 200/250 for rooms.

### Places to Eat
Rolla Square and Al-Ghazali Rd (parallel to Al-Arouba Rd but one block closer to the sea) have a plethora of cheap Indian eateries. Try the *Zumruda Restaurant* on Al-Ghazali Rd with biryanis at Dh 6 to Dh 7.

The *Geetar Restaurant*, at the corner of Al-Arouba Rd and Boorj Ave, and *Al-Anqood Restaurant* on the edge of Rolla Square, are vegetarian Indian restaurants. Further up Rolla Square try the *Thriveni Restaurant* and the slightly fancier *Satkar Restaurant* immediately above it. The Satkar offers good Thali set meals (a selection of vegetables with bread and rice) from as little as Dh 6. The surroundings are nicer and the view out over the square is worth the extra dirham or two.

### Entertainment
Sharjah's Emir banned alcohol in 1985 and all of the emirate's discos were closed. Aside from the Al-Jazeera amusement park on the road to Dubai, the main form of entertainment is the cinema. The fare is mostly subcontinental though the Al-Hamra Cinema on Al-Arouba Rd often has English films.

### Things to Buy
There are a few antique shops scattered in among all that scaffolding and reconstruction work in the old souk. A couple of antique dealers have also set up in the Central Market. The selection tends to be an eclectic blend of Chinese and Pakistani curios and Arab jewellery, mostly from Oman.

**Persian Carpets** Sharjah is one of the best places in the Gulf to buy Persian carpets. Most of the carpet shops are in the Central Market and they can arrange shipping. There are no export taxes. Prices vary wildly depending on your bargaining skills and the size and quality of the carpet. It is also useful to have some knowledge about Persian carpets because the salespeople will definitely try to rip you off – we *are* talking about carpet shopping in the Middle East here.

### Getting There & Away
**Air** Sharjah International Airport definitely lives in the shadow of Dubai, but it's putting up a good fight. The idea of raffling off expensive cars to departing and transit passengers with only 1000 tickets sold per car and free delivery anywhere in the world for the winner, now a standard feature at Abu Dhabi, Dubai and Sharjah, originated here. Sharjah Airport has also become the major point of entry for tourists coming to the UAE. The airport is 15 km from the centre. The phone number for airport information is 581111. Some of the scheduled carriers serving Sharjah are:

Syrian Arab Airlines
    Al-Ghazali St, Downtown (☎ 357203)
Air India
    Kanoo Group Building, one block south of Al-Arouba Rd, near the Giant Supermarket (☎ 356635)
Iran Air
    Al-Arouba Rd (☎ 350000)
Air China
    Al-Arouba Rd (371029)

Gulf Air
  Al-Arouba Rd, near the flyover and intersection
  with Al-Soor Rd (☎ 371366)
EgyptAir
  Al-Mina St, near the intersection with Al-Arouba
  Rd (☎ 352163)

**Bus** There is no bus service to, from or through Sharjah. If you don't have a car you'll have to get a taxi.

**Service Taxi** Sharjah has three service-taxi stations. Taxis for Umm Al-Qaiwain (Dh 7) and Ras Al-Khaimah (Dh 15) leave from the lot on Al-Arouba Rd across from the Al-Hamra cinema. Taxis for Dubai (Dh 4) depart from a stand next to the vegetable souk, and taxis for Abu Dhabi and Al-Ain (Dh 30 to either city) depart from a station on Al-Ittihad Square near the King Faisal mosque. It's worth noting that the Abu Dhabi and Al-Ain taxis rarely fill up – the stand seems mostly to be overflow space for the Dubai taxi stand. You are far better off taking a taxi to Dubai and travelling on to Abu Dhabi or Al-Ain from there.

Ajman, for travel purposes, is regarded as an extension of Sharjah so there are no service taxis going there.

**Car** In addition to the international car rental companies in the big hotels, there are a number of small firms along Al-Mina St, near the flyover.

### Getting Around
Since Sharjah has no bus system getting around without your own car means either taking taxis or walking. The taxis are without meters and trips around the centre should cost Dh 5 to Dh 10 (agree on the fare before you get in). If you hire a taxi by the hour expect to pay around Dh 20 per hour, though you might be able to bargain that down a little. When the heat is not too debilitating Sharjah's centre can be covered on foot quite easily.

## AROUND SHARJAH
### Dhaid
Dhaid is a medium-sized oasis town, 50 km east of Sharjah to which it belongs. In the days before air-conditioning it was a popular getaway spot for Sharjah's elite. It certainly looks inviting. If you are approaching the town from Sharjah it appears as a spot of green set in a sea of sand dunes. There's nothing to see but it is a good place to stop for lunch or to spend an hour or two wandering along the tracks which crisscross the oasis.

The *Al-Waha Market Restaurant* in the new souk building has cheap Indian chicken and mutton biryanis and tikkas. A meal should cost about Dh 10. Outsiders stopping for anything other than petrol are still a bit rare in Dhaid so be prepared to be stared at.

## AJMAN
The smallest of the seven emirates, Ajman is hardly the mere extension of Sharjah that some people imagine. The emirate occupies a small stretch of coast between Sharjah and Umm Al-Qaiwain and also has two inland enclaves. One is Masfut, at the western edge of the Hajar mountains, and the other is Manama, in the north-central interior on the road from Sharjah to Fujairah.

### Orientation & Information
Ajman's central square is within walking distance of pretty much everything, including the museum, Ajman's lone hotel, a couple of small restaurants and the coastline. Leewara St follows the section of the coast containing most of the city's few sites other than the museum. The local government offices, GPO and telephone office are all on Shaikh Khalifa St. The gift shop at the museum has an excellent map of the city for Dh 10.

There is no tourist office. The place marked on maps as Ajman Tourist Centre is a combination video arcade and coffee shop.

The telephone code for Ajman is 06.

### Ajman Museum
Ajman's museum occupies the old police

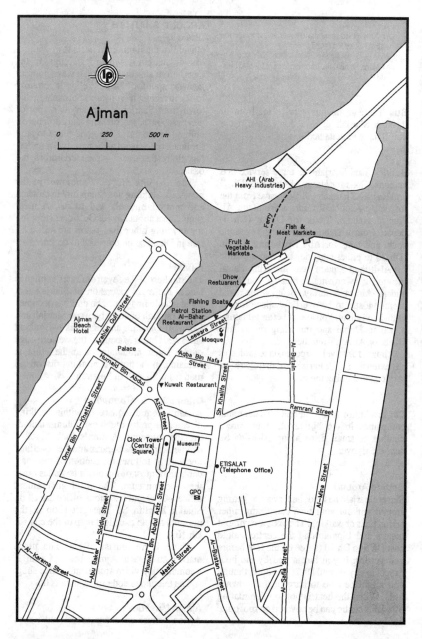

fort on the emirate's central square. It is open Sunday to Thursday from 9 am to 1 pm and daily (ie, including Friday) from 4 to 7 pm. It is closed Saturday. Fridays are reserved for families and Mondays are reserved for women and children, though this appears to be only loosely enforced. Admission is Dh 2 and children under six are admitted free. Photography is permitted but you will have to buy a camera ticket for Dh 5 for still cameras, Dh 10 for videos.

The fort was built in the late 18th century and served as the ruler's palace and office until 1970. From 1970 to 1978, it was Ajman's main police station. The police moved out of most of the complex in 1978 (they still occupy a few buildings attached to the fort but opening onto Shaikh Khalifa St) and renovation work on the building began. It was opened as a museum in 1981. It is one of the best museums in the UAE and is well worth the drive from Dubai.

The museum is very well laid out. The displays include a collection of manuscripts, weapons, archaeological finds and reconstructions of traditional rooms. Also on display are gifts and decorations the Emir has received over the years. Everything is labelled in both Arabic and English, except for one section of the Police Exhibit which deals with capital punishment and includes before and after photos of someone facing a firing squad.

Until fairly recently, Ajman issued its own passports. Some of these are on display, including Ajman Passport No 1 which belonged to the present Emir's father, Sheikh Rashid. It is a diplomatic passport.

There is also a quite effective reconstruction of a traditional street in a souk. It's at the far edge of the main courtyard, opposite the museum entrance.

Immediately to your right as you come in through the gate is a reconstructed tomb from the Umm Al-Nar civilisation. The tomb was excavated in the Mowaihat area and moved to the museum after suffering water damage.

The museum shop is worth a look both for its map of the city and its small collection of local handicrafts. They also sell a guide to the museum for Dh 5.

### Beaches

There are several public beaches in Ajman town, particularly around the Ajman Beach Hotel. A smaller public beach can also be found on Arabian Gulf St, just south of the Ajman Tourist Centre.

### Souks

Fruit and vegetables and meat and fish are sold in two purpose-built souk areas along the coast, off Leewara St. The best time to come is early in the morning, around 7 or 8 am, when the fishers are back in port with the day's catch and the fish souk is at its busiest.

### Places to Stay & Eat

The only place to stay in Ajman is the *Ajman Beach Hotel* (☎ 423333). It has decent singles/doubles for Dh 145/210.

The *Kuwait Restaurant*, at the junction of Humaid Bin Abdul Aziz St and Abu Baker Al-Siddiq St, has good biryanis for Dh 6. A few other Indian food items are also available. You'll find a number of similar places along Leewara St. The *Dhow Restaurant* is actually a coffee house in a traditional barasti shelter along the waterfront. It's a nice place for a cup of coffee or tea late in the afternoon. Look for the blue-and-white sign with three coffee pots on it.

### Getting There & Away

Ajman has no bus service and there's no taxi stand. But taxi drivers on the Sharjah route don't mind travelling here as it's only a few extra km. After dropping a passenger off they'll cruise around the centre looking for passengers and then head back to the taxi stand in Sharjah. From Sharjah a taxi ride to Ajman costs Dh 20 or Dh 30.

### AROUND AJMAN
### Manama

This Manama is an enclave of Ajman lying near the junction of the southbound road from Ras Al-Khaimah and the east-west road linking Dubai and Sharjah with the east

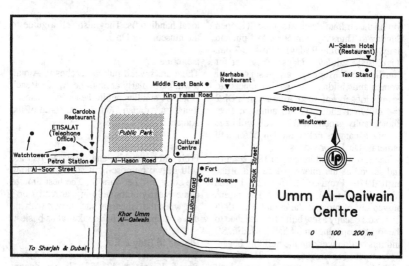

coast. It is an oasis town in the midst of a heavily agricultural area.

The town is mainly the set of shops bordering on the roundabout with the miniature Eiffel Tower. It consists of a few small Indo-Arab restaurants and grocery stores, a couple of garages and a petrol station.

The only thing to see is the **fort** near the main roundabout. It is quite well preserved, probably because the police still use it. It is not open to the public. Steer well clear of the red fort on the edge of town and do not attempt to photograph it. It is part of an army base.

## UMM AL-QAIWAIN

With a population of around 40,000, Umm Al-Qaiwain (Umm Al-Quwain, Umm Al-Qawain) is the least populous of the seven emirates.

When the British announced that they would withdraw from the Gulf in 1971, all of the emirs initially wanted complete independence. After Bahrain and Qatar pulled out of a proposed federation, it was largely British pressure that convinced the emirs of the Trucial States that they could not each go it alone.

Today the attraction of this small and relatively remote emirate is its very isolation. More than any other place in the UAE, Umm Al-Qaiwain provides a glimpse of what life throughout the country was like not so long ago. There are no high-rise buildings in the town centre and the pace of life is still unhurried. It's definitely worth the hour or so drive from Dubai.

## Orientation & Information

Umm Al-Qaiwain lies on a narrow peninsula of sand jutting north from the main road linking Dubai and Sharjah with Ras Al-Khaimah. The old town and the emirate's small business district are at the northern tip of the peninsula, particularly along King Faisal Rd after it splits into a loop. Most of the streets are not signposted but it is hard to get lost in a place this small.

The post office is south of the centre near the stadium. The ETISALAT office is in the centre at the junction of Al-Hason Rd and the main road from Sharjah and Dubai, though a new telephone office is under construction several km to the south near the Hospital Roundabout. The telephone code for Umm Al-Qaiwain is 06.

## Things to See & Do

The small **fort** at the intersection of Al-Hason Rd and Al-Lubna Rd is not much to look at and it's usually closed as well. The **mosque** next to the fort is a bit more interesting. It has a largely open design. An inscription over the doorway dates its construction to circa 1869 (1286 AH). Along the coast the fort and mosque you can see a few dhows and fishers but there is not a lot left of the old harbour atmosphere. A few old **watchtowers** are scattered around town, including two near the ETISALAT office.

For activities, the Marine Club & Riding Centre (☎ 666644, 665446) offers water-skiing, windsurfing and horseback-riding.

## Places to Stay & Eat

Both of Umm Al-Qaiwain's hotels are south of the centre, and neither is cheap. On the peninsula's eastern side, the *Pearl Hotel* (☎ 666672), about five km south of the town centre, has singles/doubles for Dh 225/250. Another km back toward the centre and on the western side of the peninsula is the *Umm Al-Quwain Beach Hotel* (☎ 666647), a slightly musty place which rents bungalows by the bedroom: one bedroom for Dh 350 per night, two bedrooms for Dh 500. To get there, turn right at the T-junction after you get off the main road.

Both of the hotels have restaurants. The centre also has a collection of tiny places serving kebabs and Indian biryanis. Try the *Cardoba Restaurant* next to the ETISALAT office on King Faisal St.

## Getting There & Away

Without your own car the only way in or out of Umm Al-Qaiwain is by taxi. The taxi stand is on King Faisal Rd, across from the Al-Salam Hotel (which is actually a restaurant). A seat in a shared taxi to Dubai, Sharjah or Ajman costs Dh 7. If you want to go to Ras Al-Khaimah, you will have to take the taxi 'engaged' (ie, by yourself and paying for all seven seats in it). With some bargaining this will probably cost about Dh 50.

You could, in theory, get from Dubai to Umm Al-Qaiwain and back the same day by service taxi (with your own car you could do it in under two hours), but there does not seem to be a lot of action at the taxi stand in Umm Al-Qaiwain, and taxis bound for Umm Al-Qaiwain do not fill up quickly in Dubai either. Be prepared both for a long wait and for a possible engaged ride back to Dubai.

## RAS AL-KHAIMAH

Ras Al-Khaimah is one of the most beautiful spots in the UAE. It is the northernmost and the most fertile of the emirates. Much of its land has been carefully irrigated and the result is an area of abundant greenery on the edge of both the mountains and the desert. The city is relaxing, has its share of interesting sites and is a good base for exploring the countryside. Ras Al-Khaimah is a favourite weekend getaway for people from Dubai and is also increasingly popular with package tourists from Scandinavia.

## History

Flints and potsherds found near the Khatt Hot Springs indicate that Ras Al-Khaimah has been inhabited since the 3rd millennium BC. For much of its history the region's main town was Julfar, a few km to the north of the modern city of Ras Al-Khaimah.

By the 7th century AD, Julfar was an important port and the 12th century Arab geographer Al-Idrisi mentions it as a pearling centre. Pottery and other finds from this era indicate that Julfar had significant trade links with both China and India. In the 15th century Julfar was the birthplace of Ahmed Bin Majid, the great Arab sailor whose books on navigation are still studied and who was hired by Vasco de Gama to guide him to India in 1498.

In the early 16th century, the Portuguese occupied Julfar where they built a customs house and, in 1631, a fort. No trace of either of these remains today and their exact location is uncertain. The Portuguese abandoned the fort and the town in 1633 after a series of attacks by both the local tribes and the British and Dutch navies. By the time they left, Julfar was apparently in ruins because its

Arab inhabitants moved to Ras Al-Khaimah despite the fact that they had won the war.

The Al-Qasimi family rules both Ras Al-Khaimah and Sharjah, tracing its ancestry to an 18th century sheikh from Ras Al-Khaimah. Throughout the 18th century the Qawasim, as the ruling clan was known, were the most powerful rulers in the lower Gulf and by the beginning of the 19th century they had a large fleet. The early 19th century British raids on the Qawasim-controlled coast were partly in retaliation for attacks on British shipping, but they were also prompted by a belief that the Qawasim posed a threat to Oman's independence. Britain had a treaty with the Omanis and regarded Oman's independence as crucial to the protection of its own supply lines to India.

In 1809, the British raided Ras Al-Khaimah and briefly occupied it. Ten years later, they again invaded and occupied the town, besieging the inhabitants of both Ras Al-Khaimah and Rams at Dhayah. The hilltop fortress at Dhayah, to which the inhabitants retreated, can still be seen. The British withdrew after imposing a General Treaty of Peace on the sheikhs of the coast in 1820 and the Qawasim never quite recovered their previous power and status.

It was with this history in mind that Ras al-Khaimah initially chose to stay out of the UAE when the federation was formed in December 1971. Three months later the ruler changed his mind, apparently after concluding that the emirate couldn't survive as an independent state. Small quantities of oil were discovered in Ras Al-Khaimah in 1976 but the revenues from this have never amounted to much.

Today, Ras Al-Khaimah's economy is based mainly on agriculture (particularly vegetables and citrus fruits), and it is sometimes referred to as the breadbasket of the UAE. There are also relatively small cement and petrochemical plants and an increasingly important tourism industry.

Ras Al-Khaimah is said to have the largest number of indigenous Arabs of any of the emirates. It has no long-established Indian or Persian merchant communities like Dubai or Sharjah. It is the only place in the UAE where, as in Saudi Arabia, all shops are required to close at prayer time.

## Orientation

Ras Al-Khaimah is really two cities. Ras Al-Khaimah proper, which is the old town on a sandy peninsula along the Gulf coast, and Al-Nakheel, the newer business district on the other side of Ras Al-Khaimah's creek. There is a bridge across the creek and another road to the south which skirts the water's edge. Only a few of the streets in either town have names and there are no street signs.

Aside from the museum and the Old Town's souk, there isn't very much to Ras Al-Khaimah proper. Most of the hotels and services, and even the city's lone traditional coffee house, are in Al-Nakheel.

Most of Al-Nakheel's shops and offices are on Oman St, between the Hospital Roundabout and the Cinema Roundabout. This area includes the city's one cheap hotel and a number of small restaurants.

## Information

You can find out what's happening by checking the activities boards in the lobby of the Bin Majid Beach Hotel or the Ras Al-Khaimah Hotel. These are also the best places to go if you want to book a tour.

You can change money at any of the many banks along Al-Sabah St in Ras Al-Khaimah or Oman St in Al-Nakheel.

The GPO is on King Faisal St, a short distance north of the Bin Majid Beach Hotel. The ETISALAT office is one km east of the Cinema Roundabout in Al-Nakheel. It is open Saturday to Thursday from 7 am to 8 pm and Friday from 9 am to 8 pm. The telephone code for Ras Al-Khaimah is 07.

## Ras Al-Khaimah Museum

The museum is in the old fort on Al-Hosen Rd, next to the police headquarters. It is open from 8 am to noon and from 4 to 7 pm daily except Tuesday. Thursdays are for women only and admission is Dh 2. All the signs are in both Arabic and English and a good guide-

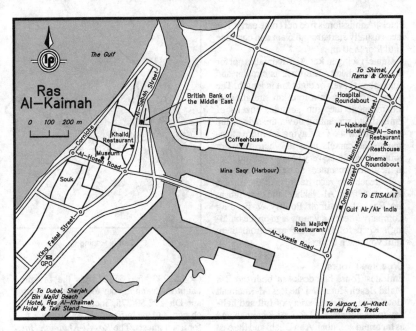

book is on sale at the gate for Dh 10. The fort was built in the mid-18th century. Until the early 1960s it was the residence of the ruling Al-Qasimi sheikhs.

One room on the ground floor has a particularly good display of Arabian silver jewellery and another room features a collection of sea shells from all over the UAE. The lower floor also includes exhibits on Ras Al-Khaimah's archaeology and ethnography and the region's natural history. The highlight of the upper floor is the working wind tower, beneath which you should definitely take a moment to sit. A few of the other rooms upstairs are also open to the public though they are not furnished. The upper floor also houses a display on the ruling family and the museum offices.

### The Old Town

Ras Al-Khaimah's old town is a wonderful place to stroll around. The souk area, south of the museum, has a number of small tailors'

shops but the main attraction is the unspoiled atmosphere. Ras Al-Khaimah welcomes tourists without bending itself out of shape to cater to them. The other part of the old town worth seeing is the km or so of coast immediately north of the bridge, including the old fishing port.

### Activities

**Water Sports** Water sports are being promoted by both the Bin Majid Beach Hotel and the Ras Al-Khaimah Hotel. If you are staying in one of these places they can provide you with more information on windsurfing, water-skiing, diving, etc.

**Camel Racing** Ras Al-Khaimah's camel race track is one of the best in the country. It is in Digdagga, about 10 km south of town. Races usually take place on Fridays during the winter and sometimes also on Tuesday or Wednesday. The schedule is irregular, so ask locally or check with the tour operators at the hotels. Admission is free but come early. The races usually start around 6 am and continue until 9 or 9.30 am.

Camel racing in Ras Al-Khaimah is not for the faint of heart. The track is circular and huge, about seven or eight km in length. The races take place on a four-km straight and, the moment the gun sounds, dozens of Emiratis go screaming down the side of the track in their 4WDs, paying far more attention to the camels than to where they are going. It would be *very* easy to get run over in these circumstances so be careful.

To reach the race track, take the airport road south from Al-Nakheel and turn right at the Ras Al-Khaimah Poultry & Feeding Company (there's a yellow sign on the building). Keep following the road from there until you reach the track.

### Organised Tours

Emirates Tours has desks in both the Bin Majid Beach Hotel and the Ras Al-Khaimah Hotel. They offer a variety of full and half-day tours both around Ras Al-Khaimah and as far afield as Dubai, Abu Dhabi and the east coast. They can also arrange desert camping safaris. Call 225611 or 335611 and then wait for them to call you back (both are pager numbers).

### Places to Stay

There are four hotels in Ras Al-Khaimah. The one cheapie is the *Al-Sana Restaurant & Resthouse* (☎ 224849), a great place run by a friendly Filipino named Rojier who is also the head of the local Filipino club. The rooms are spotless and a few have kitchenettes. Singles/doubles are Dh 60/80. You'll find it behind the Al-Nakheel Hotel, between Oman and Muntaser Sts in Al-Nakheel.

The *Al-Nakhel Hotel* (☎ 222822), on Muntaser St in Al-Nakheel, has the cheapest bar in town but not much else to recommend it. Rooms are Dh 100/150.

The two top-end hotels can both arrange visas for tourists, though if you're coming in through the airport of Dubai or Sharjah it would be a good idea to give them two weeks or more warning. The *Bin Majid Beach Hotel*

Camel Racing

(☎ 352233, fax 353225) is the favoured haunt of Scandinavian tour groups. Rooms are Dh 192.50/275, including the service charge, and the buffet lunch on Friday is free for hotel guests. The *Ras Al-Khaimah Hotel* (☎ 352999, fax 352990) has rooms for Dh 264/374, including service, during the week and only for Dh 125/175 on Thursday and Friday nights. At the weekend rate it is a very good deal.

### Places to Eat

Even if you are not staying there I highly recommend the *Al-Sana Restaurant & Resthouse*. They have Western, Chinese and Filipino food. Meals should not run to more than Dh 15 to Dh 20. In the Old Town, try the *Khalid Restaurant* on Al-Sabah St for cheap Indian fare.

For a more up-market meal don't miss the *Ibin Majid Restaurant*, an excellent Lebanese place on Al-Muntaser St in Al-Nakheel just north of the junction with Al-Juwais Rd.

You should also drop in at the *Coffeehouse*, the last of Ras Al-Khaimah's old-style coffee houses. It is in an unmarked barasti structure near Mina Saqr, next to the garish *Tourists Cafeteria*. Very sweet tea costs 50 fils a cup.

## Entertainment

There's a disco at the Bin Majid Beach Hotel, and lounge acts will assault your ears in the bars at all three of the more up-market hotels. The Ras Al-Khaimah Hotel's Piano Bar is probably the least offensive of the lot while the bar at the Al-Nakheel certainly wins the local prize for tastelessness. The clientele is largely a combination of British expats and Scandinavian tourists down from the Bin Majid for a change of scenery.

## Getting There & Away

**Air** Ras Al-Khaimah's small airport is 22.5 km south of Al-Nakheel. Three airlines operate international services to Ras Al-Khaimah. Gulf Air has weekly flights from Ras Al-Khaimah to Bahrain, Bombay, Doha, Karachi and Muscat. Air India flies once a week to Bombay and EgyptAir has a weekly flight to Cairo. For airport information ring 448000. Their addresses in Ras Al-Khaimah are:

Air India
    Oman St, Al-Nakheel, between Al-Juwais Rd
    and the Cinema Roundabout (☎ 227536)
EgyptAir
    Al-Sabah St, Ras Al-Khaimah Old Town
    (☎ 335000)
Gulf Air
    Oman St, Al-Nakheel, between Al-Juwais Rd
    and the Cinema Roundabout (☎ 221531)

**Service Taxi** Ras Al-Khaimah's taxi stand is on King Faisal St, just south of the Bin Majid Beach Hotel and on the same side. Taxis leave when full, taking either five or seven passengers. Taxis to Dubai and Sharjah charge Dh 15 per person. For the same price, the driver might drop you off in Ajman or Umm Al-Qaiwain if you ask nicely. Taxis to Abu Dhabi charge Dh 50. Fujairah taxis cost Dh 20 though unless you have a group of people large enough to fill the taxi, you will probably have to take it engaged. Taking a taxi engaged to Dubai costs Dh 100.

Local service-taxi destinations north of Ras Al-Khaimah include Rams, Dh 6; Khor Khowair, Dh 8; and Sham, Dh 9.

Taxis into Ras Al-Khaimah's centre are Dh 2 shared and Dh 10 engaged.

**Car** You can rent cars in the hotels or from one of the small agencies along Oman St in Al-Nakheel.

## Getting Around

Taxis are without meters. Fares within Ras Al-Khaimah town or within Al-Nakheel are about Dh 5 engaged and Dh 1.50 to Dh 2 shared. Between Ras Al-Khaimah and Al-Nakheel, expect to pay Dh 10 (engaged) and Dh 2 (regular).

## AROUND RAS AL-KHAIMAH

Ras Al-Khaimah is a perfect base for exploring the northern tip of the UAE. Several interesting archaeological sites and the Khatt Hot Springs are within easy driving distance. In fact, it would not be too hard to cover everything listed here in one day provided you get an early start. None of the archaeological sites listed here are fenced in so you can approach them throughout the day. To visit most of these places, you'll need to have a car or to hire a taxi.

## Shimal

The village of Shimal, five km north of Ras Al-Khaimah, is the site of some of the most important archaeological finds in the UAE. The area has been inhabited at least since the 2nd millennium BC when, excavations have shown, it was one of the largest settlements in this part of Arabia.

The main attraction is the **Queen of Sheba's Palace**, a set of ruined buildings and fortifications spread over two small plateaus overlooking the village. On a clear day the view is great. Despite its name, the palace was not built by the Queen of Sheba who is generally thought to have come from what is now Yemen. It may, however, have been visited by Queen Zenobia who ruled a sizeable chunk of the Near East in the 4th century AD from Palmyra in modern Syria. The fortifications are known to have been in use as recently as the 16th century. What is visible today apparently sits on top of an older structure.

To reach the site go north for 4.5 km from the Hospital Roundabout (which is just a set of traffic lights) in Al-Nakheel and turn right onto a paved road. There are three signs in Arabic pointing toward various places in Shimal. Look for a white sign with the UAE crest and a big red arrow (for those who read Arabic, the sign points to the Shimal Health Centre). Follow this road for about 1.5 km until you reach a roundabout and take the first right turn out of the roundabout. Follow the road for another 2.3 km and take the first paved turn to the left. After about 400 metres the pavement ends; keep going straight on a dirt track through the village. You'll pass a small mosque after which the track forks; take the right-hand track. After a few hundred metres you will come to a hill which is lighter in colour than the higher hills behind it. You will see a fence around the hill and a locked gate immediately in front of you. Keep going in the same direction, keeping the hill on your right. About one km after the place where the road ended you'll come to a parking area in the village and an opening in the fence. Park here.

Getting to the top of the hill involves a fairly easy five or 10-minute climb. As you start up the hill you will see a ruined cistern which looks like a stone box. Once you've passed it, head for the wall across the cleft in the hill.

## Rams

A quiet village 12 km north of Ras Al-Khaimah, Rams has a nice coastline and a few old **watchtowers**. Rams has played an important role in Ras Al-Khaimah's history. It was one of the sites at which the British fleet landed in 1819 during the invasion of the lower Gulf which led, the following year, to the area coming under de facto British rule.

Coming from Ras Al-Khaimah, the easiest way to access the town is by taking the second Rams turn-off.

Service taxis between Rams and Ras Al-Khaimah cost Dh 6 per person.

## Dhayah

Another 3.5 km beyond Rams is Dhayah, a small village beneath a ruined fort. It was here that the people of Rams retreated in the face of the advancing British in 1819 and surrendered after a four-day siege.

The **fort** sits atop a sharp, cone-shaped hill behind the modern village. It takes 15 to 20 minutes to climb the hill, longer if you stop to collect some of the numerous sea shells which blanket the slopes. Be careful, however, the rock is very loose and it's easy to slip. The easiest approach is from the west side of the hill (the side facing the sea), moving toward the south side as you ascend. Once you get to the top the only easy way into the fort is through the south wall.

To reach the hill, turn right off the road from Ras Al-Khaimah immediately after you pass Dhayah's new white mosque and the Lehamoodi Grocery, both of which are also on the right (the turn is 14.5 km north of the Hospital Roundabout). If you pass a sign saying 'Sha'm 15 km', you have gone too far. Leaving the main road you follow a dirt track which swings around to the right behind the village. After about 500 metres you'll see the Al-Adal Grocery; keep to the left of this and continue for another 300 metres. When the main track swings around to the left continue straight on a smaller track toward an old watchtower which you pass on your left. From there the track twists around for another 400 metres; take a right turn and then proceed for another 300 metres straight toward the hill and park on its north side.

There are some more ruined fortifications just south of the hill.

## Khatt Hot Springs

The popular Khatt Hot Springs are open daily from 5.30 am to 10.30 pm. Admission is Dh 3. The scenery on the drive is quite nice. Head south out of Al-Nakheel following the signs for the airport; you'll see signs for Khatt further along the road. The spring is just over eight km from the centre. When you reach the roundabout in the village of Khatt, turn left. The spring is another 800 metres down the road.

# The East Coast

The east coast is the most beautiful part of the UAE. Fujairah, the only emirate without any territory on the Gulf, dominates the east coast. However, several of the area's towns, including Khor Fakkan, are part of the Sharjah Emirate. There is even a small enclave of Omani territory between Fujairah and Khor Fakkan which is entirely surrounded by the UAE.

## FUJAIRAH

Fujairah is the youngest of the seven emirates – it was part of Sharjah until 1952. Its youth and location overlooking the Gulf of Oman distinguishes Fujairah from the other emirates. Fujairah is not cheap but it is attractive and a good base for exploring the east coast.

## Orientation

Fujairah is quite spread out but most of the services travellers will need are in a fairly compact area. The main business area is Hamad Bin Abdulla Rd, between the Fujairah Trade Centre and the coast. Along this stretch of road you will find the main post office, several banks and, at the intersection with the coast road, the central market. There is a concentration of good, cheap restaurants near the Hilton hotel.

The coastal road changes its name three times, which can be confusing. Passing through the city from south to north it is called Regalath Rd, Gurfah Rd and Al-Faseel Rd, in that order.

## Information

**Money** There are a number of banks on or near the roundabout at the intersection of Shaikh Zayed Bin Sultan and Hamad Bin Abdulla Rds.

**Post & Telecommunications** The GPO is at the intersection of Al-Sharqi and Hamad Bin Abdulla Rds. It is open Saturday to Wednesday from 8 am to 2 pm and 3 to 9 pm,

Thursday from 8 am to 1 pm and 2 to 7 pm, and Friday from 8 to 11 am. The ETISALAT office is on Al-Nakheel Rd, between Fahim Rd and Shaikh Zayed Bin Sultan Rd. It is open daily from 7 am to 9 pm.

The telephone code for Fujairah is 09.

## Fujairah Museum

Fujairah's museum is the newest in the UAE, having opened to the public at the end of 1991. The museum, at the intersection of Al-Nakheel and Madab Rds, is open daily from 8 am to noon and 4 to 6 pm. Admission is Dh 2. It has an archaeology gallery and an ethnographic display. The former is much the more interesting of the two.

Most of the items displayed in the archaeology gallery come from the digs at Badiyah, Qidfa and Bithna. Particularly interesting is the container made from an ostrich egg, found intact at Qidfa, 18 km north of Fujairah. Everything in the archaeology gallery is labelled in both Arabic and English.

The ethnographic display has a collection of old photographs, weapons, clothing, tools and household articles. There are also a few unusual items, such as the portable rope, wood and leather contraption which was used to haul water from wells. The signs in the ethnographic gallery are mostly in Arabic.

In the museum's courtyard you will find a full-scale barasti house, complete with a 'laundry' that has been hung out to dry.

## The Old Town

Spooky might be the best word to describe the Old Town, which consists of a fort at least 300 years old overlooking the ruins of old Fujairah. The fort has been partially restored but little else here seems to have been touched since the inhabitants moved south to the site of the modern city a generation or so ago.

## Ain Al-Madab Garden

On the edge of town, this park-cum-hotel is a pretty sorry sight as none of the kiddie rides dotted around the park looked as if they had

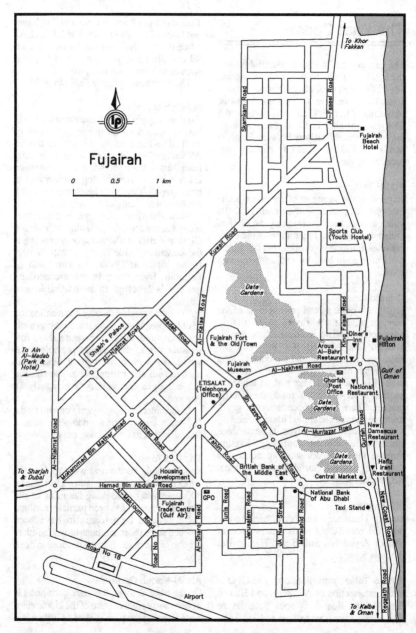

Fujairah

been used in a very long time. Only the swimming pools seem to be in regular use. The garden is open during daylight hours and admission is Dh 2. They also rent out rooms at Dh 100/200 for singles/doubles in mobile homes which serve as a hotel.

## Kalba

The largely residential town of Kalba, just south of Fujairah, is part of the Sharjah emirate. It has nice beaches and a hotel (see Places to Stay).

## Places to Stay

Fujairah's *Youth Hostel* (no telephone) on Al-Faseel Rd is OK at Dh 15 per bed. However, they cater mostly to local teenagers travelling in groups and it appears that they are not used to tourists (the management seemed a bit put off by the idea of accommodating a foreigner). You'll need to have a hostel card and, as elsewhere in the UAE, it's for men only.

There are only two hotels in Fujairah and neither is cheap. The *Fujairah Beach Hotel* (☎ 228054) is several km north of the centre. It is a good, if slightly musty, place where teenage Emirati boys hang out in the bar and use the hotel's stereo system to play at being rap DJs. Single/double rooms cost are Dh 150/200. The *Fujairah Hilton* (☎ 222411, fax 226541) has the sort of facilities you would expect at a Hilton. Rooms are Dh 310/380. They sometimes offer cheap weekend packages on Thursdays and Fridays. The Hilton will sponsor visas for tourists with 15 days notice.

In Kalba, the *Marine Hotel* (☎ 778877, fax 776769) is 13 km south of Fujairah on the coast road. Rooms are Dh 250/300. Note that Kalba is part of the Sharjah Emirate so the hotel does not serve alcohol.

## Places to Eat

The *Diner's Inn* on Al-Faseel Rd, across from the Hilton, has good cheap Indian and Chinese food served in reasonably large

helpings. Meals can cost as little as Dh 8 to Dh 10. Nearby, also on Al-Faseel Rd but on the other side of the intersection with Al-Nakheel Rd, the *National Restaurant* has cheap chicken, rice and biryani dishes. The *Hafiz Irani Restaurant* on Gurfah Rd offers an Iranian menu though it looks a lot like the fare at the National. Just up the street the *New Damascus Restaurant* has pretty much the same menu, only here it's called 'Arab'. A meal at any of these places costs about Dh 10.

A bit more up-market is *Arous Al-Bahr*, a medium-priced Lebanese restaurant with mezza at Dh 5 to Dh 15 and main dishes from Dh 10 to Dh 25. It is at the intersection of Al-Nakheel and Al-Faseel Rds.

## Getting There & Away

**Air** Fujairah International Airport is served by Gulf Air (two weekly flights to Bahrain and two to Muscat) and Air India (one flight a week to Bombay). It is on the southern edge of town. Gulf Air's office (☎ 226969) is in the Trade Centre on Hamad Bin Abdulla Rd. Air India (☎ 222524) is on Al-Faseel Rd across from the Hilton.

**Service Taxi** The taxi stand is on Regalath Rd. The fare to Dubai, Sharjah or Ras Al-Khaimah is Dh 25 per person (though don't hold your breath waiting for taxis to Ras Al-Khaimah to fill up). Seats to Abu Dhabi and Al-Ain are Dh 50; Dibba, Dh 15; and Khor Fakkan, Dh 5. The only places to which taxis seem to travel with any regularity are Dubai, Sharjah, Khor Fakkan and Dibba. There are no inter-city buses to or from Fujairah.

## Getting Around

**Car Rental** Dubai Rent-A-Car has an office opposite the Hilton hotel. A smaller place, Omar Rent-A-Car, is on the north side of the same building.

**Taxi** There are no local buses in Fujairah, so if you don't have a car you are at the mercy of the taxis which have no meters. Fares around town should not exceed Dh 5. Hiring a taxi by the hour should cost about Dh 20.

## BITHNA

The village of Bithna, in the mountains about 12 km from Fujairah, has several interesting archaeological sites. It is an easy trip from Fujairah (even by taxi it should not be too expensive) and well worth the effort. Before coming to Bithna, try to visit the Fujairah museum as it has a particularly detailed display on the T-Shaped Site. You can also ask at the museum about arranging a visit to the site.

The **T-Shaped Site**, or the Long Chambered Tomb, is fenced-in though part of the excavations are visible. The tomb was excavated in 1988 and is thought to have been a communal burial place. Its main period of use appears to have been between 1350 and 300 BC but the tomb itself may date from an earlier period. About 10 skeletons were found during the excavation, and there was evidence that the tomb had been reused several times.

The other site of note in Bithna is the **Fort** which is more impressive than its counterpart in Fujairah. The fort was important until fairly recently because it controlled the main pass through which the highway now cuts into Fujairah.

To reach the sites take the main road from Fujairah inland toward Sharjah and Dubai. About 12 km out of Fujairah, turn right at the exit marked 'Bithnah'; the town will be to the right of the road. After about 250 metres, the street becomes a dirt road in front of a small building containing a tailor's shop and a laundry. Keep following the straightish dirt road for about 300 metres and then go down over the lip of the hill and turn right. Follow the road for another 600 metres, keeping left in the two places where it forks. After going up a final small, steep slope you'll see the fort on the right.

The tomb is fleetingly visible from the main road as you approach the town from Fujairah. It is easily identified by the makeshift sun shade covering the site. To reach it, take the Bithna exit and make a 90° turn to

the right instead of going straight toward the tailor's shop and laundry. Follow the track through the village, keeping roughly parallel to the main road (as though headed back toward Fujairah) until you reach the site.

## QIDFA

Near this village, 18 km north of Fujairah on the road to Khor Fakkan, you will notice a turn on the inland side of the road (on the left if you are coming from Fujairah) with a sign welcoming you to the Omani Governate of Musandem. This marks the boundary of a small Omani enclave completely surrounded by the UAE.

## KHOR FAKKAN

One of Sharjah's enclaves and the largest town on the east coast after Fujairah, Khor Fakkan is a large port with a long, scenic corniche. It's also a trendy weekend resort, but while the port has proved to be a roaring success, the development of tourism has been somewhat held back by Sharjah's ban on alcohol.

The four-km-long corniche is bounded by the port at the south end and the luxury Oceanic Hotel to the north with lots of nice beaches in between. The swimming is good but all those tyre tracks in the sand are a dead giveaway about the favourite pastime of the local male teenagers: roaring up and down the beach in their 4WDs. Need I advise caution? Other activities, such as sailing and water-skiing, are largely concentrated at the Oceanic which has a fence around its stretch of beach largely, the manager told me, to keep away the 4WD brigade. There is very little to see except for a few lonely looking watchtowers perched on the hills above the city. The fort which once dominated the coast is long gone.

Singles/doubles at the *Oceanic Hotel* (☎ (09) 385111) cost Dh 253/330, including the service charge. On Thursday and Friday the rates drop to Dh 192.50/253. The only other place to stay in Khor Fakkan is the *Al-Khaleej Hotel* (☎ (09) 387336), about 3.5

km inland on the road to Fujairah. Coming from Fujairah it is one of the first buildings you will see upon entering Khor Fakkan. It's on the right. They only have doubles which cost Dh 100.

There are lots of small restaurants on the road from Fujairah between the Al-Khaleej hotel and the corniche. On the corniche there are two seaside restaurants north of the roundabout which marks both the corniche's midpoint and the junction with the road from Fujairah. The *Lebanon Restaurant* is rather the better of the two, with both Lebanese mezza and the usual cheap Indian fare of biryanis and tikka dishes. The restaurant on the top floor of the Oceanic is expensive but try to drop in for a cup of coffee and a chance to admire the view over the bay.

## BADIYAH

Badiyah, eight km north of Khor Fakkan but in the Fujairah Emirate, is one of the oldest towns in the Gulf. Archaeological digs have shown that the site of the town has been settled more or less continuously since the 3rd millennium BC. There is evidence that tombs of that era which have been found here were reused down into Hellenistic times (ie, as recently as the 1st century BC), though no inhabited sites from that era have been discovered so far in the Fujairah area.

Today, Badiyah is known mainly for its **mosque**, a small whitewashed structure of stone, mud-brick and gypsum which is the oldest mosque in the UAE. Its exact date of construction is uncertain but was probably not much more than a few hundred years ago. The mosque is still in use. It is built into a low hillside along the main road just north of the village. On the hillside above and behind the mosque are several ruined **watchtowers**.

There is no place to stay in Badiyah but six km to the north, near the village of Al-Aqqa, there's the *Sandy Beach Motel* (☎ (09)

445354). Singles/doubles are Dh 300/450 in bungalows near the sea.

## DIBBA

Dibba's name lives in Islamic history as the site of one of the great battles of the Ridda Wars, the reconquest of Arabia by Muslim armies in the generation after the death of the Prophet. The Muslims were fighting against a number of tribes and towns which had sworn allegiance to Mohammed during his lifetime but did not feel themselves bound to the new religion following his death. The victory at Dibba in 633, a year after the Prophet's death, traditionally marks the end of the Muslim reconquest of Arabia.

Today, Dibba is a quiet set of seaside villages. In fact, there are three Dibbas, each belonging to a different ruler: Dibba Muhallab (Fujairah), Dibba Hisn (Sharjah) and Dibba Bayah (Oman). As at Al-Ain, you can walk or drive freely across the Omani border and explore some of the Omani villages at the southern edge of the spectacular Musandem Peninsula. However, this does not seem to be formalised and accepted to the extent that it is at Buraimi, and the Omani police may turn you back if they spot you. If driving, remember that once you are across the border your UAE car insurance is invalid. Also remember that use of seat belts is mandatory in Oman.

Dibba is a really nice spot. The *UAE – A MEED Practical Guide* compares the area to an Italian fishing village, which may be over-doing it a bit. There is nothing to see except the **fort** in Dibba Hisn, which is still used by the police, and there are no hotels but the quiet pace of life makes it worth the trip. Since Dibba is only 145 km from Dubai, a popular weekend excursion is to make a loop from Dubai via Fujairah, Khor Fakkan, Badiyah and Dibba.

# Index

## Keep in touch!

We love hearing from you and think you'd like to hear from us.

The Lonely Planet Newsletter covers the when, where, how and what of travel. (AND it's free!)

*When...is the right time to see reindeer in Finland?*
*Where...can you hear the best palm-wine music in Ghana?*
*How...do you get from Asunción to Areguá by steam train?*
*What...should you leave behind to avoid hassles with customs in Iran?*

To join our mailing list just contact us at any of our offices. (details below)

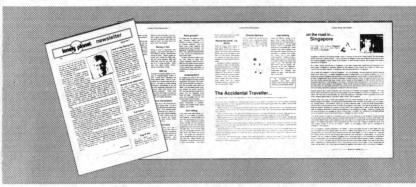

*Every issue includes:*

- *a letter from Lonely Planet founders Tony and Maureen Wheeler*
- *travel diary from a Lonely Planet author - find out what it's really like out on the road*
- *feature article on an important and topical travel issue*
- *a selection of recent letters from our readers*
- *the latest travel news from all over the world*
- *details on Lonely Planet's new and forthcoming releases*

**Also available Lonely Planet T-shirts. 100% heavy weight cotton (S, M, L, XL)**

## LONELY PLANET PUBLICATIONS
**Australia:** PO Box 617, Hawthorn, 3122, Victoria (tel: 03-819 1877)
**USA:** Embarcadero West, 155 Filbert Street, Suite 251, Oakland, CA 94607 (tel: 510-893 8555)
**UK:** Devonshire House, 12 Barley Mow Passage, Chiswick, London W4 4PH (tel: 081-742 3161)

# Guides to the Middle East

### *Egypt & the Sudan - a travel survival kit*
This guide takes you into and beyond the spectacular pyramids, temples, tombs, monasteries and mosques, and the bustling main streets of these fascinating countries to discover their incredible beauty, unusual sights and friendly people.

### *Iran - a travel survival kit*
The first English-language guide to this enigmatic and surprisingly hospitable country written since the Islamic Revolution. As well as practical travel details the author provides background information that will fascinate adventurers and armchair travellers alike.

### *Jordan & Syria - a travel survival kit*
Two countries away from the usual travel routes, but with a wealth of natural and historical attractions for the adventurous traveller...12th century Crusader castles, ruined cities, the ancient Nabatean capital of Petra and haunting desert landscapes.

### *Turkey - a travel survival kit*
This acclaimed guide takes you from Istanbul bazaars to Mediterranean beaches, from historic battlegrounds to the stamping grounds of St Paul, Alexander the Great, the Emperor Constantine, King Croesus and Omar Khayyam.

### *Trekking in Turkey*
Explore beyond Turkey's coastline and you will be surprised to discover that Turkey has mountains with walks to rival those found in Nepal.

### *Yemen - a travel survival kit*
The Yemen is one of the oldest inhabited regions in the world. This practical guide gives full details on a genuinely different travel experience.

### *West Asia on a shoestring*
Want to cruise to Asia for 15 cents? Drink a great cup of tea while you view Mt Everest? Find the Garden of Eden? This guide has the complete story on the Asian overland trail from Bangladesh to Turkey, including Bhutan, India, Iran, the Maldives, Nepal, Pakistan, Sri Lanka and the Middle East.

### *Also available:*
**Arabic (Egyptian)** phrasebook, **Arabic (Moroccan)** phrasebook and **Turkish** phrasebook.

# Lonely Planet Guidebooks

Lonely Planet guidebooks cover every accessible part of Asia as well as Australia, the Pacific, South America, Africa, the Middle East, Europe and parts of North America. There are five series: *travel survival kits*, covering a country for a range of budgets; *shoestring guides* with compact information for low-budget travel in a major region; *walking guides*; *city guides* and *phrasebooks*.

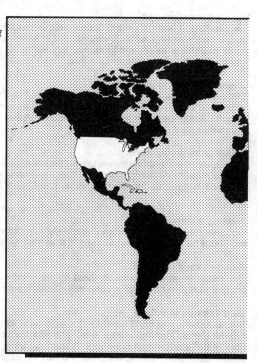